Yes Africa Can

Yes Africa Can

SUCCESS STORIES FROM A DYNAMIC CONTINENT

EDITORS
PUNAM CHUHAN-POLE AND MANKA ANGWAFO

THE WORLD BANK
Washington, D.C.

ISBN: 978-0-8213-8745-0
eISBN: 978-0-8213-8746-7
DOI: 10.1596/978-0-8213-8745-0

Cover design: Naylor Design, Inc.

Library of Congress Cataloging-in-Publication Data

Yes Africa can : success stories from a dynamic continent / editors: Punam Chuhan-Pole, Manka Angwafo.
    p. cm.
  Includes bibliographical references.
  ISBN 978-0-8213-8745-0 — ISBN 978-0-8213-8746-7 (electronic)
    1. Africa—Economic policy. 2. Africa—Economic conditions—1960- 3. Africa—Economic conditions—21st century. 4. Africa—Social conditions. 5. Africa—Politics and government—21st century. I. Chuhan-Pole, Punam. II. Angwafo, Manka.

HC800.Y47 2011
330.967—dc22
                                                             2011014918

CONTENTS

FOREWORD

In April 2011, a study entitled "Hiding the Real Africa" documented how easily Africa makes the evening newscasts and newspaper headlines in the West when a major famine, pandemic, or violent crisis breaks. For example, over a five-month period from May 2010, more than 245 articles on Africa published by the 10 most-read US newspapers focused on poverty. Only five of them mentioned wealth and growth.

The tendency to dwell on Africa's challenges, long-standing problems, and failures rather than on its opportunities and successes is one of the continent's most enduring stereotypes. Despite an acceleration of economic growth over the past 10 years and a growing army of African middle-class consumers, the narrative about Africa has remained one of poverty, disease, and conflict.

This suggests that changing the narrative on Africa requires not only sustained economic progress in the continent, but also a collaborative platform for telling the story in a compelling way.

Economic growth has spurted, averaging 5 percent a year from 1998 to 2008. Despite a sharp slowdown in the wake of the recent global financial crisis, growth has rebounded and is back on track. Africa's private sector is showing signs of dynamism, attracting growing amounts of investment from domestic and foreign investors. Africa's poverty rate declined by about 1 percentage point a year, from 59 percent in 1995 to 51 percent in 2005. Primary completion rates are rising faster in Africa than anywhere else. More girls are in school, as educational opportunities for girls have expanded across the region. The death of children aged five or younger continues to decline.

Undeniably, much remains to be done: nearly 400 million people still live in extreme poverty; human capital is low; the production structure of African economies is largely undiversified, heavily concentrated in primary commodities; and governance remains weak.

To harness the recent growth and dynamism in the continent to address these long-term challenges, we need to understand what was behind Africa's resurgence. This book documents some of the success stories in Africa. The 26 case studies, which have been prepared by local and international academics, analysts, and practitioners, take an in-depth look at economic and social development achievements across countries, themes, and sectors. Some of these are well known, such as Mauritius's economic growth experience and the information, communications, and technology revolution in Africa. But others are not: the transformation of Rwanda's coffee sector and the shift to high-quality coffee production; Lesotho's success in boosting apparel exports; Mozambique's rapid economic growth (averaging more than 8 percent a year from 1993–2009); and the progress in combating malaria. In addition to documenting the nature of the successes, the case studies identify the reasons and draw lessons for other countries on the continent and elsewhere.

I expect *Yes Africa Can: Success Stories from a Dynamic Continent* to stimulate the interest of both the media and filmmakers to seek out and tell more of Africa's many success stories; to help put Africa's positive achievements on the map; and to inspire a vigorous discussion on how Africans can do more to unleash the full economic potential that is needed to transform one of the world's fastest growing regions.

Obiageli Katryn Ezekwesili
Vice President, Africa Region
The World Bank

ACKNOWLEDGMENTS

This volume was prepared by a team led by Punam Chuhan-Pole under the general guidance and direction of Shantayanan Devarajan, Chief Economist of the World Bank's Africa Region. Several of the case studies included in this volume were written by local researchers and practitioners based in Sub-Saharan Africa.

The team contributing to the book consisted of: overview—Punam Chuhan-Pole, Shantayanan Devarajan, Manka Angwafo and Dana Vorisek; chapter 1—David Robinson, Matthew Gaertner, and Chris Papageorgiou; chapter 2—Sarah Ssewanyana, John May Matovu, and Evarist Twimukye; chapter 3—Antonio Nucifora and Luiz A. Pereira da Silva; chapter 4—Michael Lewin; chapter 5—Ali Zafar; chapter 6—Jonathan Kaminski; chapter 7—Vishal Gujadhur; chapter 8—Vivek Srivastava and Marco Larizza; chapter 9—Jean-Paul Azam; chapter 10—Yéyandé Sangho, Patrick Labaste, and Christophe Ravry; chapter 11—Karol Boudreaux; chapter 12—Shashi Kolavalli and Marcella Vigneri; chapter 13—Mallika Shakya; chapter 14—Hannah Nielson and Anna Spenceley; chapter 15—Aliou Diagne, Soul-Kifouly Gnonna Midingoyi, Marco Wopereis, and Inoussa Akintayo; chapter 16—Joshua Ariga and T.S. Jayne; chapter 17—Andrew Dorward, Ephraim Chirwa, and T. S. Jayne; chapter 18—I.V. Sijali and M. G. Mwago; chapter 19—Kaoru Kimura, Duncan Wambogo Omole, and Mark Williams; chapter 20—Ignacio Mas and Dan Radcliffe; chapter 21—Anton Eberhard and Katharine Nawal Gratwick; chapter 22—C. Sekabaraga, A. Soucat, F. Diop, and G. Martin; chapter 23—Anne-Maryse Pierre-Louis, Jumana Qamruddin, Isabel Espinosa, and Shilpa Challa; chapter 24—Nejmudin Kedir Bilal, Christopher H. Herbst, Feng Zhao, Agnes Soucat, and Christophe Lemiere; chapter 25—Mona Sharan, Saifuddin Ahmed, John May, and Agnes Soucat; and chapter 26—B. Essama-Nssah.

Many people provided guidance in identifying potential success stories. Notably, Cecilia M. Briceno-Garmendia, Donald F. Larson, Hannah Messerli, Vincent Palmade, Markus Moeller, Agnes Soucat, and Hassan Zaman. Discussions with Jorge Saba Arbache, Christopher Paul Jackson, and Stephen Mink were also useful in selecting case studies. Laurent Wagner made a central contribution in the early phase of the study.

The report benefited from input by peer reviewers: Rocio Castro, Vandana Chandra, Quy-Toan Do, Elena Ianchovichina, Hannah Messerli, Celestin Monga, Blanca Moreno-Dodson, Claudia Paz Sepulveda and Hassan Zaman. Comments were also received from Fabiano Bastos, Jaime Biderman, Maya Brahmam, Mukesh Chawla, Delfin Go, Monica Das Gupta, Kenechukwu Maria Ezemenari, Errol George Graham, Jane Wangui Kiringai, Patrick Labaste, Karen Mcconnell Brooks, Moussa Diarra, Motoky Hayakawa, Maureen Lewis, Christine Lao Pena, Anne M. Pierre-Louis, Kofi Nouve, Rojid Sawkut, Shahzad Sharjeel, Toni Sittoni, Yutaka Yoshino, and Ali Zafar.

Participants at the April 2010 forum provided useful insights and perceptives that helped shape the output. Excellent editorial review was provided by Dana Vorisek, Barbara Karni, and Martha Gottron. Ann G. Karasanyi and Kenneth Omondi provided administrative support throughout the project, particularly during the forum. The Web site featuring the stories was produced by Michael Matovina and Yohannes Kebede. Mapi M. Buitano and Odilia Renata Hegba managed the communication and dissemination activities. Book design, editing, production, and printing were coordinated by Steven McGroarty, Rick Ludwick, and Denise Bergeron of the World Bank Office of the Publisher.

Finally, the production of this volume was made possible by the World Bank Office of the Publisher.

Punam Chuhan-Pole
Manka Angwafo
Editors

ABBREVIATIONS

ACT	artemisinin-based combination therapy
BPO	business process outsourcing
CPR	contraceptive prevalence rate
DHS	Demographic and Health Survey
ECOWAS	Economic Community of West African States
FAO	Food and Agriculture Organization
FMOH	Federal Ministry of Health
GDP	gross domestic product
GSM	Global System for Mobile Communications
HEP	Health Extension Program
ICT	information and communications technology
IDA	International Development Association
IT/ITES	information technology/information technology–enabled service
MOES	Ministry of Education and Sports
NERICA	New Rice for Africa
NGO	nongovernmental organization
PC	personal computer
PIN	personal identification number
PMA	Plan for the Modernization of Agriculture
SADC	Southern Africa Development Community
SMS	short messaging system
TFR	total fertility rate
UNFPA	United Nations Population Fund
USAID	U.S. Agency for International Development
WAEMU	West African Economic and Monetary Union
WHO	World Health Organization
	(all dollar figures are U.S. dollars)

Overview

Punam Chuhan-Pole and Shantayanan Devarajan

WHY STUDY AFRICAN SUCCESSES?

Over the past decade Sub-Saharan Africa has seen a remarkable turnaround in economic performance. After years of stagnation, economic growth has spurted—gross domestic product (GDP) grew from an annual average rate of less than 2 percent in 1978–95 to nearly 6 percent over 2003–08. Inflation is half its level of the mid-1990s. Private capital flows have risen to $50 billion, exceeding foreign aid. Exports are growing, as is private sector activity. The number of democratic regimes has risen and the security situation has improved. The poverty rate is falling by 1 percentage point a year. Countries such as Ethiopia, Ghana, Mauritania, and Rwanda are on track to reach many of the Millennium Development Goals. Nine African countries have achieved or are on track to achieve the target for extreme poverty (World Bank and IMF 2011). Among other encouraging trends are more fair and effective leadership, an improving business climate, increasing innovation, a more involved citizenry, and growing reliance on home-grown solutions. More and more, Africans are driving African development.

This increased dynamism in Sub-Saharan Africa is evident across a broad swath of countries. It has created optimism that Africa's favorable development performance will be long lasting and that it could dramatically transform countries in the region. Along the way, the prevailing discourse on Africa's economic development has shifted from *whether* the region will develop to *how* the region is developing.

Yet, there are still causes for concern. For one thing, performance across countries varies substantially. Also worrying is that, historically, Africa's performance has been volatile—with short periods of acceleration followed by long periods of deceleration and decline brought on by recurrent crises (Arbache and Page 2007). Moreover, the pattern of progress underscores serious shortfalls in some areas, notably, in the economic diversification of many countries and in the integration of African economies into the global economy (UNIDO 2009). African countries also need to correct large infrastructure deficits, dramatically expand the skills base of their labor forces, and improve their ability to absorb technical knowledge in the private sector to improve their global standing in the years ahead.

With the lingering specter of past failures, continued economic development challenges in Sub-Saharan Africa have led to questions of whether improved performance in recent years is sustainable. This book attempts to answer these questions by documenting and better understanding some of the impressive achievements that have occurred in recent years. By systematically identifying and assessing positive outcomes, it is possible to draw out lessons regarding what has worked in practice and why. These lessons will in

We wish to thank Manka Angwafo and Dana Vorisek for their excellent contributions.

turn inform our judgment about whether Africa's growth is sustainable.

After a review of the major recent economic developments in Africa, this overview describes the approach and methodology used in the study of African successes. We then present a framework for understanding the 26 case studies, a framework that is based on the balance between overcoming market failures and overcoming government failures. We conclude that the way in which African governments have been increasingly addressing government failures—with impressive results—bodes well for the sustainability of Africa's decade-long growth.

A CHANGING ECONOMIC LANDSCAPE

After lackluster economic performance for decades, during which the gap between Sub-Saharan Africa and the rest of the developing world widened, the region's economies have seen a visible turnaround that began in the mid-1990s. The most visible evidence is the acceleration in output growth from under 2 percent in 1978–95 to nearly 6 percent in 2003–08.[1] Oil exporters have seen an especially steep rise, but growth has been widespread (figure 1). Indeed, 21 non-oil countries, home to over 40 percent of the region's population and accounting for nearly a quarter of the region's GDP, have posted annual economic growth of more than 4 percent during 1995–2008. Many of these 21 countries face the additional challenge of being land-locked. Within this overall improvement in the growth trend, some countries are lagging, but their numbers are small and declining.

In a remarkable break from historical performance, not only has growth accelerated, but the acceleration has been sustained for a longer period than in the past. For example, Mozambique, Tanzania, and Uganda have experienced growth rates above 5 percent in every year during 2001–08. Arbache et al. (2008) find that growth accelerations were more frequent in 1995–2005, whereas growth decelerations were more common in the preceding two decades: the likelihood of a growth acceleration was 0.42 in 1995–2005 but 0.21 in 1985–94.

Strong output growth has lifted per capita incomes as well. Per capita incomes fell in 1975–84 at an average annual rate of 0.88 percent, and at an even faster pace (1.13 percent) in 1985–94. By contrast, per capita income expanded at nearly 2 percent a year in 1995–2008, in step with growth rates in other developing regions (figure 2).

African exports are growing as well but remain highly concentrated (figure 3). After stagnating in volume and value terms in the 1980s, exports doubled in volume and rose fivefold in value in the period 1994–2008. Nevertheless, exports of goods (excluding oil) account for less than 20 percent of GDP (reflecting little change over the previous decades), and Africa's share of world exports remains low, after falling for more than half a century. Export growth has been led by extractive resource exports, fueled by a commodity boom (figure 4). Africa's exports continue to be dominated by extractive and agricultural commodities. In many cases, commodity dependence seems to have intensified. Manufacturing exports have grown slowly, and much of the region has yet to break into the global industrial market (UNIDO 2009). The diversity and sophistication of exports has changed very little. Whereas the mostly upward trend in extractive commodity prices has provided revenues to finance much needed infrastructure and social spending, it also presents challenges of avoiding the "resource curse" and converting the revenues into sustained development.

Improving economic prospects have attracted foreign direct investment (FDI) to the region (figure 5). FDI grew by more than 17 percent a year between 1995 and 2008. Although extractive industries account for the bulk of the FDI inflows, significant amounts—especially greenfield investments—are being recorded in the construction, communications, and banking sectors. Emerging market countries such as China and India are becoming important sources of FDI.

A notable feature of the transformation under way in Africa is the upsurge in agricultural output and productivity. Agricultural GDP growth averaged nearly 3 percent a year over 1980–2004, but growth per capita averaged only 0.9 percent, between one-third and half that of other developing regions (World Bank 2008). This average hides considerable variation across countries and over time. For example, per capita growth in agricultural output was negative in the 1980s and early 1990s, before turning positive. A recent study (Fuglie 2010) finds that the pickup in agricultural growth in the 1990s and 2000s resulted from expansion of land under agriculture. Block (2010) finds that agricultural total factor productivity growth declined in 1960s and 1970s, but productivity picked up over the last two decades. Signs of change in African agriculture are evident in the successes documented in this book, such as the expansion in maize production in Kenya that was driven by liberalization of the local fertilizer market, in cotton in West Africa, and in cassava and rice production in many countries, boosted by improved varieties. In a region where two-thirds of the population is rural and 70 percent of the poor derive their livelihood from agriculture, the favorable trend in agriculture is encouraging. Robust growth in agriculture

Figure 1   Average Real GDP Growth Rates in Sub-Saharan Africa: 1995–2008

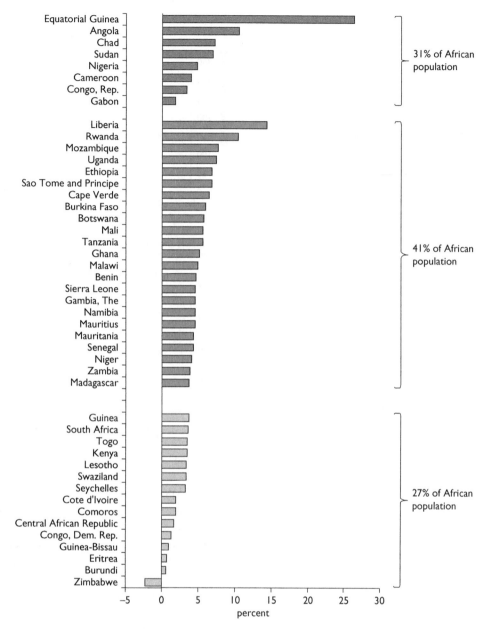

Source: World Development indicators, World Bank.

holds the promise of enhancing food security and facilitating broad-based economic growth and poverty reduction.

As stagnation in African economies has given way to growth, poverty has begun to decline. The incidence of extreme poverty—the share of people living on less than $1.25 a day—fell from 59 percent in 1995 to nearly 50 percent in 2005, a decline of 1 percentage point a year in the poverty rate. Several African countries are likely to achieve the MDG of halving income poverty by 2015 (Goal 1). Overall, however, the region lags other regions in attaining Goal 1 of the MDGs.

Education and health indicators have also improved (figure 6). For example, primary school enrollment has jumped 14 percentage points, from about 59 percent in

Figure 2 Average per capita income growth by country groups: 1975–2008

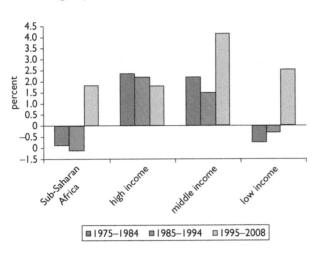

Source: World Development indicators, World Bank.
Note: Middle and low income includes Sub-Saharan Africa.

Figure 3 Trends in Export Volumes and Values, Sub-Saharan Africa, 1970–2010

Source: World Development indicators, World Bank.

Figure 4 Trends in Commodity Prices and Terms of Trade in Sub-Saharan Africa

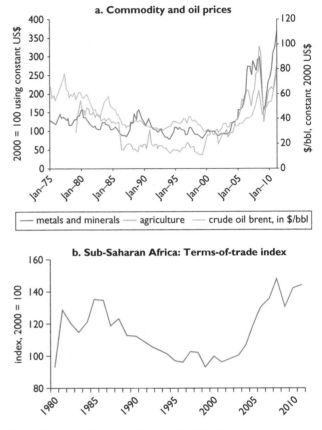

Source: World Development indicators, World Bank.

2000 to 73 percent in 2008—the fastest improvement of any region. More girls are attending school. Some significant gains have also been made in the area of health, where progress has admittedly been mixed. For example, child deaths (under-five mortality rates) have declined from 181 per 1,000 births in 1990 to 132 per 1,000 in 2009, with some of the poorest countries, such as Eritrea and Malawi, showing remarkable progress. Maternal mortality rates are also trending down, though not fast enough, and the region is beginning to make inroads in halting the spread of communicable diseases.

Since the mid-1990s African countries have made strides in the area of economic management and structural policies. Combined with debt relief, these reforms have helped to redress external and fiscal imbalances and rein in inflation. Median inflation has fallen from double-digit levels in the 1970s and 1980s to well below 10 percent in 1996–2007. In 1995 nearly a third of countries had inflation rates above 20 percent; in 2008 this figure had dropped to one-tenth

Figure 5   Foreign Direct Investment in Sub-Saharan Africa

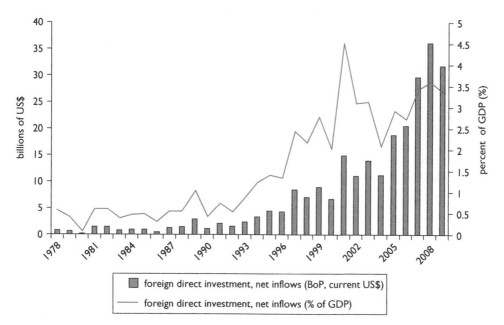

Source: World Development indicators, World Bank.

Figure 6   Progress in Human Development in
Sub-Saharan Africa

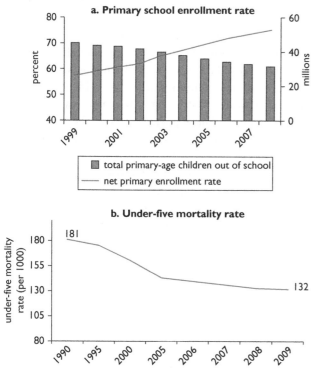

Source: World Development indicators, World Bank.

(figure 7). Exchange rates have also been maintained at competitive levels, including the one-time devaluation of the CFA franc in 1994.

Over the past several years, many African countries have moved to liberalize trade, and reforms have brought down tariff rates. Average most-favored-nation (MFN) applied tariff rates more than halved from 1981 to 2009 and are comparable to those of developing countries in other regions (figure 8). But improvements in trade facilitation have lagged. In a bid to enhance competitiveness, African countries have also made progress in recent years in implementing reforms to support the investment climate. Because of reforms, Rwanda is now one of the fastest places in the world to start a business (11th overall according to the World Bank's 2010 *Doing Business* report). There are also indications that the quality of governance is improving in some countries (figure 9). But, overall, weak governance remains a problem in Africa, especially in fragile states and resource-rich countries, and exerts a drag on long-term development.

APPROACH AND METHODOLOGY

A number of major academic and policy studies published in recent years have examined trends related to

Figure 7   Inflation Patterns in Sub-Saharan Africa

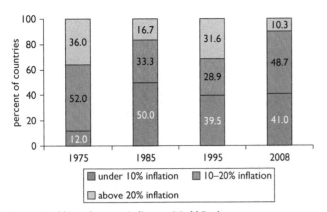

Source: World Development indicators, World Bank.
Note: The figure shows the share of countries in each inflation range.

Figure 8   Trends in Average MFN Applied Tariff Rates,
Sub-Saharan Africa, 1981–2008

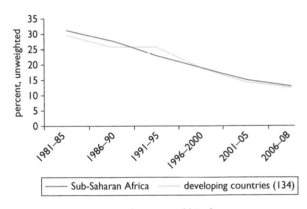

Source: World Development indicators, World Bank.

Figure 9   Trends in Political Rights and Civil Liberties in
Sub-Saharan Africa

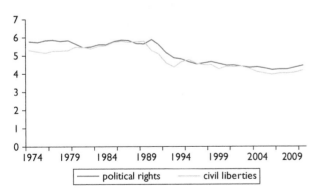

Source: Freedom House.
Notes: Political rights and civil liberties are measured on a one-to-seven scale, with one representing the highest degree of freedom and seven the lowest.

economic development in Sub-Saharan African countries. In *Can Africa Claim the 21st Century?*, released in 2000, authors from four multilateral institutions conclude that the emergence of three favorable trends—greater political participation (the basis for more accountable governments), a changing view of Africa in the wake of the end of the cold war, and the increasing presence of globalization and information technology—hold the promise of accelerating development and moving Africa out of poverty. At the same time, the book indicates that strengthening governance, investing in people, increasing competitiveness, and reducing aid dependence are crucial to development paths in African economies.

Ten years later, Radelet, in his book *Emerging Africa: How 17 Countries Are Leading the Way*, finds that an improving governance environment, stronger economic policies, a changed relationship with the international donor community, the increased accountability provided through new technologies, and a new generation of business leaders and policy makers have been indispensable in bringing about progress in the 17 African countries where a turnaround has been most evident.

Drawing on the existing knowledge of African development presented in these and other publications,[2] *Yes Africa Can: Success Stories from a Dynamic Continent* takes an in-depth look at 26 economic and social development successes in Sub-Saharan African countries—20 from individual countries and 6 that occurred regionwide.[3] The successes manifest at the project, provincial, subnational, national, or regional level and cut across themes, programs, and sectors. The overall goal of the research is to address how Sub-Saharan African countries have overcome major development challenges. The approach straddles the development debate that Cohen and Easterly explore in *What Works In Development?: Thinking Big and Thinking Small*. That is, should one adopt a big-picture approach that focuses on the role of the quality of institutions and macroeconomic and structural policies or an approach that focuses on microeconomic interventions such as conditional cash transfers and bed nets, whose impact can be measured through impact evaluations?

The case studies were chosen through a stocktaking exercise that included consultation with experts inside and outside the World Bank. To qualify for selection, each case study had to meet several criteria. First, the achievement identified in the case study had to be observable and measurable. Second, the achievement had to represent an outcome perceived as desirable in the literature on development. Third, there must have been existing analytical work—impact evaluations, assessments (including against relevant regional or sectoral benchmarks), and reports—regarding the achievement. And fourth, the achievement must have been sustained over time. In light of the above criteria, and because of the potential lessons that can be learned, there was a focus on critically evaluating well-recognized success stories in addition to those that are less well known. Where possible, the case studies attempt to identify achievements that have the potential to be scaled up or that have elements of transferability.

The coverage of development successes is selective rather than comprehensive. Indeed, some achievements were not examined because of resource constraints and timely availability of experts who could undertake the studies. A notable example that was not studied in detail is the success of Kenya's horticulture industry in becoming a major supplier of cut flowers to the European Union.

The 26 case studies presented in *Yes Africa Can: Success Stories for a Dynamic Continent* cover six broad topical areas:

SUCCESSFUL GROWTH EXPERIENCES. Both a high rate of growth and the quality of growth are central to achieving poverty reduction.

- *Sustaining strong economic growth.* High and sustained economic growth is needed if countries are to substantially reduce poverty and achieve the MDGs. A few African countries have grown at a brisk pace over many years. What explains these long periods of growth accelerations? What has been the role of a strong business environment in unleashing growth? Has growth been inclusive?
- *Quality of growth—industrial development.* Empirical evidence shows that countries with more diversified production and more sophisticated production sectors have stronger growth. Africa's industrial development has been disappointing. Yet, there are glimmers of progress. How have some African countries achieved more broad-based production?

POSTCONFLICT SITUATIONS: BUILDING INSTITUTIONS AND GOVERNANCE. Institutions and governance are central to the development process anywhere, but they are particularly vital in postconflict situations. How have some postconflict countries established better governance and transparency?

EXPANDING EXPORTS. Increasing competitiveness and diversifying exports is important if a country is to integrate in the global economy and benefit from globalization. How have some countries managed to diversify exports away from

traditional goods? How have some countries been able to build capacity so as to respond to quantity and quality needs of the global market, including compliance with international standards?

BOOSTING AGRICULTURAL EFFICIENCY AND OUTPUT THROUGH TARGETED INTERVENTIONS AND REFORMS. The vast majority of Africa's poor are concentrated in rural areas and are heavily dependent upon agriculture for their livelihoods. Spurring agricultural development will be vital for achieving the MDGs in Africa. Raising agricultural productivity is important for stimulating growth in other sectors as well. What are some of the ways in which countries have succeeded in boosting agricultural production, commercial agriculture, and productivity?

ENGAGING THE PRIVATE SECTOR TO UPGRADE INFRASTRUCTURE. Africa has large unmet infrastructure needs: the latest estimates point to a financing gap of more than $30 billion a year (World Bank 2010). Closing the infrastructure gap will require more private investment and operation. But the region has been slow to mobilize private resources, partly because of governance, institutional, and regulatory issues. How have some countries managed to attract private participation in delivering infrastructure services? One important area where African countries have seen rapid progress is in the mobile telecommunications segment of the information and communications technology (ICT) sector. Deployment of this technology holds the potential for large benefits—for example, connecting people and firms to formal financial markets and linking farmers to output markets. The African private sector has responded to competition in this market in unprecedented ways. What is behind the vibrancy of this market and what is the scope for scaling up innovative uses of ICT in African countries?

IMPROVING HUMAN DEVELOPMENT OUTCOMES WITH INNOVATIVE POLICIES. Sub-Saharan Africa lags on all the health and education MDGs. Yet, some countries have made significant progress in improving health and education outcomes. How have these countries achieved rapid progress? What policies and approaches have worked and why? What has been the role of public and private donors in improving service delivery?

Each case study includes: a description of the achievement and the elements that qualify the outcome as successful; an assessment of the main policies, interventions, actions, and other factors that contributed to the positive outcome; a presentation of the lessons learned and the contribution to the discourse on African development; and, where, possible insights on the transferability of the achievement and potential for scaling up the interventions and actions. Individual case studies also examine the role of the key stakeholders—the government, donors, or private investors—in facilitating and promoting the achievement.

In examining government contributions to successful outcomes, the focus is on the quality of economic policies and actions—that is, whether public action relieved constraints to growth—whether they provided macroeconomic stability, improved the investment climate, enhanced competitiveness or eased access to markets, promoted human development, or leveraged the global economy. How well strategies and policies adjusted in response to changes in the local and external economic environment is also addressed in many of the case studies. The narrative avoids being prescriptive because there are several policy combinations for achieving desirable goals.

MAIN FINDINGS OF THE CASE STUDIES

There has been no shortage of narratives about Africa's many failures, giving rise to academic titles such as *Africa's Growth Tragedy*, or *The Bottom Billion*, not to mention relentless media coverage of poverty, conflict, disease, and famine on the continent. While the proximate causes of African countries' failure to thrive are quite different—hyperinflation in Zimbabwe, civil war in Sierra Leone, desertification in the Sahel, and HIV/AIDS in South Africa, to name a few—they can be boiled down to two main sources: market failures, such as the common-property externalities associated with desertification, and government failures, often created by state intervention to correct market failures. For instance, governments throughout the world have central banks to manage monetary policy because markets alone cannot do that; but Zimbabwe's central bank started issuing so much money to finance the fiscal deficit that the currency became worthless, resulting in hyperinflation and many years of hardship.

Market failures can be corrected by implementing a tax or subsidy or by generating a public good, such as improved infrastructure or a better public health care system, for which the government can take credit. Overcoming government failures is more difficult, because the source of the problem is usually powerful people who are benefiting from the intervention. Correcting the problem involves undermining these people's rents. In some cases, governments fail to correct a market failure—another form of government failure—because vested interests are benefiting from the distortion (think of politically connected monopolists).

The 26 case studies in this book—all policy success stories from Sub-Saharan African countries—illustrate the many ways Africa has avoided or overcome market and government failures. That these countries have surmounted failures and generated economic and social progress benefiting millions of poor people is testament to the innovation, dynamism, and spirit of the African people. But the case studies do more than inspire: they teach us about the nature of government and market failures, and how they can be prevented or corrected.

To learn from the studies, it is useful to classify them into four categories: overcoming or avoiding massive government failure, rebuilding or creating a government, rationalizing government involvement in markets, and listening to the people (table 1). Regardless of which category each of the case studies falls into, as a group, they demonstrate that the African landscape is dotted with success stories. The sectoral and geographical diversity of the case studies illustrates that there are many ways to overcome Africa's challenges. To paraphrase Tolstoy, African failures are all alike; but each success is successful in its own way.

Overcoming massive government failure or bad policies

In all the case studies in this group, existing policies were standing in the way of growth, either at the sectoral or economywide level. In Ghana's cocoa sector, Rwanda's coffee sector, Kenya's agricultural sector, Burkina Faso's cotton sector, and Tanzania's wider economy, the willingness of the government to allow liberalization has paid off. In Uganda and Mozambique, postconflict reforms have paved the way for impressive improvements in economic performance. Across Sub-Sahara Africa, governments are grappling with opening up the power sector to private sector participation. Finally, the case study on Botswana proves that the resource curse can successfully be avoided even in an economy that is highly dependent on diamond mining. All of these cases show that the timing and nature of reforms is key to their success. But the specifics of each case offer important lessons.

Long an integral part of Ghana's economy, the cocoa industry faced near collapse in the early 1980s, battered by several forces. For one, Ghana was experiencing hyperinflation and an overvalued exchange rate (the market exchange rate was approximately 44 times the official rate in 1983), making selling its cocoa at official rates almost worthless. As much as 20 percent of Ghana's cocoa harvest was smuggled into Côte d'Ivoire for export. At the same time, an aging tree

Table 1   Categorizing Successes: Overcoming Government and Market Failure

Overcoming or avoiding massive government failure	Liberalization of the exchange rate and other reforms to revive the cocoa sector in **Ghana**
	Removing barriers to trade and creating incentives for entrepreneurship in the coffee sector in **Rwanda**
	Liberalization of the fertilizer market in **Kenya**
	Liberalization of the cotton sector in **Burkina Faso**
	Facilitating private partnerships in the power sector across Sub-Saharan Africa through **independent power producers**
	Wide-ranging economic liberalization in **Tanzania**
	Reforming the economy in a postconflict environment in **Uganda** and **Mozambique**
	Good timing and good luck for diamond mining in **Botswana**
Rebuilding a government or creating a government where none existed	Rebuilding government following civil wars in **Liberia** and **Sierra Leone**
	Using traditional systems for collective action in **Somaliland**
Rationalizing government involvement in markets	Development of a system of air, rail, and road transport and cold storage to support mango exports in **Mali**
	Provision of textile and apparel industry infrastructure in **Lesotho**
	Catalytic government role in private sector development in **Mauritius**
	Using input subsidies to improve agricultural output in **Malawi**
	Provision of gorilla reserves to boost tourism revenues in **Rwanda**
	Shifting the government role in the **ICT sector** from monopoly provider to regulator across Sub-Saharan Africa
	Success in **malaria control** across Sub-Saharan Africa
Listening to the people	Performance-based financing in the health sector in **Rwanda**
	Abolishment of fees to achieve free universal primary education in **Uganda**
	Training and deploying extension workers to improve access to health care in **Ethiopia**
	Lowering fertility through **family planning programs**
	Developing new varieties of rice, **NERICA**, to increase yields and decrease food insecurity
	Using **Moneymaker pumps** to support innovation and diffusion of technology in the agricultural sector
	Using mobile phones to improve financial access in Kenya via **M-PESA**

stock and the spread of plant diseases made Ghana's cocoa crop increasingly unproductive and investment in the cocoa sector unattractive. Ghana's proportion of global cocoa production fell by half between the mid-1960s and the early 1980s, from 36 percent to 17 percent. Starting in 1983, within the context of a wider economic recovery agenda that devalued the Ghanaian cedi and increased the farm gate prices paid to farmers for commodities (thus decreasing the incentive to smuggle cocoa out of the country), the government undertook a specialized program intended to revive the cocoa sector. Among other reforms, the program compensated farmers for replacing ailing cocoa trees (often with better-performing hybrid varieties), shifted responsibility for cocoa procurement to privately licensed companies, and provided subsidies to increase the usage of fertilizer on cocoa crops. Cocoa production and exports boomed. The amount of cocoa produced per hectare doubled between 1983 and 2006 as a result of increased fertilizer application and better production practices. A greater share of cocoa sales is now passed on to the 700,000-plus cocoa farmers, reducing poverty and improving prospects for cocoa-producing households.

In Rwanda, where the vast majority of people depend on agriculture for their livelihoods, major transformation of the coffee sector came about more quickly than it did in Ghana's cocoa sector. As of the late 1990s farmers were producing a small amount of mediocre-quality coffee that attracted little attention from discriminating importers and consumers, while the economic destruction of the country during the genocide in 1994 remained a serious impediment to markets. The first wave of reforms was introduced in the late 1990s—several barriers to trade were removed, a network of coffee-washing stations that allowed producers to shift from semiwashed to fully washed (higher-value) coffee was implemented, and incentives to foster entrepreneurship in the coffee industry were introduced. As a result, both the quality and quantity of coffee produced in Rwanda increased, allowing the government to launch, in subsequent years, a successful strategy to boost Rwandan producers' participation in the international specialty-coffee market. Between 2003 and 2008, the average export price of green coffee originating in Rwanda nearly doubled, from $1.60 to $3.10 a kilogram, leading to important improvements at the household level. The coffee washing stations, which had created 4,000 jobs as of 2006, also appear to have led to improved economic cooperation among people using them.

Like cocoa in Ghana, cotton has long been integral to the economy of Burkina Faso. Cotton accounted for 60 percent of the country's exports between 1994 and 2004 and contributed to Burkina Faso's good economic performance. A series of institutional reforms implemented in the cotton sector during the 1990s and 2000s—including the formation of a national cotton union and the partial privatization of the national cotton parastatal, SOFITEX—have succeeded in opening the sector. The Burkinabe reform model is unique among Sub-Saharan African countries, because it addressed government failures and local realities within the existing institutional framework, adopted reforms using a cautious, piecemeal approach, and built the capacity of producers and upgraded institutions within the commodity chain while the government withdrew from most of its activities. But it is also clear that Burkina Faso's dependence on cotton makes economic growth and performance in the country quite volatile, because cotton earnings are dependent on international markets. In the years ahead, the country will need to seek avenues by which to diversify the economy.

In Kenya, as in Sub-Saharan Africa as a whole, fertilizer use traditionally has been quite low, meaning that overall productivity in the agricultural sector is also quite low. Combined with the price volatility brought about by unpredictable weather and poor infrastructure, this low productivity has contributed to food insecurity in Kenya. For decades, the Kenyan government addressed this food insecurity through direct, monopolistic involvement in the markets for a wide array of agricultural products. This changed in the 1980s, when the government began relaxing its hold on agricultural markets, allowing the private sector to compete with state agencies and easing trade restrictions on fertilizer and maize. A more complete liberalization of the fertilizer market occurred in 1993. This change in policy, coupled with liberalization of the foreign exchange regime in 1992, encouraged the entry of a significant number of private sector firms in importing, wholesaling, distribution, and retailing of fertilizer. Government price controls and import licensing quotas were ultimately eliminated, and fertilizer donations by donor agencies were phased out. Kenya now stands as a notable departure from the Sub-Saharan African average in terms of fertilizer usage, which almost doubled between 1992 and 2007. Much of the increased use has been among smallholder farmers. Largely as a result of the increase in fertilizer usage, maize yields in Kenya increased 18 percent over 1997–2007.

Efforts to overcome bad policies in the power sector have been effective in some Sub-Saharan African countries. The case study on independent power producers (IPPs) focuses on the seven countries that have had the most experience with IPPs. As of the early 1990s, virtually all major power producers in Sub-Saharan Africa were publicly owned. They had been performing poorly for decades, and public financing for new projects (from both domestic and international sources) was drying up. Governments needed to develop a new tactic. Starting in Côte d'Ivoire in 1994, they experimented with opening power generation to the private sector. Ghana, Kenya, Nigeria, Senegal, Tanzania, and Uganda, among other countries, followed suit shortly thereafter. While the presence of IPPs has not solved the electricity deficit on the continent—only 25 percent of the population has access to electricity—IPPs have added several gigawatts of capacity to Sub-Saharan Africa's electric grid, complementing incumbent state-owned facilities. It is also clear that a sound policy framework (namely, adequate legislation), a good investment climate, and local availability of cost-competitive fuel can all contribute to the success of IPPs. When these elements are not in place, IPPs are much more likely to be untenable.

The case study on Tanzania addresses long-term market reforms that have gone far beyond a single sector. Following independence, the country's economy languished for more than two decades, held back by loss-making public enterprises, deteriorating infrastructure, and mismanagement of terms of trade and weather shocks, among other things, while poverty increased. Starting in 1986, a series of structural reforms focusing on liberalization was implemented, many of which were similar to the reforms put in place by Uganda in the same time period (see below). Trade and exchange rate regimes were liberalized; marketing boards for agricultural products were dismantled; and parastatals, the financial sector, and the civil service began to be reformed. The reform cycle continued into the 1990s, supported by a significant amount of debt relief from international donors, which freed budgetary resources for other purposes. By the mid-1990s Tanzania was on the cusp of a decade-long growth take-off, with real GDP growth averaging around 6 percent from 1996 to 2008. Despite a difficult external environment, Tanzania has maintained economic stability in recent years. Aside from the fact that fiscal and monetary authorities have succeeded in putting the economy on much better footing than existed decades ago, two other factors—low reliance on exports for growth and low levels of foreign exposure within the banking sector—allowed Tanzania to weather the global financial crisis relatively unscathed. And while poverty among Tanzania's population remains high, the country is on track to meet several of the targets laid out under the Millennium Development Goals.

In Uganda sustained, carefully sequenced macroeconomic reforms in a postconflict environment have produced remarkable outcomes. At the end of decades of political instability and civil war in 1986, Uganda's economy was in disarray and its population was struggling with a very high incidence of poverty. The reform agenda, begun in 1987 and implemented in stages, focused on stabilization, liberalization, and structural reforms: prices controls were loosened, a floating exchange rate regime was adopted, marketing boards were abolished, parastatals were abolished or privatized, the civil service was reformed, and efforts were made to stimulate private investment. These steps were followed by a wide-ranging poverty reduction plan that started in 1997. The performance of Uganda's economy in the 1990s and 2000s suggests that the reform policies worked. Growth averaged 7.7 percent a year over 1997–2007. Increased international confidence in the economy spurred substantial aid and foreign direct investment inflows and reversed capital flight. Poverty figures have also improved dramatically, so much so that Uganda will be one of the few Sub-Saharan African countries to achieve the first Millennium Development Goal of halving extreme poverty by 2015. At the same time, the Uganda case strikes a cautionary note: despite strong growth, income inequality has increased and the formal sector employment rates are very low, particularly among youth.

Having emerged from 16 years of devastating civil war in 1992 as one of the poorest countries in the world and with the second-lowest Human Development Index score, the economic situation in Mozambique was bleak. As in Uganda, Mozambique implemented a series of macroeconomic and structural policy reforms shortly after the war ended, in addition to encouraging support from the international donor community. The turnaround in Mozambique between 1993 and 2009 was profound: growth averaged more than 8 percent a year (compared to 0 percent from 1981 to 1992), the poverty rate dropped dramatically, and social indicators improved. Double-digit growth has been observed in mining, manufacturing, construction, electricity, gas, and water. Sound macroeconomic management allowed Mozambique to attract an increasing amount of foreign direct investment, which increased from an average of 1.5 percent of GDP in 1993–98 to 5.2 percent of GDP in 1999–2010. While progress has been impressive, in the years ahead, Mozambique will need to determine how to create

more jobs (particularly outside the agricultural sector, where most people are still employed) and widen the productive base in order to create an economy in which wealth is more broadly shared.

Policy choices in Botswana, like those in Tanzania, have been key to long-term economic progress. At the time of independence in 1966, Botswana's per capita income was among the lowest in the world. Many of its human development indicators were equally abysmal: life expectancy was 37 years, and the primary school completion rate was less than 2 percent. The country's outlook was not encouraging. But Botswana's economic performance in the years since has proven those expectations wrong: per capita income growth, for example, averaged 7 percent a year between 1966 and 1999. Without a doubt, Botswana met with a good bit of luck along the way—the discovery of large deposits of diamonds just after independence. In the decades since, diamonds have fueled solid economic growth and a rapid increase in per capita annual income. But effective, transparent governance and good economic management have been crucial to Botswana's success; they helped Botswana avoid the resource curse experienced by other Sub-Saharan African countries. In addition, the policies Botswana did *not* adopt also appear to have contributed to its economic success. Botswana did not follow an import substitution policy, and it did not expand state-owned enterprises, which employ only a small percentage of the workforce. In the ensuing decades, economic and social indicators in Botswana outperformed those of Sub-Saharan Africa as a whole by a wide margin. Life expectancy in Botswana was 60 years as of 1990, 10 years above the African average, while the under-five mortality rate had fallen to about 45 per 1,000, compared with 180 for Africa as a whole.[4]

Creating or repairing government

The second set of case studies details how countries have recovered from what is arguably the biggest government failure of all—civil conflict. In Liberia and Sierra Leone, governments have been successfully rebuilt from the rubble of devastating wars. In Somalia, on the other hand, which has existed without an internationally recognized central government since 1991, traditional power structures have been used in the breakaway region of Somaliland to strengthen infrastructure.

A long, violent conflict that ended in 2003 left Liberia in a state of collapse. Corruption was rampant, external debt was approximately 800 percent of GDP, the government's ability to manage public finances had essentially disintegrated, and the Liberian people received among the lowest amounts of per capita public spending in the world—approximately $25 a year. In the years since, the country's reform agenda has vastly improved the governance and economic environment. Liberia's situation took a solid turn for the better at the beginning of 2006. Under the direction of the newly elected president, Ellen Johnson Sirleaf, and in conjunction with a host of international donors, Liberia embarked upon a broad-ranging recovery and reform plan. Improving revenue collection and establishing an effective national expenditure process were the initial areas of focus. A unique feature of the program was its cosignatory arrangement, under which no major public financial transactions could take place without first being scrutinized by both a Liberian manager and an international advisor. This element of balance was fundamental to the functioning of the overall reform program. While the outcomes have been generally positive—revenue collection and expenditure management has improved dramatically—a final lesson is that a lot of capacity building still has to be done in the area of economic governance in Liberia.

Neighboring Sierra Leone was in a situation similar to that in Liberia. More than a decade of civil war in Sierra Leone came to a close in 2002, leaving the little infrastructure the country had in shambles, measures of human development among the worst in the world, and capacity for economic and political governance virtually nonexistent. The process of restoring (and indeed, improving) the system of political governance in Sierra Leone was a crucial part of the country's postconflict reform program, because marginalization of people living outside the capital, Freetown, was a main cause of the conflict. A national reform program, begun in 2004, focused on devolving political, fiscal, and administrative power to local governments. In some respects, the reform process has been quite successful—access to quality health services has improved dramatically, for one, and previously marginalized groups, such as women and ethnic minorities, have benefited from the new space for political participation. But in other areas positive results are less clear. In addition, recent developments within the central government indicate there may be increasing pressure to pull back from the decentralization, potentially reducing the future successes of the initiative.

Finally, the case study on Somaliland is an illustration of traditional structures playing the role of government where no formal system of government existed. Following the collapse of the central government of Somalia in 1991, much of the country fell into the domain of bandits and warlords,

making transporting goods through and out of the country a risky ordeal. But Somaliland, which unilaterally declared its secession from Somalia the same year the central government collapsed, has made admirable progress in improving its infrastructure to foster trade—namely, in expanding the port of Berbera, on the Gulf of Aden, and in ensuring the usability and security of the highway that leads to the port. Travel on the road is now reliable enough that Ethiopia transports a large portion of its exports along it before shipping them from Berbera. Somaliland's success in building up its infrastructure stands in sharp contrast to the situation in the rest of Somalia, which remains tense and dangerous. Factors contributing to Somaliland's success were twofold: use of the traditional social structures to control violence, and successful political cooperation in order to instill the level of security needed to allow development and operation of the port. While Somaliland is an extreme case, it is undoubtedly representative of scores of cases across Sub-Saharan Africa in which local communities succeed in providing leadership the official government is unable or unwilling to provide.

Rationalizing government involvement in markets

The third set of case studies illustrates how governments have successfully intervened to correct market failures—and no more. In the cases of mangoes in Mali, gorilla tourism in Rwanda, and apparel production in Lesotho, the respective governments stepped in to provide the elements necessary for the private sector to thrive. Responding to the possibility of profits, private entrepreneurs took on the bulk of the work to develop the sectors in question. In Malawi measured government involvement in agriculture has produced positive outcomes, while in Mauritius strategic government involvement in several sectors over the course of three decades played a catalytic role in the country's private sector development. Across Sub-Saharan Africa, the government's pullback from the power and information and communication technology sectors has allowed more people to take advantage of those services. The ICT sector, especially, has experienced a dramatic take-off. In all of these cases, the governments provided services essential for private sector success and then stepped back to allow private sector actors to carry out sectoral development. Even in difficult sectors such as health, initiatives that balance private and public sector involvement have produced truly impressive results, as discussed in the case study on malaria control.

In the 1970s Mali, where the vast majority of the population works in agriculture, began to explore opportunities to export its fresh mangoes. Malian mangoes quickly found a market in specialty stores in France and elsewhere in Europe. But Mali is landlocked, so traditionally, it either depended on neighboring countries for road, rail, and port infrastructure for export purposes or shipped goods from within its own borders via expensive air freight. By the early 1990s, with demand for mangoes in Europe increasing and countries such as Brazil (where shipping costs were lower because of good ocean transport options) becoming bigger producers, Mali grew increasingly uncompetitive in the global market for mangoes. Less expensive, more efficient methods of transportation were needed. Starting in 1995 the government in partnership with the private sector—farmers, farmer groups, and other businesses—launched an innovative response: a multimodal supply chain overhaul that used temperature-controlled containers to transport mangoes and improved road, rail, and sea links with neighboring countries. The level of government involvement in the mango sector turned out to be ideal, and the efficiency improvements have led to a host of positive outcomes: a 150 percent increase in the price mango producers receive for their products, a 1,000 percent increase in the tonnage of mangoes exported between 1993 and 2008, and a reduction in the average transit time for mangoes between Mali and Europe, from 25 to 12 days.

Another landlocked country in Sub-Saharan Africa, Lesotho, was also struggling to export in the 1990s, thanks to its limited transportation infrastructure, underdeveloped factor markets, and inadequate backward and forward industrial linkages and technical expertise. The solution came in the form of an international mandate, the U.S. African Growth and Opportunity Act (AGOA). In the early 2000s Lesotho launched a series of aggressive investment and export promotion strategies that positioned it to capitalize on the apparel industry benefits of AGOA. One notable aspect of Lesotho's experience is the government's decision to combine an apparel industry competitiveness initiative with a series of early-stage incentives for investors (they were offered publicly owned factory shells at subsidized rents). The tactic has yielded positive results—namely, that Lesotho's apparel exports to the United States, at $177 per capita in 2009, are higher than in any other apparel-producing country in Sub-Saharan Africa.

In Malawi a government initiative in the agricultural sector has had positive results within just a few years. Launched by the Malawian government in 2005 in response to severe food security difficulties in the early 2000s, the agricultural input subsidy program was intended to reverse the low productivity and high price of maize, a staple food for the

country and an important source of jobs. While intervention in the maize market, including input subsidies, has been a longstanding—though often contentious—feature of government and international donor strategies to promote agricultural productivity and food security in Malawi, the 2005 program went further than past efforts in its scale and scope. Vouchers for maize fertilizers were provided to more than half of Malawi's farm households. Additional vouchers were distributed for improved maize seeds and tobacco fertilizers. The core objective of the program was twofold: improving farmers' ability to achieve food self-sufficiency, and boosting farmers' incomes through increased crop production. Without a doubt, Malawi's input subsidy program has had positive impacts: maize production is estimated to have increased by 26–60 percent under the program, while food availability has improved and real wages in the agricultural sector have increased. But doubts about the effectiveness and appropriateness of the program have also been raised—namely, that the fiscal costs of the program are high, as are its opportunity costs (in terms of crowding out other needed public investments), and that it may be impeding the development of sustainable commercial agricultural input markets.

With the specter of the genocide still looming in the background in 1994, the Rwandan government embarked upon a national recovery strategy that included the redevelopment of the tourism sector. The goal was to focus on attracting high-end, conservation-oriented tourists interested in viewing Rwanda's gorilla population. The strategy also included an international marketing campaign intended to improve Rwanda's image in the world. Importantly, it also called for near-complete privatization of the hotel and leisure sector. The results have been impressive. Tourism has emerged as Rwanda's top foreign currency earner, ahead of the coffee and tea sectors. The number of visitors to Rwanda's national parks has increased exponentially—from 417 in 1999 to 43,000 in 2008. Moreover, it is clear in the case of Rwanda that initial actions by the government to revive the tourism sector have encouraged active involvement of the private sector: 86 percent of all new tourism-related projects in the country are locally owned.

The case study on Mauritius discusses government involvement in markets not over several years but several decades. Much has been made of the Mauritian "miracle," whereby the island transformed itself from a poor, sugar-dependent economy at independence in 1968 into what it is today: a fast-growing, much more diversified economy with one of the highest per capita income levels in Africa. Along the way, human development indicators such as life expectancy (73 years in 2008, compared to 62 years in 1970) have registered impressive improvements. And unlike in many other fast-growing economies, income inequality in Mauritius has declined solidly over the past 40 years. Aside from prudent fiscal, monetary, and exchange rate policies, Mauritius' economy has benefited from vibrant partnership between the public and private sectors. Among the most visible of the results of these partnership efforts has been the establishment of export processing zones (EPZs) to push along development of the light manufacturing sector in the 1980s and policies supporting growth in the financial services and ICT sectors in recent decades. Another important key to success in Mauritius has been the country's ongoing efforts to forge consensus between the Franco-Mauritian business elite and the Indo-Mauritian political elite.

In the health sector, too, an appropriate level of government participation in markets has produced positive outcomes in Sub-Saharan Africa. One example is in the battle against malaria. Governments, communities, donors, and individuals are increasingly coordinating their responses to the disease, reducing duplicative efforts, increasing the capacity to mobilize resources, raising awareness of the problem, and creating a network of technical and implementation experts. Efforts under the umbrella of the Roll Back Malaria Partnership, for example, have been a key in reducing the incidence of malaria in numerous Sub-Saharan African countries, such as Eritrea, Ethiopia, Rwanda, and Zambia by promoting the use of insecticide-treated bed nets, managing malaria vector breeding sites, and providing widespread diagnostic and treatment services. In Eritrea, for example, malaria morbidity dropped from about 100,000 cases in 2000 to about 8,000 in 2008. In Zambia the percentage of under-five children with malaria parasite prevalence fell from 22 percent in 2006 to 10.2 percent in 2008; the number of deaths caused by malaria declined 47 percent over the same years. These emerging successes notwithstanding, more remains to be done to control malaria in Sub-Saharan Africa.

Finally, the information and communication technology revolution that has occurred across Sub-Saharan Africa since the late 1990s is the result of government moving out of the way of the private sector. With demand for mobile phones increasing, most governments in Africa switched from being the monopoly provider (as they were for landlines) to being only the regulator in the mobile phone industry. As a result, the private sector was able to move in, increasing competition and reducing costs. The number of mobile phone subscribers grew exponentially, from 4 million in 1998 to 259 million in 2008, dramatically improving the ability of people across Sub-Saharan Africa to communicate. Phone services are now affordable to the majority of Africans rather than a privileged few. Private sector involvement in the ICT sector has also allowed innovative, mobile-based services in the banking, agricultural, and health sectors to take hold quickly.

Listening to the people

The final category of case studies examines policies and innovations that were successful in part because end users were consulted in the process of developing them. Two of the case studies in this section discuss how the provision of tangible products—human-powered water pumps and new varieties of high-performing hybrid rice—have contributed to a reduction in food insecurity across Sub-Saharan Africa. Four other cases studies detail important successes at the country level: abolishing school fees to achieve universal primary education in Uganda; providing health services in underserved rural areas in Ethiopia; implementing a performance-based financing system to improve health coverage in Rwanda; and reducing the cost of transferring money in Kenya through M-PESA, a mobile-phone-based electronic payments system. In some cases, similar innovations had been previously attempted but failed. The difference this time around was the way governments went about policy making. Rather than assuming they understood what worked well for their people and implementing policy from the top down, governments elicited feedback from the public in the course of formulating and implementing the policy. They adopted bottom-up approaches. As a result of being included in the policy-making process, people were much more likely to benefit from the final product or service. Finally, the case study on family planning programs illustrates that the responsiveness to users of family planning services is a prerequisite to reducing fertility.

Founded in Kenya in 1991, KickStart International's mission is to promote economic growth and employment creation in Sub-Saharan Africa by developing and promoting technologies that can be used to establish and operate profitable small-scale businesses, including its range of low-cost, human-powered pumps that allow farmers to irrigate their land. In turn, pump users are able to increase their yields (providing more food for their families), earn additional income, and create agricultural jobs. An important part of KickStart's model is the participatory fashion in which products are developed, with farmers advising on marketing and, in the case of the SuperMoneyMaker pump, the design itself. This element has been key in attracting pump customers and, as a result, improving agricultural returns.

That participatory spirit also contributed to the successful uptake of the New Rice for Africa (NERICA) hybrid varieties in the 1990s. The rationale behind developing the hybrids was quite clear. Though rice is the third-highest source of caloric intake and the fastest-growing food staple in Africa, up to 40 percent of rice is imported. From the start, the developers of NERICA, the Africa Rice Center and a consortium of partners, intended for it to increase food security and farmers' incomes. Importantly, the team consulted extensively with farmers in the course of developing the new varieties. That extra step ensured active adoption of the new varieties in a relatively short time frame. Initial empirical evidence from five Sub-Saharan African countries indicates that NERICA has had positive impacts on yields—especially in Benin and The Gambia—and on household income. Female farmers, in particular, have profited from cultivating NERICA varieties.

In Uganda free primary education was abandoned in the 1980s because the government's money was not reaching schoolchildren. Budgetary leakages were ubiquitous, and teacher performance abysmal. But after more than a decade, it was clear that charging school fees was not working either. When Uganda reintroduced free primary education in the 1997, it not only provided an incentive for parents to send their children to school but also publicized the amount of money each school district was receiving as a way for the citizens to hold the government accountable for the program. By quantitative measures, the universal primary education initiative in Uganda has been a resounding success. Net primary enrollment rose from 57 percent to 85 percent in a single year, from 1996 and 1997, and to 90 percent in 1999. Importantly, poor children, girls, and rural residents have benefited disproportionately from the increase in access. Over time, the quality of primary education in Uganda has also improved: between 2003 and 2010, for example, the numeracy rate among students at the Primary 3 level rose from 42 to 72 percent, while the literacy rate increased from 36 to 58 percent. That said, there is still considerable space for improvement in Uganda's education sector, particularly in reducing overcrowding in schools, ensuring adequate supply of teachers and materials, and reducing the number of over-age students in primary schools.

Cases in which governments acted with sensitivity to the people have also brought dramatic improvements in the health sector. In Ethiopia, a country of 80 million people, mostly in rural areas, more than half lived more than 10 kilometers from a health services facility as of 2005. Yet the rural poor in Ethiopia, where maternal and child mortality ratios were among the highest in the world and the number of trained health workers was inadequate, desperately needed better health services. Seeking innovative ways to respond to this challenge, policy makers came upon the idea of creating a national network of health extension workers who could address the basic health needs of the rural population. The program, launched in 2003, involved training and deploying more than 34,000 (predominantly female) community health workers who provide essential services covering hygiene, disease control and prevention, family planning, and health education. Although full implementation of the program was completed only in 2010, the outcomes thus far have been extremely promising. Childhood vaccination coverage has increased dramatically: 62 percent of children were fully immunized as of 2010, representing an average annual increase of 15 percent since 2006. Prenatal and postnatal maternal health coverage has improved. Women who previously desired family planning services but were unable to find them now have access to those services. Use of insecticide-treated bed nets increased 15-fold between 2004/05 and 2009/10, so that 68 percent of households in malaria-affected areas are now protected by at least one bed net or indoor residual spray; the reduction in malaria incidence in recent years is attributable to expanded coverage of these malaria interventions.

In Rwanda, too, listening to what people need has worked in the health sector. In addition to broad health sector reform and fiscal decentralization, Rwanda made use of two innovative policy tools—community-based health insurance and performance-based financing—to increase access to health services. The first policy made health services more available in rural areas and available at a lower cost. Under the second policy, Rwanda pays doctors a bonus depending on the number of children immunized or the number of pregnant mothers examined, more closely linking rewards with performance. Rwanda's innovative policy tools have contributed to the profound improvements in health indicators in recent years. Under-five mortality, for example, dropped from 196 to 103 per 1,000 live births between 2000 and 2007, and the maternal mortality ratio fell by more than 12 percent each year from 2000 to 2008. Rwanda is on track to reach the maternal health Millennium Development Goal by 2015. Improvements among the most vulnerable segments of the population have been particularly evident.

In crafting family planning programs, being responsive to the needs of users is a prerequisite to reducing fertility. Sub-Saharan Africa has the highest total fertility rate in the world, but some countries in the region are undergoing dynamic and unprecedented fertility transitions. In countries in which the greatest progress has been made, some of the key ingredients of success have been a high level of political commitment, strong country-level institutions, and effective family planning service delivery strategies. Family planning programs that have delivery points throughout the country; provide a range of contraceptive methods; ensure easy availability of contraceptives; adopt a reproductive health approach; and reach adolescents, men, and unmarried people are most likely to accelerate progress toward fertility decline in Africa. Many countries in Africa have tried community-based distribution of contraceptives to extend family planning to hard-to-reach populations, particularly in rural areas. Community depots, mobile clinics, women's groups, and both paid and volunteer village health workers are some modes of service delivery utilized by such programs.

The phenomenal success of M-PESA's mobile payments system is the quintessential example of (the private sector, in this case) providing a service that poor people in Kenya sorely needed—the ability to transfer small sums of money to people in remote areas at a low cost. Built on a mobile phone platform, M-PESA filled that niche, enabling customers to send money and store money through a simple interface. The service has been wildly successful. Launched in 2007, the number of subscribers surpassed 9 million in late 2009. Recent figures indicate that M-PESA handles $320 million in person-to-person transfers a month, or roughly 10 percent of Kenya's GDP on an annualized basis.

WHY DID REFORM HAPPEN AND WHY WAS IT EFFECTIVE?

The above findings beg two important questions: what prompts change in policies, and why did policy reforms work? In all but one of the cases of correcting massive government failure, existing policies were standing in the way of growth. How then did change come about? How were the obstacles to correcting government failure overcome? To address these issues one needs to understand why failed policies were present to begin with. Central to this issue is political context—that is, the political economy factors that induced the prior bad policies. There is a vast literature examining the political economy of poor policies, and studying it could help countries recognize when reforms could work and how to design reforms. Although an assessment of the political economy dimension is outside the scope of this study, some observations can be made based on the findings.

From a political economy perspective, poor policies persist because the preferences of those in power are not aligned with those of the public, and the former use bad or inefficient policies for political purposes or financial gain, or both (either politicians are beholden to interest groups or politicians create interest groups that are beholden to them). Individuals and groups who expect to lose economic rent from policy correction are likely to resist change or weaken its effects. Accountability mechanisms—checks and balances—on policy makers are designed to reduce incentives for opportunistic behavior and distortionary policies. But coordination and collective action problems prevent the establishment of strong accountability mechanisms. The weaker the constraints on politicians, the less likely reforms are to occur. Conversely, where political constraints are strong, bad policies will not persist, so the scope for reform to have a major improvement is low (Acemoglu et al. 2008).

However, policy change can occur in an environment of weak political constraints when there is a big change in political power.[5] Such a change disrupts the existing status quo and shifts power from existing interest groups to new ones and possibly to a broader group of people. That is what seems to have happened in the case of several countries is the study.

For example, in Ghana there was a shift from military rule to democracy. Under military rule the government had an incentive to keep agricultural and import prices low because its power base was the urban elite, including the army. But when democracy came, politicians needed the rural vote, so it was in their interest to liberalize the exchange rate and allow agricultural prices to rise. In Rwanda the situation was different. The liberalization of the coffee sector was part of the postgenocide government's attempt at restoring growth and rebuilding trust in government among all the people.

Likewise, in Uganda and Mozambique, both of which had been devastated by decades of political instability and civil war, major political reforms occurred in a postconflict environment. In both cases the new stability allowed new governments to adopt broad-based reforms to reverse economic decline and boost economic development.

Botswana, on the other hand, represents a case where the country was able to avoid bad policies after independence, despite the discovery of resource riches. One reason why the elite did not capture resource rents was the presence of traditional institutions—the Tswana tribal tradition of consultation, known as *kgotla*—which emphasized that the government exists to serve the people and promote development and is not the instrument of one group or individuals for the purpose of getting hold of the wealth. Tswana tradition also respected private property; the fact that many of the tribal leaders who helped usher in modern government were also large cattle owners may have reinforced this respect. These traditional institutions promoted respect for property rights and the rule of law, reducing incentives for distortionary policies.

Although transformation or creation of functioning institutions takes time, Radelet (2010) finds strong evidence of improved governance and more accountable governments in African countries that have achieved steady economic growth and lower poverty rates since the mid-1990s. As noted above, stronger constraints on politicians reduce incentives for inefficient policies.[6] It would thus appear that strengthening institutions can be extremely effective in bringing about change. Many of these countries are also identified in our study as experiencing successful growth episodes (table 2).

The range of reforms—exchange rate liberalization, opening up of trade, reduction of barriers to market entry, and liberalization of input and output markets—are not new. But why do these reforms work in some cases and fail in many other instances? Country context is one reason: it is central to understanding what works. A few insights are provided by the case studies. One possible factor could be that the reform was part of a broader set of reforms. This meant that successful policy reform in one area was not being largely offset or negated by reforms elsewhere—what Acemoglu et al. (2008) call a "seesaw" effect. The seesaw occurs when successful policy reform in one area is largely offset by reforms elsewhere as powerful interest groups opposed to the reforms attempt to thwart their effect. Simultaneous reforms that were complementary meant that the effect of any one reform was likely to be enhanced.

Another factor is the level of commitment to reform. Here, it is important to consider what prevents the reform from being reversed. The case studies on growth find that policy makers were generally able to commit to appropriate reforms—especially macroeconomic stabilization. One could reasonably argue that a benign global environment of strong growth, rising commodity prices, and low interest rates provided an enabling environment for sensible macroeconomic and structural reforms.

CONCLUDING REMARKS

Whether viewed through aggregate indicators or the case studies in this book, Africa's growth and development over the past decade has been impressive. The question on everyone's mind is: Will it be sustained? By showing that progress has come about through a combination of policy reform and active government interventions—balancing market failure and government failure—the 26 case studies included here give cause for optimism. If, as seems to be the case, African governments are reforming large, distortionary policies, and replacing them with selective interventions where there is genuine market failure and, more important, intervening with the feedback of the ultimate beneficiary to avoid government failure, then there is a good chance that the continent's strong economic performance of the last decade will be sustained.

NOTES

1. Several studies find a shift in trend beginning in the mid-1990s.

2. World Bank 2005; Growth Commission 2008; IFPRI 2009; Center for Global Development 2007.

3. The National Bureau for Economic Research Africa Project, which is ongoing, identifies and analyzes a large number of economic development successes in the region— 35 cases have been already selected for in-depth study and 40 are anticipated—to better understand the factors behind the positive experiences and to evaluate the sustainability of the successes and their transferability to other African countries. The study covers four broad topics: macroeconomic dimensions of growth; microeconomic aspects of growth; the intersection of health and growth; and cross-regional comparisons. The full findings of the 4.5 year project (2007–12), which is being supported by the Gates Foundation, will be available in a few years.

Table 2	Countries with Strong Economic Performance Saw an Improving Trend in Institutions			
	Freedom House 1.0 = best score 7.0 = worst score		Polity IV Score 10 = best score −10 = worst score	
Country	1989	2008	1989	2008
Botswana	1.5	2.0	7	8
Burkina Faso	5.5	4.0	−7	0
Liberia	5.5	3.5	−6	6
Mozambique	6.5	3.0	−7	6
Rwanda	6.0	5.5	−7	−3
Sierra Leone	5.5	3.0	−7	7
Tanzania	6.0	3.5	−6	−1
Uganda	5.0	4.5	−7	−1

Source: Radelet 2010.
Note: Polity IV measures qualities of executive recruitment constraints on executive authority, and political competition. Freedom House measures political rights and civil liberties.

4. Life expectancy and health indicators have deteriorated in the face of the HIV/AIDS epidemic.

5. Politicians can also adopt reforms when their earlier policies prove to be utterly ruinous to the economy and changing course seems to be the only viable option to avoid political change. Jones and Olken (2007) find empirical evidence that assassination of autocrats affects institutional change—specifically, a move toward democracy.

6. Where there is competition, inefficient institutions will be eliminated (Kingston and Gonzalo Caballero 2008).

REFERENCES

Acemoglu, Daren, Simon Johnson, Pablo Querubin, and James A. Robinson. 2008. "When Does Policy Reform Work? The Case of Central Bank Independence." *Brookings Papers on Economic Activity* (Spring): 351–418.

Arbache, J., D. Go, and J. Page. 2008. "*Is Africa's Economy at a Turning point?*" In *Africa at a Turning Point? Growth, Aid, and External Shock* ed. D. Go and J. Page, 13–85. World Bank. Washington, DC

Arbache, J. and J. Page 2007. "More Growth or Fewer Collapses? A New Look at Long-Run Growth in Sub-Saharan Africa." Policy Research Working Paper 4384. World Bank, Washington, DC.

Block, S. 2010. "The Decline and Rise of Agricultural Productivity in Sub-Saharan Africa Since 1961." NBER Working Paper 16481, National Bureau for Economic Research, Cambridge, MA.

Center of Global Development. 2007. *Case Studies in Global Health: Millions Saved.*" Washington, DC.

Cohen, Jessica, and William Easterly, eds. 2009. *What Works In Development?: Thinking Big and Thinking Small.* Brookings Institution, Washington, DC.

Fuglie, Keith. 2010. "Agricultural Productivity in Sub-Saharan Africa." U.S. Department of Agriculture, Washington, DC.

Commission on Growth and Development. 2008. *The Growth Report: Strategies for Sustained Growth and Inclusive Development.* Washington, DC: World Bank.

Devarajan, Shantayanan, David Dollar, and Torgny Holmgren. 2001. *Aid and Reform in Africa: Lessons from Ten Case Studies.* World Bank, Washington, DC.

IFPRI (International Food Policy Research Institute). 2009. *Millions Fed: Proven Successes in Agricultural Development.* Washington, DC.

Jones, B., and B. Olken. 2007. "Hit or Miss? The Effect of Assassinations on Institutions and War." NBER Working Paper 13102. National Bureau for Economic Research, Cambridge, MA.

Kingston, C., and G. Caballero. 2008. "Comparing Theories of Institutional Change." *Journal of Institutional Economics* 5: 151–80.

Radelet, Stephen. 2010. *Emerging Africa: How 17 Countries Are Leading the Way.* Washington, DC: Center for Global Development.

UNIDO (United Nations Industrial Development Organization). 2009. *Industrial Development Report 2009: Breaking In and Moving Up.* Vienna: UNIDO.

World Bank. 2000. *Can Africa Claim the 21st Century?* Washington, DC: World Bank.

———. 2005. *Scaling Up Poverty Reduction: Learning and Innovating for Development: Findings from the Shanghai Global Learning Initiative.* Washington, DC: World Bank.

———. 2008. World Development Report 2008: Agriculture for Investment. Washington, DC: World Bank.

———. 2010, Africa's Infrastructure: A Time for Transformation. Washington, DC: World Bank.

World Bank and IMF (International Monetary Fund). 2011. *Global Monitoring Report: Improving the Odds of Achieving the MDGs.* Washington, DC: World Bank.

PART I

Tracking Successful Growth Experiences

Tanzania: Growth Acceleration and Increased Public Spending with Macroeconomic Stability

David O. Robinson, Matthew Gaertner, and Chris Papageorgiou

In the space of a few decades, Tanzania moved from colonialism to independence—including the union of two states (Tanganyika and Zanzibar)—to socialism to a market-oriented developing economy. Each of these stages involved significant change, with different economic institutions and economic incentives.

Tanzania has emerged from this period of significant economic transition as one of the most rapidly growing economies in Sub-Saharan Africa. For the first time since independence, it has broken out of the cycle of short-lived accelerations in growth that has characterized many low-income countries, enjoying strong uninterrupted growth since the mid-1990s. During the period between 1992/93 and 2008/09, inflation remained in single digits; the debt burden fell dramatically; the level of public spending increased significantly, permitting expansion of public services; and international reserves rose sharply (annex figures 1.A1 and 1.A2).

Achieving and sustaining rapid growth while preserving macroeconomic stability represents a major achievement, and significant improvements have taken place in many aspects of development. But Tanzania remains a low-income country, with per capita gross domestic product (GDP) of only $550 in 2009, and it is on track to meet only about half of the Millennium Development Goals (MDGs). The challenge is to harness the country's enormous potential to increase growth and thus to provide opportunities for all to enhance living standards.[1]

TANZANIA'S GROWTH TAKE-OFF

Sub-Saharan Africa enjoyed relatively rapid growth over the decade leading to the 2009 global financial crisis. After many years of poor performance, it grew faster than developed countries between 1995 and 2005.

Tanzania experienced sustained growth acceleration over this period (figure 1.1). This section examines when and why this acceleration occurred.

Most low-income countries exhibit frequent phases of growth, stagnation, and decline (Pritchett 2000), even where key policies and country characteristics have been relatively stable (Easterly et al. 1993). A technique developed by Bai and Perron (1998) can be employed to identify structural "up" and "down" breaks in economic growth trends, capturing this "stop and go" behavior of economic growth in low-income countries. A break in growth is identified as the point after which the average growth rate is above or below the previous average growth rate. Berg, Ostry, and Zettelmeyer (2008) extend this methodology to identify "growth spells" by modifying the procedure to determine sample-specific critical values when the time dimension is 30 years or less, the typical time horizon in low-income countries growth series. This methodology was used here to identify episodes of growth acceleration for all countries in Sub-Saharan Africa for which sufficiently long data series were available (table 1.1). The results reveal a large number of countries with growth accelerations in the 1990s (11 of 25).[2]

Figure 1.1   Real GDP Growth in Tanzania, 1970–2009

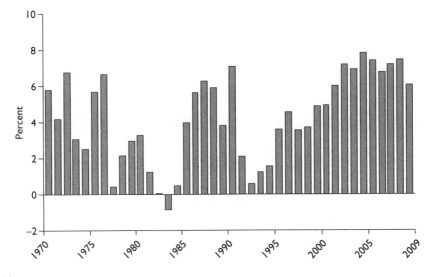

Source: Tanzanian authorities.

Table 1.1   Countries in Sub-Saharan Africa Experiencing "Growth Spells" in the 1990s

Country	Year of acceleration
Burkina Faso	1998
Cameroon	1994
Djibouti	1998
Equatorial Guinea	1994
Ghana	1997
Liberia	1994
Mozambique	1995
Namibia	1998
Rwanda	1994
South Africa	1995
Tanzania	1996

Source: Authors' compilation, based on data from Berg, Ostry, and Zettelmeyer 2008.

Tanzania's growth take-off was spurred by several key factors, including the significant structural changes that occurred as the basic institutions of a market economy—a private banking system, the unification of the exchange rate, and price liberalization—were introduced. Relative to other countries that have experienced growth accelerations, Tanzania stands out in two respects. First, the extent of the reforms was much broader and larger than the average of other countries that saw growth accelerate. Second, there was a long lag between key reforms and the realization of the growth acceleration. The role of macroeconomic policy

making during this period was to balance the need to create a supportive environment for growth against the need to contain the potential vulnerabilities that have derailed economic booms in the past, in Tanzania and elsewhere. Tanzania's macroeconomic record has been remarkably successful during a period that has seen both external shocks (sharp fluctuations in global commodity prices, such as oil and food, and a global financial crisis) and domestic shocks (periodic droughts, bank failures, and governance scandals). Navigating such shocks without major macroeconomic disruption is a reflection of strong institutions and responsible policy making.

In addition, Tanzania's move to a higher growth trajectory came following a period of substantial economic reform. Three distinct phases in economic policy making can be identified (figure 1.2).[3] The first, which began at the time of the Arusha Declaration in 1967, was the period of Ujamaa socialism, which created a one-party system with state control of the economy and nationalization of all major enterprises. This period ended in the mid-1980s, with attempts to gradually introduce key components of a market-oriented economy.

The pace and breadth of key reforms—both absolutely and relative to the rest of the world—can be highlighted by using newly constructed indexes of structural reforms developed by the Research Department of the International Monetary Fund (IMF) covering several kinds of real (trade, agriculture, and networks) and financial (domestic finance, banking, securities, and capital account)

Figure 1.2   Chronology of Transformation of Tanzania's Economy, 1967–2009

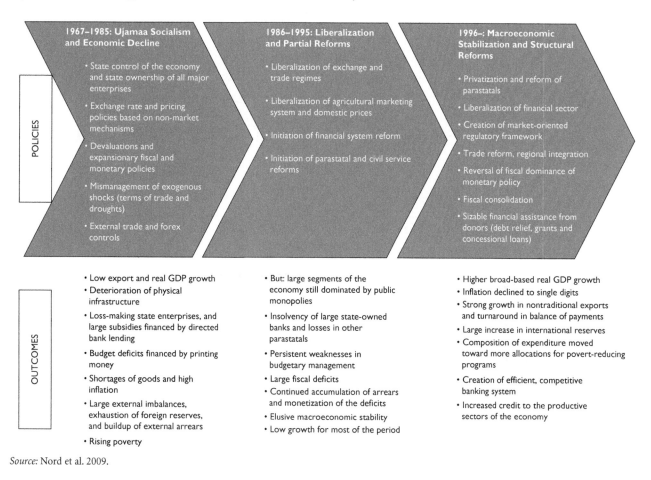

Source: Nord et al. 2009.

indicators. The indexes, which date back as far as the 1970s, are summarized in annex C and in Prati, Onorato, and Papageorgiou (2010).

There was a broad trend across much of the world toward greater structural reform and liberalization during the 1990s. Tanzania implemented significant reforms in the real and financial sectors beginning in the early 1990s and continuing into the late 1990s, reaching levels well above the averages for Sub-Saharan Africa (an exception is the capital account index, which lagged the region as a whole). Clear standouts are current account and domestic financial reforms (annex figure D1), which show extraordinary improvements in a very short period. Figures 1.3 and 1.4 document the association between reforms (especially in trade and finance) and growth breaks.

Various factors may explain this pattern. First, given the nationalization of all private property that occurred in 1967, a credibility gap probably existed regarding the irreversibility of reforms. Second, given the physical size of

Tanzania and the limited means of communication, it took time to convey information on the reforms throughout the country and to translate the legislative reforms into actual change on the ground. Third, as discussed in Mwase and Ndulu (2008), failure to address key bottlenecks prevented the realization of gains from other reforms. The exchange market was unified only in 1994, for example, removing a severe obstacle to trade, including access to needed imports (figure 1.5).

SUSTAINING GROWTH FOLLOWING THE INITIAL ACCELERATION

Tanzania's economy has grown by 3.5–7.8 percent a year since 1996, averaging 6.0 percent, well above the rates for Sub-Saharan Africa as a whole. These rates represent a substantial increase over earlier growth rates in Tanzania and, unlike previous accelerations in growth, have been maintained over a sustained period of time (figure 1.6).

Figure 1.3 Indexes of Real Sector Reform in Tanzania and Other Countries Experiencing Growth Acceleration

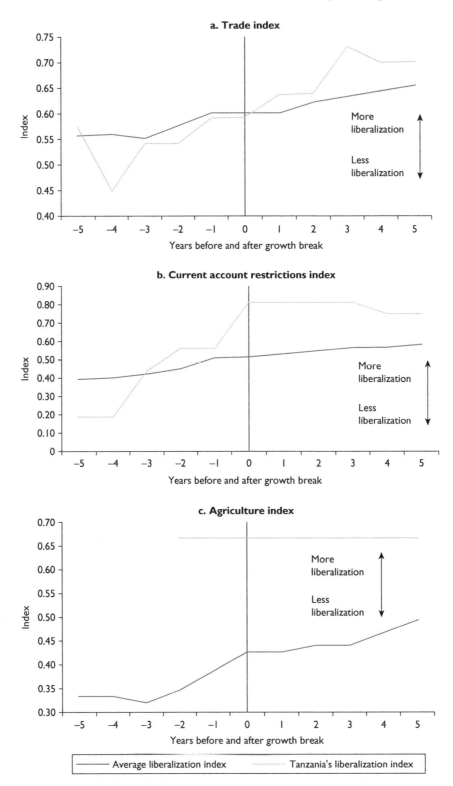

Source: Authors estimates using GDP data from IMF 2010d.

Note: The number of countries used to compute each average varies across indexes, based on data availability. See annex B for a list of countries included in sample.

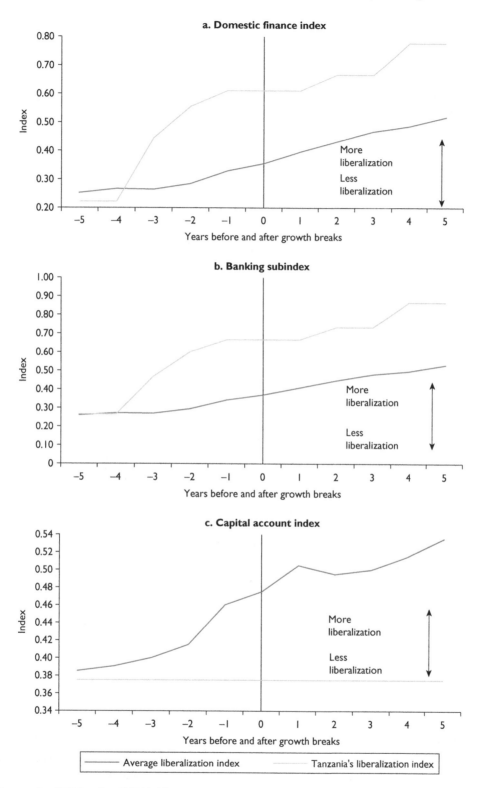

Source: Authors estimates using GDP data from IMF 2010d.
Note: The number of countries used to compute each average varies across indexes, based on data availability. See Annex B for a list of countries included in sample.

Figure 1.5   Official and Parallel Market Exchange Rates in Tanzania, 1970–95

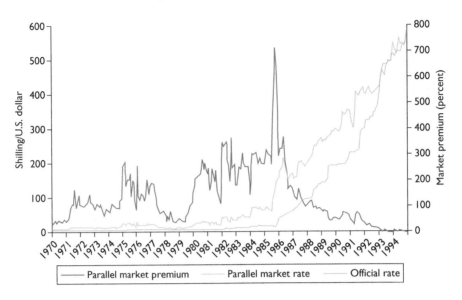

Source: Nord et al. 2009.

Figure 1.6   Real GDP Growth in Tanzania, 1970–2008/09

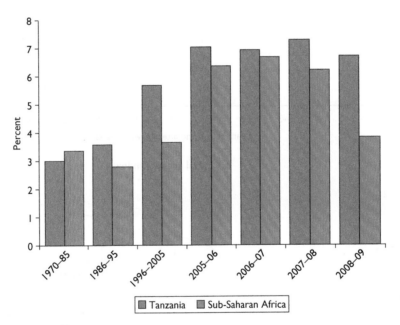

Sources: Tanzanian authorities and IMF staff estimates.

Several patterns are evident from Tanzania's growth performance (figures 1.7 and 1.8 and table 1.2):

■ Acceleration has been driven by domestic demand, not exports. Large increases in both consumption and investment have been recorded, in both cases reflecting significant increases in public spending.

■ The key sectors contributing to growth have been services and, to a lesser degree, industry; agriculture has not contributed to growth. Within the service sector, particularly rapid growth has been experienced in construction, telecommunications, financial services, and mining—all subsectors that have been liberalized. The limited contribution of agriculture—in a country where

Figure 1.7   Contributions to Real GDP Growth in Tanzania by Type of Expenditure and Production, 1999–2009

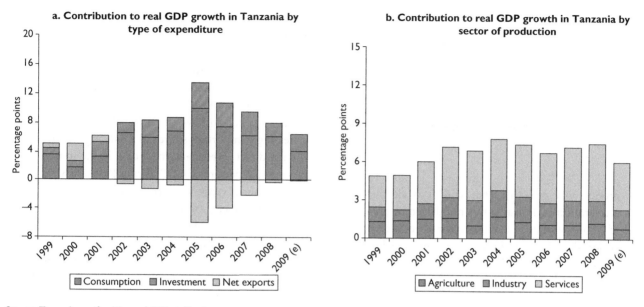

a. Contribution to real GDP growth in Tanzania by type of expenditure

b. Contribution to real GDP growth in Tanzania by sector of production

Consumption   Investment   Net exports

Agriculture   Industry   Services

Sources: Tanzanian authorities and IMF staff estimates.

Figure 1.8   Contribution to Real GDP Growth in Tanzania of Labor, Capital, and Total Factor Productivity, 1995–2008

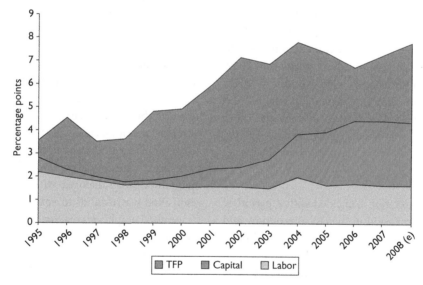

TFP   Capital   Labor

Sources: Tanzanian authorities and IMF staff estimates.

about three-quarters of the population resides in rural areas, where poverty is concentrated—is a concern. It also represents an opportunity, because international experience suggests that the sector can respond rapidly if the right incentives and supporting infrastructure are put in place.

■ The acceleration in growth can be traced to a combination of higher investment and increases in productivity. Growth decomposition is always subject to interpretation, particularly regarding the estimation of the capital stock (and therefore the contribution of investment and the interpretation of the residual as

Table 1.2 Factor Contributions to Real GDP Growth in Tanzania, 1986–2008
(percent)

Item	1986–90	1991–95	1996–2000	2001–08
Real GDP growth	5.3	1.8	4.3	7.1
Labor force	2.2	2.5	1.7	1.7
Capital	0.9	1.3	0.3	1.9
Total factor productivity	2.2	−2.0	2.3	3.5

Source: Tanzanian authorities and IMF staff calculations.

productivity growth). That said, it is clear that the acceleration in Tanzania was not driven by greater use of labor.[4] Studies of the agricultural sector during this period show little or no improvement in yields for the sector as a whole, with increased output coming from an increase in land under cultivation.

Although exports did not lead the growth acceleration—indeed at just 25 percent of GDP in 2008/09, they remain at a low level—the composition of exports has seen significant changes (figure 1.9). Traditional exports (cotton, coffee, and tea) have declined significantly in importance, partly reflecting the reorientation of the sector toward meeting the consumption needs of a rapidly growing local population. At the same time, gold exports went from zero in 1999 to $1.4 billion (nearly 40 percent of export receipts) in 2009, making Tanzania the fourth-largest gold exporter in Africa after South Africa ($6.3 billion), Ghana ($2.6 billion), and Mali ($2.0 billion). The service sector—tourism and other services, such as transport—has also grown at a steady rate.

The external environment

Tanzania's growth acceleration coincided with a period of both unprecedented expansion in the global economy and significant volatility in commodity prices and capital flows (private and official, including both aid and debt relief) that have posed challenges for macroeconomic management. Given its low level of exports, Tanzania has been insulated from fluctuations in prices and demand for exports and the boom-bust cycles such fluctuations have created in other commodity-dependent countries. However, significant impacts have been felt on the import side. The sharp increase in oil prices during the 2000s resulted in an oil import bill of $1.7 billion in 2007/08, almost 9 percent of GDP. Recent spikes in the price of fertilizer, most of which is imported, have constrained the government's ability to

stimulate agricultural production. Disruptions in the global rice market in 2008 hit Zanzibar hard, contributing to inflation that reached 27 percent a year in September 2008 before declining to 5 percent a year later.

Fairly broad restrictions on capital account transactions remain in place—preventing, for example, foreign portfolio inflows to the domestic government securities markets or private capital outflows into neighboring securities markets. Private capital inflows are nevertheless becoming an increasingly important source of financing for investment. Foreign direct investment, most of it in the mining sector, averaged 3.5 percent of GDP during 1996–2008. Before the global financial crisis, loan syndications were being used to finance investment, mostly in the telecom sector.

Official capital inflows have been important sources of financing for Tanzania since independence. Official development assistance peaked on average during 1986–92 (it represented almost 25 percent of GDP in 1992) before declining through the 1990s and then rising again, to about 17 percent of GDP in 2007. The component of aid that goes through the budget has been rising, albeit with significant year-on-year variability (table 1.3).

In addition to the absolute level of aid inflows, two other aspects of aid have had macroeconomic impacts. First, the composition of aid inflows has shifted. In line with the government's stated preferred modality, aid has increasingly been provided in the form of general budget support—cash that goes directly into the budget—rather than project support. Such aid gives the government more control over the use of resources provided by development partners and can be used to better meet national rather than externally driven (foreign) priorities. However, the use of general budget support also places a heavier burden on government processes to ensure the effective allocation of budgetary resources and maintain a broad dialogue with development partners on results and use of funds to ensure continued access to aid. Its use also complicates macroeconomic management, making it critical to ensure that the spending of aid does not induce undesirable macroeconomic consequences, such as a sharp appreciation of the exchange rate. An early evaluation of the impact of general budget support in Tanzania noted that it facilitated the government's ability to implement policies to which it was committed without discernable adverse macroeconomic consequences, but that it was less effective in securing commitment to policies (Lawson et al. 2005).

Significant aid has been provided in the form of debt relief. Tanzania qualified for the Heavily Indebted Poor Countries Initiative in 2001, receiving debt relief of about

Figure 1.9 Composition of Exports of Goods and Services in Tanzania, 1996/97–2008/09

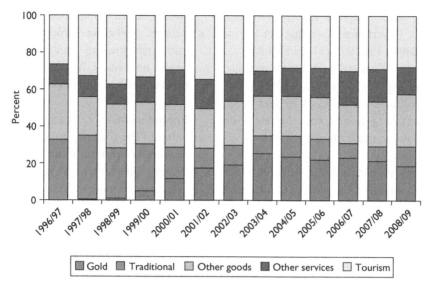

Source: Tanzanian authorities.

Table 1.3 Gross External Program and Project Assistance in Tanzania, 1996/97–2007/08

| Year | Program assistance[a] | | Project assistance | | Debt service relief | Total assistance |
	Grants	Loans	Grants	Loans		
1996/97	1.7	0.9	3.0	3.2	0.0	8.7
1997/98	1.7	1.3	2.6	2.2	0.0	7.8
1998/99	1.7	1.2	2.5	1.9	0.0	7.3
1999/00	1.7	0.7	2.8	2.8	0.0	8.1
2000/01	1.6	0.5	3.2	2.1	0.4	7.8
2001/02	2.4	0.9	2.8	1.1	0.6	7.8
2002/03	3.2	1.3	2.3	1.1	0.6	8.5
2003/04	3.4	1.7	2.6	2.0	0.6	10.2
2004/05	4.2	1.3	2.7	2.1	0.5	10.7
2005/06	3.5	2.0	2.0	1.9	0.7	10.1
2006/07	3.3	1.7	1.2	2.2	1.2	9.7
2007/08	3.5	2.4	3.0	2.2	0.9	12.1

Source: Tanzanian authorities and IMF staff estimates.
a. Includes both general budget support and basket funds.

$3 billion. In 2006 the IMF, the World Bank, and the African Development Bank implemented the Multilateral Debt Reduction Initiative, providing debt relief of an additional $3.5 billion.

Debt relief has substantially reduced the debt burden in Tanzania, freeing up budgetary resources for alternate uses. It has also left the country with a low level of debt—in absolute and especially net present value terms, given the highly concessional nature of much of the outstanding stock—generating a low risk of debt distress in conventional debt sustainability analyses (see, for example, the joint Bank/Fund debt sustainability analysis in IMF 2010c) and

making Tanzania a potentially attractive destination for capital inflows. Cognizant of the difficulties that arose from the very high debt burden, in 2004 lawmakers introduced a formal minimum concessionality requirement in external borrowing by the government, initially established at 50 percent but subsequently reduced to 35 percent.

Fiscal policy

The most striking feature of fiscal policy between 1992/93 and 2008/09 was the expansion in public spending. After falling to 15–17 percent of GDP in the mid-1990s as inflation was brought under control, spending increased sharply in 2001/02, reaching more than 25 percent of GDP in 2008/09 (even higher figures were budgeted for 2009/10 and 2010/11) (figure 1.10). Government spending per capita increased from about $40 in 1998/99 to $150 in 2008/09.

How was this spending financed without endangering price stability or increasing debt sustainability? Where did the money go? Expenditures are financed by increasing revenues, obtaining financing from abroad (as loans or grants), or borrowing domestically. Tanzania has used all three sources (figure 1.11).

Revenue performance has been striking. After an initial dip in the second half of the 1990s, revenues increased strongly, from just 10 percent of GDP in 1999/2000 to almost 16 percent in 2008/09. The improvement reflects a combination of tax policy and administration.

Tax policy has focused on reorienting the tax system to reflect the changing economic structure, as parastatals were gradually privatized; trade (internal and external) was liberalized; and a private sector, often informal, emerged. Key changes included the following:

- A value added tax (VAT) was introduced in July 1998, providing about one-third of government revenues. The rate was reduced to 16 percent in July 2009, bringing it into line with most other East African countries.
- Income taxes, which also provide about one-third of government revenues, were progressively modernized, with the maximum rates reduced to 30 percent, down from 70 percent rate in 1991.

Figure 1.10   Government Expenditure in Tanzania as Percent of GDP, 1992/93–2008/09

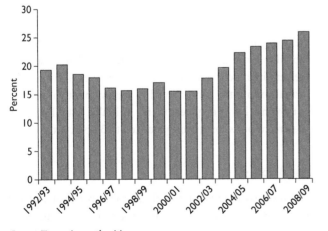

Source: Tanzanian authorities.

- The tax system was simplified, through restrictions on the range of taxes subnational authorities can impose and the repeal of numerous low-yielding taxes.
- Relative stability was achieved in key tax rates. Following initial reforms, the rates of the major taxes were left largely unchanged, in part because they were linked to regional tax harmonization initiatives.[5]

Improvements in tax administration have been no less important. The first step in strengthening administration came with the creation of the Tanzania Revenue Authority, in 1998/99. The Tanzania Revenue Authority has been able to progressively modernize tax collections, by introducing self-assessment procedures and electronic filing and payments and by carefully allocating its own human resources into high-return areas. Indeed the Large Taxpayer Department introduced in 2003 now collects almost three-quarters of domestic taxes, with the number of enterprises covered rising from 98 to more than 370.

There is still scope for improving tax policy. In addition to its revenue-raising role, tax policy has been used as a component of the broader development strategy to provide incentives for specific economic activities in an attempt to attract investment. Exemptions, such as tax holidays, are provided for qualified investments and for companies established in designated export-processing zones or special economic zones. A special regime was also created for mining activities, based on a tax/royalty regime but with additional relief from VAT and other taxes, such as the fuel levy. The efficacy of such incentive regimes for attracting investment is the subject of a fierce debate and beyond the scope of this chapter. Recent budgets have also introduced VAT exemptions for specific industries or products, thereby eroding the tax base and complicating tax administration.

Reliance on domestic financing—initially largely from the central bank, later from commercial banks and social security funds—has decreased significantly, in part out of a desire to contain the rate of monetary growth to bring down inflation. For several years in the mid-2000s, budgets were anchored on a zero net domestic financing target, which provided continued support for inflation stabilization, eased interest rate pressures, and increased room for banks to lend to the private sector. Where there were shortfalls in foreign financing, limited resort was made to domestic financing in order to avoid disruptions in expenditure programs.[6]

Even with this dramatic improvement in revenues, donor dependency has not declined. Government revenues

Figure 1.11   Sources of Fiscal Expenditure in Tanzania, 1992/93–2008/09

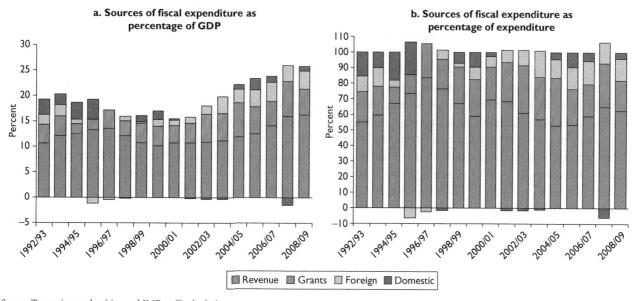

Source: Tanzanian authorities and IMF staff calculations.

still cover only about 50–60 percent of government expenditures—less than the level of recurrent spending (see figure 1.11).

Weak domestic revenue perpetuates reliance on foreign support, potentially adding both uncertainty and volatility to the government's ability to deliver its programs. Alternatively, the low share of government revenues to expenditures can be interpreted as an effort by the government to exploit the availability of cheap financing sources to expand delivery of public services beyond the level possible from domestic resources alone. The key is to ensure that efforts are under way to build a broad tax base capable of sustaining the desired level of public services in the event that donor funds diminish over time, that these efforts are not reduced by the presence of aid inflows, and that the additional public spending is used wisely.

The higher spending has appropriately been focused on priorities related to the National Strategy for Growth and Reduction of Poverty (known by its Swahili acronym, MKUKUTA). The 2009/10 budget allocates 71 percent of expenditures to MKUKUTA priorities. At the sectoral level, the two sectors receiving the largest budget allocations are education and health, which together account for about 30 percent of budgetary spending. The impact of the spending is difficult to gauge. In education, for example, substantial investment in construction of new classrooms has supported an expansion in primary school enrollment

to about 95 percent, up from about 60 percent a decade earlier. But issues remain with unfilled vacancies for teachers, particularly in rural communities; uneven financial transfers; and concerns about the quality of education, with pass rates in standardized examinations declining. In the health sector, a recent value-for-money study identified sharp regional differences in activity levels and performance, with no linkage to resource allocations (National Audit Office 2010).

Monetary and exchange rate policies

The primary objective of the Bank of Tanzania is to maintain domestic price stability conducive to balanced and sustainable growth of the national economy. A secondary objective is to support the integrity of the financial system. With inflation reduced to single digits and a financial system that has grown rapidly in recent years, the Bank of Tanzania appears on track to meet both objectives.

It has not been an easy transition. In the late 1980s Tanzania had one of the least developed financial systems in the world. Credit was allocated centrally; all of the major financial institutions were state owned; there were no capital or money markets, so the Bank of Tanzania simply printed money to finance the fiscal deficit and provide liquidity to insolvent banks; and foreign exchange was rationed, with a substantial spread between the official and black market rates.

Interest rates and foreign exchange markets were progressively liberalized starting in 1991, but the initial distortions—the legacy constraints—took time to resolve and served to shape economic policy options for most of the decade. In particular, with minimal foreign exchange reserves, central bank interventions in the market were initially targeted at accumulating reserves while smoothing seasonal volatility in the exchange rate. As the government was able to rein in its domestic financing needs and donors increasingly moved to providing budget support, the availability of foreign exchange increased, allowing the Bank of Tanzania to accumulate reserves, reducing upward pressure on the exchange rate (figure 1.12). It did so at the cost of assigning the burden of liquidity management to Treasury bill sales, however, resulting in rising domestic debt and upward pressure on nominal interest rates.

This unbalanced monetary policy mix, with high yields on government securities, low inflation, and exchange rate stability, proved difficult to sustain, however, particularly given the shallow domestic financial market with a small number of key players (Abbas, Ali, and Sobolev 2008). In late 2007 the central bank issued a press release indicating that its foreign exchange operations were limited to smoothing short-term volatility and that the exchange rate could appreciate. Only thereafter did markets become more balanced.

Private banks

Private banks were formally permitted in 1992, but none began operations until 1994. All of the large state-owned banks were privatized, but the process was lengthy and the former state-owned banks—CRDB (privatized in 1996), NBC (privatized in 2000), and NMB (privatized in 2005)—continue to dominate the financial system. Indeed, only since about 2000 has the private sector been able to access credit from the banking system.

Credit has grown rapidly since then (figure 1.13). Entry of new banks has accelerated in recent years, with 41 banks licensed as of the end of June 2010. Access to financial services remains limited, however—only 11 percent of adult Tanzanians held a bank account at end-2009—with financial services in rural areas increasingly shifting to mobile telephone systems.

Financial sector supervision has evolved along with the changing role of Tanzania's financial institutions. The government and the Bank of Tanzania developed a risk-based supervisory framework that provides sufficient authority to the body responsible for supervising and regulating the banking system. A bank intervention and resolution framework is in place, supported by a deposit insurance scheme. These institutions facilitated the closure of four private banking institutions, including two foreign-owned, without major disruptions to the banking system and with full compensation for individual depositors.[7] The legislative foundation for supervision of the broader financial system—chiefly pension funds and insurance companies—has been put in place, but implementation needs to be enhanced to guard against the buildup of potentially large fiscal liabilities.

Figure 1.12 Foreign Exchange Reserves in Tanzania, 1992/93–2008/09

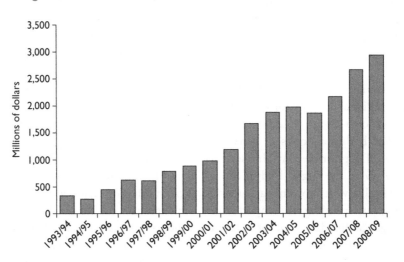

Source: Tanzanian authorities.

Figure 1.13   Private Sector Credit as Percent of GDP in Tanzania, 1992/93–2008/09

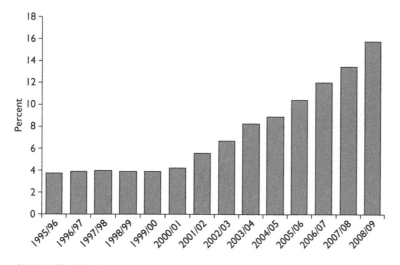

Source: Tanzanian authorities and IMF staff calculations.

USING THE NEWFOUND POLICY SPACE: COUNTERCYCLICAL POLICY RESPONSE TO THE GLOBAL FINANCIAL CRISIS

The degree to which Tanzania, and many other countries in Africa, have changed in terms of both economic structures and macroeconomic policy space was clearly demonstrated during the global financial crisis. Past global slowdowns have been very difficult for Africa: as documented in IMF (2010a), in previous global slowdowns, Africa suffered both a deeper slowdown and a more gradual recovery. This crisis has been different, with Sub-Saharan Africa as a whole seeing a large but short-lived dip in economic growth (figure 1.14).

Another key difference is that, for the first time, many countries in Sub-Saharan Africa were in a position to pursue countercyclical policies in the face of an adverse shock. In response to previous shocks, African countries generally pursued procyclical macroeconomic policies, largely out of lack of choice: high debt burdens, limited sources of financing, and low levels of international reserves provided few options for easing fiscal or monetary policy in the face of a growth slowdown. In addition, changes in the structure of the global economy—specifically the increased role of China and India, both of which are key trading partners for much of Sub-Saharan Africa and which were able to contain the damage to their economies—mitigated the external demand shock experienced by countries in Sub-Saharan Africa from the global financial crisis.

Despite initial concerns that contributed to a request for financing from the IMF under the exogenous shocks facility, Tanzania has managed to contain the impact of the global financial crisis through a macroeconomic policy response supported by interventions at the microeconomic level, all laid out in an economic recovery plan launched in June 2009. At the macroeconomic level, both fiscal and monetary policies were eased to help sustain the growth momentum. On the fiscal side, easing of more than 2 percent of GDP was envisaged, including a reduction in the VAT rate from 20 percent to 18 percent, partial government guarantees for loan restructurings in troubled sectors, expanded agricultural input subsidies, expanded investments in energy and road sectors, and temporary exemptions from royalties for tanzanite and diamond miners. The interventions were specifically targeted to sectors expected to be hardest hit by the crisis. The fiscal easing was financed in part by development partners, several of which were able to advance funding from future years, but also in part from domestic sources, with a modest increase in the volume of sales of Treasury bills and exceptional direct credits from the central bank. As elsewhere, commercial banks became more risk averse, with credit growth to the private sector falling sharply and high demand for government obligations serving to push interest rates to record lows. Although the crisis is not yet over, preliminary estimates for 2009 point to growth slowing to 6.0, rising to 6.5 percent in 2010.

Figure 1.14 Real GDP Growth in Sub-Saharan Africa and the World, 1992/93–2008/09

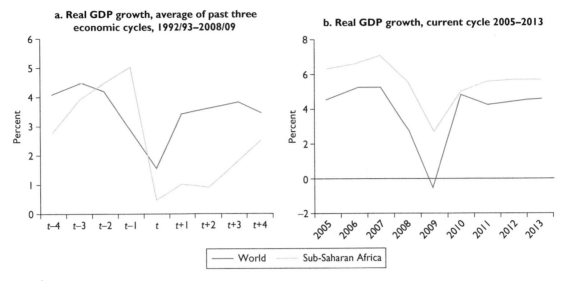

Source: IMF 2010d.
Note: t = trough in the cycle.

WHAT'S NEXT?

Tanzania has managed to achieve and sustain rapid growth while preserving macroeconomic stability for the past 15 years. Despite this achievement, it is on track to achieve only about half of the MDGs (table 1.4) (United Republic of Tanzania 2009b). What needs to be done in the years ahead? What macroeconomic policies would be beneficial?

Accelerating pro-poor growth

Constraints to growth in Tanzania are similar to those seen in most countries: inadequate infrastructure, regulatory bottlenecks, skill shortages, and deficiencies in the legal environment. These weaknesses constrain the realization of income opportunities at all levels—from the smallholder farmer trying to get surplus crops to market to the large foreign investor.

The past few years have seen little progress in several indicators of the business environment. Tanzania's rank in the Doing Business Index has been slipping, reaching 131 in 2010, as other countries have taken more determined strides to make their economies more business friendly. Tanzania scores particularly poorly on basic bureaucratic requirements involving numbers of procedures and permits and the time spent to receive them. The importance of addressing this slowdown in these broader areas of structural reform is reinforced by a key result of the literature on growth spells: although macroeconomic and financial

reforms can drive a growth up-break, they are not sufficient in isolation to sustain one (Hausmann, Pritchett, and Rodrik 2005).

Infrastructure is a constraint across Africa. But Tanzania lags even other countries in Africa (table 1.5).

Where will growth come from? Studies of potential growth drivers for Tanzania (Mbelle et al. 2010, for example) highlight a combination of agriculture, tourism, transport, and mining, with a focus on developing manufacturing and value addition activities. The identified sectors largely reflect physical and geographical endowments, with existing activities in these sectors fairly nascent—only a small portion of Tanzania's natural resource endowments are being exploited—and often characterized by low productivity. In many countries developing agriculture has been key to ensuring sustained progress toward the MDGs (World Bank 2005). Tanzania has decided to emphasize agriculture, having launched the Kilimo Kwanza (Agriculture First) campaign designed to accelerate reforms in the sector, including expanding input subsidy programs and significant investments in irrigation.

Meeting macroeconomic challenges

Addressing the infrastructure deficit will be expensive and will likely require funding beyond that likely to be available on the highly concessional terms at which Tanzania has been borrowing. The additional funds could come from many potential sources, including donor-financed projects,

Table 1.4 Projected Progress toward Selected MDG Targets by Tanzania

Target	1990	2000	2008	2015	Likely to achieve target?
Population below basic needs poverty line (percent)	39.0	36.0	33.6	19.5	No
Under-five underweight (percent)	28.5	29.5	22.0	14.4	No
Under-five stunted (percent)	46.6	44.4	38.0	23.3	No
Primary school net enrollment rate	54.2	58.7	97.2	100.0	Yes
Under-five mortality rate (per 1,000 live births)	191.0	153.0	112.0	64.0	Yes
Infant mortality rate (per 1,000 live births)	115.0	99.0	68.0	38.0	Yes
Maternal mortality rate (per 100,000 live births)	529.0	—	578.0	133.0	No
Births attended by skilled health personnel (percent)	43.9	35.8	63.0	90.0	No
HIV prevalence, 15–24 (percent)	6.0	—	2.5	< 6.0	Yes
Access to potable water (percent of rural population)	51.0	42.0	57.1	74.0	No
Access to potable water (percent of urban population)	68.0	85.0	83.0	84.0	Yes

Source: United Republic of Tanzania 2009a.
Note: — Not available.

Table 1.5 Infrastructure Indicators in Selected Countries in Sub-Saharan Africa

Country or country group	Households with fixed telephone (percent of households)[a]	Mobile phones (subscribers per 100 people)[b]	Households with electricity (percent connected to network)[a]	Roads (km per 1,000 km^2 of land)[c]	Access to improved sanitation (percent of the population)[a]	Access to improved water source (percent of the population)[a]
Ghana	8	32	44	187	10	80
Kenya	12	30	13	111	42	57
Rwanda	1	7	5	568	23	65
South Africa	27	92	63	300	59	93
Tanzania	10	21	11	62	33	55
Uganda	3	18	8	385	33	64
Zambia	4	21	20	50	52	58
Sub-Saharan Africa	7	16	29	—	31	58
Sub-Saharan Africa low income[d]	6	19	26	—	15	25
Sub-Saharan Africa middle income[d]	19	36	55	—	41	66

Source: World Bank Africa Infrastructure Country Diagnostic Database and World Bank various years.
Note: — Not available.
a. Data are from Demographic and Health Surveys, latest available year for 2001–08.
b. Data are for 2006.
c. Data are for latest available year 2001–08.
d. Income groups are based on World Bank classification.

local or international bonds, and public-private partnerships (Ter-Minassian, Hughes, and Hajdenberg 2008). Countries in Sub-Saharan Africa are increasingly accessing international capital markets, in several cases in the context of IMF-supported programs (Redifer 2010). Whatever the source of financing, it will be critical to ensure strong government processes for project selection, planning, and implementation and effective debt management to maximize the probability of a strong economic return while containing macroeconomic risks. Additional capacity to monitor risks in public-private partnerships will also be important to avoid the emergence of potentially significant contingent liabilities (the track record of such partnerships in Tanzania and more generally in Sub-Saharan Africa is littered with examples of projects in which the host government ended up either simply taking over the project or having to renegotiate in order to provide better terms for the private sector partner) (Gratwick and Eberhard 2008).

Fiscal pressures—not just from infrastructure spending but also from growing demand for public services as a result of high population growth—could be eased by mobilizing additional domestic resources. Estimates of tax potential suggest that revenues could reach 21 percent of GDP, almost 5 percentage points more than current collections (IMF 2010c).[8] A big part of the revenue loss stems from exemptions, which amounted to 30 percent of tax collections (3.5 percent of GDP) in 2007/08, according to estimates by the Tanzania Revenue Authority, making Tanzania's VAT one of the least efficient in the region (table 1.6). A possibly substantial upside is natural resource revenues: the mining sector is expanding rapidly and, as exemptions are reined in and those for the more established mines expire, the tax take can be expected to increase significantly. Close cooperation and transparency in the granting of exemptions will also need to be tackled in the context of regional integration efforts, in order to avoid a race to the bottom, with potential investors able to induce neighboring governments to compete against one another on the physical location of activities, resulting in the erosion of the tax base.

The exchange rate may also pose challenges. To date, the flexibility in the exchange rate, the apparent absence of resource capacity constraints in the economy, and productivity growth have all served to avoid the emergence of a misalignment of the exchange rate (see Hobdari 2008). Going forward, in the event of the planned scaling up of both public spending and private sector investment, emerging capacity constraints will need to be monitored carefully, and it will be important to ensure that public spending is channeled into productivity-enhancing investment to support the competitiveness of the economy. Similarly, the move to a common currency for the East African Community—which could generate additional growth opportunities—will need to address the issue of how individual national economies will adjust to localized shocks once they relinquish the ability to adjust through the exchange rate.

Limiting vulnerabilities but preparing for the worst

Even with the best macroeconomic policies and monitoring systems, bad outcomes can happen. Timely policy responses are often critical for containing the impact of bad outcomes. Being able to craft them requires having appropriate systems in place before the shock occurs.

In the financial sector, Tanzania's basic crisis resolution framework, together with a deposit insurance scheme, was able to handle failures of individual banks. That framework should be continuously reviewed to ensure that it can meet potential risks; there is room to further strengthen banking supervision, including risk analysis and enforcement of prudential requirements, while addressing staffing constraints (IMF 2010b).

The absence of effective oversight of pension funds is a critical deficiency in the current regulatory framework. Little information is available on the financial position of pension funds, their role in capital markets, and potentially large fiscal liabilities.

With the increasing integration of the financial system of the East African Community, there is also a need to ensure that a coordinated policy response or intervention can be orchestrated in the event of, say, pressure on a systemic institution. The initial difficulty in agreeing on a coordinated response was perhaps one of the key features of the global financial crisis.

More generally, a well-defined social safety net can help protect the most vulnerable in the event of economic downturns. All of these responses require policy flexibility. Retaining the policy buffers that were used to such good effect during the global financial crisis is critical for the conduct of countercyclical policy and the ability to prevent an adverse shock from derailing the economy's growth momentum.

CONCLUSION

Tanzania has seen unprecedented sustained growth acceleration since 1996. Several major (real and financial) reforms played a pivotal role in the take-off. Maintaining macroeconomic stability was a critical component in

Table 1.6   VAT Revenue and Revenue Productivity in Selected Countries in Sub-Saharan Africa, 2009/10

Country	Current standard VAT rate (percent)	VAT revenue (percent of GDP)[a]	Revenue productivity (percent)[b]
Kenya	16.0	6.0	37.5
Malawi	16.5	6.0	37.0
Rwanda	18.0	6.0	33.3
South Africa	14.0	5.7	40.5
Tanzania	18.0	4.6	25.5
Uganda	18.0	4.0	22.2
Unweighted average	16.8	5.4	32.7

Source: IMF VAT database and staff projections.
a. Projection for 2009/10.
b. Total VAT revenue, as percent of GDP, divided by the standard rate.

sustaining growth. Navigating the post–1996 period has involved the development of new policy instruments, as the nature of the economy changed and legacy constraints were eased.

Is another 15 years of uninterrupted growth likely? Untapped growth potential clearly remains, and the policy space that has been developed over the past decade or so can provide needed support.

ANNEX I.A MACROECONOMIC PERFORMANCE

Figure I.A1 Macroeconomic Performance in Tanzania and Sub-Saharan Africa, 1970–2009

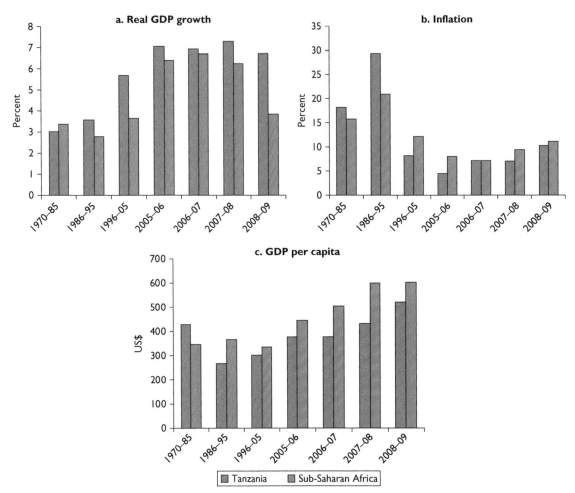

CHAPTER 1: TANZANIA: GROWTH ACCELERATION AND INCREASED PUBLIC SPENDING WITH MACROECONOMIC STABILITY

Figure I.A2 External Sustainability Indicators in Tanzania, 1970–2009

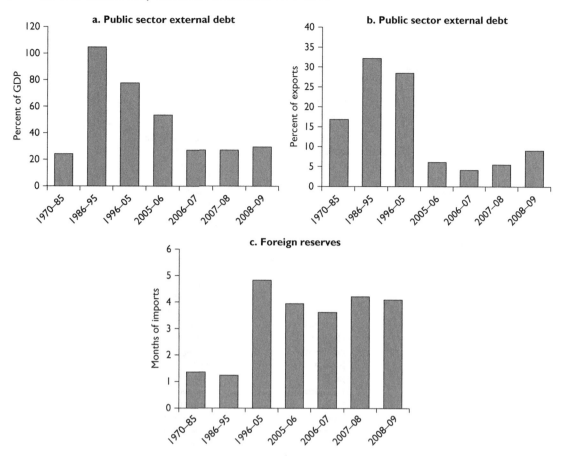

Table I.BI   List of Countries in the Sample

Low income	Middle income	High income
Bangladesh	Albania	Australia
Burkina Faso	Algeria	Austria
Côte d'Ivoire	Argentina	Belgium
Ethiopia	Azerbaijan	Canada
Ghana	Belarus	Czech Republic
India	Bolivia	Denmark
Kenya	Brazil	Estonia
Madagascar	Bulgaria	Finland
Mozambique	Cameroon	France
Nepal	Chile	Germany
Nigeria	China	Greece
Pakistan	Colombia	Hong Kong SAR, China
Senegal	Costa Rica	Ireland
Tanzania	Dominican Republic	Israel
Uganda	Ecuador	Italy
Uzbekistan	Egypt, Arab Rep. of	Japan
Vietnam	El Salvador	Korea, Rep. of
Zimbabwe	Georgia	Netherlands
	Guatemala	New Zealand
	Hungary	Norway
	Indonesia	Portugal
	Jamaica	Singapore
	Jordan	Spain
	Kazakhstan	Sweden
	Latvia	Switzerland
	Lithuania	Taiwan, China
	Malaysia	United Kingdom
	Mexico	United States
	Morocco	
	Nicaragua	
	Paraguay	
	Peru	
	Philippines	
	Poland	
	Romania	
	Russian Federation	
	South Africa	
	Sri Lanka	
	Thailand	
	Tunisia	
	Turkey	
	Ukraine	
	Uruguay	
	Venezuela, R. B. de	

Source: World Bank classification.

ANNEX I.C MEASURES OF REFORM

Table I.C1 Measures of Reform

Measure	Description	Source	Start year	End year	Coverage MIN # of countries in any year	Coverage MAX # of countries in any year
Real Indices						
Trade Openness						
Tariff Rates	Average tariff rates, with missing values extrapolated using implicit weighted tariff rates. Index normalized to be between zero and unity: zero means the tariff rates are 60 percent or higher, while unity means the tariff rates are zero.	Various sources, including IMF, World Bank, WTO, UN, and the academic literature (particularly Clemens and Williamson, 2004)	1960	2005	47	142
Current-Account Restrictions	An indicator of how compliant a government is with its obligations under the IMF's Article VIII to free from government restriction the proceeds from international trade in goods and services. The index represents the sum of two sub-components, dealing with restrictions on trade in visibles, as well as in invisibles (financial and other services). It distinguishes between restrictions on residents (receipts for exports) and on non-residents (payments for imports). Although the index measures restrictions on the proceeds from transactions, rather than on the underlying transactions, many countries in practice use restrictions on trade proceeds as a type of trade restriction. The index is scored between zero and 8 in half-integer units, with 8 indicating full compliance.	Quinn (1997), and Quinn and Toyoda (2007; forthcoming).	1960	2005	50	65
Product Markets						
Telecom and Electricity Industries	Simple average of the electricity and telecom markets sub-indices, which are constructed, in turn, from scores along three dimensions. For electricity, they capture: (i) the degree of unbundling of generation, transmission, and distribution; (ii) whether a regulator other than government has been established; and (iii) whether the wholesale market has been liberalized. For telecom, they capture: (i) the degree of competition in local services; (ii) whether a regulator other than government has been established; and (iii) the degree of liberalization of interconnection changes. Indices are coded with values ranging from zero (not liberalized) to two (completely liberalized).	Based on legislation and other official documents.	1960	2003	106	108

(continued next page)

Table 1.C1 (continued)

Measure	Description	Source	Coverage		Coverage	Coverage
			Start Year	End Year	MIN # of countries in any year	MAX # of countries in any year
Real Indices						
Agriculture	Given that developing countries constitute most of our sample, the degree of regulation in agriculture, which continues to account for a large part of many of these economies, is an essential aspect of product market competition. Index aims to capture intervention in the market for the main agricultural export commodity in each country. As data limitations preclude coding separate dimensions of intervention, the index provides a summary measure of intervention. Each country-year pair is assigned one of four degrees of intervention: (i) maximum (public monopoly or monopsony in production, transportation, or marketing); (ii) high (administered prices); (iii) moderate (public ownership in relevant producers, concession requirements); and (iv) no intervention.	Based on legislation and other official documents.	1960	2003	96	104
Financial Indices						
Capital Account Openness: Aggregate	Qualitative indicators of restrictions on financial credits and personal capital transactions of residents and financial credits to nonresidents, as well as the use of multiple exchange rates. Index coded from zero (fully repressed) to three (fully liberalized).	Abiad and others (2008), which follows the methodology in Abiad and Mody (2005). The original sources are mostly various IMF reports and working papers, but also central bank websites, etc. Resident/nonresident-specific indices are based on Quinn (1997), and Quinn and Toyoda (2007).	1973	2005	72	91

Capital Account Openness: Residents (nonresidents) only

Measures the extent to which residents (nonresidents) are free from legal restrictions to move capital into and out of a country.

Domestic Financial Liberalization

The index of domestic financial liberalization is an average of six subindices. Five of them relate to *banking*: (i) interest rate controls, such as floors or ceilings; (ii) credit controls, such as directed credit, and subsidized lending; (iii) competition restrictions, such as limits on branches and entry barriers in the banking sector, including licensing requirements or limits on foreign banks; (iv) the degree of state ownership; and (v) the quality of banking supervision and regulation, including power of independence of bank supervisors, adoption of a Basel I capital adequacy ratio, and framework for bank inspections. The sixth subindex refers to the regulation of *securities markets*, including policies to encourage the development of bond and equity markets, and to permit access of the domestic stock market to foreigners. The subindices are aggregated with equal weights. Each subindex is coded from zero (fully repressed) to three (fully liberalized).

Source: Prati, Onorato, and Papageorgiou (2010).

Table I.C2 Description of Reform Indices

Reform indices	Description	Source	Start year	End year	Coverage	
					MIN # of countries in any year	MAX # of countries in any year
Financial Sector						
Domestic Financial Sector Liberalization	The index of domestic financial liberalization is an average of six subindices. Five of them relate to *banking*: (i) interest rate controls, such as floors or ceilings; (ii) credit controls, such as directed credit and subsidized lending; (iii) competition restrictions, such as limits on branches and entry barriers in the banking sector, including licensing requirements or limits on foreign banks; (iv) the degree of state ownership; and (v) the quality of banking supervision and regulation, including power of independence of bank supervisors, adoption of Basel capital standards, and a framework for bank inspections.	Abiad and others (2008), following the methodology in Abiad and Mody (2005), based on various IMF reports and working papers, central bank websites, and others.	1973	2005	72	91

The sixth subindex relates to *securities markets* and covers policies to develop domestic bond and equity markets, including (i) the creation of basic frameworks such as the auctioning of T-bills, or the establishment of a security commission; (ii) policies to further establish securities markets such as tax exemptions, introduction of medium and long-term government bonds to establish a benchmark for the yield curve, or the introduction of a primary dealer system; (iii) policies to develop derivative markets or to create an institutional investor's base; and (d) policies to permit access to the domestic stock market by nonresidents. The subindices are aggregated with equal weights. Each subindex is coded from zero (fully repressed) to three (fully liberalized).

	Description	Source				
External Capital Account Liberalization: Aggregate	Qualitative indicators of restrictions on financial credits and personal capital transactions of residents and financial credits to nonresidents, as well as the use of multiple exchange rates. Index coded from zero (fully repressed) to three (fully liberalized).	Abiad and others (2008), following the methodology in Abiad and Mody (2005), based on various IMF reports and working papers, central bank websites, and others.	1973	2005	72	91
External Capital Account Liberalization: Residents vs. Nonresidents	Indicators measuring the intensity of legal restrictions on residents', respectively nonresidents', ability to move capital into and out of a country. Index originally coded from zero (fully repressed) to 50 (fully liberalized).	Based on the methodology in Quinn (1997) and Quinn and Toyoda (2007), drawing on information contained in the Fund's AREAER.	1960	2005	50	65
Real Sector						
Trade Liberalization						
Tariff Rates	Average tariff rates, with missing values extrapolated using implicit weighted tariff rates. Index normalized to be between zero and unity: zero means the tariff rates are 60 percent or higher, while unity means the tariff rates are zero.	Various sources, including IMF, World Bank, WTO, UN, and the academic literature (particularly Clemens and Willamson, 2004).	1960	2005	47	142
Current-Account Restrictions	An indicator of how compliant a government is with its obligations under the IMF's Article VIII to free from government restriction the proceeds from international trade in goods and services. The index represents the sum of two subcomponents, dealing with restrictions on trade in visibles, as well as in invisibles (financial and other services). It distinguishes between restrictions on residents (receipts for exports) and on nonresidents (payments for imports). Although the index measures restrictions on the proceeds from transactions, rather than on the underlying transactions, many countries in practice use restrictions on trade proceeds as a type of trade restriction. The index is scored between zero and 8 in half-integer units, with 8 indicating full compliance.	Based on the methodology in Quinn (1997) and Quinn and Toyoda (2007) drawing on information contained in the Fund's AREAER.	1960	2005	50	65

(continued next page)

Table 1.C2 (continued)

Reform Indices	Description	Source	Coverage			
			Start Year	End Year	MIN # of countries in any year	MAX # of countries in any year
Product Markets						
Telecom and Electricity Industries	Simple average of the electricity and telecom markets subindices, which are constructed, in turn, from scores along three dimensions. For electricity, they capture: (i) the degree of unbundling of generation, transmission, and distribution; (ii) whether a regulator other than government has been established; and (iii) whether the wholesale market has been liberalized. For telecom, they capture: (i) the degree of competition in local services; (ii) whether a regulator other than government has been established; and (iii) the degree of liberalization of interconnection changes. Indices are coded with values ranging from zero (not liberalized) to two (completely liberalized).	Based on various existing studies and datasets as well as national legislation and other official documents.	1960	2003	106	108
Agriculture	The index captures intervention in the market for the main agricultural export commodity in each country. As data limitations preclude coding separate dimensions of intervention, the index provides a summary measure. Each country-year pair can take four values: (i) zero (public monopoly or monopsony in production, transportation, or marketing, e.g., export marketing boards); (ii) one-third (administered prices); (iii) two-thirds (public ownership of relevant producers or concession requirements); and (iv) one (no public intervention).	Based on IMF commodities data, various existing studies and datasets, and national legislation and other official documents.	1960	2003	96	104

Source: Prati, Onorato, and Papageorgiou (2010).

A discussion of structural reforms, their determinants, and their economic impact requires solid data on structural policies and how they have changed (IMF 2009). A new dataset was compiled by the Research Department of the IMF that brings together information on a variety of structural reforms in both the real and financial sectors of the economy. The dataset spans about 30 years (1973–2005) and 90 countries, selected on the basis of data availability. The key advantage of these new indexes over those used in previous work, such as IMF (2004), is that they cover both a long sample period and a broad range of countries, including advanced and developing economies.

Among the indicators of real sector reforms, two separate indexes measure trade openness. The first covers average tariff rates; the second covers restrictions on other current account transactions, including payments and receipts on exports and imports of goods and services.[9] Two separate indexes measure product market liberalization. The first covers the network industries, specifically the degree of liberalization of the electricity and telecom markets. The second covers the agriculture sector. It aims to capture public intervention in the market for the main agricultural export commodity in each country.

Among the indicators of financial sector reforms, the index of capital account openness measures restrictions on

financial transactions of residents and nonresidents, as well as the use of multiple exchange rates. The index of domestic financial liberalization is an average of six subindexes, covering credit controls, such as directed credit; interest rate controls, such as floors or ceilings; entry barriers in the banking sector, such as licensing requirements or limits on foreign banks; competition restrictions, such as limits on branches; the degree of state ownership; and aggregate credit ceilings. All indicators were rescaled to range between zero and one, with higher values representing greater liberalization. Differences in the values of each index across countries and over time provide useful information on the variation in the absolute degree of economic liberalization within each sector. Instead, differences in the value of the indexes across sectors are not a precise quantitative measure of whether one sector is more liberalized than another because of the different methodology used to construct each index. For instance, a positive difference between the trade index and the financial index does not necessarily mean that trade is more liberalized than the financial sector.

As illustrated in figure 1.D1, all indexes trend upward over time toward a high degree of liberalization. At a sectoral level, the global liberalization of international trade, capital movements, and the domestic financial sector has been fairly steady and gradual over the past three decades,

Figure I.DI   Indexes of Structural Reform, 1973–2003
(*All countries*)

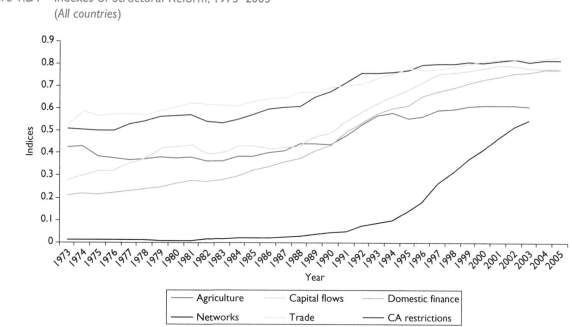

Source: IMF 2009.
Note: Data are based on sample of 90 countries for which data were available.

whereas product market liberalization started only about 1990. There have been no global setbacks in the average degree of liberalization in any sector. Liberalization measures display significant differences across regions, but all sectoral indexes have converged across income levels, pointing to imitation and "catch-up" effects.

NOTES

1. This chapter draws heavily on Nord et al. (2009). The authors are grateful to Daehaeng Kim, Saul Lizondo, Roger Nord, Laure Redifer, and World Bank reviewers for helpful comments.

2. To the authors' knowledge, this is the first time Tanzania has been formally shown to have had an "up-break" in 1996. Previous studies (Hausmann, Pritchett, and Rodrik 2005; Berg, Ostry, and Zettelmeyer 2008) failed to identify a break, probably because they used shorter time series.

3. Excellent descriptions of the reforms undertaken during these periods from varying perspectives can be found in Maliyamkono and Mason (2006), Mtei (2010), Mwase and Ndulu (2008), and Nord et al. (2009).

4. A World Bank (2007) study identifies increases in higher education attainment as an important contributor to growth.

5. The tax system has not been fully predictable for investors, because of fairly frequent changes in administration—often designed to close loopholes—and the existence of a large number of tax exemptions granted to particular sectors, subcategories of investors, and specific enterprises.

6. Government programs during this period, supported by the IMF (first under the Poverty Reduction and Growth Facility, subsequently under the Policy Support Instrument), were designed in such a way that a shortfall in foreign program financing automatically triggered the possibility of resort to high domestic financing subject to a pre-agreed upper limit; in the event that foreign program financing exceeded targets, the government was unconstrained in its ability to spend the additional financing received.

7. The bank closures were Meridien Bank (in 1995), Tanzania Housing Bank (in 1995), Greenland Bank (in 1999), and Delphis Bank (in 2003). Depositors were fully compensated in all cases, with the resolutions of both Meridien Bank and Delphis Bank facilitated by the transfers of deposits to other banks operating in Tanzania.

8. The models predict tax potential through a regression of the tax to GDP ratio on observable structural characteristics of the economy, such as the size of the agricultural sector.

9. This index—measuring how compliant a country is with its obligations under the IMF's Article VIII to free from restrictions the proceeds from international trade in goods and services—captures only some nontariff barriers to trade. For other nontariff barriers, such as quotas and subsidies, there is not a sufficiently long time series to be used in the analysis.

REFERENCES

Abbas, S., M. Ali, and Y. Sobolev. 2008. "High and Volatile Treasury Yields in Tanzania: The Role of Strategic Bidding and Auction Microstructure." IMF Working Paper 08/81, International Monetary Fund, Washington, DC.

Bai, J., and P. Perron. 1998. "Estimating and Testing Linear Models with Multiple Structural Changes." *Econometrica* 66: 47–78.

Berg, A., D., J. Ostry, and J. Zettelmeyer. 2008. "What Makes Growth Sustained?" IMF Working Paper 08/59, International Monetary Fund, Washington, DC.

Drummond, Paulo, A. Mrema, S. Roudet, and M. Saito. 2009. *Foreign Exchange Reserve Adequacy in East African Community Countries.* African Departmental Paper 09/01, International Monetary Fund, Washington, DC.

Easterly, W., M. Kremer, L. Pritchett, and L. H. Summers. 1993. "Good Policy or Good Luck? Country Growth Performance and Temporary Shocks." *Journal of Monetary Economics* 32 (3): 459–483.

Gratwick, K. N., and A. Eberhard. 2008. "An Analysis of Independent Power Projects in Africa: Understanding Development and Investment Outcomes." *Development Policy Review* 26 (3): 309–38.

Hausmann, R., L. Pritchett, and D. Rodrik. 2005. "Growth Accelerations." *Journal of Economic Growth* 10 (4): 303–29.

Hobdari, Niko. 2008. "Tanzania's Equilibrium Real Exchange Rate." IMF Working Paper 08/138, International Monetary Fund, Washington, DC.

IMF (International Monetary Fund). 2004. "Advancing Structural Reforms." *World Economic Outlook* (April), Washington, DC.

———. 2009. *Structural Reforms and Economic Performance in Advanced and Developing Countries.* Occasional Paper 268, Washington, DC.

———. 2010a. "Sub-Saharan Africa: Back to High Growth?" Regional Economic Outlook, April, Washington, DC.

———. 2010b. *Tanzania: Financial System Stability Assessment Update.* IMF Country Report 10/177.

———. 2010c. *Tanzania: Seventh Review under the Policy Support Instrument, Second Review under the Exogenous Shocks Facility, and Request for a New Three-Year Policy Support Instrument.* IMF Country Report 10/173, Washington, DC.

———. 2010d. *World Economic Outlook*, April. Washington, DC.

Lawson, A., D. Booth, M. Msuya, S. Wangwe, and T. Williamson. 2005. *Does General Budget Support Work? Evidence from Tanzania.* Overseas Development Institute, London.

Maliyamkono, T. L., and H. Mason. 2006. *The Promise.* Dar es Salaam: TEMA Publishers.

Mbelle, A. V. Y., L. Rutasitra, B. Makenda, R. Lokina, A. Naho, and Y. Aikaeli. 2010. "Analytical Study on the Drivers of Growth and Implications for Growth Strategy for Mainland Tanzania," University of Dar es Salaam, Dar es Salaam.

Mtei, Edwin. 2009. *From Goatherd to Governor.* Dar es Salaam: Mkuki na Nyota Publishers.

Mwase, Nkunde, and Benno Ndulu. 2008. "Tanzania: Explaining Four Decades of Episodic Growth." In *The Political Economy of Economic growth in Africa 1960–2000, vol 2., Country Case Studies,* ed. Ndulu, B, S. O'Connell, J. P. Azam, R. Bates, A. Fosu, J. Gunning, and D. Njinkeu. Cambridge: Cambridge University Press.

National Audit Office. 2010. *A Performance Audit Report on Health Care Centres Efficiency in Tanzania.* www.nao.go.tz

Nord, Roger, Yuri Sobolev, David Dunn, Alejandro Hajdenberg, Niko Hobdari, Samar Maziad, and Stephane Roudet. 2009. *Tanzania: The Story of an African Transition.* International Monetary Fund, Washington, DC.

Ostry, J. D., A. Prati, and A. Spilimbergo. 2009. *Structural Reforms and Economic Performance in Advanced and Developing Countries.* IMF Occasional Paper 268, Washington, DC.

Prati, Alessandro, Massimiliano Onorato, and Chris Papageorgiou. 2010. "Which Reforms Work and under What Institutional Environment? Evidence from a New Dataset on Structural Reforms." International Monetary Fund, Washington, DC.

Pritchett, Lant. 2000. "Understanding Patterns of Economic Growth: Searching for Hills among Plateaus, Mountains, and Plains." *World Bank Economic Review* 14 (2): 221–50.

Redifer, Laure. 2010. "New Financing Sources for Africa's Infrastructure Deficit." *IMF Survey* July 21, Washington, DC.

Selassie, Abebe Aemro. 2008. "Beyond Macroeconomic Stability: The Quest for Industrialization in Uganda." IMF Working Paper 08/231, International Monetary Fund, Washington, DC.

Ter-Minassian, Teresa, Richard Hughes, and Alejandro Hajdenberg. 2008. "Creating Sustainable Fiscal Space for Infrastructure: The Case of Tanzania." IMF Working Paper 08/256, International Monetary Fund, Washington, DC.

United Republic of Tanzania. 2009a. "Millennium Development Goals Report, Mid-Way Evaluation: 2000–2008." www.tzdpg.or.tz/external/mkukuta-mkuza-review/studies-tors-cvs.html.

———. 2009b. *MKUKUTA Annual Implementation Report 2008/2009, Success in the Midst of Turbulence.* Dar es Salaam.

———. 2010. *Public Expenditure Tracking Survey for Primary and Secondary Education in Mainland Tanzania.* Dar es Salaam.

World Bank. Various years. *World Development Indicators.* Washington, DC: World Bank.

———. 2005. *Agriculture and Achieving the Millennium Development Goals.* Report 32729-GLB, Agriculture and Rural Development Department, Washington, DC.

———. 2007. *Tanzania: Sustaining and Sharing Economic Growth.* Country Economic Memorandum, Washington, DC.

———. 2009. *Doing Business 2010, Tanzania.* Washington, DC: World Bank.

Building on Growth in Uganda

Sarah Ssewanyana, John Mary Matovu, and Evarist Twimukye

Over the past two decades, Uganda has seen a remarkable turnaround in economic performance, with growth averaging about 7.7 percent a year over the 1997–2007 period. Equally impressive has been the sharp decline in poverty rates, which fell about 15 percentage points over this period. Improved macroeconomic management and economic reforms contributed to the country's strong growth performance.

Although growth and poverty reduction have been impressive, Uganda has experienced worsening income distribution; a decline in the relative importance of agriculture to overall gross domestic product (GDP); a growing youth population, with increasing unemployment; and a low rate of urbanization. There has also been limited structural transformation of the economy, a reflection that growth has come largely from the services sector, which employs the highly skilled, rather than from the agricultural sector, which still employs 70 percent of the population. Notwithstanding the considerable progress in diversifying its export base away from coffee, Uganda still remains a primary commodity exporter, with limited value addition to its major exports.

GROWTH EXPERIENCE

Uganda achieved impressive economic growth over the past two decades, with positive per capita GDP growth since 1987 and stronger growth than the continent as a whole (figure 2.1 and table 2.1). Despite this improvement,

Uganda's per capita GDP at purchasing power parity remains about half that of Sub-Saharan African as a whole.

During the decade following the end of political instability and civil war in 1986, Uganda's economy grew at an average rate of 7.7 percent a year. (Economic growth declined by 1.4 percentage points between 2008/09 and 2009/10.) Initially, economic growth was driven by postwar recovery and reconstruction. Since the early 1990s it has been driven by comprehensive macroeconomic and structural reforms. Investment growth also remained strong, with private investment rising by an estimated 17 percent and public investment rising 15 percent (table 2.2). Private investment growth was led by construction (AfDB 2009).

Economic growth has been export led, with the share of exports in GDP rising over the past two decades. The expanding regional market for Uganda's food and manufactured products has boosted exports during the past five years, a reflection of the dividend enjoyed by Uganda's neighbors, whose demand for Ugandan goods has increased.

Growth has been driven by the services sector, which has accounted for almost half of GDP since 2001/02 (table 2.3). Before the global financial crisis, the key subsectors driving growth in the services sector included financial services, transport and communications, public administration, and defense (see annex table 2.A1). The agricultural sector grew more slowly than the other sectors between 2001/02 and 2009/10, accounting for about 24 percent of annual GDP on average over the period (table 2.3).

Figure 2.1   Annual GDP Growth in Uganda, 1983–2007

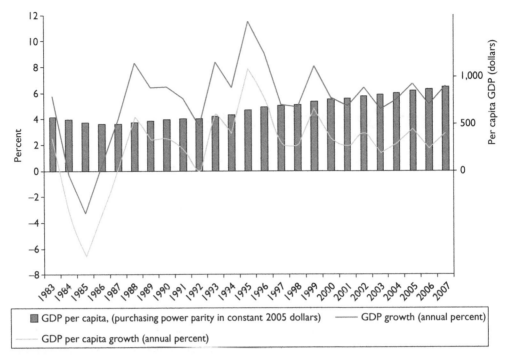

Source: World Bank 2009.

Table 2.1   Annual GDP Growth in Selected Countries in Sub-Saharan Africa, 1997–2009

Year	Ghana	Kenya	Mauritius	Mozambique	South Africa	Tanzania	Tunisia	Uganda	Sub-Saharan Africa
1997	4.20	0.47	5.69	10.24	2.65	3.53	5.44	5.10	3.58
	(1.59)	(−2.23)	(4.37)	(7.26)	(0.32)	(0.84)	(4.00)	(1.94)	(0.87)
1998	4.70	3.29	6.07	10.78	0.52	3.71	4.78	4.91	2.42
	(2.15)	(0.59)	(4.96)	(7.96)	(−1.82)	(1.12)	(3.46)	(1.77)	(−0.24)
1999	4.40	2.31	2.61	8.12	2.36	3.53	6.05	8.05	2.46
	(1.90)	(−0.33)	(1.31)	(5.39)	(−0.08)	(0.97)	(4.68)	(11.11)	(−0.19)
2000	3.70	0.60	9.03	1.09	4.15	5.10	4.70	3.14	3.53
	(1.24)	(−1.98)	(7.96)	(−1.52)	(1.61)	(2.46)	(3.52)	(−0.01)	(0.87)
2001	4.00	3.78	2.57	11.9	2.74	6.24	4.92	5.18	3.62
	(1.56)	(1.11)	(1.46)	(8.93)	(0.65)	(3.53)	(3.73)	(1.92)	(1.00)
2002	4.50	0.55	2.11	8.82	3.67	7.24	1.65	8.73	3.45
	(2.07)	(−2.03)	(1.24)	(5.92)	(2.25)	(4.46)	(0.53)	(5.31)	(0.87)
2003	5.20	2.93	3.66	6.02	2.95	5.67	5.56	6.47	4.23
	(2.79)	(0.29)	(2.59)	(3.21)	(1.65)	(2.84)	(4.94)	(3.09)	(1.67)
2004	5.60	5.10	5.75	7.88	4.55	6.73	6.04	6.81	6.19
	(3.23)	(2.40)	(4.84)	(5.08)	(3.33)	(3.88)	(5.05)	(3.39)	(3.60)
2005	5.90	5.91	1.24	8.39	5.28	7.37	3.98	6.33	5.72
	(3.58)	(3.17)	(0.44)	(5.66)	(4.09)	(4.46)	(2.98)	(2.92)	(3.15)
2006	6.40	6.32	3.95	8.68	5.60	6.74	5.66	10.78	6.17
	(4.13)	(3.56)	(3.14)	(6.04)	(4.43)	(3.79)	(4.63)	(7.23)	(3.59)
2007	6.46	7.01	5.52	7.28	5.49	7.15	6.33	8.41	6.60
	(4.24)	(4.22)	(4.87)	(4.75)	(4.34)	(4.15)	(5.32)	(4.92)	(4.02)
2008	8.43	1.55	5.09	6.74	3.68	7.44	4.64	8.71	5.26
	(6.20)	(−1.09)	(4.41)	(4.29)	(2.54)	(4.39)	(3.60)	(5.21)	(2.72)
2009	4.66	2.59	2.14	6.33	−1.78	5.50	3.13	7.06	1.65
	(2.52)	(−0.08)	(1.62)	(3.96)	(−2.83)	(2.48)	(2.10)	(3.62)	(−0.80)

Source: World Bank 2010.
Note: Figures in parentheses are per capita growth rates.

CHAPTER 2: BUILDING ON GROWTH IN UGANDA

Table 2.2 Components of GDP Growth in Uganda, 2001–09
(percent, in 2002 prices)

Component	2001	2002	2003	2004	2005	2006	2007	2008	2009
Consumption									
Private	6.3	6.1	2.8	3.4	8.1	12.3	2.9	8.2	11.5
Public	2.9	5.2	5.2	3.7	4.5	3.7	−1.5	1.7	−1.9
Investment									
Private	10	14.1	16.1	14.6	23.5	10.3	14.6	12.0	1.1
Public	0.3	−8.1	2.3	11.6	9.3	13.5	19.6	−15.3	28.8
Trade									
Exports	17.2	7	6.6	20.9	21.5	−6.3	53.8	45.0	−12.0
Imports	12.8	7.5	6.2	9.6	16.8	17.2	15.7	17.6	4.6

Source: Uganda Bureau of Statistics 2010.

Table 2.3 Sectoral Contributions to GDP and Growth Rates in Uganda, 2001/02–2008/09
(percent, in 2002 prices)

Item	2001/02	2002/03	2003/04	2004/05	2005/06	2006/07	2007/08	2008/09	2009/10
Sectoral contributions to GDP (in current prices)									
Agriculture	23.1	22.1	21.1	20.2	24.1	22.3	21.4	23.1	23.9
Industry	22.0	22.6	22.8	24.0	22.8	25.1	25.8	24.7	24.6
Services	48.3	48.6	49.1	49.0	47.2	47.0	46.9	46.4	45.4
Growth rate									
Total GDP	8.5	6.5	6.8	6.3	10.8	8.4	8.7	7.2	5.8
Per capita GDP	5.1	3.1	3.4	3.0	7.3	5.0	5.3	3.8	2.4
Agriculture	7.1	2.1	1.6	2.0	0.5	0.1	1.3	2.5	2.1
Industry	7.4	9.5	8	11.6	14.7	9.6	8.8	5.8	8.9
Services	11.0	7.4	7.9	6.2	12.2	8.0	9.7	8.8	5.8

Source: Uganda Bureau of Statistics 2010.

The contribution of industry to GDP—which ranged from 22.0 to 24.6 percent over the period—is well below the 35 percent benchmark for countries graduating from low- to middle-income status (Bevan and others 2003). Growth in the sector fell from 9.1 percent in 2007/08 to 5.8 percent in 2008/09, largely as a result of the global economic crisis, which reduced the remittances that had fueled a construction boom in Uganda. The decline caused the share of the construction subsector in GDP to fall from 10.8 percent in 2007/08 to 3.7 percent in 2008/09 (see annex table 2.A1). The slowdown was also a result of the increase in the costs of imported inputs arising from the depreciation of the Ugandan shilling. The contribution of the manufacturing subsector to overall GDP was well below that of the construction subsector.

Structural transformation of the economy

Uganda's economy has been growing rapidly, but growth has failed to create enough jobs for the ever-increasing labor force. Evidence from the Uganda National Household Surveys shows that as a result of impressive economic growth during the 1990s, the population experienced important broad-based welfare gains in terms of consumption increases. The gains were not equally distributed across social groups and spatially. Overall, the pattern of growth has been skewed, with growth taking place in subsectors such as telecommunications and finance, which employ highly skilled people, not the poor.

The mismatch between the contribution of the different sectors to GDP and the proportion of the population that derives its livelihood from the sectors has serious implications for the level of unemployment and underemployment in Uganda. Although the contribution of agriculture to overall GDP has remained lower than that of services or industry, its share in employment remains high. Services, which account for almost half of GDP, employ only about 24 percent of the population. Employment in industry, which accounts for more than a quarter of GDP, is also very minimal, at about 8 percent of the population (table 2.4).

Agricultural performance

Because more than two-thirds of Ugandans work in agriculture, development of the Ugandan economy is closely linked to transformation of the agricultural sector. Agriculture in Uganda is still characterized by low productivity, mainly as a result of poor inputs, undeveloped value chains, and low public and private investment in the sector. The lack of sustained agricultural growth and the slow process of diversification in agriculture pose serious threats to poverty reduction efforts.

The reforms of the early 1990s, especially the dismantling of the agricultural public enterprises and liberalization of the economy, led to greater participation of the private sector in marketing agricultural produce. The agricultural reforms implemented since the mid-1990s, however, have largely benefited only a small fraction of farmers, particularly richer and better-educated farmers, who have been able to diversify their agricultural production. Once these efficiency gains were exploited, other innovations were needed to maintain growth in the sector (Okidi and others 2007).

Only 50 percent of agricultural production in Uganda is sold on markets. With the exception of coffee farmers and farmers engaged in other tradables or niche markets (vanilla, fruit, tomatoes), most smallholders in Uganda are still engaged in subsistence farming. For the most part, Ugandan farmers remain poor and out of mainstream economic activity.

Export performance

Exports as a share of GDP have increased over time in Uganda (see figure 2.2). Before the liberalization of the economy and the emphasis on import substitution and export diversification in the 1990s, Uganda depended mainly on coffee as its main export. This dependence on a single commodity was a major constraint to terms-of-trade growth, especially when world coffee prices dropped, as they did in the mid-1990s.

To insulate the economy from adverse terms of trade and instability in export earnings associated with commodity concentration, the government adopted a policy shift in 1987 that sought to diversify the exports base to include nontraditional (mainly agricultural) exports. Since

then, Uganda has diversified its exports base to include larger shares of flowers, fishing, and other agricultural exports (see annex table 2.A2). Revenue from noncoffee exports increased by more than sixfold between 1997/98 and 2008/09, rising from $189.6 million to $1,199.6 million (figure 2.3).

Trade liberalization was designed to reverse and even eliminate the trade deficit by increasing export earnings and curtailing the demand for imports. Incentives for export-oriented trade and market-determined exchange rate policies were expected to encourage both traditional and nontraditional exports. Nevertheless, merchandise exports continued to decline throughout the liberalization period (1987–92), partly because the manufacturing sector had shrunk as a result of the economic mismanagement of

Figure 2.2   Exports as Percentage of GDP in Uganda, 1998/99–2008/09

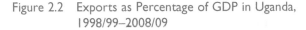
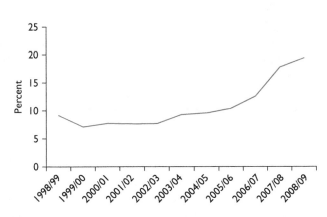

Source: Bank of Uganda 2009.

Figure 2.3   Coffee, Noncoffee, and Total Exports from Uganda, 1997/98–2008/09

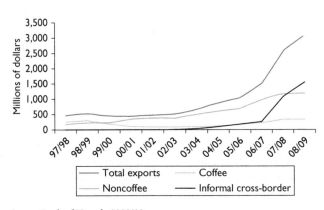

Source: Bank of Uganda 2008/09.

Table 2.4	Distribution of Employment in Uganda, by Sector and Gender, 2003 (*percent*)		
Sector	**Women**	**Men**	**Total**
Agriculture	76	62	69
Industry	5	10	8
Services	19	28	24

Source: World Bank 2009.

earlier regimes. Since then, the value of exports has improved markedly.

Alongside the increase in noncoffee exports has been a huge increase in the importance of informal cross-border trade, which rose from 1.3 percent of total exports in 2002/03 to 50.2 percent by 2008/09—a significant development in the wake of the global financial crisis, which was beginning to affect traditional exports, especially coffee. Including informal cross-border trade, the share of industrial products in total exports increased from 43.8 percent in 2007/08 to 54.9 percent in 2008/09 (figure 2.4). As new emerging export markets within the region stabilize, it will be difficult for Uganda to sustain the recent rate of industrial product export growth.

Most primary commodities earn a fraction of what they would earn if they had been processed. Consequently, although the shilling depreciated against the U.S dollar in real terms (from U Sh 558 per dollar in 1987 to U Sh 2,000 in 2008), implying higher domestic producer prices in Uganda shillings, the trade deficit ballooned, from $446.7 million in 1997/98 to $936.3 million in 2008/09. The increase in the trade deficit reflected the low returns from exports caused by the deteriorating terms of trade and the large increase in the value of imports caused by the depreciation of the shilling. The trade deficit as a share of GDP has declined since 2005/06 (figure 2.5).

Uganda will potentially benefit from the expanded East African Common Market, estimated at 120 million people, which allows unimpeded movement of labor, capital, and other services across borders within Burundi, Kenya, Rwanda, Tanzania, and Uganda. However, trade with the largest economies in the union (Kenya and Tanzania) has been one sided, with limited exports from Uganda to the two countries. Uganda's trade has been boosted mainly by

Figure 2.4 Industrial Products as Percentage of Total Exports in Uganda, 1997/98–2008/09

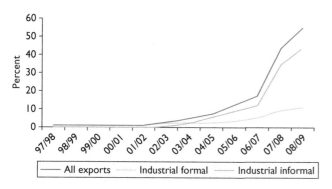

Source: Bank of Uganda 2008/09.

Figure 2.5 Trade Deficit as Percentage of GDP in Uganda, 1998/99–2008/09

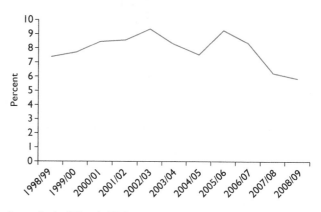

Source: Bank of Uganda 2009.

trading with postconflict economies in the region, including Southern Sudan, the Democratic Republic of Congo, and Rwanda. As these countries stabilize, the trade deficit of Uganda with its major East African Community partners will have to be addressed by increasing exports to Kenya and Tanzania.

Impact of growth on poverty reduction and other millennium development goals

Uganda is one of the few Sub-Saharan African countries to achieve the first MDG of halving extreme poverty before 2015 (annex table 2.A3). The proportion of the population living below the absolute poverty line declined from 56.4 percent in 1992/93 to 31.1 percent in 2005/06 and to 24.5 percent in 2009/10 (table 2.5).[1] Income poverty remains a key development challenge, however, with the absolute number of poor people declining only marginally, from 9.8 million in 1992 to 8.4 million in 2005/06 and to 7.5 million in 2009/10, as a result of a population growth rate of 3.2 percent a year. The majority of the poor live in rural areas, in particular in northern Uganda (Ssewanyana and Okidi 2007; Uganda Bureau of Statistics 2010).

The regional ranking of other poverty measures in Uganda is identical to that of the headcount index, although there are growing differences in the poverty gap between northern Uganda and the rest of the country. Overall, the poverty gap dropped faster than the poverty headcount, implying rising mean consumption by Uganda's poor. The recovery in the agricultural sector, especially the food crop subsector; return to peace in northern Uganda and some parts of the eastern region; and resettlement of the

Table 2.5 Poverty Headcount and Income Inequality Estimates for Uganda, 1992/93–2005/06

Region	Poverty headcount				Gini coefficient			
	1992/93	2002/03	2005/06	2009/10	1992/93	2002/03	2005/06	2009/10
National	56.4	38.8	31.1	24.5	0.365	0.428	0.408	0.426
Rural	60.3	42.7	34.2	27.2	0.328	0.363	0.363	0.375
Urban	28.8	14.4	13.7	9.1	0.396	0.483	0.432	0.447
Central	45.6	22.3	16.4	10.7	0.395	0.460	0.417	0.451
East	58.8	46.0	35.9	24.3	0.327	0.365	0.354	0.319
North	73.5	63.0	60.7	46.2	0.345	0.350	0.331	0.367
West	52.7	32.9	20.5	21.8	0.319	0.359	0.342	0.375

Source: Ssewanyana and Okidi 2007; Uganda Bureau of Statistics 2010.
Note: The poverty headcount is the percentage of people estimated to be living in households with real private consumption per adult equivalent below the poverty line for their region.

internally displaced persons partly accounted for the decline in poverty between 2005/06 and 2009/10.

Although absolute income poverty fell during the past two decades, the distribution of income worsened. Income inequality as measured by the Gini coefficient increased from 0.365 in 1992/93 to 0.408 in 2005/06. Growing income disparities are evident between 2005/06 and 2009/10, when the Gini coefficient reached 0.426. Growth rates for consumption grew more rapidly among the richer quintiles, increasing inequality (Ssewanyana and Okidi 2007; Uganda Bureau of Statistics 2010). Income inequality between rural and urban areas and between regions widened between 2005/06 and 2009/10.

Increasing inequality has slowed the rate of poverty reduction in Uganda. For every 1 percent decrease in growth, the percentage of people living below the poverty line will increase by 2 percent, holding income distribution constant (Ssewanyana 2009). This means that the economy has to grow by at least 7 percent and household consumption has to rise at least 4 percent if Uganda is to avoid reversals in its poverty reduction efforts.

Uganda is likely to attain MDG 3 (promoting gender equality and empowering women), MDG 6 (combating HIV/AIDS), MDG 7 (ensuring environmental sustainability), and MDG 8 (developing a global partnership for development). The stagnation in net primary school enrollment since 2003 at about 85 percent is a clear indication that intensified efforts are required if Uganda is to meet MDG 2, however, and attainment of MDG 4 (reducing child mortality) and MDG 5 (improving maternal health) is unlikely even with improved policies, institutions, and funding (UNDP 2010).

REFORMS DRIVING GROWTH

The past two decades have seen tremendous economic transformation in Uganda, fueled mainly by good policies involving careful sequencing and determined implementation. The World Bank has referred to Uganda's efforts as "the most far-reaching stabilization and structural reform program in Africa, and one of the most comprehensive reform efforts in the world" (World Bank 2007, 4).

The first reform was the Economic Recovery Program, introduced in 1987, with support from the World Bank and International Monetary Fund (IMF), which focused on price stabilization and liberalization. Policies under this program included currency reform, devaluation, liberalization of domestic prices, and conversion to a floating exchange rate regime (in 1993).

The next set of reforms involved the adoption of the structural adjustment program that was meant to free up markets and create price incentives, stimulate private investment, and encourage competition. Reforms under this program included the abolition of marketing boards, the privatization or abolition of parastatals, and the establishment of the Uganda Investment Authority. This period was characterized by sustained macroeconomic stabilization, adjustment, and structural reform efforts that affected almost all sectors of the economy. Policies mainly involved the macroeconomic stabilization process, price liberalization, financial sector liberalization, public enterprises reform, and civil service reform. In addition to changing and stabilizing the structure of the economy, reorientation of pricing and marketing policies, restarting of economic growth, and strengthening the institutional framework constituted the major cornerstones of the program. To achieve these ends, the Economic Recovery Program focused on ensuring macroeconomic stability; liberalizing the foreign exchange system, trade, prices, and marketing systems; improving the incentive structure and business climate to promote savings mobilization and investment; and rehabilitating the economic, social, and institutional infrastructure.

With the economy back on its footing, in 1997 the government introduced the Poverty Eradication Action Plan (PEAP), a multisectoral program aimed at reducing poverty. Policies in this program included the Plan for the Modernization of Agriculture (PMA), which sought to address agricultural constraints to production and to turn agriculture commercial. The plan has not been as successful as envisaged, mainly because it was too broad and in some cases ambiguous, with several programs having too many pillars when the focus should have been on enhancing agriculture productivity. The National Agricultural Advisory Services, the flagship agricultural productivity enhancement program within PMA, was beset by inefficiencies and other implementation problems that limited its impact on agriculture.[2]

Other sectoral reforms that contributed to the liberalization and stabilization of the economy included the Medium-Term Competitive Strategy for the Private Sector, the Strategic Export Program, and the Strategic Export Intervention Program. These policies were accompanied by important institutional reforms, such as decentralization efforts, the abolition of state-owned marketing boards, and the restructuring of the public administration.

The 1990s saw a substantial reversal in the decline of the economy that had characterized the 1970s and early 1980s, suggesting that reform worked. Confidence in the economy was restored, spurring substantial inflows of aid and foreign direct investment and a reversal of capital flight (figure 2.6). Most economic indicators rebounded, and by 1996 the economy had recovered to its nominal 1971 dollar per capita GDP (World Bank 2007).

To sustain rapid economic growth, the government needed to reorient expenditures toward social sectors and increase spending on infrastructure. Social policy spending was aimed at spurring growth as well as the level of productivity of assets of poor people. Policies undertaken under the framework of the PEAP included universal primary and secondary education, intended both to raise education indicators and to remove the financial burden of education from parents as a means of reducing poverty. Efforts were also made to increase health coverage, by constructing health centers in all subcounties and parishes.

Examination of the composition of the public budget for most of the 1990s and 2000s reveals that total government expenditure steadily increased, from about 18.6 percent of GDP in 1992/93 to about 32.0 percent in 2008/09. Evidence suggests that increased funding to social services has benefited the poor, especially in rural areas (Kappel, Lay, and Steiner 2005).

With reasonable progress in the social sectors, in the late 2000s the government began addressing the infrastructural constraints that have dogged the country since independence. Since 2007/08 substantial resources have been committed to the rehabilitation and construction of roads and hydroelectric dams. The government has prioritized the building of roads in the medium and long term, with more than 20 trunk roads planned or in the process of being built in the next 20 years (MFPED 2009). The share of total central government budget allocated to works and transport rose from 10.0 percent in 2005/06 to 18.4 percent in 2009/10, and the share of the budget allocated to energy and mineral development rose from 3.5 to 10.3 percent. Taken together, allocations for works, transport, and energy represented almost a third of the 2009/10 budget—a substantial figure given Uganda's historically low investments in infrastructure. Although issues about absorption capacity and quality of infrastructure remain, there is a perception that the government's tightened focus on improving infrastructure will help reduce Uganda's perennial infrastructural shortages, giving the economy a major boost.

CHALLENGES TO DEVELOPMENT

Policy makers need to address a variety of challenges in reducing poverty and spurring growth. In addition to the challenges identified in this section, they need to ensure that growth is inclusive. Failure to achieve equity is likely to exacerbate unemployment and lead to social unrest.

Slow progress in reducing poverty and slowing population growth

Although Uganda has already achieved MDG 1 (halving extreme poverty), poverty remains high, especially in the

Figure 2.6   Official Development Aid as Percentage of GDP in Uganda, 1998/99–2008/09

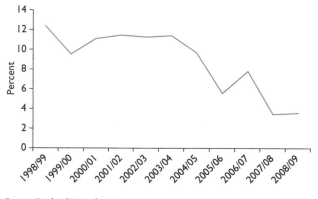

Source: Bank of Uganda 2009.

northern region. Poverty reduction interventions, especially the Peace and Reconciliation Development Plan (PRDP), in this part of the country need to be restructured to ensure that they reach and benefit vulnerable groups.

Even at the average GDP growth rate of 6.9 percent attained during the 1990s, it would take Uganda about 20 years to double average per capita income. With population growth rate at 3.2 percent a year, one of the highest population growth rates in the world, it is going to be very difficult to reduce poverty (World Bank 2007).

Uganda's 3.2 percent annual population growth thwarts development, especially in social services provision and social outcomes. Unless efforts at reducing the high population growth rates are intensified, many of the MDGs will be difficult to achieve.

Inadequate transformation of the agriculture sector

Land reform is a critical factor that will ensure sustainable agricultural productivity and facilitate commerce and agriculture. Such reform would involve the government buying out landlords in order to consolidate the small plots on which many rural farmers depend to enable commercial agriculture. The government could also try to draw the rural population to urban centers through more planned urban development.

Other factors explaining low agricultural productivity include poor inputs, undeveloped value chains, and low public and private investment in the sector. The issue of low productivity in agriculture will need to be addressed by, for instance, accelerating the creation of on-farm and off-farm processing zones to add value to agricultural commodities, financing activities along the entire value chain as opposed to funding on-farm activities only, and land reforms that will allow commercial agricultural production as articulated in the National Development Plan (Republic of Uganda 2010).

Weak infrastructure

Uganda's infrastructure is among the worst in the world (Republic of Uganda 2010; World Bank 2007). The National Development Plan identifies weak infrastructure as one of the key binding constraints in Uganda. Roads, power and railways are all below those of Uganda's neighbors, with grave implications for the economy.[3] The National Development Plan identifies the most challenging infrastructural impediments as power, transport, and access to and the high cost of finance, in that order. Efforts to address infrastructure constraints by increasing sector funding represent a move in the right direction and should be followed by prudent use of the resources by responsible agencies to avoid leakages, which have often derailed service delivery. Regional infrastructure also remains a key challenge, especially for boosting regional trade.

Lack of sufficient private sector development

Private sector growth has been impressive since liberalization, but Uganda's economy remains dominated by small firms that usually employ fewer than five people, making it difficult to absorb the growing number of graduates and exacerbating the youth unemployment problem. In addition, although the private sector has played a significant role in areas such as education and health services, it has not been prominent in other sectors that require significant investments, such as energy, and even in sectors in which the private sector is active, the impact of its activities on employment creation has been limited. Enlarging the role of the private sector calls for more active participation of the government under private-public partnership arrangements.

Government development programs and successive generations of Country Strategy Papers have emphasized the development of the private sector as a major goal for the country. But progress has been slow in this area, partly because of weak human and institutional capacity, which limits private sector participation in execution of contracted or self-initiated projects. Further limiting the growth of the private sector is the poor state of the financial sector, which limits access to credit. Equity finance is also lacking, and small businesses have limited access to commercial banking facilities. It is important that the government expedites the recapitalization of the Uganda Development Corporation and the Uganda Development Bank to make private sector access to credit easier.

Narrow export base and terms-of-trade vulnerability

Despite the diversification of its export base, Uganda remains heavily dependent on primary commodities. Diversification of the export base is of paramount importance. The factors that continue to constrain export diversification include the primary and low-value-added nature of Uganda's exports, poor product quality, and poor regulation standards, which inhibit competition in marketing and export of primary commodities.

Low tax revenue

Tax revenue in Uganda is low, the result mainly of untaxed sectors, especially informal businesses and some agricultural activities, and tax evasion (Sennoga, Matovu, and Twimukye 2009). The lack of revenue has translated into an unending dependence on foreign aid, which accounted for about 32 percent of the budget in 2008/09. In 2007/2008 tax revenue amounted to about 12 percent of GDP. This figure is low relative to Uganda's neighbors (tax revenue was about 17 percent of GDP in Tanzania and about 27 percent of GDP in Kenya for the same period). Lack of adequate tax revenues constrains government operations and weakens economic management. It also increases government reliance on foreign aid to finance development, making economic management more difficult.

The recent discovery of oil in Uganda could significantly boost the resources mobilized domestically, widening resources available to finance Uganda's development agenda. The government could also try to expand the tax base, by targeting sectors that are currently untaxed, especially the informal sector, and setting up regulation to reduce tax evasion.[4]

Corruption and weak governance

The government has made numerous efforts to strengthen good governance, by allowing civil society organizations to participate more in planning and budgeting and by setting up institutions to strengthen accountability. Such initiatives included the creation, in 2008, of the anticorruption court to handle corruption-related cases and the value-for-money audit unit in the Auditor General's office to check on government spending at all levels. Uganda has also adopted a national anticorruption strategy.

These efforts notwithstanding, the perception remains that corruption is rampant, and the government has come under pressure from several quarters to show more political will to address the problem. Uganda's ranking on the Ibrahim Index of African governance improved from 27th in 2007 to 19th in 2008. But in May 2009, Transparency International ranked Uganda the third most corrupt country in the world. And although there has been considerable progress in tax administration with the formation of the Uganda Revenue Authority in 1991, tax policy and administration remain issues as they relate to revenue mobilization, partly because of corruption within the tax body. In 2010 Transparency International ranked Uganda's revenue authority the second most corrupt tax body in East Africa (Transparency International 2010).

More needs to be done to improve governance in Uganda, where civil society organizations are weak and the legislature often fails to rein in Uganda's powerful executive. Unless governance is strengthened, even increased resources may fail to bring meaningful development to Uganda.

Weak human and institutional capability

Uganda's Five-Year National Development Plan 2010–15 identifies weak human and institutional development as one of the economy's key binding constraints. Most public sector departments are characterized by coordination failures, corruption, endemic malaise, and weak institutional linkages among relevant stakeholders, including the Ministry of Finance Planning and Economic Development, sector line ministries, and the private sector. As a result, budgeting processes are inefficient, and scarce investment resources are not allocated rationally. Problems are particularly acute at the local government level. The central government needs to address these problems as it devolves planning, delivery, and management of basic services to local governments (EPRC 2010). There is a need to increase human and institutional capacity to meet the growing needs of local governments as the scope of their functions broadens.

CONCLUSION

Uganda has experienced relatively strong growth and poverty reduction since the 1990s. The growth period was characterized by sustained macroeconomic stabilization, adjustment, and structural reform efforts, which had a large impact on most sectors. Efforts included price liberalization, financial sector liberalization, public enterprises reform, and reform of the civil service.

Growth has been accompanied by rising inequality and very high unemployment levels, however, especially among youth. Moreover, growth has been registered in sectors (particularly services) whose contribution to employment is limited. More needs to be done to translate impressive performance at the macro level into improvements in the welfare of the majority of Uganda's people, especially the rural poor.

Looking forward, Uganda needs to address several issues in order to enjoy equitable growth. First, policy makers need to increase the pace of transformation of the agricultural sector and strengthen the sector's weak link to industry, where outputs from agriculture can be used as inputs. Given that the sector employs 70 percent of the workforce, doing so would spur equitable growth and reduce high unemployment.

Second, policy makers have to find new ways to mobilize domestic revenues to finance the budget. To address the growing trade deficit, Uganda should continue diversifying its export base into higher-value-added products. Third, policy makers also need to address other key challenges, including weak human and institutional capability, a weak private sector, poor infrastructure, poor governance, and high population growth rates.

ANNEX 2.A

Table 2.A1 GDP in Uganda, by Economic Activity, 2001/02–2008/09
(percent, at constant 2002 prices)

Item	2001/02	2002/03	2003/04	2004/05	2005/06	2006/07	2007/08	2008/09	2009/10
GDP at market prices	8.6	6.6	6.8	6.3	10.8	8.4	9.0	7.2	5.8
Agriculture, forestry, and fishing	7.1	2.1	1.6	2.0	0.5	0.1	1.3	2.5	2.1
Cash crops	12.5	3.2	7.3	−5.5	−10.6	5.4	9.0	5.6	−2.9
Food crops	5.7	2.2	−1.5	−0.2	−0.1	−0.9	2.4	2.6	2.7
Livestock	4.0	3.5	4.7	3.0	1.6	3.0	3.0	3.0	3.0
Forestry	6.8	5.2	3.1	6.5	4.1	2.0	2.8	6.3	2.4
Fishing	13.8	−4.3	9.6	13.5	5.6	−3.0	−11.8	−0.7	2.6
Industry	7.4	9.5	8.0	11.6	14.7	9.6	9.1	5.8	8.9
Mining and quarrying	12.2	12.8	1.7	27.2	6.1	19.4	3.0	4.3	12.8
Manufacturing	6.7	4.4	6.3	9.5	7.3	5.6	7.6	10.0	5.9
Formal	7.7	4.6	8.3	11.8	7.8	4.9	9.2	12.0	6.1
Informal	4.5	4.0	1.7	3.6	6.0	7.7	3.3	4.4	5.5
Electricity supply	−1.7	3.7	7.7	2.1	−6.5	−4.0	5.4	10.6	8.9
Water supply	3.0	3.9	4.2	3.9	2.4	3.5	3.8	5.7	2.7
Construction	10.1	14.6	10.0	14.9	23.2	13.2	10.8	3.7	10.9
Services	11.0	7.4	7.9	6.2	12.2	8.0	10.2	8.8	5.8
Wholesale and retail trade; repairs	7.4	5.1	6.3	7.2	12.3	10.4	14.7	9.7	−0.3
Hotels and restaurants	2.8	8.2	9.5	6.5	8.7	11.3	10.7	4.5	4.5
Transport and communications	17.8	14.9	15.8	9.8	17.1	17.7	21.3	14.3	15.1
Road, rail, and water transport	6.0	5.6	8.9	6.7	12.8	9.5	20.8	12.9	2.8
Air transport and support	0.5	5.8	13.8	19.4	6.9	13.8	17.8	−3.6	−1.2
Posts and telecommunication	76.5	40.4	28.6	11.8	26.2	29.1	22.6	19.8	30.3
Financial services	32.6	13.2	0.0	13.0	31.7	−11.9	17.1	25.4	21.1
Real estate activities	5.4	5.5	5.5	5.5	5.6	5.6	5.6	5.7	5.7
Other business services	11.6	7.6	7.0	9.2	12.5	8.0	10.8	12.4	10.4
Public administration and defense	20.4	3.6	7.7	−5.4	15.8	−6.3	12.1	5.5	3.9
Education	14.2	7.2	9.1	4.4	9.4	10.6	−6.5	4.3	−0.5
Health	18.0	13.7	0.9	5.6	12.9	2.7	−4.8	−3.2	11.0
Other personal services	8.5	8.5	16.1	15.0	14.1	13.4	12.8	12.3	11.8

Source: Bank of Uganda 2009.

Table 2.A2 Composition of Uganda's Exports, 1997/98–2008/09
(percent)

Year	Coffee exports	Noncoffee exports	Informal cross-border exports
1997/98	58.7	41.3	0.0
1998/99	55.9	44.1	0.0
1999/2000	42.0	56.6	1.3
2000/01	24.5	75.5	0.0
2001/02	18.1	81.9	0.0
2002/03	20.8	77.9	1.3
2003/04	17.0	78.4	4.6
2004/05	16.3	71.4	12.3
2005/06	16.6	67.3	16.0
2006/07	15.2	67.4	17.4
2007/08	13.4	45.4	41.2
2008/09	10.9	38.9	50.2

Source: Bank of Uganda.

Table 2.A3 Poverty Headcount, Poverty Gap, Poverty Severity, and Income Inequality Estimates, 1992/93–2005/06

Region	Poverty headcount					Poverty gap					Severity of poverty					Gini coefficient				
	1992/93	2002/03	2005/06	2009/10	1992/93	2002/03	2005/06	2009/10	1992/93	2002/03	2005/06	2009/10	1992/93	2002/03	2005/06	2009/10
National	56.4	38.8	31.1	24.5	20.9	11.9	8.7	6.8	10.3	5.1	3.5	2.8	0.365	0.428	0.408	0.426
Rural	60.3	42.7	34.2	27.2	22.6	13.1	9.7	7.6	11.2	5.7	3.9	3.1	0.328	0.363	0.363	0.375
Urban	28.8	14.4	13.7	9.1	8.7	3.9	3.5	1.8	3.7	1.6	1.4	0.6	0.396	0.483	0.432	0.447
Central	45.6	22.3	16.4	10.7	15.3	5.5	3.6	2.4	7	1.9	1.3	0.8	0.395	0.46	0.417	0.451
East	58.8	46	35.9	24.3	22	14.1	9.1	5.8	10.9	6	3.4	2.1	0.327	0.365	0.354	0.319
North	73.5	63	60.7	46.2	30.3	23.4	20.7	15.5	15.8	11.5	9.2	7.3	0.345	0.35	0.331	0.367
West	52.7	32.9	20.5	21.8	18.7	8.5	5.1	5.4	9.0	3.3	1.8	2.0	0.319	0.359	0.342	0.375

Source: Ssewanyana and Okidi 2007.

Note: The poverty headcount is the percentage of people estimated to be living in households with real private consumption per adult equivalent below the poverty line for their region. The poverty gap is the sum over all individuals of the shortfall of their real private consumption per adult equivalent and the poverty line divided by the poverty line. Severity of poverty is the squared poverty gap (the sum over all individuals of the square of the shortfall of their real private consumption per adult equivalent and the poverty line divided by the poverty line).

MDG/target/indicator	1990	2005/06	2009/10	2007/08 PEAP target	2013/14 PEAP target	2015 MDG target	Target possible at current trend?	Target possible with better policies, institutions, and additional funding?
1. Eradicate extreme hunger and poverty: Halve, between 1990 and 2015, the proportion of people whose income is less than $1 a day								
1.1 Poverty headcount ratio (percent)	56	31.1	24.5	n.a.	28	28	Met	Yes
1.2 Prevalence of child malnutrition (percent of children under five)	23	23	n.a.	n.a.	n.a.	12	No	Yes
2. Achieve universal primary education: Ensure that, by 2015, children everywhere, boys and girls alike, will be able to complete a full course of primary schooling								
2.1 Net primary enrollment ratio (percent of children 6-12)								
Boys	58	84	82.4	90	100	100	Yes	Yes
Girls	48	85	83.2	89	100	100	Yes	Yes
2.2 Primary completion rate (percent of boys and girls)	n.a.	56	n.a.	69	n.a.	100	No	Yes
3. Promote gender equality and empower women: Eliminate gender disparity in primary and secondary education, preferably by 2005, and in all levels of education no later than 2015								
3.1 Ratio of girls to boys in primary education (percent)	83	99	n.a.	100	100	100	Met	Yes
4. Reduce child mortality: Reduce by two-thirds, between 1990 and 2015, the under-five mortality rate								
4.1. Under-five mortality rates (per 1,000)	177	152	n.a.	n.a.	n.a.	53	No	Uncertain
4.2 Infant mortality rate (per 1,000 live births)	98	88	n.a.	68	n.a.	32	No	Uncertain
4.3. Immunization against DPT (percent of all children)	45	83	n.a.	90	n.a.	n.a.	n.a.	
5. Improve maternal health: Reduce by two-thirds, between 1990 and 2015, the under-five mortality rate								
5.1 Maternal mortality ratio (modeled estimate, per 100,000 live births)	n.a.	505	n.a.	354	n.a.	126	No	Uncertain
5.2 Deliveries in health care centers (percent of all deliveries)	n.a.	24	n.a.	50	n.a.	n.a.	Met	Yes
6. Combat HIV/AIDS, malaria and other diseases: Have halted by 2015 and begun to reverse the spread of HIV/AIDS								
6.1 Prevalence of HIV, total (percent of adult population)	20	6.2	n.a.	5	n.a.	<20	Met	Yes
7. Ensure environmental sustainability: Integrate the principles of sustainable development into country policies and programs and reverse the loss of environmental resources								

(continued next page)

Table 2.A4 (continued)

MDG/target/indicator	1990	2005/06	2009/10	2007/08 PEAP target	2013/14 PEAP target	2015 MDG target	Target possible at current trend?	Target possible with better policies, institutions, and additional funding?
7.1 Forest area (percent of total land area)	n.a.	24	n.a.	27	30	>24		
7.2 Access to safe water (percent of population)								
Urban	45	86.8	92.3	100	n.a.	90	Yes	Yes
Rural	45	63.6	69.5	90	n.a.	90	Yes	Yes
7.3 Access to improved sanitation (percent of population)								
Urban	n.a.	65	n.a.	100	n.a.			
Rural	n.a.	55	n.a.	80	n.a.			
7.4 Tilled land (percent of land)	n.a.	13	n.a.	17	25			
8. Develop a global partnership for development								
8.1 Debt service (percent exports of goods and services)		305		238	187		Yes	Yes

Source: 2004 PEAP; Uganda Bureau of Statistics various years.
Note: n.a. is not applicable. PEAP is Poverty Eradication Action Plan.

NOTES

1. Some reversals in the decline occurred during this period: the share of poor people rose from 34 percent in 1999/00 to 38 percent in 2002/03 (Appleton and Ssewanyana 2004).

2. The program targeted relaxation of marketing infrastructure constraints, production and dissemination of technology, removal of financial constraints, improvement of land tenure and policy, formation of farmers organizations, improvement of human resources and information, promotion of on-farm and off-farm storage, and efforts to reduce environmental degradation and mitigate the effects of HIV/AIDS.

3. Electricity coverage stood at 8 percent of the population in 2009, far below coverage in other low-income countries, which stands at 35 percent. At 190 meters per square kilometer, the density of roads in Uganda is much higher than in the average low-income country (where the average is 126 meters per square kilometer), but the roads are of poor quality, with only 4 percent of the road network paved. Only 26 percent of the railway network in Uganda is functional. Access to improved water stands at 51 percent of the population, far below the 64 percent for the average of a low-income country (Republic of Uganda 2010).

4. Taxing the informal sector could be implemented by taxing small establishments based on characteristics such as turnover, profits, and location of business.

BIBLIOGRAPHY

AfDB (African Development Bank). 2009. "Uganda Economic Outlook 2009/10." *Africa Economic Outlook 2009/10.* Tunis.

Appleton, S., and S. Ssewanyana. 2004. "Poverty Estimates from the Uganda National Household Survey of 2002/03." Economic Policy Research Centre, Kampala.

Bank of Uganda. 2009. *Annual Report* 2008/09. Kampala.

Bevan, D., C. Adam, J. Okidi, and F. Muhumuza. 2003. "Economic Growth, Investment and Export Promotion." Paper prepared for Uganda's Poverty Eradication Action Plan Revision, 2002/03.

Collier, P., and R. Reinikka. 2001. "Reconstruction and Liberalization: An Overview." In *Uganda's Recovery, The Role of Farms, Firms and Government,* ed. R. Reinikka and P. Collier, 15–48. Washington, DC: World Bank.

Dijkstra, A. G., and J. K. Van Donge. 2001. "What Does the 'Show Case' Show? Evidence of and Lessons from Adjustment in Uganda." *World Development* 29 (5): 841–63.

EPRC (Economic Policy Research Centre). 2010. *Corruption Trends in Uganda: Using Data Tracking Mechanism.* Kampala.

Kappel, R., J. Lay, and S. Steiner. 2005. "Uganda: No More Pro-poor Growth?" *Development Policy Review* 23 (1): 27–53.

MFPED (Ministry of Finance Planning and Economic Development). 2009. "Budget Speech for Financial Year 2009/2010." Delivered at the Fourth Session of the Eighth Parliament of Uganda, June 11.

Okidi, J. A., S. Ssewanyana, L. Bategeka, and F. Muhumuza. 2007. "Uganda's Experience with Operationalising Pro-Poor Growth, 1992–2003." In *Delivering on the Promise of Pro-Poor Growth: Insights and Lessons from Country Experiences*, ed. T. Besley and L. J. Cord, 169–98. Washington, DC: Palgrave Macmillan and World Bank.

Republic of Uganda. 2010. *National Development Plan 2010/11–2014/15*. Kampala.

Senoga, E., J. M. Matovu, and E. Twimukye. 2009. "Tax Evasion and Widening the Tax Base in Uganda." EPRC Research Series 63, Economic Policy Research Centre, Kampala.

Ssewanyana, S. 2009. "Growth, Inequality, Cash Transfers and Poverty in Uganda." Country Study 19, International Policy Centre for Inclusive Growth, United Nations Development Programme, Brasilia. http://www.ipc-undp.org/pub/IPCCountryStudy19.pdf.

———. 2010. "Combating Chronic Poverty in Uganda: Towards a New Strategy." EPRC Research Series 67, Economic Policy Research Centre, Kampala.

Ssewanyana, S., and J. A. Okidi. 2007. "Poverty Estimates from the Uganda National Household Survey of 2005/06." EPRC Occasional Paper 34, Economic Policy Research Centre, Kampala.

Transparency International. 2010. www.transparency.org

Uganda Bureau of Statistics. 2009. *Statistical Abstract*. Kampala.

———. 2010. *Uganda National Household Survey 2009/10: Socio-Economic Module*, Abridged Report. Kampala.

UNDP. 2010. *Uganda MDG Progress Report*, Kampala.

World Bank. 2007. "Uganda, Moving beyond Recovery: Investment and Behavior Change for Growth." Country Economic Memorandum Volume II: Overview, Report 39221-UG, Africa Region, Poverty Reduction and Economic Management Unit, Washington, DC.

———. 2009. *World Development Indicators. 2009*. Washington, DC.

———. 2010. *World Development Indicators. 2010*. Washington, DC.

CHAPTER 3

Rapid Growth and Economic Transformation in Mozambique, 1993–2009

Antonio M. D. Nucifora and Luiz A. Pereira da Silva

Mozambique's economic growth after 1992 and the poverty alleviation achieved since then constitute an extremely successful development take-off. Average real GDP growth rate soared from 0 percent (1981–1992) to 8.1 percent (1993–2008), making Mozambique the fastest-growing non-oil economy in Sub-Saharan Africa over the period (AfDB 2009) (figure 3.1). As a result, per capita GDP has doubled since 1992 (figure 3.2). The poverty headcount dropped rapidly during the early years of this process, falling from 69 percent in 1996 to 54 percent in 2002.

The political stability brought about by the end of the armed conflict in 1992, a first wave of structural reforms coinciding with responsible macroeconomic policies, and the support of the international donor community have been the bedrock of Mozambique's transformation. They have enabled the country to better face the development challenges that lie ahead—in particular, how to tap into the country's resources (labor and land) and the entrepreneurial drive of its people to promote strong, sustainable, and inclusive economic growth. Large mineral resources and the recent growth in extraction activities is allowing Mozambique to expand further its development strategy. On the one hand this new revenue source can allow the country to become less dependent on foreign aid and define with more independence new elements of its development agenda. On the other, it raises a number of textbook challenges such as how to trigger externalities (e.g., job creation) in other sectors and how to effectively employ these revenues, while improving governance and accountability.

This chapter provides a brief overview of Mozambique's profound economic transformation and highlights the major drivers of change and the challenges ahead. It does not discuss the macroeconomic policies and performance that underpinned the economic transformation over the past two decades (for a detailed discussion of macroeconomic and stabilization issues in Mozambique, see Clement and Peiris 2008).

GROWTH DRIVERS AND ECONOMIC TRANSFORMATION

Sound macroeconomic environment allowed donors to contribute substantial amounts of aid to Mozambique, averaging about 14 percent of GDP a year since 1993 (figure 3.3). That aid inflows have remained fairly constant as a percentage of GDP over the period, during a period when the economy grew at an average annual rate of more than 8 percent, reflects the rapid growth in aid inflows in U.S. dollar terms. These large inflows financed investments in education and health, as reflected in the rapid improvements in human development indicators (table 3.1).[1] They also financed substantial investments in rebuilding the country's roads, ports, and railways, which had been shattered by 16 years of war.

Figure 3.1   Real GDP Growth in Mozambique and Sub-Saharan Africa, 1981–2005

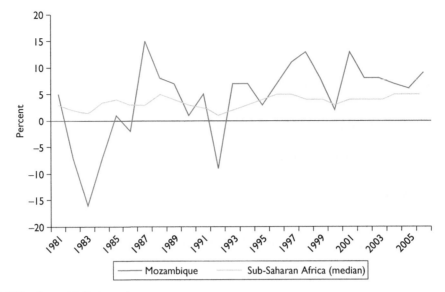

Source: World Bank *World Development Indicators* various years.

Figure 3.2   Per Capita GDP in Mozambique and Sub-Saharan Africa, 1980–2006

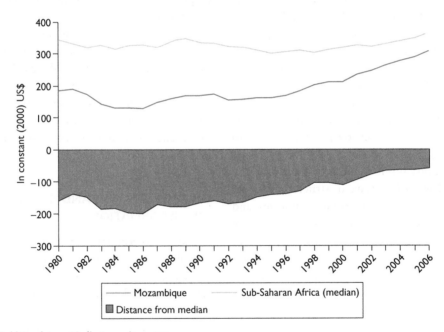

Source: World Bank *World Development Indicators* various years.

Good macroeconomic management also attracted substantial foreign direct investment (FDI). FDI inflows increased from an average of 1.5 percent of GDP in 1993–98 to an average of 5.2 percent of GDP in 1999–2010 (figure 3.4). In 2009 and 2010 FDI reached an estimated $900 million, about 9 percent of GDP. A large part of these

inflows has funded large investment projects in the mining sector, underpinning recent export performance in Mozambique.

From a supply-side perspective, capital accumulation, higher quality–adjusted labor input, and positive aggregate productivity performance were important determinants of

Figure 3.3   Gross Annual Aid Inflows to Mozambique, 1998–2010

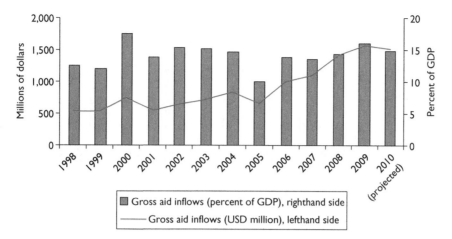

Gross aid inflows (percent of GDP), righthand side
——— Gross aid inflows (USD million), lefthand side

Source: Bank of Mozambique, IMF, and World Bank.

Table 3.1   Selected Social Indicators for Mozambique, 1990–2008

| Indicator | Latest single year | | |
	1990–1996	2000–03	2006–08
Primary school enrollment (net %)	43.000	56.000	96.000
Primary school enrollment (gross %)	61.000	84.000	105.000
Ratio of girls to boys in primary and secondary education (%)	72.000	75.000	85.000
Under-5 mortality rate (per 1,000 live births)	212.000	178.000	138.000
Infant mortality rate (per 1,000 live births)	145.000	122.000	93.000
Life expectancy at birth (years)	27.000	42.000	42.000
Physicians per 1,000 people	0.012	0.024	0.030
Inmunization, DPT (% of children under 12 months)	60.000	72.000	72.000
Inmunization, measles (% of children under 12 months)	58.000	77.000	77.000
Access to improved water sources (% of population)	39.000	42.000	48.000
Access to sanitation facilities (% of population)	22.000	27.000	31.000

Source: World Bank staff, based on data from Instituto National de Estatistica.
Note: Latest single year means the latest year for which data are available in a given period.

growth in Mozambique. Growth accounting exercises indicate that physical investments partly associated with mega-projects and significant improvements in education led to growth dynamics heavily influenced by the accumulation of human (quality-adjusted) and physical capital between 1993 and 2008. Figure 3.5 shows the average capital contribution to growth strengthening from 1999 onward, a result consistent with the timing of mega-projects. Aggregate productivity growth (total factor productivity)—measured as the residual of output growth after labor and capital contri-

butions are subtracted—was also important. Figure 3.6 suggests roughly balanced growth of inputs and productivity.[2] Productivity increases contributed about a third to overall growth between 1993 and 2008. These results are broadly consistent with those of Jones (2006) and Vitek (2010).[3] Jones presents evidence suggesting a positive contribution (crowding in) of public capital accumulation in the aftermath of the civil war, which opened the door for private investment to play an increasingly important role in Mozambique's growth.

Figure 3.4   Foreign Direct Investment in Mozambique, 1993–2010

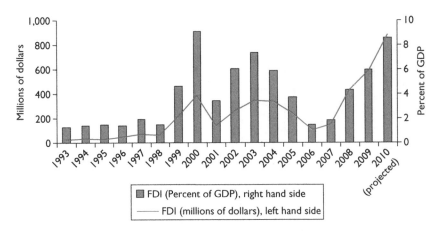

Source: Bank of Mozambique.

Figure 3.5   Decomposition of Growth in Mozambique by Factors, 1993–2008

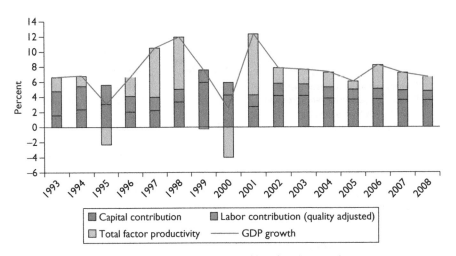

Source: World Bank staff calculations based on *World Development Indicators* (World Bank various years).

Figure 3.6   Average Factor Contributions to Growth in Mozambique, 1993–2008

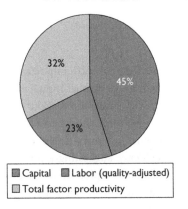

Source: World Bank staff calculations based on *World Development Indicators* (World Bank various years).

A level change in aggregate investment from mega projects triggered strong export and import activity from 1999 onward, with direct impact on aggregate demand. The expenditure components of output (figure 3.7) indicate that GDP and consumption have been trending up since the end of the civil war but that growth after 1999 has been different. Strong investment performance starting in 1999—which matured into strong export performance from 2001 onward—allowed for continued increases in output and consumption at the same time that imports were growing. This pattern inaugurated a different growth model for Mozambique, whereby strong exports, though offset by accompanying imports, reflected stronger private sector activity.

More recently, as a result of sharp increases in the price of aluminum from 2004 onward, the pace of profit repatriation

Figure 3.7   Components of GDP Expenditure in Mozambique, 1993–2006

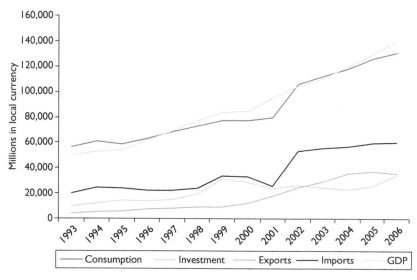

Source: World Bank 2010a.

Figure 3.8   Gap between GDP and GNP in Mozambique, 1994–2007

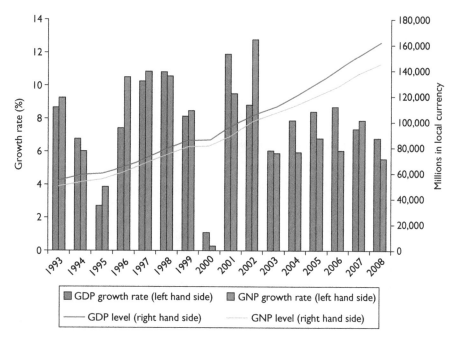

Source: World Bank 2010a.

associated with mega-projects has widened the gap between GNP and GDP (figure 3.8). This stylized fact is a reminder of a key challenge for the country: the need to compliment the current export drive based on mega–projects with a diversification strategy that activates a broader set of growth drivers and taps more effectively into Mozambique's more

abundant factors of production, particularly labor, land, and entrepreneurial drive.

Although the private sector has spearheaded large mega-projects in the mining sector, its role in economic growth over the past decade should not be overemphasized. Sonne-Schmidt, Arndt, and Magaua (2008) developed a methodology to evaluate the direct contribution of three key operational mega-projects (Mozal, Sasol, and Moma) to growth at factor cost. They conclude that the direct effects of these mega-projects were an increase in the average annual growth rate between 1996 and 2006 of about 1 percentage point (average annual growth rate was about 8 percent). Moreover, as foreign-owned, capital-intensive, export-oriented companies benefiting from fiscal exemptions, mega-projects made only a small contribution to job creation, tax revenue, use of domestic intermediate inputs, and profit reinvestment in Mozambique.

Benito-Spinetto and Moll (2005) present similar results. Using a computable general equilibrium (CGE) model to replicate the performance of the Mozambican economy, they find that about half of the 8 percent average GDP growth during 1994–2004 was driven by catch-up growth in the agricultural sector (as people returned to the fields following the end of the war), a quarter was driven by the growth in aid inflows (and the resulting investments in social and physical infrastructure sectors), and a quarter was equally divided between mega-projects and growth in other private sector activities. Clearly, the initial bet on mega-projects, despite the usual uncertainty in quantifying their precise economic effects, rested more on their capacity to generate immediate revenue rather than truly create downstream externalities (especially jobs and demand for industrial and services inputs).

Indeed, the positive total factor productivity reflects the reshuffling of labor resources and a rapid transformation in the output structure of the economy. In a postwar context—where reconstruction efforts, a first wave of structural reforms, and a stabilized macroeconomic environment spurred private sector activity—the Mozambican economy posted double-digit growth rates in mining, manufacturing, construction, electricity, gas, and water. Sectoral output shares experienced substantial changes between 1993 and 2006, especially in agriculture, which nearly halved its output participation, despite the positive contributions of agriculture to overall economic growth (figures 3.9 and 3.10). Sectoral output reflects a deep transformation to more productive sectors that generated positive composition effects in aggregate productivity.[4] Nevertheless, although economic growth has been strong and has underpinned the process of economic transformation, the structure of the economy still remains narrowly based on subsistence agriculture and a few isolated, albeit large, mega-projects. Agriculture, which employed about 78 percent of the economically active population, accounted for 25 percent of GDP in 2009. It was followed by manufacturing (12 percent, two-thirds of which was accounted for by one large aluminum smelter); trade and retail services (11 percent); transport and communications (10 percent); financial services (7 percent); and extractive industries (1 percent). Going forward, a key

Figure 3.9   Sectoral Contribution to Growth in Mozambique, 1994–2006

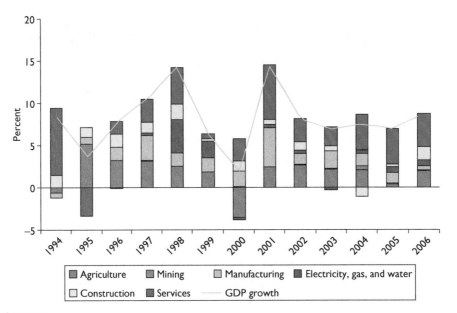

Source: World Bank various years.

CHAPTER 3: RAPID GROWTH AND ECONOMIC TRANSFORMATION IN MOZAMBIQUE, 1993–2009

Figure 3.10   Changes in Sectoral Output Share in Mozambique, 1993–2008

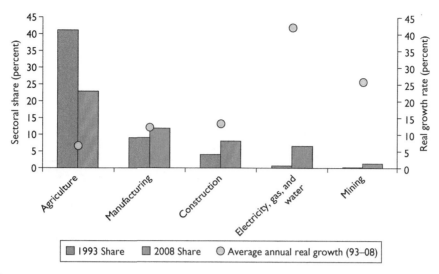

Legend: ■ 1993 Share   ■ 2008 Share   ○ Average annual real growth (93–08)

Source: World Bank various years.

challenge is not only to support the continuation of intersectoral (structural) transformations but to ensure within-sector productivity gains by addressing impediments to microeconomic efficiency (World Bank 2008a).

Economic transformation in Mozambique entailed a profound rebalancing of sectoral roles, with the (private) service sector absorbing labor at a particularly strong pace. Agriculture displays the lowest level of labor productivity of all sectors (figure 3.11). Between 1996 and 2003 its output contribution to GDP fell by 6 percentage points (to 27 percent), and its share of employment in the total labor force fell by 8 percentage points (to 82 percent) (figure 3.12). Although output shares were gained primarily by the industry sector, employment shares were gained by the private service sector.

While the increase in the employment share of the private service sector has benefited the poor (World Bank 2008b),[5] the challenge to generate an even greater number of jobs at higher levels of the value chain remains. The overwhelming concentration of employment (more than 78 percent) remains in agriculture. In urban areas, retail trade and vehicle repair employ a quarter of all workers; manufacturing industries employ 7.5 percent (table 3.2).

Formal employment generation has been very limited in recent years and is confined to a few large companies. Establishment-level data from a sample of 600 firms suggest that large firms (more than 100 employees) and some medium-large firms (about 100 employees) were responsible for the majority of jobs created in the manufacturing, services, con-

struction, and transportation sectors between 2003 and 2006 (table 3.3).[6] The dominance of large companies in formal employment generation reflects the lack of growth in small and medium enterprises. The "entry margin" (creation of formal jobs through new firms) also appears considerably more stifled for micro and small firms than for medium and large firms, perhaps a reflection of the fact that entry costs and overall business environment constraints impinge more severely on smaller producers.

The concentration of the economy in a few large companies is also reflected in export patterns. The export basket remains extremely limited, with only 15 products registering exports of more than $1 million a year. More than half of Mozambique's exports remain concentrated in the Mozal aluminum smeltering enclave (figure 3.13), virtually all of whose production goes to the European Union. Electricity and gas are also important export products (bought largely by South Africa).

Overall, Mozambique's exports increased significantly (in real terms), with average annual growth rates of 14.9 percent over 1995–99 and 19.8 percent over 2000–08. Most of this growth, however, was driven by exports from the mega-projects; although excluding mega-projects, exports grew at an average rate of 10 percent a year during 2000–08, which represents a reasonable performance. Progress in penetrating Southern Africa Development Community (SADC) countries continues; Mozambique should position itself to exploit non–SADC markets as well. Mozambique exploits only 2 percent of the potential

Figure 3.11 Labor Productivity in Mozambique by Sector (Relative to Agriculture), 1996 and 2003

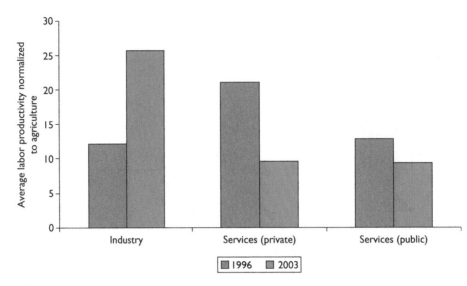

Source: World Bank 2008b.
Note: Figures are normalized to agriculture.

Figure 3.12 Changes in Employment versus Output Shares in Mozambique, by Sector, 1996–2003

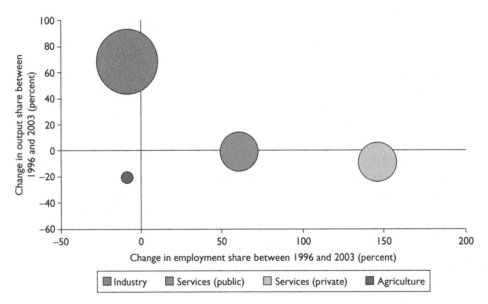

Source: World Bank 2008b.
Note: Services (private) include trade, and transport. Services (public) include health, education, and public administration. The larger the bubble, the higher the labor productivity.

bilateral flows for all the products it exports (Gillson 2008).[7] Although this is comparable to other countries in the region, it is far lower than the levels achieved by more advanced and better integrated economies (such as South Africa) (figure 3.14).[8]

A STRATEGY FOR BROADLY SHARED ECONOMIC GROWTH

Rapid economic growth was accompanied by significant strides in reducing poverty during the stabilization phase, after the peace accords and up to 2003.[9] Household survey

Table 3.2 Distribution of Employment in Mozambique, by Sector, Gender, and Location, 2004/05
(percent)

Sector	Total	Men	Women	Urban	Rural
Agriculture and fishing	78.5	68.0	87.3	40.1	92.7
Extractive industries	0.3	0.6	0.0	0.4	0.2
Manufacturing industries	3.1	5.4	1.2	7.5	1.5
Electricity, water, and construction	1.2	2.6	0.1	3.5	0.4
Retail trade and vehicle repair	9.2	11.7	7.0	25.9	3.0
Transport and communication	0.8	1.6	0.1	2.6	0.1
Financial services and rental	2.9	3.9	2.0	9.5	0.5
Administration	1.7	2.9	0.7	5.3	0.4
Education	1.6	2.3	1.0	3.5	0.9
Health and social work	0.7	0.8	0.5	1.6	0.3

Source: INE 2006.

Table 3.3 Number of Full-Time Employees in Sample of 600 Firms in Mozambique, by Firm Size, 2003 and 2006

Firm size	Growth rate in number of employees between 2003 and 2006 (percent)	Number of employees in 2003	Number of employees in 2006	Change in number of employees between 2003 and 2006	
				In firms created before 2003	In firms created after 2003
Micro	63	408	666	190	68
Small	35	2,064	2,803	493	246
Medium	36	4,630	6,323	992	701
Large	60	2,922	4,685	772	991
Total	44	10,024	14,477	2,447	2,006

Source: World Bank 2010b.

Note: Full-time employment in 2003 was used to determine firm size. For firms created after 2003, employment in 2006 was used to determine firm size.

Figure 3.13 Mozambique's Main Exports, 2008

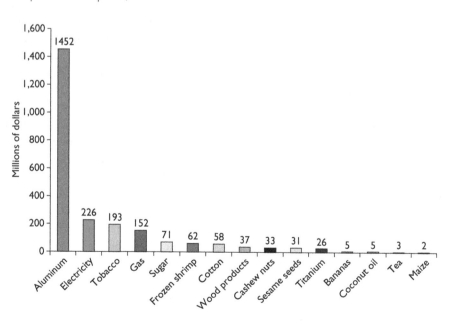

Figure 3.14 Mozambique's Export Market Penetration, by Country, 2006

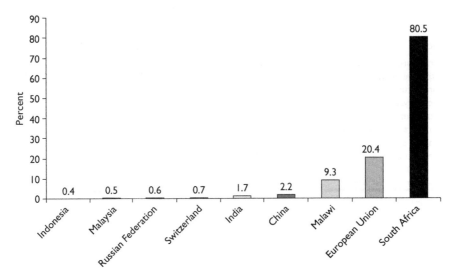

Source: UN COMTRADE (various years); Gillson 2008.

data indicate that the national poverty headcount fell rapidly, from 69 percent in 1996 to 54 percent in 2003 (MPD 2004). Reduction in rural poverty was even more pronounced, declining from 71 percent to 55 percent during the same period.

The pace of poverty reduction appears to be slowing, however, now that the post-war reconstruction effort and the agriculture catch-up has been exhausted, and the existing pattern of economic growth is not generating a sufficient number of jobs. The preliminary results of the 2009 nationally representative household budget survey are mixed. Although there was significant progress on many nonmonetary poverty indicators (such as access to education and health services, increase in asset ownership by households, and improvements in housing quality), the poverty headcount suggests that poverty may have stagnated at about 55 percent during 2003 and 2009 (MPD 2010). Urban poverty continued to decline, although at a much slower rate, reaching 50 percent, but rural poverty increased to 57 percent.[10] Although the food and fuel crisis played a role in this outcome, the stagnation of poverty reduction while the economy continued to grow at high rates suggests that growth has become less inclusive in the past few years.

These results are important because they seem to corroborate what many academics in Mozambique (see, among others, Castel-Branco 2002; Castel-Branco and Ossemane 2009) have been arguing for a number of years: that even though GDP growth rates have been very high in Mozambique, the current development strategy is lagging behind

expected promises. The model—which focuses on maintaining macroeconomic stability, making public investments in infrastructure and increasing access to public services (education, health, water, and electricity), and attracting capital-intensive mega-projects (which are capital intensive)—is still not bringing the increase in jobs and productivity required to set the economy on a more diversified growth pattern and eventually to reduce poverty by more than under the current strategy. In addition, lack of progress on the good governance agenda is putting strain on Mozambique's relationship with some of its development partners, and raising further questions about the sustainability of Mozambique's development strategy (box 3.1).[11]

A more inclusive, labor-intensive economic growth strategy is needed to reduce poverty and improve living standards (World Bank 2010a). Diversifying the economy into labor-intensive sectors (including agriculture, agroprocessing, manufacturing, and tourism) and increasing the competitiveness of domestic production to replace imports and diversify exports requires a new strategy focused on eliminating barriers to private investment (both domestic and foreign). Such a strategy would attempt to reduce excessive regulation; simplify the trade and tax regime; reduce the costs of hiring and firing workers; improve labor force skills; eliminate the rigidity in the land tenure system (freeing up access to land use rights and allowing their tradability); strengthen transport logistics and facilitate better services/articulation for exports; address the lack of standards; and maintain sound fiscal, monetary, and exchange rate policies. A number of constraints have to be addressed through a

CHAPTER 3: RAPID GROWTH AND ECONOMIC TRANSFORMATION IN MOZAMBIQUE, 1993–2009

Aid flows needed to finance public investments and expand service delivery are becoming increasingly uncertain in Mozambique but also for other Low Income Countries. This is due, in part, from the budgetary consequences of the 2008 global financial crisis in ODA allocation in many OECD countries.

OECD donors have been considering Mozambique an emblematic success story since the 1990s, especially since the end of the Civil War (1992). Official development assistance flows were significant and relatively stable both for projects and for direct budget support, given the country's good performance and "donor-agencies" high ratings. Throughout the early 2000s changes occurred in Mozambican politics: from a relatively strong showing in the first, post–Civil War elections in 1994, RENAMO's electoral results declined subsequently and posed a lesser threat to FRELIMO-dominated politics. Changes also affected the FRELIMO leadership, rotating toward a more business-oriented framework. With more investment opportunities brought by macroeconomic stabilization, positive donor sentiment, and increased aid inflows, among other things, a shift toward a market-oriented framework took place, accentuated by the discovery in the mid-2000s of significant mineral resources that triggered private sector interest and investment. In recent years, the discovery of such sizable reserves of minerals began to engender business interest in the country by global players, triggering expectations of large, private sector-led investments in these areas but also in the accompanying infrastructure for export corridors.

Inevitably these prospects brought more attention to issues of economic governance such as the relationship between an emerging class of businesses and entrepreneurs with the dominant political elite. Following several years of unhappiness about mixed progress in the good governance agenda and fears that increasing growth of non-aid revenue would allow Mozambique to become less aid-dependent. Some OECD donors in late 2009 threatened to "cut budget support" if very specific actions on political reforms were not urgently undertaken. While the 2009–10 standoff has since been largely resolved, some of the reasons and the political dynamics that led to the impasse appear to signal a structural change in Mozambique's relationship with the budget support donors. Many donors, however, consider such interference in the country's political affairs as unwarranted and refrain from entering into this type of conditionality. In fact, the government has also started to consider different possible scenarios to reduce its political vulnerability to aid-dependence, ranging from the possibility of revising some contracts with some mega-projects that benefit from generous tax incentives, or turning to some of BRIC countries for support, in addition to the need to expand the tax collection base and diversify revenues, among other strategies.

mix of simultaneous policy reforms, investments, and strengthening of institutions. They can be categorized as business environment, factor markets, trade logistics, and export-supporting institutions.

Aggressive reforms are required to improve the business environment and entice potential investors. First, the regulatory environment is very unfriendly to small and medium enterprises, and licensing, inspections, and red tape are a heavy burden. This is arguably the most important priority needing attention to unleash private sector potential, starting with domestic investors. Second, the Mozambican tax and tariff system is characterized by many different exemptions whose cumulative effects are unclear. Additionaly, small entrepreneurs normally do not benefit from current exemptions, because they cannot afford the fixed cost involved in applying for them. The standard statutory tax regime (excluding incentives) continues to place a substantial burden on investors, notably small domestic entrepreneurs. The combination of a statutory tax regime with relatively high tax rates with a generous system of tax incentives influences investment decisions and the allocation of resources in a way that is not immediately visible but distortionary in the long run. One widely recognized distortion is that the past tax regime encouraged industries that used more capital rather than labor. Mozambique's fiscal climate could be significantly improved by simultaneously reducing fiscal incentives and the number and level of tax rates without compromising government revenues. Third, despite progress in recent years, tax administration remains another impediment to Mozambique's competitiveness and productivity. A large number of the firms interviewed in the recent Investment Climate Assessment (World Bank 2010b) reported that tax administration is a major or severe obstacle to doing business. Reducing the number of taxes on the books and simplifying compliance with tax legislation would reduce transaction costs of businesses.

Factor markets—land, labor, and capital—need to allocate resources to their most productive uses. The 1997 Land Law is generally considered to be exemplary in Africa. However, 10 years after its approval, its implementation is weak, and the reality on the ground is one of extensive extralegal land markets, multiple claims to the same pieces of land, and a lack of guidance on how to protect or compensate customary and good-faith occupation rights. This situation has led to extensive land speculation and corruption, potentially leading to land conflicts and landlessness in the future. In the short run, the land situation acts as a deterrent to investors, particularly in tourism and agribusiness. Access to land for productive purposes needs to be improved. The new labor law approved in 2007 has substantially improved labor regulations for new investments. However, the labor market could and should be allowed to work even better to attract more domestic and foreign investment and sustain high growth rates.

In addition, despite significant progress, education levels in Mozambique are still very low and constitute a structural constraint for job creation in the formal sector. Quality of education is key for inclusive growth. Professional services (such as engineering, auditing, legal, and medical services) are expensive and in short supply in Mozambique; at the same time, many highly skilled Mozambicans are emigrating because they can earn more money abroad. This paradox of not having enough supply of skills (making professional services very expensive) while at the same time not having enough demand for them (leading to emigration) needs to be analyzed carefully to come up with an appropriate package of policy reforms. Inappropriate standards often stifle demand for services in areas such as engineering and accounting. Professional associations can play a key role in creating, with government support, a framework for regulation and appropriate standards, and also monitor quality and skills development. Immigration rules for qualified specialists who can provide managerial and technical expertise to Mozambican enterprises are still very restrictive, particularly for companies providing professional services. In the short run, a more liberal policy of granting work visas to skilled foreigners would help to develop the market for professional services in Mozambique and would enable Mozambican companies to compete better with foreign companies providing such services.

Legislation for the financial sector has been evolving continuously, and all banks were privatized in the 1990s. However, capital markets remain very shallow. The banking system is now sound and highly profitable. Exceptionally high ratios of capital adequacy (17 percent on Basle I) and liquidity (55.4 percent) of commercial banks raise a legitimate question as to whether there is sufficient financial intermediation for a fast-growing economy. Only a quarter of all districts have any kind of banking service, housing finance faces big constraints, and trade finance is still underdeveloped.

Trade logistics remain a serious constraint. Mozambique has the potential to be a major outlet for southern Africa based on its strategic location and congestion in Durban port, provided that it becomes more logistics friendly. Maputo port is the closest route for the largest mining and manufacturing region of South Africa, while Beira and Nacala are the closest ports for the other neighboring countries. Yet corridor traffic potential remains mainly untapped. Traffic going to and from Gauteng and Mpumalanga provinces equals at least 700 million tons. If Maputo could capture 1 percent of this traffic, its total throughput would be doubled and port revenues would be increased by several tens of millions of dollars. Despite a rather successful concession process, transit traffic at Maputo port remains relatively low, and the port operates at less than 30 percent of its capacity. Beira port has also operated at less than 40 percent capacity for the past five years. Mozambique's main deficiencies for trade mostly derive from logistics problems and low transport reliability. Low ratings in the logistic performance index (LPI) (2.29) and in the timeliness index (2.83) put Mozambican ports at a disadvantage compared with the port of Durban (with an LPI of 3.53 and a timeliness index of 3.78). The World Bank's 2008 *Doing Business* report highlights a web of procedures taking 27 days for exports and 38 days for imports. Some large South African shippers are still reluctant to shift their transport routes from Durban to Maputo because they still perceive the business climate there as unpredictable, including a higher incidence of bribe payments for the port of Maputo than for Durban (World Bank 2010a). Also, the poor integration of trucking services with the rest of the subregion explains why South African shippers are still reluctant to use Mozambican ports. High transport unpredictability is closely linked to low traffic volumes. As a result, shipping lines do not call directly in Maputo and cargo has to be transshipped in Durban or Mombasa. Physical investments and reforms of customs procedures should be carried out simultaneously to reach a critical mass in port transport volume. At that point, international shipping lines will make direct calls, which will greatly improve predictability. Constructing the "one-stop border post" in Ressano Garcia for trade with South Africa is of highest priority and should be quickly emulated in other large border posts. At the same time, all the customs clearance procedures including at the dry ports have to be revised. Long truck immobilization creates unnecessary delays and costs for shippers and transporters. Capital dredging of the Beira port is also very important, as is the reconstruction of the road between Nampula City and the border of Malawi.

Strengthening specialized export-supporting institutions that can assist small- and medium-size exporters is important for product and market development. Needed are a national system for standards and quality controls; an ICT-based proactive trade information system; product ID cards, and CITEs (centers supporting knowledge, innovation, and technology transfer and services otherwise not available). In addition, more "articulators" are needed to connect Mozambican businesses and products with regional and global markets. For a country where production is highly fragmented, such articulation initiatives are critical to secure scale benefits and knowledge transfer. There are already a number of ongoing articulation efforts in Mozambique through nongovernmental organizations, producer associations, private sector firms, and government agencies. But more needs to be done to get the benefits of economies of scale.

CONCLUDING REMARKS

The government of Mozambique has consistently pursued sound fiscal, monetary, and external policies, demonstrating a clear understanding of the benefits of a solid underlying macroeconomic framework for fostering further private sector-led growth. Mozambique's stable macroeconomic environment has allowed the economy to undergo significant transformation over the past two decades, in part supported by a stable source of ODA funding. Sectoral output composition has witnessed significant changes, with the participation of agriculture in output diminishing as more productive sectors grow. Although employment is still overwhelmingly concentrated in agriculture, job growth in the private sector (mostly informal) has led to increased participation of private services in output. Nevertheless, Mozambique's current growth model is not creating enough jobs or widening the productive base in order to create an economy in which wealth is broadly shared. However, the strategy implemented since the discovery and exploitation of large

mineral resources has produced positive results. The country has achieved high growth rates, is getting significant amounts of export revenue and has begun to reduce its aid-dependency, especially vis-a-vis traditional Western donors. However, the trickle-down effect of such a bet has not (yet) produced the expected impact on local businesses and labor markets. Moreover, uneven income distribution in urban areas and rising food prices during the last global commodity price cycle triggered protests.

Shifting growth dynamics toward a more inclusive pattern based on economic diversification and increased participation of small and medium enterprises will require policy action. Businesses' interest in expanding and initiating operations in Mozambique is palpable. This ongoing diversification of productive activities is bound to spur transformations in the economic landscape. Economic diversification and increasing engagement of small and medium enterprises leveraged by sustained efforts to participate in world markets represent a strategic orientation in the Mozambican growth model that is required to accelerate growth and reduce poverty. Harnessing such transformations for economic development will require strategic policy steps. By promoting competition and trade integration measures, the government should induce further private sector demand for Mozambique's factors of production, diversifying the economy and achieving shared and sustained economic growth.

A more balanced growth path, that would rely on local business initiatives, is fundamentally about creating the right incentives and necessary underlying conditions to foster entrepreneurial drive. These conditions can be achieved through policies to improve the business environment, the functioning of factor markets and land allocation, and the trade infrastructure, aiming to strengthen or create the institutions necessary for more absorption of labor, in particular helping small and medium enterprises to succeed. Such a shift requires political commitment and attention to new institutional bottlenecks and implementation capacity.

The bet that Mozambique has taken is showing some positive results. It was perhaps, given its chronic aid-dependency during most of its post-independence history, the only possible way to depart from it. This bet is not exempt from risks, and there are several indications that the political leadership is fully aware of many of them. Losing too soon significant portions of ODA would certainly be harmful to both macroeconomic stability and the quality of policies, although it should be acknowledged that the country has fully owned and implemented the standard agenda aimed at stability. The benefits from the export windfall could be captured by vested interests and not reinvested into the rest of the economy. There could be a substitution of aid-dependency by an excessive reliance on the business interests of large private groups.

Nevertheless, it is overall quite a success story, despite these risks and perhaps because of these risks. To the extent that the country understands these challenges and works to address them, especially in the efficient allocation of windfalls to development purposes, chances are that Mozambique could be a bright spot in terms of a successful strategy that overcame a civil war, instabilities of all sorts, lack of initial resources, lack of human capital, poverty and excessive dependency on external assistance.

NOTES

1. In primary education (grades 1–7), the number of children more than tripled, from about 1.3 million in 1992 to 4.2 million in 2008. Net enrollment rates in primary education doubled, from 45 percent in 1998 to more than 96 percent in 2008, with rates for girls rising from 40 percent to 93 percent. The number of primary school teachers increased from 30,000 in 1992 to 73,900 in 2008. The gross enrollment rate in lower secondary education (ES1) increased from 4.8 percent in 1998 to 28.0 percent in 2008. The gross enrollment rate for upper secondary school (ES2) increased from 1.3 percent in 2008 to 8.0 percent in 2008. Under-five mortality rates decreased from 212 per 1,000 live births in 1996 to 178 in 2003 and 138 in 2008. Infant mortality decreased from 145 per 1,000 live births in 1996 to 122 in 2003 and 93 in 2008. Maternal mortality fell from an estimated 1,000 per 100,000 live births in the early 1990s to 408 in 2003 and 340 in 2007. The share of the population with access to an improved water source increased from 39 percent in 1995 to 48 percent in 2008. Although the rate of HIV prevalence remains very high, the capacity of the health system was expanded to start providing free antiretroviral treatment for HIV infection.

2. The methodology applied to obtain the decomposition was based on a Cobb-Douglas production function with capital and quality-adjusted labor as inputs. Shares of the inputs were considered fixed at 0.4 and 0.6. Data from the Instituto National de Estatistica (INE 1998, 2004) were used to adjust for labor quality.

3. Jones (2006) provides a thorough discussion of growth accounting in Mozambique between 1980 and 2004. He considers alternative and more flexible functional forms for the production function; discusses perils of the growth accounting exercises with specific Mozambican data constraints in mind; and reviews results from other authors, such as Sulename (2001); Benito-Spinetto and Moll (2005); IMF (2005); Tahari, Akitoby, and Aka (2004); and Ndulu and O'Connell (2003). Vitek (2010) provides a growth accounting exercise in Mozambique between 1990 and 2008.

4. The shrinking of the labor force in agriculture in favor of other more productive sectors is a general pattern in the development process of many other advancing economies and should not be viewed as a negative phenomenon.

5. Job creation in the nonagricultural informal sector between 1997 and 2003 was also an important determinant of poverty reduction (World Bank 2008b). It provided economic opportunities to the poor and led to economywide productivity gains.

6. The enterprise survey of 600 firms was carried out in 2008 by the World Bank for the Investment Climate Assessment (World Bank 2010b). Each firm in the sample was visited to collect employment information on 2003 and 2006.

7. The index essentially compares each product Mozambique exports with all importing countries of the product from all world sources. By tracing all bilateral flows for each exported good, Gillson (2008) proposes a measure that captures the extent to which markets have been penetrated by Mozambican products. For instance, if country A exports good X only to country B, but good X is also imported by countries C and D only from country E, then country A is exploiting one of three (or one-third of) bilateral flows for good X.

8. Market penetration measures disaggregated by largest export partners indicate that Mozambique is already exploiting 80 percent of its potential bilateral flows to South Africa.

9. This section draws heavily on the recent Country Economic Memorandum on "Reshaping Growth and Creating Jobs through Trade and Regional Integration" (World Bank 2010a).

10. These results should be treated with caution, however. Substantial underreporting of food consumption has been identified in the 2008/09 household survey data, which could affect both the poverty levels and their trend over time. The data problem also affects the 1996/97 and 2002/03 household surveys, albeit to a different extent. Additional analytical work is required to test the robustness of the poverty analysis in Mozambique by correcting for the data problems.

11. The considerable amounts of aid and the presence of a great number of aid agencies led to the establishment of donor coordination mechanisms that were considered best international practices until recently. A number of donor-government working groups were established during a "golden era" for coordination that brought benefits to both

donors and the government—in terms of transaction costs—and culminated with the adoption of the Paris and Accra Declarations. In parallel, a distinction began between donors providing direct budget support (such as a regrouping into a group of nineteen OECD countries or the G-19) and those involved in more traditional project activities. While important donors (such as the United States) concentrated efforts in specific sectors (like health and clean water), the G-19 elaborated a memorandum of understanding to define quasi-contractual rules for disbursing budget support, considered as a sign of a more mature relationship with recipient governments. In fact, while Mozambique's success led the country to benefit from larger shares of aid under direct budget support (by the G-19), this theoretically more "advanced" form of aid, adequate for countries with a solid track record, also makes the country more dependent on the political and budgetary cycles of OECD donors (see box 3.1).

REFERENCES

AfDB (African Development Bank). 2009. *African Development Indicators 2009*. Tunis.

Benito-Spinetto, M., and P. Moll. 2005. "Macroeconomic Developments, Economic Growth and Consequences for Poverty." Background Paper for the 2005 Country Economic Memorandum. World Bank and International Monetary Fund, Washington, DC.

Castel-Branco, Carlos Nuno. 2002. "Mega projectos e estratégia de desenvolvimento." http://www.iese.ac.mz/lib/cncb/Mega_projectos_Moz_texto.pdf.

Castel-Branco, Carlos Nuno, and Rogéio Ossemane. 2009. "Crises cíclicas e dasfios de transformação do padrão de crescimento económico em Moçambique." In *Desafios para Moçambique 2010*, ed. L. Brito, C. Castel-Branco, S. Chichava, and A. Francisco, pp. 141–82. Maputo: Instituto de Estudos Sociais e Económicos (IESE).

Clement, Jean A. P., and Shanaka J. Peiris, eds. 2008. *Post-Stabilization Economics in Sub-Saharan Africa*. Washington, DC: International Monetary Fund.

Gillson, Ian. 2008. "Mozambique's Export Market Penetration." World Bank, Poverty Reduction and Economic Management (PREM), Africa Region, Washington, DC.

IMF (International Monetary Fund). 2005. *Republic of Mozambique: Selected Issues and Statistical Appendix*. IMF Country Report 05/311, Washington, DC.

INE (Instituto National de Estatistica). 1998. *Relatório final do inquérito sobre orçamento familiar (IOF), 1996/7*. Maputo.

———. 2004. *Relatório final do inquérito aos agregados familiares sobre orçamento familiar (IAF), 2002/3*. Maputo.

———. 2006. *National Labor Force Survey 2004/5*. Maputo.

———. 2010. *Relatório final do inquérito sobre orçamento familiar (IOF), 2008/9*. Maputo.

Jones, Sam. 2006. *Growth Accounting for Mozambique, 1980–2004*. Discussion Paper 22E, Ministry of Planning and Development, National Directorate of Studies and Policy Analysis, Maputo.

MPD (Ministry of Planning and Development), Government of Mozambique. 2004. *Second National Poverty Assessment*. Maputo.

———. 2010. *Third National Poverty Assessment*. Maputo.

Ndulu, B., and S. O'Connell. 2003. *Revised Collins/Bosworth Growth Accounting Decompositions*. AERC Growth Project, African Economic Research Consortium, Nairobi.

Sonne-Schmidt, C., C. Arndt, and M. Magaua. 2008. *Contribution of Mega-Projects on GDP*. Ministry of Planning and Development, Direcção Nacional de Estudos e Análise de Políticas (DNEAP), Maputo.

Sulename, Jose. 2001. "Economic Decline: A Study with Reference to Mozambique." Ph.D. diss., Department of Economics, University of Notre Dame, South Bend, IN.

Tahari A., B. Akitoby, and E. Aka. 2004. "Sources of Growth in Sub-Saharan Africa." IMF Working Paper 04/176, International Monetary Fund, Washington, DC.

UN COMTRADE (various years). United Nations Commodity Trade Statistics Database. http://comtrade.un.org/db/

Vitek, Francis. 2010. "Economic Growth in Mozambique: Experience and Policy Challenges." International Monetary Fund, Africa Department, Washington, DC.

World Bank. 2008a. *Expanding the Possible in Sub-Saharan Africa: How Tertiary Institutions Can Increase Growth and Competitiveness*. Poverty Reduction and Economic Management (PREM), Washington, DC.

———. 2008b. *Mozambique, Beating the Odds: Sustaining Inclusion in a Growing Economy. A Mozambique Poverty, Gender, and Social Assessment*. Poverty Reduction and Economic Management (PREM), Washington, DC.

———. 2010a. *Mozambique Country Economic Memorandum: Reshaping Growth and Creating Jobs through Trade and Regional Integration*. Washington, DC.

———. 2010b. *Mozambique Investment Climate Assessment 2010*. Washington, DC.

———. Various years. *World Development Indicators*. Washington, DC.

CHAPTER 4

Botswana's Success: Good Governance, Good Policies, and Good Luck

Michael Lewin

Over the past 60 years, Botswana's economy has been one of the most successful in the world. The country's achievement is remarkable, because at independence, in 1966, its prospects were not encouraging.

ECONOMIC AND SOCIAL INDICATORS

Botswana is a sparsely populated, arid, landlocked country; at independence it was also one of the poorest countries in the world, with per capita income of just $70 a year. In the first few years of independence, about 60 percent of current government expenditure consisted of international development assistance. There were only 12 kilometers of paved roads, and agriculture (mostly cattle farming for beef production) accounted for 40 percent of gross domestic product (GDP).

By 2007 Botswana had 7,000 kilometers of paved roads, and per capita income had risen to about $6,100 ($12,000 at purchasing power parity), making Botswana an upper-middle-income country comparable to Chile or Argentina. Its success is also evident in other measures of human development. At independence, life expectancy at birth was 37 years. By 1990 it was 60, 10 years above the African average. Under-five mortality had fallen to about 45 per 1,000 live births in 1990, compared with 180 for Africa as a whole. Development assistance has shrunk to less than 3 percent of the government budget, and agriculture currently accounts for only about 2.5 percent of GDP. Major strides have also been made in infrastructure and education.[1]

Annual growth in per capita income averaged 7.0 percent between 1966 and 1999 (table 4.1 and figure 4.1). The country's performance is particularly impressive compared with that of other African economies (figure 4.2).

Critics have argued that the social gains from this growth have been somewhat limited. In fact, in addition to the gains in health and life expectancy noted above, there have been gains in poverty reduction and education. The proportion of poor people fell from about 50 percent in 1985 to 33 percent in 1994, and the proportion of people completing at least primary school rose from less than 2 percent at independence to about 35 percent in 1994 (Leith 2005).

Not all indicators are as positive: income distribution in Botswana remains very unequal (the Gini coefficient was about 0.55 in 1994).[2] Unemployment remains high, reflecting to a large extent rural to urban migration, although it too has fallen, dropping from about 21 percent in the 1990s to about 17 percent in 2008.

DIAMONDS AND DEVELOPMENT

Botswana's extraordinary growth was fueled by minerals, particularly diamonds. At independence, beef, the country's main export and largest sector, contributed 39 percent of GDP. From independence until the 1970s, international aid dominated the government budget and was the main source of foreign exchange. At that time the mineral sector, mainly diamonds, began to take off and soon became the dominant

Table 4.1	Annual Growth in per Capita Income in Selected Economies, 1966–99
Economy	**Average growth rate**
Botswana	7.0
Chile	2.1
Hong Kong SAR, China	4.6
Indonesia	3.8
Ireland	4.1
Korea, Rep. of	6.1
Singapore	6.2
Thailand	4.6

Source: Adapted from Leith 2005.

Figure 4.1 Average Annual Growth in per Capita Income in Botswana, 1980–2008

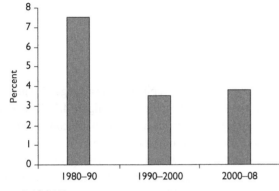

Source: Leith 2005.

Figure 4.2 Average per Capita Income in Africa and Botswana, 2001–09
(purchasing power parity at current dollar prices)

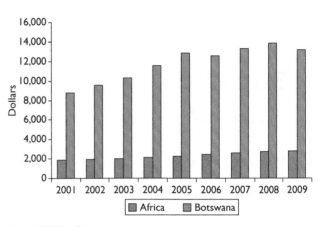

Source: OECD n.d.

sector. Income growth and the growth of the mining sector accelerated in tandem from about 1974/75 until recently.

Luck—the discovery of diamonds as well as other important minerals—was clearly an element of Botswana's success. However, there is considerable disagreement over whether the discovery of minerals in a developing economy generally brings good luck or bad (box 4.1).[3] Indeed, many countries in Africa, including Zambia, Nigeria, the Democratic Republic of Congo, Sierra Leone, and others, have squandered vast amounts of their natural wealth. One does not have to be persuaded that natural resources are necessarily a curse to conclude that they certainly are not sufficient for economic success or even a good predictor of it. In the case of Botswana, minerals turned out to be lucky, but other key ingredients in the recipe for success were present, including good governance and good economic management.

Avoiding the bad governance curse

Mineral-based countries seem to be prone to bad government, a phenomenon Acemoglu and others have termed

"good economics, bad politics." In almost all developing countries, the government owns the mineral resources and is therefore the main recipient of the revenues from their extraction. This concentration of revenues with the government as the conduit of benefits to the rest of the economy can lead to a host of problems, including rent-seeking, corruption, and the efficiency losses that result from them. It is not surprising that, with easily accessible wealth concentrated in the hands of the government, malignant dictatorships and predatory regimes often thrive. There also seems to be a greater tendency for armed civil conflict in mineral-based economies (Collier and Hoeffler 2004). These "bad politics" are extremely costly.

Botswana has avoided these manmade disasters. Part of its success may reflect luck: Botswana's relatively homogeneous population has less potential for ethnic polarization, which when combined with mineral rents can be particularly combustible. Still, most of the credit must be given to the leadership, which, since independence, has designed and fostered the conditions of governance that have ensured stability and social and economic progress. The government established respect for property rights and the rule of law. It maintained a high degree of transparency, which was reinforced by continuing the Tswana tribal tradition of consultation. These consultative institutions, known as *kgotla*, created a degree of trust in the government—the sense that government exists to serve the people and promote development and is not the instrument of one group or individuals for the purpose of getting hold of the wealth. Tswana tradition also

Box 4.1   The Resource Curse

The counterintuitive notion that the endowment of natural resources is a curse rather than a blessing has become received wisdom. Sachs and Warner (1995) report regression results showing that being a natural resource or mineral exporter reduces a country's development prospects. Many other researchers find evidence to support this claim (see for example, Auty 2004 and the references therein). The fact that most of the East Asian tigers (the Republic of Korea; Taiwan, China; Hong Kong SAR, China; and Singapore) plus Japan are resource poor has added to the perception that endowed wealth is an obstacle to growth and development.

There is certainly evidence that a disproportionate number of the poorest countries are dependent on mineral exports. The direction of causality, however, is far from clear: does mineral dependence retard development, or does retarded development create mineral dependence?

Accounting for the endogeneity of mineral dependence overturns the Sachs-Warner conclusions. Countries that fail to develop remain resource *dependent*, but resource *abundance* may be correlated with higher growth (see, for example, Brunnschweiler and Bulte 2008; Alexeev and Conrad 2009). Many rich countries—including Canada, Australia, Norway, the United States, and Latin America's top performer, Chile—were or are mineral dependent. In Africa the two richest countries, South Africa and Botswana, owe much of their wealth to gold and diamonds.

In short, resources are not necessarily a curse, but many countries have squandered their resources, and in some cases, the presence of mineral resources may have contributed to economic stagnation or decline. What is it about mineral endowments that can make things go wrong?

Dutch Disease

Dutch disease refers to the deleterious effects that purportedly result from the real appreciation of the currency caused by a booming resource export sector (Corden and Neary 1982). The discovery of minerals or an increase in their international price leads to an increase in income and expenditure. As long as some of the increased expenditure goes to domestically produced goods, there will be a real appreciation of the currency, which causes productive resources to move from nonmineral traded goods, the output of which declines, to nontraded goods, the output of which increases. The resulting excess demand for tradables

can be financed by the revenue from the mineral exports.

Because the entire process is initiated by an increase in income, expenditure, and consumption, it is not clear why it should be thought of as a disease. One reason given is the presence of positive externalities in the declining sector. The declining traded goods sector is thought to have spillover effects that contribute to long-run growth and industrialization. Hence, the real appreciation caused by mineral exports is said to cause "deindustrialization," contributing to poor long-run performance. Of course, in Africa and Botswana in particular, the declining traded goods sector was agriculture, not industry (there was no significant industry to deindustrialize). Some might argue that mineral exports prevent the real depreciation needed to industrialize. Additionally, it is argued, the mineral sector fails to stimulate the nonmineral sector through linkages to the rest of the economy.

Against this effect, one must weigh the advantages that minerals bring in terms of increased saving and hence investment, which should offset any loss of competitiveness caused by the real exchange rate. Moreover, because government is usually the chief beneficiary of the resource revenues, the increase usually eases constraints on public goods, such as infrastructure, education, and health, which should contribute to growth and industrialization. If private investment or public goods expenditure fails to materialize, the problem lies not in the real exchange rate but rather in the failure of financial markets to allocate the saving and investment productively or of government to invest wisely.

The Volatility Curse

Mineral prices tend to be volatile, which, it is argued, destabilizes the economy (Hausmann and Rigobon 2003). This volatility affects the economy through the exchange rate, which appreciates in the boom and depreciates in the bust, and through fiscal policy, which tends to be procyclical, leading to inefficient "stop-go" provision of government services and infrastructure projects.[a] It is argued that the perceived riskiness that this volatility engenders leads to lower investment, particularly foreign direct investment, which seeks out safer markets. In addition, governments tend not only to increase spending when current revenues rise but often also to believe that revenues will continue to rise; they therefore borrow against future revenues. Instead of being able to use accumulated assets to help in the bust,

(continued next page)

Box 4.1   (continued)

economies find themselves contending with debt overhang.

It is possible to insulate the domestic market from the volatility of the commodity markets. Because the government is the conduit of the cycle to the economy, it is also the solution. The key is to delink expenditure and revenue, essentially by saving all or part of the revenues, thereby replacing a volatile income stream with a more stable one. Expenditure can then be based on this more stable, permanent income. In this way, consumption can be smoothed over time, in some cases over generations. Many countries, including Botswana, Chile, Kuwait, Norway, Qatar, and Saudi Arabia, have successfully applied such an expenditure-smoothing policy.

The Governance Curse

In most developing countries the government claims ownership of all minerals. If government institutions are weak to begin with, there is a strong likelihood that the resources will be squandered. In addition, the presence of the resources may weaken and corrupt government. The relative ease with which mineral revenues are collected can lead to a lack of transparency and accountability. The resulting interdependence of government and the mining industry reinforces this tendency. Government itself is seen as the means to acquiring wealth, which typically leads to rent seeking and corruption. There is also evidence that in many cases mineral wealth provokes or fuels internal conflicts (Collier and Hoeffler 2004).

In an ironic metaphor, underground minerals are often referred to as one of the "commanding heights" of the economy. Postindependence governments claimed the need to control these commanding heights for the benefit of all the governed. One of the unforeseen consequences of this policy was the perception that control of government is the path to wealth, which in turn, unsurprisingly, has often led to regional and ethnic conflict for control of these resource rents (Collier and Hoeffler 2004).

Exhaustibility

Minerals are a windfall, even in the long run, in the sense that they are finite and that when they are depleted an economic slump will occur. That a blessing does not last forever hardly makes it a curse, however. If at least some of the windfall is saved, in the form of physical and human capital or financial assets, future generations will benefit from it. Moreover, the depletion usually does not occur suddenly. With some foresight, the adjustment and transition can be cushioned by accumulated saving.[b]

How Has Botswana Fared?

To a large extent, Botswana overcame the threat of the resource curse:

1. Dutch disease was avoided, most significantly by government investment in public goods and infrastructure. The government also took measures to help boost productivity, by limiting parastatals and avoiding import substitution policies.
2. The volatility curse was overcome by unlinking public expenditure from revenue. The government established savings funds and avoided typical procyclical behavior and real exchange rate volatility.
3. The governance curse was avoided, through a series of actions described in the chapter. Botswana's success in this regard is exceptional.
4. The question of whether the exhaustibility challenge has been met remains unclear. If current predictions are correct, diamond revenues will begin declining in 2016 and could be exhausted by 2029. Botswana has adopted many of the appropriate policies to prepare for the depletion of its mineral base, by accumulating funds for the future, building infrastructure, and investing in health and education. However, the growth of the nonmineral traded goods sector, which has remained flat at about 5 percent of GDP, will need to accelerate to avoid balance of payments problems as diamond revenues begin to decline.

a. Rather than being procyclical, in most developing countries, the government initiates the cycle because it is the recipient of the rents. The boom therefore begins with government expansion and the bust with its contraction. Hence, real exchange rate variability is also the result of volatile government expenditure.

b. A full discussion of mineral resource management in the context of intertemporal and intergenerational allocations goes beyond the objectives of this chapter. Essentially, the optimal management of resource rents requires expenditure smoothing not only to avoid cyclical volatility but also to spread the benefits of the windfall over time. Like a rational household, an optimizing government will attempt to base its long-run expenditure on some calculation or estimate of its "permanent" or stable revenue rather than on its current or transitory revenue. For some calculations of permanent income in the case of Botswana, see Basdevant (2008).

respected private property; the fact that many of the tribal leaders who helped usher in modern government were also large cattle owners may have reinforced this respect.

Acemoglu and Robinson (1999) emphasize that property rights and the rule of law are the key factors explaining development success. They also emphasize the importance of the preindependence colonial regime in determining the adoption of these institutions after independence. More heavily settled colonies tended to establish institutions to maintain the rule of law and enforce property rights; in sparsely settled colonies, the colonial regimes tended to be more "extractive" or "exploitative," unconstrained by law and respect for property. Although Botswana's colonial past is not typical of the kind of regime that usually led to a postindependence government constrained by law and property rights, its unique colonial history had the same effect.[4] Before independence, Botswana was a British protectorate, the colonial power having been "invited" in. Because Botswana was not colonized for economic or strategic advantage, the colonial rulers, it is argued, did not impose the extractive-type regime often found in other sparsely populated areas. Thus the regime that evolved after independence was one that respected the law and property and was dedicated to development.

More controversial is the role of democracy. Botswana has maintained a parliamentary democracy since independence. To be sure, its democracy is not perfect: the country has had one-party rule since independence, women's representation is limited, and there has been some criticism that minorities (particularly the San people) are not treated equally. Nevertheless, the government functions in a democratic manner, elections are "free and fair," and the government is responsive to the electorate and transparent in its dealings.

Is democracy a positive factor for economic growth and development? None of the miracle East Asian economies or Latin America's high performer (Chile) was democratic during the first years of rapid growth and development, leading many commentators to conclude that property rights and the rule of law are more important than democracy (Acemoglu, Johnson, and Robinson 2003). For some observers, democracy is actually a hindrance to economic development. Although this conclusion is probably unwarranted, the fact that many democracies (such as India) have not fared well economically undoubtedly means that democracy is neither sufficient nor necessary for growth and development.[5]

In the case of mineral-rich countries like Botswana, democracy may be an important catalyst. Mineral-dependent economies seem to spawn the predatory type of dictatorship rather than the relatively benevolent ones of East Asia's past. Although this notion is largely speculative, it seems that a democratic government dependent on mineral wealth is more likely than a dictatorial one to be responsive to development needs, to settle disputes peacefully, and to respect the rule of law. Very few, if any, mineral-rich countries in Africa have been ruled as peacefully and productively as Botswana; it is hard to escape the conclusion that the democratic institutions established at independence are an important part of the explanation.

Social science cannot rigorously assess the relative importance or contribution of leadership in the evolution of successful institutions. However, in the case of Botswana, leadership, particularly that of its first president, Seretse Khama, may have been crucial, especially in the areas of mineral exploitation and the rights of the state versus those of the tribes. The discovery of minerals can easily lead to civil war and the dissolution of the state. To prevent this from happening, even before independence, Khama's party, the Botswana Democratic Party (BDP), wrote into its platform its intention to assert the state's rights to all mineral resources. After independence, the government reached agreement on ownership of mineral resources with the tribal authorities. Although the largest diamond deposits were discovered in Khama's own district of Bamangwato, he chose the country over his tribal land, thus helping limit the possibility of conflict.

Implementing good policies

All mineral-based economies face the issue of an appreciating real exchange rate (box 4.2). The well-known possible harmful consequences of this are often referred to as Dutch disease (see box 4.1). Prevention of Dutch disease in Botswana consisted of three key components: fiscal saving, a surplus on the current account of the balance of payments, and heavy government investment in infrastructure and human capital. Together these policies limited the erosion of domestic productivity and competitiveness that can result from the appreciation of the real exchange rate. High fiscal saving limits current consumption, reducing pressure on domestic price inflation, a typical problem in natural resource booms. Some of the government saving took the form of offshore investments, which directly limited real exchange rate depreciation and diversified the sources of future foreign exchange revenues. The accumulation of reserves is a form of self-insurance against short-run declines in mineral revenues as well as long-run reductions

Box 4.2   Windfall Economics 101

The mechanism by which mineral resource flows affect the real exchange rate depends on the nominal exchange rate regime maintained by the country. Botswana has a fixed exchange rate system. Initially, it pegged its currency to the U.S. dollar. When the South African rand depreciated relative to the dollar, Botswana suffered from the appreciation of the pula (Botswana's currency) relative to the rand (the currency of its main trading partner).[a] The pula is therefore now pegged to the rand.

In a fixed-rate regime, the first effect of a resource windfall is the creation of an excess supply of foreign exchange. To maintain the peg, the monetary authority must accumulate reserves. Doing so will inject domestic money into the economy, however, resulting in domestic price inflation, which will eventually erode local competitiveness until the balance of payments surplus is eliminated. This is the effect of real appreciation when the nominal rate is fixed. To prevent this from happening, the government has to sterilize the effects of the resource rents on the domestic money supply. In the medium to long run, the fiscal authority can do so by absorbing the excess domestic money through fiscal budget surpluses. This policy of twin surpluses—a balance of payments surplus in tandem with a fiscal budget surplus—is essentially the policy that Botswana has followed. (Some analysts have argued that China has followed a similar policy to maintain an undervalued currency.)

a. In contrast, Argentina maintained a dollar peg after the devaluation of the Brazilian real. Many analysts consider this a key element leading to the Argentine crisis.

---

in these revenues as a result of mineral depletion. The instruments of public saving took the form of the Public Service Debt Management Fund and the Revenue Stabilization Fund. These funds have proved to be successful mechanisms for managing fiscal saving; income from the Revenue Stabilization Fund is now a stable source of government revenue.

Another part of the fiscal saving was channeled to domestic assets, combating the effect of the loss of competitiveness by raising productivity. When this investment is focused on public goods (for example, infrastructure, health, and human capital), it will contribute to growth without crowding out private sector investment and development. Public sector saving was positive in every year between 1975 and 1996, fluctuating between 10 and 40 percent of GDP. Public sector investment was fairly constant at about 10 percent of GDP.[6] However, if one counts expenditure on health and human capital as investment, government investment has consistently remained about 20 percent of GDP. The capital budget focused on basic infrastructure with about 30 percent devoted to water, electricity, roads, communication, and transportation. Twenty percent of the capital budget, on average, went to education and around 30 percent of recurrent expenditures was devoted to education and health.[7] While quantifying the effectiveness of public expenditure on growth and development is notoriously difficult, particularly in resource-based economies where soft budget constraints may lead to overinvestment, the emphasis on infrastructure, health, and education seems to have served Botswana well. As noted above, the number of paved roads increased from around 20 kilometers in 1970 to 2,300 in 1990; 90 percent of the population had access to safe water (compared with 29 percent in 1970); and the number of telephone connections rose from around 5,000 in 1970 to 136,000 in 2001.[8] Similarly, in educational achievement Botswana leads Africa. For example, adult literacy, male and female, is around 80 percent compared with 69 percent and 50 percent, respectively, for the rest of sub-Saharan Africa.[9]

As a result of its prudent fiscal policy, Botswana has enjoyed relative macroeconomic stability and avoided the boom-slump cycles that characterize many mineral-based economies. Monetary policy was also restrained: for most of the postindependence period, inflation was moderate, averaging about 10 percent (Maipose n.d.). The periodic slowdowns in the diamond industry have thus by and large not been passed on to the rest of the economy. By withholding some of the benefits from the economy during the booms, the government has, to some extent, been able to insulate it from the busts.[10]

Shunning import substitution and parastatals

Two things Botswana did not do are also significant. Unlike many African countries, it did not adopt a policy of import substitution, and it did not expand the extent of state-owned productive entities, which employ only about 5 percent of the workforce in Botswana (figure 4.3).

Source: Leith 2005.

Being part of the South African Customs Union (which required cooperation with the then odious regime in South Africa) meant maintaining a fairly low tariff regime and provided a steady stream of government revenue. Avoiding an activist import-substituting policy and maintaining limited government involvement in production seems to have paid off for Botswana by allowing it to avoid many of the inefficiencies and structural deficits that so often arise from such policies.

Trade policy is also an area where good governance and good policies reinforce one another. A government rich with mineral revenues is an inviting target for rent seekers and worse; restricting the avenues for rent seeking and corruption thus helps preserve the efficiency and integrity of the government. Even if the theoretical merits of import substitution or the existence of state-owned enterprises seem persuasive, in practice both often result in inefficiency and drain fiscal resources.

Good fiscal policies by themselves may not be sufficient for success. Many mineral-based economies with high rates of investment have not enjoyed the positive results that Botswana has. The quality of investment is evidently as important as the quantity. Moreover, in the hands of the venal and corrupt, government savings funds can easily turn into slush funds for the favored elites. There may be a lesson in this from Botswana: good governance will aid the effectiveness of good policy, and good policy encourages better government. Policy formulators should therefore not ignore the political economy consequences of economic policy.

Botswana's combination of policy and governance evidently helped it avoid the worst effects of the resource curse.

PLANNING FOR A FUTURE WITHOUT MINERALS

Botswana is still a mineral-based economy: it has not succeeded in significantly diversifying its economy away from diamonds. Government remains the largest employer (employing 30 percent of the active workforce); other than minerals (which employ a relatively small share of workers), most production is in nontraded goods. This pattern is typical of mineral-dependent economies. Real GDP and mining income have moved in tandem since 2000 (figure 4.4), and mining consistently accounts for about 40 percent of GDP, completely dwarfing the contributions of manufacturing and agriculture (figure 4.5).[11] Minerals, mostly diamonds,

Figure 4.4 Mining Revenues and Real GDP in Botswana,
2000–09

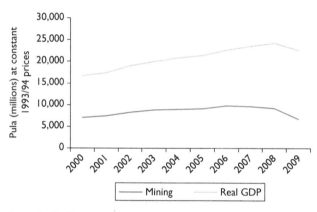

Source: Bank of Botswana 2010.

Figure 4.5 Contributions of Mining, Manufacturing, and
Agriculture to Botswana's GDP, 2000–09

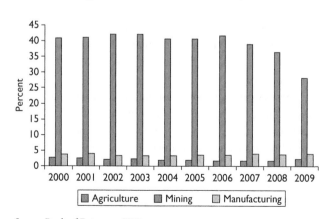

Source: Bank of Botswana 2010.

comprise about 85 percent of exports, and mineral revenues account for about 50 percent of government revenues (Bank of Botswana 2008).[12]

The diamond industry is expected to decline in the near future, with revenues projected to begin falling in 2016 and to be depleted by 2029 (Basdevant 2008). If these projections are correct, adjustment is inevitable and unlikely to be painless, although Botswana's prudent policies—particularly regarding saving and investment—have left it in a relatively strong position to facilitate a soft landing. For most years, domestic saving has been above 40 percent and investment about 35 percent of GDP. (The difference is the surplus on the current account of the balance of payments.) This implies that from the perspective of the economy as a whole, all revenue from minerals is being saved rather than consumed, because total saving from national income is roughly equal to mineral income. When mineral revenues begin to decline, some of the adjustment could thus be absorbed by saving rather than consumption. Thus, even if growth slows, consumption growth can be maintained as the proportion of consumption to income rises.

The government has also been a big saver. Central bank profits and other income from accumulated assets now make up about 30 percent of government revenue, most of it income from the accumulated saving of mineral revenues. At times, the overall fiscal surplus rose to more than 30 percent of GDP (Maipose n.d.), and public sector investment (as noted) has been consistently about 10 percent of GDP. If investment is defined more broadly to include human capital and health, public investment rises to about 20 percent of GDP, which meets the IMF benchmark for sustainability (Basdevant 2008). The government has used this accumulated savings to smooth expenditure over the business cycle, thus providing the economy with a short-run shock absorber. However, as argued in box 4.1, the accumulated saving is also a long-run shock absorber, because it has built up human and physical capital and financial assets that should serve the economy well during the adjustment period. In addition, the accumulated foreign assets managed by the Bank of Botswana now amount to about 40 months of imports.

These advantages notwithstanding, Botswana faces serious challenges. Dependence on mineral exports is the key weakness of the current economic outlook and diversification of the traded goods sector is the most important policy objective. Accumulated foreign assets and the income from them can ease the welfare cost of adjustment, but it cannot eliminate it. Barring a miraculous jump in productivity, some real depreciation of the pula and the consequent hard-

ships this may cause, will be necessary to create the competitiveness needed to replace falling mineral exports.

In 2009 manufacturing contributed less than 5 percent of GDP (see figure 4.5). This share will have to rise if Botswana is to avoid decline. The fact that manufacturing has been flat as a proportion of income conceals its growth, because just keeping pace with Botswana's growing economy has required rapid growth.[13] However, manufacturing growth will have to accelerate if Botswana is to raise or even maintain its standard of living in the long run.

Key to such growth will be Botswana's ability to attract foreign direct investment (FDI). Although FDI fell between 2002 and 2007 (Bank of Botswana 2010), Botswana's reputation as a stable country and successful economy should help it attract FDI in the future.[14] Policy makers should examine the country's overall investment environment with a view to attracting desirable investment.[15]

Clouding Botswana's smooth transition to a more diversified economy is HIV/AIDS, which hit Botswana harder than any country in Africa (with the possible exception of South Africa). The epidemic has reversed many of the impressive gains in health indicators achieved over the past 100 years and reduced productivity. The number of deaths from AIDS began declining in about 2003 (World Bank 2009), but the costs and consequences of the epidemic will persist for many years.

CONCLUSION

Landlocked Botswana seems to have defied the odds by creating a successful economy. Poverty has been reduced, education has become more widespread, and health indicators had improved before the HIV/AIDS epidemic undid some of that progress.

The country's vast natural resources played a key role in this accomplishment, but the mere endowment of resources is clearly not the whole story. In much of Africa—and in other parts of the world—natural resources have not always been conducive to growth and development; in many cases they seem to have brought out the worst in countries, in the form of conflict and predatory governments.

Studying the effect of mineral wealth on economic outcomes is timely, because the increase in the prices of natural resources as a result of the rise of China and India is likely to result in windfalls for many African countries. How can countries turn these windfalls into long-run growth and development? In Botswana's case, the key to successfully harnessing natural resources lay in good governance and good policies. Governance has not been perfect in Botswana, but it has been good. Botswana has been largely free of kleptocracy and civil conflict; it has maintained a transparent, law-abiding government; and it has implemented good policies, including a hyper-prudent fiscal policy, which has done much to diversify foreign exchange earnings and prevent the volatility that typifies many resource-based economies. Investments in human and physical capital and vast improvements in infrastructure have also raised Botswana's productivity, which, together with its substantial financial reserve in the form of foreign assets, should help ease the transition to a more diversified economy.

NOTES

1. For discussions of Botswana's success, see Maipose (n.d.), Acemoglu and Johnson (2003), and Leith (2005).

2. Leith (2005) notes that when measured accurately, taking into account social, health, and educational services provided by the government to the poor, this measure falls to about 0.53. No measure of inequality is without serious analytical problems; the Gini coefficient is probably the best available and most widely used index. The coefficient ranges from 0 (perfect equality) to 1 (perfect inequality). The higher the index, the more unequal the society. An index above 0.5 is thought to denote an unequal distribution (Leith 2005).

3. See, for example, Auty (2004) and Sachs and Warner (1995). For a contrary view, see Stevens (2003) and Brunnschweiler and Bulte (2008). See also Lederman and Maloney (2007).

4. The analysis is based on the idea that some colonial regimes were mostly "extractive"—that is, the regime existed to reap the maximum out of the colony's economy. Other regimes, usually ones in which there were more colonial settlers, were less extractive. They often established institutions that put more constraints on the extractive and arbitrary powers of government. These constraining institutions often carried over into independence.

5. All of the high-performing developing countries mentioned have established strong democratic institutions. The question therefore arises whether the causality runs the other way, from growth to democracy. It can also be argued that democracy is necessary to sustain a high-income economy (see Barro 1997).

6. Isham and Kaufmann (1999) estimate this proportion (10 percent of GDP) to be the likely ceiling for public investment to remain productive. Beyond this they find public sector investment is likely to be detrimental to growth.

7. Lange and Wright (2002) point out that the only single "nonproductive" item of comparable weight in the budget

was defense expenditure, which average about 11 percent of total expenditure. While this is high relative to most countries Botswana arguably had good reason to do this.

8. World Bank cited in Lange and Wright, 2002, 32.

9. World Bank 2009. Botswana, however, lags other upper middle income countries in these categories.

10. Botswana has not been able to escape the effects of the current global crisis: GDP declined 4 percent in 2009, and for the first time in many years, Botswana had fiscal and balance of payments deficits. However, the economy appears to have weathered the worst, with the Bank of Botswana projecting real growth of more than 3 percent for 2010 and 2011.

11. Mining's share fell in 2009 because of the slump in world trade, not because of the declining importance of the sector.

12. Between 2005 and 2008, before the effects of the global slump set in, exports grew by about 40 percent. The share of diamonds fell from about 75 percent in 2005 to about 65 percent in 2008. Total mining remained more or less constant, however, at about 85 percent of total exports. The share of diamonds fell because of rising copper and nickel exports (Botswana Central Statistical Office 2009).

13. Other areas of interest are services, including financial services; downstream diamond processing and trading; and tourism, which represented about 10 percent of GDP in 2008 and is a potential growth sector for export earnings.

14. FDI rose again in 2008. It is too early to tell whether this is a trend.

15. Botswana had the best ranking in Africa on Transparency International's corruption perception index in 2011 and ranked 33rd worldwide. (See http://www.transparency .org/policy_research/surveys_indices/cpi/2010.) On the World Bank's 2010 Ease of Doing Business index, Botswana ranked 3rd regionally but only 52nd worldwide, indicating some room for improvement (see http://www.doingbusiness .org/rankings).

REFERENCES

Acemoglu, D., S. Johnson, and J. A. Robinson. 2003. "An African Success: Botswana." In *In Search of Prosperity: Analytical Narratives on Economic Growth*, ed. D. Rodrik. Princeton, NJ: Princeton University Press.

Acemoglu, D., and J. A. Robinson. 1999. "On the Political Economy of Institutions and Development." *American Economic Review* 91 (4): 938–63.

Alexeev, Michael, and Robert Conrad. 2009. "The Elusive Curse of Oil." *Review of Economics and Statistics* 91 (3): 586–98.

Auty, R. (ed.) 2001. "Resource Abundance and Economic Development." Wider Studies in Development. Oxford University Press, Oxford, UK.

Bank of Botswana. 2008. *Annual Report*. Gabarone.

———. 2010. *Botswana Financial Statistics*. Gaborone. http://www.bankofbotswana.bw/index.php/content/2009110615035-botswana-financial-statistics.

Barro, R. 1997. *Determinants of Economic Growth: A Cross-Country Empirical Study*. Cambridge, MA: MIT Press.

Basdevant, O. 2008. "Are Diamonds Forever? Using the Permanent Income Hypothesis to Analyze Botswana's Reliance on Diamond Revenue." IMF Working Paper, International Monetary Fund, Washington, DC.

Botswana Central Statistical Office. 2009. *External Monthly Trade Digest* January. Gaborone. http://www.cso.gov.bw/.

Brunnschweiler, C. N. and E. H. Bulte. 2008. "The Resource Curse Revisited and Revised: A Tale of Paradoxes and Red Herrings." *Journal of Environmental Economics and Management* 55: 248–64.

Collier, P., and A. Hoeffler. 2004. "Greed and Grievance in Civil War." Oxford Economic Papers 56, Oxford University, Oxford, UK.

———. 2005. "Democracy and Resource Rents." Oxford University, Oxford, UK.

Corden, W. M., and P. J. Neary. 1982. "Booming Sector and Deindustrialization in a Small Open Economy." *Economic Journal* 92: 825–48.

Hausmann, R., and R. Rigobon. 2003. "An Alternative Interpretation of the 'Resource Curse': Theory and Policy Implications." NBER Working Paper 9424, National Bureau of Economic Research, Cambridge, MA.

Isham, J., and D. Kaufmann. 1999. "The Forgotten Rationale of Policy Reform: The Productivity of Investment Projects." *Quarterly Journal of Economics* 116 (1).

Lange, G., and M. Wright. 2002. "Sustainable Development in Mineral Economies: The Example of Botswana." Ceepa Discussion Paper Series, University of Pretoria, Pretoria, South Africa.

Lederman, D., and W. F. Maloney, eds. 2007. *Natural Resources: Neither Curse nor Destiny*. Washington, DC: World Bank.

Leith, J. C. 2005. *Why Botswana Prospered*. Montreal: McGill-Queen's University Press.

Maipose, G. n.d. *Policy and Institutional Dynamics in Sustained Growth in Botswana*. University of Botswana, Gaborone.

OECD (Organisation for Economic Co-operation and Development). n.d. *Africa Economic Outlook*. http://www.africaneconomicoutlook.org/en/countries/southern-africa/botswana/.

Sachs, Jeffrey D., and Andrew M. Warner. 1995. "Natural Resource Abundance and Economic Growth." NBER Working Paper W5392, National Bureau of Economic Research, Cambridge, MA.

Stevens, P. 2003. "Resource Impact: Curse or Blessing? A Literature Survey." *Journal of Energy Literature* 11 (1): 3–42.

World Bank. 2009. *Country Partnership Strategy for the Republic of Botswana*. Washington, DC.

CHAPTER 5

Mauritius: An Economic Success Story

Ali Zafar

In 1961 James Meade, a Nobel Prize recipient in economics, famously predicted a dismal future for Mauritius because of its vulnerabilities to weather and price shocks and lack of job opportunities outside the sugar sector. The small island nation in the Indian Ocean of approximately 1.3 million people has defied those predictions, transforming itself from a poor sugar economy into a country with one of the highest per capita incomes among African countries.[1] Mauritius's combination of political stability, strong institutional framework, low level of corruption, and favorable regulatory environment has helped lay the foundation for economic growth, while its open trade policies have been key in sustaining growth. The government functions as a parliamentary democracy, and the country has an efficient administration that is both technically competent and adaptive to changing global economic circumstances. Mauritius's financial sector is sufficiently well developed that it has begun to position itself as a platform for investment linking East Africa with India and China.

Headline figures related to Mauritius's economic performance are impressive. Growth of real gross domestic product (GDP) has averaged more than 5 percent a year since 1970, and annual growth in real per capita income has likewise been strong. GDP per capita increased about sevenfold between 1976 and 2008, from less than $1,000 to roughly $7,000. Imports and exports have boomed; together, they reached more than 100 percent of GDP during the late 1990s and early 2000s. At the same time, efforts at economic diversification have been successful, allowing the country to move from sugar to textiles to a broader service economy. Mauritius's reliance on trade-led development has helped the country achieve respectable levels of export performance. Along the way, measures of human development have improved substantially.

Despite being a small island economy vulnerable to exogenous shocks, Mauritius has been able to craft a strong growth-oriented developmental path. Natural disasters and terms-of-trade shocks have never prevented the economy from having strong and regular growth. Constrained at inception by a monocrop sugar economy, low amounts of arable land, and a high rate of population growth, Mauritius has emerged as a regional entrepôt and tourism destination as well as the top-ranked African country in the World Bank's Doing Business survey (in 2010, it ranked 20th of 183 countries).

Although a variety of explanations have been advanced to explain Mauritius's growth, the country's focus on international trade has been, without doubt, a critical element of that performance.[2] Mauritius's preferential access to trading partners, particularly the European Union (EU), in the sugar, textile, and clothing sectors resulted in subsidies for

Ali Zafar is a macroeconomist in the World Bank Group.

the export sector and provided important foreign exchange for the economy. Preferential trading deals accounted for strong growth in Mauritius's total exports between the 1970s and the 1990s. Although imports tariffs in Mauritius were kept high, they have never been high enough to interfere with the overall trade regime. For example, the average tariff for manufacturing was 86.2 percent in 1980, but it fell to 30.1 percent in 1994 (Wignaraja and O'Neil 1999). Simultaneously, Mauritius pursued a very liberal investment regime and used incentives to attract foreign direct investment (FDI). Mauritius also offset the burdens on its exporters with tariff-free access for productive inputs, with tax incentive subsidies and relaxed labor market regulations in the export sector. Furthermore, it has used export processing zones (EPZs) to export key manufacturing goods, mostly apparel and textiles. Mauritius's overall trade and investment policy has been based on a managed embrace of globalization and cultivation of market access.

Aside from its trade and investment policy, Mauritius has benefited from prudent fiscal, exchange rate, and monetary policy, the latter of which has also been beneficial to export performance. To compensate for the myriad disadvantages of limited scale, Mauritius has developed a plethora of strong institutions and good governance. Additionally, the public and private sectors maintain a vibrant partnership that manifests itself in a range of areas.

Finally, Mauritius has always displayed receptivity to new ideas and adaptability. At various points in its history, Mauritius has used intervention, subsidies, and targeting to adapt to shifting economic circumstances. Although Mauritius benefited from the sugar protocols, the government also recognized early on the advantages of diversification. As a result, it relied heavily on EPZs but ensured that there was no anti-export bias. Mauritius has also proven very adept at embracing new sectors, particularly light manufacturing, offshore banking and financial services, and service-related information and communication technology (ICT). It has adapted and transformed its ethnic pluralism into a tangible economic force.[3] It has forged a vibrant democracy with competing parties, a strong electoral system, and an open media.[4] In sum, Mauritius's impressive economic performance has not been an accident, but rather the result of careful planning and policies. During and in the aftermath of the biggest exogenous shocks to its economy in recent times—the phasing out of the Multifibre Arrangement governing textiles, significant reductions in EU sugar protocol prices, the 2008 food and fuel crisis, and the 2008–09 global financial crisis—Mauritius's economy has displayed strong resilience.

THE GROWTH STORY

Since the 1970s Mauritius has recorded very high growth rates and sustained increases in human development indicators through a combination of good macroeconomic policies and strong institutions (table 5.1). With the advent of the sugar preferences and the EPZs in the 1970s and 1980s, Mauritian authorities have succeeded in

Table 5.1   Major Economic Indicators for Mauritius 2006–09

Indicator	2006	2007	2008	2009
National income (%)				
Real GDP growth	3.9	5.4	4.2	1.5
Consumer prices	11.8	8.7	6.8	4.0
Unemployment	9.1	8.5	7.2	8.3
Fiscal (% of GDP)				
Revenue	19.3	22.0	22.5	21.1
Expenditure	23.6	25.7	26.1	25.6
Fiscal balance	−4.6	−4.0	−3.4	−4.5
Total external debt	6.1	4.6	6.1	8.0
Total domestic debt	46.6	45.6	43.8	42.0
External (%)				
Import	16.4	6.0	20.6	−24.5
Export	8.9	−4.7	7.3	−23.5
Current account (% of GDP)	−9.4	−5.6	−10.4	−8.1
Terms of trade	−5.8	−1.0	−1.1	1.6
Domestic investment (% of GDP)				
Public	6.9	6.4	5	6.1
Private	17.3	18.7	19.6	20.2
Nominal GDP ($ billions)	6,507	7,521	9,321	8,527

Source: IMF (2010); Government of Mauritius.

transforming the economy and laying the foundation for stable growth in the future. Sugar and textile revenues have been used to facilitate service-sector development and contribute to socioeconomic progress and higher living standards.

A well-managed economic regime

Proper macroeconomic management—fiscal discipline during boom times, monetary management that kept inflation in the single digits and that produced interest rates that encouraged domestic savings, and an exchange-rate policy that maintained flexibility and competitiveness for exporters—have all been key to Mauritius's economic success. At the same time, flexible public policy, especially in the form of experiments creating EPZs in the 1980s and embracing the ICT industry in the 2000s, was also an important feature. Trade reforms, the development of a social welfare system, and policies that favored human capital development also played a part. The result has been manageable fiscal and current account deficits, high rates of private investment, and respectable and stable growth rates.

A very successful economic trajectory

Between 1977 and 2009, and despite the volatility caused by exogenous shocks during those years, real GDP in Mauritius grew on average by 5.1 percent annually, compared with 3.2 percent for Sub-Saharan Africa (figure 5.1). The growth rate accelerated in the 1980s as a result of the macroeconomic reforms instituted in response to protracted balance of payments and fiscal troubles. Following the reforms,

Mauritius experienced steady growth, low inflation, and increased employment. GDP per capita, meanwhile, increased approximately sevenfold between 1976 and 2008, from less than $1,000 to nearly $7,000 (figure 5.2). At the same time, consumer price inflation in Mauritius has remained in the low single digits through the 1990s and early 2000s, and the country's debt stock has been manageable.[5] Windfalls from sugar and textile preferences have been used wisely to help promote diversification and boost growth. The structural transition away from agriculture and into manufacturing and services shows the success of the government's efforts at economic diversification.

Favorable international comparisons

Both a cursory examination of economic indicators and detailed diagnostics show that Mauritius has been one of the best-performing and most stable economies in Sub-Saharan Africa in recent decades, even in the presence of terms-of-trade and oil shocks. Using purchasing power parity (PPP) data for 44 Sub-Saharan African countries, Arbache and Page (2008) examine country-level dynamics of long-run growth between 1975 and 2005 and conclude that Mauritius was one of the best performers, both in per capita growth performance and in low volatility of growth, alongside Botswana, Cape Verde, Gabon, Namibia, the Seychelles, and South Africa.

Decomposing the standard deviation of GDP per capita and economic growth into within-country and between-country components, one finds that Mauritius's growth stability was much higher than that of many oil economies, such as Angola and Nigeria, and of many resource-poor

Figure 5.1   Real GDP Growth in Mauritius, 1981–2009

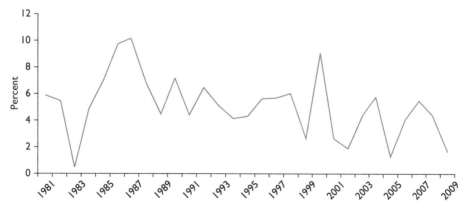

Source: Government of Mauritius.

Figure 5.2   GDP per Capita in Mauritius, 1976–2008

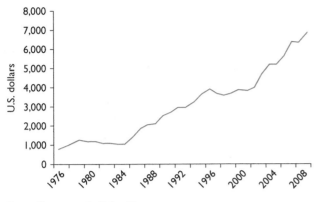

Source: Government of Mauritius.

economies, such as Burundi and Central African Republic, in Sub-Saharan Africa. While Mauritius was growing, much of Sub-Saharan Africa was not. In 1975–94 growth decelerations were twice as frequent as accelerations: 29 percent versus 14 percent of all country-year observations in the Arbache-Page dataset.

The role of total factor productivity

Empirical work decomposing total factor productivity (TFP) in Mauritius during different time periods shows the strong role of factor accumulation. As in many countries in East Asia, the principal drivers of growth in Mauritius have been capital and labor accumulation, with TFP growth making a significant but varying contribution.

In a paper using a growth accounting framework analysis for Mauritius and highlighting the performance of the 1980s and 1990s, Subramanian and Roy (2001) uncover diverse performance in the two periods. For the period 1982–99, productivity growth in the EPZ sector was 3.5 percent, substantially more than double the 1.4 percent for the economy as a whole. In the first period (1982–90), economic growth was rapid and driven predominantly by the growth of inputs—capital and labor—which together accounted for more than 80 percent of the annual average rate of GDP growth of 6.2 percent. During this period, employment growth averaged 5.2 percent a year, reflecting a sharp decline in the unemployment rate from 20 percent of the total labor force in the early 1980s to 3 percent in the late 1980s. TFP growth was respectable at more than 1 percent, but capital accumulation was the main driver of growth. The authors find that economic growth from 1991 to 1999, however, was driven less by capital accumulation

than in the past and to a greater extent by productivity growth, with TFP growth during this period averaging more than 1 percent a year.[6] Their estimates suggest that in the EPZ sector, TFP grew by 5.4 percent from 1991 to 1999.

In another study, Rojid and Seetanah (2009) provide evidence that TFP gains in Mauritius have reached a plateau. TFP growth averaged 1.4 percent in the 1980s, 1.0 percent in the 1990s, and 0.7 percent in the 2000s, but the TFP contribution to overall growth varies depending on the different growth rates (table 5.2). For the entire period 1980–2007, TFP contribution to growth in Mauritius averaged 1.0 percent annually, considerably higher than the 0.3 percent average in Common Market for Eastern and Southern Africa (COMESA) countries over the same years. The TFP change in Mauritius resulted from economic reforms and human capital improvements.

Structural transformation

Over time the sectoral composition of the Mauritian economy has changed profoundly. Between 1976 and 2010 the share of primary-sector production declined from 23 percent of the overall economy to 6 percent, while the secondary sector (including manufacturing, electricity, water, and some construction) increased from about 23 to 28 percent (with manufacturing making an even bigger jump). The tertiary sector, which includes tourism and financial services, grew from just over 50 percent to nearly 70 percent of GDP (figure 5.3). Projections by the Mauritian government suggest further expansion of the tertiary sector as a share of the economy in the future. In general, the share of manufacturing output increased in the 1980s because of the presence of EPZs but stagnated as the sector faced adjustment in the 1990s and 2000s. Table 5.3 shows patterns for specific industry groups and subgroups between 1990 and 2010. Sugar, which represented more than 20 percent of Mauritius's GDP in 1976, accounted for approximately 4 percent of GDP in 2009. At a disaggregated sectoral level (whether at current prices or constant prices), there has been a strong structural change, with the decline in sugar, a rise of financial services and real estate, and a mixed performance of textiles as the service sector has strengthened (figure 5.4) By the 2000s the service sector had become the dominant feature of the economy in terms of contribution to output. This noteworthy structural transformation has helped the country deal with decreasing returns to scale of capital accumulation at the sectoral level. The various economic pillars in Mauritius have thus contributed to growth and mitigated output volatility.

Table 5.2 Total Factor Productivity Decomposition and Contribution to Growth

Economy/	Years	Growth rate (percent)	Contribution to the Growth Rate		
			Capital (percentage points)	Labor (percentage points)	TFP (percentage points)
Mauritius	1980–1990	6.3	3.0	2.0	1.3
	1991–2000	5.6	2.5	2.1	1.0
	2001–2007	4.1	2.5	0.9	0.7
	1980–2007	**5.3**	**2.6**	**1.7**	**1.0**
COMESA	1980–1990	3.1	1.5	1.7	−0.2
	1991–2000	2.4	0.7	1.6	0.1
	2001–2007	4.5	2.1	1.5	0.9
	1980–2007	**3.3**	**1.5**	**1.6**	**0.3**

Source: Rojid and Seetanah 2009.

Note: Percentages are rounded to nearest tenth.

Figure 5.3 Sectoral Composition of GDP in Mauritius, 1976–2010

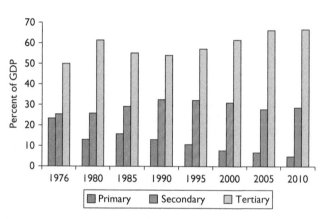

Source: Mauritius authorities; World Bank 2009.

Improvement in human development indicators

In contrast to many Sub-Saharan African and comparator economies, rapid economic growth in Mauritius has occurred in parallel with substantial improvement in human development indicators and a decrease in income inequality. Life expectancy at birth, for example, increased from 62 years in 1970 to 73 years in 2008, while infant mortality dropped from 64 per 1,000 live births in 1970 to 15 in 2008 (figure 5.5). The Gini coefficient, a measure of income inequality in which 0 represents perfect equality among households and 1 represents perfect inequality, declined from 0.5 in 1962 to 0.37 in 1986–87 and was stable at 0.38 in 2008. Following heavy government investment in education improvements in the 1980s and 1990s, primary school enrollment rates reached very high levels, averaging more than 90 percent in the 1990s and 2000s, although challenges remain.[7]

Poverty levels in Mauritius have also fallen significantly. In 1975, 40 percent of Mauritian households were below the presumed poverty line, according to the government's Central Statistics Office.[8] By 1991/92 the proportion had fallen to 11 percent, and by 2010 absolute poverty was less than 2 percent. The poverty decline was achieved with no exacerbation of inequality. Significant improvements in gender equality have resulted from the massive inflow of women into the labor market starting in the 1980s. The country recently ranked 11th of 102 countries in the OECD Social Institutions and Gender Index. Mauritius's housing stock has also improved, both in quality and quantity, as a result of government investment. Finally, Mauritius has developed a sophisticated pension system covering retirement benefits and general social security.

MACROECONOMIC MANAGEMENT

Prudent, proactive fiscal policy

A hallmark of economic management in Mauritius in recent decades has been prudent fiscal policy, which has helped maintain macroeconomic stability and contributed to growth. Fiscal policy has focused on ensuring that spending remains linked to resource availability. While there have been fiscal imbalances, there is no history of the government borrowing from the central bank or from aid agencies. The strong growth in the 1980s led to a decrease in recourse to foreign financing. The budget deficit, which was at 3 percent in 1983, turned into a budget surplus by 1987, as current expenditures shrank from 26 percent of GDP to 21 percent in 1987 while government revenues remained flat, around 24 percent over the same period. On the expenditure side, the government withdrew from subsidies on food items and kept the wage bill under control during that period.

Table 5.3 GDP by Industry Group at Current Basic Prices, 1990–2010
(percent)

Industry group	1990	1995	2000	2005	2010[a]
Agriculture, hunting, forestry, and fishing	**12.9**	**10.4**	**7.0**	**6.0**	**4.3**
Sugarcane	8.0	5.7	3.6	3.2	1.6
Other	4.8	4.6	3.4	2.8	2.7
Mining and quarrying	**0.2**	**0.2**	**0.2**	**0.1**	**0.0**
Manufacturing	**24.4**	**23.0**	**23.5**	**19.8**	**19.1**
Sugar	3.4	1.6	0.8	1.0	0.5
Food, excluding sugar	0.0	—	4.1	5.1	6.6
Textiles	0.0	—	12.0	6.7	5.2
Other	0.0	—	6.6	7.0	6.8
Electricity, gas, and water supply	**1.5**	**2.4**	**1.7**	**2.1**	**2.5**
Construction	**6.7**	**6.4**	**5.6**	**5.6**	**7.1**
Wholesale and retail trade; repair of motor vehicles, motorcycles, and personal and household goods	**13.0**	**12.8**	**12.2**	**12.1**	**11.9**
Wholesale and retail trade	12.6	12.3	11.7	11.4	11.1
Other	0.4	0.5	0.5	0.7	0.8
Hotels and restaurants	**3.9**	**5.1**	**6.5**	**7.7**	**7.5**
Transport, storage, and communications	**10.4**	**11.4**	**13.0**	**12.6**	**10.8**
Financial intermediation	**4.9**	**6.5**	**9.7**	**10.3**	**12.3**
Insurance	1.5	2.1	2.3	2.9	2.9
Banks[b]	0.0	4.4	6.6	6.2	8.0
Other	0.0	—	0.8	1.2	1.4
Real estate, renting, and business activities	**8.9**	**8.5**	**8.9**	**10.2**	**11.9**
Owner-occupied dwellings	6.4	5.3	4.5	5.0	5.0
Other	2.5	3.2	4.4	5.2	6.9
Public administration and defense; compulsory social security	**6.4**	**6.7**	**6.7**	**7.1**	**6.5**
Education	**4.1**	**4.4**	**4.5**	**4.8**	**4.6**
Health and social work	**2.5**	**2.8**	**3.0**	**3.4**	**3.8**
Other community, social, and personal service activities and private households with employed persons	**2.0**	**2.8**	**3.3**	**3.7**	**4.7**
Financial intermediation services indirectly measured (FISIM)	**−1.8**	**−3.3**	**−5.7**	**−5.5**	**−7.0**
GDP at basic prices	**100.0**	**100.0**	**100.0**	**100.0**	**100.0**
Manufacturing industries previously operating with an EPZ certificate	**11.9**	**11.4**	**11.9**	**7.4**	**6.7**

Source: Central Statistics Office, Government of Mauritius.
Note: Figures may not add up to the totals due to rounding. — = not available. Data are at current prices.
a. Forecast figures.
b. For years 1991 to 1996, figures for other financial intermediation are included in banks.

Figure 5.4 Major Economic Sectors in Mauritius, 1976–2009

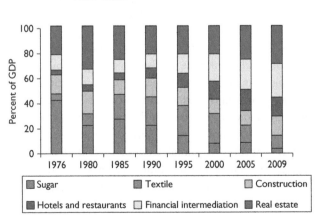

Source: Mauritius authorities; World Bank 2009.

Similarly, in the 2000s, the government built up reserves that allowed it the freedom to expand fiscal policy in the aftermath of the 2008–09 global financial crisis. Moreover, the stock of international and domestic debt has remained well below an unsustainable threshold (total public debt was projected to be 60.4 percent of GDP at the end of 2010). Excluding a period in the early 1980s, current expenditures have never much exceeded 20 percent of GDP and have been used mostly for wage policy, with a small amount devoted to food subsidies. Taken together, the composition of current expenditure has been mostly oriented in recent decades to the outlays for wages and subsidies, but there has been little expansion of the federal apparatus as a share of GDP because fiscal profligacy has been an anathema to the Mauritian policy makers. In the first four years of the 1980s, the ratio of current expenditure to GDP was close to 25 percent but it steadily dropped to around 20 percent by the mid 1980s, and that ratio has stayed relatively constant, in contrast to that of many developing countries. Capital expenditures, which have averaged less than 5 percent of GDP since independence, have been used productively to invest in infrastructure—especially roads—and to provide a necessary operating environment for EPZs.[9] Mauritian policy makers have been remarkably fiscally prudent to avoid any macroeconomic instability. In sum, fiscal policy has helped lay the foundation for management of volatility and robust growth.

In terms of both revenue management and expenditures, fiscal policy in Mauritius has been proactive. International trade taxes anchored the system's revenue system, accounting for close to 50 percent of GDP during the 1970s, 1980s, and 1990s. High import tariffs and export levies on sugar helped give the government resources during the early years, although the introduction of a value added tax (VAT, which replaced the sales tax) in 1998 has played an important role in improving tax buoyancy at the level of direct and indirect taxes and has allowed the fiscal system to evolve.[10] As a result, the tax system has not been affected by import tariff liberalization in recent years. In addition, in 2007 the implementation of a flat tax of 15 percent on corporate and personal incomes streamlined tax administration. By 2008 tax revenue amounted to 19 percent of GDP, of which 20 percent came from income taxes, more than 35 percent from the VAT, and slightly less than 5 percent from international trade taxes. The diversified stream of revenue helped the fiscal system absorb shocks and provide stable revenue flows to the government.

Monetary policy as an anchor for economic growth

In tandem with fiscal policy, monetary policy in Mauritius has helped anchor economic growth and ensure competitiveness. Since its creation in 1967, the Bank of Mauritius has been concerned with ensuring the competitiveness of the country's export sectors and, secondarily, with price stability. In important ways, a series of exchange rate decisions early on had ripple effects on economic activity. As part of the liberalization program, the Mauritian rupee (MUR) was devalued by 30 percent in 1979 and readjusted by 20 percent in 1981, when the rupee was officially delinked from the IMF's special drawing right and pegged to a trade-weighted basket of the currencies of its major trading partners. By the mid-1980s the Bank of Mauritius was intervening to smooth currency fluctuations, and the country has maintained a managed float since the mid-1990s. Figure 5.6 shows the path of the real effective exchange rate (REER) of the rupee (base year is 1970 = 100). The results of the managed float exchange rate regime have been favorable to the economy, with the trade-weighted REER depreciating on average by more than 5 percent a year from 1981 to 2007.[11] Although inflation has been higher in other Sub-Saharan African countries than in Mauritius, the central bank allows the accommodation of these inflation differentials by letting the nominal exchange rate slide in order to keep the REER competitive. The policy has worked well in terms of being flexible and being sensitive to the country's export sector.

Figure 5.5 Social Indicators in Mauritius, 1970 and 2008

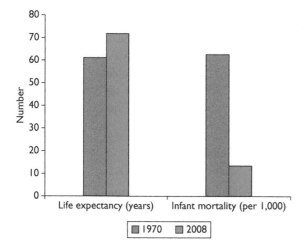

Source: World Bank 2010, UNICEF.

Figure 5.6 MUR Real Effective Exchange Rate, 1981–2009

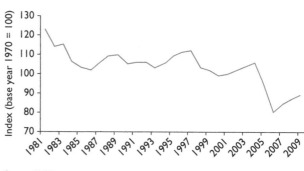

Source: IMF.

As inflation fell in other parts of the developing world in the 1990s, Mauritius adopted an informal inflation targeting approach. Over time, monetary policy in Mauritius has evolved from a strong reliance on direct monetary instruments, such as credit ceilings, to a gradual introduction of market-based instruments such as weekly auctions of Treasury and Bank of Mauritius bills. In practice, monetary management has been oriented to ensure a positive interest rate differential relative to major currencies while reacting to domestic inflation when it is above a certain level. Interest rate policy has been used successfully to provide savers with positive real rates of return in order to mobilize domestic capital and to help sterilize excess liquidity. As a result, national savings has consistently exceeded investment expenditure since the mid-1980s.[12]

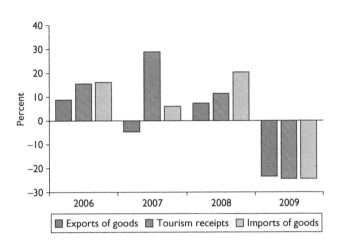

Figure 5.7   Trade and Tourism Growth, 2006–09

Source: IMF 2010.

Effective response to economic shocks

A tribute to Mauritius's successful macroeconomic management can be seen in the response to the global financial crisis and the various shocks that preceded it. The combination of the phasing out of the Multifibre Arrangement starting in 2004, the reduction in sugar price guarantees from the European Union starting in 2006, and dramatic increases in world commodity prices (especially for food and fuel) had already started to act as a brake on the country's growth trajectory and current account and fiscal positions when the financial crisis began. The financial crisis hit the small, open economy of Mauritius hard. The country experienced a sharp decline in demand for tourism and textile exports (figure 5.7). Labor-intensive sectors, especially construction and textiles, contracted as the crisis made its way to Mauritius.

As a result of the crisis, growth slowed to 4.2 percent in 2008 and to less than 2 percent in 2009, while unemployment increased from 7.2 percent in 2008 to 7.7 percent in 2009. Through prudent macroeconomic management, however, international reserves continued to expand and the fiscal deficit was kept below 5 percent of GDP. Morisset, Bastos, and Rojid (2010) find that the country's resilience to the shocks derived from a combination of four factors: reforms to sustain long-term growth, which accelerated in 2006; a timely, targeted, and temporary short-term response to the crisis; institutional arrangements to face the crisis that promoted private sector collaboration; and strong relationships with development partners.

In response to the global financial crisis, Mauritius passed a fiscal stimulus and monetary easing package of about 5 percent of GDP over 2009–10. The plan focused on infrastructure spending, providing financial relief to the firms hit hardest by the global crisis, and social and job protection measures. At the same time, the government introduced offsetting measures that are expected to bring the primary budget into surplus by the end of 2011, and a public debt management act was passed limiting public sector debt to 60 percent of GDP, with a goal of reducing it to 50 percent by 2013. The government has also been using special "rainy day" funds to help finance the stimulus. These funds had been prudently put aside in previous financial years (to the tune of 3 percent of GDP), reducing current debt financing needs. Monetary policy in Mauritius was also loosened, the key discount rate at the central bank was cut by 250 basis points, and reserve requirements were reduced.

In addition to easing fiscal and monetary policy, Mauritius introduced measures to assist the private sector in the wake of the crisis. Firms facing liquidity difficulties were given temporary financial relief (conditional on credible restructuring plans), with costs shared by banks, the government, and the firm's shareholders.[13] A tax suspension program was also introduced for the labor-intensive and vulnerable tourism, construction, and real estate sectors.

A TALE OF THREE SECTORS: SUGAR, EPZs, AND TOURISM

At various times in Mauritius's history, sugar, EPZs, and tourism each have been a mainstay of the economy, and the interaction among the three sectors has been essential for the country's economic take-off. As a small, open economy with a high ratio of trade of goods and services to GDP (averaging more than 50 percent from 1970 to 2010), Mauritius has long been well positioned to embrace globalization. Over the years Mauritius has used trade policy as a means both to protect domestic industry and to launch export growth.

The sugar sector

In its heyday in the 1970s the sugar sector in Mauritius accounted for close to one-third of employment, one-third of export earnings, and one-quarter of GDP. Through smart negotiations and building on a preexisting relationship with the United Kingdom, Mauritius succeeded in obtaining preferential treatment from the European Economic Community (EEC) through the Sugar Protocol of the Lomé Convention in 1975, under which it received more or less free access for its sugar exports to the EEC.[14] Mauritius sold its sugar to the EEC at a premium—three times the international market price, on average. For years Mauritius's export quota was fixed at more than 500,000 metric tons annually, the largest quota share among African, Caribbean, and Pacific (ACP) countries. Even with these international trade agreements in place, however, the collapse in international sugar prices in the mid-1970s hit Mauritius's sugar sector hard, leading to balance of payments difficulties and recourse to external assistance. Nevertheless, by 2005, in the aftermath of the World Trade Organization's ruling that the above-market prices paid to sugar producers constituted unfair trade, the European Union ended the preferential deals by slashing sugar prices.

Import substitution industrialization (ISI) and restrictive trade policies following the colonial period

Following the establishment of a development certificate scheme by colonial authorities in 1964 to promote import substitution industrialization and provide incentives for local manufacturers through concessions and tariffs, Mauritius invoked a series of protectionist measures in an effort to develop local industry. Besides providing government with some revenue and helping to incubate entrepreneurial talent, these policies, which were concentrated in the EPZs, had a marginal impact on the local economy. Subramanian and Roy (2001) find that Mauritius's trade policy was highly protective during the 1970s and 1980s. In 1980 average effective protection exceeded 100 percent, although this fell to 65 percent by the end of the 1980s. During the 1970s and 1980s, there were extensive quantitative restrictions in the

form of import licensing, which covered nearly 60 percent of imports, and an extensive system of exemptions and concessions. Protection was especially high in the clothing, footwear, furniture, and rubber sectors, all of which had tariffs above 50 percent, while tariffs for electronics and plastics averaged more than 40 percent. Corporate taxes were also very high, and bureaucracy was quite heavy. Protectionism faded through the course of the 1980s, however, and by the early 1990s import licensing was eliminated on all but a limited list of items subject to health, sanitary, or strategic controls, while export licensing was abolished for most products.

The rise of EPZs in the 1970s and 1980s

Having studied the success of export processing zones in East Asia, a group of visionary policy makers in Mauritius put forth the idea that the country's small economic size and distance from large developed markets presented a potential opportunity to develop an export-oriented textile industry. In 1970 Mauritius passed the Export Processing Zone Act, which provided powerful incentives to manufacturers that catered to foreign markets. The EPZ was not restricted to one physical location but was envisaged as a fiscal regime that encompassed the entire island, and the idea was to develop a fast-track approval for all administrative procedures in the EPZ. Ambitious and well-crafted legislation provided the underpinnings for the new regime. Key components of the new legislation included protective import duties and quotas for infant industries, suspension of import duties on materials and equipment for industrial use that were not locally available, rebates of import duties on other raw materials and components for specified industries, duty drawback schemes, and favorable long-term loans. The granting of duty-free inputs for manufactured exports was key in expanding Mauritius's export competitiveness on world markets, while tax incentives helped subsidize exports. Firms within EPZs also benefited from the availability of relatively cheap labor, drawn from unemployed workers and women who were outside the labor force at the time. According to interviews with textile executives located in the EPZs, 80 percent of workers in the EPZs in the 1980s were women. The rate has decreased somewhat in the 1990s and 2000s, but more than 60 percent of the workers in the zones are women. The lower wages that were paid to the workers in the EPZs in the early years allowed the firms to accumulate capital and reinvest the earnings into the firms' expansion.[15] However, over time the wages in the EPZ became higher than those in the non-EPZ economy.

Also important, Mauritius did not restrict EPZs to one geographical location, and the government invested heavily in the infrastructure needed to set up EPZs. Finally, it is important to note that the government provided strong institutional support for marketing EPZ products.

By the 1980s EPZs had exceeded the expectations of even visionary policy makers in Mauritius. The zones accounted for more than 60 percent of Mauritius's gross export earnings and employed one-third of the Mauritian labor force. Goods produced in EPZs more than tripled as a share of GDP between 1980 and 1988, from 4 percent to more than 14 percent (figure 5.8). More people worked in EPZs than in the agricultural sector by the end of the 1980s. The growth rate of the EPZs' value added was close to 30 percent annually between 1983 and 1988. Most of the goods produced in EPZs were exported to Europe under a preferential regime. Notably, there was significant interaction between the sugar sector and EPZs. Much of the start-up capital for EPZ firms, as well as technical and managerial expertise, came from the well-established sugar companies in the aftermath of the sugar boom in the 1970s. Together with the sugar sector, the textile sector provided the capital accumulation that allowed Mauritius to decrease reliance on foreign capital and start down the path to becoming a middle-income economy.

Several additional factors contributed to Mauritius's success with EPZs. First, the country took advantage of the depth of EU and U.S. demand for textiles and apparel, which provided a solid base for expansion. Second, Mauritius's timing was good, as its initial entry into the U.S. market got a boost from investors based in Hong Kong SAR, China, who were seeking to move capital and factories out of Hong Kong SAR, China, in anticipation of the 1997 reunification with China. Third, there was a strong political stability, proper governance, and a clear legal and institutional demarcation between the ISI and the EPZ regimes.

Fourth, quotas on Asian textile exports into Western markets led investors to look to alternate production countries. Those investors brought capital, marketing networks, and technological know-how to Mauritius's nascent textile sector. Greenaway and Milner 1989, however, find that the decision to grant Mauritius trade preferences in garments through the Multifibre Arrangement was more important in giving the country privileged access to developed markets relative to established Asian producers. Fifth, EPZs benefited from the inflow of local capital and of indigenous managerial capacity, which had partly been incubated under import substitution policies. Bheenick and Schapiro (1989) find that local participation in EPZ equity in Mauritius was roughly half, a much higher ratio than in EPZs in other developing countries. And finally, Mauritius benefited from a strong entreprencurial class and a trainable labor force, that together with the political class, had a strong ownership in the success of the EPZs. In turn, the job opportunities offered by EPZs played a significant part in unemployment falling from 20 percent to less than 5 percent between the mid-1970s and 1990. Over time the EPZs have helped the country's exports match the imports, although the proportion of service exports has increased in recent years as the economy has changed (see figure 5.8).

Post-EPZ economic drivers: Tourism, business process outsourcing, and financial services

Although EPZs brought dramatic economic improvements to Mauritius, the textile and apparel sectors have met challenges in more recent years. Not least of these was the phasing out of the Multifibre Arrangement, which started in 2004 and led to a contraction of 30 percent in value added of the products produced in EPZs. The number of Mauritians employed in EPZs fell by about 25,000 people between 2005 and 2010.[16] In parallel, the European Union's reduction of sugar prices by more than 50 percent starting in 2005 and continuing onto 2010 was a significant blow to the Mauritian economy, given that from 1975 to 2005, about 90 percent of its sugar production was exported to the European market. The European Union's decision to end price guarantees on raw sugar for all countries has thus been a shock for the $10 billion Mauritian economy. In short, both the sugar and textile and apparel sectors are in the process of adjustment in order to remain globally competitive, with the textile sector making inroads into fully integrated activities (for example,

Figure 5.8 Value of Mauritian Exports and Imports, 1980–2009

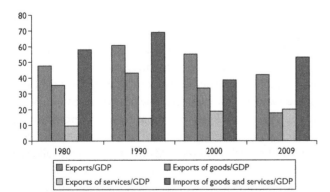

Source: Mauritian authorities.

spinning and weaving) and higher-end manufacturing and the sugar sector increasing its focus on refined sugars.

As the sugar and EPZ sectors in Mauritius have struggled in recent years, the tourism sector has expanded rapidly, backed by a master plan reflecting the government's dislike for mass tourism and high-rise buildings. Public sector efforts to expand tourism have been complemented by the promotional activities of the hotels and by Air Mauritius. Indeed, Mauritius's combination of beautiful beaches, a multiethnic society, and excellent hotels dotting the coastline has been quite effective in attracting tourists. According to the Mauritius Chamber of Commerce, tourist arrivals reached 240,000 in 1988, 400,000 in 2000, and 900,000 in 2008. An estimated 1 million tourists were expected to visit the country in 2010. Tourism is also among the strongest foreign exchange–earning sectors of the Mauritian economy.

In addition to tourism, the government of Mauritius has also encouraged diversification of the economy into business process outsourcing (BPO), financial services, and information technology. According to government figures, the BPO industry has been growing 70 percent a year and is currently worth $1.6 billion, employing more than 100,000 people. Offshore banking was introduced in 1988 as a first step toward developing Mauritius into an international financial center, and the offshore sector is now emerging as a growth vehicle for the economy.[17] Development of the information technology sector, meanwhile, is intended to transform Mauritius into "a cyber island" by creating a high-tech, multi-story tower that provides a home to companies from all over the world to set up BPO operations, including data management, e-commerce, and call centers. The government has also encouraged use of Mauritius as a transshipment center and a re-export base and, more recently, as an international medical hub and regional knowledge center. As a result of these efforts, the Ministry of Finance finds that the services sector showed consistent growth over 2006–09, with financial intermediation growing by 10.1 percent in 2008.

Lessons of the three sectors

The story of the three sectors in Mauritius offers a number of lessons. Most important, the constant search for new drivers of economic growth reflects a desire by policy makers to adapt to the future rather than wait for and respond to shocks. The central lesson here is that the public sector can effectively formulate and implement sectoral policies to stimulate the private sector. In the case of sugar, the protocols were signed and the private sector rushed into the activity. In the case of EPZs and tourism, a well-articulated policy framework led to a strong private sector response. And in all cases, the government acted as a facilitator of private sector expansion.

DYNAMIC INSTITUTIONS AND ADAPTABILITY TO CHANGE

Aside from its success in macroeconomic management, one of the keys to Mauritius's economic success has been its rich web of trade links, effective institutions, and history of public collaboration. In surveys of institutional quality, Mauritius repeatedly ranks high relative to comparator countries, particularly in measures of governance, rule of law, and control of corruption. The combination of political stability, democratic legacy, rule of law, and quality of judicial institutions sets Mauritius apart from many Sub-Saharan African countries. Moreover, a set of informal and formal mechanisms guide the interaction between the public and the private sector, with the result that the private sector plays a seminal role in the policy formulation process (all Mauritian delegations to international organizations, for example, have a private sector member). Indeed, cooperation between the public and private sectors has a long history in Mauritius.

For decades, Mauritius served as a trade hub for Chinese and Indian traders and an entrepôt for shipping across the Indian Ocean, and its inhabitants were known for their entrepreneurship. Over time those trade links coalesced into formal trade associations and entities, some of which came to be represented at the political level. At the same time, Mauritius has been quite effective at promoting its trade links on the international level.

The importance of forging consensus

The search for consensus is one of the remarkable features of the Mauritian political economy. Essentially, the Mauritian state is modeled on the British system of government, with a cabinet headed by a prime minister and a legislative assembly serving as the law-making body. As in the United Kingdom, the system of government in Mauritius is based on the principle of separation of power between the legislature, the executive, and the judiciary. Gulhati and Nallari (1990) argue that since no single political party has ever secured a majority in the assembly, which would allow it to form a government on its own, there has always been a need to work together across party lines, putting a distinctive stamp on economic policy process. Despite being based on loose agglomerations of ethnic and economic interests, political parties in Mauritius have not been vehicles for eth-nic separation. To the contrary, political parties have long recognized that building consensus is necessary to avoid adverse economic effects in a small economy.

The nexus between the public and private sectors

A paramount role in state-business relations in Mauritius is played by the Joint Economic Council (JEC), which occu-pies a central place in the country's institutional landscape and represents an umbrella association of a number of sector-specific groupings. As such, it carries a certain amount of institutional weight, meeting with the prime minister on a regular basis and providing input on major policy decisions. Being funded entirely by the private sector, it also has a degree of financial autonomy. The overarching goal of the JEC is to ensure private sector representation in all key government economic decisions. It also ensures that its members' ideas are conveyed to political leaders.

Another example of public-private sector cooperation is the establishment of the EPZs, which would not have been possible without support from several key public sector institutions. Central among these were the Mauritius Export Development and Investment Authority (MEDIA), the Export Processing Zone Authority (EPZDA), and the Devel-opment Bank of Mauritius (DBM). MEDIA was formed in 1985 as a public trade and investment promotion agency (with some private sector membership) and was a pivotal institution behind the country's drive for export growth and industrial upgrading. Providing overseas marketing support for exports and arranging buyer-seller meetings, it helped explore niches for Mauritian garments in European and American markets. Formed in the early 1970s, the EPZDA helped represent the interests of firms in the EPZs, while the Development Bank of Mauritius provided much of the credit and start-up capital for the economy as it was taking off from its narrow monocrop base. More recently, the Board of Investment has played a role in helping to promote Mau-ritius as an international investment, business, and service center, providing counseling on investment opportunities in Mauritius and helping in setting up businesses.

BUSINESS CLIMATE AND INVESTMENT

Alongside successful trade policy and adaptability, another major reason for Mauritius's economic success has been its business climate and incentives for foreign companies to locate there. Mauritius has no capital controls, a relatively stable currency, a low flat corporate tax rate of 15 percent,

and a large number of double taxation avoidance agree-ments; together, these attributes sometimes make Mauri-tius more attractive than larger financial sectors for busi-nesses. International rankings consistently give Mauritius high marks for business and investment climate. The main lesson from Mauritius in this regard is that geography is not destiny and that policies to improve investment cli-mates can have large positive multiplier effects.

Business climate improvement in recent years

The World Bank's *Doing Business 2010* ranks Mauritius as the best country in which to do business in Africa. Overall, Mauritius is ranked 20th of 183 countries included in the 2010 survey, up from 24th of 183 in 2009. Currently, Mauritius is among the top-performing developing coun-tries in starting a business, paying taxes, and protecting investors, and it has been a consistent reformer since it began being included in *Doing Business* in 2005. More broadly, Mauritius has taken steps to improve business facilitation since the late 1990s. In earlier years, while the private sector was thriving in certain sectors such as sugar and textiles, the climate for domestic firms in the non-EPZ sector was unfavorable. A study by Lall and Wignaraja (1998) found several major obstacles for enterprises oper-ating in Mauritius at the time: high interest rates; heavy bureaucratic procedures resulting in delays in obtaining foreign investment approvals; difficulty getting loan approvals from the Development Bank of Mauritius; delays in receiving refunds on import duties; difficulty obtaining work permits for foreign technical staff; lack of access to finance for small enterprises; and high sea-freight costs. Government reforms have helped alleviate all of these obstacles in the years since.

One major piece of legislation, the Business Facilitation Act 2006, provided a new, streamlined legal framework for business operations in Mauritius. The legislation facilitates doing business and acquisition of properties by foreigners and, among other things, enables small enterprises to start business activities within three working days. As a result, the private sector and foreign investors can more easily venture into new sectors, such as real estate and financial services, in which growth rates are eclipsing traditional sectors. Between 2006 and 2010, the share of private sector invest-ment, mainly in infrastructure projects such as commercial and office buildings, hotels, and resorts, grew to account for more than 80 percent of gross domestic capital formation. While infrastructure deficiencies and difficulties obtaining credit remain for small firms, along with a lack of skilled labor for larger firms, the thrust of the reforms has been to alleviate these constraints.

The role of foreign direct investment

FDI inflows to Mauritius have increased rapidly in the past several years, attracted by reforms such as the removal of the tax on capital account transactions and the waiving of the requirement that foreign investors need approval of the Bank of Mauritius to carry out activity. In addition while the corporate tax rate is a low 15 percent, foreign firms receive a subsidy of close to 10 percent, leading to an effective tax rate of 5 percent. The country attracted more FDI during 2004–07 than the cumulative stock of FDI during the previous 25 years (figure 5.9). Importantly, FDI inflows are accompanied by new business ideas, technologies, and managerial skills. Most FDI inflows have gone to the hospitality and tourism, property and real estate, banking and finance, information technology, health, and education sectors. The main FDI source countries are France, South Africa, and the United Kingdom, although total FDI inflows are equally divided between developed and emerging countries. Interestingly, Mauritius has also been a beneficiary of a high inflow of FDI into India. Because of special tax treatment given to investments that come through Mauritius to India,[18] Mauritius has become a quasi-tax haven for foreign funds invested in India, and currently, about 80–90 percent of foreign direct investment into India flows through Mauritius through private equity, hedge, and mutual funds. Under the current double taxation treaty between India and Mauritius, capital gains on Indian shares that are held by a Mauritian company are not subject to Indian tax laws and rates, an issue that has been vexing to Indian regulators and policy makers. Simply put, Mauritian companies are taxed according to Mauritius tax laws, which are extremely favorable, compared to Indian laws. There is some chance that India will try to amend the treaty in 2011 to try to capture more of the revenue from this activity. Nevertheless, FDI from Mauritius to India, which has been mostly in the electrical equipment, cement, telecommunications, and financial sectors, has helped Mauritius establish the attributes needed to compete globally in high-value service sectors.

THE ECONOMIC FUTURE OF MAURITIUS

The long-term challenge for the government of Mauritius is to maintain its unique combination of resilience in the face of changing economic circumstances and adaptability to new paths for growth. A number of key lessons can be learned from Mauritius's experience. First, the forging of consensus between the Franco-Mauritian business elite and the Indian political elite has provided a sound foundation for economic growth. Consensus building was mapped into the management of ethnic interests while the country opportunistically moved forward with growth strategies.

Figure 5.9   FDI Inflows to Mauritius, 2002–08

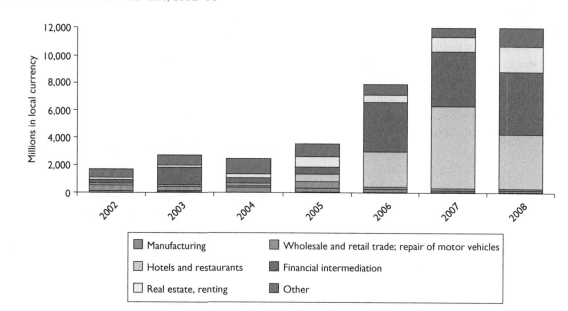

Source: World Bank 2009.

Even an occasionally contentious political environment has not jeopardized the continuity of state policies and administrative stability. The combination of adaptable institutions and a rich interface between the public sector and private sectors has ensured effective economic policy. The important role the private sector plays in the formulation of economic policy, especially through the Joint Economic Council, is relatively unparalleled in Africa.

Second, Mauritius benefited from pragmatic macroeconomic management that was supportive of long-term growth aspirations. The rents generated within the system during the 1970s and 1980s were used to finance capital accumulation rather than consumption. The real exchange rate was kept competitive, fiscal discipline was maintained, and debt burdens were kept at respectable levels, while there was a willingness to correct external and internal imbalances when needed.

Third, Mauritius recognized the benefits of economic openness at an early stage, implementing effective sectoral polices and building a good investment climate. The policy framework was used to facilitate private and foreign investment, particularly in the textile and tourism industries. The interplay between the relatively closed import substitution industrialization on one hand and export-driven initiatives on the other (particularly the EPZs) provides a fascinating tale. In general, though, Mauritius's openness, which allowed it to successfully penetrate developed markets through exports, has been unrivaled by countries in Africa and the Middle East. Through smart tax policy, the country has become a source of a large portion of FDI flows into India. Throughout, Mauritius has demonstrated a capacity to capitalize on good international relationships.

While its future success is not guaranteed, Mauritius has proven that it has the right instruments to weather a range of economic shocks. Its history is one of adaptability, innovation, and anticipating global changes. Its combination of good leadership, consensus building, sound macroeconomic management, and positive policies for the private sector will serve it well in the future.

NOTES

1. Careful empirical work by Subramanian (2009) shows how initial conditions in Mauritius—especially the income level, geography, and commodity dependence—have hurt long-term growth, while favorable demography and high levels of human capital have been mitigating factors. For example, Mauritius is disadvantaged by being at least 25–30 percent more distant from world markets than the typical African country. Statistical analysis shows that on balance, the disadvantages outweigh the advantages: initial conditions have slowed growth by about 1 percentage point a year relative to the average African country and by nearly 2 percentage points relative to the fast-growing developing economies of East Asia.

2. See Sachs and Warner 1995, 1997; Meade 1961; Rodrik 1999; Romer 1993; and Subramanian and Roy 2001, among others.

3. Mauritius has three ethnic groups: Mauritian Creoles, Indo-Mauritians, and Franco-Mauritians. The Creoles (African) were brought to Mauritius as slaves to work for owners of sugar cane fields. Indo-Mauritians came to Mauritius as indentured laborers after slavery was abolished in 1835 and eventually became the country's political elite. And Franco-Mauritians were the French who remained in Mauritius after the British took over in 1810 to look after their large sugar estates and other businesses, including trading and banking.

4. Mauritius's legislative system is based on a classic parliamentary Westminster system. Legislative power is vested in the National Assembly, which is composed of 62 elected and up to 8 designated representatives. The four main current political parties in Mauritius are the Labour Party (PTR), the Movement Mauricien Militant (MMM), the Mauritius Socialist Militant (MSM), and the Parti Mauricien Xavier Duval (PMXD).

5. Although Mauritius's public debt is relatively high, at about 60 percent of GDP, most of it is held domestically by the National Pension Fund and commercial banks.

6. Note that TFP calculations are very sensitive to the start and end year.

7. One challenge Mauritius faces is the large proportion of young people who are unable to access secondary education because of the very competitive system for moving from primary to secondary schools and who thus cannot contribute to the skilled labor force required by the economy. Almost 35 percent of students fail to pass the completion-of-primary-education examination and drop out of the school system at the age of 12.

8. Mauritius does not have a national poverty line; poverty figures are derived by the Central Statistics Office using census and survey data.

9. It should be noted that capital expenditures are underestimated in the Mauritian budget, because many public investments take place through parastatals, while expenditure classifications are detailed for the central government. As a result, some capital expenditures may be classified as current expenditures.

10. The VAT was introduced in Mauritius in September 1998, close to six months ahead of schedule, and its performance has exceeded expectations.

11. The IMF (2008) finds that using the macroeconomic balance approach and the single-equation equilibrium exchange rate approach, the real exchange rate at the end of 2007 was broadly in line with its equilibrium value (as determined by economic fundamentals).

12. Since the mid 1980s private sector investment has also exceeded private sector savings.

13. Technically, the Mechanism for Transitional Support for the Private Sector (MTSP) under the Additional Stimulus Package (ASP) was a combination of equity support, liquidity/working capital (including guarantees for bank support), and asset purchases and swaps. Between mid-December 2008, when the mechanism began functioning, and September 2010, 11 companies had received assistance under the MTSP, to which the government contributed MUR 140 million (36 percent of the total MTSP support for these companies; the remainder was provided by banks and shareholder equity) in the form of debentures at 5 percent interest.

14. The Sugar Protocol was negotiated as a condition of the United Kingdom's membership in the EEC to protect the developing countries from which it had traditionally imported sugar under the Commonwealth Sugar Agreement.

15. Firms within EPZs were subject to general labor laws (including minimum wages) but were free to fire workers, to demand compulsory overtime work, and to penalize workers heavily for absenteeism.

16. Despite the challenges, the government has supported the restructuring of EPZ textile firms in order to avoid a possible collapse of the sector. These efforts include establishing the Textile Emergency Support Team initiative in July 2003 and encouraging the National Productivity and Competitiveness Council to carry out a diagnostic study of textile firms to assess their cost structure and point to areas in need of improvement.

17. At the end of October 2002, the number of companies registered in the offshore sector reached 20,111. The Mauritius Freeport, the duty-free zone in the port and airport, aims at transforming Mauritius into a major regional distribution, transshipment, and marketing center.

18. India has double taxation avoidance agreements with approximately 65 countries, including France, Germany, Japan, the United Kingdom, and the United States, although Mauritius is the most preferred route for FDI inflows.

BIBLIOGRAPHY

Arbache, J., and J. Page. 2008. "Hunting for Leopards: Long-Run Country Income Dynamics in Africa." Policy Research Working Paper 4715, World Bank, Washington, DC.

Bheenick, R., and M. O. Schapiro. 1989. "Mauritius: A Case Study of the Export Processing Zone." EDI Development Policy Case Studies 1, World Bank, Washington, DC.

Greenaway, D., and C. Milner. 1989. "Nominal and Effective Tariffs in a Small Industrializing Economy: The Case of Mauritius." *Applied Economics* 21 (8): 995–1009.

Gulhati, R., and R. Nallari. 1990. "Successful Stabilization and Recovery in Mauritius." EDI Development Policy Case Studies. World Bank, Washington, DC.

IMF (International Monetary Fund). 2008. "Mauritius: Selected Issues." Washington, DC.

———. 2010. "Mauritius Article IV Consultation Staff Report." Washington, DC.

Lall, S., and G. Wignaraja. 1998. "Mauritius: Dynamizing Export Competitiveness." Commonwealth Secretariat, London.

Meade, J. E., et al. 1961. *The Economics and Social Structure of Mauritius: Report to the Government of Mauritius.* London: Methuen.

Morisset, J., F. Bastos, and S. Rojid. 2010. "Facing Off a Man-Made Disaster: Global Financial Crisis and Policy Response in the Small Tropical Island of Mauritius." World Bank Note, Africa Region, Washington, DC.

Rodrik, D. 1999. *The New Global Economy and Developing Countries: Making Openness Work,* London: Overseas Development Council.

Rojid, S., and B. Seetanah. 2009. "Using Growth Accounting to Explain Sources of Growth: The Case of COMESA." *International Journal of Business Research.*

Rojid, S., B. Seetanah, and R. Shalini. 2009. "Are State Business Relations Important to Economic Growth: Evidence from Mauritius." DFID/University of Mauritius working paper.

Romer, P. 1993. "Two Strategies for Economic Development: Using Ideas and Producing Ideas." In *Proceedings of the World Bank Annual Conference on Development Economics.* Washington, DC: World Bank.

Sachs, J., and A. Warner. 1995. "Economic Reform and the Process of Global Integration: Comments." *Brookings Papers on Economic Activity,* 1: 1–118.

———. 1997. "Sources of Slow Growth in African Economies." *Journal of African Economies* 6 (3): 335–76.

Subramanian, A. 2009. "The Mauritian Success Story and its Lessons." Research Paper 2009/36, United Nations University–World Institute for Development Economics Research, Helsinki.

Subramanian, A., and D. Roy. 2001. "Who Can Explain the Mauritian Miracle: Meade, Romer, Sachs, or Rodrik?" IMF working paper, WP/01/116, Washington, DC.

Wignaraja, G., and S. O'Neil. 1999. *SME Exports and Public Policies in Mauritius.* Commonwealth Trade and Enterprise Paper. London: Commonwealth Secretariat.

World Bank. 1989. Mauritius Country Economic Memorandum, Washington, DC.

———. 2009. *Mauritius Investment Climate Assessment.* Washington, DC.

———. 2010. World Development Indicators Database. Washington, DC.

CHAPTER 6

Cotton Dependence in Burkina Faso: Constraints and Opportunities for Balanced Growth

Jonathan Kaminski

Burkina Faso experienced more than a decade of robust growth in gross domestic product (GDP) following the devaluation of its currency in 1994. Average growth of 6 percent a year—nearly double the growth of the previous decade—was led largely by the cotton sector, which accounted for about 60 percent of exports. GDP per capita in Burkina Faso rose from $214 in 1997 to $260 in 2007 ($430 in real terms). Reforms in the cotton sector contributed to rapid growth of this sector, but spillover in terms of structural transformation of the economy has been slow, especially because the increase in cotton production was not productivity-based. While reforms that led to management improvement and institutional upgrading in the cotton sector were necessary, they were not sufficient to translate productivity increases in the cotton sector into economic consolidation, structural transformation, and diversification. Instead, the economy's dependence on cotton has exacerbated growth volatility and vulnerability to exogenous shocks. Despite this, Burkina Faso's economic prospects remain positive due to record cotton prices in the world market, a growing level of gold exports, effective government-led growth strategies, and continuing improvement of the business environment.

ECONOMIC GROWTH IN BURKINA FASO

Burkina Faso's average annual GDP growth rate accelerated from an average 3.8 percent in the 1980s to 6 percent during 1994–2008. The agricultural sector, which accounts for

85 percent of Burkina Faso's active labor force, has been the main driving force of growth. Within agriculture, the cotton sector has shown particular dynamism. The cotton boom during the 2000s lifted cotton's share of GDP from around 4 percent in the 1980s to 12 percent in 2008, contributing to higher GDP growth (figure 6.1).

As cotton production in Burkina Faso posted unprecedented growth in the 2000s, the share of cotton earnings in export revenues shot up from less than 40 percent in the 1990s to 85 percent in 2007. At the same time, increased export dependency on cotton has exacerbated vulnerability to exogenous shocks over the past decade, which was characterized by a pattern of falling world cotton prices and rising input prices; a decline in local profitability and farm productivity; and poorly performing cotton firms that lack the ability, information, and resources to adjust to evolving international markets.

Although cotton represents a large proportion of Burkina Faso's exports, its contribution of export earnings to GDP is small (10 percent) and trade openness is limited. Most of the country's growth is from domestic demand.[1] Limited export earnings highlight the unsustainable growth path that Burkina Faso is currently on. Although the country's terms of trade have recovered since the early 2000s, structural deficiencies have led to persistent trade deficits (Savadogo 2009).

EFFECT OF GROWTH ON DEVELOPMENT

Sustained growth has had only a limited effect on poverty reduction in Burkina Faso (World Bank 2009a). Despite

Figure 6.1   Annual Changes in Cotton Production and GDP in Burkina Faso, 1980–2008

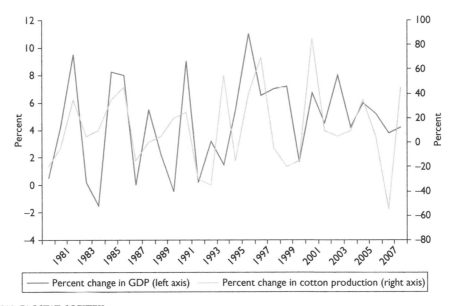

Source: World Bank 2010; FAOSTAT, SOFITEX.

sustained annual per capita GDP growth of about 2–3 percent between 1994 and 2003, the national poverty headcount index remained about 45 percent at the end of that period. Granted, estimation of poverty measures has been subject to controversies (including methodological), but no significant effect of growth on poverty reduction has been found at the aggregate level (Lachaud 2005, 2006; Grimm and Gunther 2004). Grimm and Gunther (2004) show that only cotton-producing households increased their expenditures significantly between 1995 and 2003, a finding that attests to the pro-poor growth effect of smallholder cotton production. Several studies find that the impact of Burkina Faso's GDP growth was mostly neutralized by its population growth, which limited scaled-up investments in infrastructure, education, and health.

Several pieces of research show evidence of poverty reduction in the mid- to late 2000s: the incidence of poverty fell from 46 percent in 2003 to 38.5 percent in 2007; the incidence of poverty in rural areas fell from 52 percent to 44 percent over the same years. There is no evidence, however, that cotton-producing regions had lower incidence of poverty than other rural areas (Grimm and Gunther 2004). The apparent contradiction between pro-poor cotton growth on one hand and the absence of rapid poverty reduction in cotton-producing areas on the other reflects both the effect of political and economic turmoil in Côte d'Ivoire (which reduced remittances to Burkina Faso) and

some amount of poverty convergence across the West African region as a result of the migration of less productive and poorer farmers in cotton regions to more marginal lands (Gray and Kevane 2001). In addition, the increase in cotton production reduced poverty largely among households that were able to increase their per capita agricultural incomes through more productive assets and factors. There was no significant poverty reduction effect as a result of the decline in cereal prices or spillovers into the local economy led by higher domestic demand (Kaminski, Headey, and Bernard 2009).

As global food and fuel price increases took hold in 2007, the purchasing power of households in Burkina Faso declined and the incidence of poverty began to rise again. Cotton households did not escape these negative impacts, and in subsequent years, negative shocks such as flooding have hurt cotton-producing households even more. At the same time, the deceleration in economic growth had a dramatic effect on poverty, alleviation of which requires higher rates of economic growth, mainly in the rural sector (cotton and livestock). Measures of the depth and severity of poverty in Burkina Faso have also increased since 2007.

Although poverty is much higher in rural areas than in urban areas, unemployment in Burkina Faso is largely an urban problem that disproportionately affects women, youth, and highly skilled workers.[2] The urban unemployment rate fell to 8.6 percent in 2007, down from 13.8 percent in 2003

CHAPTER 6: COTTON DEPENDENCE IN BURKINA FASO: CONSTRAINTS AND OPPORTUNITIES FOR BALANCED GROWTH

(16 percent for the labor force ages 15–25, down from 30 percent in 2003). According to the World Bank (2009a), the quality of jobs has not improved, however, and a large proportion of the workforce remains employed in low-paying jobs and jobs that do not provide social benefits. Absorbing young graduates in professional jobs remains a major challenge for the government in the coming years. A new law that promotes more flexibility in the labor market went into effect in 2008, but creation of new jobs has been hampered by the economic slowdown.

Other indicators of social welfare and development have exhibited encouraging signs over the past decade. Education-related infrastructure has been scaled up, with the number of classrooms increasing by 9 percent annually since 2006. Primary school enrollment rates have also risen, reaching 78 percent in 2009. Although regional disparities are significant, gender disparities in enrollment rates have narrowed. These results have been achieved thanks to long-term policy frameworks, substantial increases in public investment in education in the 2000s, and partnerships with the private sector (which has contributed about 15 percent of investment in education infrastructure).

In the health sector, the prevalence of HIV/AIDS has fallen, and progress has been made in containing epidemic and endemic diseases. Both morbidity and mortality rates decreased between the mid-1990s and mid-2000s.

REFORM OF THE COTTON SECTOR

Since the early 1990s Burkina Faso's dependence on cotton has grown as a result of the implementation of institutional reforms, which have brought new land and producers to cotton production (Kaminski and Thomas 2009). Table 6.1 details the chronology of the reforms.

The cotton sector provides income for 15–20 percent of the active labor force of Burkina Faso, supporting 1.5 million–2 million people. It is composed mostly of small farms and smallholders, with a small number of large farms led by rural elite. In 2005 Burkina Faso became the leading West African producer of cotton, ahead of Mali, producing 500,000 to 800,000 tons of seed cotton between 2005 and 2010. In 2006 and 2007, Burkina Faso was the leading cotton producer and exporter among all African countries.

Table 6.1   Chronology of Cotton Reforms in Burkina Faso, 1992–2008

Year(s)	Development
1992–93	Formal commitment made by Societé Burkinabé des Fibres et des Textiles (SOFITEX), the national cotton parastatal company, to let producers' representatives participate in reform debate. Contrat-Plan Etat SOFITEX, in which the state committed not to interfere with management of SOFITEX, established a plan to streamline accumulated debts of producers and the parastatal.
1994	Laws pertaining to establishment of farmer groups amended.
1996–99	Free membership introduced in formation of groups of local cotton farmers; the groupements villageois were replaced by market-oriented organizations (groupements de producteurs de coton) at the subvillage level, with implementation of new local governance rules.
1996–2001	National cotton union (Union Nationale des Producteurs du Coton du Burkina, or UNPCB) is established with support of l'Agence Française de Développement, the Burkinabe government, and SOFITEX, based on membership of local groups and their integration into regional unions.
1998	Accord Interprofessionnel signed by SOFITEX, the state, UNPCB, donors, and financial consortium (Caisse Nationale du Crédit Agricole; Banque Internationale pour le Commerce, l'Industrie, et l'Agriculture; Banque Internationale du Burkina), replacing the Contrat-plan and defining the reallocation of responsibilities.
1999	State partially withdraws from the sector through partial privatization of SOFITEX; half of government's share in SOFITEX is transferred to UNPCB.
2000–06	Economic activities—including provision of cereal input credit; management assistance of cotton groups; and participation in quality grading, financial management, and price bargaining—progressively delegated from SOFITEX and the government to UNPCB. The state downsizes support of research and extension services.
2002–06	New players—including private input providers, new regional private cotton monopsonies (SOCOMA, FASOCOTON), and private transport companies—begin operating in the sector.
2004–06	Interprofessional association (AICB) is established with cooperation of cotton farmers, banks, private stakeholders, the government, and research institutes. Association of cotton firms (APROCOB) established to interact with UNPCB.
2006–08	Price-setting mechanism changed to better reflect world price levels; new smoothing fund managed by an independent organization becomes operational in 2008.

Source: Kaminski, Headey, and Bernard 2009.

A partial equilibrium analysis based on estimation of counterfactuals suggests that cotton reforms explain two-thirds of the threefold increase in production from 1996 to 2006, which enabled farmers to cultivate more land, raise their incomes, and improve food security (Kaminski, Headey, and Bernard 2009). Figure 6.2 compares average production of seed cotton in Burkina Faso and neighboring West African countries with that in the Southern African countries of Zambia and Zimbabwe, in which conventional privatization and reforms were pursued (table 6.2). As shown in figure 6.2, the volume of cotton production growth in Burkina Faso has been substantially higher than in comparator countries since 2000.

Importantly, increased cotton production in Burkina Faso in recent years was not based on significant productivity increases but rather on accumulation of factors such as land, labor, and inputs. Rising cotton yields also hide the negative dynamic effect resulting from the entry of less able farmers and land in cotton production. Hence, stagnant (even slightly increasing) yields mean that individual performance increased over the last decade. Overall competitiveness of cotton farmers and of the cotton industry increased much more rapidly than in neighboring countries and has been hampered only by low world market prices (which include the depreciating effect of U.S. cotton subsidies) and the appreciation of the euro.

Nevertheless, cotton-led growth faces several challenges. Kaminski, Headey, and Bernard (2009) point out the lack of sustainability of cotton reforms as well as the limitations of the factor-driven Burkinabe economy, especially with regard to the underlying environmental constraints to extensive agricultural growth and the need for the intensification of sustainable agricultural. The cotton sector also faces environmental challenges, including the threat of soil impoverishment and emerging conflicts regarding access to land (Gray and Kevane 2001). These problems notwithstanding, the reform has led to upgraded institutional arrangements between producers and other stakeholders and helped farmers organize in more professional-oriented associations to carry out a growing number of responsibilities (World Bank 2004). All these factors improved the overall management of the sector. The reform has resulted in higher profit-sharing for farmers, better extension services, fairer quality grading, and better access to agricultural inputs with improved credit repayment mechanisms (Kaminski 2007).

The Burkinabe reform model is unique in Sub-Saharan Africa in that it addresses government failures and local realities within the current institutional framework,

Figure 6.2 Seed Cotton Production in Selected Sub-Saharan African Countries, 1980–2010

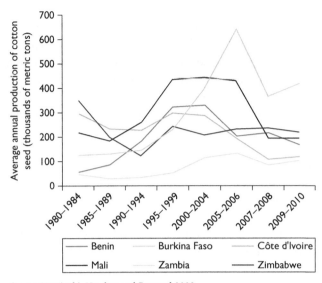

Source: Kaminski, Headey, and Bernard 2009.

adopting reforms using a cautious, piecemeal approach (Kaminski, Headey, and Bernard 2009). The approach differs substantially from the conventional approaches of other countries, which ignored the specificities of the institutional set-up (Jayne and others 1997). Reinforcing the institutional framework has ensured better market coordination along the value chain and higher levels of contract self-enforcement, the main bottleneck to better performance of cotton industries in the region.[3] The reforms in Burkina Faso also countermanded several government interventions and policies that had directly contributed to inefficiency, while reallocation of activities among the new institutions and tightened vertical coordination improved efficiency in the cotton sector.

Burkina Faso's success in creating an efficient cotton value chain stems from the institutional capacity for improved contractual coordination and collective action—something that was achieved through the creation of professional (under free membership principles) cooperatives of cotton growers, which substantially improved cotton marketing and input credit repayment, yielding significant operational cost savings. The improved institutional framework has allowed cotton firms to provide better-quality technical extension services and research in the course of sectoral privatization and ensured coordination of the delivery of public goods, quality control, picking and ginning, and marketing activities. At the same time, access to

CHAPTER 6: COTTON DEPENDENCE IN BURKINA FASO: CONSTRAINTS AND OPPORTUNITIES FOR BALANCED GROWTH

Table 6.2   Reforms and Outcomes in Benin and Mali, 1992–2010

| | Benin | | Mali | |
Period	Development	Outcome	Development	Outcome
1992–99	Supervised liberalization of input distribution; progressive establishment of professional and interprofessional associations	Production increased by more than 50 percent	Traditional integrated commodity chain experienced financial troubles and embezzlement	Production increased by more than 50 percent
2000–05	Quasi-competition and dismantlement of parastatal, emergence of several farmers' networks, establishment of financial clearinghouse, disappearance of former professional associations; institutional failures	Slight increase in production; problems in input recovery governance	Producer boycott, opening of reform dialogue; establishment of cotton cooperatives (but limited adoption de facto)	Stagnation, with periodic declines as result of farmers' collective action
2006–10	Move toward a private monopolistic organization with new public regulation and new institutional framework for public-private partnership	Yields and production decreased, stabilizing only recently	Reform process under way, with privatization and convergence toward zoning approach (splitting of parastatal into four private territorial entities linked through newly established interprofessional body)	Production plummeted as a result of delays in and uncertainties surrounding reform; farm profitability declined

Source: Kaminski, Headey, and Bernard 2009.

finance and inputs has been eased for smallholder farmers, and transportation services are now provided by the private sector. Figures 6.3 and 6.4 present the main organizational changes.

In the long term, mitigating vulnerability requires that the main stakeholders improve their risk-management strategies and that the government increase the quality of agricultural services provided to farmers (research, extension, and quality grading). There is also a need to invest in human capital in a number of areas. To deal with world market volatility, the new price-determination mechanism—which has suffered from lack of adjustment—has been supplemented by an independently managed smoothing fund. Price and weather risk-management instruments are currently in development. Another risk-mitigation strategy is to moderate U.S. dollar–euro exchange rate volatility (using, for example, the holistic approach proposed by the World Bank 2009a). Input price risk is another substantial risk faced by cotton sector participants. In response, stakeholders are exploring the possibility of establishing an input fund that could lead to as much as 20 percent savings on input procurement costs. Last, stakeholders are working to provide a more adequate set of microfinancial and micro-insurance instruments to farmers to stimulate small-scale farm investment and protect against production risks, including those related to weather. With the sustainable management of smoothing schemes and risk-mitigation

strategies, most of the income vulnerability of cotton could be removed.

Although the Burkinabe cotton story is largely one of removing institutional constraints, further reforms and new policy frameworks are needed. The growth in cotton areas in the early 2000s reflects the lack of alternative (crop) solutions, combined with a strong comparative advantage for cotton growing in a very constrained market environment.[4] Farmers need a secure access channel to output markets, because marketing is typically too costly for them to do on their own—or they lack the human capital to do so. Because of market failures (incomplete or missing input and rural credit markets), Burkinabe farmers must establish contractual arrangements with downstream stakeholders (processors and traders) to access inputs and credit.[5] Effective contractual arrangements involve a high degree of market coordination and trust-building relationships. At the same time, Burkina Faso's challenging business environment and poor overall institutional framework discourages entrepreneurs from investing in agrifood or large-scale trade because of unmanageable risks and hidden costs. This lack of investment limits the scope for developing other high-value commodity chains, even where the potential exists. The unsatisfactory outcome is that most tradable agricultural output markets are tied to the cotton sector for accessing inputs and credit, increasing the vulnerability of rural income to changes in the cotton market.

Figure 6.3   Prereform Organizational Model of the Cotton Sector in Burkina Faso

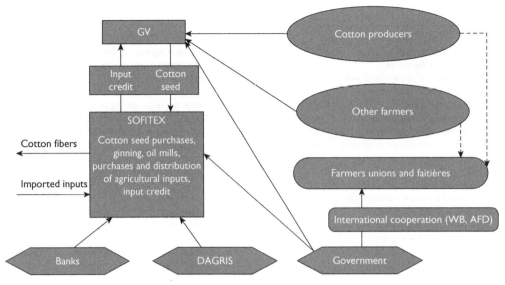

Source: Kamınski 2008.
Note: GV are village groups; AFD is Agence Française de Développement; DAGRIS is Développement des Agro-Industries du Sud (DAGRIS), a French parastatal involved in the agroindustrial sectors of many French-speaking countries.

Figure 6.4   Postreform Organizational Structure of the Cotton Sector in Burkina Faso in 2007

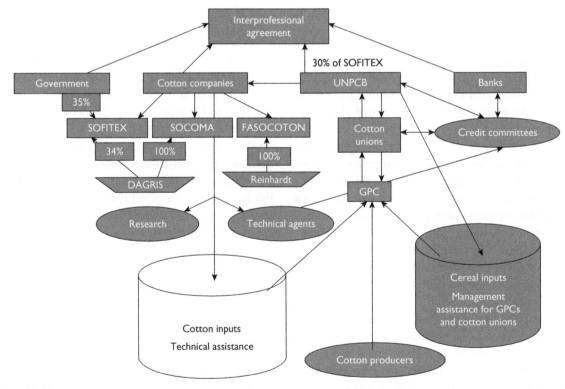

Source: Kaminski 2008.
Note: SOCOMA and FASOCOTON are the regional cotton firms that were granted regional monopolies in the more marginal center and eastern cotton-producing regions. UNPCB is Union Nationale des Producteurs de Coton du Burkina Faso; GPC is Groupement de Producteurs de Coton . DAGRIS is no longer operating in Burkina Faso after its withdrawal from SOFITEX shareholding in 2008. The sector then went through financial restructuring with state recapitalization, which resulted in a substantial reduction of producers' shares in cotton companies' capital (from 30 percent to around 10 percent for SOFITEX).

DRIVERS OF COTTON GROWTH; MARKET AND INSTITUTIONAL ADVANTAGES

Structural characteristics of rural markets partly explain why the Burkinabe economy has remained so dependent on its cotton sector. Historically, the cotton sector has been better supported by institutions, stakeholders, and infrastructure than cereal sectors, which face enormous logistical constraints and high transport costs. The cotton sector in Burkina Faso has benefited from better social organizations of farmers, better public and private institutions, and better infrastructure, ensuring better-functioning markets (Bassett 2001). Infrastructure is funded by cotton revenues through private (local public goods) and public investments. Since the 1980s investments in the cotton sector have also fostered technology adoption, thanks to high-quality research, cooperation between French and local researchers, farmer organizations, and top-down implementation policies.

Technological progress in agricultural sectors is more likely to diffuse when land becomes increasingly scarce (Boserup 1965). Constraints in the farmer environment (liquidity and market failures) hamper the adoption of technology, notably for the poorest households that seek to meet their food-security objective and minimize production risks (Abdoulaye and Lowenberg-DeBoer 2000). Fertilizer use is constrained by lack of experience, access to inputs and capital markets, and learning (Abdoulaye and Sanders 2005).[6] These problems suggest the need for more extension services, quality control, and research to foster fertilizer use on higher-value crops and efforts to reduce the risk associated with fertilizer use through training and quality standards for lower-value crops. As a result of demographic pressure in and migration into cotton areas, as well as the relatively high value of cotton compared to other crops, cotton has attracted increasing levels of technology, capital, and inputs.

The advantages of growing cotton (rather than other crops) include better access to rural finance and agricultural inputs, thanks to interlinked transactions with powerful agribusinesses (contract farming and other contractual arrangements) and the ability to overcome inherent market failures in the realms of input and rural credit markets. The strong position of these agribusinesses ensures contract self-enforcement (in that it prevents significant room for side-selling). This is not the case in the cereal sector, which is characterized by small traders who lack physical capital.

In Burkina Faso, most reforms in the cotton sector addressed government failures and institutional weaknesses by building the capacity of producers and upgrading institutions within the commodity chain while the state withdrew from most of its activities. Although most of the other key sectors of the economy—the agricultural input supply chain, energy and other public utilities, and a portion of the financial sector—remained at least partially state controlled until the early 2000s, they have been progressively privatized and liberalized in the years since. All banks are now privately controlled, as are some public utilities and input markets. This completed the privatization and liberalization process that occurred in the trade, transport, and cereals sectors. The evolution of organizational structures in the cotton sector also has created better incentives for farmers and manufacturers and allowed them to benefit from profit-sharing. Apart from these improvements, stakeholders in other agricultural sectors had to incur more economic risks in the course of liberalization (in terms of the profitability of different marketing channels, processing, and retailing activities), although they stand to reap potentially higher financial margins.

Cotton producer organizations have benefited rural civil society and revitalized rural communities in Burkina Faso and neighboring countries (SWAC Secretariat and OECD 2007). Such organizations help farmers establish professional structures and participate as political actors. Governance structure and management capacities are critical to this success, in addition to local social conservatism and other social norms at the village level. As Bernard and others (2008) show, community-oriented organizations are often captured by traditional authorities and local elites; in contrast, when elaborate administrative rules are established, market-oriented organizations are much more democratized and efficient. In the cotton sector, market-based cooperatives of cotton farmers have been established and producers have become significant players in policy making and the public debate. In other rural sectors, by comparison, institutional constraints remain more or less unchanged at the farmer level.

Importantly, cotton provides better risk-management arrangements to producers than do other sectors, especially with regard to price, outlets, and marketing. Cotton producer prices are administratively determined at the beginning of the cropping season and the pricing formula allows for *ristournes* (after-harvest bonus payments) to farmers. In addition, cotton farmers have better access to market information than farmers in other sectors, thanks to their effective organizations and national union, expansion of local infrastructure, and increased use of mobile phones in cotton-producing areas. Better information sharing can also help agribusiness entrepreneurs provide insurance schemes to farmers.

Despite several shortcomings (including the weakness of the farmers' union, corruption, and adjustment lags in the price determination mechanism), the revamped cotton policy framework in Burkina Faso has contributed to an increased concentration of cotton exports and dependency on cotton production at both the national and farm levels. Consensus building was forged by top-down establishment of the cotton union, state authoritarianism, trust-building with foreign partners, and accumulation of social capital at the village level (Kaminski and Bambio 2009). Consensus building followed by institutional innovations built partnerships along the supply chain with the professionalizing of farmers' groups and reinforced their bargaining power. As a result of upgraded institutional and policy frameworks, profit-sharing has evolved in favor of producers, while the management, input procurement and cost recovery, and overall market coordination of the sector has become more efficient, even in the face of the decline in the world price of cotton and the appreciation of the euro against the U.S. dollar. A larger profit share for farmers reinforced production incentives once coordination was improved, contributing to the impressive cotton growth pattern observed in the 2000s (figure 6.5).

Aside from these positive outcomes, the state bailout of SOFITEX and the lack of political sustainability of the cotton policy framework have reduced sectoral efficiency and led to failures in market coordination once the world price fell in the late 2000s. As a result, smallholders' profitability is threatened and trust in the newly established arrangements and partnerships declined from 2007 to 2009. Indeed, due to a misapplication of the pricing formula in 2006–07, the smoothing fund was depleted and farm gate prices were adjusted downward in 2007–08 once the formula started to be rigorously applied. In addition to growing deficits, SOFITEX had trouble paying farmers and delivering inputs to them on time. Some observers point to management problems in SOFITEX once DAGRIS left the shareholding and the company was recapitalized by the state. But the recent spike in cotton prices, even in the face of higher marketing costs attributable to the political crisis in Côte d'Ivoire, means that financial prospects are optimistic in the mid-run. The expectation of good financial prospects is all the more true since the price-determination mechanism has been in effect (and rigorously applied) over the past five production cycles. Burkinabe farmers' profitability is tightly linked to world prices—with predefined pricing at the beginning of the crop season, they receive roughly 60 percent of the world price of cotton for their crops.

In sum, while growth strategies aimed at economic diversification should be pursued within an adequate policy framework, governance, management, and institutional improvements are still required in the cotton sector if it is to remain a sustainable pillar of the Burkinabe economy.

Figure 6.5   Farm Gate and World Price Indexes of Seed Cotton, 1990–2009

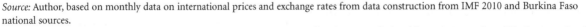

Source: Author, based on monthly data on international prices and exchange rates from data construction from IMF 2010 and Burkina Faso national sources.
Note: The Liverpool cotton price index is the index of world cotton prices. All series were calculated from averages of monthly data covering the period February–January, the production year for Burkina Faso's cotton sector.

COMMODITY DEPENDENCE AND ECONOMIC VULNERABILITY

Over the past decade, GDP growth in West African countries has been derived largely from agriculture (export crops in coastal countries and livestock in landlocked countries) and mining. As many economists, including Hausman, Hwang, and Rodrik (2007), note, export sectors are key to economic growth, as they typically have a cascade of effects on other sectors. However, export earnings cannot compensate for weak internal conditions for sustained growth.

The problematic issue here is commodity dependence. Because of few absolute advantages, poor countries such as Burkina Faso often experience unbalanced growth patterns driven by a restricted number of export commodities traded on very volatile world markets. Furthermore, these commodity markets are characterized by distortive policies and barriers to entry or participation for farmers in developed countries. In addition, production is subject to climatic variability (droughts and floods) and problems of soil fertility. Relying on a few commodities with uncertain profitability leads to economic vulnerability and calls for an in-depth examination of viable economic alternatives.

Globally, the outlook for cotton profitability is uncertain because of enduring institutional and governance limitations (despite recent improvements in both areas) and volatile world markets. In addition, cotton sectors sometimes still serve political ends—for example, offering good prices to producers before elections, even if these offers tend to vanish, and ensuring a minimum amount of agricultural inputs to the noncotton agricultural sectors.

The cotton-led growth of Burkina Faso has been negatively affected by volatile world cotton prices (competing synthetic fibers, cotton subsidies in the United States and Europe) and the appreciation of the euro (World Bank 2009a).[7] Moreover, increases in production have been driven mainly by increases in factors of production (labor, land, inputs) rather than through increases in total factor productivity. Economic vulnerability from commodity dependence has thus been exacerbated by the nonintensive pattern of growth, which has had a limited effect on overall economic transformation and limited spillovers through domestic demand-led growth. Due to environmental and demographic limitations, this growth path looks to be unsustainable in the long run. In general, the Burkinabe economy is still highly agriculture-oriented with a growing importance of cotton during the late 2000s and increasing importance of the mining sector. Figure 6.6 compares the economic growth of each economic sector over the past decade.

Economic diversification is one of Burkina Faso's national priorities, as stressed in recent official strategic documents. Of particular importance is diversification in the rural sector toward higher-value agricultural exports, such as fruits and vegetables. In the medium term, diversification to manufactured products does not appear necessary for growth. In contrast, increases in the production of higher-value natural-resource-based products are required. Such a shift may raise income levels by developing capacities

Figure 6.6   Real GDP Average Growth, by Economic Sector, 1994–2008

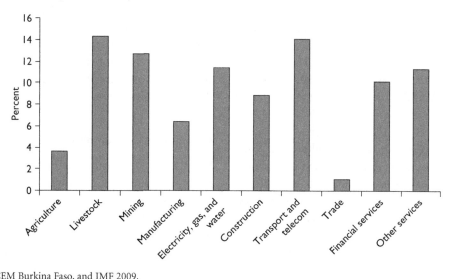

Source: World Bank, CEM Burkina Faso, and IMF 2009.

for manufactured goods together with the capacities of marketing and exporting a diversified basket of primary products. The application of technology to increase cotton profitability should also be encouraged.

Although growth of the cotton sector has been accompanied by some amount of economic diversification, that diversification has not been sufficient to stimulate structural transformation through macroeconomic spillovers. Although cotton provides skills to the other agricultural sectors, the growth of the cotton sector has not brought improvement in labor and land productivity and has not enabled sufficient redistribution of public goods such as education and health. In addition, spillovers of cotton activities to other economic sectors in Burkina Faso are restricted because of the limited industrial nature of cotton growing and its limited size in the rural sector (not more than 20 percent). A natural way to encourage spillovers would be to scale up textile activities. Finally, it is important to recognize that the increase in demand for agricultural inputs from cotton growers themselves has not been met by corresponding increases in local supply. Most agricultural inputs and nonfood goods are produced abroad, limiting transmission of demand increases in the rest of the economy.

Constraints to economic diversification

A number of factors constrain the diversification of Burkina Faso's economy.[8] Inefficient and incomplete policy reforms, institutions, and investments (in infrastructure, capacity-building, and public goods, for example) are all hindrances to diversification. Yet diversification is clearly a necessity for more sustainable and balanced growth. Macroeconometric studies (Berthelemy 2005) show that diversification indicators positively influence GDP growth rates, notably through increases in total factor productivity.

In general, there is a U-shaped relationship between economic concentration in exports (the Herfindahl index) and per capita income (World Bank 2009a). In the low part of the curve (where the relationship is negative) stand low-income countries such as Burkina Faso, characterized by export earnings derived mainly from agriculture (Imbs and Wacziarg 2003). The key role of diversification is to smooth export earnings derived from volatile (agricultural and resources) world markets in developing countries (Massel 1970), which fosters economic structural changes and consolidation. A more sustainable and balanced growth path can be attained by economic diversification and a set of policies and institutions that accompanies the process of

diversification by establishing facilitating conditions. This process involves general policies aimed at building institutions, providing necessary public goods, and loosening economic constraints in areas such as public administration, market imperfections and transaction costs, fiscal and trade policies, and weak governance. Such policies should be combined with sectoral policies according to absolute and comparative identified advantages, emerging champions (World Bank 2009a), and the structural role of key economic sectors (Hirschman 1958). Hence, diversification and specialization may exist side by side because of segmentation of the economy. This is the case for most West African countries, where there is a lack of economic integration between the primary sector (agriculture and mining) and the industrial sector.

The most important challenge for spurring sustainable growth in Burkina Faso lies in increasing total factor productivity, which depends to a large extent on the investment climate. Policies that make it easier to do business, reduce the burden borne by entrepreneurs, and upgrade the institutional framework are worth considering. From an investment climate perspective, Burkina Faso has improved significantly over the past decade, placing it in the midrange of African countries in the World Bank's Doing Business rankings (World Bank 2009b) and other indexes. Yet important bottlenecks remain, such as lack of access to finance and electricity, high tax rates, unfair (on fiscal grounds) practices in the informal sector, corruption, inadequate transportation, lack of access to land, ineffective bureaucracy, lack of technology, inadequate health services, and lack of an educated labor force. These constraints raise labor costs, limiting producers' competitiveness. Large firms in Burkina Faso, however, are roughly as productive as smaller ones (World Bank 2009a), implying that differences in labor productivity are not necessarily a matter of scale efficiency but rather rely on higher capital intensity for larger firms. Indirect and "invisible" costs account for an estimated 8.2 percent of firms' sales in Burkina Faso (table 6.3).

Constraints to technology adoption and diffusion

Promising technologies exist in the rural sector, but low levels of technology adoption and diffusion hamper the process of diversification.[9] Several underlying constraints are at play. First, diffusion of a new technique or technology requires complementary techniques and inputs, for which extension services and sustainable arrangements to ensure the provision of inputs are needed. Given the market

Table 6.3 Indirect and Invisible Costs as Share of Firms' Sales, Selected Sub-Saharan African Countries *(in percent)*

Country/year	Indirect costs				Invisible costs			Total indirect and invisible costs
	Transport	Telecommunications	Customs	Losses due to power outages	Cost of manager's time to deal with regulations	Cost of corruption (informal payments to get things done)	Cost of security measures	
Burkina Faso 2006	2.23	0.70	1.63	1.20	0.05	1.48	0.86	8.20
Benin 2004	—	—	0.48	1.16	0.06	4.27	0.57	6.55
Mali 2007	1.96	0.86	0.26	1.39	0.05	0.24	0.12	4.60
Uganda 2006	1.08	0.50	0.52	28.16	0.06	2.18	0.43	32.93
Zambia 2007	0.61	0.71	0.68	1.79	0.04	0.05	0.93	4.81

Source: World Bank Enterprise Surveys, 2004–07.

Notes: Estimates are based on at least 15 observations. — = not available.

failures affecting rural credit and agricultural inputs in Burkina Faso, it is understandable that technology diffusion may be constrained.

Apart from institutional and market constraints, technology diffusion and adoption need a clear and consistent policy framework for new marketing strategies, risk-mitigation strategies, or export promotion set-ups to be sustainable and provide the necessary incentives for long-term investment. In the rural sector, Abdoulaye and Sanders (2006) have shown that new marketing strategies (such as the Intsormil project[10]) do not ensure sufficient investment incentives if food security policies are inconsistent and do not allow a greater number of farmers to derive more profits during adverse years (removing export quotas, for instance). Technology adoption also relies on comprehensive exchange rate and trade reforms. In the manufacturing and services sectors, policy frameworks are also critical. The needed reforms combined with long-term commitment of the public sector in export promotion and investment strategies should, in turn, facilitate technology diffusion and diversification in higher-value production and exports.

Market constraints: Missing and incomplete markets in the rural sector

Agricultural producers face missing and incomplete markets for their goods. This is especially true for cereal producers. Cereal markets are still characterized by high transaction costs, ineffective institutions, and discriminatory policies, maybe because of their low value to weight ratio and logistical disadvantages (information access, inland freight cost). This notably contrasts with the dynamics of cotton markets. Hence, the transport cost component

of cereal profit margins is significant, meaning variability at producers' gate prices when combined with low market integration. Public investments in market infrastructures have been low, and only some rural cotton producing areas have been unlocked thanks to cotton benefits and the interests of agribusinesses. Not surprisingly, the most integrated cereal markets are the ones located close to the most productive cotton markets, because they benefit from better infrastructures and institutions.

After the liberalization of cereal markets in Burkina Faso, many small-scale traders coexisting with larger private traders have replaced government marketing. However, because of information asymmetries with farmers and the lack of access to reliable information services, traders have a comparative advantage and better information regarding local and central markets, retailers, and processing facilities. Even if this has created competitive emulation, there has been an associated lack of investment in human capital and innovation, few long-term contractual relationships with agribusinesses, and no significant change in access to financial markets. Due to several market failures and institutional weaknesses (contract enforcement), informal traders rely on social networks, rendering competition imperfect (Barrett 1997). In addition, Burkina Faso's network economy— retention of profits among insiders—tends to limit business expansion, as noted by Badiane and others (1997).

Not only do producers face constraints in output markets, which slows down diversification, but they also face constraints with respect to input markets. Hence, the potential for income-enhancing diversification of the rural sector is limited. Input market imperfections result from structural deficiencies such as high transaction costs, liquidity constraints of producers, and asymmetric information.

Lack of well-maintained and high-quality infrastructure also impedes market integration in Burkina Faso, translating into higher market risks borne by producers and traders, together with capacity constraints (risk-management and storage).[11] Cost-effective ways to provide infrastructure may use existing infrastructures with the involvement of user communities (mainly for maintenance with own-managed funds). Productivity benefits could be achieved by improving off-road transport and intermediate means of transport with capital-savings techniques for road construction or using labor-based techniques to overcome usual problems related to equipment use and availability in the region. Soft infrastructure, such as information, is also in short supply. Diversification from cotton to other agricultural commodities needs to rely on better market information services and farmer literacy to foster adoption of more profitable crops and techniques.

Institutional constraints

A country's institutional environment is composed of market and nonmarket relationships between different stakeholders. The role of institutions is all the more crucial in Burkina Faso given that markets are subject to structural deficiencies and constraints for participants. Nonmarket institutions define social rules and norms that, in turn, overcome the other market and institutional imperfections. But informal institutions, such as social networks and personal relationships, have been shown to be less efficient than formal ones, and they severely restrict the degree of competition, information, and business expansion.

SUPPLY CHAINS AND VERTICAL RELATIONSHIPS (REGULATORY, INFORMAL INSTITUTIONS, CONTRACT ENFORCEMENT, INFORMATION ASYMMETRIES). In the formal realm, the institutional structure of many supply chains was deeply reconfigured in the course of structural adjustment plans and sectoral reforms. Vertical relationships now entail more specific arrangements between stakeholders and more coordinated provision of public goods. Stakeholders face more options as marketing channels may be potentially beneficial for them if stakeholders can improve their capacities (information, management, bargaining, storage, infrastructures). However, competition in several sectors can be detrimental because of the persistence of other market failures (Lipsey and Lancaster 1956) and the fact that it can lead to coordination problems regarding the provision of certain public goods,

such as agricultural or industrial innovation and quality grading.

In Burkina Faso organizational structures rely on formal and informal institutions to coordinate the decisions of major players and to regulate the industry. Formal structures include state rules and formal regulations or collective organizations such as producers' associations, partnerships, and farmer unions. The evolution of the regulatory framework in Burkina Faso can be qualified as uneven. Overregulation in several sectors has been quite counterproductive and has notably contributed to restrictive environments, such as in the trade sector. Despite several improvements, there is a persistent lack of confidence in formal institutions, including the legal system. There are no effective institutions dedicated to investment and export promotion, indicating the absence of a long-term strategic vision for economic development and diversification. In contrast, standardization and quality promotion systems are being developed, and business associations are beginning to adopt quality control systems within their marketing systems. Continued improvements in these areas would benefit the whole set of private investors and business expansion.

THE INSTITUTIONAL ENVIRONMENT. Because formal institutions in Burkina Faso face a lack of credibility, many producers and private stakeholders rely on informal institutions, social networks, and personal relationships. However, this poses a problem, since the prevalence of informal institutions weakens the credence of the formal ones.

Informal village norms—such as those for credit, risk, or access to land—also enable local actors to overcome several market constraints. In matters of land access, however, informal norms often entail exclusion of some ethnic groups or difficult access to the fertile or accessible land for some societal groups. Political and ethnic biases in the allocation of land imply allocation inefficiencies. Informal and traditional risk-sharing arrangements provide only imperfect assurance of low effectiveness.

The decentralization of rural development policies in Burkina Faso, together with more participatory approaches, has contributed to a democratization process whereby responsibilities have been gradually transferred from national institutions to newly established local institutions. However, capacity constraints are still very strong.

To improve the business environment, national stakeholders in Burkina Faso have begun exploring various options: public-private partnerships, business associations and interprofessional bodies, information services, and consensus-building institutions. While all of these options have the potential to improve vertical and contractual relationships within supply and value chains, the experience of building the interprofessional association in the cotton sector was especially encouraging in that it provided a credible institutional framework to the main stakeholders and ensured market coordination while being limited by the predominant position of SOFITEX, which can sometimes impose some decisions on collective management issues (quality grading, input distribution system or regulation, and so on).

RISK MANAGEMENT. Along with being a market constraint, risk is an institutional constraint. Inefficiencies in the current institutional arrangements in Burkina Faso require mitigation of business and production risks as well as economic ones. For example, minimizing production risks for all agricultural commodities and livestock requires a better institutional framework. The development of new microinsurance schemes may help farmers facing external shocks to production. Indeed, improved transmission of information about weather conditions would help in the development of weather index microinsurance schemes (as already achieved in Southern Africa), providing farmers with producers' incentives. Another innovative insurance scheme that could be applicable is parametric insurance. Although the development of markets in innovative insurance schemes requires a strong financial framework to be established, enhancing information access through new technologies for information and communication could help spread these schemes.

Political constraints

Constraints to economic diversification also include the ones that come from policy making and that contribute to market and institutional failures. Most of them can be classified as government failures: public governance problems, transparency, democratization, nonbenevolence, corruption, and lack of foresight. Despite substantial improvements in the political environment in Burkina Faso over the past decade, enduring political practices hamper the effectiveness of upgraded policies and the questions of democratization and authoritarianism remain.

COMMODITY REFORMS AND THE POLITICAL ECONOMY OF COTTON-CEREAL REFORMS. Although commodity reforms in many Sub-Saharan African countries have been the subject of criticisms (Akiyama and others 2001), Burkina Faso has been viewed as a positive experience. These successes can be attributed to a consistent policy framework in which the state gained credibility with its economic partners, farmers' groups were strengthened, and private arrangements (such as contract farming) were not hindered by second-generation controls. Policy inconsistency remains in the cereal sector, however, in the form of food security policies (lowering agricultural profits of the most efficient farmers), protectionist trade policies (lowering incentives for diversified exports), and restrictions on input markets. Fortunately, these short-lived interventions that were common in the past are increasingly less evident. If needed, they should be decided upon harmoniously at the regional level, one of the purposes of the Comprehensive Africa Agriculture Development Programme (CAADP), an initiative of the New Partnership for Africa's Development (NEPAD) that calls for more harmonized agricultural and trade policies at the regional level in West Africa.

Sufficient agricultural extension services remain a challenge in Burkina Faso. Currently, there is a lack of means, training, and funding for extension services, along with lack of involvement by the state.

POLITICAL ECONOMY, SOCIAL CONTRACTS, AND THE URBAN BIAS. The political economy of agricultural policies explains the persistence of contradictory policies and incomplete market reforms. Compared to neighboring countries, Burkina Faso stands between the situation of Mali—steady adherence and commitment to market reforms—and that of Benin—de jure reforms and de facto state control with regard to noncotton sectoral policies (the reverse with regard to cotton policies). Private incentives in Burkina Faso have been jeopardized by entrepreneurs' fear of government intervention and by the somewhat volatile political environment. Fewer private sector opportunities create scope for a larger government involvement in markets, which, in turn, fuels this pattern. Therefore, political economy conditions have contributed to constraining agricultural diversification while favoring the cotton sector. These political conditions also apply to the services and industrial sectors in Burkina Faso.

THE POLITICAL ENVIRONMENT. Despite several improvements, the political environment in Burkina Faso continues to present constraints in the form of enduring political practices resulting in weak or poor governance, collusion of interests between officials and executives, and lack of political and democratic accountability of political leaders.

CONCLUSION

From an overarching perspective, cotton continues to account for a significant share of exports in Burkina Faso's very concentrated economy. Future global demand for cotton, however, does not appear consistent with an economic strategy in Burkina Faso that relies heavily on cotton exports as a driver for growth, not least because world cotton demand is expected to remain at volatile levels because of imperfect substitution among textile fibers and rising oil prices (oil is used in the production of synthetic fibers). But in the short run, there is a need to maximize cotton revenues and benefit from the historic price swings on the world markets.

A useful approach for Burkina Faso would be to examine other sectors with significant export growth potential, such as gold and livestock. Ramping up exports in these sectors may reduce dependence on cotton incomes. Expanded production and export of other agricultural products (vegetables, fruits, poultry, and rice) and nonprimary commodities may also serve to reduce the economic concentration on cotton.

Even with the potential expansion of other sectors, cotton is likely to continue providing livelihoods for a significant share of Burkina Faso's rural population and to remain important in the national economy. The most urgent concern is to tackle the issue of "sustainable intensification" at the farm gate, together with increasing the cost-effectiveness of cotton firms. Overall, there is a need to consolidate the cotton sector in the course of ongoing reforms and institution building, and to initiate a significant process of economic diversification through the formulation and implementation of growth-enhancing policies aiming to overcome the most relevant constraints. Nonmarket factors, such as the quality and effectiveness of institutions, are also at play, meaning that improvements in the business environment and investment climate would not automatically lead to a scale-up of nontraditional export industries as a prerequisite for structural transformation of the economy.

While policies are moving in the right direction—generalization of GM Bt cotton (genetically modified cotton with *Bacillus thuringiensis* inserted into the seeds) and diffusion of improved agricultural productivity practices (such as irrigation) and soil conservation, improved business environment, implementation of more adequate risk-management instruments and the new accelerated growth strategy, explicit support to growth poles as a means to create faster growth and diversification—removing the constraints described in this study in Burkina Faso are still of crucial importance. This calls for a policy-led economic transformation induced by structural changes, a consistent policy framework, and institutional innovations. Innovation needs to take place in a range of sectors: agriculture and livestock, mining, trade, tourism, and the food industry.

In the mining sector, the Burkinabe government has recently established a mining law to improve incentives for cost-effectiveness, export promotion, and for informal *orpailleurs*. In the agricultural sector, income-enhancing options exist and are achievable but would not lead to significant changes in the current environment of smallholders and traders, partly because of enduring market imperfections, structural deficiencies, and macroeconomic instabilities. Higher-value production is also of potential interest and has already driven growth and diversification in India and in several countries in Eastern Africa (for example, in horticulture, fruits, and nuts). A strategic set of sequenced actions could be led by officials and local leaders.[12]

Another area in which Burkina Faso has space for reform is trade. Currently, the trade environment in the country is characterized by high tariffs and low market integration. Burkina Faso would also benefit from diversifying its primary products, the production of which is constrained by the scope of development of manufacturing industries (for example, the food industry). Reasons typically invoked for the limited scope of manufacturing in the country include its abundance of land, scarcity of skilled labor, insufficient or poor-quality infrastructure, lack of policy reform, high transaction costs, and mismanaged or uninsured risks (Collier 1998, 2002; Habiyaremye and Ziesemer 2006; Collier and Gunning 1999). A consistent policy framework toward structural transformation should deal with these constraints.

Several of the issues raised in this study are already being addressed by officials and foreign donors in policy formulation and project implementation. Stylized facts, in fact, show that policy makers have been successful in bringing about change in several areas:

- Established priorities: food security, poverty reduction, private investments, and public-private partnerships in infrastructure and human capital.
- Policies for emerging and developing economic sectors
- On-going reforms
- Strategic action plans with donors: special economic zones and planning for employment, competitiveness, and diversification of economic growth poles

- Capacity to improve the institutional framework (for example, the cotton reform) even in the face of external shocks (declining world cotton prices and economic and political crisis in neighboring Côte d'Ivoire)
- Accumulated experience
- Government capacity to react to shocks and resistance to economic turmoil while maintaining the pace of reforms.

The outlook for Burkina Faso—albeit promising—could be made more secure with scaled-up investments in crucial sectors, and deepening market and political reforms. As such, the road is half-traveled. Burkina Faso is still at the stage of establishing policy and institutional frameworks. Governance has mixed records, despite progress in areas such as public investments. Demographic growth is a key challenge but the way government is responding to it, rather than hiding behind cultural values and norms, may be viewed as a success. Creating and using fiscal space in the near future, coping with demographic growth, and pursuing reforms will all be crucial. Key investments in infrastructure (first priority) and in human development (second priority) will be the cornerstone of subsequent development. While progress thus far has been in the right direction, it must be complemented by sector-specific policies in line with structural economic change and better promotion of private investment and exports. Several further improvements in the public administration and the political systems are also expected. Indeed, internal political sustainability of the policymaking and decision processes is a necessary condition for successful policy-led development and reforms (Rodrik 1996).

Finally, in the course of market reforms in Burkina Faso, policy makers should bear in mind that removing market imperfections (with investments in infrastructure to reduce transaction costs) needs to be done very carefully. As Lipsey and Lancaster (1956) note, the persistence of other market failures may have an adverse effect even after imperfections are removed. Timing of market and institutional reforms and infrastructure investment should proceed accordingly.

NOTES

1. Other significant sources of export earnings are livestock and gold.

2. The higher incidence of poverty in rural areas is disputable, because the official poverty line established by the Institut National de la Statistique et de la Démographie (INSD) in 2003 places too much weight on the prices of necessary goods (such as staples and water) relative to the weights used to construct the urban CPI (Grimm and Gunther 2004).

3. Market coordination is essential to ensure the delivery of crucial public goods (inputs and credit) in an incomplete marker environment. More competition broadens the scope for strategic defaulting on input credit and side-selling (selling outside the contractual arrangement to another company) and reduces the incentives to provide public goods, such as research or extension services.

4. This phenomenon explains the rise in the Herfindahl index from 0.2 to 0.6.

5. Cotton inputs are provided by ginning companies, which also directly purchase and gin seed cotton; inputs have been subsidized lately by the government.

6. The use of fertilizer increases with roads and rainfall.

7. Cotton production still ensures most cash earnings for farmers as well as most of their inputs and credit for other crop productions. Cotton earnings also provide funds for increasing capacities of smallholders' unions, agricultural extension services and research. The strong linkages between cotton and other crop productions must be borne in mind while not forgetting agronomic and economic complementarities that are harnessed in a very constrained environment for farmers.

8. *Economic diversification* is defined here as the process of progressive enlargement of the number of goods produced in an economy without a decline in productivity.

9. Promising technologies include integrated livestock-crop farming systems; soil conservation; regreening programs; small-irrigation schemes; intercropping and alley cropping; pest management; early cultivars for rain-fed rice, millet, and sorghum; and new generations of maize varieties (Kaminski 2008).

10. They involve the widespread use of inventory credit, agroprocessing of traditional cereals such as millet, producers-processors contracts in the poultry industry. and so on.

11. As noted by Platteau (1996), infrastructural constraints are a major cause of the low long-run supply response of farmers to price incentives, notably for transport and communications. Although tax reforms and infrastructure investment both compete for public funds, their effects are complementary and differently impact producers.

12. The mitigation of agricultural incomes' vulnerability to weather and external shocks is a key strategy through income-enhancing diversification under intensified farming systems for selected products (comparative advantages and market/trade potential), an improved business environment to encourage private sector investment (decreasing transaction, financial, labor, and energy costs), and an improved trade environment (infrastructures, export promotion, market integration, and quality standards).

BIBLIOGRAPHY

Abdoulaye, T., and J. Lowenberg-DeBoer. 2000. "Intensification of Sahelian Farming Systems: Evidence from Niger." *Agricultural Systems* 64 (2): 67–81.

Abdoulaye, T., and J. H. Sanders, 2005. "Stages and Determinants of Fertilizer Use in Semiarid African Agriculture: The Niger Experience." *Agricultural Economics* 32: 167–79.

———. 2006. "New Technologies, Marketing Strategies and Public Food Policy for Traditional Food Crops: Millet in Niger." *Agricultural Systems* 90: 279–92.

African Economic Outlook. n.d. "Burkina Faso." http://www.africaneconomicoutlook.org/en/countries/west-africa/burkina-faso/.

Akiyama, T., J. Baffes, D. Larson, and P. Varangis. 2001. *Commodity Markets Reforms: Lessons of Two Decades.* Washington, DC: World Bank.

Badiane, O., F. Goletti, M. Kherallah, P. Berry, K. Govindan, P. Gruhn, and M. Mendoza. 1997. *Agricultural Input and Output Marketing Reforms in African Countries: Final Report.* Washington, DC: International Food Policy Research Institute.

Barrett, C. B. 1997. "Food Marketing Liberalization and Trader Entry: Evidence from Madagascar." *World Development* 25 (5): 763–77.

Bassett, T. 2001. *The Peasant Cotton Revolution in West Africa, Côte d'Ivoire, 1880–1995.* Cambridge: Cambridge University Press.

Bernard, T., M-H. Collion, A. de Janvry, P. Rondot, and E. Sadoulet. 2008. "Do Village Organizations Make a Difference in African Rural Development? A Study for Senegal and Burkina Faso." *World Development* 36 (11): 2188–204.

Berthelemy J-C. 2005. "Commerce international et diversification économique." *Revue d'Economie Politique* 115 (5): 591–611.

Boserup, E. 1965. *The Conditions of Agricultural Growth: The Economics of Agrarian Change under Population Pressure.* Chicago: Aldine.

Boughton, D., and T. Reardon. 1997. "Will Promotion of Coarse Grain Processing Turn the Tide for Traditional Cereals in the Sahel? Recent Empirical Evidence from Mali." *Food Policy* 22: 307–16.

Collier, P. 1998. "Globalization: Implications for Africa." In *Trade Reform and Regional Integration in Africa*, ed. Z. Iqbal and M. S. Khan. IMF Institute, International Monetary Fund, Washington, DC.

———. 2002. *Primary Commodity Dependence and Africa's Future.* Washington, DC: World Bank.

Collier, P., and J. W. Gunning. 1999. "Why Has Africa Grown Slowly?" *Journal of Economic Perspectives* 13 (3): 3–22.

Conley, T. G., and C. R. Udry. 2000. "Learning about a New Technology: Pineapple in Ghana." Yale Economic Growth Center Working Paper 817, New Haven, CT.

Coulter, J., A. Goodland, A. Tallontire, and R. Stringfellow. 1999. *Marrying Farmer Cooperation and Contract Farming for Agricultural Service Provision in a Liberalizing SSA.* ODI Natural Resources Perspectives, 48, Overseas Development Institute, London.

Fafchamps, M. 2004. *Market Institutions in Sub-Saharan Africa: Theory and Evidence.* Cambridge, MA: MIT Press.

Foster, A. D., and M. R. Rosenzweig. 1995. "Learning by Doing and Learning from Others: Human Capital and Technical Change in Agriculture." *Journal of Political Economy* 103 (6): 1176–1209.

Gray, Leslie C., and Michael Kevane. 2001. "Evolving Tenure Rights and Agricultural Intensification in Southwestern Burkina Faso." *World Development* 29 (4): 573–87.

Grimm, M., and I. Gunther. 2004. "How to Achieve Pro-poor Growth in a Poor Economy? The Case of Burkina Faso." Working paper, University of Göttingen, Germany.

Habiyaremye, A., and T. Ziesemer, 2006. "Absorptive Capacity and Export Diversification in Sub-Saharan African Countries." UNU-MERIT Working Paper Series. United Nations University, Maastricht Economic and Social Research and Training Centre on Innovation and Technology, Maastricht, the Netherlands.

Hausmann, R., J. Hwang, and D. Rodrik. 2007. "What You Export Matters." *Journal of Economic Growth* 12 (1): 1–25.

Hausmann, R., and B. Klinger. 2006. "Structural Transformation and Patterns of Comparative Advantage in the Product Space." CID Working Paper, Center for International Development, Harvard University, Cambridge, MA.

Hirschman, A. 1958. *The Strategy of Economic Development.* New Haven, CT: Yale University Press.

Imbs, J., and R. Wacziarg. 2003. "Stages of Diversification." *American Economic Review* 93 (1): 63–86.

IMF (International Monetary Fund). 2007. *Burkina Faso. Propositions de réformes fiscales: Simplification, équité et efficacité.* Washington, DC.

———. 2008. *Burkina Faso: Third Review Under the Three-Year Arrangement under the Poverty Reduction and Growth Facility.* Washington, DC.

———. 2009. Burkina Faso: "Third Review under the Three-Year Arrangement under the Poverty Reduction and Growth Facility. Staff Report." Press Release on the Executive Board Discussion. IMF Country Report No. 09/38, Washington, DC (January).

Jayne, T., and S. Jones. 1997. "Food Marketing and Pricing Policy in Eastern and Southern Africa: A Survey." *World Development* 25: 1505–27.

Jayne, T., J. D. Shaffer, J. M. Staatz, and T. Reardon. 1997. "Improving the Impact of Market Reform on Agricultural Productivity in Africa: How Institutional Design Makes a Difference." MSU International Development Working Paper 66, Michigan State University, East Lansing, MI.

Jones, S. 1998. *Liberalised Food Marketing In Developing Countries: Key Policy Problems.* Oxford Policy Management.

Kaminski, Jonathan. 2007. "Interlinked Agreements and the Institutional Reform in the Cotton Sector of Burkina Faso." Working paper, Atelier de Recherche Quantitative Appliquée au Développement Économique, Toulouse School of Economics, Toulouse, France.

———. 2008. "Cotton-Cereal Systems in West and Central Africa: Opportunities and Constraints for Revenue-Raising Diversification and Marketing Strategies." FAO All-ACP Background Paper, European Union, Rome.

Kaminski, J., and Y. Bambio. 2009. "The Cotton Puzzle in Burkina Faso: Local Realities versus Official Statements." Paper presented at the annual meeting of the African Studies Association, New Orleans, LA.

Kaminski, J., D. Headey, and T. Bernard. 2009. "Navigating through Reforms: Cotton in Burkina Faso." In *Millions Fed: Proven Successes in Agricultural Development.* Washington, DC: International Food Policy Research Institute.

Kaminski, J., and A. Thomas. 2009. "Land Use, Production Growth, and the Institutional Environment of Smallholders: Evidence from Burkinabe Farmers." CAER-LERNA Working Paper, Hebrew University, Jerusalem, and Institut National de la Recherche Agronomique, Toulouse School of Economics, Toulouse France.

Labaste, Patrick. 2009. Background paper for the Country Economic Memorandum. World Bank, Washington, DC.

Lachaud, J-P. 2005. "A la recherche de l'insaisissable dynamique de pauvreté au Burkina Faso. Une nouvelle évidence empirique." Document de travail 117, Centre d'Economie du Développement de l'Université Montesquieu Bordeaux IV, Bordeaux, France.

———. 2006. "La croissance pro-pauvres au Burkina Faso. L'éviction partielle de l'axiome d'anonymat en présence de données transversales." Document de travail du département de l'école d'économie du développement, l'Université Montesquieu Bordeaux IV, Bordeaux, France.

Lipsey, R. G., and K. Lancaster. 1956. "The General Theory of Second Best." *Review of Economic Studies* 24 (1): 11–32.

Massel, B. F. 1970. "Export Instability and Economic Structure." *American Economic Review* 60 (4): 618–30.

McMahon, G., and N. J. Ouédraogo. 2009. "Ouagadougou, Burkina Faso." Draft mining chapter for Country Economic Memorandum. World Bank, Washington, DC.

Moseley, W. G., and L. Gray, eds. 2008. *Hanging by a Thread: Cotton, Globalization, and Poverty in Africa.* Athens, OH: Ohio University Press.

Newbery, J. 1989. "The Theory of Food Price Stabilization." *Economic Journal* 99: 1065–82.

Pinkney, T. C. 1993. "Is Market Liberalization Compatible with Food Security? Storage, Trade, Price Policies for Maize in Southern Africa." In *Agricultural Policy Reforms and Regional Market Integration in Malawi, Zambia and Zimbabwe,* ed. A. Valdés and K. Muir-Leresche. Washington, DC: International Food Policy Research Institute.

Platteau, J-P. 1996. "Physical Infrastructure as a Constraint on Agricultural Growth: The Case of Sub-Saharan Africa." *Oxford Development Studies* 24 (3): 189–219.

———. 2007. "Constraints on African Economic Growth: The Institutional Legacy." Paper presented at the first IERC conference, "The Economic Performance of Civilizations: Roles of Culture, Religion, and the Law," University of Southern California, Los Angeles.

Reardon, T. 1993. "Cereals Demand in the Sahel and Potential Impacts of Regional Cereals Protection." *World Development* 21 (1): 17–35.

Reij, C., G. Tappan, and M. Smale, 2009. "Re-Greening the Sahel: Farmer-Led Innovation in Burkina Faso and Niger." In *Millions Fed: Proven Successes in Agricultural Development.* Washington, DC: International Food Policy Research Institute.

Rodrik, D. 1996. "Understanding Economic Policy Reform." *Journal of Economic Literature* 34 (1): 9–41.

Savadogo, K. 2009. Le contexte macroéconomique. Background paper for the Burkina Faso Country Economic Memorandum. World Bank, Washington, DC.

Stringfellow, R., J. Coulter, A. Hussain, T. Lucey, and C. McKone. 1997. "Improving the Access of Smallholders to Agricultural Services in Sub-Saharan Africa." *Small Enterprise Development* 8 (3): 35–41.

Stringfellow, R., J. Coulter, T. Lucey, C. McKone, and A. Hussain. 1996. *The Provision of Agricultural Services through Self-Help in Sub-Saharan Africa.* Research report R6117CA, Natural Resources Institute, Chatham, United Kingdom.

SWAC Secretariat, and OECD (Organisation for Economic Co-operation and Development). 2007. "Economic and Social Importance of Cotton Production and Trade in West Africa: Role of Cotton in Regional Development, Trade and Livelihoods." Working Paper, Paris.

Teravaninthorn, S., and G. Raballand. 2008. *Transport Prices and Costs in Africa. A Review of the International Corridors.* Washington, DC: World Bank.

Tschirley, D., C. Poulton, and P. Labaste, eds. 2009. *Organization and Performance of Cotton Sectors in Africa.*

Learning from Reform Experience. Washington, DC: World Bank.

World Bank. 2004. "Cotton Cultivation in Burkina Faso: A 30-Year Success Story." Paper presented at the conference "Scaling up Poverty Reduction, a Global Learning Process," Shanghai.

————. 2007a. *Burkina Faso: The Challenge of Export Diversification for a Landlocked Country. Diagnostic Trade Integration Study for the Integrated Framework Program.* Washington, DC.

————. 2007b. *World Development Indicators.* Washington, DC: World Bank.

————. 2008. *World Development Indicators.* Washington, DC: World Bank.

————. 2009a. *Burkina Faso: Country Economic Memorandum. Promoting Growth, Competitiveness and Diversification.* Washington, DC.

————. 2009b. *Doing Business 2009.* Washington, DC: World Bank.

————. 2010. *World Development Indicators.* Washington, DC: World Bank.

————. Various years. *Enterprise Surveys.* Washington, DC.

Yanggen, D., K. Kelly, T. Reardon, and A. Naseem. 1998. "Incentives for Fertilizer Use in Sub-Saharan Africa: A Review of Empirical Evidence on Fertilizer Response and Profitability." Michigan State University Working Paper 70, East Lansing, MI.

PART II

Post Conflict Situations – Building Institutions and Governance

CHAPTER 7

Postconflict Economic Governance Reform: The Experience of Liberia

Vishal Gujadhur

When Ellen Johnson Sirleaf began her tenure as president of Liberia in January 2006, she took charge of a country facing enormous challenges. It had been more than two years since the signing of the Accra Comprehensive Peace Agreement that brought an uneasy end to a conflict that killed more than 250,000 Liberians and left more than 500,000 others displaced. The scale and intensity of the violence had destabilized the region politically and economically, making Liberia a global exemplar of a failed state.

Chief among the president's many challenges was restoring public trust in economic governance. As the country collapsed during the conflict, so did government finances and management of those finances. By 2005 revenue was less than $95 million a year, with public spending only about $25 a year on each citizen, one of the lowest levels in the world. Corruption was rampant. Liberia's external debt ballooned to $4.7 billion, or roughly 800 percent of GDP and 3,000 percent of export in 2005. Domestic debt and arrears exceeded $600 million by 2006, largely due to weak government spending controls that allowed ministries and agencies to spend without central authorization. Economic mismanagement and the uncertainty surrounding public finances was reflected in the continuation of UN sanctions on the export of Liberian diamonds and timber.

The low level of trust in the government's economic management capabilities was even more significant given

that poor economic governance during the 1970s and 1980s was one of the causes of the conflict. Corruption and mismanagement of the economy worsened dramatically during the war and prolonged the conflict, as corruption grew out of control and there was little political will for a well-run government. Sound economic policies were therefore, crucial for Liberia's long-term prospects for peace.

Initial steps toward reform of economic governance in Liberia were taken during the transitional period between the end of the civil war and start of the new administration. Among these was the launch of the Governance and Economic Management Assistance Program (GEMAP) several months before the January 2006 elections. A partnership between the government of Liberia and a group of international donors, GEMAP was intended to improve the accountability and transparency of fiscal management in Liberia. President Sirleaf continued the implementation of GEMAP after her election, and in addition she committed to making further economic governance reforms. Five years on, Liberia's recovery in terms of public finances and responsible public policy is striking. Annual government revenue has nearly tripled since the start of the Sirleaf administration and substantial inroads have been made in the budgeting and expenditure processes. Civil servants are now paid on time, the government has accumulated no new domestic arrears, and it has reached the completion point in

Vishal Gujadhur is a former Center for Global Development Scott Fellow at the Ministry of Finance in Liberia.

the enhanced Heavily Indebted Poor Countries (HIPC) process, allowing more than $4 billion of external debt to be written off. Liberia's international reserves also increased, reaching $108 million in December 2008 and $312 million in December 2009.[1] At the same time, Liberia has climbed the ranks of Transparency International's Corruption Perceptions Index, moving from 137 of 158 countries in 2005 to 97 of 180 countries in 2009. The nation has also adopted the Kimberley Process Certification scheme for sourcing diamond exports, established new forestry regulations, and is now fully compliant with the Extractive Industries Transparency Initiative (EITI). Thanks to the improvements in economic governance, the UN-imposed ban on diamond and timber exports from Liberia has been removed.

Liberia's success at gaining control over public finances in a postconflict environment has prompted a closer look at the factors underpinning the turnaround. Establishing a simple causal story is difficult because two major policy changes happened nearly simultaneously: the start of President Sirleaf's administration and the implementation of GEMAP. The story is further complicated by a general lack of data resulting from the realities of a postconflict country and the difficulty of measuring outcomes related to economic governance.

Many observers have been quick to credit GEMAP for the economic governance successes that have taken place in Liberia in recent years. While GEMAP played a useful role, it also had shortcomings, and an understanding of the context in Liberia and the efforts of the Sirleaf administration is necessary to establish a more complete story of the recovery and the reform effort in Liberia.

THE CONTEXT BEHIND ECONOMIC GOVERNANCE REFORM

Several major events in Liberia's recent history lie behind the country's need for economic governance reform, namely, the long period of conflict; a difficult economic recovery following the conflict; and the start of a new, democratically elected administration.

Descent into war and emergence from conflict

Liberia's economic problems began before the first outbreak of conflict in 1989. Even then, the country was marked by deep social and economic divisions, and Samuel Doe's coup d'état in 1980 began a decade of gross mismanagement until his assassination in 1989. Between 1987 and 1995, Liberia's gross domestic product (GDP) fell by an astonishing 90 percent, and by the time elections took place in 2005, average income in Liberia was one-fourth of what it had been in 1987 and one-sixth of what it had been in 1979.

Finally, after 14 years of instability covering two civil wars, the Accra Comprehensive Peace Agreement signed in August 2003 provided for a National Transitional Government of Liberia (NTGL) to guide Liberia toward elections in late 2005. The country faced enormous reconstruction needs, and international donors stepped in to help set Liberia on the path to recovery. The transitional government took several initial steps toward addressing economic governance issues. The chairman of the NTGL signed Executive Order No. 2, which consolidated all government accounts at the Central Bank of Liberia (CBL). The government requested audits of practices under the past regime. The Results-Focused Transitional Framework (RFTF), meanwhile, set out a comprehensive reconstruction framework. The transitional government also partnered with the World Bank, the International Monetary Fund (IMF), and the European Community (EC) to work on issues related to governance, economic revitalization, and financial management.

Persistent fiscal problems and the genesis of GEMAP

Following a hopeful start, doubts surfaced at the end of 2004 about the NTGL's commitment to improving economic governance and fighting corruption, while Liberia's overall economic recovery remained sluggish. A group of international partners known as the International Contact Group (ICG) expressed concern that the lack of economic progress would threaten peace. Audits commissioned by the EC in early 2005 revealed widespread corruption, not just during the time of the Taylor regime but also during the NTGL. At a review of RFTF progress in May 2005, many international partners focused on the mismanagement of public resources as a primary reason for the sluggish recovery, kick-starting negotiations with the NTGL for a more robust international engagement on public financial management in Liberia.[2]

The NTGL was reluctant to submit to international partners' recommendations. For the NTGL, the two main points of contention were the submission of GEMAP for UN Security Council endorsement and the international recruitment of the chief administrator of the CBL. Only after repeated threats of halting all international aid did the NTGL representatives agree to GEMAP. In the end, explicit linkage to the UN was removed, although the exit from GEMAP was now linked to Liberia reaching the Enhanced HIPC Completion Point. This had the benefit of both tying the completion of GEMAP to a significant incentive (clearing Liberia's enormous debt burden) and providing detailed triggers that could be determined at a later date, because the triggers in a HIPC program generally relate to public financial management and goals that are in concert with GEMAP.

Broadly, GEMAP targeted transparency in public financial management and revenue collection, expenditure controls, and government procurement and concession practices. Thus conceived, GEMAP ambitiously sought to accomplish six objectives: securing Liberia's revenue base, improving budgeting and expenditure management, improving procurement practices and granting of concessions, establishing effective processes to control corruption, supporting key institutions, and capacity building.

A key innovation undertaken as part of GEMAP was the system of internationally recruited financial controllers posted alongside Liberians in key agencies. This system was meant to enable the controllers to help establish transparent financial procedures, train and build local capacity from within the agencies, and report on revenue and spending. The centerpiece of GEMAP design, for which it is known internationally, is the cosignatory authority these experts wielded, which ensured that no major financial transactions could take place without being scrutinized by both a Liberian manager and an international adviser. The basic GEMAP goal was to "ensure that all revenues due to the government are collected, and [that] those revenues are spent according to a budget," all in an environment of increasing transparency.[3]

Although GEMAP was intended to be an interim plan for the body of international partners involved in postconflict reconstruction in Liberia, in practice it provided an embedded control system to maintain a transitional economic governance framework. The intention was to ensure that government and donor resources were secured and channeled through the budget, but the overall setup was one of increased oversight. In the end, it would be up to the government to put in place the internal systems and use the space that this oversight afforded in order to set up long-term systems.

Elections and the Sirleaf administration

Liberia's Economic Governance Steering Committee (EGSC) held its inaugural meeting in October 2005, one month after the signing of GEMAP. There was little progress on GEMAP implementation at that point, because Liberia was focused on the elections. The IMF, which had cut off relations with Liberia during the war, began discussions about providing assistance to the country and possibly instituting a staff-monitored program.

At her inauguration in January 2006, Ellen Johnson Sirleaf acknowledged the scale of the challenge of rebuilding the war-torn country. Toward this end, the administration announced its "150-Day Action Plan" shortly thereafter. The plan detailed the objectives and deliverables that both it and the donor community would assume upon taking office. The 150-Day Action Plan organized the administration's work into four pillars: expanding peace and security, revitalizing economic activity, strengthening governance and the rule of law, and rebuilding infrastructure and providing basic services.

Revitalizing economic activity and strengthening governance, in particular, are both closely related to the areas covered by GEMAP. While the capacity for overlap between the administration's 150-Day Plan and GEMAP was certainly possible—as was the possibility, at the time of GEMAP's creation, that the new administration would not want to work within the GEMAP framework—the scenario played out otherwise. A passage from President Sirleaf's inauguration speech addresses the issue directly:

"If we are to achieve our development and anti-corruption goals, we must welcome and embrace the Governance and Economic Management Program (GEMAP) which the National Transitional Government of Liberia, working with our international partners, has formulated to deal with the serious economic and financial management deficiencies in our country.

We accept and will enforce the terms of GEMAP, recognizing the important assistance which it is expected to provide during the early years of our government. More importantly, we will ensure competence and integrity in the management of our own resources and insist on an integrated capacity building initiative so as to render GEMAP nonapplicable in a reasonable period of time." (Sirleaf 2006)

In short, the new administration recognized that with scarce government resources and limited capacity, the international community would play a prominent role in Liberia's reconstruction and economic governance reform.

KEY COMPONENTS OF THE APPROACH TO ECONOMIC GOVERNANCE REFORM

The simultaneous timing of the GEMAP implementation and the change in administration in Liberia is an important one, because the government of Liberia is both the driver of interventions and the target of change. Clearly, this duality complicates assessments of causality. In addition, GEMAP's broad objectives and multiple actors mean that it is "difficult to trace the boundaries of GEMAP assistance," as noted in a midterm GEMAP evaluation (Morsiani et al. 2008, 13). Finally, GEMAP and the change in administration were necessarily complementary from the start, with GEMAP providing a set guideline the government could rely on but would also be constrained by. Indeed, GEMAP was meant to provide a transitional economic governance system and enable long-term systems to be put in place. The key question to focus on then is the appropriateness of the GEMAP interventions and their effect on government policy initiatives.

While GEMAP was an extensive initiative, its essential thrust was clear. As stated in an early World Bank/UN joint review, "GEMAP is notable for three key features: the scope and intrusiveness of its key features, the consistency of its features throughout the negotiating process, and a lack of detail on funding and implementation" (Dwan and Bailey 2006, 19). The "intrusive" key feature referred to the cosignatory authority for state-owned enterprises (SOEs), the Ministry of Finance, the Bureau of the Budget, and the CBL; the position of chief administrator was created in each of these agencies to be the cosignatory with the international financial expert. Additionally, linking the exit from GEMAP to Liberia achieving HIPC completion shows the imposition of forces outside Liberia on the program, despite GEMAP's mentions of the "full respect for the sovereignty of Liberia." (Government of Liberia 2005).

Other GEMAP features, such as support for Liberia's General Auditing Commission and the Public Procurement and Concession Commission, are also important. Those features, however, do not differ substantively from international postconflict reconstruction programs in other countries, and much of the work process related to them could be completed outside the general framework of GEMAP. Indeed, the other interventions contain much less detail about how they are to be implemented, underlining the centrality of the cosignatory aspect of GEMAP.

Establishing space for reform was also a key component of GEMAP. At the time of its formulation, an optimistic outcome for GEMAP would have been its full utilization by an incoming administration. At the least, though, it could have been a fail-safe within the government and a way for external agencies to place some checks on corruption in the absence of domestic impetus. That said, GEMAP also left ample room for domestic authorities to implement it in either more extensive or more limited ways, partly through the vagueness of such areas as capacity building, but also in the possibility that GEMAP would enable more resources to be channeled through the budget.

The Sirleaf administration approached its governing plans thoughtfully and outlined its key goals and tactics from the start. These plans can be traced to the 150-Day Action Plan, a framework similar to Poverty Reduction Strategy Papers prepared by IMF and World Bank member countries. That framework, which was announced at the start of the Sirleaf administration, would continue to form the overall strategic governance platform as the administration embarked on an iterative process that moved from the 150-Action Plan to an Interim Poverty Reduction Strategy Paper in 2007 to a full Poverty Reduction Strategy Paper in 2008. The administration also used the poverty reduction strategy program as an opportunity to set out annual plans for economic governance reforms. In fact, it could be argued that the government's iterative planning process, including efforts such as the IMF's Staff Monitored Programs and the Poverty Reduction and Growth Facility, are part of the GEMAP process insofar as they are linked to the Enhanced HIPC Completion Point.

From the start, the Sirleaf administration exerted bold political leadership and made concerted efforts to work with donors collaboratively and ensure coordination. In particular, the administration supported a series of locally sourced and targeted interventions in key ministries and agencies, while making use of donor resources and coordination. Also key in the administration's plans was its effort to make effective use of donor resources. Given the ravaged state of the country at the end of the war, the administration recognized from the start that the reconstruction of Liberia would require significant external assistance. The challenge was to channel the resources effectively, no easy task given the multitude of partners, projects, and methods of funding. Flow of donor information was poor, and only in the 2009/10 national budget were preliminary estimates of total aid to Liberia collected by the government.

The Sirleaf administration introduced a new mechanism to coordinate government and donor activities: the Liberia Reconstruction and Development Committee (LRDC). The LRDC's Steering Committee was initially kept small, to allow decisions to be made more quickly and easily, and resembled a subcabinet group chaired by the president. Members of the Steering Committee included four ministers, each with responsibility for one of the reconstruction pillars, and representation by the four largest donors (the United States, United Nations, World Bank, and the European Commission). Representatives of the Economic Community of West African States (ECOWAS) and of the IMF joined meetings, as did other donors and ministers when appropriate. The Steering Committee met every two weeks at the start of the Sirleaf administration, reflecting the large amount of work to be done, before moving to monthly meetings.

The LRDC resembled, in some ways, the Economic Governance Steering Committee envisioned by GEMAP. By adopting an administrative structure that mirrored the substantive pillars of the government's own comprehensive action plan, as well as including key donors, a small group of decision makers was able to make policy decisions and ensure coordination across efforts. The LRDC also allowed problems to be addressed as they emerged, permitting donors to see and participate in the decision-making processes of the government and understand the realities the politicians faced. The strength of this arrangement was ultimately reflected in the decision in 2009 to merge the EGSC gatherings into the LRDC.

At their core, both GEMAP and the incoming Liberian administration's plans attempted to accomplish the same goals. GEMAP provided an external oversight and control function, while the government was responsible for carrying out the actual reforms. After several years, it is now possible to investigate the underlying efforts and examine their gains. As discussed earlier, GEMAP's objectives were broad and ambitious, which has made it difficult to take stock of the program's effectiveness. Further fuzziness around the program's edges is the result of programs undertaken by GEMAP's international partners on behalf of the government of Liberia but not explicitly outlined within GEMAP. Given the broad scope of public financial management and establishing fiscal accountability and transparency, the focus in the future will need to be on two priority areas: securing Liberia's revenue base and establishing an effective expenditure process.

Improving revenue collection

Securing Liberia's revenue base was a primary initial goal of both the Sirleaf administration and GEMAP. Indeed, first on the list of GEMAP components is financial management and accountability. As described in the GEMAP agreement, "It is critical to protect the revenue streams of key revenue generating agencies and institutions, as well as to secure the revenues from customs duties, import levies and taxes" (Government of Liberia 2005). For the administration, procedures to improve tax collection were included in the 150-Day Plan under the banner of "economic revitalization," while increased revenues were central to its ability to begin to fulfill its campaign promises.

The scale of the revenue collection problem was enormous. In fiscal year 2004/05, the government received only $75 million in taxes, although it had spent more than $85 million a year between 2000 and 2005. Corruption affected public spending at all levels of government. Spending per capita of only about $25 was already among the lowest in the world, and for the government to begin showing peace dividends and deliver urgently needed services to its citizens, revenue had to be raised quickly. The international community noted in the GEMAP that progress on increasing revenue collection was not fast enough under the NTGL, saying that "large leakages were taking place due to difficulties in fiscal administration, absence of verifiable mechanisms for financial control, and malfeasance" (Government of Liberia 2005). GEMAP designers also focused on the need to enforce the NTGL Executive Order mandating that all revenue due to the government be consolidated by the CBL.

While financial management was weak across government, GEMAP noted that "SOEs present particularly large risk given their weak management and operational structures and systems" (Government of Liberia 2005). This concern was reflected in GEMAP's primary instrument for enforcing financial management and accountability. Perhaps influenced by the audits of the SOEs that had been conducted by the EC during the NTGL, GEMAP led to the imposition of management contracts and international controllers for several SOEs (the National Port Authority, Roberts International Airport, the Liberia Petroleum Refinery Corporation, the Forestry Development Agency, and the Bureau of Maritime Affairs) and backed an adviser in the Bureau of Customs and Excise and a new post of chief administrator in the CBL.

In hindsight, the focus of GEMAP on placing experts at SOEs may have been misdirected, because the SOEs were somewhat peripheral to the central government's operations. The Forestry Development Authority, which would have been the focal point for forestry revenues, was not as important after the implementation of UN sanctions on timber exports. That was also true for SOEs as a whole, because in the absence of profits that can be turned over as dividends, there was little financial connection between the central government and SOEs. In fact, the only transfer to the government from SOEs during the first few years of the administration was $1.7 million from the LPRC in 2007. As a GEMAP evaluation report noted, total revenue collection by the Ministry of Finance in fiscal year 2006/07 was $139 million—approximately four times the combined gross revenues of the four SOEs with GEMAP controllers (Dod and Nelson 2008).

As for the Bureau of Customs and Excise at the Ministry of Finance, which collects over half of government revenue, the improvement in revenue performance has not been a result of GEMAP. An evaluation of the first short-term expert working in those two agencies found him to be of substandard quality, and three years after the signing of GEMAP there had been no systematic donor support under GEMAP auspices (Morsiani et al. 2008). In fact, government action and IMF support were much more salient in improving revenue collection, as evaluations have concluded. A U.S. Agency for International Development (USAID) report, however, has noted that while there have been efforts under GEMAP to support systemic improvements in revenue collection in Liberia, particularly in the customs arena, the assistance was "not being fully utilized for the benefit of Liberia" and has produced little follow-up for functions that had been installed (Dod and Nelson 2008).

How, then, was the Liberian government able to have a nearly instantaneous effect on revenue collection? The 150-Day Plan announced a target of increasing revenues by at least 15 percent year-on-year, and indeed, the overall revenue from international trade increased by 35 percent in the first five months of the Sirleaf administration (Dod and Nelson 2008). This was accomplished largely by better use of solutions already proposed. As the new government came to office, customs payments were collected in an "unwieldy and complex manual system," according to a GEMAP assessment (Dod and Nelson 2008). To address this, a technical expert from the U.S. Treasury designed an electronic computerized receipt system during 2005 in collaboration with USAID, the Ministry of Finance, and the CBL. However, the system was not fully used and reconciliation of the CBL/Ministry of Finance account did not begin until the new administration took office. By the end of January 2006, before any GEMAP advisers had been deployed across government, the newly installed Liberian authorities accepted only computer-produced receipts at the CBL. Liberian authorities also began to ensure more stringent preshipment inspections for goods moving through the port, and began to eliminate noncash tax payments—previously, the government had accepted "in kind" payments. This sort of insistence on adherence to existing rules and use of systems already in place allowed the government to produce the dramatic 35 percent increase in revenue collection, and in the process demonstrated newfound political will.

The government's success in increasing revenues was not limited to collection of customs duties; in fact, it was real and sustained across several areas of the government. Customs duties nearly doubled in the first year of the Sirleaf administration, from $35.3 million in fiscal year 2005/06 to $69.9 million in 2006/07. This is all the more impressive considering that the percentage increase in imports during this time was much smaller (imports rose from $294 million in 2005 to $418 million in 2007). The government also began to reorganize its methods for collecting income taxes. Efforts in this area paid off immediately, with actual tax revenues increasing 19 percent between February and June 2006 (IMF 2006). GEMAP experts did not arrive in Liberia until mid-April 2006.

Table 7.1 shows that the increase in Liberian revenues was not limited to customs duties (shown in the table as international trade taxes). The deputy minister of revenue of the Ministry of Finance, in tandem with the IMF, introduced a

Table 7.1   Revenue Collection in Liberia
         (millions of dollars)

Revenue	2003/04	2004/05	2005/06	2006/07	2007/08	2008/09
Total revenue	56.0	79.3	84.6	146.8	200.8	211.3
Total tax revenue	55.3	75.7	81.0	140.0	168.8	190
International trade tax	24.3	30.2	35.3	69.9	79.1	87.9
Income tax	9.4	28.4	25.1	42.5	52.6	65.8
Goods and services tax	21.3	16.9	20.3	26.1	34.9	33.7
Other	0.3	0.3	0.3	1.4	2.2	2.6
Nontax revenue	0.8	3.6	3.6	6.9	32.0	21.4
From SOEs	0	0	0	1.7	0	0
Grants	3.0	1.0	1.0	1.5	0	23.6

Source: IMF Liberia Program Reviews.

series of actions aimed at both short- and medium-term revenue collection. A partial list of actions includes computerization of the tax payment system; strengthening customs administration and steadily reducing exemptions; increasing penalties for not undergoing preshipment inspection, reorganizing the tax collection system into large, medium, and small taxpayer units, with an emphasis on the large taxpayer units; and increasing the excise tax on beer and cigarettes. The turn away from exemptions and short-term fixes that had been common during the periods of instability in favor of modernization of tax collection and rules-based collection is reflected in an increase in the income tax revenue take of more than 50 percent during the first year of the Sirleaf administration.

Another central platform in the GEMAP effort to increase revenue collection in Liberia was the institution of the chief administrator position at the Central Bank of Liberia. The original idea was for the administrator to serve under the guidance of the governor of the CBL, to possess binding cosignatory authority on operational and financial matters, to advise on banking operations and to emphasize internal controls and audits. These plans never came to fruition, however, because the governor of the CBL considered the cosignatory arrangement unacceptable and the first GEMAP adviser found it difficult to work within the system and left the position after 15 months. After this, a GEMAP adviser was placed at the CBL in a revamped position, focused more on operational matters.

The second GEMAP adviser was able to contribute significantly to improvements in the CBL system. The CBL was able to register surplus in its financial position, introduce a travel policy harmonized with the rest of the government, and increase its dollar reserves from $6.4 million at the start of 2006 to $35.1 million in 2007. The midterm GEMAP evaluation, though, recommended "a careful scrutiny in the effectiveness of GEMAP assistance to CBL given the fact that the conflicts it creates are not conducive to the achievement of results" (Dod and Nelson 2008).

Despite their successes, GEMAP efforts were a relatively small part of the overall task of improving revenue collection in Liberia, primarily because of GEMAP's targeting of SOEs. During the war and the NTGL period, resources continued to flow to SOEs and agencies, while the central government remained weak. Centralization of government accounts significantly reduced opportunities for leakage. Although GEMAP's support to SOEs was useful in improving those institutions' performance, it was peripheral to the revenue recovery led by government efforts and non-GEMAP-related donor support. This finding is echoed in evaluation reports, which found that GEMAP performed "unremarkably" in regard to the improvement of central banking and securing revenue at the Bureau of Customs (Morsiani et al. 2008).

Establishing an effective expenditure process

Just as important as improving revenue collection in Liberia was increasing the transparency and effectiveness of public spending. One of the stated aims of the government was to "restore the government's credibility in using the country's scarce resources efficiently and effectively," while a primary GEMAP objective was to improve the controls in public expenditures. Gains in effective expenditure, however, are more difficult to isolate than gains in revenue collection, because metrics of the quality and efficiency of spending are generally not objective or are unavailable in Liberia.

During the NTGL period, the meager amounts of revenue the government collected were not spent effectively, and reports were widespread in the Liberian media of corruption and similar accusations among various factions in the NTGL. Because the Bureau of Budget was initially operationally independent from the Ministry of Finance, the structure required cooperation and collaboration in budget formulation and execution. Past governments, meanwhile, had kept the national budget secret and allowed unlimited transfers between line items at the executive branch's whim. Procurement did not follow standardized procedures. In short, the structure the Sirleaf administration inherited did not fit its aims.

As an interim measure, foreign policy advice and technical assistance during the NTGL established a cash-based balanced budget with budget execution handled through the Cash Management Committee (CMCo), which consisted of the Bureau of Budget and Ministry of Finance officials, who approved all government expenditures. To introduce better procurement practices, international partners helped draft a new Public Procurement and Concessions Act. By the time of the 2005 IMF Article IV consultation, however, IMF staff found that "significant expenditures were still made without the committee's prior authorization" and that the CMCo was "not operating as intended" (IMF 2005). Reviews of the Ministry of Finance found that it "operated in constant crisis mode, with the CMCo under constant and enormous pressure to clear payments," while "poor documentation, thirty stages of voucher review, lack of information and opaqueness regarding prioritization exacerbated [problems]" (Morsiani et al. 2008). With no reliable estimates of budgetary receipts and balances, it was hard for line ministries to learn of their budgetary allotments, and the lack of commitment controls led to a buildup of government liabilities. By the end of 2004 the government had approximately $12 million in domestic arrears, roughly 15 percent of the total budget.

GEMAP interventions aimed at improving budgeting and expenditure management consisted of the establishment of an Integrated Financial Management Information System and the placement of advisers with cosignatory authority in the Bureau of Budget and Ministry of Finance. The incoming government also took action in this area, indicating in its 150-Day Action Plan that the CMCo should be effectively operational upon the start of the new administration in January 2006. In this case, the work done by GEMAP and the government were mutually reinforcing.

Expenditure controls first took root through the CMCo, which quickly began to function effectively and arguably became one of the successes of GEMAP and the government. Under GEMAP's commitment control system, all purchase orders and expenditure vouchers from line ministries were submitted to the CMCo, which verified that each proposed expenditure was consistent with the spending agency's monthly expenditure allocation and compliant with the procurement law. The CMCo also ensured that there were sufficient funds in the government's accounts at the CBL. The system in which payments required CMCo authorization prevented expenditure arrears and unauthorized government purchases. Although similar systems had been in place beforehand, they were cumbersome, had little political support, and consequently were rarely enforced.

In a September 2006 review, IMF staff found that Liberia's commitment control system had been well implemented. From the start of the administration, no new arrears accumulated and all expenditure authority was consolidated with the CMCo. Through public notices, the government made it clear that commitments not accompanied by CMCo vouchers were not legal claims on the government. Although the foreign adviser at CMCo likely played a significant role, CMCo also had a foreign adviser during the NTGL period. What changed with the Sirleaf administration was not the presence of a foreign adviser but the political environment and support for that adviser.

Within the Bureau of the Budget, complementary improvements were implemented. Even before the GEMAP-recruited adviser began to work with the Bureau of the Budget in April 2006, there was increased communication with ministries to ensure that commitments did not exceed available revenues. The task of the Bureau of the Budget, however, was complicated by the importance of both short- and medium-term targets: the monthly allotments and current budget had to be executed appropriately, while the following year's budget had to be prepared simultaneously. The arrival of the GEMAP adviser brought increased focus on both immediate controls in terms of cosigning of allotment requests and capacity building through training of staff at the Bureau of the Budget. The importance of the adviser was also discernible in reports noting instances of abuse when the adviser was temporarily absent (Dod and Nelson 2008).

In the lead-up to the merger of the Bureau of the Budget and the Ministry of Finance, reactivation of Liberia's interagency National Budget Committee led to improved coordination and oversight of both budget policy formulation and expenditure. In addition, the budget preparation process became more open and participatory, particularly during the fiscal year 2007/08 budget cycle, when both the GEMAP adviser and local staff began to focus on long-term planning and processes. This sequenced intervention—first providing for the immediate stabilization of the procurement system and then moving toward long-term planning—was an example of effective implementation of the GEMAP.

A key enabling factor for Liberia's success in establishing an effective expenditure program was senior management at both the Ministry of Finance and Bureau of the Budget. Given the political nature of a budget in a democracy, this also involved strong links with Liberian civil society, and the lengths to which the administration went to work with civil society were rewarded with a relatively high Public Expenditure and Financial Accountability (PEFA) score of "B" by 2007.[4]

While Liberia should be lauded for its success in managing its budget and expenditures, it should also be noted that the Integrated Financial Management Information System did little to improve Liberia's budget and expenditure reform process. As of 2010 the system still had not been implemented. On the other hand, the Resource Management Unit, the pool of donor money originally intended to fund technical assistance and support for the system, was able to be used to attract talent to and finance a management training school and an aid management unit within the Ministry of Finance. In fact, the RMU became an adaptable method of ensuring that the Ministry of Finance received technical assistance for its changing needs and could fill immediate capacity gaps where advisers had direct operational responsibilities. With this flexible setup, Liberian leaders were able to implement their own programs and initiate the day-to-day operational work needed to get Liberian institutions running effectively again.

Overall, evaluation reports are favorable for GEMAP on securing and stabilizing revenue collection and improving expenditure management, despite the fact that the processes were not fully in line with what was intended at program conception. That said, the GEMAP-appointed advisers at the Ministry of Finance and Bureau of the Budget had a positive impact, and reports suggest cosignatory authority was useful in these cases, although the advisers were also significantly enabled by the leadership in various ministries. In both expenditure management and budget coordination, GEMAP was able to play a role in stabilizing the system and creating capacity for more significant reforms to take place. How this capacity would be used, however, is another question. Several additional accomplishments made under GEMAP are illustrated in box 7.1.

THE LINK BETWEEN THE GOVERNMENT OF LIBERIA AND GEMAP

While it is difficult to assess how the Liberian government would have performed in the absence of GEMAP, it is clear that without government buy-in, GEMAP would have operated very differently. In the case of revenue collection, the Liberian government acted almost independently of GEMAP, driving the reform process, whereas in establishing expenditure and budgeting controls GEMAP had a larger role in helping the government stabilize the system. The commitment and actions of the government in Liberia to the changes in public accountability are striking, yet many stock-taking reviews have focused only on the role of GEMAP. Any overall report card for the administration's performance, on economic governance or otherwise, is perhaps complicated by the government of Liberia being both an agent and target of change. Still, the effect of the change in political leadership in the sequence of reform is undeniable. Figure 7.1 provides an overview of the timeline of economic governance reforms in Liberia.

Without a doubt, the shift between the NTGL period and the Sirleaf administration in terms of economic management was marked. President Sirleaf was democratically elected, selected members of her government, and had a comprehensive plan to rebuild Liberia. She signaled a clear break with the policies of the past, and one of the first agenda items in the new administration's 150-Day Action Plan was to dismiss all NTGL political appointees from the Ministry of Finance. She also endorsed GEMAP in her inaugural speech and included GEMAP implementation benchmarks in the 150-Day Action Plan. Political leadership, then, was clearly important to both the functioning of GEMAP and the change in economic governance. GEMAP evaluators recognized this. Indeed, without this change in leadership, GEMAP's operations would necessarily have been vastly different.

All of this said, the openness of Liberian politicians to receiving technical assistance and accepting foreign advisers working alongside them is also striking. In part, it reflects the scale of work that needed to be accomplished. It likely also reflects a country in which both the president and the minister of finance were international technocrats with significant policy-making experience. Either way, it made for a collaborative process that helped to drive economic governance reform forward.

Government buy-in was particularly important in Liberia's case because at its core, GEMAP established only a

---

Box 7.1   Other Accomplishments under GEMAP

GEMAP consisted of six pillars. In addition to the pillars focused on improving revenue collection and establishing effective expenditure processes, the GEMAP pillars focused on supporting key institutions and establishing effective processes to control corruption.

These two pillars had contrasting outcomes. In the first case, the evaluation teams appointed by GEMAP to support the General Auditing Commission were successful, playing a strong role in rebuilding institutional and capacity building. The European Community provided long-term technical support, financed an auditor general position (currently held by a Liberian) and the refurbishment of the General Auditing Commission, and provided general advisers. The result has been an independent General Auditing Commission that provides, in a very public manner, an ex post check on fraud and support for accountability.

By contrast, the Liberia Anti-Corruption Commission has yet to take off. Although donors explicitly outlined an Anti-Corruption Commission in the GEMAP document, the legislation to establish such a commission did not pass until 2008, and then donor funding support proved to be lacking.

Figure 7.1 Economic Governance Reform Timeline

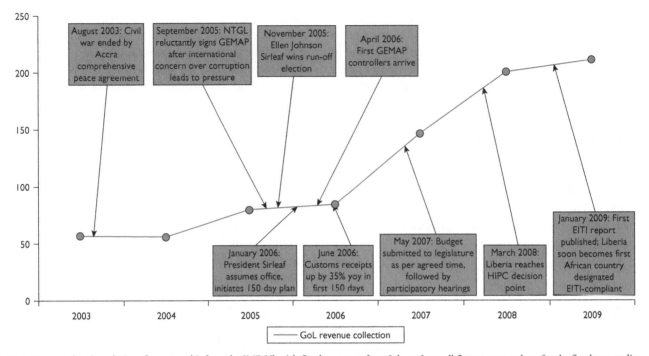

Note: Revenue data is exclusive of grants and is from the IMF. Liberia's fiscal year runs from July-to-June, all figures reported are for the fiscal year ending in June (i.e., 2003 is for the fiscal year 2002/2003)

transitional economic governance framework that merely created the space for the government to carry out the more operational aspects of reform. While a GEMAP-style program might work in the case of a hostile recipient government, such a situation is unlikely. One program, the USAID-sponsored "Liberia Economic Stabilization Support Program," which strongly resembled GEMAP, can serve to inform the feasibility of GEMAP under a different governance regime. Implemented in 1989, that program sought to improve revenue collection and expenditure control by giving 17 experts financial control over government accounts (Dwan and Bailey 2006). Its failure in less than a year underscores the importance of dynamic leadership and political will.

GEMAP certainly complemented the government's efforts and put in place a stop-gap system, but questions still surround the mix of its activities. Although GEMAP's intention, in part, was to lay the foundations for reform, the activities carried out under it concentrated on keeping the system moving forward as constructed. The implementation of the CMCo and financial controllers, for example, while successful, left most of the heavy lifting in terms of

long-term building of systems to the government. So, while the interim controls carried out under GEMAP were successful in helping to prevent new arrears and rooting out opportunistic corruption, their effectiveness resulted in a top-heavy structure that led to a difficulty in allowing a more successful rollout of spending.

By 2008 it was apparent to both the government and its international partners that a lack of capacity at the line ministry level was hindering the effective implementation of the government's agenda. Difficulties implementing the procurement law led to a slowdown in critical government spending that GEMAP's stop-gap, concentrated measures were not equipped to address. The capacity building that GEMAP was supposed to deliver could possibly have removed this bottleneck but did not materialize in a significant way. Instead, the focus on the immediate controls reduced the long-term relevance and effectiveness of GEMAP, leaving the government to drive the capacity-building agenda with donors.

In addition to enabling GEMAP to be a success, the political leadership in Liberia also took independent actions to improve financial management and transparency from the start. In her inaugural speech, President Sirleaf promised that there would be actions taken "so as to render GEMAP unnecessary," implying that she intended for the new administration to target not just GEMAP actions but also the larger economic governance areas that GEMAP covered. In the end, the Liberian government's drive for reform outgrew the outlines of GEMAP assistance once the system had stabilized.

FURTHER CAPACITY FOR ECONOMIC GOVERNANCE REFORM

Despite significant progress since 2005, Liberia is still a fragile state, and much work remains to be done. That said, criticism of the government or of donor interventions should not downplay the enormity of the tasks before it just five years ago, and many of the concerns today were not of top priority during the initial launch; when stabilizing the economy was the government's unique focus.

Liberia's most problematic economic governance shortfall continues to be capacity building, the most vaguely defined objective in the GEMAP program document, which noted the other components would be accompanied by "a plan and resources to enable major progress for capacity building" (Government of Liberia 2005). In general, capacity building has never been a priority under the GEMAP program. A two-year capacity-building training program at the Ministry of Finance, though useful, is the only explicit capacity-building initiative conducted under GEMAP auspices. More informal programs took place in other ministries.

One GEMAP evaluation reported that even though line ministries and agencies were committed to economic governance improvements, their lack of capacity severely limited their performances. This shortcoming was exacerbated by a new public procurement law that, while necessary, decentralized procurement without first building capacity to facilitate its implementation. Overall, however, the will to retrain Liberian government workers on new procedures and regulations has been lacking, and the role of GEMAP in capacity-building initiatives has not always been constructive.

In hindsight, GEMAP should have paid closer attention to capacity building from the start. Rather than allowing its focus to pivot as needed based on the situation in Liberia, it appears that GEMAP efforts focused on form, rather than function, with too much focus on SOEs, despite GEMAP reviews suggesting a change in focus. One evaluation noted that, "When best practices are in place, cosignature arrangements are not a function of control but complement capac-

ity and institutional building" (Morsiani et al. 2008) and recommended a transition from a focus on immediate controls to longer-term system building.

The Sirleaf administration made its views clear early on. In a paper prepared for the Liberian Partners Forum in February 2007, the administration gently noted that donors continued to focus on the short term: "Previous breakdowns in governance led to considerable focus being placed on the 'cosignatory' aspects of GEMAP. Considering the progress and positive changes that have taken place in the leadership of the country, [the government of Liberia] has encouraged partners to focus on the development of attitudes, systems and procedures that can promote and sustain integrity, rather than on a transient policing role" (Government of Liberia 2007).

While this focus on stabilization was appropriate and useful to economic governance reform in an immediate postconflict situation, a second phase was needed to deepen upstream and downstream controls on spending, including building up internal and external audits and increasing the public procurement capacity in spending agencies, a task that GEMAP frequently bypassed. The controls introduced under GEMAP were at best transitory, and it is possible that they were actually a hindrance to establishing deeper, more strategic reforms. Indeed, despite GEMAP efforts to strengthen systems, most donors have yet to trust Liberia with budget support. Like GEMAP's transitional systems, donors continue to intervene in Liberia in an ad hoc fashion, from providing project support to multidonor trust funds to contributing to a variety of parallel implementation units designed to work around the Liberian system rather than build it up.

As further confirmation of the need for sustained capacity-building efforts in Liberia, the national capacity development plan currently being formulated under the auspices of GEMAP (the same report discusses progress on the implementation of Liberia's poverty reduction strategy) finds that capacity building is the primary constraint to faster progress on economic governance reform in Liberia. Without the capacity to implement, the long-term systems upon which sustained success depends will remain elusive.

KEY LESSONS LEARNED FROM THE LIBERIAN ECONOMIC GOVERNANCE EXPERIENCE

Despite the difficulties in attributing causality to governance policy interventions given the two policy changes that took place in early 2006, it is possible to draw lessons from Liberia's public financial management gains.

- **Placing international advisers in postconflict environments can be useful in some cases.** The GEMAP program was primarily aimed at top-down controls, and this target was appropriate and valuable in the Ministry of Finance and SOEs in the initial transitional NTGL period given the situation at the time. Building up systems, however, requires more than top-down checks on abuse. For the most part, stationing advisers in the ministries both helped Liberia fill immediate capacity gaps and established controls and set examples for those willing to follow them. This was dependent, however, on local authorities being open to the process. The cosignatory process was useful in some cases, but GEMAP tended to be a focus on the process itself, rather than the function the reforms were to intended to carry out.

- **Finding the appropriate role for international partners is key.** In 2005 a key question in the process of economic governance reform appeared to be whether discipline could be imposed from the outside. While it is simplistic to view governance interventions on a continuum between international trusteeship and full country ownership, most people familiar with the situation in Liberia considered that a significant amount of external assistance was needed. In the case of Liberia, however, the government had changed by the time GEMAP was formulated, complicating assessment of how effectively GEMAP fulfilled its intentions. Indeed, GEMAP helped improve economic governance in Liberia, but only after the new administration changed the parameters of its operation.

- **Partners must strike a balance between capacity building and delivery.** Under GEMAP, international controllers were to serve two roles in Liberia. First, they were to impose temporary controls and give the government the necessary breathing space to put long-term systems into place. Second, they were to help fill in for the lack of capacity and help to build up the long-term systems from the inside. While those two roles are interrelated, the distinction between the two continues to matter. GEMAP was ostensibly designed to cover both, but the focus ended up being on delivery. Once Liberia's top-level governance problems were resolved, capacity became the binding constraint to fully rebuilding government institutions, and by some accounts, GEMAP did not do enough to address that.

- **Provisions must be made for flexibility.** The timing of GEMAP, which was signed during the transitional government in Liberia, required that donors be flexible in their support of the incoming government. An economic

governance reform program should, for example, be able to provide for rapid-progress scenarios. Although GEMAP met with success in several of its interventions, it focused on the control process and did not go much beyond it, which lessened its impact in terms of building institutions that go beyond the initial stabilization of the system.

In terms of revenue collection, for example, the initial GEMAP interventions targeted SOEs, which were important but not especially relevant for long-term fiscal gains in Liberia. More generally, as pointed out in one evaluation, "assistance provided by GEMAP partners outside GEMAP arrangement were . . . more relevant to the specific needs of the various institutions" (Morsiani et al. 2008).

- **Supporting local leaders can improve economic governance outcomes.** Ultimately, success in economic governance reform depends on local efforts, and leadership in particular was a key ingredient in Liberia's success. Additionally, local leaders took charge of programs through constant dialogue with donors and took ownership of the reform process. Although it was impossible to know at the time GEMAP was signed whether the new administration would fully support the program, the new administration found GEMAP to be, in the words of President Sirleaf, "a necessary intrusion." Indeed, the reform progress under GEMAP was only a start for the government, and the impetus provided by the new government in addressing economic governance, implementing strong expenditure controls, and securing and expanding revenue cannot be underestimated. In the end, strong leadership may be both the most relevant point and the hardest to replicate.

NOTES

1. Special SDR allocation included.

2. For more detailed discussions on the genesis of GEMAP, see Dod and Nelson (2008).

3. Retrieved from http://www.gemapliberia.orsg/pages/accomplishments.

4. www.pefa.org.

REFERENCES

Dod, D., and E. Nelson. 2008. "USAID Activities under GEMAP in Liberia: Impact Assessment Report." U.S. Agency for International Development, Washington, DC.

Dwan, R., and L. Bailey. 2006. "Liberia's Governance and Economic Management Assistance Program (GEMAP): A

Joint Review by the Department of Peacekeeping Operations' Peacekeeping Best Practices Group and the World Bank's Fragile State's Group." United Nations, Department of Peacekeeping Operations, New York.

Government of Liberia. 2005. "Government and Economic Management Assistance Program." Monrovia.

———. 2007. "Progress under GEMAP." Monrovia.

IMF (International Monetary Fund). 2005. "Liberia: Article IV Consultation: Staff Report." Country Report 05/166. Washington, DC.

———. 2006. "First Review of Performance under the Staff-Monitored Program." Country Report 06/412. Washington, DC.

Morsiani, G., et al. 2008. "Mid-term Evaluation of the Governance and Economic Management Assistance Program." GEMAP, Monrovia.

Sirleaf, Ellen Johnson. 2006. Inauguration Speech Transcript. www.emansion.gov.lr/doc/inaugural_add_1.pdf).

CHAPTER 8

Decentralization in Postconflict Sierra Leone: The Genie Is Out of the Bottle

Vivek Srivastava and Marco Larizza

When Sierra Leone emerged from more than a decade of conflict in 2002, it was one of the poorest countries in the world. It faced huge development challenges, with much of its infrastructure having been destroyed during the war.

The areas outside Freetown had traditionally been excluded and marginalized. In fact, the overcentralized system of rule, which excluded the majority of the population, was one of the key causes of the conflict. There were internal and external pressures on the government to be more inclusive to establish its legitimacy and reverse the conditions that led the country to conflict (Truth and Reconciliation Commission 2004; Hanlon 2005; Kieh 2005).

The reestablishment of local governments, through the Local Government Act of 2004, was an important initiative in this direction undertaken by the Sierra Leone People's Party (SLPP) government of Abdul Tejan Kabbah. The legislative framework provided by the act and the associated regulations for political, fiscal, and administrative decentralization (with some exceptions) provided a robust foundation for the establishment of decentralization through devolution of key functions from the central government to local councils. They also provided a simple and easily understood system for intergovernmental transfers.

With financial support from donors and through the efforts of a set of donor-supported agencies established within government, a functioning system is now in place. Although the process has been somewhat slower than desired, there has been a steady devolution of functions and

finances, and local councils are now fully staffed. Each council has a core staff of development planners, internal auditors, monitoring and evaluation officers, and procurement officers with requisite capacity for managing their service delivery functions. Both the legislation and its implementation leave open the possibility, however, of the center dominating and manipulating the subnational governments by playing off the traditional authorities (chieftaincies) against the local authorities through a "divide and rule" strategy and by minimizing the autonomy of the local councils over the control of financial and human resources.

This chapter examines the devolution of power in Sierra Leone since the end of armed conflict. The first section briefly reviews the history of decentralization in Sierra Leone and discusses the incentives and motivations that may have influenced the government's decision to decentralize in 2004. The second section highlights the key features of fiscal, administrative, and political decentralization by comparing the legal (de jure) provisions of the Local Government Act with the actual (de facto) implementation experience during the period 2004–10. The third section summarizes the major achievements of decentralization to date, focusing on the impact on service delivery and local governance. Addressing the politics of decentralization, the fourth section identifies potential threats and emerging evidence that suggests that the national government may be trying to regain control and manipulate local politics in a way that would be optimal for the center. The last section summarizes the main arguments and suggests politically feasible options available for development partners to move the decentralization agenda forward and prevent a reversal.

THE LEAD UP TO THE ESTABLISHMENT OF LOCAL GOVERNMENTS

Under colonial rule, the British authorities established a strong political and administrative divide between the Colony (Freetown and the Western Areas) and the Protectorate (the rest of the country, which was divided into three provinces) (figure 8.1). The Colony was ruled by an elected local government and a British governor representing the monarch. The Protectorate was administered through a system of "indirect rule" in which traditional authorities (the chieftaincy) were appointed by the state for the collection of revenue, the maintenance of law and order, and the resolution of local disputes.

After independence, outside of Freetown the local administration retained many of the features of the British colonial indirect rule system, but elected local councils also functioned until 1972, when President Siaka Stevens abolished them, moving their responsibilities to the central government (Fanthorpe et al. 2006). Management committees superseded local town councils, but they focused largely on the collection of market dues. They became grossly over-

staffed, with employment provided as a reward for political support, and accountability for service delivery was undermined. This dramatic retraction of local government, which coincided with the period of the All People's Congress (APC) single-party rule, meant that traditional authorities represented the only form of governance in the provinces. Although chiefs became increasingly active in the collection of revenues on behalf of the central state, they had no service delivery or development functions.

This reliance on chiefs, who were often repressive, and a lack of formal state structures in most of Sierra Leone led governments to start considering decentralization as a viable option to mitigate popular discontent. Following multiparty elections in 1996, the new government prepared a national document entitled the "Good Governance and Public Sector Reform Strategy." The document focused on decentralization as a major instrument for reform, especially in deprived rural areas. It suggested that decentralization could help rebuild service delivery and improve quality; improve resource allocation, by moving resources to the service delivery level; ensure greater citizen engagement in the processes of government; and involve the community in its own development by enhancing citizens' participation in the planning and implementation of development strategies and the setting of priorities.

Figure 8.1   Territorial Organization of Sierra Leone

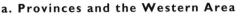

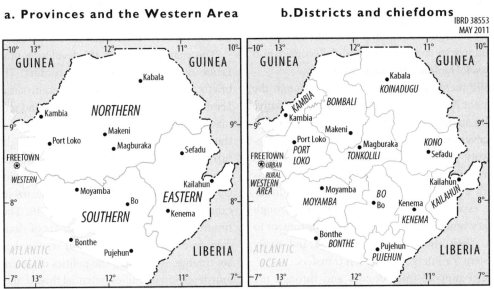

Source: Zhou 2009.

Note: The Republic of Sierra Leone is composed of three provinces (the Northern, Southern, and Eastern Provinces) and a region known as the Western Area, which is governed by a rural council and a city council for Freetown, the nation's capital. The provinces are divided into 14 districts, which are divided into chiefdoms.

In 2004 the government embarked on a nationwide decentralization reform program, with the official goal of addressing some of the root causes of civil war and improving the delivery of basic services. The decentralization program was officially launched in 2004, when the Parliament passed the Local Government Act and its related statutory instruments. The process of decentralization was designed around two major components: the re-creation of the local councils, which had been abolished in 1972; and an attempt to re-create and re-legitimize the institutions of the chieftaincy, which had suffered greatly during the period of one-party rule and the civil war. The government and its development partners viewed the revival of subnational political institutions—which had existed before the period of one-party rule—as a primary strategy with which to build popular legitimacy, sustain political stability, and reverse the massive urban/central bias that was a feature of Sierra Leone's postcolonial politics and led the country into war.[1]

Although the efficiency gains normally associated with decentralization may have played a role in determining the government's decision to decentralize, their influence was probably of secondary importance.[2] The dominant factors in the choice of this strategy were the political and economic interests of national politicians in the SLPP government, who supported decentralization for two main reasons.[3]

First, the SLPP was the prime victim of prewar political economy: the dismantling of local councils went hand in hand with the concentration of power in Freetown and the consolidation of APC power in Sierra Leone (Reno 1995). The SLPP decision to decentralize in 2004 may have been part of a more general attempt to reconfigure political institutions in a way that reduced the urban/central bias and the potential for a return to the prewar political economy, which tended to benefit the APC more than the SLPP.

Second, the SLPP may have perceived decentralization as a good opportunity to meet popular expectations, enhance the government's legitimacy, and increase political support for the ruling party—all likely outcomes given that a key source of popular discontent before the war was the "local despotism" (Richards 1996) of the paramount chiefs. The SLPP addressed that discontent by reestablishing the institution of local councils, which reduced the authority of the paramount chiefs. The SLPP president, Ahmad Tejan Kabbah, had been a district commissioner himself and often made public his view of local councils as cornerstones of democratic life and citizens' participation in local politics.[4]

DECENTRALIZATION IN PRINCIPLE AND IN PRACTICE

The Local Government Act and its statutory instruments provided the legislative framework governing decentralization in Sierra Leone. With some exceptions, the act laid down a robust framework for political, fiscal, and administrative decentralization in Sierra Leone. The framers of the document took a pragmatic approach, putting in place a framework that included "transitional" provisions that were acceptable in the absence of a policy on decentralization. Policies on decentralization and chiefdom governance were to be prepared subsequently. The act recognized the need for change and identified the period up to 2008 as the first phase of the arrangements for fiscal decentralization.

An important area on which the act did not bring closure is the relationship between the local councils and the chieftaincy. Although by law the chiefdoms are subordinate to the local councils, chiefs have not accepted this hierarchy, and ambiguity on the part of the national government persists. In particular, the issue of the revenue domain was not satisfactorily resolved with respect to the local tax. Under existing law, the tax rate and the share of the local tax ("precept") to be paid to the council are to be determined by the councils. The Chiefdom Councils are required to collect this tax, presumably on behalf of the local councils, and to hand over the precept to the local councils.[5] Moreover, the identification of the chiefdoms as a lower unit of administration and of local councils as the highest political authority at the local level is not acceptable to the chiefs, creating continuing tensions between the two institutions. The various laws governing the chieftaincy have not been repealed. The delay in addressing this issue leaves open the possibility of manipulation by the national government to pursue a "divide and rule" strategy (Robinson 2010; Acemoglou, Robinson, and Verdier 2004), thereby keeping the local councils weaker than they could be.

Several other laws are inconsistent with the Local Government Act 2004 or duplicate its provisions. Four laws in particular place more control in the hands of the ministries of education, health, and energy and power than envisaged in the Local Government Act 2004.[6]

Political decentralization

The Local Government Act of 2004 identifies local councils as the highest political authority in their jurisdiction. The legislation sets out a detailed political framework covering the election and composition of councils; the qualifications of councilors; procedures for the election of mayors (urban) and chairpersons (rural); powers to make and execute bylaws; the role and responsibilities of ward committees; and provision for citizen participation, transparency, and accountability. The act also recognizes the laws and regulations governing the chieftaincy and chiefdom administration, which were not repealed. Chiefdoms are identified as the lowest unit of administration. The Local Government Act provides paramount chiefs representation in councils and membership in the ward committees.

Local elections in 2004 and 2008 were successfully completed, and transitions were peaceful. Elections were fairly competitive. In 2004, 1,112 total candidates registered with the National Electoral Commission for the 394 constituencies. In 84 constituencies (21 percent), councilors were elected unopposed. Elections in urban areas were more competitive than in rural areas, and the elections were more competitive in 2008 than in 2004, with the number of uncontested wards dropping from 84 to 38 (less than 10 percent of all constituencies). There was a significant turnover of councilors between the two elections, creating a new class of local politicians, perceived by the population as "the young generation of leaders on the political scene" (Zhou 2009, 105). These trends suggest that channels of political accountability are taking root at the local level, with citizens willing to reward or punish politicians based on their performance.

Fiscal decentralization

The Local Government Act provides a framework for fiscal decentralization for a first phase (2004–08).[7] With the exception of the point regarding local taxes noted earlier, it clearly lays down the revenue domain of the local councils. Three sources of financing exist for local governments in Sierra Leone: central government transfers for devolved functions and administrative expenses; local councils' own revenues from taxes, fees, licenses royalties, mining revenues, and other sources; and loans and grants from other sources.[8] The act recognizes that in the short term, own revenues are unlikely to finance the functions devolved to the subnational level. It therefore provides for a "first-generation" system of intergovernmental transfers to fill the gap.[9]

The act provides for tied grants to the local councils to carry out the functions devolved to them and to meet their administrative costs. The law separates the grant arrangements for a first phase (2004–08) from those for the period after 2008. The description of the goals and bases for grants is different for the two periods. For the period up to 2008,

the grant for each devolved function was to be sufficient to provide the service at the standard at which it was provided before devolution. The act did not provide a rule or formula for determining the vertical pool of resources to be devolved; in practice, each sector allocation was determined through negotiations with the line ministry, intermediated by the Local Government Finance Department (LGFD).[10] Allocation across councils was to be determined on the principal of "equity." Equity was not defined in the law but, in practice, transparent formulas based on population and existing infrastructure were devised and are being used for the horizontal allocation of grants for devolved functions. Additional administrative grants were provided based on expenditure needs and fiscal capacity and indexed to inflation.[11]

For the period after 2008, the law indicates that the volume of grants should allow councils to provide devolved services "at an appropriate standard" and that the annual changes must grow at least as fast as the total budgetary appropriation made to government ministries. For all grants for devolved functions, parliament retains the authority to specify the functions on which these tied grants must be spent. Horizontal distribution is expected to depend on the expenditure needs and revenue-raising capacity of local councils (the specific relationships are not articulated).

Transfers are significantly tied not only to sectors but to specific activities and programs, making for a large number of separate grants. Although the formulas for the horizontal allocation of grants are transparent, there is scope for simplification and improvement. The design of a "second-generation" grant system has been delayed and is currently ongoing.

Budgeted transfers to local councils increased from Le 19 billion in 2005 to Le 34 billion in 2009, an increase of 44 percent (figure 8.2). With the exception of 2007 (a national election year), actual transfers increased during the same period by 150 percent, reflecting the fact that the ratio of actual to budgeted transfers rose from about 70 percent in 2005 to about 98 percent in 2009. The provisional figures for 2010 indicate that the budgeted amount for 2010 was more than 50 percent higher than for 2009 and that the actual transfers were higher than the budgeted amounts. This is a remarkable achievement for a country with a history of centralization. Transfers as a share of central government's nonsalary, noninterest expenditures also increased, from 4.9 percent in 2005 to 11.9 percent in 2009 On average, however, actual transfers remain low, and local councils are still underfunded relative to the functions that

Figure 8.2   Budgeted and Actual Transfers to Local
Councils, 2005–2010

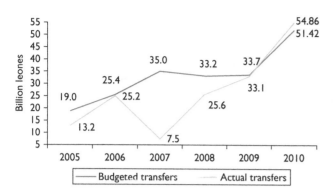

Source: IRCBP 2010b.
Note: Figures for 2010 are provisional.

Figure 8.3   Local Council Own Revenues as Share of
Total Revenues, 2005–2010

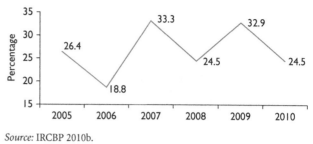

Source: IRCBP 2010b.
Note: Figures for 2010 are provisional.

have been devolved to them. Given these circumstances, the move to a more rational "second generation" of grants is long overdue.

Not surprisingly, revenue generation by the local councils continues to be weak, with local councils on average able to finance only about 25–30 percent of their expenditures from their own revenues (Searle 2009). Local taxes and property taxes are the sources of revenues for the local councils. The main sources of nontax revenues are market dues, business registrations, license fees, and mining royalties (in selected councils).

Local council revenues as a percentage of total revenues indicate that limited and uneven improvements have taken place over time (figure 8.3). This trend is slightly more positive if one considers revenues in absolute terms: in 2008 the local councils collected Le 8.3 billion, a substantial increase over the Le 4.7 billion collected in 2005. Revenues in 2009 were Le 16.2 billion, an increase of 95 percent over 2008.[12] There was a further increase of about 10 percent between 2009 and 2010 although the share of own revenues in total revenues fell due to the significant increase in the total volume of transfers.

Administrative decentralization

The statutory instrument accompanying the Local Government Act 2004 provided a detailed framework and timetable for devolving functions housed in 17 ministries, departments, and agencies to the local councils. The functions that were to be devolved between 2005 and 2008 included primary and mid-secondary education, primary and secondary health facilities, feeder roads, agriculture, rural water, solid

waste management, youth and sport activities, and some fire and social welfare functions. Central ministries and agencies retain responsibility for strategic planning, setting of standards, quality control, and monitoring, as well as procurement of certain priority commodities, such as textbooks and drugs. Central government also retains administrative control over staff responsible for performing devolved functions.

The devolution of functions has been slower than expected, with varying degrees of responsiveness. Although the act envisioned completion of the transfer of authority by 2008, by mid-2010 only 46 of 80 functions had been formally devolved to local councils (Decentralization Secretariat 2010). Important areas such as the devolution of feeder roads remain politically contentious.

Each local council has a political head (mayor and deputy) and administrative head (chief administrator) (figure 8.4). The chief administrator is responsible for management and all administrative and technical matters. In addition, each of the local councils now has its complement of core technical staff under the supervision of the chief administrator. However, staff for devolved functions continue to remain under the administrative control of the central ministries, departments, and agencies. Under the new decentralization policy (Government of Sierra Leone 2010a), staff for devolved functions are to be fully devolved to the local councils by 2016. In the interim, it is proposed that administrative control of local councils over such staff will be enhanced through "letters of deployment."

MAJOR ACHIEVEMENTS OF DECENTRALIZATION

Sierra Leone's success in reestablishing local government in a fragile postconflict environment is notable. Despite some

Figure 8.4 Intergovernmental Relationships under Decentralization

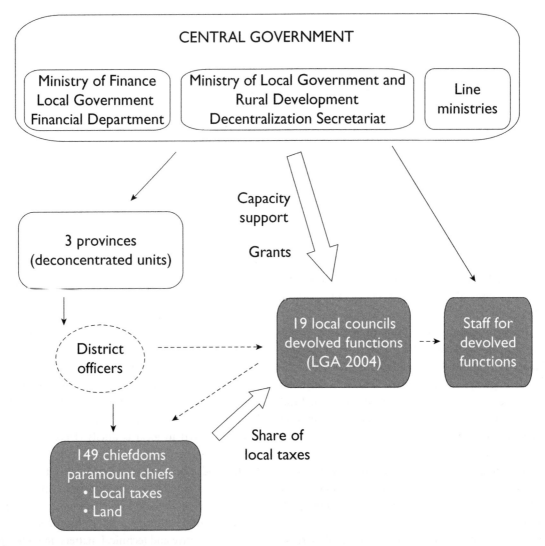

Source: Authors.
Note: The shaded boxes identify central government institutions and deconcentrated units (provinces, district officers). The dashed box identifies the key actors of decentralized administration. The solid arrows indicate a clear relationship of authority across levels of government. The dotted arrows denote the lack of clarity in defining relationships between government institutions, including the recently re-introduced district officers and local councils; local councils and chiefdoms; and local councils and local staff, who are formally accountable to the local councils but appointed by the central administration. The hollow downward-slanting arrow indicates the flows of resources from the central government to local councils (resources come from capacity support from the Ministry of Local Governance and grants from the Ministry of Finance). The hollow upward-slanting arrow indicates the flows of resources (share of local taxes) from chiefdoms to local councils. Historically, there were 149 chiefdoms established under the Chiefdoms Councils Ordinance 1938 (and subsequent amendments). A local council thus has more than one chiefdom within its jurisdictions.

of the shortcomings outlined above, decentralization is now well established, arguably more strongly on the political dimension than on the others. Two council elections have been completed; all local councils have the core staff to carry out planning, budgeting, accounting, and procurement functions; a system of intergovernmental transfers is in place; and, although there is scope for improvement, local governments are able to work with centrally managed frontline staff to manage service delivery in the areas devolved to them. The pace at which local councils assumed full identity as democratic, effective, and legitimate political actors and institutionally oriented themselves to discharging devolved functions has been a notable feature of the decentralization process.

Service delivery

With all councils decentralizing at the same time, it is difficult to rigorously establish the extent to which improvement in services is a result of decentralization.[13] That said, on average the quality of services did not decline, and in some cases there have been significant improvements, according to data from a series of national public service and sector (health and education) surveys carried out by the evaluation unit of the Institutional Reform and Capacity Building Project Evaluation Unit (IRCBP) together with the Abdul Latif Jameel Poverty Action Lab (table 8.1).[14]

Communities far from Freetown but close to a district capital saw the biggest improvements in services, even holding constant the remoteness of these communities. A reduction in "distance from power"—a direct byproduct of decentralization—thus appears to have had a positive impact on service delivery.

These improvements are remarkable if one considers the short time since the launch of decentralization and the fact that local government performance continues to be constrained by several factors, including the incomplete devolution of functions and line staff, the relatively small size and tied nature of the transfers, and the unresolved tensions between local councils and the traditional authorities.

HEALTH. Health is the sector that has progressed furthest on devolution, with about $3 million, just less than one quarter of the national health budget, budgeted to grants to local councils as early as 2006. Access to and quality of health services have improved dramatically since 2005, with most of the gains taking place between 2005 and 2006. Clinic infrastructures, availability of drugs, and numbers of staff have all improved, with the result that public satisfaction with health services improved from 81.0 percent to 90.6 percent (see table 8.1). Between 2006 and 2008 the largest gains were in the number of staff, particularly senior staff. Although progress is being made in filling vacant positions, the percentage of clinics open fell between 2006 and 2008, from 88 percent in 2006 to 82 percent. Also, the percentage of clinics receiving supervision by Ministry of Health and local council members declined after 2005. Despite decentralization, local councilors in particular do not appear to be taking a strong supervisory role, with only one in four clinics receiving a visit from a councilor in the year preceding the survey. These trends suggest that more effective supervision by the local councils and ministry staff, rather than more hiring, should be the main focus moving forward.

EDUCATION. Education has seen less devolution than other sectors. Because only one detailed survey of school quality has been undertaken by the IRCBP, it is harder to assess gains in education. Household surveys show that more rural Sierra Leoneans are within reach of a primary school than they were in 2005. The percentage of households with access to a school within 30 minutes' walking distance increased from 68.3 percent in 2005 to 74.3 percent in 2008 (see table 8.1). Overall public satisfaction with primary schools has improved. Informal school fees remain high, however, a key reason why children are not in school. Although only 3 percent of schools were reported to be closed, teacher absenteeism was estimated at 22 percent in 2005, highlighting the lack of adequate supervision.

AGRICULTURE. Access to drying floor and storage space improved sharply between 2005 and 2007, although most households still lack access. Only 18 percent of households had contact with an extension worker in 2007, down from 23 percent in 2005. Nearly half of farmers sell their produce

Table 8.1   Quality of Service Delivery Reported in Household Surveys, Selected Years (percent of respondents)

Service indicator	2005	2007	2008
Access to school within 30-minute walking distance	68.3	73.9	74.3
Satisfaction with primary schools	87.7	94.4	90.3
Satisfaction with health clinic	81.0	90.9	90.6
Spoke to an extension worker in past year	23.0	17.8	9.0
Access to sufficient storage space (farming households only)	8.4	11.8	14.3
Drivable road within 30-minute walking distance	67.1	73.2	77.5
Market area within 60 minutes	31.9	45.8	50.9
Water source within 15 minutes	61.0	73.4	80.9

Source: IRCBP 2010.

to traders who come to the village, a third sell at the market themselves, and the rest sell to a trader at market.

OTHER SECTORS. Although the Local Government Act was supposed to devolve responsibility for the rehabilitation and maintenance of roads to local councils, devolution has not yet taken place, and no money has been transferred from the central government to the local councils for this function. Resistance by the powerful Sierra Leone Roads Authority is the main reason for this delay.[15]

No central government agency is responsible for markets, another area in which local councils do not yet receive transfers. Local councils have, however, spent a significant share of their discretionary funding on roads and markets, which are perceived as key means to increasing the efficiency of the agriculture sector.

Access to markets in rural areas remains weak, with half of the rural population having to travel more than an hour to reach a market. As indicated in table 8.1, however, there have been significant and steady improvements: in 2005 only 32 percent of rural respondents had a market less than 60 minutes away. In 2008 this figure increased to 51 percent. Road access also improved, but the percentage of respondents having access to regular public transport declined between 2005 and 2008. Access to water and water sources saw significant improvements: in 2008 about 81 percent of respondents had access to a water source within 15 minutes, a sharp increase from the 2005 baseline (61 percent).

Local governance

A central argument in support of decentralization is that it brings government closer to the people. By expanding the political space, decentralization is expected to allow greater government accountability and citizen participation to public affairs, hence strengthening state legitimacy (Bardhan and Mookherjee 2006).

In Sierra Leone national elections tend to become "winner takes all" games focused on region-based ethnic identities. The role of ethnicity is likely to be less relevant at the local level, where voters are more likely to share a common ethnic background. Decentralization may provide citizens with greater opportunities to monitor the performance of local authorities on service delivery and hold them accountable through elections. The experience of Sierra Leone suggests that decentralization is indeed contributing to better local governance by providing greater scope for citizens' participation and engagement with local authorities, especially in rural communities and areas without transport or telecommunications (IRCBP 2010).

ACCOUNTABILITY AND PARTICIPATION. Provisions of the Local Government Act stipulate that councilors must declare their assets and councils must maintain an inventory of assets, print receipts, and maintain other accounting documents. Notice boards are also to be maintained in wards and at the council displaying financial information and strategic documents, such as development plans and procurement contracts, to enhance accountability and information sharing with the community. To ensure greater accountability and support a participatory approach to the decision-making process, ward committee members participate in council meetings and review the council's development plan. It is the responsibility of the ward committee to prioritize the community's development needs, which are then finalized and passed at the council meeting.

Evidence suggests that local communities are becoming increasingly active in demanding services and holding local authorities accountable, looking at local elections as a means to achieve the promise of development.[16] Participation in local elections remains moderately high—albeit lower than in national elections—with civic activism tending to be higher in remote areas than in urban areas.[17]

Marginalized groups, such as women and ethnic minorities, have been the largest beneficiaries of the new space for political participation. In 2004 women occupied about 13 percent of council seats in council elections; in 2008 this share increased to 18 percent, more than three times the 5 percent share of seats that women have in the national Parliament (IRCBP 2010). In 2004 and 2008 representatives from minority ethnic groups such as the Kono, Loko, and Sherbro, were elected to local councils (Zhou 2009)—a remarkable achievement given Sierra Leone's history. Decentralization has thus made significant contributions to promoting prospects of political stability by allowing greater participation and power-sharing dynamics.

PERFORMANCE OF LOCAL COUNCILS. In 2006 the Decentralization Secretariat, supported by the IRCBP, designed a Comprehensive Local Government Performance Assessment System (CLoGPAS) tool to serve as a sustainable local council management accountability mechanism for the local councils.[18] The first assessment was carried out in June 2006. A follow-up assessment was conducted in early 2008. The results show that performance of local councils is improving in several development and management functions.

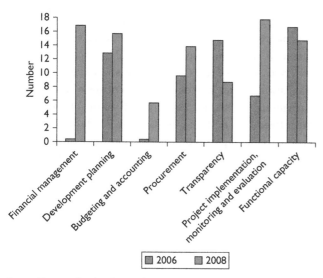

Source: Decentralization Secretariat 2007, 2009.

Figure 8.5 shows the number of councils that fully met the seven "minimum conditions" of the CLoGPAS.[19] It indicates that the number of local councils that met the minimum conditions rose between 2006 and 2008 in all but two areas (transparency and, to a lesser extent, functional capacity). Local councils hold regular meetings and produce minutes, citizens participate in meetings, participatory development planning has taken root (although there is scope for improving its quality), accounts are completed on time, and regularly audited and financial information is disclosed. These promising trends have been confirmed by the latest (draft) report on public expenditure and financial accountability (Government of Sierra Leone 2010b), which assesses the performance of central and subnational government authorities across various dimensions of public financial management.[20] According to the report, in 2010 local councils received the highest scores on key dimensions of budget execution (namely, competition, value for money, and controls in procurement) and accounting practices (namely, timeliness and regularity of accounts reconciliation), scoring higher on these dimensions than the national government. This performance is remarkable in view of the fact that local councils were established as recently as 2004.

CITIZENS' TRUST IN PUBLIC INSTITUTIONS. Results from National Public Services surveys indicate that public confidence in local councilors has increased over time, with local councils making the largest gains among political institutions between 2007 and 2008 (table 8.2). Together with chiefdom officials, local (political) authorities are more trusted by citizens than national government officials. These trends are encouraging, although some of the findings may partly reflect a temporary boost from the publicity surrounding the July 2008 local council elections. This line of argument seems to be (indirectly) confirmed by the findings of the 2008 National Public Services survey that trust in local councils is higher among citizens who are more actively engaged with local politics.

THREATS AND CHALLENGES

Six years after the decentralization initiative was launched, it has arguably taken firm root, leading several observers to suggest that it would be very hard to reverse the process and concentrate power in Freetown again. Thus, from a Freetown-centric perspective, decentralization is a "genie" that is out of the bottle. Recent developments, however, suggest that pressures might be building to weaken decentralization, casting some doubt on the central government's intentions to unequivocally move the agenda forward. Ironically, this apparent weakening may well be a result of the successes of the initiative. Rather than empowering local councils further, national elites seem to be following a strategy of "divide and rule," preventing local councils from becoming strong enough to seriously challenge the political hegemony of the center.

Stance of the national government

Tensions between the local councils and the chieftaincy result largely from a lack of clarity about their respective domains (Fanthorpe 2005; Sawyer 2008). It is difficult to judge whether this situation is intentional or reflects simple

Table 8.2   Citizens' Trust in Public Institutions, 2007 and 2008
(percent of respondents)

Type of official	2007	2008
Justice sector		
Police	36	38
Local court	41	45
Magistrate court	34	37
Political authorities		
Central government	42	44
Chiefdom	47	51
Local council	33	49

Source: IRCBP 2010.

delays in decision making, although some evidence suggests that it is intentional. A national decentralization policy has recently been drafted, but a critical companion piece—the policy on chiefdom governance—has not been prepared. The Chieftaincy Act of 2009 codifies and adds to customary law on the election and removal of chiefs. With the enactment of this law, any reforms aimed at the democratization of the chieftaincy are unlikely, at least in the medium term. Under the law, the central executive has effective leverage over the chieftaincy, because it plays an important role in the election and removal of paramount chiefs. The ministry responsible for local government has traditionally dealt with the chiefs and even today is much more comfortable with this function than with its new role with respect to the local councils.[21] These links are important for the national elections because, by some estimates, the chiefs are able to influence 10–20 percent of voters in their jurisdictions.

In 2009, contrary to the provisions of the Local Government Act 2004, the minister for local government advised the chiefs not to share local tax revenues with the local councils. Since then, also contrary to the provisions of the law, the ministry has played a role in determining the amount of the local tax precept, establishing a range of 0–20 percent for different classes of chiefdoms. Until 2008 most chiefs were paying a precept of 60 percent. This ministry action will undermine the fiscal autonomy of the local councils.

The National Decentralization Policy approved by the cabinet in September 2010 provides strong support to the hypothesis of a containment strategy by the center to limit political power of local governments. According to the policy, "Local councils shall continue to exist as the highest development and service delivery authority" (Government of Sierra Leone 2010a). This policy is inconsistent with the Local Government Act (2004), which defines local councils as the highest political authority at the local level. The policy also reintroduces the position of district officers.

In June 2010 the APC government decided to reintroduce the post of district officers, who traditionally represented the national government in the districts and provided the links with the chieftaincy. The official explanation is that there is a need to establish a stronger channel of communication between the national government and the chiefs. Representatives from the SLPP opposition and civil society groups, however, have articulated the concern that the district officers—acting as representatives of the central government at the local level—will try to influence decision making by the local councils, which may further reduce the councils' financial autonomy and increase the control of the ruling party as the 2012 elections draw closer. Several

senior government functionaries have remarked that the local councils—whose key function is development—were becoming political. Although these actions by the central government may be a response to real political change engendered by decentralization, they represent a potential threat to the autonomy of the local councils and, more generally, to prospects for further strengthening decentralization in Sierra Leone. The incentives of members of parliament (MPs) are aligned with those of the central executive. The national election of 2002 was based on proportional representation and the MPs did not have geographical constituencies. With the change in 2007, MPs represent single-member constituencies and now see the local councils as competitors.

Champions of change

The Decentralization Secretariat (Dec Sec) and the Local Government Finance Department (LGFD) have played critical roles in implementation and have been strong advocates for decentralization. Both are extragovernmental agencies created under the Institutional Reform and Capacity Building Project financed by the International Development Association (IDA) and a multidonor trust fund financed by the European Commission and the U.K. Department for International Development. Although, in principle the Dec Sec is an arm of the Ministry of Local Government and Rural Development and the LGFD is a unit in the Ministry of Finance and the secretariat to the Local Government Finance Committee (LGFC), all of the staff and expenses associated with these agencies are currently financed by the IRCBP.[22] With the project due to close soon, it is not entirely clear how and how well their functions will be integrated into government. Without the mainstreaming of these functions, the future of decentralization in Sierra Leone will be in jeopardy. If progress on this issue of mainstreaming continues to be slow, donors will need to make a judgment fairly soon about whether the government is genuinely handicapped by financial and capacity constraints or whether this lack of progress reflects apathy toward the decentralization agenda.

Dependence on national government

The local councils are highly dependent on grants from the national government. Although the volume of these grants has increased over time and a larger proportion of budgeted amounts are now being transferred, the lack of financial autonomy leaves the local councils very vulnerable to the whims of the national government. The lack of control over frontline staff weakens the ability of the local councils to influence the quality of services. Both of these risks are exacerbated by the fact that the national government appears to want to keep the local councils weak.

LESSONS LEARNED AND CONCLUDING REMARKS

Decentralization has had a significant positive impact on the political landscape in Sierra Leone. The sharing of political power beyond Freetown is unprecedented; on this dimension alone, the initiative can be viewed as a major success.

There is scope for improving the capability of local councils to deliver on development outcomes. The volume of resources available to the local councils remains small, and the relatively low level of own revenues and dependence on central grants undermines accountability, limits autonomy, and makes the local councils vulnerable to manipulation by the center.

Functioning and effective local governments provide a viable and promising alternative to the persistent patrimonial nature of Sierra Leone's national politics for a shift toward public goods and better service delivery to the poor.[23] In particular, the local councils are in a position to contribute to the improvement of services and the provision of public goods in the social sectors and in those aspects of infrastructure (water and sanitation, feeder roads, off-grid power) that can efficiently be provided at the subnational level.

Although it is unlikely that any government will openly seek to recentralize power in Freetown, as the APC led by Siaka Stevens did in 1972, there are risks that the center will try to undermine the emerging political power at the subnational level. The reintroduction of the district officers and the downgrading of the political status of the local councils provide some evidence of a new containment strategy designed to protect the interests of the national elites. These efforts by the national government to undermine the autonomy and strength of local councils may be the ultimate outcome of an effective decentralization process—the "paradox of success"—implicitly suggesting that local governments are indeed emerging as important players in the political and development landscape of Sierra Leone. The risks associated with the containment strategy of the center suggests that donors and civil society groups will need to play an important role, however, if decentralization is to succeed and central government efforts to undermine it are to be neutralized. Continuing engagement by donors and key national stakeholders is crucial to support decentralization

and help local authorities in their ongoing efforts to meet citizens' demands and perform the functions devolved to them. Donors have played an important role so far. The main instrument has been the IRCBP, which, through the Dec Sec and LGFD, has supported the establishment of a simple but robust intergovernmental grant system; made resources available for small capital works; and, probably most important, supported the development of capacity in the local councils to enable them to perform their core functions and become established as credible governments. On some dimensions, such as procurement, capacity is rated to be better at the subnational level than at the national level. Continuing support for strengthening service provision at the local level and enhancing the resources and autonomy of the local councils is being provided through the $20 million IDA–financed Decentralized Services Delivery Project (DSDP). This second-generation project—which tilts the balance toward significantly augmenting the grants provided by the central government while providing support for a "maintenance" level of capacity development—is expected to attract additional donor contributions. An increasing allocation of donor resources to the subnational level through well-designed projects will strengthen both the autonomy and the capacity of local councils and help mitigate countervailing pressures from the national government. In the authors' view, there is a continuing need for building technical capacity beyond what was originally envisaged in the DSDP and, more important, for dialogue and advocacy.

These donor initiatives will need to be complemented with additional reform efforts to improve the prospects of decentralization and create the conditions for a greater impact on service delivery:

■ A second-generation system of grants needs to be designed and implemented as soon as possible to enhance predictability and autonomy and provide incentives for efficiency. The divisible grant pool needs to be determined based on a set of well-understood forward-looking criteria, the allocation across councils should be based on an agreed philosophy for equalization, and grants need to be gradually untied to provide greater discretion to the local councils.

■ Local councils need to be gradually provided with greater administrative control over frontline staff associated with service delivery. As noted, the provisions of the new national decentralization policy identify a vision for 2016, when comprehensive devolution of staff to the local councils should have taken place and interim arrangements made during which authority is gradually handed over to the local councils. While this is, in principle, a sensible approach the transfer of responsibility to local councils will have to be carefully balanced with local council capacity to undertake this responsibility.

- Issues concerning the functions and jurisdictions of subnational institutions need to be resolved to ensure that local councils and paramount chiefs work better together.[24] This strategy would enable subnational political actors to present a more united front, which would be effective in strengthening the decentralization process while mitigating the risk of manipulation from the center. The national government needs to take the lead in clarifying functions and jurisdictions.

- Across all devolved functions, improved supervision and monitoring of service delivery by local councils and central ministries is needed to ensure that implementation meets required standards.

- As more resources become available at the subnational level, the risk of rent-seeking behavior and corruption will increase. Close watch will need to be kept to contain opportunities for corruption and elite capture; additional resources and autonomy will have to be complemented with robust accountability arrangements involving the ward committees and citizens' participation.

Key country stakeholders and donors took advantage of the window of opportunity that became available after 2002 by supporting the enactment and implementation of the Local Government Act. They did so knowing that it was not a perfect document and that several loose ends needed to be resolved. Their actions helped to establish a system that is reasonably robust and to create a new class of subnational actors that is gaining central prominence in shaping new political and economic dynamics. The genie is now out of the bottle. The question is whether it will be able to work its magic or whether it will be "contained" by the center. Donors, together with civil society and other stakeholders, will have to play a critical role in maintaining momentum along the trajectory that has been established, including advocacy initiatives and continuous policy dialogue with the government. Any letup in effort at this stage could jeopardize the initiative and compromise the remarkable progress achieved since 2004.

NOTES

1. This massive bias not only created large socially undesirable biases in resource allocation, it also led to political instability, by raising the stakes of politics, making the center attractive to capture in a zero-sum game.

2. The standard arguments about the benefits of decentralization focus on the efficiency of service delivery. The basic idea is that by bringing representatives closer to the people, decentralization leads to socially more desirable service provision, because local politicians are more accountable and because they have better information about people's preferences and what needs to be done. Arguments that link decentralization to better service delivery may be particularly compelling in situations in which there are important ethnoregional divisions in a society, making it difficult to reach agreement about which policies to adopt or public goods to supply (Robinson 2010; see also Bardhan 2002 and Eaton, Kaiser, and Smoke 2010 for a review of this argument).

3. An additional factor that may have driven the SLPP to decentralize can be found in the use of decentralization as an electoral strategy to ensure political survival at the local level in the event of a loss of power at the national elections. Although theoretically plausible and historically relevant in other contexts (O'Neill 2003), this kind of electoral incentive was hardly a dominant factor in Sierra Leone. Historical evidence suggests that at the time decentralization was launched (2004), the SLPP was confident of remaining in power and that it remained confident of doing so until early 2007, when the sudden realization of possible electoral loss prompted uncoordinated and ineffective actions (see Kandeh 2008 for an excellent analysis of the 2007 elections).

4. At the launch of the Local Government Reform and Decentralization Programme, on February 20, 2004, President Kabbah remarked, "People have the right to elect the leaders, men or women, who are supposed to serve them at the national level, in Parliament. They also have the right to choose those who should serve them at the district and other local levels. This, in my view, is what the principle of democratic decentralization is all about. It should and must remain a cornerstone of the process of nation-building in the country."

5. The Local Taxes Act of 1975 identified the "local" tax as a tax to be collected by the "local authority" and paid into the Consolidate Revenue Fund/Accountant General. Under this act the rate of the tax was to be determined by the minister for internal affairs. Under this formulation, the local tax is collected by the "local authority" on behalf of the national government. Section 45 (4) of the Local Government Act 2004 made the "precept" payable to the local councils but did not make any reference to the Local Taxes Act 1975, which is still on the statute books.

6. The laws are the Education Act, the Hospitals Board Act, the SALWACO Act, and the Local Tax Act.

7. See Fox 2009 and Searle 2009 for detailed discussions of fiscal decentralization in theory and practice.

8. Under section 65 of the Local Government Act 2004 and section 17 of the Public Debt Management Bill 2010 (gazetted but not enacted at the time of writing), local governments can borrow domestically up to limits agreed with the Minister of Finance. This borrowing need not be guaranteed by the central government. So far, local governments have not used this option as a source of financing and local government debt is not currently a problem.

9. We refer to the grant arrangements envisaged under the Local Government Act 2004 for the period 2004–2008 as the "first generation" system of intergovernmental transfers. The design of a "second generation" system is ongoing and has not been completed.

10. The LGFD is a unit in the Ministry of Finance that performs the secretariat functions for the Local Government Finance Committee (LGFC), the entity that determines the volume and distribution of grants under the law.

11. In practice the administrative grants are in two parts. The first part covers the sitting fee and transport allowances of councilors and is based on the number of councilors. The second part finances their general administrative expenses; it is positively related to expenditure needs for undertaking revenue collection and administering devolved functions and negatively related to fiscal capacity.

12. Several factors (beyond decentralization) may have driven the positive results in 2009; considered alone, this sharp improvement is not sufficient to establish a trend.

13. For example, the fact that satisfaction with health improved more sharply than satisfaction with education does not necessarily reflect the fact that health decentralized earlier than education. It may be that health decentralized more rapidly than education because there was greater capacity in the Ministry of Health and that satisfaction with health improved more because of that capacity.

14. The National Public Services survey was administered three times between 2005 and 2008. The quality of services at health clinics was surveyed three times, and a baseline for education quality was created in 2005. The surveys include large, nationally representative samples of households, clinics, and primary schools; the data collected can be compared over time.

15. The Sierra Leone Roads Authority is a powerful independent statutory body established in 1993 responsible for policy formulation and implementation in the roads sector.

16. A household survey by GoBifo (Sierra Leone's community-driven development project) and the IRCBP in 2009 in the Bonthe and Bombali districts asked respondents their main reasons for voting. It found that in national elections, voters ranked political party as the most important

and development second; for local elections the promise of development was the priority (Zhou 2009).

17. According to the latest National Public Services survey data, respondents were significantly more likely to report voting in national (87 percent) than local council (77 percent) elections. Official electoral data show substantially lower participation rates in local elections, indicating a decrease from 55 percent in 2004 to 39 percent in 2008.

18. The design and implementation of CLoGPAS involves the setting up of a multidisciplinary task team comprising technical staff of IRCBP and the Ministry of Internal Affairs, Local Government and Rural Development.

19. The minimum conditions deal with aspects of local council management accountability and examine functional capacities of the local councils in terms of their preparedness to take over devolved functions and deliver services at acceptable standards. They also assess/review the compliance of local councils with existing laws and regulations that guide the decentralization process.

20. More precisely, the public expenditure and financial accountability report "first examines the credibility of the Budget as a tool for implementing government policy, and then looks at two key crosscutting issues relating to Public Financial Management (PFM), the comprehensiveness and transparency of PFM systems. It then rates performance through the four key stages in the budget cycle: budget formulation, budget execution, accounting and reporting and finally external scrutiny and audit. Under each dimension, a set of performance indicators is identified, and scoring criteria is set out" (Government of Sierra Leone 2010b).

21. In 2004 the ministry was known as the Ministry of Local Government and Community Development. In 2007 it became the Ministry of Internal Affairs, Local Government and Rural Development. In November 2010, Internal Affairs was hived off, so the ministry is now the Ministry of Local Government and Rural Development.

22. The IRCB Project was launched in mid-2004, with a World Bank credit of $25.1 million. Financing was extended in 2006 with an additional $25 million provided by the Department for International Development and the European Union through a multidonor trust fund.

23. See Robinson (2008) for a compelling analysis of the sources of patrimonialism in Sierra Leone. Robinson (2010) further elaborates on the political economy of decentralization, analyzing the reasons why local governments are expected to be less subject to the capture of patrimonial politics.

24. Fanthorpe and Sesay (2009) make a number of well-informed and constructive recommendations for how to reform the chieftaincy and make it work better with local councils.

REFERENCES

Acemoglu, Daron, James A. Robinson, and Thierry Verdier. 2004. "Kleptocracy and Divide-and-Rule: A Model of Personal Rule." *Journal of the European Economic Association* 2 (2–3): 162–92.

Bardhan, Pranab K. 2002. "Decentralization of Governance and Development." *Journal of Economic Perspectives* 16 (4): 185–205.

Bardhan, Pranab, and Dilip Mookherjee, eds. 2006. *Decentralization and Local Governance in Developing Countries: A Comparative Perspective.* Cambridge, MA: MIT Press.

Decentralization Secretariat. 2007. *Comprehensive Local Government Performance Assessment System (CLoGPAS): 2006 Summary Report.* Freetown.

———. 2009. *Comprehensive Local Government Performance Assessment System (CLoGPAS): 2008 Summary Report.* Freetown.

———. 2010. *Status Report on the Devolution of Functions to the Inter-Ministerial Committee.* Freetown.

Eaton, Kent, Kai Kaiser, and Paul Smoke. 2010. *The Political Economy of Decentralization Reforms in Developing Countries: A Development Partner Perspective.* World Bank, PRMPS, Washington, DC.

Fanthorpe, Richard. 2005. "On the Limits of the Liberal Peace: Chiefs and Democratic Decentralization in Post-War Sierra Leone." *African Affairs* 105 (418): 27–49.

Fanthorpe, Richard, and Mohamed Gibril Sesay. 2009. *Reform Is Not against Tradition: Making Chieftaincy Revelation in 21st Century Sierra Leone.* Campaign for Good Governance, Freetown.

Fanthorpe, Richard, Taylor Brown, Janet Gardener, Lansana Gberie, and M. Gibril Sesay. 2006. *Sierra Leone: Drivers of Change.* IDLgroup, London.

Fox, William F. 2009. "Devolution and Grant Structures for Local Councils in Sierra Leone." World Bank, AFTPR, Washington, DC.

Government of Sierra Leone. 2010a. *National Decentralization Policy.* September. Freetown.

———. 2010b. *Public Expenditure and Financial Accountability (PEFA) Sub-National Government Summary Report.* Freetown.

Hanlon, Joseph. 2005. "Is the International Community Helping to Recreate the Preconditions for War in Sierra Leone?" *The Round Table: The Commonwealth Journal of International Affairs* 94 (381): 459–72.

IRCBP (Institutional Reform and Capacity Building Project Evaluation Unit). 2010. *Report on the IRCBP 2008 National Public Services Survey: Public Services, Governance, and Social Dynamics.* Freetown.

IRCBP (Institutional Reform and Capacity Building Project Evaluation Unit), and J-PAL (Abdul Latif Jameel Poverty Action Lab). 2009. *Basic Services and Decentralization in Sierra Leone: Trends and Lessons.* Abdul Latif Jameel Poverty Action Lab, Massachusetts Institute of Technology, Cambridge, MA.

Kandeh, Jimmy. 2008. "Rogue Incumbents, Donor Assistance and Sierra Leone's Second Post-Conflict Elections of 2007." *Journal of Modern African Studies* 46: 603–35.

Kieh, George. 2005. "State-Building in Post-Civil War Sierra Leone." *African and Asian Studies* 4 (1–2): 1.

O'Neill, Kathleen. 2003. "Decentralization as an Electoral Strategy." *Comparative Political Studies* 36 (9): 1068–91.

Reno, William. 1995. *Corruption and State Politics in Sierra Leone.* New York: Cambridge University Press.

Richards, Paul. 1996. *Fighting for the Rainforest: War, Youth and Resources in Sierra Leone.* Oxford: James Currey.

Robinson, James. 2008. *Governance and Political Economy Constraints to World Bank CAS Priorities in Sierra Leone.* World Bank, AFTPR, Washington DC.

———. 2010. *The Political Economy of Decentralization in Sierra Leone.* World Bank, AFTPR, Washington, DC.

Sawyer, Edward. 2008. "Remove or Reform? A Case for. Restructuring. Chiefdom Governance in Post-Conflict." *African Affairs* 107: 387–403.

Searle, Bob. 2009. *Sierra Leone: Issues in Fiscal Decentralization.* World Bank, AFTPR, Washington, DC.

Truth and Reconciliation Commission. 2004. *Final Report of the Truth and Reconciliation Commission of Sierra Leone.* Freetown.

Zhou, Yongmei, ed. 2009. *Decentralization, Democracy and Development: Recent Experiences from Sierra Leone.* World Bank, AFTPR, Washington, DC.

CHAPTER 9

Transport Infrastructure and the Road to Statehood in Somaliland

Jean-Paul Azam

How can economic success emerge in the midst of political chaos and civil war? This is the question raised by the experience of Berbera, a successful port located on the southern shore of the Gulf of Aden, in the former British protectorate of Somaliland. Berbera's traffic has been rising steadily over the past decade. For example its traffic of import containers has nearly doubled between 2003 and 2007 (MNPC 2010). This port's promising position is confirmed by the fact that Bolloré Africa Logistics, the biggest port operator in Africa, has recently announced its plan to invest massively in Berbera's port and its transport corridor with the Ethiopian capital city, Addis Ababa.[1]

Somaliland's small population, estimated at about 3.5 million people, benefits from two main kinds of physical assets: its pastoral assets of grazing land and livestock, on the one hand, and its transport infrastructure, on the other hand. The latter includes mainly the port of Berbera and, to a lesser extent, the airport of Hargeysa, its capital city, as well as their connecting roads. The nomadic herdsmen need the port of Berbera for exporting their livestock to the Arabian Peninsula and other Middle Eastern countries, which provide their main outlet. Moreover, Berbera is ideally located to give a convenient access to the Indian Ocean to neighboring landlocked Ethiopia, and there is a main road between the two countries.[2]

Ethiopia's Ogaden province across the border is also peopled by Somali-speaking herdsmen, and that border is traditionally fairly porous, as might be expected in a land mostly devoted to nomadic pastoral activity. Refugees have crossed this border back and forth over the past decades, depending on the changing intensity of fighting during the Ethiopian civil war, which ended in 1991, and the ongoing one in Somalia that began in 1991. The best grazing land, called the *Haud*, straddles this border, which nomadic herdsmen also routinely cross (Doornbos 1993, map 6.1, 101). While ethnically homogenous, these Somali-speaking people of Djibouti, Ethiopia, Kenya, Somalia, and Somaliland are traditionally affiliated with different clans that straddle these countries' borders and that at times enter into violent conflict with one another. The chaos that prevails in most of Somalia, which has been engulfed in warlordism and banditry ever since the collapse of the state in 1991, testifies to the threat of violence that looms over these people. Siyad Barre's military government had launched an unsuccessful invasion of Ethiopia's Ogaden region in 1978 and eventually signed a peace agreement with the Mengistu regime in 1988, which was perceived as a disgrace by many Somalians. Many military officers from the north, mainly from the Isaaq clan, which is the largest one in Somaliland, accused Siyad Barre of having mishandled the operation. They felt that the conquest of a more limited area in the Ogaden, including mainly the grazing land of the Isaaq clan, could have been a success. The peace agreement with Ethiopia triggered a full-blown civil war in Somalia, because many clans wanted to hang on to the pan-Somali project, and a coup d'état toppled the military regime in 1991. Chaos ensued, and Somalia collapsed into a stateless entity. Nevertheless, in the nearly two decades since Somaliland seceded from Somalia, it has managed to develop the port of Berbera and to enforce an acceptable enough level of security on the paved road linking it to Ethiopia for the traders to adopt this route. A large share of Ethiopia's international trade is now shipped through this port. This achievement stands in sharp contrast to the chaotic remainder of Somalia.

This chapter presents a framework for analyzing this unexpected success and draws some lessons for understanding state formation in general. A very simple model is presented that shows how the political equilibrium that emerged in Somaliland is fundamentally rooted in the need to provide security to the traders who provide most of Berbera's activity. This is a *sine qua non* for the traffic through Berbera to be active and flourishing. This model sheds some light on the fairly unusual political institutions that emerged from less than two decades of self-rule by Somaliland. Although some limited fighting occurred for a while in the early 1990s, this former British colony quickly engaged in a political process that led to the creation of a fairly successful democracy in about a decade.

What seems very important when looking at the experience of Somaliland is that this gradual buildup of a functioning state started from the grassroots, with very little outside interference. Eubank (2010) emphasizes that the Somaliland Republic has not been recognized internationally, which makes it ineligible for foreign aid. In his view, this is an asset rather than a liability, because it forced the Somalilanders to develop accountable political institutions and to engage in state formation in a non-Eurocentric fashion. The aim of this chapter is to go one step further in analyzing the type of government that resulted and in particular to explain clearly why the "fiscal decentralization" that Eubank is looking for does not exist in Somaliland. The model argues instead that the redistribution of fiscal resources from the government to the different regions lies at the heart of these peaceful and democratic institutions. The key role of redistribution in peaceful state-building in Africa has been emphasized in particular by Azam (2006). In Somaliland this redistribution of fiscal resources has mainly funded a significant expansion in the education sector in all regions of the country. Between 1997 and 2006 the number of primary schools rose from 165 to 516, while the number of universities increased from 1 to 5 (MNPC 2010).

The model presented later argues that the Somaliland Republic shares many features of the "indirect rule" system

that was widely used in the days of the British Empire and that has been used in many developing countries since their independence. In particular, Boone (2003) shows how this system was applied quite successfully in several parts of postcolonial Francophone West Africa, where the central government delegated the task of controlling some areas to some local traditional authorities, in return for some transfers. I argue here that this system cuts through a vexing "bootstrap" problem that faces all new states: a state needs to have fiscal resources to extend its control to various parts of its territory, but the state needs to have a fairly serious level of control to be able to raise those fiscal resources in the first place. This problem explains to a large extent why the control many African states exert is in fact extremely limited, leaving de facto large parts of their country without any effective state presence, as emphasized by Herbst (2000). I argue that Somaliland was put on the fast track to solve this problem thanks to two of its preexisting assets. First, this country inherited a valuable transport infrastructure, which only required establishing an efficient political regime to become competitive in the Horn of Africa. I suggest that "ports are the taxman's best friends," because they provide a "choke point" where taxable resources are concentrated and make revenue collection relatively cheap. Second, the traditional institutions of this nomadic pastoral society had not been destroyed by either British colonial rule, or the subsequent "modernizer" national government of post-colonial Somalia, despite the brutal attacks by the Mogadishu government in the final years of Siyad Barre's rule in the late 1980s (Lewis 2008). That indiscriminate violence against civilians and soldiers alike probably helped the Somalilanders to achieve a consensus on the project to secede from Somalia and build a state of their own. The clans with which Somali nomadic herdsmen are affiliated are themselves subdivided into kinship groups, which are subject quite informally but firmly to the leadership of the elders. There is no real "chiefdom" among the Somali, unlike in many other African societies (Lewis 2008), but the elders exert a significant level of authority.

This power was successfully harnessed to the emerging Somaliland Republic by creating a House of the Elders, called *Gurti* in Somali, in addition to a more standard elected House of Representatives. This upper house is playing a part in Somaliland's bicameral system close to that played by the House of Lords in Britain's Westminster system, allowing the traditional authorities to be involved directly in running the country's affairs. I argue that this is one of the fundamental pillars of this country, because it is the key to establishing—at a low up-front cost—the required level of security for making the port of Berbera an economic success and hence a reliable source of fiscal revenues. The emerging Somalilander government is in fact delegating to the elders the task of controlling violence and banditry, with a view to protecting the traders who then pay taxes in return for the transport services of Somaliland and its port. Then, the redistribution of fiscal revenues pointed out by Eubank (2010), as mentioned above, is the natural compensation for the investment made by the elders in providing the key public good that makes this lucrative trade possible. Hence, my approach to Somaliland's state-building shares some features of the so-called "property rights" approach to the theory of the firm (Hart 1995). The returns to the transport infrastructure inherited by Somaliland thus depend crucially on the "relationship-specific investments" (Hart 1995) made by the elders in controlling violence and banditry, which is in turn rewarded by some redistribution of fiscal revenues. Similarly, Hart's theory rests on "incomplete contracts theory," which assumes that only a fraction of the observable information can be used as part of an enforceable contract, while the rest is not verifiable by a court, although it is observable by the parties to the contract. My model pushes this to the extreme, because there is no third party that can be called upon to enforce any agreement between the government and the clans' elders.

The solution offered here to this fundamental commitment problem brings out the key theoretical contribution made by the current model relative to Alesina and Spolaore's theory of the size of nations (Alesina and Spolaore 2003). These authors define the government as a country's monopoly producer of a public good that affects its people differentially. They then raise serious doubts about the possibility of compensating people for these differential benefits by transfers, because of the lack of commitment of the democratic government that they assume. In the model presented here, the government is unable to produce the public good alone and must rely on the traditional authorities that are in a position to control violence and banditry, provided their participation is satisfied through a transfer. Then, the promise of this transfer can be made credible in a repeated-game framework because the recipients can punish any deviation by the government by reducing drastically its payoff in case of cheating. This implicit threat is credible because the recipient of the transfer is incurring a positive opportunity cost in delivering its part of the deal. Hence, what looks like a transfer is in fact the price paid for a productive service sold to the government.

More generally, the state-formation theory sketched below views the state as a means to internalize some key externality that has the potential to enlarge the opportunity set of the players, provided a fair compensation is paid to the investors. This is why redistribution plays such a key role in African state-building, as mentioned above. The reason for this result is that the basic negative externality that plagues African states is the threat of civil war or, more generally, the threat of violence. If I become armed, then your expected welfare goes down, because there is a non-zero probability that I will use these weapons to attack you. This is what the "social contract" aims at preventing, by providing a fair and credible compensation for giving up one's weapons (Azam and Mesnard 2003). In Somaliland the threat was more directed at the economy, because any insecurity felt by the traders would have brought the port of Berbera to a halt. Nevertheless, this implicit threat was overcome through a gradual bottom-up process leading to the emergence of the democratic regime.

A MODEL OF TRADERS UNDER THREAT

After the breakup of Somalia, law and order collapsed, and the country became prey to roving bandits and warlords, making trade highly risky. However, Somaliland itself managed to isolate a relative safe haven for traders. The following model aims at bringing out the two levels of political organization that made this possible. I first analyze how the traditional system of social control was mobilized for reining in uncontrolled violence. The next section shows how a higher level of political cooperation was needed to create the required level of security for making Berbera a success.

The traders

A very simple model was chosen for capturing the key part played by security in determining the level of trade going through Somaliland and Berbera. Let V be the value of the goods transported through the country by the traders. The traders potentially incur three types of costs while moving across the country. First, there is a resource cost involved in trucking the shipments, including fuel and labor. Second, there is a possibility that bandits might rob the trader along the way, leaving him without anything to sell at the port; the probability that this happens is denoted as π. Last, I assume that the lucky traders who have not been raided have to pay a tax on the goods leaving the country at the fixed rate τ. On the export side, I thus assume that the tax is paid at the port, and on the import side, at the end of the trip, that is, mainly at the border for the transit trade to Ethiopia. We assume that the government controls corruption well enough so that the tax rate is fixed before other agents make their decisions and does not respond to the observed trade flow coming through its control points. All the parameters of the model are assumed to be common knowledge, so that all the players can correctly anticipate the decisions made later on by the other players. The traders are assumed to play last, that is, to make their decision to start the trip or not while taking τ and π as given.

It is realistic to assume that there is no free entry in the trading business, mainly because of the limited warehouse capacity and restricted credit that is typical in poor countries. In Africa long-distance traders usually belong to some long-established family networks (Grégoire and Labazée 1993). Assuming for the sake of simplicity a quadratic cost function, then the representative trader chooses Berbera rather than any other port of the Red Sea or the Gulf of Aden area if:

$$E = \max_{v}(1-\tau)(1-\pi)\overline{v} - \frac{v^2}{2\overline{v}} \geq r \qquad (9.1)$$

where r is the trader's reservation profit, which he could expect to earn while using an alternative trade route and $\overline{v}$ is the maximum carrying capacity of this route. From the first-order condition, the amount of trade going through the country if the weak inequality in (9.1) holds, is:

$$v = \overline{v}(1-\tau)(1-\pi). \qquad (9.2)$$

Substituting back into (9.1), I find that a positive level of trade will go through the country if:

$$(1-\tau)(1-\pi) \geq \left(\frac{2r}{\overline{v}}\right)^{1/2}. \qquad (9.3)$$

Assuming that $\overline{v} > 2r$, (9.2) and (9.3) jointly imply that when this is profitable, the level of trade will be such that:

$$(2r\overline{v})^{1/2} \leq v \leq \theta. \qquad (9.4)$$

Otherwise, it will fall to zero. This simple setting thus captures the idea that the competitiveness of the port of Berbera depends first on two parameters, namely, r and $\overline{v}$, which determine respectively the profitability of doing business with the competitors and the physical transport cost inside the country, and then on two choice variables, π and τ, which are determined by two key players, respectively, the bandits and the tax authority. In the following, I assume that $\overline{v}$ is much larger than $2r$, in order to capture the geographical advantage of Berbera over its competitors. Then, Berbera should win, provided the two key players manage to coordinate their decisions efficiently.

The potential bandits and the government

How would the potential bandits behave in a hypothetical society where the traditional clan authorities would fail somehow to organize their activity? I assume that there are N bandits who sequentially choose whether or not to raid a shipment. I make the simplest assumption regarding the cost of raiding the traders, namely, that a fraction $0 < \gamma < 1$ of the shipment is lost in each raiding. This might capture the collateral damage of any fighting between the bandits and the traders, or any other form of cost that the bandits incur in raiding. This assumption is the simplest, but most results below are robust to several extensions. Given this cost function, a given bandit $i \in \{1, \ldots, N\}$ takes the decision $x_i \in \{0,1\}$ to raid a trader to maximize his expected profit simply defined as:

$$B_i = \max_{x_i} x_i p(1-\gamma)v_i, \qquad (9.5)$$

where p is the probability a raid is successful once undertaken and v_i is the value of the traffic faced by bandit i, which takes value 0 if the trader has been successfully raided earlier, and v otherwise.

This expression implies that the bandits incur no cost at all if $x_i v_i = 0$ either because there is no traffic to attack, or because they have chosen not to undertake any raiding. Otherwise, they loose a constant fraction of the catch when they raid a trader. When the bandits are not organized, they do not take into account the externality that they inflict on other bandits when performing an attack, namely, that this will in turn reduce the level of traffic that can be raided. Thus, any bandit has an incentive to raid a trader, which implies that the probability of a successful raid eventually converges to 1 as the number of bandits grows large: $\pi_N = 1-(1-p)^N$ and $\lim_{N \to \infty} \pi_N = 1$.

Thus, the resulting expected value of the trader's shipment converges to zero:

$$\lim_{N \to \infty} v_N = 0. \qquad (9.6)$$

Against this background, I can now analyze the first contribution made by the assembly of elders in the Somali clan society in reducing banditry. In this nomadic society, where the young men are spread all over the land in search of fodder for their flocks, collective identity is not defined so much by reference to a territory as by genealogy. Moreover, in this potentially violent society, where herdsmen could fight over grass or water at any time without any witnesses, escalation is prevented by the widespread use of "blood compensation," or *diya* in the Somali language. This is a clever system for creating joint liability within the group of origin of the perpetrator of a violent crime, because the whole group is responsible for paying the compensation required by the victim's group for settling the issue. According to Bradbury (2008), the *diya* for the murder of one man is 100 camels (half of this for one woman), which is a very high cost for the group. If the *diya* is not paid, then the aggrieved group is committed to launch a war against the criminal's group. This provides a strong incentive for those involved to exert some control over their fellow clan members, so that any man found guilty of a crime against a member of another clan would potentially be punished by his own clan, thereby avoiding interclan violence as far as possible. Hence, an important service delivered by the clan is to control the violence that could be perpetrated by its own members against both the clan's members and the members of the other clans. This gives the elders a key role in the Somali society's control of violence. This power was gradually aggregated in Somaliland during the political buildup toward democracy by organizing first a large series of local meetings of elders, which then developed in a kind of pyramidal fashion, culminating with the creation of the national assembly of the elders at the *Gurti*. This process is well documented by Bradbury (2008). The most striking point about this process is that it was mainly organized and funded by the diaspora of Somalilanders who had fled the repression under the Siyad Barre regime. The diaspora played a key role in many other parts of Somaliland's political development and the emergence of democracy there.

What can such a consolidation process deliver within my model society of traders and bandits? Quite obviously, such a consolidation process would end up creating a kind of syndicated banditry, which could internalize the negative externality involved because an increase in the raiding activity against traders would reduce the size of the trade flow itself. Now, instead of problem (9.5), this coalition would choose the number of raids or, equivalently given equation (9.6), the probability of a successful raid so to maximize:

$$B^S = \max_{\pi} \pi (1 - \gamma) v, \qquad (9.7)$$

such that (9.2) holds.

It can be readily checked that this "syndicated banditry" equilibrium yields the following levels of raiding and traffic:

$$\pi^S = 1/2 \text{ and } v^S = \bar{v}(1 - \tau)/2. \qquad (9.8)$$

This implies that the mere fact of forming a coalition of clans is not sufficient in general to explain why raiding would stop. Nevertheless, the model predicts that the creation of an institution that helps the traditional clan

authorities to coordinate their action makes a positive contribution toward efficiency by reducing raiding. This institution helps the clans' leaders to internalize the negative externalities that they would inflict on one another by raiding the traders without control, inducing them to reduce their raiding activity.

Now, absent any political arrangement that could help the government and the potential bandits to coordinate their action, the government would simply maximize its expected fiscal revenues, taking into account the traders' best-response function (9.2) and the bandits' best choice:

$$G = \max_{t,x} \tau (1 - \pi^s) v, \text{ s.t. (2) holds.} \qquad (9.9)$$

Proposition 1 below describes the resulting Nash equilibrium that prevails in this model when the two players do not coordinate their actions through some political arrangement.

PROPOSITION 1: *The uncoordinated Nash equilibrium choice of π and τ by the government and the syndicated bandits, respectively, is:*

$$\tau^N = \pi^N = 1/2, \qquad (9.10)$$

entailing a level of traffic:

$$v^N = \bar{v}/4, \qquad (9.11)$$

and the following payoffs for the bandits and the government, respectively, are:

$$G^N = \bar{v}/16 \text{ and } B^N = (1 - \gamma)\bar{v}/8. \qquad (9.12)$$

The next section shows how a more inclusive political arrangement can harness this social control mechanism provided by the traditional clan authorities to improve efficiency still further and reduce raiding to zero.

REDISTRIBUTION IN THE EFFICIENT POLITICAL EQUILIBRIUM

In a clan society, genealogy is the essence of social identity, as mentioned above. It is then natural to assume that the elders have a strong interest in the continuation of the clan and thus care for the welfare of the next generation. This can be captured by using a dynastic family model à la Barro (1974). In this kind of model, each generation is affected by intergenerational altruism, such that the next generation's welfare is an argument in the current generation's utility function. Choi and Bowles (2007) have coined the expression "parochial altruism" to describe such an intergenerational externality and have shown how these links across generations are an important asset for the survival of human groups in a violent society within an evolutionary framework. Hence, the dynastic family assumption seems especially appropriate for describing the behavior of a traditional clan society like the Somali one. In this case, it is natural to assume that the players have an infinite horizon, because their concern for the next generation creates a chain of intergenerational links up to infinity. I thus discuss the political setting in which banditry and warlordism can be eradicated by embedding the simple model of the previous section within an infinite-horizon repeated game framework. I then show how Somaliland's political institutions cater for the key mechanisms brought out by this model.

To capture their common ethnic heritage in Somaliland, assume that the potential bandits and the government have the same discount factor $0 < \delta < 1$. Then, assume that the government can offer at each period the following contract to the potential syndicated bandits: "I will give you g > 0 if you refrain from raiding the traders and enforce $\pi = 0$". This contract clearly entails that the potential syndicated bandits play first and the government second, after having observed whether the raiding was avoided or not. Moreover, no third party is available to enforce the promise made by the government to deliver the transfer once the potential bandits have refrained from raiding the traders. I define an efficient political equilibrium as an efficient outcome that can be sustained ad infinitum in the repeated game between the government and the potential bandits.

DEFINITION 1: An efficient political equilibrium is a triplet $\{\tau, \pi, g\}$ that lies on the Pareto frontier in the game between the government and the potential syndicated bandits and that can be sustained by a standard trigger-strategy equilibrium.

In this simple setting involving a transfer, the Pareto-efficient $\{\tau, \pi\}$ pair of actions by the two players can be derived by solving the following problem:

$$\max_{t,\pi}\left[\tau(1-\pi)+\pi(1-\gamma)\right]v, \text{ s.t. (2) holds.} \quad (9.13)$$

Using standard maximization techniques (Kuhn and Tucker theorem), one finds easily that the Pareto-efficient outcome is a corner solution that implies the following:

$$\pi* = 0, \tau* = 1/2 \text{ and } v* = \bar{v}/2. \quad (9.14)$$

The intuition for this result is pretty straightforward. Because of the unit cost $\gamma > 0$, raiding is an inefficient way of collecting revenues from the traders. The government thus will perform all the tax collection in the efficient equilibrium,

knowing that it will redistribute part of the resulting revenue, as explained below, to compensate the potential bandits for their restraint. Moreover, the chosen tax rate is the same as in the Nash equilibrium of the previous section, at the level that maximizes the Laffer curve $\tau(1-\tau)$. Then, the traffic level is twice as large in this equilibrium as in the uncoordinated Nash equilibrium of the previous section.

We can now prove the following:

PROPOSITION 2: *There exists at least one efficient political equilibrium with $\pi* = 0$, $\tau* = 1/2$ and:*

$$(1-\gamma)\bar{v}\left(\frac{4-3\delta}{8}\right) \le g* \le \frac{3\bar{v}\delta}{16}, \quad (9.15)$$

if:

$$\delta \ge \underline{\delta} = \frac{(1-\gamma)8}{9-6\gamma}. \quad (9.16)$$

The proof is rejected in the appendix, while figure 9.1 helps the reader understand proposition 2 intuitively. The downward sloping line represents the left-hand part of condition (9.15). All the points located above this line are acceptable for inducing the potential syndicated bandits to cooperate. The required transfer is lower, the more patient the potential bandits are. The upward sloping line represents the right-hand part of this condition; all the points located below it are acceptable for inducing the government to cooperate. The government is willing to pay more, the more patient it is. Then, the figure makes it clear that the triangle on the right labeled "acceptable triangle" is the set of

Figure 9.1   The Efficient Political Equilibrium Set

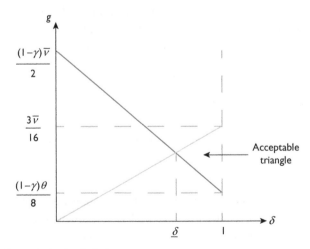

Source: Author's calculations.

all the points that are acceptable to induce cooperation by both players. Notice that $\underline{\delta}$, whose value is given at (9.16), is strictly lower than 1. This means that the set of acceptable $\{\delta, g*\}$ is not empty, ensuring existence of at least one possible efficient political equilibrium point. Moreover, $\underline{\delta}$ is a decreasing function of γ, so that cooperation is easier to achieve, the higher is the unit cost of raiding. Hence, (9.16) defines a credibility frontier in the $\{\delta, \gamma\}$ space, which is used in the next section. The intuition for this result is that the stronger the comparative advantage of the government at collecting revenues, the easier it is for it to buy off credibly the potential bandits with a transfer for producing security for the traders. The next section exploits this intuition to diagnose why a solution similar to Somaliland's did not emerge elsewhere in Somalia.

WHY NOT THE REST OF SOMALIA?

The foregoing modeling exercise begs the question of why such an efficient political equilibrium did not emerge in the rest of Somalia. One easy answer is given by Eubank (2010), who claims that foreign aid played a detrimental role there, by relaxing the need to build accountable institutions in that part of the country. Nevertheless, it is worth going into more detail to look at the missed opportunities in eastern and southern Somalia in order to bring out the kind of diagnosis that the model above is pointing out. It emphasizes some more structural characteristics.

The first point to notice is that without declaring secession formally, the northeastern part of Somalia also built a bottom-up institutional solution known as the "New Puntland State of Somalia," which was founded at a conference in Garowe in 1998. This promising solution started among some Darod clans, in particular the Mijerteyn (Lewis 2008), but it was missing two of the key ingredients of Somaliland's success. First, that part of the country did not inherit an infrastructure asset of the same caliber as the port of Berbera. In fact, the Puntland ruling elite never lost sight of the nearby formal capital city of Mogadishu in the south. That is where the infrastructural assets are naturally located, despite the massive destruction brought about by the war. Mogadishu has two ports, one new and the other old, and an international airport. Moreover a road to Addis Ababa, called the "Strada Imperiale," could be restored. Hence, the Puntlanders never severed their links to the rest of Somalia, realizing probably that they would never be in a position to levy the fiscal resources required to cement a Puntlander social contract similar to the one prevailing in Somaliland. Their strategy was clearly leaning in the opposite direction, suggesting that they were just regarding the "New Puntland State" as a mere building block to reconstruct Somalia. Second, they did not build any institutional representation of the elders, because they created a unicameral parliament, which did not have many resources in any event. In terms of the model described above, this lack of resources might be blamed on the lack of significant transport infrastructures and thus on the lower need for internal security. This is illustrated by the fact that piracy is quite active off the coast of Puntland, imposing some negative externality on all the ports of the Red Sea and the Gulf of Aden. However, the failure to give the elders a large enough role in the New State of Puntland is also probably due to the towering figure of Colonel Abdillahi Yusuf, who assumed first the presidency in Puntland, up to 2001, and then won the federal presidency in Mogadishu, which is in fact an empty shell. Abdillahi obviously did not draw the lessons of the failure of Siyad Barre's military regime to create top-down a viable state in Somalia, because he tried also to impose his authoritarian rule on the New State of Puntland. However, imposing the "rule of fear" also requires resources, which are dramatically lacking in Puntland, while they are somewhat higher in Mogadishu, if only because of foreign aid as mentioned above.

Southern Somalia once had the resources to support the strong authoritarian government led by Siyad Barre, who for a while was aligned with the Soviet Union, which was playing a complicated game in the Horn of Africa. Then alliances switched, and the United States became involved. Although southern Somalia inherited a valuable infrastructural asset, in addition to the sovereignty rent due to international recognition and foreign aid, it was facing a more complicated political problem than Somaliland. While the latter is very homogenous, with most of its population involved in nomadic pastoral activity, the former has a sizable agricultural area, between the Shabelle and Jubba rivers. The Somali clans living there have a distinct sedentary culture, in which territory matters at least as much as genealogy, so the elders have a weakened role in social control. Moreover, there are some Bantu farmers in the midst of this Somali population, loosening further the ethnic ties in that part of Somalia. Hence, the traditional authorities are too weak in that part of Somalia to deliver the kind of social-control services available in Somaliland, on the one hand, while the government was too authoritarian to make credible promises of redistribution, for lack of checks and balances, on the other hand.

Figure 9.2 summarizes the foregoing discussion within the analytical framework presented earlier. It represents

Figure 9.2   Why Not the Rest of Somalia

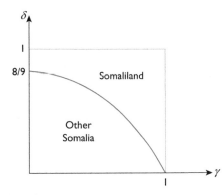

Source: Author's depiction.

condition (9.16) as the downward sloping frontier represented in the $\{\delta, \gamma\}$ space. This is the credibility frontier defined above. The parameter γ measures the cost advantage enjoyed by the Somalilander government over the potential bandits in collecting revenue, thanks to the preserved stock of infrastructure inherited from colonial days, and enhanced over the recent past by some investment. In the case of Puntland, no such stock is available, as explained above, suggesting that γ is small there, because the government is not in a position to collect revenue much more efficiently than the potential bandits. In Southern Somalia, γ is potentially much larger, because of the infrastructure available in Mogadishu, although the latter needs massive investments to recover its potential efficiency. However, the mixed ethnic composition of the population living between the Jubba and the Shabelle rivers, as well as the sedentary culture of the Somali agriculturists living there, suggest that δ is much lower there than in Somaliland. Hence, this analysis emphasizes that Somaliland exploited the two-dimensional edge that it had over the rest of Somalia for creating its efficient political equilibrium. This is captured in figure 9.2 by noting that Somaliland's efficient political equilibrium prevails for a $\{\delta, \gamma\}$ pair lying above the frontier, while the other parts of Somalia are found below that frontier.

This finding also suggests that simply trying to export the solution that worked in Somaliland to the rest of Somalia would probably not bring about the same benefits. Some additional imagination is surely needed to devise an appropriate system for the rest of Somalia with a view to create a lasting peace there. Nevertheless, the analysis presented here points to the two dimensions where economic and political innovation is required: enhancing the relative efficiency of the government at collecting revenue, relative to warlords and bandits; and making credible the necessary

redistribution mechanisms for compensating the latter for giving up their highly lucrative violent activities.

CONCLUSION

This case study of the emerging Somaliland Republic provides a natural experiment that sheds some useful light on the theory of state-building. It shows that the Hobbesian Leviathan is not the only path available for controlling violence and building up a peaceful state. It suggests that a Lockean "horizontal social contract" model may be a viable solution in some circumstances, for "breaking up" a state of anarchy, using the expression coined by Hirshleifer (1995). In Somaliland, one observes a separation of the power to control violence, which belongs to the clans' elders, on the one hand, and the power to tax and to produce some of the public goods that a modern state is expected to provide, on the other hand. Among other things, this study thus shows the benefit that political economists can gain from using the work of the social anthropologists for understanding the political economy of developing countries. In return, the modeling exercise demonstrates the key part played by an inherited infrastructural asset, namely the port of Berbera and the road that links it to Ethiopia.

This model sheds some light on the political institutions that have been put in place in Somaliland. The key problem to be solved was for the business-oriented elite to delegate to the traditional authorities the task of controlling violence and banditry effectively so that Berbera became an attractive outlet for the traders from Ethiopia as well as for exporting the output of the livestock sector. The first step was to help the clans' elders to cooperate by organizing several local conferences. But the model shows that this is not enough to provide the incentives for reducing banditry to zero. The second step was aimed at making credible the promise of redistributing the enhanced fiscal resources resulting from the increased trade flow to the clans. A bicameral system was put in place to ensure that the elders had a key role to play in the law-making process, by giving them a direct access to the required information, as well as some veto power in the implicit bargaining problem. As noted, the redistribution of the fiscal resources was focused on the development of the education sector in all the regions, as one would expect in a country where genealogy is the key social identifier that determines each person's affiliation to a clan. The dynastic family model thus seems to apply perfectly in this case and explains why people felt compensated for their efforts by seeing their children going to school and to university.

This model may thus be viewed as an extension of Hart's "Property Rights Approach" to the theory of the firm (Hart 1995). The clan authorities can invest in providing security, an asset that enters the production function for transport services as a complement to infrastructure. This insight is fundamental for understanding why a bicameral democratic institution lies at the heart of Somaliland's political institutions, for providing a balanced representation of both the traditional authorities and the business-oriented modern actors. Hence, Somaliland's experience provides a fruitful line of arguments in favor of a qualified support for the traditional "project aid" doctrine, with its emphasis on funding infrastructural projects, which has inspired the action of the World Bank and other development agencies

for decades. The qualification brought out by this case study is that a correct political setting is required, aimed at making the redistribution of the benefits from cooperation among the different actors credible. This redistribution is the compensation due to the potential bandits for refraining from raiding the traders and thus participating in the efficient political equilibrium. This suggests that the inability to set up a correct political system, partly because of external interference, is what makes the infrastructural assets of southern Somalia, like Mogadishu's old and new ports, its airport, and the "Strada Imperiale" road that links them to Addis Ababa, as well as the rent to sovereignty provided by access to foreign aid that comes with international recognition, largely useless for producing peace.

APPENDIX PROOF OF PROPOSITION 2

Assume that both players adopt the standard trigger strategy (see, for example, Gibbons 1992). If they choose to cooperate and refrain from raiding the traders with a view to receiving the transfer g from the government, the potential syndicated bandits receive the following present value:

$$V^C = \frac{g}{1-\delta}. \qquad (A9.1)$$

If they choose instead to deviate and attack the traders, the syndicated bandits will be punished first within the same period, as the government withholds the transfer g, and the static Nash equilibrium outcome will then prevail ever after. Assuming that this deviation is not expected by the traders, this yields the following present value:

$$V^D = \frac{(1-\gamma)\bar{v}}{2} + \frac{\delta(1-\gamma)\bar{v}}{8(1-\delta)}. \qquad (A9.2)$$

The potential syndicated bandits will thus choose to refrain from raiding the traders if $V^C \geq V^D$, that is, if:

$$g \geq (1-\gamma)\bar{v}\left(\frac{4-3\delta}{8}\right). \qquad (A9.3)$$

On its part, if the government chooses to cooperate, that is, to deliver the agreed amount g when observing $\pi = 0$, it receives the following present value:

$$W^C = \frac{\bar{v}-4g}{4(1-\delta)}. \qquad (A9.4)$$

If it chooses instead to deviate and to withdraw its transfer despite the potential bandits' compliance with the promised $\pi = 0$, then the government will first keep the whole fiscal revenue in the current period, and then get its Nash-equilibrium payoff G^N from then on. This yields the following present value:

$$W^D = \frac{\bar{v}}{4} + \frac{\delta\bar{v}}{16(1-\delta)}. \qquad (A9.5)$$

Then, the government will choose to cooperate if $W^C \geq W^D$, that is, if:

$$g \leq \frac{3\theta\delta}{16}. \qquad (A9.6)$$

Then (A9.3) and (A9.6) together make (9.16). Last, $\underline{\delta}$ is computed as the value of δ such that the range of values of $g*$ defined at (9.15) is just empty, as illustrated in figure 9.1.

NOTES

1. "Bolloré proposes Berbera-Addis Ababa Transport Corridor." *WorldCargo News online.* December 10, 2009.

2. Markakis (1992) provides a regional perspective on the ports in the Horn of Africa.

REFERENCES

Alesina, Alberto, and Enrico Spolaore. 2003. *The Size of Nations.* Cambridge, MA: MIT Press.

Azam, Jean-Paul. 2006. "The Paradox of Power Reconsidered: A Theory of Political Regimes in Africa." *Journal of African Economies* 15 (1): 26–58.

Azam, Jean-Paul, and Alice Mesnard. 2003. "Civil War and the Social Contract." *Public Choice* 115 (3): 455–75.

Barro, R. J. 1994. "Are Government Bonds Net Wealth?" *Journal of Political Economy* 81: 1095–1117.

Boone, Catherine. 2003. *Political Topographies of the African State: Territorial Authority and Institutional Choice.* Cambridge, U.K.: Cambridge University Press.

Bradbury, Mark. 2008. *Becoming Somaliland.* London: Progressio.

Choi, Jung-Kyoo, and Samuel Bowles. Samuel. 2007. "The Coevolution of Parochial Altruism and War." *Science* 318 no. 5850: 636–40.

Doornbos, Martin. 1993. "Pasture and Polis: The Roots of Political Marginalization of Somali Pastoralism." In *Conflict and the Decline of Pastoralism in the Horn of Africa*, ed. John Markakis, 100–121. Basingstoke, U.K.: Macmillan.

Eubank, Nicholas. 2010. "Peace-Building without External Assistance: Lessons from Somaliland." Working Paper 198, Center for Global Development, Washington, DC.

Gibbons, Robert. 1992. *Game Theory for Applied Economists.* Princeton NJ: Princeton University Press.

Grégoire, Emmanuel, and Pascal Labazée, eds. 1993. *Grands Commerçants d'Afrique de l'Ouest.* Paris: Karthala-Orstom.

Hart, Oliver. 1995. *Firms, Contracts, and Financial Structure.* Oxford, U.K.: Oxford University Press.

Herbst, Jeffrey. 2000. *States and Power in Africa. Comparative Lessons in Authority and Control.* Princeton, NJ: Princeton University Press.

Hirshleifer, Jack. 1995. "Anarchy and its Breakdown." *Journal of Political Economy* 103 (1): 26–52.

Lewis, Ioan M. 2008. *Understanding Somalia and Somaliland* New York: Columbia University Press.

Markakis, John. 1992. "The Regional Significance of Sea Ports in the Horn of Africa." In *Beyond Conflict in the Horn*, eds. Martin Doornbos, Abdel Gaffar M. Ahmed, and John Markakis, 130–31. London: James Currey.

MNPC (Ministry of National Planning and Coordination). 2010. *Somaliland in Figures 2009.* Hargeysa.

PART III

Leveraging Sectoral Advantages to Expand Exports

Growing Mali's Mango Exports: Linking Farmers to Market through Innovations in the Value Chain

Yéyandé Sangho, Patrick Labaste, and Christophe Ravry

Although less than 4 percent of land in Mali, a landlocked country in West Africa, is arable, agriculture accounts for 45 percent of the country's economy and employs 80 percent of its workforce. Industry represents 17 percent of the country's gross domestic product (GDP), with food processing, construction, and phosphate and gold mining as the principal industrial activities. Mali's main agricultural export is cotton, followed by livestock. The fact that Mali is landlocked, however, has always made it dependent on the transport infrastructure and other logistical arrangements of its neighbors for trade and exports.

Thanks to excellent geographical and weather conditions prevailing in the southern part of the country, mangoes have always been abundant in Mali, particularly in the Bamako and Sikasso regions. The fruit was traditionally sold in the domestic market. In the 1970s Mali was the first country in West Africa to explore opportunities to export fresh mangoes. These exports were shipped exclusively by air freight to a niche market—high-end retail shops in France selling tropical fruits—and reached a volume of between 1,000 and 1,500 metric tons a year

Starting in the early 1990s Mali undertook several transformations in its mango subsector that have allowed the country to overcome logistical dependencies and constraints, expand exports of fresh mangoes, and make

major leaps toward developing a competitive horticulture export sector.

MALI'S EXPORT DIVERSIFICATION STRATEGY

A key objective of Mali's poverty reduction strategy over the past two decades has been—and still is—to increase rural incomes and employment opportunities by promoting agricultural diversification and developing exports of high-value commodities. In the early 1990s the government of Mali recognized a need to design policies to diversify exports and foreign exchange earnings, which had been heavily dependent on only three export products: gold, cotton, and livestock. These products, however, are quite susceptible to fluctuations. For example, cotton exports dropped dramatically in 2008 to less than half of their previous level; also, because of several years of financial crisis, the contribution of the sector to fiscal revenues has been negative throughout the whole decade.

Striving for diversification

In the face of these fluctuations, the government of Mali began, in the 1990s, to focus on high-value and nontraditional agricultural products as a means to generate income and achieve greater diversification of exports, based on the

Yéyandé Sangho is Senior Operations Officer at the World Bank. Patrick Labaste is Lead Agriculture Economist at the World Bank. Christophe Ravry is Senior Agribusiness Specialist at the World Bank. This paper builds on an early draft and research work done by Malick Antoine at the World Bank in 2006.

country's comparative advantages. Besides offering small-holder farmers the opportunity to diversify the source of their livelihoods, high-value and nontraditional agricultural products also offer countries the opportunity to diversify away from low-value bulk commodities.

Several horticulture crops were considered as possible targets for these diversification efforts, including cashews, tomatoes, shallots, and mangoes. Mangoes were a prime candidate both because of the excellent agroclimatic conditions for growing them in the southern regions of Bougouni and Sikasso and because of the fast-growing demand for mangoes in European markets (figure 10.1). Furthermore, because mangoes were already being produced by small-holder farmers throughout the country, the subsector had the potential to contribute to rural livelihood improvements. However, despite the high quality of Mali's fresh fruit and vegetables, the high cost of air freight was severely limiting marketing and exportation. In fact, significant volumes of Mali's mangoes were purchased and processed for export by operators based in Côte d'Ivoire, thus leaving little potential for value addition in Mali.

Early efforts toward agricultural diversification

In 1992 Mali's Ministry of Agriculture prepared a national rural development strategy, the *Schéma Directeur du Développement Rural* (SDDR), emphasizing commercial agriculture, export promotion, and value addition, and the government began directing resources toward those ends using financing from international donors such as the World Bank and the U.S. Agency for International Development (USAID).

Figure 10.1   Imports of Mangoes into the European Union, 2004–08

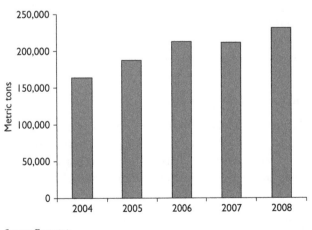

Source: Eurostat.

In 1996 the government of Mali used $6 million in World Bank financing for an agricultural trading and processing pilot project, PAVCOPA (*Project d'appui à la valorisation et à la commercialisation des produits agricoles*). The project sought to promote agribusiness and exports. Specifically, it aimed to "improve the enabling environment needed to enhance private sector business opportunities and encourage [state] disengagement from commercial activities, improve technical support to producers through effective research and extension aimed at enhancing and diversifying production and improving the international competitiveness of Malian exports, and boost private investment in agricultural trading and processing" (World Bank 1996). In addition, the PAVCOPA project aimed at supporting producers, processors, and traders in the Sikasso, Segou, and Koulikoro regions and the Bamako district, providing technical and promotional assistance (including price information) and organizing commercial forums, supporting professional associations, and carrying out studies on the markets for high-value crops.

The Agricultural Value Chain Promotion Agency (APROFA, by its French acronym), established by the government in 1993, was designated as the project executing agency for PAVCOPA. APROFA's goal was to create sustainable growth in the agrifood sector by increasing exports to the European and African regional markets and establishing import substitution activities. Further, the agency was to support the improvement of the technical, managerial, organizational, and professional capacities of public and private actors engaged in agribusiness.

The global market for fresh mangoes

Demand for mangoes in the European Union (EU) has grown significantly in recent years, increasing by approximately 55 percent between 2001 and 2008, from 136,000 tons to more than 230,000 tons respectively (table 10.1). The leading exporter countries, in order, are Mexico, Brazil, Peru, India, Pakistan, and the Philippines; together, they represent around 75 percent of the market. Although African mango exports grew by 69 percent during the same period, export volumes remain far lower than those of the leading producers. In 2007, for example, Mexico was exporting a total of 236,000 metric tons of mangoes, while the entire African continent recorded 46,300 metrics tons of exports only (FAOSTAT).

Within Africa, leading producers, in order, are South Africa, Côte d'Ivoire, Sudan, Kenya, the Arab Republic of Egypt, and Mali. Historically, Côte d'Ivoire has exported

Table 10.1 Mango Imports to the European Union, by Country, 2004–09
(*metric tons*)

Country	2004	2005	2006	2007	2008	2009[a]	Growth 2004–08 (percent)	
							Annual	Total
Brazil	69,319	82,293	84,858	82,993	96,870	69,590	9	40
Peru	19,817	26,394	41,027	36,854	50,756	25,062	27	156
Pakistan	10,938	12,306	10,120	13,224	12,941	12,913	4	18
Israel	8,059	12,548	11,181	14,808	12,261	12,606	11	52
Côte d'Ivoire	11,426	9,856	14,428	14,706	11,249	11,659	0	–2
United States	7,612	6,894	5,971	7,404	7,516	5,536	0	–1
Senegal	2,810	3,011	6,194	4,702	6,034	6,219	21	115
Costa Rica	3,983	6,271	7,545	4,664	5,360	5,685	8	35
Mali	2,096	2,560	3,477	4,317	4,902	3,480	24	134
Dominican Rep.	1,228	1,591	1,618	2,767	4,307	4,179	37	251
India	915	1,720	2,472	2,425	2,577	2,470	30	182
Burkina Faso	928	1,164	2,152	3,191	2,406	1,957	27	159
Other	23,516	20,035	19,786	19,003	13,209	12,893	–13	–44
Total	**162,646**	**186,643**	**210,829**	**211,057**	**230,388**	**174,248**	**9**	**42**

Source: Eurostat.
a. January to November.

significantly higher volumes of mangoes than its closest competitors on the continent, apart from South Africa. In the early 2000s, before political disturbances in the country, Côte d'Ivoire exported around 11,000 metric tons; the next closest African rival was Burkina Faso with 3,500 metric tons exported. That same year Mali reported 900 metric tons of exports (FAOSTAT).

THE CHALLENGES

Identifying market opportunities

The large amount of mango exports from Côte d'Ivoire can be partly explained by the fact that the country was working with buying agents from Mali in the 1980s and 1990s. Mango exporters in Côte d'Ivoire operated pack houses in the northern part of the country, sourcing mangoes from growers across the border in Mali. The arrangement led to a surge of mango exports, sold under an Ivorian label.

Malian mango producers did not anticipate the increasing demand for mangoes in the European market, which was moving from a luxury, niche market to a volume market. Mangoes, like some other tropical fruits, such as bananas and pineapples some decades earlier, became a fruit that was in high demand all year round by European customers.

In an attempt to increase its mango exports, Mali sought alternatives to air freight that would increase its competitiveness and market share. Mali's landlocked status posed a serious challenge to that effort, however, and logistics and transport issues prevented an initial substantive scaling up of exports.

Overcoming transport and logistics constraints

High transportation costs made Malian mangoes uncompetitive in the global market. Whereas competitors in Latin America could take advantage of more economic sea freight, Mali's producers were limited to the more expensive air freight option, which reduced their exports and relative position as a mango exporter in West Africa (table 10.2).

Historically, Mali relied on Côte d'Ivoire as a link to port facilities. Cotton lint and other products, for example, were exported through the port of Abidjan. In addition to relying on its neighbor's ports, Mali also relied on its neighbor's infrastructure to move its export products to the ports. Until the 1990s the only rail line in Mali with international links was run inefficiently, leading to significant high prices and delays. This protracted transport process was especially detrimental to those Malian agricultural products that have high spoilage and shrinkage rates. A research report (CARANA Corporation 2004) also points out that producers' logistical costs were negatively affected by the cost of the consolidation of goods and poor business practices.

Other challenges

Although infrastructure was the most serious constraint to Malian exports of fresh produce, inadequate access to finance and land; a poor business climate; inadequate

Table 10.2 Mango Exports to the European
Union, 1970–95
(*metric tons*)

	Mali	Burkina Faso	Côte d'Ivoire
1970	35	122	—
1980	1,172	2,116	281
1990	1,300	2,700	1,000
1995	850	714	7,107

Source: FAOSTAT.
Note: — = not available.

management, harvesting, and handling techniques; and little investment in mass production further weakened producer export capacity.

LACK OF MARKET INFORMATION AND ORGANIZATION. Malian producers and exporters did not have a good grasp of the requirements of the intensely competitive European market. In addition, poor organization and coordination between producers, government inspection officials, and exporters led to inefficiencies affecting the industry's ability to meet international orders on time.

LACK OF PROPER HARVESTING PRACTICES AND POSTHARVEST HANDLING TECHNIQUES. Buying agents typically visited orchards once a season and harvested all of the fruit at once, regardless of its ripeness. In addition, many growers did not manage their orchards, did not prune undergrowth, and did not clean the ground under the trees, creating a good habitat for fruit flies.

LITTLE INVESTMENT AT THE PRODUCTION LEVEL. Investment in mango production—including the establishment of commercial orchards—is important because it provides producers and exporters a degree of organization and efficiency. Traditionally, Malian farmers saw mango production as mainly a subsistence activity, a business opportunity. Even though orchards were smaller than five hectares, as much as 50 percent of total mango production was wasted each year (Club du Sahel/OECD 1998), and little investment was made in increasing production. Additionally, because Malian mangoes were exported through Ivoirian pack houses, Malian producers received little return from their crop and thus had even fewer incentives to invest in commercializing crop production.

AN UNINVITING INVESTMENT CLIMATE. Foreign investors, unfamiliar with Mali's policies and procedures for conducting business, perceived investment in the country as high risk. In addition, limited foreign direct investment in the country and poor enforcement of fair business practices further reduced competitiveness.

POOR LAND TITLING AND A NONEXISTENT LAND MARKET. Bureaucratic inefficiencies and land tenure rules kept Malian producers from owning large tracts of land, thereby creating another barrier to large-scale horticulture. Until the Agriculture Orientation Law of 2006, there were no provisions for the establishment of commercial-scale irrigated plots, nor could producers purchase irrigated land that could be used as collateral against which to secure loans.

INADEQUATE WORKING CAPITAL AND LACK OF SUPPLY CHAIN FINANCING. With limited working capital, Malian production and subsequent exports were constrained because exporters were required to finance the cost of shipping. This problem was of particular urgency to exporters, who did not always receive payments from previous shipments before they needed to send additional shipments.

In short, not only did Mali need to make changes that would enable it to improve its main constraint—infrastructure—it also needed to undertake a series of transformations improving technical capacity and business regulatory practices in the mango sector (box 10.1).

INTERVENTIONS

Supporting agricultural diversification

The transformation of Mali's mango export sector began in the mid-1990s with PAVCOPA, the pilot project funded by

---

Box 10.1 The Mango Export Value Chain before Reforms

Before reforms in the sector, the value chain included producers, intermediaries, and exporters.

- Producers sold produce to buying agents, called "*pisteurs*," independent traders who select, harvest, wash, sort, package, and transport the fruit from orchard to pack house.
- Agents worked exclusively for a particular exporter.
- Quality control was undertaken by exporters, who selected fruit that were of export quality and returned the second-grade fruit to the *pisteur* for sale on the domestic market.

Source: Authors.

the government of Mali and the World Bank. Initially, Malian buying agents used existing facilities at the Bamako airport, to export about 1,500 metric tons of mangoes to the European market each year. In the early 1990s, however, as demand in Europe increased, competition intensified among producers as South American exporters, notably Brazil, began exporting sea-freighted mangoes to Europe on a large scale. Even though air freighting allows mangoes to be picked at a more advanced stage of maturity (resulting in sweeter fruit), it also comes at a significantly higher cost.

In addition to the government and World Bank initiatives, USAID contributed to jump-starting initial work in Mali's mango subsector through support to the Office de la Haute Vallée du Niger (OHVN) project, that also focused on high-value agriculture and food products (HVAFs). This program served as a pilot project while the preparation of PAVCOPA was ongoing. Aid organizations continued to be involved in Mali's agriculture sector for over 15 years following the initial project in 1993.

Rethinking and redesigning the mango export value chain

The first step that triggered the agricultural export reform process in Mali occurred when a small but critical mass of stakeholders were brought together to thoroughly analyze and assess opportunities for diversification into higher-value crops. Initial implementation of PAVCOPA was not unsuccessful; however, the preparation of its midterm review in January 2000 provided an opportunity to restructure the project and create a new business plan.

Another critical point was reached when APROFA and its technical team of advisors began analyzing what had made Côte d'Ivoire successful in developing sea-freighted mango exports. Although Mali had been exporting mangoes for years, the industry was not broadly based but rather limited to a narrow market targeting an exclusive club of exporters on the periphery of Bamako.

Observing and understanding the success of Côte d'Ivoire entailed a thorough analysis of the global market demand and its trends, and an assessment of the supply chain in Côte d'Ivoire. This evaluation suggested that three critical steps were necessary to change the mango industry in Mali. The industry had to penetrate and compete in the growing market for fresh mangoes (that is, the sea-freighted trade to major European ports and hubs such as Rotterdam, Antwerp, Algesiras, and London); establish the drivers of change and a value chain within the system to improve competitiveness; and identify and implement solutions to

overcome poor access to international ports while developing alternate and effective transport routes.

A key innovation: Introduction of multimodal transport in the export value chain

The design and implementation of a multimodal transportation system in 1995 was a key innovation for the Malian mango industry that eased transportation logistics constraints and costs. Through this new system, mangoes are loaded into temperature-controlled containers and driven into Ferkessedougou, Côte d'Ivoire. There, the containers are transported by rail to Abidjan and shipped to Europe. The containers are maintained at 5 degrees Celsius. Transit times per shipment between the mango-producing regions of Sikasso and northern Europe have declined from 25–30 days to approximately 12–15 days (Danielou, Labaste, and Voisard 2003). As figure 10.2 illustrates, multimodal transit also allowed large volumes of mangoes to be exported from Mali at an affordable cost. The existence of this uninterrupted cold chain (refrigerated containers) greatly decreases the rate of spoiling of mangoes during transit.

Designing the innovation and testing the system

To hedge risks involved with the new system, APROFA negotiated and signed a partnership agreement with a privately owned Ivorian company, SN Tropical Expressions (SNTE), that split the costs, profit margins, and risks associated with the first shipment of 200 tons. SNTE was responsible for both the logistics and packaging involved in shipping the produce to their ultimate port of destination in Europe. A profit margin was built into the fixed price to ensure that both parties respect their mutual costs objectives. If the average selling price is greater than the fixed price, APROFA and SNTE share the difference. This partnership resolved the problem of lack of finance for exporters because SNTE had the necessary working capital to fund the operation.

Under the same agreement, APROFA was able to obtain a guarantee from a local bank enabling SNTE to lease an existing pack house in Sikasso with the necessary equipment for precooling fruit pallets. In addition, SNTE seconded two experienced managers to operate the Sikasso facility. Precooling the mangoes at the pack house stage is critical for the continuous cold chain. The establishment of continuous cold chains in the export of horticulture and other high-value crops remains one the most serious challenges to the expansion of exports from other Sub-Saharan African countries.

Figure 10.2 Supply Chains for Fresh Mango Exports from Mali

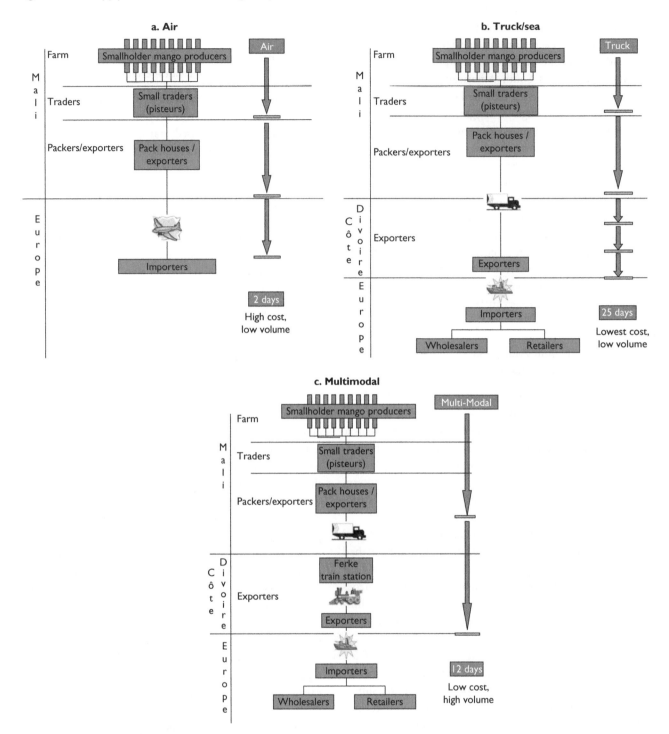

Source: Geomar International.

Early success

The test carried out by APROFA and SNTE was a great success from many points of view, particularly in terms of quality: none of the 63,000 cartons of mangoes shipped to the Netherlands was rejected. To the contrary, there were demands for steady shipments of Malian mangoes. The validation of the feasibility and profitability of the new value chain for mango exports represented a critical breakthrough and opened completely new horizons for the mango business in Mali.

Despite sociopolitical turmoil in Côte d'Ivoire, Mali's cold chain transportation system remained uninterrupted. The pilot project helped Malian producers and exporters address the three major constraints of Mali's export supply chain: finance, management, and infrastructure. Producers were able to receive a higher price for their mangoes at the farm gate—125 CFA francs versus 50 before, a 150 percent increase. Similarly, exporters increased the volume of fruits they were able to ship from Mali, which translated into increased revenues. The impact of the pilot project has been far reaching and has encouraged entrepreneurs to engage in similar ventures within and outside the mango sector.

Although the full export potential of Malian mangoes is yet to be determined, APROFA conducted a number of studies to produce estimates of such figures. In the Sikasso region, for instance, where production in 2001 was estimated at 48,000 metric tons, it is expected that the region could export 14,400 metric tons (under the assumption that only 30 percent of the mangoes would be of export quality). APROFA estimates that with total production of approximately 200,000 metric tons, Mali would be able to export 50,000 metric tons (25 percent) of its mangoes.

Consolidating success and transforming agricultural exports in Mali

In 2005 the government of Mali launched the Agricultural Competitiveness and Diversification Project, a six-year investment project, funded by a $46.4 million World Bank credit. The project's goal is to increase revenues and competitiveness for a range of agricultural products with growing (yet mostly untapped) markets and strong demand, thus diversifying the economy's foreign exchange earnings. In addition, its development objective is to improve the performance of supply chains across a range of nontraditional agricultural, livestock, fisheries, and produce in which Mali enjoys a strong competitive advantage, including mangoes, cashews, shallots, potatoes, dairy products, beans, papayas, sesame, and shea nuts.

The project includes five components: demonstration and dissemination of irrigation, postharvest, and value-adding technologies; improvement of the performance of existing and developing supply chains; facilitation of access to finance for producers and operators; investment in key collective, market-oriented infrastructure; and management, monitoring, and evaluation of project implementation.

Using a series of analytical tools and data, the project team identified value chains for export markets, providing a basis for prioritized interventions that would ultimately create value and improve livelihoods of Malian small farmers. The analysis used five modules to assess the competitiveness of a range of nontraditional agricultural value chains (box 10.2). Each module built on the previous one and progressed from a comprehensive list of sectors to those with true marketability, competitive advantage, and comparative advantage. This process also took into account the demand in existing end markets and identified new potential end markets, regional climate and growing factors, production capacity, access to finance, and infrastructure, among other determinants.

Improving quality by investing in infrastructure and technical assistance

Mali's revised surface transport system vastly increased the country's export capacity for mangoes. In fact, once the new transportation system was established and proven economically efficient and reliable, the government pursued additional

---

Box 10.2   The Strategic Profile Approach

The approach that was followed to identify and prioritize value chain interventions in Mali entailed the following sequence of modules, each one comprising several steps:

- Module 1: Defining Mali's Broad Portfolio of Agricultural Sectors
- Module 2: Analyzing Market Demand and Market Entry Conditions
- Module 3: Analyzing the Competitiveness of Potential Malian Offerings
- Module 4: Defining Priority Sectors
- Module 5: Competitiveness Planning: Putting the Analysis into Action

Through this process, a series of operational tools was developed for each of the selected value chains—the Strategic Development Plan, the Competitiveness Plan, and the Priority Action Plan. PCDA is now in the process of implementing these action plans with the respective value chain stakeholders.

Source: Authors.

interventions to increase the quality and quantity of mangoes exported. A number of successive agricultural diversification projects were thus started during the 2000s: USAID's Centre Agro-Entreprise (CAE), Trade-Mali, the Initiatives Intégrées pour la Croissance Economique du Mali (IICEM) program, and the World Bank's Programme Compétitivité et Diversification Agricoles (PCDA). Interventions covered by these programs included infrastructure cold-chain and conditioning improvements, phytosanitary improvement programs (especially the control of fruit fly infestation), certification programs, traceability programs, training in orchard management practices, and postharvest handling training programs. Figure 10.3 summarizes the continuum of projects and initiatives that supported the development of the mango industry in Mali between 1993 and 2009.

To strengthen human and physical capacity and to improve the competitiveness of mango exports, a pack house and logistics facility known as the PLAZA (Périmètre Logistique Aménagé en Zone Aéroportuaire), with capacity to handle 2,000 tons of fresh produce a year, was built in 2007 (box 10.3). The PLAZA has been integral in helping mango exporters (mainly sea-freight exporters) prepare their products for export with precooling and storage rooms, meet international standards for quality and safety, and train staff. The PLAZA is the only modern pack house

Figure 10.3   The Stages of Development of the Mango Export Industry in Mali

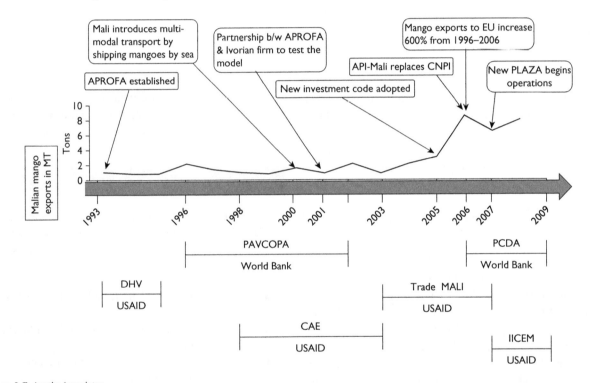

Source: J. E. Austin Associates.
Note: DHV, API and CNPI are all project acronyms.

for horticulture in Mali. A precooling and shipping facility in Sikasso is also being considered.

With assistance from the donor community, the government has provided technical assistance and training in phytosanitary issues. Continuous tightening of the EU food safety regulations, coupled with stricter demands in terms of traceability, are making it necessary to devise and deliver substantial interventions in agricultural export countries. Figure 10.4 illustrates the general stages of horticulture export quality requirements.

Phytosanitary requirements are still a challenge for Malian produce and several other West African countries. In the past, many shipments of mangoes were rejected once they reached Europe because of fruit fly infestations or other phytosanitary concerns. These problems arise partly from a lack of proper harvest and postharvest handling techniques. Since the fruit fly problem is a regional one, several regional initiatives have been established to eliminate the flies. Over the past three years, the West African Fruit Fly Initiative (WAFFI), jointly financed by the World Bank, the European Union, and the World Trade Organization (WTO), has been piloting fruit fly surveillance and mitigation protocols in West African orchards, including those in Mali. The knowledge and experience gained thus far has led to the design of a West African Regional Action Plan to control fruit flies. Once the substantial funding required to implement this program (€25 million) is gathered, the large-scale interventions planned by the program should translate into much-reduced prevalence of fruit flies in Malian orchards, thus improving the quality of the marketed fruit.

Figure 10.4   Continuum of Commercial and Regulatory Horticulture Export Requirements

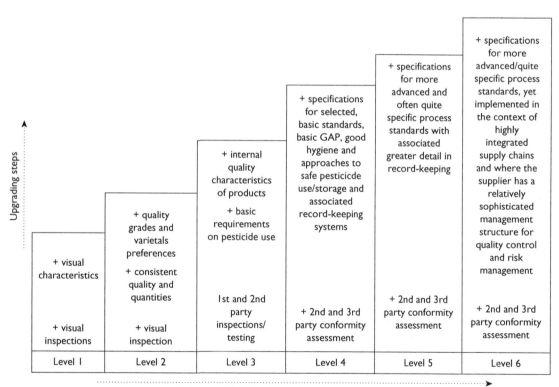

Source: Jaffee 2009.

Phytosanitary issues are closely linked to the certification process. Recognizing that many of its mangoes are sold in supermarket chains in Europe, Mali has pursued several certifications, including GLOBAL G.A.P. certifications. Streamlining the export process at the airport has contributed to the success of Mali's certification programs.

Improving orchard management and postharvest handling interventions

Orchard management and postharvest handling interventions have been very important in Mali as well. To have high-quality fruit to export, quality improvement must begin at the orchard level. Training in such improvements has been provided by several institutions in recent years, including the government, international partners, and even exporters themselves. Training has been comprehensive, with topics ranging from harvesting best practices, transport handling aimed at reducing damage to the product, and grafting techniques to improve the varieties and productivity of trees. Over time, training has increased the capacity of mango producers, allowing for continued success in the subsector.

Supply chain financing

Through the PCDA project, local banks and other financial institutions have regained trust and interest in Malian horticulture. In 2008 CFAF 150 million were lent to operators in the subsector, a record level compared with the past 10 years. This loan was disbursed in the form of credit for the import of shipping material (CFAF 56 million) and seasonal credit (CFAF 94 million) for three exporters. Between 2007 and 2008, PCDA provided a guarantee to a commercial bank to fund the import of transport boxes from Côte d'Ivoire; the bank held them in bond through a third party, releasing them on credit terms when the exporters needed to prepare an export shipment. In 2009 the same banks agreed to pre-finance the import of boxes directly to the exporters. PCDA has established its credibility in this area and continues to play an important facilitative role between farmers, exporters, and professional operators on the one hand, and the banks and financial institutions on the other hand.

Business training

Capacity building has been critical for the transition from subsistence mango farming to commercial farming. Producers received training in crop husbandry and best harvest practices, developing tools and linking value chain actors to financing. International partners have also provided assistance in small business development techniques.

As part of PCDA, for example, the Dutch firm Bakker Barendrecht teamed with five exporters operating at the PLAZA to teach the exporters how to reach European markets with their products. Bakker invests in knowledge in mango production and pays a minimum on the fruit if the exporters abide by a code of practice detailed in the contract. Varieties, ripeness, size, and other details are agreed upon with exporters for the entire season, with the possibility of payment of premiums if the mangoes sell well.

RESULTS AND IMPACTS

Mali's development agenda places a high priority on agricultural growth and diversification. The achievements realized through the PAVCOPA and PCDA projects have made a direct and tangible contribution to this agenda. A whole range of stakeholders participating in the value chain—small farmers, traders, agroprocessors, exporters, service providers (technicians, financiers, and accounting specialists), and input and equipment providers—have been involved since project launch and are benefiting from the expansion and improvements brought about by these projects.

Quantitative results

Results achieved after 15 years of reform in Mali's mango subsector are summarized in table 10.3. In many cases, the improvements are significant. The volume of mangoes exported, for example, reached 11,995 tons in 2008, an all-time record with a growth rate of 24 percent a year. (figure 10.5). Mango exports generated revenue of CFAF 9.7 billion ($25 million) in the same year, a significant proportion of the earnings generated by Mali's traditional exports, such as cotton lint. A range of stakeholders—farmers, harvesters, processors, and exporters—are benefiting from expansion in mango trade and improvements along the value chain. This means increased market share, value creation, and improved prices at all stages of mango production. The price producers receive for their mangoes at the farm gate increased by 150 percent between 1993 and 2008. That price increase has allowed for additional capacity for other on-farm activities as farmers became aware of the margins to be gained from horticulture production.

1993	2008	Impact
1,050 metric tons exported	11,995 tons exported	1,042%
Marginal sea-freighted mango exports; exports not recorded as originating in Mali	Sea-freighted exports total 4,600 tons	460%
$460,000 of revenue generated by mango exports	Value of mango exports reached $3.4 million in 2007	639%
25-day transit time from Sikasso to northern Europe	12-day transit time from Sikasso to northern Europe	−13 days
Farm gate price of CFAF 50	Farm gate price of CFAF 125	150%
237 tons of European imports	European imports increased to 4,560 tons	1,824%

Source: Author research; revenue contribution figures from FAOSTAT.

Figure 10.5 Mali Mango Exports, 1993–2008

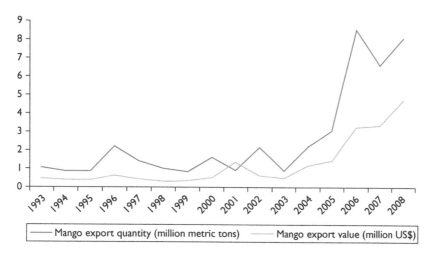

Source: FAOSTAT and J. E. Austin.

The average quality of fruit exported from Mali has improved. The number of sea container rejections due to fruit flies, for example, dropped from 14 containers in 2007 to 5 containers in 2008. Backward linkages at the production level also have improved tremendously, as have relationships between exporters and farmers. Mali has also been able to set a foothold on the Fair Trade niche market (box 10.4). Exporters provide support services to farmers such as helping to manage their plantations, working to reduce fruit flies, and implementing certification or traceability programs on the plantation. In return, exporters purchase farmers' final product—often without a contract. The trust established by these interactions allows exporters to obtain a higher-quality product, because farmers are more willing to respect phytosanitary controls when provided assistance. In fact, trust among all actors in the mango value chain has increased over time.

Box 10.4 Fair Trade Market Opportunities

Recent data from the Fairtrade Labelling Organizations show that about 8,000 tons of fair-trade-certified fruit were sold in Europe in 2005, including pineapples, mangoes, avocados, and citrus and deciduous fruits (excluding bananas). By volume, the United Kingdom accounted for more sales than any other country, with 4,700 tons of fruit. On a per capita basis, however, spending was highest in Switzerland. Sales of fair-trade products have grown strongly since 2005.

As a brand, fair trade is making its way into the mainstream and is being taken up by supermarkets. The sector already has the same performance requirements as conventional products: year-round supply and quality and price guarantees are to be expected.

Source: Authors.

In addition to improvements within Mali, regional cooperation also has improved. For example, mango exporters in Mali have organized to obtain multicountry support from donors to fight against fruit flies, and the multimodal transport initiative involved coordination among several stakeholders across borders. These efforts have led to an improved value chain not only in Mali but in Côte d'Ivoire, Senegal, and other countries.

Qualitative changes

The initial, and now sustained, take-off in the growth of mango exports has led to a complete transformation of the subsector, not only in quantitative terms but also qualitatively. The expansion of the subsector has brought about a progressive and likely irreversible change in business practices in the sense of increased professionalism and attention to product quality, better compliance with trade standards, and increasing interest in private investment.

For one, major players in the mango business are now present in Mali and have an interest in expanding their operations and making long-term investments in the country. AHOLD, a major Dutch supermarket retail chain, has operated in Mali since the PLAZA and has been providing technical assistance to Malian exporters and PCDA. In addition, substantial work has been undertaken on the upstream/production level of the production chain. Mango production is now considered a legitimate agricultural activity, not just fruit collection. (PCDA, for example, has invested in a study that aims to map tree crop plantations using satellite imaging.) Financial institutions have also shown renewed interest as demonstrated by the increasing volume of credit to the subsector, the low default rates, and the emergence of innovative financing instruments, such as input prefinancing. Finally, Mali's Mango Task Force has been active for some years to improve coordination in the subsector, develop an agenda for collective action between professionals, and provide a platform to address issues of common interest with the public sector.

THE WAY FORWARD

While the mango industry in Mali has grown in recent years, it will continue to develop in the years ahead. Mali has given priority to a number of areas, including market positioning, improving quality and quantity, attracting capital, adding value to mango exports, improving transportation infrastructure, and potentially establishing more links at the regional level.

Improving market positioning and diversifying market outlets

While Mali has succeeded in increasing sea-freighted exports since the 1990s, there is still room for better market positioning and diversification of market outlets. First, Mali, whose mangoes represent only 2 percent of the total mango imports to the European Union, is still a marginal player in the global market for mangoes (figure 10.6). Second, the European Union and other importing markets are dynamic, meaning that there is constant need for adjustment and improvement to meet market demand. Mali is currently supplying the EU market based on the seasonality of its production, which is concentrated between mid-May and early July, after Burkina Faso but before Senegal (figure 10.7).

Going forward, it will be important for Mali to extend its harvest season and develop markets other than Europe. To address this, PCDA is testing the irrigation of mango orchards, which may offer opportunities to induce flowering and fructification at a different period of the year. Local exporters also have begun seeking market opportunities in the Middle East and North Africa, among other places. Mali has begun to export mangoes to Morocco. There are also substantial opportunities in other Sub-Saharan country markets.

Continuing to invest in quality and product differentiation

In recent years Mali has focused on obtaining certifications that will allow mangoes to enter the European market, such

Figure 10.6 Volume of Mango Imports to the European Union, by Country of Origin, 2008

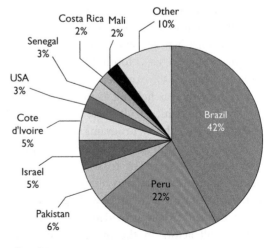

Source: Eurostat.

Figure 10.7 Seasonality of Mango Imports to the European Union, by Country of Origin, 2008 (*metric tons*)

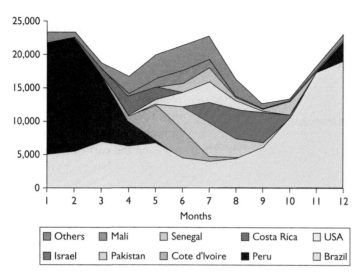

Source: Eurostat.

as GLOBAL G.A.P. the certification required by supermarkets in the European Union. Collaboration along the value chain led exporters to assist producers to achieve certification through training, with the support of PCDA. Some producers have even obtained certification of their mangoes as organic. The market for organic fruit and vegetables is a growing one, particularly in countries of northern Europe and Switzerland.

Ensure compliance with standards and phytosanitary requirements

The constant evolution of EU food safety regulations toward more stringent phytosanitary requirements, coupled with demands for traceability, make it necessary to devise and deliver specific interventions in the produce-exporting countries to meet market requirements. Recently PCDA financed an intervention by the Comité de liaison EU-ACP pour les fruits et légumes (COLEACP) specific to the mango value chain aimed at building capacities in health and phytosanitary risks control. A series of workshops, which brought together mango stakeholders of Mali and Burkina Faso, were held to train participants on risk assessment and mitigation. This training led to the creation of a guidebook for the mango value chain that is now followed in both countries.

Continuing to focus on improvements in quantity and quality

Although estimates vary greatly, some experts estimate that Mali could export between 20,000 and 50,000 metric tons

of mangoes a year with improved management of existing mango plantations. Effective management includes introduction of new varieties, improved grafting and replanting of new trees for increased yields and quality, additional investments in pack houses and cold storage, renewed efforts in the control of fruit flies, and procurement of technical advisory services. However, in 2009, against an initial export program of 104 containers, the PLAZA could finally ship only 42 containers because of the lack of mangoes of exportable quality.

Attracting capital

Developing commercial value chains is a private sector business. It requires capital and know-how. If an economic sector does not manage to attract investors and capital, both national and foreign, sustaining growth will be difficult. In general, governments should encourage commercial farming by facilitating access to land concessions. In Mali's mango subsector, the government should make financing more readily accessible and provide incentives to banks to lend to stakeholders. These actions would stimulate private sector investment into value-addition activities such as drying, canning, and juice production. Burkina Faso has had some success in producing dried mangoes, and Mali has the potential to achieve similar success.

Diversify to better utilize the PLAZA terminal

To maximize the use of the PLAZA and ensure sustainability, commercial operations must be able to cover PLAZA operating costs by the end of 2012, when the public funding stops. Several exporters are looking at opportunities to export green beans and other vegetables that could be packed at the terminal. To ensure profitability and competitive pricing for its members, there are plans for a strong professional organization to eventually take over management of the PLAZA.

Further invest in marketing infrastructure

A mechanical grading line is being installed to improve turnover at the PLAZA, enhancing the ability to quickly meet demand quantity and quality in the European market. The equipment was ordered by PCDA, and the calibrating machine should be installed for the 2010 season. Assuming an adequate fruit harvest, the PLAZA should now be able to handle over 100 containers in the 12- to 14-week mango season.

Adding value to consolidate the achievements

Strengthening and diversifying the value chain, in addition to valorizing the large mango surplus that is not exportable, is critical for the future growth of the mango subsector. While fresh mango exports were an entry point for Mali to reach the EU market (and indeed, demand for fresh mangoes is expected to continue in the foreseeable future), fresh mangoes may not be extremely profitable in the long run, and Malian professionals need to seek different ways to add value in the mango subsector. PCDA has been working on several clear opportunities: processing, increasing the range of products offered, expanding other value chains (papaya), and establishing new value chains.

A recent study (Royal Tropical Institute 2010) shows the potential for exports of dried mango from Mali to European markets, provided the product meets the expected quality standards. For dried mangoes, Mali has an advantage over Burkina Faso in the sense that it is relatively unencumbered by an obsolete technology and enjoys a large surplus of mango varieties that are not exportable as fresh. Recently, PCDA agreed to take up one of the study's recommendations and finance a pilot project to produce dried mangoes based on technology established in South Africa, which currently meets the quality standards in EU markets.

Further improving transport and fostering cluster development

The inefficiencies the Bamako-Dakar railway and at the Dakar port are resulting in higher costs, longer wait times,

and higher risks as Malian exporters operate through Côte d'Ivoire. Improvements in alternative transport routes would certainly benefit the mango subsector. Mali could also improve the road-to-rail corridor in order to reduce transport times and increase quality.

To develop a vibrant and competitive export horticulture sector, Mali also needs to encourage the development of related industries and services, such as certification, packaging material, and inputs. These related industries are key to improving the competitiveness of the value chain(s) by reducing the cost of inputs, technology, and services, and also by providing an important source of revenue and employment in Mali.

Joining forces at the regional level

Finally, when examining trade figures, it is evident that the competition for West African mango sectors does not come from neighboring countries, but from Central and South America. The concentration of mango exporters within the West African region, however, suggests advantages from coordinating the production and export of mangoes to Europe at a subregional level. Mali could reap significant advantages from coordinating mango production and export with Côte d'Ivoire, Burkina Faso, and Senegal. Such coordination could result in an increase in the scale of export and greater efficiencies in shipping and standardized quality control, better handling of traceability, and branding. All these factors would contribute to increased volumes of exported mangoes and, ultimately, to increased revenues for producers. One possibility would be to create a West Africa brand for mangoes.

LESSONS AND REPLICABILITY

The driving forces behind Mali's experience in developing its mango sector, as well as the lessons learned during the development process, are useful to point out for other countries in the course of such a transition.

Drivers of success

INNOVATION IS CRITICAL IN TRIGGERING AND DRIVING CHANGE. In the case of mango exports from Mali, the key initial innovation was in transport and logistics. Together, these changes created greater opportunity to access the large EU market. The innovations also created the dynamics of change and initiated a learning process. There is no universal formula for achieving innovation, however; innovation derives from a combination of factors that depend on the specific country and sector context. In the case of the mango subsector of Mali, two key resources, expertise and entrepreneurship, were brought together to improve the export capacity of the industry. Additionally, creativity in funding mechanisms is another important lesson learned in the case of Mali.

TIME IS OF THE ESSENCE. Building capacity—human, physical, or otherwise—in a new or small industry requires sustained efforts over time, especially when starting from scratch or from a very low base, as was the case in Mali.

HIGH-QUALITY TECHNICAL WORK IS KEY. The importance of market research, value chain cost analysis, benchmarking, and assessment of industry constraints cannot be overstated. This work is critical in identifying and designing action plans, programs, and business solutions. In the case of Mali, it was perhaps the most critical factor contributing to launching the reforms.

PRIVATE SECTOR LEADERSHIP IS ALSO IMPORTANT. Even though private sector involvement in the mango sector in Mali was weak at the start of the transition, it was necessary to work with the existing private operators and eventually bring in new ones, such as the Ivoirian company that conducted the pilot export test. In the case of Mali, the partnership with SN Tropical Expressions was unique and provided a good model of what public-private partnerships can achieve.

KNOWLEDGE AND FUNDING MUST BE PACKAGED AND DELIVERED PROPERLY. Building capacities in emerging subsectors and industries takes not only time and perseverance but also the ability to deliver investments in "hardware" (infrastructure and other means of production) and "software" (training and knowledge transfer) in a flexible manner. In the case of Mali, capital investments such as PLAZA were imperative to the success of the mango subsector. Training alone could not bring about such a transition. Improvements to cold chain, transportation, and conditioning facilities within the horticulture sector significantly improved Mali's capacity to export quality mangoes.

Lessons learned

A TARGETED, ORGANIZED APPROACH IS NECESSARY TO SECTOR REFORM. Sector and value-chain analysis are essential

tools in identifying opportunities and articulating operational strategies to create greater value in agriculture and agribusiness. It is also essential to find a key entry point that responds to market demand and helps increase scale. For Malian mangoes, this meant finding a more effective way to get the product to the market, while innovations in transport and logistics system allowed farmers and exporters to achieve the economies of scale they needed. A structured, holistic approach is required.

SUSTAINING DEVELOPMENT EFFORTS OVER TIME IS NECESSARY. Mali could not have successfully transformed its mango sector if activities had not been pursued year after year. Building an industry takes years, not months. The lesson here for governments and development partners is that if they not prepared to dedicate time and resources to a reform over a long period of time, it is probably better not to start at all. That said, early success in the reform process, such as what Mali achieved through the positive outcome of the multimodal export pilot launched by APROFA in 2000, can serve as a foundation on which to build momentum for further reforms.

AID FUNDS CAN PLAY A CATALYTIC ROLE IN CHANGE PROCESSES. Project aid has the capacity to provide both financial resources and know-how to share risks in order to facilitate innovation. In Mali, technical assistance programs targeting postharvest handling, supply chain finance, export, and other areas have helped improve the performance of the mango value chain and are now doing the same for other agricultural and nonagricultural sectors. Technical assistance by aid organizations can also help address market failures and can be combined in a proactive fashion with efforts and interventions by the private sector.

COLLABORATION AND PARTNERSHIPS ARE PART OF THE SOLUTION. Public-private partnerships (between donor agencies and government, or between the private sector and government), such as the arrangement to build and manage the PLAZA, are key in developing infrastructure that will, in turn, help a country expand a specific sector. In Mali the emergence of the Mango Task Force helped provide a space for public-private cooperation, as well as an opportunity for exporters to coordinate their respective shipments through a common buyer. In addition, the use of "Mali mango" logo on boxes created closer cooperation among shippers.

A FAVORABLE INVESTMENT CLIMATE AND INVESTMENT POLICIES REMAIN IMPORTANT. Thus far the government of

Mali's commitment to reform in its mango sector has been carried out through diversification, donor financing, and improved technical expertise. The industry, however, is now experiencing a new generation of issues that will require significant reforms in the general business environment by promoting private sector investment, and improving access to land. Recent difficulties in implementing a Foreign Investment Advisory Service (FIAS) technical assistance program on agribusiness do not bode well in terms of the determination of the government to move to the next stage of development of agribusiness value chains.

Scalability and transferability

Two general lessons from Mali's experience with mangoes can be applied to other countries. First, designing market-led strategies and investing in applied value-chain analysis is necessary if the objectives of creating higher value in agriculture, raising incomes, and lifting the rural population out of poverty are to be achieved. While general, cross-cutting agricultural support programs are necessary, they are in themselves not sufficient to make a difference. Specific information and analysis must be generated on the issues to be addressed throughout the value chain(s).

Second, it should be kept in mind that sustainable market inclusion requires multiple interventions. As demonstrated by a recently completed research program funded by the U.K. Department for International Development called "Re-governing Markets," inclusion of small farmers in modern agricultural value chains does not happen by itself. In fact, inclusion requires interventions by multiple actors, as summarized in figure 10.8. The study indicates that three major categories of actors need to be involved: farmers and

farmer groups, receptive businesses, and a facilitating public sector. Actors in all categories must be willing and able to play their role, and even then establishing sustainable market inclusion needs a public sector body to facilitate the process. This is the role that APROFA and its successive projects have played for the mango subsector in Mali and the role that such projects are still playing for a number of other emerging value chains in the country (papaya, cashew, sesame, potato, and onion).

CONCLUSION

Since the early 1990s Mali has achieved a spectacular increase in its exports of fresh mangoes, seizing opportunities offered by an increasing market demand in Europe and finding solutions to overcome significant physical hurdles. The initiatives taken in the mango sector in Mali clearly demonstrate that even a physical constraint as immutable as being landlocked can be overcome to some extent through innovative solutions. In Mali the entry point was the identification and economic validation of a new transport and logistics arrangement that allowed mangoes to be exported in large volumes and in good condition.

Mali currently is focusing on consolidating and expanding its initial success by strengthening stakeholder involvement and private sector partnerships to ensure growth and sustainability. The Mango Task Force has emerged as the sector's professional organization, with potential to become a permanent trade/business association capable of handling the new issues facing the horticulture industry in Mali.

BIBLIOGRAPHY

Antoine, M. 2005. "Growing Malian Mango Exports: How New Business Models Translate to Increased Opportunities for West African Producers." World Bank.

APROFA (Agricultural Value Chain Promotion Agency). 2002a. "Mango Exports to Europe out of Sikasso-Mali: Multimodal Shipping and Cross-border Partnerships." Bamako.

———. 2002b. "Note sur l'expérience de Sikasso concernant l'amélioration des revenus des petits planteurs de mangues. " Bamako.

———. 2002c. "Projet de diversification des filières agricoles et de l'horticulture : Livrable 1.1: Diagnostic des principales filières agricoles (mangue, haricot vert, pomme de terre et oignon)." Bamako.

Birthal, P., A. Jha, and H. Singh. 2007. "Linking Farmers to Markets for High-Value Agricultural Commodities." *Agriculture Economics Research Review* 20: 425–39.

Figure 10.8   Multiple Actors Necessary for Sustainable Markets

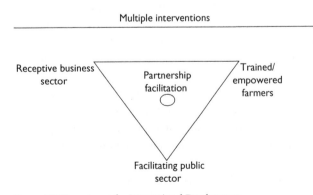

Source: UK Department for International Development.

CARANA Corporation. 2004. "Impact of Transport and Logistics on Mali's Trade Competitiveness." Washington, DC.

Chemonics International. 2003. "Mali SEG Projet Centre Agro-Entreprise: Final Report Deliverable 4." Washington, DC.

Club du Sahel/OECD (Organisation for Economic Co-operation and Development). 1998. "L'économie locale de Sikasso." Paris.

Danielou, M., P. Labaste, and J.-M. Voisard. 2003. "Good Practice Note: Linking Farmers to Markets: Exporting Malian Mangoes to Europe." Africa Region Working Paper 60, World Bank, Washington, DC.

IF (Integrated Framework for Trade-Related Technical Assistance to Least-Developed Countries). 2004. "Expanding and Diversifying Trade for Growth and Poverty Reduction: A Diagnostic Trade Integration Study." http://www.integratedframework.org/files/mali_dtis_17nov04.pdf.

Ezzine, A. 2009. "Etude des corridors pour l'export des mangues du Mali et du Burkina Faso vers l'Union Européenne." World Bank, Washington, DC.

Fairbanks, M., and S. Linsay. 1997. "Plowing the Sea: Nurturing the Hidden Sources of Growth in the Developing World." Harvard Business School Press, Cambridge, MA.

Geomar International and PCDA. 2006. "Strategic Profile of Mali's Agricultural Exports." Geomar International, Montreal.

Gulati, A., N. Minot, C. Delgado, and S. Bora. 2007. "Growth in High-Value Agriculture in Asia and the Emergence of Vertical Links with Farmers." In *Global Supply Chains, Standards and the Poor,* ed. J. Swinnen, pp 91–108. Wallingford: CABI Publishing.

Hallam, D., et al. 2004. "The Market for Non-Traditional Agricultural Exports." Food and Agriculture Organization, Rome.

Jaffee, S. 2009. "African Smallholders, Higher Value Agri-Food Markets and Measures to Achieve Compliance with Emerging Standards." World Bank, Washington, DC.

Jaffee, S., and S. Henson. 2004. "Standards and Agro-Food Exports from Developing Countries: Rebalancing the Debate." Policy Research Working Paper 3348, World Bank, Washington, DC.

Jaffee, S., P. Labaste, R. Kopicki, and I. Christie. 2003. "Modernizing Africa's Agro-Food Systems: Analytical Framework and Implications for Operations." Africa Region Working Paper 44, World Bank, Washington, DC.

Jones, C., and G. Livingston. 2009. "Supporting Agribusiness Investment in Mali." J. E. Austin Associates, Arlington, VA.

PCDA (Programme Compétitivité Diversification Agricoles). 2007. "Mango Value Chain Competitiveness Plan." Bamako.

Rey, J.-Y., et al. 2004. "La mangue en Afrique de L'Ouest Francophone: variétés et composition variétale des vergers." *Fruits* 59 (3): 191–208.

Royal Tropical Institute. 2010. "L'amélioration des performances de la filière des produits séchés de la mangue au Burkina Faso et au Mali." Amsterdam.

USAID (U.S. Agency for International Development). 2002. "Mali Trade Capacity Needs Assessment—Sub Sector Analysis." Technical Report, Washington, DC.

World Bank. 1995. "Staff Appraisal Report, Agricultural Trading and Processing Promotion Pilot Project." Washington, DC.

———. 1996. "Mali Agricultural Trading and Processing Promotion Pilot Project." Project Appraisal Document 25884, World Bank, Washington, DC.

———. 2003a. "Implementation Completion Report Republic of Mali Agricultural Trading and Processing Promotion Pilot Project." Washington, DC.

———. 2003b. "Mali: Exporting Mangoes to Europe." Washington, DC.

———. 2004. "Project Appraisal Document on a Credit and Proposed Grant to the Government of Mali for the Transport Corridors Improvement Project." Washington, DC.

———. 2005. "Project Appraisal Document on a Proposed Credit to the Republic of Mali for an Agricultural Competitiveness and Diversification Project." Washington, DC.

Economic Liberalization in Rwanda's Coffee Sector: A Better Brew for Success

Karol C. Boudreaux

I n 2008 Solberg and Hansen, a Norwegian importer of
high-quality specialty coffee, bid just under $40 a kilo-
gram (more than 21,000 Rwandan francs) for a load of
coffee from Rwanda.[1] While this bid was exceptional—
specialty coffee normally sells for between $3 and $4 a
kilogram—it also represents a real and positive transformation within Rwanda's coffee sector. In the not-too-
distant past, the country was known as a producer of
mediocre coffee that attracted little attention from discriminating importers or consumers.[2] Today, Rwandan
coffee is increasingly recognized as a high-quality product, one for which importers such as Solberg and Hansen
and, in turn, consumers are willing to pay a premium.
Although the Rwandan economy is diversifying, agriculture continues to be the primary source of livelihood for
the vast majority of the population. The overwhelming
majority of agricultural workers are subsistence farmers.
Just over 10 percent of these farmers planted coffee in
2008, and the crop remains a major source of export revenue for Rwanda, generating more than 36 percent of
total export revenue in 2009.

The evolution of coffee production in Rwanda

The transformation of Rwanda's coffee sector happened relatively quickly. In 2000 Rwandan farmers were producing
semi-processed coffee for sale on world markets. Farm gate
prices paid to farmers were low (60 Rwandan francs a kilogram), and prospects for farmers and exporters to increase

income or profits were limited. Starting in the late 1990s, the
government liberalized the sector, removing a variety of
barriers to trade, creating new incentives for groups and
individuals to invest in coffee production, and facilitating
entrepreneurship in the coffee industry.

Working with the private sector and international
donors, the government of Rwanda has reshaped the coffee
industry: the regulatory framework for production has been
modified; more than 100 coffee-washing stations have been
built; donors have supported the development of market
links between producers and foreign buyers; cooperatives
have formed; and smallholder farmers are working together
in an effort to improve the quality, marketing, and branding
of their coffee.

These changes have had important effects on the ground
in Rwanda. Coffee continues to generate important export
revenue for the country: just over $47 million in 2008, com-
pared to $35 million in 2007. Higher incomes benefit farm-
ers, their families, and their communities in a variety of
ways: farmers can improve a home, pay medical expenses
or school fees, or better ensure food security. And when
cooperatives earn a profit they are able to hire workers,
purchase capital, and support community projects such as
improved schools.

The transformation of the Rwandan coffee sector may be
creating social benefits in addition to economic benefits.
Working together at coffee-washing stations—typically
located in the rural, hilly, and relatively inaccessible areas
where coffee grows and where little other commercial

infrastructure exists—farmers have new opportunities to interact with other Rwandans. These repeated interactions may reduce the sense of ethnic distance among members of Rwandan society. As farmers and other workers at coffee-washing stations experience the increased economic satisfaction that comes with higher income earned from coffee, they may also feel greater levels of trust toward people with whom they interact and thus develop more positive attitudes toward reconciliation. And because coffee in Rwanda is grown by poor, smallholder farmers who make up 90 percent of the population, these positive changes have the potential to benefit a broad swath of Rwandan society.

Challenges and concerns

Despite this good progress, the coffee sector faces a number of serious challenges. To start, Rwanda's landlocked geographical status and poor infrastructure mean that coffee producers face high transport costs. Moving coffee cherries quickly over Rwandan roads is difficult, as is moving processed beans out of the country in a timely and cost-effective manner. Other concerns are related to the costs in the industry. Production costs remain high. Many of the newly built coffee-washing stations are operating at much less than full capacity, and labor costs are higher than in neighboring countries. Rwandan farmers are also less productive than farmers in neighboring countries. Although some have received support and training from nongovernmental organizations (NGOs), regular visits from extension agents are limited.

In addition, a variety of management concerns have plagued the cooperatives that many coffee farmers join. One specialist of Rwanda's cooperatives observed, "After five years of extensive cooperative capacity building, Rwanda's coffee cooperatives remain surprisingly fragile, unorganized, and dysfunctional" (SPREAD 2007). Some cooperatives have mishandled loans, while others have failed to fulfill contracts in a timely manner or have encountered trouble marketing their products. Some of these problems are the result of a lack of training or financial management skills.

Other challenges involve the broader institutional environment. As Rwanda implements a new land law, some smallholder farmers may face uncertainty about the rights to the land that they work. Women, in particular, may be especially vulnerable. The government, NGOs, and other stakeholders are taking measures to deal with these various challenges, however. If capacity issues can be addressed, marketing and sales problems resolved, incentives strengthened to produce higher-quality beans, and harmful government interference avoided, then the positive gains of the past several years should continue, and Rwanda's smallholder farmers can look forward to earning more income from coffee production. This income should, in turn, filter through local economies to spread benefits to other Rwandans.

REFORMING A VITAL SECTOR

Government control and limited markets

In many developing countries, governments are heavily involved in the agriculture sector, and that certainly holds true in Rwanda, where coffee has been a major export for decades. The Belgian government as well as the two independent, pre-genocide governments controlled important aspects of the coffee trade for their political and financial gain. Through compulsory production, export taxes, and a monopsony export control agency, these regimes captured the profits of mostly poor coffee farmers, and used the funds to help maintain political power (Bates 1981). Producers had little incentive to invest in the production of high-quality coffee, and so for decades Rwandans produced a small volume of low-quality coffee.

Significant government involvement in Rwanda's coffee sector began in the 1930s, when the Belgian colonial government launched a series of "coffee campaigns." Government authorities built nurseries and supplied seeds, but they also required Rwandan farmers to plant coffee trees (Dorsey 1983). The government also introduced price restrictions, imposed mandatory quality guidelines, and issued special licenses that allowed only some firms to purchase coffee. Export taxes were imposed on coffee sales, and individual income taxes were imposed on producers, who at the time were mostly Hutu farmers. Tutsi chiefs collected these taxes, which helped support them and the colonial government.

Following Rwanda's independence, the Kayibanda government (1962–73) retained most of these policies because it had limited alternatives for raising revenue. A government marketing board (OCIR, subsequently OCIR-Café), together with a monopsony export company, Rwandex, purchased, and then sold on world markets, the vast majority of coffee grown in Rwanda. The farm gate price was set by the government.[3] Middlemen bought beans from farmers and sold them to Rwandex, which in turn sold them to foreign buyers. The locations where smallholders brought their beans for purchase acted as "the economic arm of the Gitarama (that is, Kayibanda) regime" (Verwimp 2003).

Heavy government involvement in the coffee sector continued under the Habyarimana regime (1973–94). During the 1970s and 1980s, as world coffee prices rose, coffee exports provided between 60 and 80 percent of Rwanda's export revenue (Berlage, Capéau, and Verwimp 2004). President Habyarimana ensured control of these important rents by appointing relatives and political supporters to positions of authority at OCIR-Café.[4]

Crisis and response

During the early and mid-1980s, rising coffee prices allowed the government to modestly increase the price it paid to farmers for their beans. Verwimp (2003) indicates that high market prices for coffee had another effect—they "allowed the [Habyarimana] regime's elite to increase both its personal consumption and its power over the population" (p. 172). The government then used the additional revenue to buy support in rural areas (through higher farm gate prices for coffee and subsidized agricultural inputs) and to spend more on monitoring the population.

Tumbling coffee prices in the late 1980s meant reduced government revenue. For a few years, the government attempted to keep payments to farmers stable, but this policy proved unsustainable, especially after 1990, when the government needed resources to fight the invading Rwandan Patriotic Front (RPF) forces. By the early 1990s the government was forced to lower prices paid for coffee cherries to smallholder farmers. Price supports ended completely in 1992.

The fall in coffee prices, coupled with growing military expenditures, meant that the Habyarimana government faced severe fiscal constraints. Seeking alternate sources of revenue, it began confiscating property and raising taxes to supplement the budget, and there was some amount of reduction in consumption by elites. Foreign aid also became an increasingly important part of Rwanda's budget. However, the reliance upon, and competition for, foreign aid created serious problems among governing elites. As one observer puts it, "the various gentlemen's agreements which had existed between the competing political clans since the end of the Kayibanda regime started to melt down as the resources shrank and internal power struggles intensified" (Prunier 1995, 47). With its growing dependence on foreign aid, and in a bid to remain in power, the government agreed to an International Monetary Fund (IMF) structural adjustment program in 1990 that imposed further hardships on farmers.

To rebuild its popularity, the regime diverted attention from its own economic policies to the Tutsi/RPF threat and increased levels of repression within Rwandan society. The government demonized the invaders, arguing that allowing Tutsis into the country would lead to Hutus having less access to already scarce land, and used the media to foment ethnic hatred. Most repression was directed at the Tutsi minority, although some spilled over to Hutus. The ultimate results were, of course, disastrous. In the three months between April and June of 1994, approximately 800,000 people were murdered in Rwanda, mostly Tutsis but also moderate Hutus and Hutu opponents of the Habyarimana government.

Liberalization to open markets and increase opportunity

Today, the Rwandan government is less directly involved in the coffee sector. Farmers have more choice about what to grow, to whom to sell their beans, and how to market their product. Private sector investment in the sector is rising. This increased openness is part of a larger government effort to improve economic growth in the country. Rwanda's Vision 2020 is a strategic plan for economic change. This plan has, since 2003, provided a guideline for sectoral policy setting with Rwanda's ministries (Rwanda Ministry of Finance and Economic Planning 2000; IFAD 2006).

The goals created by Vision 2020, together with Rwanda's Poverty Reduction Strategy Paper (PRSP) and the subsequent Economic Development and Poverty Reduction Strategy (EDPRS), include improving the institutional environment to allow for increased private sector development and infrastructure improvements, focusing on good governance (including democratization, national reconciliation, political stability, and security), improving agricultural productivity, improving human capital through investments in health and education, creating a service-based economy with a focus on ICT (information and communication technology), reducing external support, relying more on exports, and promoting regional integration.

Some progress has been made toward achieving the Vision 2020 goals. Real GDP growth has been strong for more than a decade: 10.8 percent over 1996–2000 and 6.4 percent over 2000–06 (Rwanda Ministry of Finance and Economic Planning 2007), reaching a high of 11.2 percent in 2009 (although it was estimated to fall to under 5 percent for 2010) (Index Mundi 2010) With an emphasis on private-sector-led growth and improvements in the environment for doing business, the economy is diversifying, merchandise trade levels are rising, and the service sector is expanding. Particularly for rural Rwandans, reform in the coffee sector is playing an important part in helping thousands of farmers increase their incomes, by creating jobs and providing opportunities for new skills training. The reform measures are also strengthening human and social capital and, in the process, may also be generating valuable social benefits.

Most Rwandans—especially rural Rwandans—are still very poor, however. More than one-third of the population is unable to meet its minimum food requirements and routinely goes hungry (Rwanda Ministry of Finance and Economic Planning 2007). Although the U.K. overseas development agency, the Department for International Development (DFID), reports that the poverty rate dropped from 70 percent of the population in 1994 to less than 57 percent in 2006 (DFID 2008), the World Bank (2010) estimates that Rwanda's gross national income per capita was only $460 in 2009. Thus Rwanda has a long way to go to meet the Vision 2020 goal of transforming itself from a low-income to a middle-income society.

Modest gains and encouraging signs

Changes in the coffee sector began shortly after the genocide, when the government opened the market for coffee export to increased competition and began to focus on improving the value chain for coffee (figure 11.1). The method for pricing beans also changed. Rather than dictating a single price for the entire season, the Rwanda Coffee Development Authority (the former OCIR-Café) sets a minimum weekly reference price, in consultation with stakeholders, a basis from which a sales price per kilogram may be negotiated (Mutandwa et al. 2009).[5]

More substantial reform efforts began in 2000, when the government, working with consultants (the OTF Group has been the leader in these efforts) and donors, studied the potential to add value to Rwandan coffee through the production of higher-quality, washed, and fermented specialty coffee. Part of the catalyst for this redoubled effort came as prices for coffee of ordinary quality fell to a historic low in 1997 and farmers became increasingly unwilling to invest in the crop. The quantity of coffee produced declined as the tree stock aged and was not properly tended, soil fertility declined, and farmers battled with insects and fungal diseases. As a result, the quality of Rwanda's coffee crop tumbled: by 2000, 90 percent of Rwanda's crop was classified as low-quality, "ordinary" coffee (Rwanda Ministry of Agriculture and Animal Husbandry and Ministry of Trade and Industry 2008).

Rwanda's national coffee strategy

In 2002 the government issued a National Coffee Strategy that outlined a plan for capturing a larger share of the specialty coffee sector. A production target of 44,000 tons of coffee was set for 2010, 63 percent of which would be fully washed (figure 11.2).[6] These production targets have, however, never been met.

The shift away from low-quality coffee to high-quality specialty coffee was designed to break a perceived "low-quality, low-quantity trap." As noted, Rwandan farmers were producing low-quality coffee that sold for a low price. Low sales prices meant that farmers lacked revenue to invest in improvements. Without sufficient income, farmers could not invest in capital to improve the quality of their beans—hence, the trap.

Figure 11.1   Value Chain for Washed Coffee

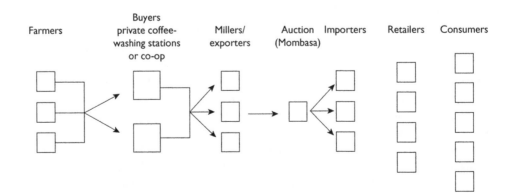

Source: Author.

CHAPTER 11: ECONOMIC LIBERALIZATION IN RWANDA'S COFFEE SECTOR: A BETTER BREW FOR SUCCESS

Figure 11.2   Targets Set Out in Rwanda's Fully Washed Coffee Strategy 2002

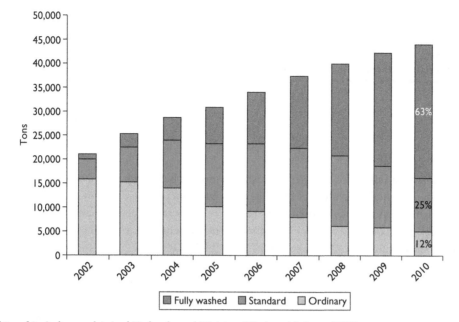

Source: Rwanda Ministry of Agriculture and Animal Husbandry and Ministry of Trade and Industry (2008).

The 2002 National Coffee Strategy was designed to break this trap, increase income and revenue, and improve price stability, because specialty coffee prices fluctuate less dramatically than does the price for semiwashed coffee. In an attempt to meet these targets, coffee-sector stakeholders focused on strengthening and supporting producer cooperatives, identifying sites for and supporting the building of coffee-washing stations, replanting aging tree stock, improving quality control throughout the industry, and strengthening the Rwandan brand globally. And as one of four focal sectors identified in its 2008–12 Economic Development and Poverty Reduction Strategy, the coffee sector remains a high priority for the government.

DIRECT ECONOMIC BENEFITS OF LIBERALIZATION

The liberalization of the coffee sector has had a number of positive effects. First, farmers now have an incentive—increased income—to shift some production from semiwashed to fully washed coffee. Entrepreneurs are investing in building coffee-washing stations, where cherries are processed for sale. Rural communities are forming cooperatives, some of which also build washing stations and process cherries. Exporters are competing for opportunities to sell Rwandan coffee to foreign buyers. Other entrepreneurs have

established cafés that feature local coffee. In other words, along a value chain, Rwandans are benefiting from the opportunity to produce and sell specialty coffee.

At the production level, thousands of Rwanda's smallholder farmers are benefiting from higher coffee prices for fully washed specialty coffee. NGOs such as PEARL and SPREAD have helped farmers establish cooperatives and have trained co-op members in quality control, processing, and marketing efforts. To date, more than 100 washing stations have been built around the country with the support of the government, donors, NGOs, and the private sector (table 11.1). As a result, Rwanda is producing more high-quality coffee and demand for the country's specialty coffee is increasing.

Incomes are rising for farmers and cooperatives

Perhaps the most important effect of the liberalization of Rwanda's coffee industry is that more of the farmers (approximately 500,000) who grow coffee have an opportunity to sell their beans for higher prices. The price that cooperatives and private sector coffee-washing stations are paying farmers for cherries rose from between 60 and 80 Rwandan francs in 2004 to between 160 and 180 Rwandan francs in 2008 (Rwanda Ministry of Agriculture and Animal Husbandry and Ministry of Trade and Industry 2008).[7] One

Table 11.1	Growth in the Specialty Coffee Sector							
	2002	**2003**	**2004**	**2005**	**2006**	**2007**	**2008**	**2009**
Number of washing stations	1	10	25	45	76	112	112	112
Tons of green specialty coffee exported	30	300	800	1,200	3,000	2,300	2,455	3,045
Number of specialty coffee buyers	2	8	16	25	30	30	—	—
Total value of specialty coffee exported ($1000s)	90	720	1,850	3,168	8,000	7,800	8,060	11,600

Source: USAID (2009).
Note: — Not available.

study finds that farmers who sell coffee cherries to washing stations increase their annual expenditures by 17 percent compared with farmers who sell lower-quality parchment coffee (Murekezi and Loveridge 2009). The same study indicates that since reform, coffee farmers have increased their food consumption and their overall household expenditures, leading to improved food security and to generally improved economic conditions for coffee farmers.

In a 2008 survey of 239 farmers and coffee-washing station workers, Tobias and Boudreaux (2011) asked farmers to identify benefits they received as a result of being a member of a coffee cooperative.[8] Farmers listed a number of direct financial benefits, such as increased prices received for their cherries, employment opportunities, and better and easier access to loans, particularly access to credit to purchase inputs such as fertilizer. Farmers also noted that their families are now better fed, that they are able to hire laborers, that they have help with marketing and sales, and that they receive some medicines for free. Some farmers also report that they benefit from access to coffee bicycles to transport coffee cherries. Less directly, farmers stated that they benefit from socializing with and learning from others. Some farmers felt their work was now easier (they no longer process cherries at home) and that they could spend time on things other than coffee production.

A 2006 analysis for the U.S. Agency for International Development (USAID) reports that "approximately 50,000 households have seen their incomes from coffee production double, and some 2,000 jobs have been created at coffee washing stations" (USAID/Chemonics 2006). An NGO involved in the USAID project (ACDI/VOCA n.d.) reports that "incomes (in the specialty coffee sector) have doubled or tripled, and business skills, labour conditions and community spirit have been enhanced." With additional income, farmers can repair their homes, buy clothes, pay school fees for their children, and get through the long

months between harvests more easily than before (personal interviews of the COOPAC cooperative 2006).

Once coffee cherries are washed, fermented, and dried, they can be sold to buyers for an even higher price. In 2004 the Maraba cooperative sold washed coffee for $3.26 a kilogram; in 2007 the cooperative was able to charge $4.08 for the same amount. The COOPAC cooperative was selling its cherries for $4.00 a kilogram in 2007, and the Rusenyi cooperative was selling in a range between $4.40 and $5.50 (Swanson and Bagaza 2008). On average, in 2007 coffee-washing stations sold their fully washed coffee for $3.60 a kilogram. In a notable achievement, importers paid a record high of $55 a kilogram (approximately $25 per pound) for the best Rwandan coffee in September 2007, a price comparable to the world's most expensive coffees (Rwanda Development Gateway 2007).

Cooperatives use the income they generate to pay individual farmers for cherries, to repay loans taken build washing stations (or for other equipment), to pay salaries for washing-station staff, and sometimes to provide other benefits to members—short-term microloans and improvements to local schools, for example.

Government revenue is increasing

The Rwandan government reports that coffee receipts increased by an average of 30 percent a year between 2002 and 2006 (figure 11.3). In February 2010 the head of Rwanda's Coffee Development Agency said that he expected 26,000 tons of coffee to be produced during the year (up from 16,000 tons in 2009) and that the value of coffee exports would increase significantly, to $69 million, from $38 million in 2009.[9]

Despite the increases in production and export value, the amount of fully washed coffee being produced in Rwanda is still below targets. It now accounts for 20 percent of the annual crop, compared with 1 percent in 2002. A greater concern is that washing stations and cooperatives need to

Figure 11.3 Average Farmer and Export Prices, 2003–08

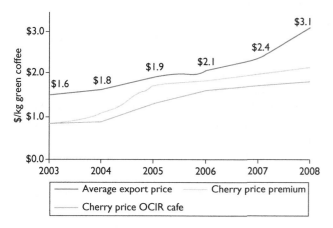

Source: Rwanda Ministry of Agriculture and Animal Husbandry and Ministry of Trade and Industry (2008).

do more improve technical capacities and operate profitably, creating incentives for more farmers to choose to sell cherries for washing rather than processing cherries themselves at home.

Identifying precisely how much coffee is being produced in Rwanda is difficult. Government figures from different sources do not necessarily coincide, and figures from the U.S. Department of Agriculture and the Food and Agriculture Organization (FAO) do not match figures produced by the Rwandan government. The government's trade statistics put the volume of coffee traded in 2008 at 18,185 tons, although a more recent news story puts that figure at 22,000 tons.[10] The news story indicates that output in 2009 was approximately 24,000 tons and that the Rwandan government projects that output would rise 13 percent in 2010, to 27,000 tons. Estimates for fully washed coffee are more solid: in 2002 Rwanda produced 48 tons of fully washed coffee, a figure that grew exponentially in by 2006, to 3,000 tons (Rwanda Ministry of Finance and Economic Planning 2007).

Rwanda's former Minister of Agriculture Anastase Murekezi has indicated that the specialty coffee industry's most successful trading partners to date, in terms of creating wealth for Rwandans, were American importers. American companies such as Starbucks and Green Mountain Coffee buy from Rwanda's producers, bringing much-needed income to smallholder farmers. Other less-well-known but highly discriminating American importers such as Intelligentsia, Thanksgiving, and Counter Culture Coffee also routinely purchase Rwandan coffee. Coffee buyers from Europe, China, and Japan also routinely visit Rwanda, bringing income to farmers and expertise that helps improve the local industry. The benefits from specialty coffee extend beyond the cooperative. Another observer notes that "[a]s income levels of the cooperative members have increased so has the flow of money in the community .... The positive feelings among community members are a reflection of increased incomes in the area (of the cooperatives)" (Goff 2006, 70).

While global growth in ordinary-grade coffee consumption remains modest, the consumption of high-quality specialty coffee (currently, 7 percent of the coffee volume in the international market) has been rising by 15 percent annually in recent years. Even with increased competition and somewhat lower prices, Rwanda's specialty coffees should continue to command a good price (Economist Intelligence Unit 2007).[11]

Increased entrepreneurship is leading to more jobs in the coffee sector

As of 2006, 4,000 jobs had been created at coffee-washing stations (USAID/Chemonics 2006). Though many of these are part-time jobs during the harvest season, others are full-time positions managing stations and cooperatives. Co-op and washing-station employees are learning valuable business skills: accounting, marketing, and negotiating. An estimated 100 Rwandans have learned to cup coffee.[12] At milling operations and at exporters, other Rwandans sort beans, operate milling equipment, and prepare beans for shipment. And as the new coffee culture grows in Rwanda, jobs are starting to be created in retail outlets such as the popular Bourbon Café in Kigali.

Although Rwanda has made good progress in the specialty coffee sector, stakeholders recognize that more must be done to consolidate these gains and to direct attention to the most pressing problems in the sector. To refocus attention, the Rwandan government issued a revised National Coffee Strategy (NCSR) in 2009. The NCSR created a modified strategy for the coffee sector, one that builds on lessons learned implementing the 2002 strategy. It sets a new, lower production target of 33,000 tons of coffee by 2012, 19,000 tons of which is to be fully washed. The government anticipates revenues of $115 million if this much coffee is produced (Rwanda Ministry of Agriculture and Animal Husbandry and Ministry of Trade and Industry 2008).

The new policy identifies five target projects: improving farming techniques, providing support to make washing stations more profitable, helping private exporters improve marketing and sales, conducting a census of all coffee-growing areas, and partnering to do toll roasting in China and the Middle East.[13] In an effort to add more value locally, the Rwanda Coffee Development Authority (RCDA) has partnered with the Hunter Foundation to build a factory to roast and package coffee locally. The hope is that this effort will produce more than 100 full-time jobs and another 2,000 indirect jobs.[14] While coffee production cannot, by itself, solve the many problems faced by the poor in Rwanda, changes in the industry are helping coffee farmers and other workers in the industry better cope with poverty, and these changes also seem to be generating positive social benefits.

INDIRECT AND SOCIAL BENEFITS OF LIBERALIZATION

The liberalization of Rwanda's coffee sector is distinguishable from other liberalization efforts, such as privatizations in Eastern Europe and land titling reforms in Kenya, that have tended to benefit elites. Because coffee sector liberalization in Rwanda has helped to raise income for the rural poor—rather than imposing costs on them—it may be less likely to promote conflict than have liberalizations in which costs are spread widely (such as when subsidies are removed) and benefits are narrowly concentrated (Collier et al. 2003).[15]

Coffee facilities are a locus of cooperation

Cooperatives and private washing stations may also serve as vehicles for increasing cooperation among members. Building on reports in the media of informal reconciliation at coffee cooperatives, Tobias and Boudreaux (2011) conducted an exploratory survey of 10 coffee-washing stations in 2008 to investigate possible social benefits associated with the liberalization of the sector.[16] A total of 239 completed surveys were obtained from a subsection of rural Rwandans associated with these stations—some were farmers with seasonal jobs at the washing stations and others were people who were at the stations to sell cherries. Statistical analysis of the surveys showed significant correlation between economic satisfaction or general perceptions of life satisfaction and more positive attitudes to reconciliation. This finding was particularly true the older a washing station was and the longer it had been a part of the local community.

The survey drew on insights from inter-group contact theory (Allport 1954). Extensive evidence indicates that positive interactions between antagonistic groups can reduce levels of prejudice and hostility. Therefore, positive contact is considered one of the most effective strategies for reducing intergroup conflict (Pettigrew 1998; Dovidio, Gaertner, and Kawakami 2003). When contact between groups in postconflict societies is intense and deep, meaning when it involves interactions at social events, helping others, or celebrating together, it can promote reconciliation and help prevent a renewal of violence (Gibson 2004; Straub 2006). If formerly antagonistic groups find ways to cooperate, they may develop a new shared identity that helps reduce prejudice and creates a sense that a more collaborative future is possible (Gaertner et al. 1990).

As noted, farmers come to coffee-washing stations either to sell beans or to do seasonal work. Seasonal employees, working side by side, help at drying tables. During the harvest season, farmers may bring cherries to a washing station several times a week. This means that farmers and seasonal workers are at the washing stations repeatedly from March or April through June or July. This organizational structure is relatively new in Rwanda (in 2000, there were only two coffee-washing stations in all of Rwanda, and as of 2009 there were more than 100), and farmers may well be experiencing a new type of contact.

Perceptions of economic satisfaction

The Tobias and Boudreaux survey explored the possible connection between perceptions of economic improvements in the lives of farmers and coffee-washing station workers and of improved interpersonal relations, comparing current levels of economic satisfaction with levels of satisfaction in the past. Economic satisfaction was measured on a four-item scale, with low scores indicating high levels of satisfaction. A high "economic satisfaction change" score indicated an improvement in economic satisfaction in recent years. Only 3 percent of participants indicated that they were very satisfied with their economic situation five years earlier, whereas 40 percent reported that they are very satisfied with their current economic situation. Forty-five percent of all participants reported a one-point improvement (on a four-item scale) in economic satisfaction in recent years, 22 percent reported a two-point increase, 10 percent reported a three-point increase in economic satisfaction, 15 percent experienced no change in economic satisfaction, and as noted, 3 percent of survey participants were more satisfied economically in the past. These respondents indicated a decrease of one or two points.

Life satisfaction ratings today and in the past were also measured. Eighty percent of participants reported a positive life satisfaction change; for 10 percent, life satisfaction remained unchanged compared with recent years. Only 7 percent indicated less life satisfaction today than in the past. These figures, like the figures for economic satisfaction, indicate that the overwhelming majority of the sample experienced positive life satisfaction gains in recent years.

To explore the impact of increased happiness among farmers and washing-station workers on other people, the survey explored possible links between perceptions of economic and life satisfaction and willingness to engage in contact with people of other ethnic groups. The findings indicate that people who are less willing to engage socially with members of another ethnic group have a greater degree of "ethnic distance" than do people who engage with others willingly and more frequently. Measures of ethnic distance were determined in the following manner: an "ethnic distance today" score was obtained by counting each of five possible interaction types from a classic social distance scale (high scores indicate low ethnic distance), and the "ethnic distance change" score was obtained by calculating the difference between a positive answer today versus a statement that in the past the participant would not have engaged in these interactions. A high numeric score for "ethnic distance change" was interpreted as a signal of less ethnic distance today than previously. In general, participants reported high degrees of reduction in ethnic distance as well as very frequent social and work-related contact.

Survey results show that meaningful contacts with members of another ethnic group are significantly correlated with low distrust and conditional forgiveness. Participants who expressed satisfaction with their economic and overall life situation had significantly correlated responses in terms of positive attitudes toward reconciliation. In particular, participants with greater economic security also reported low ethnic distance, low distrust toward the other group, and a tendency toward conditional forgiveness. Life satisfaction significantly correlated with economic security variables, and participants reporting greater satisfaction with life also expected a more positive, peaceful future in Rwanda.

Results of the survey also show that responses of participants at coffee-washing stations that had been in operation for longer periods of time are significantly correlated with a reduction in ethnic distance over time. It is reasonable to assume that positive social change in the coffee sector takes time, and the survey data support this reasoning. All of the washing stations in the study had been in operation for less than seven years, and most of them were created fewer than five years ago. If the observed pattern were to continue, however, the potential for positive social change associated with the creation of more than 100 washing stations since 2000 is substantial.

Taken together, the study's findings suggest that the enhanced entrepreneurial activities in this particular sector of Rwanda's economy not only produce positive economic change among individuals touched by this institutional change, but that they may also be triggering a chain of mediating effects linked to positive social change among people working at or with coffee-washing stations. The observed effects were not dependent on ethnicity or on the particular ethnic mix of participants in a given location. This finding suggests that forgiveness and increased levels of trust may be experienced broadly in this environment. Participants felt less ethnic distance than in the past and are now engaging in deeper social contact. It is possible that the collaboration initiated by the liberalization of the coffee sector, while difficult to quantify, is one of the most important benefits of the government's coffee sector policy reform.

CHALLENGES AND CONCERNS IN THE COFFEE SECTOR

Over the past decade, the Rwandan government has worked together with donor organizations, NGOs, the private sector (foreign and domestic), and local producers in a sustained and concerted manner to help this important sector of the economy become more competitive and, in turn, grow and expand. Political champions for these efforts existed at the highest levels of government. Donors not only supported financing and credit programs, they also facilitated programs and projects that brought individuals with a variety of technical expertise to Rwanda to share experiences and knowledge in areas of agronomy, the development of market links, coffee production, and cupping. Coffee cooperatives received support to improve their production efforts and to become competitive producers. Other donor projects supported the entry of Rwandan entrepreneurs into the market.

These joint efforts required commitments of time, resources, and talent to address weaknesses in this supply chain. This iterative process lasted for years. The manner in which the Rwandan government was able to create an effective alliance of partners to transform Rwanda's coffee sector, through these iterative efforts, from a low-volume, low-quality market to a high-quality market provides a useful example of effective policy leadership.

Although the specialty coffee industry is having positive effects in Rwanda, the smallholder farmers and the entrepreneurs who work in the sector face several challenges.

One of these is implementing strategies that create price incentives for farmers to improve both quality and washing-station management, thereby increasing production effectiveness. At the cooperative level, management needs to be improved so that costs are better controlled and members continue to benefit. The government also needs to avoid dislocations to poor Rwandans – particularly women – that may result from the 2005 Land Law. Finally, transportation costs remain high in Rwanda.

Production capacity and pricing problems

One continuing concern in the coffee sector is that farmers are not producing a sufficiently large volume of high-quality coffee to meet continuing demand. A number of factors may be contributing to this problem. First, prices paid to farmers do not provide sufficient incentives for them to focus on quality. Farmers continue to produce a much greater amount of ordinary-quality coffee than fully washed coffee. Second, farmers may lack knowledge of how best to manage their trees. Third, despite the growing number of washing stations, many farmers still have limited access to them and so process cherries at home.

As noted above, OCIR sets weekly minimum prices for the purchase of cherries at washing stations. In some areas, washing stations pay farmers amounts that fluctuate modestly to reflect changes in supply. Washing stations do not, however, seem to pay farmers a premium based on the quality of cherries they deliver. Farmers thus concentrate on quantity produced versus quality.

If there is continuing unmet demand for Rwanda's fully washed specialty coffee, washing-station operators should respond by demanding, and paying a premium for, higher-quality cherries. One possibility why this is not happening may be that washing-station personnel are unable to identify higher-quality beans. If washing stations cannot distinguish a low-quality from a high-quality cherry, they will choose to pay a low rather than a high price. Additionally, high labor and input costs also make it difficult for washing stations to operate at full capacity and as a result they generate limited income. Therefore, washing stations may lack sufficient working capital to pay farmers for higher-quality beans. Competition among washing stations could resolve this problem. At the moment, however, it is unclear how best to shift this pattern if there are no other legal impediments to paying higher prices for higher-quality beans. Although the problem of pricing is identified in the National Coffee Strategy Rwanda report, the causes of resistance are not identified, suggesting that additional research is needed to clarify this important issue.

The National Coffee Strategy Rwanda report also notes that too few farmers are familiar with and able to implement good farming practices. Farmers need good-quality inputs, such as seedlings and fertilizers, to increase their crop yields and quality, but they also need technical knowledge about how to handle seedlings, how to deal with pests and disease, and how to apply fertilizers. Although RCDA/OCIR-Café supplies farmers with fertilizer and employs agronomists, there are only a small number of these professionals, and they have a difficult time reaching all the farmers who need assistance.[17] The National Coffee Strategy Rwanda also cites a lack of coordination among agencies that further limits the effectiveness of these extension services (Ministry of Agriculture and Animal Husbandry and Ministry of Trade and Industry 2008).

Management and profitability in Rwanda's coffee-washing stations is a growing concern. Stations are operating at partial capacity, producing smaller amounts of fully washed coffee than anticipated. The government reports that operating costs associated with the stations (labor, transportation, and electricity and water) are high. In addition to these challenges, washing-station personnel often lack technical skills, particularly in finance, accounting, and management. These capacity problems can translate into difficulties securing financing and working with lenders, which in turn can translate into difficulties paying farmers in a timely fashion. The government recognizes the potential benefits of increasing coffee yields at washing stations, particularly for fully washed coffee. Farmers who sell coffee as a cash crop are projected to see their incomes grow 4 percent a year more than that of other farmers (Ministry of Agriculture and Animal Husbandry and Ministry of Trade and Industry 2008).

Concerns with cooperative management

Smallholder farmers who voluntarily join cooperatives face the difficult task of creating a culture of entrepreneurship within the cooperatives so that they become more "business minded." A key problem identified by local NGO SPREAD is the need to attract and retain more professional managers in cooperatives and, at the same time, to reduce the influence of volunteer boards of directors. An assessment of a group of Rwandan cooperatives states that "[a] professional, entrepreneurial [g]eneral [m]anager is the most important individual to a cooperative's ultimate success" (Swanson and Bagaza 2008).

However, the report's authors find that no cooperatives in the group under investigation had such a manager. The reason seems to be that the boards of directors are reluctant to pay high enough salaries to attract a professional manager. Further, boards often prefer to have to have a local representative, rather than an "outsider," fill the general manager role. Local representatives, however, are less likely to have the skill set needed to manage the cooperative effectively. Cooperatives are capable of producing very high-quality coffee, but they are experiencing real difficulties creating effective management structures.

Rwanda's coffee producers, with support from donors, NGOs, and the government, have done an impressive job of generating interest in their products. Rwandan coffee is regularly available at retailers such as Starbucks and Whole Foods across the United States and Marks & Spencer in the United Kingdom. But this good progress may stall if problems related to marketing and processing are not adequately addressed. Buyers have expressed concerns that contract terms for quality, quantity, and timely delivery are not being met (Rwanda Ministry of Agriculture and Animal Husbandry and Ministry of Trade and Industry 2008). Some buyers have reported long delays receiving shipments, and many have complained that the shipped product did not match samples. These kinds of concerns, if not addressed, will lead to loss of business for Rwanda.

A related problem is that boards of directors in Rwanda often interfere inappropriately in the daily management of the cooperative. The assessment notes that "[board members], particularly [p]residents, do not want to relinquish their authority to a strong [g]eneral [m]anager" (Rwanda Ministry of Agriculture and Animal Husbandry and Ministry of Trade and Industry 2008, 13). While it is essential that boards take seriously their fiduciary duties to create general policies and oversee management activities, the assessment recommends that they give managers increased decision-making authority and discretion.

Managers of cooperatives and boards of directors need to communicate more effectively with members so that members understand the ownership structure of the cooperative as well as their rights within the structure. To date, this has not been done effectively. Members report that they are unclear who "owns" the cooperative (Rwanda Ministry of Agriculture and Animal Husbandry and Ministry of Trade and Industry 2008). In addition, cooperatives need to develop and communicate effective business plans and to improve financial record keeping and documentation. There is a clear need for increased capacity in these areas. When members lack clear information about the financial state of the cooperative, and about likely prices for cherries and benefits of membership, the possibility of corruption and conflict over resources rises. These are especially important issues to resolve because cooperatives face increasing competition from other coffee entrepreneurs.

Cooperatives have been an important asset for Rwanda's smallholder farmers, allowing them to earn more money from coffee, develop additional skills, and work cooperatively with others in ways that may promote reconciliation. But they must address serious shortcomings in management practices and capabilities if they hope to continue playing this role in the future. Because cooperatives seem to provide a space for interaction and even informal reconciliation, further support efforts to help accomplish the goal of creating transparent and accountable management may well be justified.

Concerns with Rwanda's land law

A separate challenge in Rwanda involves use and control of land. Land is an extremely scarce and highly contested resource. More than three-fifths of families working as farmers cultivate less than 0.7 hectares, and more than a quarter cultivate less than 0.25 hectares (Rwanda Ministry of Finance and Economic Planning 2007). According to one study, "land was a factor behind social tensions before every major open conflict. Even today, more than 80 percent of all disputes in Rwanda are related to land" (Food and Agriculture Organization and Rwanda Ministry of Lands, Environment Forestry, Water and Mines 2006, 7; see also Van Hoyweghen 1999). For much of its history, Rwanda's rulers have owned most of the country's land. With control of land in the hands of government, formal land markets did not develop. Rather, transfers often took place informally, and confusion and insecurity were common. Local officials had great discretion over land allocation and favored politically powerful individuals over marginalized people who may have held traditional land use rights.[18]

In 2003 the Rwandan parliament approved a land reform decree that provides for individualized rights to property. This policy was followed, in 2005, by passage of the Organic Land Law. The law is implemented by a series of decrees, many of which are just now going into effect. The Land Law abolishes all customary forms of tenure, and in their place, establishes government-issued titles for 99-year leases. Rural land will be registered locally, and urban, commercial property will be registered in a national cadastre in Kigali. The government maintains a role in the resettling of people and in devising land use and land planning policy.

The government "sees increased security of tenure or rights of address to land, and more effective land management, as important factors for the improvement of the agricultural sector and the economy as a whole, helping to create the resources needed to reduce poverty and to consolidate peace and social cohesion" (Pottier 2005, 511). Although the government says that it wants to increase tenure security, the new law is likely to create a host of problems.

The government hopes the land law will promote consolidation of land parcels into larger units. By allowing sales of property and increasing freedom within the land market, small parcels could be sold to commercial farmers who will consolidate the land and create viable agribusinesses. However, one observer notes:

> Land fragmentation in Rwanda serv[es] as a coping mechanism in smallholder agriculture, the typical Rwandan household farms an average of five plots. Some are in the valleys, others are upland and some near the household. In some parts of southern Rwanda, a household may have up to 14 crops growing in different fragments at different seasons.... the costs of consolidation in Rwanda may not exceed the benefits of using land fragmented over the years in adopting to land scarcity (Musahara 2006, 11).

While a more open land market is desirable, the law (Organic Law No. 08.2005) contains provisions that allow the government to interfere in the market. For example, it allows the government to bar people who own less than one hectare from registering their property. More troubling is the provision that "subsistence farmers can have their land confiscated should they fail to exploit it diligently and efficiently" (Pottier 2005, 521, [Articles 62–65]). Though the government is supposed to provide compensation for such confiscations, it has not established clear standards for such payments.

The new law may pose a special problem for women smallholders and their children. Under the law, the government is supposed to register all parcels of land in the country. Only legally married women and their children, however, (not women married under customary norms and their children, or poor women who do not formally marry because of the associated costs) can register and inherit land. Further, there is uncertainty in the law regarding inheritance—specifically, whether women inherit through the inheritance law or through the land law.[19] Also of concern is the fact that local custom continues to bar women from exercising their legal rights under the land law.

Security and clarity of tenure rights, whether customary or leasehold, are essential both to avoid future conflicts and to encourage increased investment in agriculture. However, the land law raises serious concerns, especially for women and for uneducated farmers who might be dispossessed of their land. Surely, these risks are undesirable in a nation with such high levels of poverty and such strong dependence on agriculture as a livelihood.

Concerns with transportation infrastructure

Finally, as a landlocked country with limited paved roads in rural areas where most coffee is grown, transport costs in Rwanda are high. Diop, Brenton, and Asarkaya (2005) argue that Rwanda's smallholder subsistence farmers are disconnected from markets as a result of "extremely high" transport costs. The authors estimate that transport costs from farm gates to the export port of Mombasa were 80 percent of the producer price.[20] Transport within Rwanda itself was estimated at 40 percent of the producer price. If transport costs were reduced, through the development of better rural infrastructure and, in particular, more effective rural transport routes, access to markets would improve and poverty levels would likely be reduced. The authors find that a 50 percent reduction in the transport costs in rural areas would lead to a 20 percent increase in producer prices for coffee, which in turn would reduce poverty levels among coffee farmers by more than 6 percent. Given the continued emphasis on coffee production as a strategy to alleviate rural poverty, improving the rural transport system will be an important way to connect farmers to markets and to increase their household income.

CONCLUSION

Despite good economic growth and real benefits of liberalizing the coffee sector, more remains to be done to move Rwanda toward its Vision 2020 goal of becoming a stable, middle-income country. Most Rwandans remain very poor and the rural areas of the country provide few off-farm employment opportunities. Creating more employment opportunities for millions of Rwandan smallholder farmers remains a pressing challenge.

Rwanda's specialty coffee industry is helping to address some of these concerns. As a result of improvements in the sector, smallholder coffee farmers now keep more of the value of the product they grow. In turn, rising incomes for tens of thousands of farmers make them better able to feed themselves and their families, to send their children to school, to buy insurance, and to repair or improve their homes. By freeing the coffee sector from the heavy-handed involvement of the government, the Rwandan government has shifted incentives in the coffee sector and created greater scope for citizens to pursue entrepreneurial opportunities.

Though additional research needs to be done, evidence suggests that joint efforts in commercial activities related to the specialty coffee sector are providing an alternative path to postwar reconciliation in Rwanda. Initial exploratory survey data provide some supports for these claims (Tobias and Boudreaux, 2011). By working together in cooperatives and at washing stations, Rwandans are experiencing both social and economic benefits from liberalization. They feel greater economic satisfaction, which is correlated to lower levels of distrust, higher levels of forgiveness, and reduced ethnic distance.

Whether this kind of reconciliation is effective in the medium to long term in Rwanda remains to be seen. The positive experience of workers in the coffee sector, however, strongly suggests that in postconflict environments, governments should follow Rwanda's lead and promote broad-based trade liberalization that encourages commercial interaction between rival groups.

Although real concerns surround the economic viability of some coffee-washing stations and cooperatives, liberalization of the Rwandan coffee sector has created a wider and deeper space for positive entrepreneurship: a space being filled by thousands of Rwandans, from smallholder farmers to local exporters. At the same time, adding value to the coffee supply chain is producing both direct economic benefits and important indirect social benefits for individuals and communities in Rwanda.

NOTES

1. "Coffee 'Cup of Excellence' Slated for Next Year," *New Times*, September 23, 2009.

2. Traditionally, Rwandan farmers removed the fruit of their coffee cherries using either a hand-pulper or rocks. Beans would then be dried and fermented in buckets, for varying lengths of time, in water of varying quality. As a result, coffee was of lower, industrial quality. This home-processed coffee still makes up the majority of coffee being sold from Rwanda.

3. Prices were set by OCIR until 1994 and remained constant for the entire harvest season; price differences based on quality were not permitted. See Mutandwa et al. 2009 and deLucco 2006 for more information.

4. Under the Habyarimana regime, the powerful OCIR-Café agency was run by relatives of the dictator's wife, members of the *clan de Madame* (Verwimp 2003).

5. Mutandwa et al. also note that "due to the low level of production, the milling factories operate under capacity and exporters tend to lower the reference price in order to cover their relatively high milling costs" (p. 212).

6. A conflicting statement, however, can be found in the Economic Development and Poverty Reduction Strategy 2008–2012, which states that the "the proportion of fully-washed coffee production will increase from 10 percent to 100 percent ..." (p. 38).

7. See also Swanson and Bagaza (2008).

8. Survey results are available from the author of this paper.

9. Reuters, "Rwanda Sees 20010 Coffee Crop Rising 63 Pct," February 11, 2010.

10. "Coffee Output May Climb 13 Percent in 2010," *New Times*, January 8, 2010.

11. The report notes, "Stagnation in many of the traditional coffee-drinking markets of North America and Western Europe will restrict growth in demand, although demand for high-quality specialty coffees, including Rwanda's finest fully-washed Arabica, will remain more buoyant" (p. 10).

12. To "cup" coffee refers to a tasting technique used to create a flavor profile for coffee. Cuppers evaluate coffee based on fragrance, aroma, and taste, a process that helps identify defects in coffee. Fewer than half of the 100 cuppers, however, are trained and licensed to international standards. "Twenty-One Coffee Cuppers Trained on Quality," *New Times*, August 29, 2009.

13. Toll roasting involves a contractual arrangement whereby an experienced coffee roaster accepts green coffee from a client and roasts it to the client's specifications.

14. "Two Million Invested in Coffee Value Addition," *New Times*, August 7, 2009.

15. Collier et al. (2003, 53) argue that "the key root cause of conflict is the failure of economic development. Countries with low, stagnant, and unequally distributed per capita incomes that have remained dependent on primary commodities for their exports face dangerously high risks of prolonged conflict."

16. Surveys were conducted at five cooperatives and five privately owned coffee-washing stations. Surveys were administered in Kinyarwanda by students from the National University of Rwanda over a two-week period. Surveys were previously field tested in February 2008.

17. Farmers receive fertilizer from RCDA, and the agency, in turn, imposes a fertilizer fee on exporters. Exporters then choose either to pass these costs along to cooperatives and washing stations in the form of lower prices paid per kilo or they absorb the costs themselves.

18. Sales were restricted according the size of the buyer and seller's total land holdings; see Musahara (2006).

19. Dyer (2007) notes that although Rwanda's 1999 Inheritance Law gives women equal rights to men this has "yet to make any difference in practice."

20. Note these prices should now be lower as a result of Rwanda's accession to the East African Community.

REFERENCES

ACDI/VOCA. n.d. "Specialty Coffee: Increased Quality & Profits for Smallholders." http://www.acdivoca.org/852571DC00681414/Lookup/coffeebroweblayout/$file/coffeebroweblayout.pdf.

Allport, Gordon W. 1954. *The Nature of Prejudice.* Oxford, UK: Addison Wesley.

Bates, Robert H. 1981. *Markets and States in Tropical Africa: The Political Basis of Agricultural Policies.* Berkeley, CA: University of California Press.

Berlage, Lode, Bart Capéau, and Philip Verwimp. 2004. "Dictatorship in a Single Export Crop Economy." Households in Conflict Network. http://www.hicn.org/papers/dicta.pdf.

Coffeeresearch.org. "Coffee Cupping." http://www.coffeeresearch.org/coffee/cupping.htm.

Collier, Paul, V. L. Elliott, Håvard Hegre, Anke Hoeffler, Marta Reynal-Querol, and Nicholas Sambanis. 2003. *Breaking the Conflict Trap: Civil War and Development Policy.* Oxford, UK: Oxford University Press and World Bank.

deLucco, Paul. 2006. "Raising the Bar: Producing Quality Coffee in Rwanda." *World Report Spring 2006: Specialty Coffee; Improved Market Linkages & Increased Profits.* http://www.acdivoca.org/852571DC00681414/Lookup/WRSpring06-Page13-14-RaisingtheBar/$file/WRSpring06-Page13-14-RaisingtheBar.pdf.

DFID (UK Department for International Development). 2008. "Good Taxes Reduce Poverty in Rwanda." January 10.

Diop, Ndiame, Paul Brenton, and Yakup Asarkaya. 2005. "Trade Costs, Export Development, and Poverty in Rwanda." Policy Research Working Paper 3784, World Bank, Washington, DC.

Dorsey, Learthen. 1983. *The Rwandan Colonial Economy: 1916–1941.* Unpublished PhD dissertation, Michigan State University.

Dovidio, John F., Samuel L. Gaertner, and K. Kawakami. 2003. "Intergroup Contact: The Past, the Present and the Future." *Group Processes and Intergroup Relations* 6: 5–21.

Dyer, Rodney. 2007. "Land Issues in Rwanda: Drawn from DFID Technical Assistance for Land Tenure Reform, 2005–2008." http://www.oxfam.org.uk/search?q=dyer&x=17&y=19.

Economist Intelligence Unit. 2007. "Country Report: Rwanda" (February).

FAO (Food and Agriculture Organization) and Rwanda Ministry of Lands, Environment Forestry, Water and Mines. 2006. "A Case Study on the Implications of the Ongoing Land Reform on Sustainable Rural Development and Poverty Reduction in Rwanda and the Outcome Report of the Thematic Dialogue Held on the 20th January 2006." Presented at the International Conference on Agrarian Reform and Rural Development (ICAARD), Porto Alegre, Brazil, March 7–10. http://www.icarrd.org/en/icard_doc_down/case_Rwanda.pdf.

Gaertner, Samuel L., Jeffrey A. Mann, John L. Dovidio, Audrey J. Murrell, and Marina Pomare. 1990. "How Does Cooperation Reduce Intergroup Bias?" *Journal of Personality and Social Psychology* 59 (4): 692–704.

Gibson, James L. 2004. "Does Truth Lead to Reconciliation? Testing the Causal Assumptions of the South African Truth and Reconciliation Commission." *American Journal of Political Science* 48 (2): 201–17.

Goff, Samuel Neal. 2006. "A Case Study of the Management of Cooperatives in Rwanda." Unpublished master's thesis, Texas A&M University.

IFAD (International Fund for Agricultural Development). 2006. "Enabling the Rural Poor to Overcome Poverty in Rwanda." http://www.ifad.org/operations/projects/regions/Pf/factsheets/rwanda_e.pdf.

Index Mundi. 2010. "Rwanda GDP – Real Growth Rate." http://www.indexmundi.com/rwanda/gdp_real_growth_rate.html.

Murekezi, Abdoul, and Scott Loveridge. 2009. "Have Coffee Reforms and Coffee Supply Chains Affected Farmers' Income? The Case of Coffee Growers in Rwanda." Paper presented at the Agricultural & Applied Economics Association's 2009 Joint Annual Meeting, Milwaukee, WI, July 26–28.

Musahara, Herman. 2006. "Improving Tenure Security for the Rural Poor: Rwanda—Country Case Study." FAO/LEP Working Paper 7.

Mutandwa, Edward, Nathan Taremwa Kanuma, Emmanuel Rusatira, Theopile Kwiringirimana, Patrice Mugenzi, Ignatius Govere, and Richard Foti. 2009. "Analysis of Coffee Export Marketing in Rwanda: Application of the Boston Consulting Group Matrix." *African Journal of Business Management* 3 (5): 210–19.

Personal interview with Anastase Murekezi, Rwandan Minister of Agriculture. 2006 (March). Kigali, Rwanda.

Personal interviews with members of the COOPAC cooperative. 2006 (March). Gisenyi, Rwanda.

Pettigrew, T. F. 1998. "Intergroup Contact: Theory, Research and New Perspectives." *Annual Review of Psychology* 49: 65–85.

Pottier, Johan. 2005. "Land Reform for Peace? Rwanda's 2005 Land Law in Context." *Journal of Agrarian Change* 6(4): 509–37.

Prunier, Gerard. 1995. *The Rwanda Crisis: History of a Genocide.* New York: Columbia University Press.

Republic of Rwanda. Organic Law No. 08.2005: Determining the Use and Management of Land in Rwanda, Article 20. Kigali. July 14.

Rwanda Development Gateway. 2007. "Coffee Sells at Record Prices." http://www.rwandagateway.org/article.php3?id_article=6848.

Rwanda Ministry of Agriculture and Animal Husbandry and Ministry of Trade and Industry. 2008. "National Coffee Strategy Rwanda 2009–2012."http://amis.minagri.gov.rw/sites/default/files/user/National_Coffee_Strategy_Rwanda_2009-2012.pdf.

Rwanda Ministry of Finance and Economic Planning. 2000. "Rwanda Vision 2020." http://www.gesci.org/assets/files/Rwanda_Vision_2020.pdf.

———. 2007. "Economic Development and Poverty Reduction Strategy 2008-2012." http://planipolis.iiep.unesco.org/upload/Rwanda/Rwanda_EDPRS_2008-2012.pdf.

SPREAD. 2007. Annual Report. http://www.spread.org.rw/spread_project.php.

Straub, Edwin. 2006. "Reconciliation after Genocide, Mass Killing or Intractable Conflict: Understanding the Roots of Violence, Psychological Recovery and Steps toward a General Theory." *Political Psychology* 27 (6): 867–95.

Swanson, Richard, and Tom Bagaza. 2008. "SPREAD-Growers First Coffee Cooperative Assessment and 2008 Cooperative Development Work Plan." Report prepared for the Texas A&M University System, Borlaug Institute of International Agriculture and Growers First.

Tobias, Jutta, and Karol Boudreaux. 2011. "Entrepreneurship and Conflict Reducation in the Post-genocide Rwanda Coffee Industry." *Journal of Small Business and Entrepreneurship* 24 (2): 217–242.

USAID (U.S. Agency for International Development). 2009. "Rwanda." http://www.usaid.gov/rw/our_work/programs/docs/factsheets/coffee.pdf.

USAID/Chemonics. 2006. "Assessing USAID's Investments in Rwanda's Coffee Sector: Best Practices and Lesson Learned to Consolidate Results and Expand Impact."

Van Hoyweghen, Saskia. 1999. "The Urgency of Land and Agrarian Reform in Rwanda." *African Affairs* 98: 353–72.

Verwimp, Philip. 2003. "The Political Economy of Coffee." *European Journal of Political Economy* 19 (2): 161–81.

World Bank. 2010. "Country Data: Rwanda." http://data.worldbank.org/country/rwanda.

Cocoa in Ghana: Shaping the Success of an Economy

Shashi Kolavalli and Marcella Vigneri

No other country comes to mind more than Ghana when one speaks of cocoa. Likewise, one cannot think of Ghana without thinking of its cocoa sector, which offers livelihoods for over 700,000 farmers in the southern tropical belt of the country. Long one of Ghana's main exports, cocoa has been central to the country's debates on development, reforms, and poverty alleviation strategies since independence in 1957. The cocoa sector in Ghana has not been an unmitigated success, however. After emerging as one of the world's leading producers of cocoa, Ghana experienced a major decline in production in the 1960s and 1970s, and the sector nearly collapsed in the early 1980s. Production steadily recovered in the mid-1980s after the introduction of economywide reforms, and the 1990s marked the beginning of a revival, with production nearly doubling between 2001 and 2003. These ups and downs offer interesting lessons.

Various administrations in Ghana, including the colonial one, have used cocoa as a source of public revenue, and in so doing the Ghanaian experience offers a recurrent example of a policy practice followed by many other African countries: taxing the country's major export sector to finance public expenditure (Herbst 1993). Revenue extraction by the state has had varying effects on production depending on global prices, marketing costs, explicit taxes on the sector, and macroeconomic conditions such as inflation and overvaluation of exchange rates and inelasticity of cocoa supplies. Regardless of the level of extraction, the need for sound macroeconomic management, of inflation and exchange rates in particular, becomes evident for continuing to offer incentives for production. The other is the need for Ghana's cocoa pricing policy to arrive at a marketing arrangement that does not kill the goose that lays the golden eggs. Ghana appears to have achieved such as arrangement without fully liberalizing the sector as other producers in West Africa have.

OBSERVABLE ACHIEVEMENTS IN THE COCOA SECTOR

Since the introduction of cocoa in Ghana in the late 19th century, the crop has undergone a series of major expansions and contractions. Ruf and Siswoputranto (1995) suggest that cycles are intrinsic to cocoa production because cocoa is influenced by environmental factors such as availability of forest land; ecological factors such as deforestation, outbreaks of disease, and geographic shifts in production; and economic and social factors such as migration.

Shashi Kolavalli is senior research fellow and leader, Ghana Strategy Support Program, International Food Policy Research Institute. Marcella Vigneri is a visiting scholar, Department of Economics, University of Oxford.

Emergence as a leading producer

Four distinct phases can be identified in regard to cocoa production in Ghana: introduction and exponential growth (1888–1937); stagnation followed by a brief but rapid growth following the country's independence (1938–64); near collapse (1965–82); and recovery and expansion, starting with the introduction of the Economic Recovery Program (ERP) (1983 to present). Figure 12.1 shows long-term trends in levels of production.

EXPONENTIAL GROWTH (1888–1937). Cocoa was introduced in the southern region of the Gold Coast in the mid-19th century by commercial farmers from the Eastern region districts of Akuapem and Krobo, who had moved west toward the adjacent district of Akyem to purchase mostly unoccupied forest land from the local chiefs for cocoa cultivation (Hill 1963).

The conditions that encouraged these farmers to migrate and buy land for cocoa are well documented: a fall in the world price of palm oil after 1885, which pushed farmers to search for alternative export crops; a boom in rubber exports in 1890, which provided the capital for the purchase of new land; increasing population pressure in the Akuapem area, which encouraged commercial farmers to go further afield in search of alternative export agriculture opportunities; and the establishment of European produce-buying companies on the coast of West Africa that were prepared to trade the new crop (Hill 1963; Amanor 2010; and Gunnarsson 1978).

Three social classes: land-owning farmers, peasants, and laborers emerged among cocoa producers as a second wave of migrants from Akyem moved to the region. Without sufficient money with which to buy land, these migrants sharecropped with earlier settlers under a system called *abusa*, in which laborers were paid one-third of the sales price of the harvested cocoa. Simultaneously, there was a large influx of migrants from relatively distant Upper Volta (now Burkina Faso), Niger, and Mali, who were attracted by the generous remuneration that cocoa production offered in southern Ghana.

The growing population of cocoa farmers reinvested its profits in cocoa production in the western end of Ghana's Forest Zone, rapidly shifting the production frontier into the Ashanti and Brong Ahafo regions, and consolidating Ghana as the leading world producer between 1910 and 1914. Facilitated by the rapid expansion of the road and rail network which began in 1920 and the organization of cocoa marketing by Ghanaian middlemen, cocoa earnings accounted for 84 percent of the country's total exports by 1927. By the mid-1930s, production reached 300,000 tons.

STAGNATION AND GROWTH POSTINDEPENDENCE (1938–EARLY 1964). The interwar period marked a slowdown in cocoa

Figure 12.1   Ghana's Cocoa Production, 1900–2008

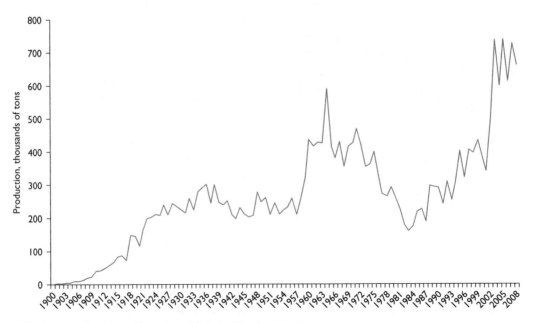

Source: Gill & Duffus Group, various issues; Ghana Cocoa Marketing Board, various issues.

CHAPTER 12: COCOA IN GHANA: SHAPING THE SUCCESS OF AN ECONOMY

production, caused by decreasing demand and growing difficulties in transport (Gunnarsson 1978). Outbreaks of pests and diseases (swollen shoot virus in particular) reduced production in the Eastern region in the early 1940s, pushing cocoa cultivation further into the western Brong Ahafo frontier (Amanor 2010). Production picked up again during the second half of the 1940s but was now concentrated in the Western region. In 1947, the colonial government established the Cocoa Marketing Board (CMB) and gave it a monopoly over the purchase of beans. Until 1951 the bulk of profit made by the CMB went into its reserves, which were then used for public investment (Brooks, Croppenstedt, and Aggrey-Fynn 2007). In 1961 a cooperative society was given the monopoly right to purchase cocoa replacing the network of private agents, brokers, traders, and middlemen who until then had controlled internal marketing.

As Beckam (1976) noted, the Convention People's Party (CPP), founded by Kwame Nkrumah, benefited from extremely favorable postwar market conditions and accumulated cocoa income on a massive scale: following the sharp increase in market prices in the 1950s, farmers were paid two to three times more than they received before the war, and between 1947 and 1965 the government collected almost one-third of the total value of cocoa export as export duties. In 1950/51 the government increased export duties and began to take a much larger share of cocoa revenue by means of a graduated ad valorem tax that increased with the increase of the average selling price per ton of cocoa. To extend its influence to the rural sector, in 1953 the Nkrumah regime also created the United Ghana Farmers' Council (UGFCC), which was mainly concentrated in the cocoa-growing regions despite its remit to cover the interest of farmers all over the country. The UGFCC was made the monopoly buyer of cocoa to create a platform for organizing the farmers behind the government and its administration.

Following the second elections in 1954, the cocoa export tax was further increased while the producer price remained at the same level for four years. This generated unrest and political agitation among cocoa farmers, ultimately forcing the government to increase the producer prices and to stabilize them during 1956–57 despite declining world cocoa prices. As a result, the share of government revenue in cocoa sales dropped from 60 percent to 13 percent between 1954/55 and 1956/57. After its third political victory of 1957, the government increased its share of cocoa revenues by reducing producer prices to the 1954 levels. It also obtained a "voluntary contribution," announced by the UGFCC on behalf of cocoa farmers, to share the burden of

the Second Development Plan at a time when the government was also receiving soft loans from the CMB. These events made it obvious that by then the CMB had been transformed into an instrument of public finance. The capturing of windfall profits from high cocoa prices had important fiscal implications. Government expenditures grew dramatically over the 1950s: in real terms total consolidated public expenditures increased almost sixfold during this period. The share of government expenditure in GDP grew from 7 percent to 18 percent over the decade, and the share of extraordinary and development expenditure grew from 27 percent to 36 percent. In 1961, a cooperative society was given the monopoly right to purchase cocoa. From 1957 to 1964 exports grew steadily, and production reached an unprecedented level of 430,000 tons despite the significant decline in world prices between 1960 and 1962.

In the early 1960s, when world prices plummeted, farmers were required to save 10 percent of their earnings in National Development Bonds, redeemable after 10 years. In 1963 this scheme was replaced by a farmers' income tax charged at a flat rate equal to previous saving deductions. The government started to rely heavily on the CMB's reserves, and the producer price was reduced from 224 to 187 new cedi per ton between 1961 and 1964. With foreign exchange reserves declining and the budget deficit rising sharply, the government introduced a number of strong restrictive measures, an increase in taxes, foreign exchange controls, and comprehensive import licensing. The austerity of these measures lost Nkrumah much of his political consent, especially from cocoa farmers who had been aggravated by declining producer prices and by the conversion of the compulsory saving scheme into an explicit export tax.

In the second half of 1964 the world cocoa price collapsed with a bumper crop in West Africa—Ghana alone reaching an unprecedented production record of 538,000 tons. After the purchasing and marketing costs of the CMB and UGFCC were covered, virtually nothing was left for the government, and the CMB's liquidity resources were nearly exhausted. To meet its expenses, the government started printing money, which ignited a 35 percent rise in inflation between October 1964 and July 1965. In the face of such pressure, cocoa producer prices were reduced to their lowest levels in years. The introduction of such highly restrictive measures represented a turning point in the fortunes of the Nkrumah government, which was overthrown in February 1966 and replaced by the National Liberation Council (NLC).

THE DOWNTURN (1964–82). The collapse of world cocoa prices in 1965 triggered another downturn (Stryker 1990).

Real producer prices dropped consistently through the 1960s because of inflation fueled by the government's printing of money to compensate for loss of revenue from cocoa and the introduction of an exchange rate policy that led to the heavy overvaluation of the *cedi*, the local currency. By 1983, market exchange rates were nearly 44 times the official rate. Between 1970s and early 1980s, it is estimated that as much as 20 percent of Ghana's cocoa harvest was smuggled into Côte d'Ivoire (Bulír 2002). Meanwhile, an aging tree stock and the continued spread of disease made investment in cocoa unattractive. Farmers in old cocoa production areas, who found that sales prices barely covered their costs, increasingly turned from cocoa to food production (Amanor 2005). Ghana's cocoa production dipped to a low of 159,000 tons in 1982/83, a mere 17 percent of the total world volume, down from the 36 percent in 1964/65.

The National Liberation Council dissolved the UGFCC and established the Producing Buying Company as a subsidiary of the CMB. Producer prices were raised and farmers were paid a bonus for top grade cocoa beans to upgrade the quality of cocoa being exported. Shortly before the Busia government came to power the cedi was devalued by 43 percent and cocoa prices were raised by 30 percent. Cocoa production stagnated in the face of unchanged real producer prices that remained at their 1950s levels. The Busia administration took advantage of windfall profits from high cocoa prices in 1970 to enable a rapid expansion of public expenditure.

In 1971 the Busia regime was replaced by the Acheampong-led National Redemption Council. Because of high world cocoa prices, this administration was initially able to offer higher prices to farmers without cutting public revenues, creating positive incentives to production. But a progressively worsening balance of payments situation fueled inflation and undermined subsequent increases in real wages, producer prices, and other real incentives.

With the fall in world cocoa prices in the mid 70's, the general macroeconomic picture began to worsen: the government budget deficit rose to 127 percent of total government revenue and inflation accelerated to 116 percent. The strong overvaluation of the cedi implied that little was left of export revenues to divide between the government and the farmers. Cocoa revenue went from 46 percent in 1974 to 23 percent in 1979 and into negative figures between 1980 and 1981 because of the exchange rate misalignment. The rising costs of the CMB further reduced government revenues.

In July 1978 the government underwent another regime change, and the cedi was devalued again, an austerity budget

was introduced, and interest rates and cocoa producer prices were raised. Cocoa production sunk to its lowest level ever in 1980–81; the world price at the official exchange rate was lower than the producer price plus marketing costs.

The domestic conditions that led to the downturn in Ghana's cocoa sector took place against an international backdrop of increasing supply of cocoa from new producers such as Indonesia and Malaysia and expanded production in Côte d'Ivoire and Brazil. By the early 1970s Ghana had also lost much of its cheap labor supply from Burkina Faso and Côte d'Ivoire, as migrant farmers, reluctant to work in the old cocoa-producing areas that had become less productive, were attracted to the neighbouring Ivorian regions, where policies granted migrants access to land at favorable terms.

THE RECOVERY AND SECOND EXPANSION PHASE (1983–2008). The turnaround in Ghana's cocoa sector began with the implementation of the ERP in 1983, which included a special program to revive the sector (the Cocoa Rehabilitation Project). Policy changes included increasing the farm gate prices paid to Ghanaian farmers relative to those paid in neighboring countries, thus minimizing the incentive to smuggle, and devaluing the cedi, thus reducing the level of implicit taxation of farmers.

As part of the Cocoa Rehabilitation Project, farmers were also compensated for removing trees infected with swollen shoot virus and planting new ones. This effort led to substantial rehabilitation, with a large number of farms planting higher-yielding cocoa tree varieties developed by the Cocoa Research Institute of Ghana. Production rebounded to 400,000 tons by 1995/96 and productivity increased from 210 to 404 kilograms per hectare. Another important reform took place in 1992, when Cocobod (as CMB was renamed in 1984) shifted responsibility for domestic cocoa procurement to six privately licensed companies (commonly known as licensed buying companies or LBCs) and reduced its staff by 90 percent between 1992 and 1995.

Growth in cocoa production became more pronounced starting in 2001, possibly driven by a combination of record-high world prices, increased share being passed onto farmers, and a set of interventions rolled out by the Cocobod to improve farming practices: mass spraying programs and high-tech subsidy packages to promote the adoption of higher and more frequent applications of fertilizer (Vigneri and Santos 2008). Some of the growth during this period may also have been due to the influx of cocoa smuggled from Côte d'Ivoire. One study estimated this amount at between 120,000 and 150,000 thousand tons in 2003/4 (Brooks, Croppenstedt, and Aggrey-Fynn 2007).

Technical change in the cocoa sector

Since 2001 a significant share of Ghana's agricultural productivity gains have been generated by export crops, with cocoa accounting for 10 percent of total crop and livestock production values (World Bank 2007a) and contributing to 28 percent of agricultural growth in 2006, up from 19 percent in 2001. At the same time, economic growth has been solid, averaging more than 5 percent since 2001 and reaching 6 percent in 2005–06. Coupled with the effects of greater access to education, health services, and land ownership (World Bank 2008), this rate of growth has contributed to the near halving of the national poverty rate since the beginning of the 1990s, from 51.7 percent in 1991/92 to 28.5 percent in 2005/06 (Breisinger et al. 2008).

Over time, cocoa farmers have changed the way they access land and labor in response to the changing production conditions of a constantly moving cocoa frontier. Until the early 1940s, when both land and labor were abundant, large farms were able to attract rural workers to establish new farms by selling them small plots of land, an arrangement that often also drew the workers' family members to establish and maintain new farms. By the second half of the 1960s, when land became scarce, sharecropping arrangements increasingly replaced land sales. During times when the cost of hiring waged workers became too high, alternative forms of labor were used—mostly, either sharecropping arrangements or informal labor groups known as *nnoboa* (Berry 1993; Blowfield 1993; Vigneri, Teal, and Maamah 2004; and Amanor 2010). Since 1990 noticeable changes have taken place in the technology of cocoa production, in particular increased use of fertilizers; the adoption of hybrid cocoa varieties, and better control of pests and diseased trees (Boahene, Snijders, and Folmer 1999; Edwin and Masters 2003; Gockowski and Sonwa 2007; Teal, Zeitlin, and Maamah 2006; Vigneri, Teal, and Maamah 2004; and Vigneri 2008).

INCREASED USE OF FERTILIZER. Fertilizer use in Ghana has increased significantly since the 1990s. Surveys of cocoa farmers in the three main cocoa-producing regions of Ghana show that fertilizer application rates increased from 9 percent in 1991 to 47 percent in 2003 (table 12.1). Although the quantity of fertilizer used decreased between 1991/92 and 1997/98, the proportion of farmers applying fertilizer increased, possibly from liberalization of input

Table 12.1 Fertilizer Use in Cocoa-Producing Regions: 1991/92–2003/04

Crop year	Ashanti	Brong Ahafo	Western	Total
Number of farmers				
1991/92	112	71	137	320
1997/98	132	54	227	413
2001/02	108	94	226	428
2003/04	108	94	226	428
Quantity of fertilizer used (50-kilogram bags)				
1990/91	0.28	0.13	0.03	0.14
Adoption rate (%)	(13)	(8)	(6)	(9)
1997/98	0.10	0.06	0.10	0.09
Adoption rate (%)	(10)	(13)	(19)	(15)
2001/02	0.35	0.17	0.74	0.52
Adoption rate (%)	(5)	(7)	(12)	(9)
2003/04	4.17	4.39	6.10	5.24
Adoption rate (%)	(57)	(52)	(41)	(47)

Source: Authors' calculations from GLSS3, GLSS4, and Ghana Cocoa Farmers Survey, 2002 and 2004 rounds.

markets in 1996/97, which eliminated subsidies but improved private distribution (Vigneri and Teal 2004).

ADOPTION OF IMPROVED VARIETIES. Hybrid cocoa varieties were introduced in 1984 through the government's Cocoa Rehabilitation Project (CRP). Hybrid varieties outperform the older "Amazons" and "Amelonado" varieties in two ways—by producing trees that bear fruit in three years compared with at least five years for the older varieties, and by producing more pods per tree.[1] But hybrid cocoa trees underperform older varieties in that they require optimal weather conditions and complementary farming practices such as the application of chemical inputs, adoption of new planting procedures, pruning, and spraying. Hybrids varieties also require that farmers make more harvest rounds at the beginning and the end of the season, something they are reluctant to do when it conflicts with other farming or trading activities (Boahene, Snijders, and Folmer 1999; Bloomfield and Lass 1992).

Despite the increased labor input for hybrid cocoa trees, farmers have increasingly adopted them. In the late 1980s only 10 percent of cocoa grown in Ghana was of the high-yielding type (Nyanteng 1993). By 2002, 57 percent of farmers in the three main cocoa-producing areas were growing hybrid trees (Vigneri 2005). Traditional varieties may have disappeared entirely from all fields planted after 1995 (Edwin and Masters 2003).

BETTER DISEASE AND PEST CONTROL. Control of disease and pests, swollen shoot virus and capsid in particular, has improved significantly in recent years. After Cocobod initiated a free mass spraying program in 2001, 93 percent of cocoa farmers who participated in a survey conducted in 2002 linked their yield improvements to the effects of the program (Steedman 2003). Similarly the cocoa farmers' panel referred to above for the crop years 2002 and 2004 suggests that nearly all farms were sprayed in 2003/04, when producers reported an average of more than four spraying applications during the crop year, of which 46 percent were carried out by the government (Vigneri 2005).

The effect of all these improved practices has been an increase in productivity of about 30 percent, which brought productivity to the levels achieved in the 1980s (figure 12.2). Productivity was stagnant until the late 1980s, with production largely related to area harvested. The first big jump in productivity occurred in the 1980s, corresponding to the year of the Cocoa Rehabilitation Program rolled out under the ERP, and the second more recently, with improved practices. The correlation between production and area harvested remains strong.

Cocoa's contribution to economic growth and poverty reduction

In the Southern Forest Belt, where cocoa is produced, aggregate figures suggest that through the 1990s, cocoa-farming households, along with those engaged in mining or timber (the other predominantly export-oriented activities) and other commercial activities, experienced improvements in their living conditions compared with food crop farmers (McKay and Coulombe 2003). Poverty reduction among cocoa farmers is clear. Household surveys indicate that poverty among cocoa-producing households dropped to 23.9 percent in 2005, down from 60.1 percent at the beginning of the 1990s (World Bank 2007b).

Reputation for high-quality cocoa

Cocoa, like many other commodities, is often differentiated by country of origin, and this in turn is associated with a reputation based on average quality. The reputation, a national public good, enables the country to earn a premium in the global market for the crop it is producing. Generally, Ghana receives a price premium for its cocoa in world markets because of the slightly higher-than-average fat content; low levels of debris, which results in higher cocoa butter yields than beans containing high levels of debris; and low levels of bean defects, which generate a cocoa liquor flavor preferred by some end users. In addition to these attributes, the reputation of the Cocoa Marketing Company (the government division in charge of all exports) in ensuring the consistency and reliability of cocoa-related shipments and documents has played a central role in establishing the country's reputation for high-quality beans (Agrisystems Ltd. 1997). Using trade NYSE Liffe cocoa market information, Gilbert (2009) suggests that Ghanaian cocoa draws a premium of 3 to 5 percent relative to Côte d'Ivoire, currently the world's largest producer of cocoa (table 12.2).

Figure 12.2   Cocoa Production, Area Cultivated, and Yields, 1961–2008

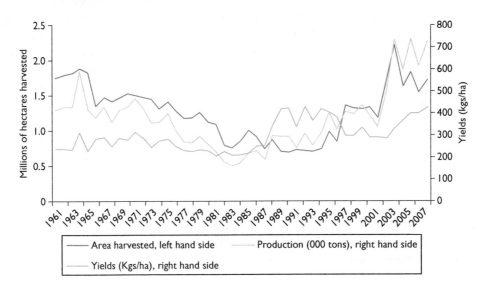

Source: FAOSTAT.

Table 12.2	Cocoa Unit Values and Terminal Market Differentials _Percent_					
	Cameroon		**Ghana**		**Nigeria**	
Period	**Unit value**	**Differential**	**Unit value**	**Differential**	**Unit value**	**Differential**
1988–1991	2.7	—	3.7	—	−0.4	—
1992–2002	−3.0	0.20	1.1	4.8	−2.1	−0.5
2003–2008	−7.8	—	5.2	4.9	−0.7	−0.9
1988–2008	−3.3	—	2.8	4.9	−1.4	−0.7

Source: Adapted from Gilbert (2009). Figures reported are relative to those of Côte d'Ivoire, the reference country.
Note: — = not available.

Characteristics that determine the quality of cocoa include content and quality of fat, consistency in the size of the beans, and their moisture content. These characteristics determine the quality of cocoa butter and cocoa liquor produced from the beans, the two ingredients that control texture, aroma, color, and flavor of chocolate. The fermentation, drying, storage, and evacuation of wet beans can alter the quality of cocoa beans dramatically, particularly in the development of the flavor of cocoa liquor. The classic "West African" cocoa flavor is obtained by fermenting beans in a heap under banana leaves for about six days with frequent manual turning and thorough drying in the sun. Drying beans slowly on raised platforms is very important for the quality of flavor because it quickly decreases the acidity level of the beans. Quality is also maintained by quickly collecting properly fermented and dried beans from smallholder farmers and promptly shipping them to avoid the buildup of moisture, mold, and free-fatty acids that can rapidly deteriorate the quality of the bean.

Partly because of its reputation for high-quality cocoa, Ghana is able to sell most of its annual production through forward contracts, which fix the price farmers are given for their cocoa for the entire crop year. The value that international firms place on Ghana's cocoa is also reflected by the amount of investment they have made in processing facilities in the country. Ghana's export earnings from processed cocoa products more than tripled between 1991 and 2004, from $32 million to $105 million (figure 12.3).[2] However, because of the limited conditions under which semiprocessed cocoa can be transported effectively (Fold 2002), it is not clear whether local value-adding efforts will be sufficiently profitable for international companies to expand their operations in Ghana. Thus far, informal discussions with the private sector participants indicate that the net benefits from processing locally may not be significant, particularly because the government allows only a limited quantity of low-quality beans to be

Figure 12.3 Share of Processed Cocoa Products in Total Cocoa Exports in West African Countries, 1990–2007

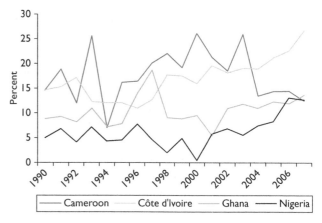

Source: FAOSTAT.
Note: Cocoa processed products include cocoa butter and cocoa paste.

used for local processing, which has resulted in considerable underutilization of existing capacity in the country.

Increased share of free on board prices going to farmers

Agricultural exports continue to be the most important source of foreign exchange for the majority of Sub-Saharan African countries (Gilbert 2009). In virtually every country in Africa with a major export crop, including Ghana, the government has intervened through state-owned marketing boards, or _caisses de stabilization_, to coordinate the production and marketing of the crop, offering farmers stable farm gate price that shield them from price volatility. Many scholars (Bates 2005; McMillan 1998; Akiyama et al. 2001) hold that marketing boards in Africa have long operated as corrupt institutions taxing farmers through the power to set prices and indirectly by maintaining overvalued exchange rates. That said, the role of governments in the agricultural sector has changed substantially since independence.

Despite granting Cocobod the monopoly over marketing, Ghana has managed to develop a marketing system that passes on an increasingly larger share of export prices to farmers. Prices received by Ghanaian producers have been a function of government interest in using the sector as a source of revenue and a balance against global prices, exchange rate distortions, and inflation. Price policies were also made ineffective by macroeconomic policies. In the early 1980s, for example, the Provisional National Defense Council (PNDC) had to choose between supporting cocoa farmers and continuing to maintain highly overvalued exchange rates (Stryker 1990).

In Ghana, the price producers are paid for cocoa is currently set at the beginning of the harvest season for the entire crop year by the Producer Price Committee.[3] The price is based on the price Cocobod expects to receive, having already sold nearly 70 percent of the crop. To this price, Cocobod adds the costs of its operations and the export tax to arrive at what it calls "net free on board (f.o.b.) price."

The share of the net f.o.b. price received by cocoa farmers in Ghana has increased to nearly 80 percent after having fallen below 20 percent before the economic reforms of the 1980s, and as low as almost 5 percent between 1975 and 1981. By 1987/88, real producer prices in Ghana had increased threefold compared with 1983/84, largely as a result of Cocobod's revised policy of paying higher prices to

the farmers, in response to pressure from multilateral organizations to streamline its operations (Brooks, Croppenstedt, and Aggrey-Fynn 2007). Figure 12.4 shows the share of f.o.b. prices paid to producers, the share retained by Cocobod (shown as direct taxation), and the share of indirect taxation imposed by the exchange rate.[4] Exchange rate distortions can further erode the share producers receive. These distortions were high in the mid-1980s but have completely disappeared.

REASONS FOR SUCCESS OF THE COCOA SECTOR

A number of factors have contributed to the success of Ghana's cocoa sector: a favorable price regime, both in terms of the f.o.b. share passed on to producers and the real price received by farmers; improved marketing through partial liberalization; and Cocobod's interventions to raise cocoa productivity.

Favorable prices

With the exception of 1998–2000 and 2003–06, world cocoa prices have steadily increased since 1990. This, combined with a higher share of the price being passed on to farmers, has offered farmers increasing real producer prices (figure 12.5). A variety of models estimating the sensitivity of production supply to farm gate prices find that

Figure 12.4 Farm Gate Prices, Direct Taxation, and Exchange Rate Taxation for Ghanaian Cocoa, 1966–2008
Percent

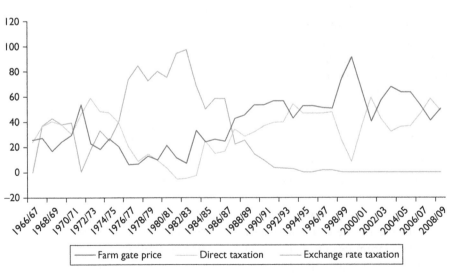

Source: Vigneri 2005.

Figure 12.5 Ghana Cocoa Production and Real Producer Price, 1990–2008

Source: Cocobod and ICCO.

small-scale cocoa producers in Ghana have responded positively to these price incentives (Bulíř 2002; Hattink, Heerink, and Thijssen 1998; and Vigneri 2005, among others).

Although strictly comparable data are not available, informed inference on the returns on cocoa farms using the results from two rural surveys, one conducted in 1996 (Agrisystems Ltd. 1997) and one in 2006 (Barrientos and Asenso-Okyere 2008), show that cocoa production has not become more profitable for farmers. In fact, calculations show that cocoa, which usually is the largest source of earnings in cocoa-producing households, accounting for more than 67 percent of revenues, has actually declined over time: net cocoa profits for cocoa-producing households were 7 percent lower in 2005 than in 1996. While the real price of cocoa increased by 47 percent between these two years, the cost of inputs increased more. These estimates, however, do not suggest a trend because they are based on observations for two specific years.

Liberalization of domestic cocoa marketing

Following pressures from multilateral organizations in the early 1980s, wide-ranging changes were introduced to improve Cocobod's efficiency: transport was shifted to the private sector, feeder road development was transferred to the Ministry of Roads and Highways, and in 1988–89 input subsidies were phased out (Brooks, Croppenstedt, and Aggrey-Fynn 2007). Following the 1992 elections more drastic measures were undertaken: Cocobod staff levels were

reduced from 100,000 in the early 1980s to 10,400 in 1999 to just over 5,100 in 2003, bringing down costs considerably. In the same year, Cocobod ended its control over all domestic purchases by allowing a number of private licensed companies to compete with its former purchasing agency, the Producing Buying Company (PBC), to buy and transport the cocoa crop from farms; the board, however, specifies a minimum price. This partial liberalization appears to have benefited producers. The internal marketing of cocoa has also become more competitive in recent years, with nearly 20 licensed buyers, along with PBC, procuring cocoa through nearly 3,000 buying stations manned by purchasing clerks or individuals from cocoa communities who purchase the crop on the buyers' behalf. Although the total number of licensed buyers is relatively large, five dominate the market: the Produce Buying Company, Kuapa Kokoo, Olam, Armajaro, and Global Haulage, a former transport company comprising three Ghanaian buyers (Federal Commodities, Transroyal, and Adwumapa) Additionally, Cocobod extends funds to producers at rates slightly below the market rate to finance their operations. It also monitors producers' operations, particularly with regard to quality of beans. Though licensed buyers are free to export, none of them has thus far because none is large enough to acquire the minimum amount needed to be eligible to export.

Zeitlin (2006) finds a positive correlation between the concentration of licensed buying companies at the village level and production. But the direction of causality is not clear, because buyers are also likely to locate themselves where large quantities of cocoa are available for purchase. The PBC continues to operate as a buyer of last resort. While Cocobod sets a minimum price that must be paid to producers, the buying companies are free to pay higher prices. Even in the absence of price competition among licensed buyers, farmers have benefited. Payments to farmers have become more reliable, and corruption, which characterized the contractual negotiations when the PBC was the only buyer, has diminished. While licensed buyers may not compete on prices, they do offer occasional price bonuses, subsidized inputs, or credit extensions for producers (Laven 2007). Because the licensed buyers buy cocoa throughout the year, however, the new buying system puts a steadier stream of money into the hands of producers (Vigneri and Santos 2008), giving farmers working capital to buy labor and other inputs when they need them.

Although the efforts at liberalization are likely to have made procurement and transport more efficient than before, it is unclear whether Cocobod's costs have been reduced by "outsourcing" procurement and transport and to what extent liberalization may have helped Cocobod pass on a higher share of f.o.b. prices to farmers. But regardless, retaining control over exports and other aspects of marketing has enabled Cocobod to support producers in ways that would not have been feasible had it devolved these responsibilities to other organizations.

Cocobod's impact on productivity

Importantly, Cocobod's continued involvement in the cocoa sector in Ghana has allowed surpluses generated in good years to be used to finance deficits during years when prices were low. Similarly, Cocobod has invested in research, disease control, and credit programs that are of general benefit to the cocoa industry (Stryker 1990). In 2001 the Cocoa National Disease and Pest Control Committee was established to develop strategies to control capsid and black pod through a nationally coordinated spraying program under which Cocobod, through a network of regional offices, undertakes spraying of all cocoa fields at no cost to the producers.[5] By Cocobod's estimates, the scheme has had a positive impact on national cocoa production, particularly during the 2003/04 and 2005/06 seasons. Cocobod also reports that the protection of the cocoa plants that the program offers has encouraged farmers to undertake additional spraying applications.

In 2002/03, Cocobod rolled out the "Cocoa High-Tech" program designed to encourage farmers to apply a minimum of 5 bags of fertilizer per hectare of planted cocoa, supplying

fertilizer on credit. The program collapsed after one year, however, because of poor repayment rates. Following this pilot, a private agri-input company, Wienco, tested a package of agricultural inputs and farm practices known as the "Abrabopa package." In 2003, its first year of testing, the package raised yields from 510 to 1,081 kilograms per hectare and to 2,317 kilograms per hectare after the third year.

In 2006 the Cocoa Abrabopa Association (CAA) was established, under which groups of farmers with mature trees on at least one hectare of land were given the Abrabopa package on credit and offered technical and business training. The number of farmers participating in this program reached 11,000 in 2008. An evaluation of the program in 2008 (Opoku et al. 2009) suggests that the principle of group liability employed in this program ensured, to some extent, the effective use of the fertilizer and other inputs provided by the CAA package. That said, a large proportion of farmers, nearly 40 percent, dropped out of the program, so the benefits of the CAA package reached only a small share of cocoa growers.

Cocobod's role in maintaining quality

In terms of quality practices by government marketing boards among West African cocoa-producing countries, Ghana is an exception, because maintenance of quality continues to be Cocobod's mandate even after its restructuring. In other countries, dismantling and restructuring of marketing boards in the 1980s radically reduced quality control systems (Fold 2001; Gilbert 2009). One rationale for a government role in maintaining quality is that cocoa is transported in bulk, and poor-quality cocoa beans can diminish the quality of other beans in the same shipment, thereby affecting the price of all beans in the shipment. Maintaining a government role is also important because it allows the government to control the national reputation of Ghana's cocoa and keep its premium in the world market (Fold and Ponte 2008). This quality maintenance comes at a cost, however, including the cost of ensuring that lower-quality beans are not mixed into those prepared for export and the costs of administration.

SUSTAINABILITY OF THE COCOA SECTOR

Ghana's cocoa sector faces a number of challenges. For one, productivity levels are lower than they are in other countries. Ghana also faces the possibility that its quality advantage may disappear in the coming years. In addition, Ghana must determine how to keep its cocoa sector competitive as cocoa-producing households change. Finally, the environmental impact of current farming practices may soon constrain cocoa production expansion. On the other hand, however, Ghana has been quite successful in taking advantage of niche cocoa markets.

Productivity and competitiveness

Notwithstanding the technical changes that have occurred in cocoa production, Ghana still needs to close a large productivity gap to remain competitive. The gap between observed and achievable yields is 50–80 percent (Gockowski 2007), depending on the production practices adopted by farmers (for example, thin shading and the amount of fertilizer applied). A survey conducted in the 1980s, however, indicated that Ghana was the lowest-cost producer in the world (Bloomfield and Lass 1992). Ghana's yields are low compared to those of its leading competitors, Côte d'Ivoire and Indonesia (figure 12.6). Additionally, it is not clear which technologies intended to increase productivity are attractive to farmers. For example, farmers may not have much incentive to apply fertilizers to hybrid trees, because the returns from doing so may not be higher than those achieved on traditional varieties (Edwin and Masters 2003).

On experimental farms, application of fertilizers to young trees has increased yields as much as threefold (Gockowski and Sonwa 2007). One evaluation (Opoku et al. 2009) suggests that the high dropout rate from the CAA program may result from high variability in the expected returns from fertilizer applications.

The low level of tree replanting is an additional threat to the sustainability of Ghana's cocoa production. Often, farmers find it more economical to expand their farms rather than to replace old and diseased trees (Vigneri 2005; Ruf and Burger 2001), because it takes twice as long to clear an old farm as it does to clear new forest land (Masdar Ltd. 1998). Additionally, farmers regard the expansion of land on which cocoa is planted as both an investment and a means to establish land ownership. Given that migrants and sharecroppers represent an increasing share of the cocoa-farming population, this dual view means that many farmers seek to acquire permanent land rights by expanding into uncultivated land, where land ownership is established by clearing land and planting new trees (Amanor 2010; Berry 2009; Takane 2002).[6] Further opportunities to increase production by land expansion may be limited, though, by the decreasing availability of virgin forest land.

Longevity of the quality advantage

Although Ghanaian cocoa draws a premium price for its reliable quality, this advantage may be eroded in the future

Figure 12.6 Cocoa Yields, by Country, 1990–2008

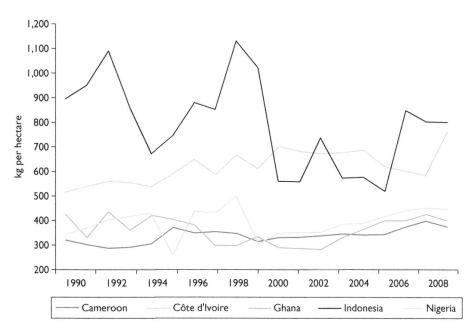

Source: FAOSTAT.

because of technological advances in processing (Agrisystems Ltd. 1997; Fold 2001). On the other hand, current quality control processes in Ghana guarantee minimum parameters that are important to large industry players like Cadbury, which is known to use Ghanaian cocoa beans exclusively in all its U.K.-retailed chocolate products. A second, potential threat is when other cocoa-producing countries improve on their quality. Currently, this is not much of a threat to Ghana, because smallholder farmers in countries such as Malaysia and Indonesia lack the institutions to support quality. In Côte d'Ivoire, the mixing of good cocoa beans with the bad ones in shipments for export results in variability in quality (Bloomfield and Lass 1992).

Competitiveness of cocoa on farms

Cocoa is a mixed crop system in which other crops may be consumed or sold. Intercropping with plantain and cocoyam, for example, provides early returns when cocoa trees are still young. Studies conducted in the 1970s and in the 1990s (Rourke 1974; Masdar 1998) report that almost all cocoa farmers grew alternative crops for subsistence and sale, mostly roots and tubers but also a variety of cereals and vegetables. Both studies also suggest that many farmers shifted to crops other than cocoa (mixed plantain and cocoyam, mixed maize and cassava, and oil palm intercropped with maize and cassava) on a scale greater than that needed to satisfy subsistence needs. This shift occurred for several reasons: the crops offered farmers greater income continuity throughout the year, and returns were perceived to be higher relative to cocoa, especially in the presence of significant problems with the rehabilitation of the existing cocoa tree stock.

More recent research has questioned the viability of cocoa on small farms. A 2001 survey conducted by the Sustainable Tree Crop Programme (STCP) in four cocoa-producing countries in West Africa shows that the top 25 percent of households (ranked by the amount of cocoa produced) have average costs of production four times lower and yields nearly four times greater than the bottom 25 percent, and that a significant share of small cocoa farms incur losses (Gockowski 2007). The study recommends the urgent adoption of policies that vary for larger, more efficient producers and poorer marginal ones as a necessary step in keeping Ghana's cocoa sector competitive and efficient.

For the larger producers, the STCP study recommends implementing innovations through the strategic distribution of improved planting material (hybrid pods) in the most densely populated regions of the cocoa belt. The study estimates that this could result in the replanting of up to 24,000 hectares of land, and that integrating this intervention with the expansion of fertilizer use would achieve productivity gains in excess of 50 percent. For less efficient cocoa producers, the STCP recommends implementing a different set of policies that would either allow these producers to exit the sector or support their transition to alternative production systems. One option for these less efficient farmers would be the conversion from a no-shade cocoa system to a partial-shade system with cocoa and non-cocoa trees intercropped, allowing producers to augment their incomes from the sale of forest products, and possibly from the additional payments for higher carbon sequestration associated with shaded tree systems.

Environmental impact of current farming practices

An issue closely related to the competitiveness of cocoa on farms is the environmental impact of existing farming practices. Since its introduction in West Africa, cocoa has been the major cause of land use change in the high forest zones of the regions in which it is grown, where it has replaced agricultural activity that incorporated fallowing to maintain land fertility (Gockowski and Sonwa 2007). Although the initial expansion of cocoa production did not entail a complete removal of the forest shade because the traditional shade-dependent and tolerant *tetteh quarshie* variety of cocoa did not require forest clearing, trees have been cut down en masse in recent years to accommodate the open-field hybrid variety, which grows in full sun conditions. In nearly three-quarters of Ghana's production area, there is little to no shade (table 12.3).

Farmers in Ghana have a strong preference for full-sun crops because their much shorter growing cycle is linked to higher short-term profits (Obiri et al. 2007). The damage to cocoa trees from capsid attacks tends to be higher for cocoa trees growing in full sun than for those in shaded systems,

Table 12.3 Shade Levels in the Cocoa Belt of Ghana (percent)

Region	None to light	Medium to heavy
Ashanti	52	47
Brong Ahafo	52	47
Eastern	50	49
Western	77	21
Ghana	72	29

Source: Adapted from Gockowski and Sonwa (2007).

however, and the carbon sequestration potential of full-sun cocoa systems is significantly less than that of traditional shaded cocoa systems (Norris 2008).

The best possible environmental alternative to the current cocoa-growing practices in Ghana would be a mixed agroforestry system, where the forest is selectively thinned and fruit trees with economic value—such as oil palm, avocado, and citrus—are grown next to cocoa trees, providing both shade for the cocoa trees and food and income for the farming household (Gockowski and Sonwa 2007). This practice, which is used in southern Cameroon, could offer farmers up to 23 percent of total revenues from their non-cocoa holdings, but it is rarely practiced in Ghana. One reason is that in the biodiversity hotspots in remote areas of the Western region, the profitable marketing of agroforestry products would not be easy. Additionally, past logging practices, in which concessionaires harvested in a way that destroyed cocoa farms with no compensation for producers, have discouraged the use of fruit and timber-producing trees in cocoa fields (Obiri et al. 2007).

Ghana's role in a changing global market for cocoa

Ghana is well positioned to expand its position in high-value markets, with Cocobod proving to be responsive to trends in international markets. The chocolate industry also has expanded into secondary markets, such as fair trade in the late 1980s. Although these markets offer strategic opportunities for countries to build competitiveness, estimated in 2000 at 2.6 percent of world cocoa bean trade (Abbott 2002), they largely remain niche markets because of their limited capacity for expansion.

Ghana's considerable progress in the fair-trade cocoa market began with the establishment, in 1993, of Kuapa Kokoo, a farmers' cooperative that operates as a private, licensed buying company. Its share in the domestic market is now estimated to be around 10 percent of total purchases, and a panel survey of farmers spanning 2002 to 2006 shows the cooperative to be farmers' second preferred outlet for selling beans (Vigneri and Santos 2008). Within Cocobod, a special channel exists for fair-trade cocoa sourced and exported from Kuapa Kokoo, although the system traces such cocoa back to the cooperative rather than to the individual farmer. The social premium earned on fair-trade exports, which in 2000 was reported to be $150 per ton (Abbott 2002), goes into a trust fund that sponsors development projects in cocoa-producing communities. Recently, the CAA became the first cocoa cooperative in Ghana to obtain certification for organic production, with more than 500 members meeting the required standards.

LESSONS FROM GHANA'S EXPERIENCE WITH COCOA

Cocoa was developed in Ghana, largely by commercial farmers, many of whom were smallholders and laborers drawing on their own savings and labor, in response to market opportunities and the development of infrastructure. Policies and institutions have played an important role. The importance of macroeconomic management, the avoidance of distortions in the exchange rate in particular, is clearly evident from the effect of its absence on farm gate prices in the mid-1980s.

Ghana appears to have emerged with an appropriate institutional mix in which competition has been introduced in internal marketing to benefit from efficiencies in procurement and transport, while the government marketing board retains control over setting minimum prices for the year, maintaining quality, and managing exports. The control it has retained over exports enables it to stabilize prices and use the surpluses to offer some services such as plant protection, research, and extension that may not be forthcoming from the private sector, as suggested by the experience of the fully liberalized producing countries in the region. Public support to farmers to rehabilitate the diseased tree stock, public research that produced new hybrids, and the continued state intervention to promote fertilizer use have all been instrumental in reviving the sector. More recently public spraying and dissemination of technical packages have spurred private action.

Would the cocoa sector have been better if it were fully liberalized? Examining the experience of liberalization of cocoa sectors in four West African countries, Gilbert (2009) suggests four criteria to address this question: (1) the level of competition achieved on both the export and import side of producing countries, (2) the ability to sustain quality standards, (3) the share of the f.o.b. price passed on to the farmers as an indication of the degree of state taxation, and (4) the extent of producer price stabilization achieved. The evidence suggests that it may not be so.

Liberalization has not resulted in competition in the value chain, particularly in exports. Local companies engaged in exports without access to global financing have withdrawn over the years, leaving exports largely in the hands of multinationals, either converters or their agents (Gilbert 2009). But, there has been greater competition in internal trade. As for the share of the f.o.b. price passed on to the farmers, the proportion is higher in countries such as Cameroon and Nigeria, but Ghana's government has made concrete efforts in the recent past to raise the share similarly. Finally, in relation to the price stabilization objective, Ghana has clearly been successful in reducing farmers' exposure to price variability during the crop year through its practice of forward sales. This, combined with the more stable inflation rate of the past decade, has de facto acted as an insurance mechanism against the variability in the world price of the commodity. Global businesses like the Ghana model because it delivers consistently high quality. Local businesses are also content because they can continue to participate in the sector (Gilbert 2009).

The interesting question is whether it is possible to arrive at this mix of public and private institutions and also be certain that a parastatal organization such as the Cocobod would operate reasonably efficiently. Ghana's experience suggests that external pressures as a part of the ERP to reform the sector were instrumental in making Cocobod liberalize some of its operations and streamline its own working to reduce costs. Ghana appears to have done enough to fend off pressures for further liberalization of the sector. To what extent it will strive to continue to pass on a higher share of prices to farmers without external pressures and whether there is a recognition of the benefits from appropriate management that survives political changes are not clear. The affairs of the Cocobod are not as transparent as they should be, and the line between cocoa revenues and government finances remains fuzzy. Whether the Cocobod will be able to stabilize prices if the world market were to become more volatile than it has been in recent years is not clear.

The pressure on the government and on its marketing institution to improve their efficiency (as measured by the share of the world price going to producers) rather than to seek full liberalization appears to have worked well in Ghana. Given the preponderance of smallholders in the sector and the risks associated with the total withdrawal of the government's services, the partial liberalization experience of Ghana's cocoa sector has so far offered a unique example of how it is possible to learn from past reforms and to continue to seek further reform to sustain the sector. However, the scope for future improvements and for further learning opportunities will require appropriate pressures from both local political processes and from external sources.

NOTES

1. Using survey data collected in 2002, Edwin and Masters (2003) show that the new tree varieties yield approximately twice as much cocoa per hectare as similar-aged fields planted with traditional trees.

2. Ghana maintains a state-owned processing plant, the Cocoa Processing Company (CMC). Historically, CMC has operated at low capacity. A five-year rehabilitation and expansion program, however, allowed it to double its annual processing capacity between 2004 and 2009.

3. The committee includes a variety of representatives from the cocoa sector: Cocobod, government officials, and representatives of cocoa buyers, the national cocoa farmers' association, and haulers and transporters.

4. Indirect taxation is measured as the difference between world prices converted using the official exchange rate and world prices converted using the market exchange rate. Direct taxation includes Cocobod's marketing costs and export duties imposed by the government (export duties have been close to 25 percent in recent years). The share of f.o.b. prices received by farmers does not correspond with global prices. For example, between 1971 and 1983, the farmer share declined sharply while global prices were rising. This period, however, coincided with acute domestic currency overvaluation in Ghana, which further eroded farmers' real producer prices. Similarly, in the mid-1990s, producers' share of world prices increased while global prices were falling.

5. How much of the program is funded by cocoa revenues and whether any of the program is subsidized by the government is not clear, however.

6. In Ghana, the distinction between land ownership and usufruct rights over what grows on land has traditionally shaped smallholders' investment choices.

BIBLIOGRAPHY

Abbott, P. 2002. "Towards more Socially Responsible Cocoa Trade." Working Paper 03-3, presented at the Annual Meeting of the International Agricultural Trade Research Consortium (IATRC), Monterey, CA, December 15–17.

Agrisystems Ltd. 1997. "Study of the Cocoa Sector to Define Interventions on Behalf of Ghana's Smallholder with Particular Reference to the Framework of Mutual Obligations." Prepared for the Stablex 1992 and 1993 Allocation.

Akiyama, T., J. Baffes, D. Larson, and P. Varangis. 2001. *Commodity Market Reforms: Lessons of Two Decades.* World Bank Regional and Sectoral Studies. Washington: World Bank.

Allman, J. M. 1993. *The Quills of the Porcupine.* Madison, WI: University of Wisconsin Press.

Amanor, K. 2005. "Agricultural Markets in West Africa: Frontiers, Agribusiness and Social Differentiation." *IDS Bulletin* 36 (2).

_____. 2010. "Family Values, Land Sales and Agricultural Commodification in Rural Ghana." *Africa* 80 (1): 104–125.

Austin, D. 1978. *Politics in Africa*. Manchester, U.K.: Manchester University Press.

Awanyo, L. 1998. "Culture, Markets, and Agricultural Production: A Comparative Study of the Investment Patterns of Migrant and Citizen Cocoa Farmers in the Western Region of Ghana." *Professional Geographer* 50: 516–30.

Barrientos, S. W., and L. Asenso-Okyere. 2008. "Mapping Sustainable Production in Ghanaian Cocoa: Report to Cadbury." Institute of Development Studies, University of Sussex, and University of Ghana.

Bateman, M. 1965. "Aggregate and Regional Supply Functions for Ghanaian Cocoa: 1946–1962." *Journal of Farm Economics* 47 (2): 384–401.

Bates, R. H. 2005. *Markets and States in Tropical Africa. The Political Basis of Agricultural Policies*. Berkeley, CA: University of California Press.

Beckman, B. 1976. *Organising the Farmers: Cocoa Politics and National Development in Ghana*. Uppsala: Scandinavian Institute of African Studies.

Berry, S. 1993. *No Condition Is Permanent: The Social Dynamics of Agrarian Change in Sub-Saharan Africa*. Madison, WI: University of Wisconsin Press.

_____. 2009 "Building for the Future? Investment, Land Reform and the Contingencies of Ownership in Contemporary Ghana." *World Development* 37 (8): 1370–78.

Bloomfield, E. M., and R. A. Lass. 1992. "Impact of Structural Adjustment and Adoption of Technology on Competitiveness of Major Cocoa Producing Countries." Working Paper 69. Paris: Organisation for Economic Cooperation and Development.

Blowfield, M. 1993. "The Allocation of Labour to Perennial Crops: Decision-making by African Smallholders." NRI-Socioeconomic Series 3, Natural Resources Institute, University of Greenwich, Kent, U.K.

Boahene, K., T. A. B. Snijders, and H. Folmer. 1999. "An Integrated Socio Economic Analysis of Innovation Adoption: The Case of Hybrid Cocoa in Ghana." *Journal of Policy Modelling* 21 (2): 167–84.

Breisinger, C., X. Diao, S. Kolavalli, and J. Thurlow. 2008. "The Role of Cocoa in Ghana's Future Development." IFPRI Background Paper 11, IFPRI, Ghana.

Breisinger, C., X. Diao, J. Thurlow, and R. M. Al Hassan. 2009. "Potential Impacts of a Green Revolution in Africa – The Case of Ghana." Paper presented at the 27th IAAE Conference, Beijing, August 16–22.

Brooks, J., A. Croppenstedt, and E. Aggrey-Fynn. 2007. "Distortions to Agricultural Incentives in Ghana." Agricultural Distortions Working Paper 47, World Bank, Washington, DC.

Bulíř, A. 2002. "Can Price Incentive to Smuggle Explain the Contraction of the Cocoa Supply in Ghana?" *Journal of African Economies* 11 (3): 413–39.

Coulombe, H., and Q. Wodon. 2007. "Poverty, Livelihoods, and Access to Basic Services in Ghana." In "Ghana Country Economic Memorandum: Meeting the Challenge of Accelerated and Shared Growth." World Bank, Washington, DC.

Edwin, J., and W. A. Masters. 2003. "Genetic Improvement and Cocoa Yields in Ghana." Working Paper, Purdue University, West Lafayette, IN.

Fold, N. 2000. "A Matter of Good Taste? Quality and the Construction of Standards for Chocolate Products in the European Union." Cahiers d'économie et sociologie rurales, 55–56.

_____. 2001. "Restructuring of the European Chocolate Industry and Its Impact on Cocoa Production in West Africa." *Journal of Economic Geography* 1: 405–20.

_____. 2002. "Lead Firms and Competition in 'Bi-polar' Commodity Chains: Grinders and Processors in the Global Cocoa-Chocolate Industry." *Journal of Agrarian Change* 2 (2): 228–47.

Fold, N., and S. Ponte. 2008. "Are (Market) Stimulants Injurious to Quality? Liberalization, Quality Changes and the Reputation of African Coffee and Cocoa Exports." In *Globalization and Restructuring of African Commodity Flows*, ed. N. Fold and M. N. Larsen. Uppsala, Sweden: Nordic Africa Institute.

Ghana Cocoa Marketing Board. Various years. "Cocoa Marketing Board Newsletter."

Ghana Ministry of Manpower, Youth and Employment. 2006. "Labour Practices in Cocoa Production in Ghana (Pilot Survey)." Accra.

Gibbon, P., Y. Lin, and S. Jones. 2009. "Revenue Effects of Participation in Smallholder Organic Cocoa Production in Tropical Africa: A Case Study." DIIS Working Paper 2009:06, Danish Institute for International Studies, Copenhagen.

Gilbert, C. L. 2009. "Cocoa Market Liberalization in Retrospect." *Review of Business and Economics* 54: 294–312.

Gill & Duffus Group. Various years. "Cocoa Statistics."

Gockowski, J. 2007. "The Analysis of Policies, Productivity and Agricultural Transformation in the Cocoa-Producing Rural Economies of West Africa." STCP Technical Report Executive Summary.

Gockowski, J., and D. Sonwa. 2007. "Biodiversity Conservation and Smallholder Cocoa Production Systems in West Africa with Particular Reference to the Western Region of Ghana and the Bas Sassandra region of Côte d'Ivoire." Draft paper, Institute of Tropical Agriculture, Ibadan, Nigeria. http://www.odi.org.uk/events/2007/11/19/434-paper-discussion-biodiversity-conservation-smallholder-cocoa-production-systems-west-africa.pdf.

Government of Ghana. 2003. "Ghana Poverty Reduction Strategy, 2003-2005: An Agenda for Growth and Prosperity."Government of Ghana, Accra.

Gunnarsson, C. 1978. "The Gold Coast Cocoa Industry 1900–1939. Production, Prices and Structural Change." PhD thesis, Department of Economic History, Lund University, Lund, Sweden.

Gyimah-Brempong, K. 1987. "Scale Elasticities in Ghanaian Cocoa Production." *Applied Economics* 19: 1383–90.

Hattink, W., N. Heerink, and G. Thijssen. 1998. "Supply Response of Cocoa in Ghana: A Farm-Level Profit Function Analysis." *Journal of African Economies* 7 (3): 424–44.

Herbst, J. 1993. *The Politics of Reform in Ghana, 1982–1991.* Berkeley, CA: University of California Press.

Hill, P. 1963. *The Migrant Cocoa Farmers of Southern Ghana. A Study in Rural Capitalism.* Cambridge, UK: University Press.

International Cocoa Organization. Various years. "Quarterly Bulletin." London.

Konings, P. J. J. 1986. *The State and Rural Class Formation in Ghana: A Comparative Analysis.* Leiden, Netherlands: African Studies Centre.

Laven, A. 2007. "Marketing Reforms in Ghana's Cocoa Sector: Partial Reforms, Partial Benefits?" Background Note, Overseas Development Institute, London. http://www.odi.org.uk/resources/download/420.pdf.

Masdar Ltd. 1998. *Socio-Economic Study of the Cocoa Farming Community.* Wokingham, United Kingdom.

McKay, A., and H. Coulombe, 2003. "Selective Poverty Reduction in a Slow Growth Environment: Ghana in the 1990s." Human Development Network, World Bank, Washington, DC.

McMillan, M. 1998. *A Dynamic Theory of Primary Export Taxation.* Discussion Paper 98-12. Department of Economics, Tufts University.

Norris, K. 2008. "Carbon, Biodiversity and Cocoa Farming in Ghana." Climate Change Unit, Forestry Commission of Ghana, Accra.

Nyanteng, V. K. 1993. "The Prospect of the Ghanaian Cocoa Industry in the 21st Century." Paper presented at the International Conference on Cocoa Economy, Bali, Indonesia, October 19–22.

Obiri, B. D., G. A. Bright, M. A. McDonald, L. C. N. Anglaaere, and J. Cobbina. 2007. "Financial Analysis of Shaded Cocoa in Ghana." *Agroforestry Systems* 71: 139–49.

Okali, C. 2010 "The Organisation of Cocoa Production on the Farm and its Evolution over Time." Unpublished paper.

Opoku, E., R. Dzene, S. Caria, F. Tea, and A. Zeitlin. 2009. "Improving Productivity through Group Lending: Report on the Impact Evaluation of the Cocoa Abrabopa Initiative." Centre for the Study of African Economies, University of Oxford, Oxford, United Kingdom. http://www.csae.ox.ac.uk/output/reports/pdfs/rep2008-01.pdf.

Piasentin, F. and L. Klare-Repnik. 2004. "Quality Matters." Global Research on Cocoa and CABI, Conservation International.

Quisumbing, A. R., E. Payongayong, J. B. Aidoo, and K. Otsuka. 2001. "Women's Land Rights in the Transition to Individualized Ownership: Implications for the Management of Tree Resources in Western Ghana." *Economic Development and Cultural Change* 50 (1): 157–81.

Rourke, B. E. 1974. "Profitability of Cocoa and Alternative Crops in Eastern Region, Ghana." In *Economics of Cocoa Production and Marketing,* ed. A. Kotey, C. Okali, and B. E. Rourke. Proceedings of Cocoa Economics Research Conference, University of Ghana, Legon, 1973.

_____. 2007a. "The Cocoa Sector: Expansion, or Green and Double Green Revolutions?" Overseas Development Institute Background Note, London.

_____. 2007b. "International Perspectives on the Cocoa Sector: Expansion or Green and Double Green Revolutions?" http://www.odi.org.uk/events/2007/11/19/434-presentation-session-1-international-perspectives-cocoa-sector-francois-ruf.pdf.

_____. 2009. "Libéralisation, cycles politiques et cycles du cacao: le décalage historique Côte-d'Ivoire-Ghana." *Cahiers Agricultures* 18 (4).

Ruf, F., and K. Burger. 2001. "Planting and Replanting Tree Crops. Smallholders' Investment Decision." Unpublished paper, Centre de coopération internationale en recherche agronomique pour le développement (CIRAD), Paris.

Ruf, F., and H. Zadi. 1998. "Cocoa: From Deforestation to Reforestation." Prepared for the First International Workshop on Sustainable Cocoa Growing, Smithsonian Institute, Panama.

_____ and P. S. Siswoputranto. 1995. *Cocoa Cycles: The Economics of Cocoa Supply.* Cambridge, U.K.: Woodhead Publishing Ltd.

Shepherd, A. W., and S. Farolfi. 1999. "Export Crop Liberalization in Africa: A Review." Agricultural Services Bulletin 135, FAO, Rome.

Sjaastad, E. and D. Bromley. 1997. "Indigenous Land Rights in Sub-Saharan Africa: Appropriation, Security and Investment Demand.'" *World Development* 25: 549–62.

Steedman, C. 2003. "Agriculture in Ghana: Some Issues." Unpublished paper, World Bank, Washington, DC.

Stryker, J. D. 1990. "Trade, Exchange Rate, and Agricultural Policies in Ghana." World Bank Comparative Studies, World Bank, Washington, DC.

Takane, T. 2002. *The Cocoa Farmers of Southern Ghana: Incentives, Institutions, and Change in Rural West Africa.* Chiba, Japan: Institute of Developing Economies and Japan External Trade Organization.

Teal, F., A. Zeitlin, and H. Maamah. 2006. "Ghana Cocoa Farmers Survey 2004: Report to Ghana Cocoa Board." Centre for the Study of African Economies, University of Oxford, Oxford, United Kingdom.

Vigneri M. 2005. "Trade Liberalisation and Agricultural Performance: Micro and Macro Evidence on Cash Crop Production in Sub-Saharan Africa." DPhil thesis, University of Oxford, Oxford, United Kingdom.

_____. 2008. "Drivers of Change in Ghana's Cocoa Sector." IFPRI-GSSP Background Paper 13, International Food Policy Research Institute, Washington, DC.

Vigneri M., and P. Santos. 2008. "What Does Liberalization without Price Competition Achieve? The Case of Cocoa Marketing in Rural Ghana." IFPRI-GSSP Background Paper 14. International Food Policy Research Institute, Washington, DC.

Vigneri M., F. Teal, and H. Maamah. 2004. "Coping with Market Reforms: Winners and Losers among Ghanaian Cocoa Farmers." Report to the Ghana Cocoa Board, Accra.

World Bank. 2007a. *World Development Report: Agriculture for Development.* Washington, DC: World Bank.

_____. 2007b. "Ghana: Meeting the Challenge of Accelerated and Shared Growth." Country Economic Memorandum, World Bank, Washington, DC.

_____. 2008. "Country Brief: Ghana." World Bank, Washington DC.

Zeitlin, A. 2006. "Market Structure and Productivity Growth in Ghanaian Cocoa Production." Unpublished paper, Centre for the Study of African Economies, University of Oxford, Oxford, U.K.

CHAPTER 13

Apparel Exports in Lesotho: The State's Role in Building Critical Mass for Competitiveness

Mallika Shakya

Lesotho, a country of 1.9 million people, has been quite successful in capitalizing on the African Growth and Opportunity Act (AGOA), the economic partnership agreement between the United States and Africa launched in 2000 to increase African exports to the U.S. market. Lesotho's experience with its apparel exports demonstrates that competitiveness is not only about firm-level costing but about developing a broader coordination mechanism through which the government delivers public goods necessary for overcoming market failures in such a way that private sector investment is triggered and sustained.

A notable aspect of Lesotho's experience is the government's decision to combine an apparel industry competitiveness initiative with a series of early-stage incentives for investors—a tactic that has yielded positive results for Lesotho thus far. The sequencing and balancing of such policy measures has differentiated Lesotho's apparel export path from those of other African countries in recent years. Its proximity to South Africa and its membership in the Southern African Customs Union offers Lesotho unique geographic and fiscal advantages that other countries may not have, but the industrial policy measures and institutional reforms undertaken by the government of Lesotho are relevant for several African countries. Lesotho's success can especially be attributed to its direct engagement with global and regional apparel buyers and an overall policy acknowledgement of the rapidly changing structure of the global apparel trade. Over time, Lesotho has started to climb the apparel value chain and overcome issues of corporate social responsibility.

To better understand the policy measures behind the success factors involving Lesotho's apparel trade, this chapter asks three main questions. First, how are spatial and economic factors balanced in pursuing a coherent competitiveness strategy in Lesotho's apparel sector? Second, what were some of the industry-specific strategies employed by the government of Lesotho in overcoming the government and market failures? How are they complemented with economywide measures and socioeconomic measures? And third, what public-private collaborative efforts have led to reforms that maximized private sector investments? How have bottlenecks related to transportation, logistics, innovation, and quality been overcome to produce the success of the apparel industry in Lesotho?

In exploring these questions, this chapter takes as a basic premise that international trade is no longer a random phenomenon where anonymous producers and buyers engage in exchange of what they produce and consume. Rather, international trade and investment decisions increasingly depend on a successful ecosystem of producers, suppliers, and providers of specialized services and infrastructure, along with cooperation from the public sector on essential issues of tax, finance, innovation, and quality control. There is a growing tendency for global apparel investors, buyers, and producers to rely on concerted public support

Mallika Shakya is Wolfson Research Fellow at the School of Interdisciplinary Area Studies, University of Oxford.

that harnesses new production methods, facilities, and logistical models. Beyond macroeconomic soundness, countries should also give attention to micro- and meso-level issues related to delivery of necessary public goods for private investment. All of these factors add up to a better business-enabling environment necessary for sustained competitiveness.

Not only is the apparel industry an entry point for a broad range of light manufacturing industries but, if managed well, it has the capacity to unleash the growth and competitiveness potential of an economy. Growth of the apparel industry makes immediate contributions to employment and creates tremendous potential for backward and forward linkages that are important to developing countries such as Lesotho.

Lesotho exported just under $350 million worth of apparel to the United States in 2008, approximately 29 percent of apparel exports (Edwards and Lawrence 2009) from all of Sub-Saharan Africa to the United States for that year (figure 13.1). Although this marks a dip from the amount exported in 2004, Lesotho still exports substantially more apparel than its closest rivals in the sector, Madagascar and Kenya. The value of Lesotho's apparel exports to the United States is about three times higher than those of Swaziland, a country that has similar geopolitical conditions and that follows Lesotho's growth path to a certain extent. Lesotho is also far ahead of neighboring Mozambique, which exported less than $400,000 worth of apparel to the United States in 2008, approximately 0.1 percent of the amount Lesotho exported.

Other African countries, such as Cameroon, Ghana, and Tanzania, lag far behind Lesotho in apparel exports,

and even middle-income countries in Sub-Saharan Africa such as Mauritius and South Africa are rapidly losing their comparative and competitive advantages in the apparel sector. Although both these countries exported amounts comparable with that of Lesotho in 2001, the situation changed dramatically in 2008, when Mauritius exported only about $100 million worth of apparel and South Africa exported a negligible amount to the United States. While South Africa exports some of its apparel to the European Union (EU) and has a significant domestic market, it is quite striking that Lesotho, a country with a very small domestic market, exports three times as much apparel than Mauritius and is decisively ahead of larger African countries Madagascar and Kenya. Even though the global financial crisis negatively affected Lesotho's apparel exports in 2008 and 2009, it is difficult to challenge the country's success between 2001 and 2007.

Figure 13.1 shows that Lesotho's apparel exports to the American market grew exponentially in the late 1990s and early 2000s, before more or less stabilizing in recent years. A brief slowdown due to the uncertainty in international trade agreements resulted in the closure of six firms and a moderate compromise on exports in 2004 and 2005, but four new firms entered the market at the same time, and there was a significant increase in total employment in the apparel industry. Despite the impact of the 2008/2009 global financial crisis recovery has been relatively quick.

The magnitude of Lesotho's apparel industry success becomes clearer when its export figures are weighed against the size of its population. While high population density and availability of cheap labor explain the success of the apparel industry in Bangladesh, China, and India, the situation is not that straightforward in Africa. As measured by apparel exports per capita, smaller countries with lower population density are outperforming larger countries with large labor forces (figure 13.2). Lesotho, in fact, outranks other apparel-producing countries in Sub-Saharan Africa, with apparel exports per capita of $177 as of 2009. Swaziland and Mauritius have the second- and third-largest per capita apparel exports, respectively, among Sub-Saharan African countries.

The apparel industry represents a significant proportion of Lesotho's gross domestic product (GDP), trade, and employment. Clothing, in fact, has represented the majority of Lesotho's total exports since the late 1990s (figure 13.3). In addition to Lesotho's successful entry into the U.S. apparel market, investors are producing higher-value-added items such as woven shirts and men's trousers and are now targeting the regional (South African) and EU

Figure 13.1   U.S. Imports of Clothing and Textiles from AGOA Countries

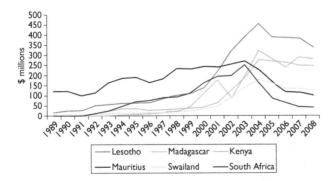

Source: U.S. Trade Development Agency.

Figure 13.2   Per Capita Apparel Exports to the
           United States

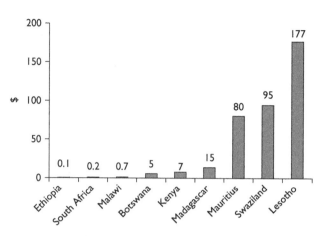

Source: Apparel data, Edwards and Lawrence 2009; population data, United
Nations database.

Figure 13.3   Composition of Lesotho's Exports

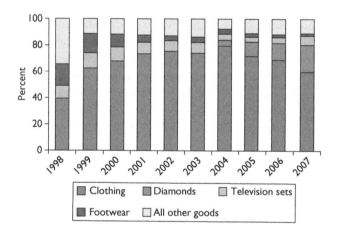

Source: Lesotho Bureau of Statistics.

markets. Lesotho has also emerged as one of the few African countries where regionally grown cotton is processed into denim and exported as part of final apparel products to the United States.

Beyond economic considerations, direct employment benefits make Lesotho's apparel industry an important part of the national economy. In 2010 just under 40,000 of a total population of 1.9 million people were employed in the apparel industry. Figure 13.4 shows the extent to which labor conditions in the apparel sector dictate the overall employment conditions in Lesotho.

Figure 13.4   Employment Trends in Lesotho

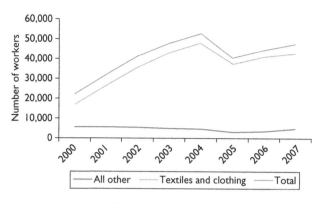

Source: Lesotho Bureau of Statistics.

GLOBAL AND REGIONAL TRADE AGREEMENTS SET THE STAGE FOR APPAREL TRADE

AGOA, which went into effect in October 2000, designated 34 "least developed" countries in Sub-Saharan Africa as eligible for specialized trade benefits in the United States.[1] Swaziland was designated as the 35th AGOA-eligible country in January 2001. Under AGOA, Lesotho's apparel exports enjoy duty-free access to the American markets until 2012, making them up to 15 percent cheaper in the U.S. market than exports from non-Sub-Saharan African countries. And because Lesotho is still categorized as a least developed country under AGOA, it is exempt from the rules of origin clause, meaning that it is free to import fabrics and other inputs from anywhere in the world.

Because it was among the first countries to put necessary systems into place, Lesotho was among the first African countries to reap the benefits of AGOA. It was not until February 2002, for example, that neighboring Mozambique was technically qualified for the U.S. apparel provision. To qualify for the AGOA, each country must ensure the United States Trade Representative's office that it has the administrative capacity to effectively monitor against possible abuse of the privileges granted under AGOA.

The period from 2000 to 2004 was a unique time for African countries seeking to seize opportunities in the global apparel market. During these years African countries not only received preferential treatment in the U.S. market under AGOA, but the preference came at a time when quota-based restrictions were being imposed on exports from large Asian countries to the United States under the Multifibre Agreement (MFA).[2] For some large Asian countries, the MFA-imposed quota meant that they could only export less than half of what they had historically exported.

The MFA quota, however, could be borrowed from the forthcoming year and any unused quota from one year could be carried over to the next. More importantly, quotas could be transferred between countries (that is, countries wishing to export more could purchase quotas from countries not using them). At times the value of quota reached up to 30 percent of the original value of apparel being traded. Over time, this quota system encouraged large Asian manufacturers to relocate their operations to less-developed countries, such as Lesotho, that could participate in preferential trade arrangements with the United States. In addition to the tariff-based preferences it offered, Lesotho's historical ties to East Asian countries made it attractive as a location for apparel manufacturing.

KEY FACTORS BEHIND LESOTHO'S COMPETITIVENESS IN APPAREL

There is no set formula to explain why some countries are more competitive than others in a given industry. In general, competitiveness stems from sophisticated firms engaging in productive ventures, supported by a policy and institutional environment in which firms are able and encouraged to forgo rent-seeking behavior and government and market failures are overcome. In this regard, competitiveness is a kind of continued filtration process through which well-performing firms and markets distinguish themselves from weaker firms.

Although a sound macroeconomic environment is necessary for increased competitiveness of a sector, that alone will not create competitiveness when the basic building blocks of industrialization, such as having a critical mass of firms that can develop a sustainable economic ecosystem, are missing, as is often the case in Sub-Saharan Africa. Development of a critical mass of firms, however, is subject to public support for necessary institutional and infrastructural mechanisms. In the case of Lesotho's apparel industry, the institutional framework was created through a coordinated public-private partnership.

To answer the question of why Lesotho succeeded in apparel while most other African countries failed, despite having equally preferential market access through AGOA, a closer examination of the costs of apparel manufacturing is needed. Beyond having the appropriate macroeconomic fundamentals in place, success in apparel manufacturing is related to labor and overhead costs, which together represent the bulk of the cost of apparel manufacturing. Figure 13.5 shows that while labor makes up as much as 49 percent of the nonmaterial costs of apparel manufacturing, overhead

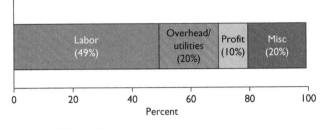

Figure 13.5 Breakdown of Nonmaterial Costs of Apparel Production in Lesotho

Source: World Bank 2006.

and utilities are 20 percent of such costs. Both of these costs are dependent on the presence of public goods that are necessary for factories' efforts to reduce cost and enhance competitiveness.

Factory market

A typical apparel factory in Southern Africa spends approximately 20 percent of total production costs in overhead and utilities, including land, electricity, and transportation. Land ownership in Southern Africa was historically under a communal system, and later a public system, hence there is no commercial land market. Availability of land is a major problem for any foreign investor seeking to start a business venture in Southern Africa. In Lesotho, even if land becomes available, the cost of renting it is sometimes as high as in developed countries, and obtaining a permit to construct a factory or other commercial building on the land takes an average of 16 months. According to the *Doing Business* report, it takes 601 days to obtain a construction permit in Lesotho, compared with the Sub-Saharan African average of 260; and 157 days in developed countries. The cost of obtaining a construction permit in Lesotho is 670 percent of per capita gross national product, compared with 56 percent in developed countries, while the unsubsidized rate of renting a factory shell in Lesotho is more than twice the rate for a comparable facility in South Africa and other developed countries.

While national land ownership systems are not likely to be reformed overnight, it seems logical for governments to offer transitional arrangements for commercial land use in the form of hassle-free leasing contracts. This point was highlighted in a study commissioned by the government of Lesotho in 2002 to develop a comprehensive apparel industry development plan. Among the 11 principal constraints to the growth of the apparel industry in Lesotho identified in the report, lack of industrial land and factory shells were the top two constraints.

To compensate for high land costs, the government of Lesotho constructed industrial zones and serviced factory shells available for rent by foreign investors, allowing investors to avoid cumbersome bureaucratic processes. Two large industrial zones—Maputsoe on 29 hectares of land and Ha on 10 hectares—were built between 1991 and 1995. Additional zones were built subsequently on the Lesotho–South Africa border areas of Mohale's Hoek, Mfeteng, and Butha Buthe. Currently these fully functional industrial zones in Lesotho together house about 60 factories and employ just under 40,000 workers (figure 13.6).

The industrial zones provide a range of real estate services to assist manufacturing and commercial enterprises, including fully serviced industrial plots, customized factory buildings, and development of commercial properties for leasing. The buildings are fully serviced with electricity, telephone, water, and sewerage. All six zones can be reached by tarred road, are within reach of the public transport system, and have access to rail links connecting them to apparel distribution hubs in Johannesburg.

Because the land tenure system in Lesotho does not provide for land being bought or sold, investors were offered long-term leases within these zones and were given the option to sublease if necessary. Rental procedures and regulatory processes were simplified and centralized so that the export promotion agency, Lesotho National Development Corporation (LNDC), could undertake all necessary administrative procedures and cater to the business needs of potential foreign investors. In fact, LNDC's success as an export promotion agency draws enormously on its success as a property developer and service provider, which catalyzed development of a critical mass of first-generation apparel manufacturing companies in Lesotho. After managing these services in house for several years, LNDC recently began subcontracting day-to-day property operation and maintenance tasks to JHI Real Estate, a prominent estate management company active in several other African countries.

Timing was crucial to the success of industrial zone construction in Lesotho, a point that is often omitted from policy discussions. After AGOA became effective in 2000, and foreign investors operating in East and South Asia

Figure 13.6   Industrial Zones in Lesotho

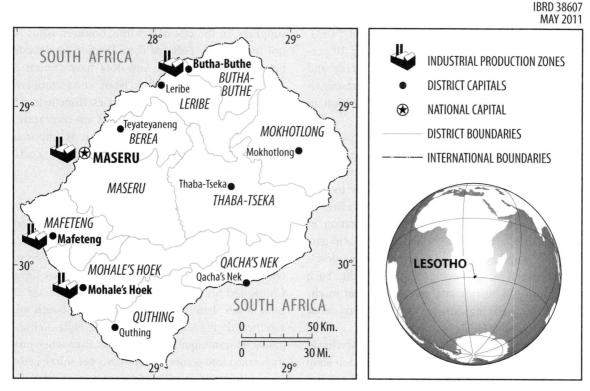

Source: Government of Lesotho.

began to operate factories in Africa, and Lesotho was among the few countries that already had industrial zones with well-equipped and serviced factory shells. As a specific response to AGOA, Lesotho offered the apparel investors subsidized rent for at least the first five years of operation. While the sustainability and macroeconomic rationale of this policy decision may be questioned, it virtually preempted the efforts of other countries in the region to attract foreign direct investment (FDI).

Export and investment promotion

Observers often claim that export and investment promotion activities have not yielded results and that they have instead become rent-seeking activities. This is true in several cases both in Africa and elsewhere in which export promotion agencies are captive to poor leadership due to heavy government involvement, inadequate funding, cumbersome bureaucracy, and lack of client orientation. At times, countries suffer from strong antitrade bias and anti-FDI sentiment. By many measures, Lesotho's success in export and investment promotion defies the general trend in developing countries. The LNDC is the main wing of the government charged with the implementation of export and investment promotion programs. Founded in 1967 by an act of parliament, LNDC was amended in 1990 and again in October 2000. LNDC is primarily owned by the government of Lesotho (90 percent); DEG, a German finance company, owns the remaining 10 percent. The LNDC is part of the Ministry of Trade and Industry, Cooperatives and Marketing, which is responsible for overall policy direction on industrialization in Lesotho.

The LNDC works with medium and large companies in the manufacturing and services sectors to strengthen Lesotho's exports and generate foreign investment in Lesotho. Rather than relying on a broad strategy to promote all exports, the LNDC focuses on nontraditional exports. Because of Lesotho's extreme concentration in apparel, the LNDC also has functioned as a de facto garment promotion agency in the past several decades, developing with it several sector-specific skills and insights. Such insights have proved instrumental in ensuring that incentive packages offered to investors are not poorly utilized or captured by rent-seekers.

In addition to the LNDC's role as real estate developer, facilitator, and service provider, it acts as a one-stop shop that covers most aspects of company operations, ranging from business inquiries, site selection, firm registration, regulation and facilitation on various aspects of production and sales, and management of government incentive schemes and tax procedures (box 13.1). Through its Investment Promotion Center (IPC), the LNDC markets Lesotho as a destination of choice to potential manufacturers. To achieve this, it has developed an information dissemination system that reaches out to potential investors within Lesotho, Southern Africa, and beyond. The LNDC has sent trade missions to South and East Asia to mobilize networks of firms that are already invested in Lesotho. One factor behind the success of Lesotho's export and investment promotion is that the IPC has adopted tailor-made strategies to attract and sustain investments from very different investors, including those from South Africa; China; Taiwan, China; and elsewhere. In recent years, the IPC has also sought to attract yarn, trim, zipper, button, bag, hanger, and carton manufacturers to Lesotho. To some extent, these specialized manufacturers can assist Lesotho in taking full advantage of AGOA and allow a structured approach to inward investment.

Labor coordination and skill development

At 49 percent, labor is the largest nonmaterial cost in Lesotho. It goes without saying that labor costs directly influence investors' decisions about where to locate their operations and buyers' decisions about where to choose suppliers. In the case of Lesotho, however, labor costs are not the primary point of consideration for investors and buyers. In other words, investors have chosen Lesotho despite its relatively higher labor costs compared with other Sub-Saharan African countries. Nonetheless, because production and sourcing dynamics are constantly changing in the global apparel market, it is important that Lesotho takes measures to reduce labor costs while improving labor productivity.

LABOR COSTS ARE HIGH IN LESOTHO COMPARED TO OTHER SUB-SAHARAN AFRICAN COUNTRIES. Hourly wages range from approximately $0.14 to $1.80 in apparel-producing African countries as well as in several non-African countries with significant apparel sectors such as Bangladesh, China, and Sri Lanka. Wages in Lesotho average $0.46 an hour, lower than those in Mauritius and South Africa but significantly higher than those in Ethiopia, Kenya, Madagascar, Mozambique, and Swaziland. Even when productivity is taken into account (labor costs per shirt), Lesotho still is an expensive manufacturer compared with Ethiopia, Kenya, Madagascar, and Mozambique (figure 13.7).

Box 13.1   LNDC as a One-Stop Shop

Company support

- Business registration procedures
- Acquisition of permits and manufacturing licenses
- License and residency paperwork for foreign workers, managers, and owners
- Arrangement of site visits and assistance in selection of suitable sites
- Key focal point for contact with relevant ministries on business regulations
- Facilitation of contact with business companies supplying services
- Facilitation of skill and technology development programs
- Industrial relations if disputes arise with workers

Management of incentive schemes

- Unimpeded access to foreign exchange
- Export finance facility

Source: Consultations with LNDC officials.

- Short- and long-term loans
- Import value added tax (VAT) credit facility for local purchase of raw materials and capital goods

Tax management oversight

- No tax on income generated from exports outside the Southern African Customs Union
- Permanent maximum manufacturing tax rate of 10 percent on profits
- No tax on dividends to local or foreign shareholders
- Free repatriation of profits
- Double taxation agreements with Germany, Mauritius, South Africa, and the United Kingdom

Investment attraction

- Information dissemination to targeted investor pools
- Trade missions to targeted markets and investor pools

LABOR UNIONS IN LESOTHO HAVE UNDERGONE A MAJOR TRANSITION. The first apparel factories were set up in Lesotho by South African companies in the 1980s, and were, for the most part, subsidiaries of bigger industrial conglomerates that had specialized for decades in the South African market. Primarily located in Maputsoe, these companies initially established higher labor standards for Lesotho. They negotiated recognition agreements with the trade union of employees at the LNDC and the Department of Labor. While those negotiations were frequently difficult and protracted, they inevitably resulted in pay increases for workers. Over the years, negotiations with trade unions became commonplace among apparel companies in Lesotho, even among those where the majority of employees were not union members.

The new generation of apparel manufacturers and buyers that moved to Lesotho in response to the MFA and AGOA provisions created a demand for a very different set of labor skills and expectations. In short, the industry became less regulated by local labor codes and more influenced by the global momentum around labor-related corporate social responsibility. The apparel industry in Lesotho underwent a major labor crisis in the 2000s as a result, one that involved policy deadlocks and street riots. On one

hand, workers were upset that job stability was no longer guaranteed; on the other, factory owners were frustrated about low labor productivity. Fueling the antagonism were several cases of exploitation of workers by foreign factory owners and foreign supervisors.

The Lesotho Clothing and Allied Workers Union (LECAWU) is the predominant union representing employees of the apparel industry. It was formed under the terms of the national labor code of Lesotho in1992 and is recognized by the government of Lesotho as the representative of labor. Historically, anti-union sentiment has made it difficult for LECAWU to organize workers; the unwillingness of management, particularly in Maseru and Thetsane, to engage in meaningful negotiation also impeded the union. Nevertheless, LECAWU membership has grown in recent years as a result of AGOA provisions, changes in apparel companies' codes of conduct, and increasing interest in labor relations among company owners and managers. The labor movement in Lesotho encouraged the government to create the legislative framework that set up the Industrial Relations Council, the Directorate for Dispute Prevention and Resolution, and the Labor Appeal Court. This important piece of legislation provides for the settling of labor disputes through mediation, conciliation, and arbitration,

Figure 13.7 a. Factory-Floor Productivity and Labor Costs in Apparel Assembly; b. Hourly Wages for Apparel Assembly
(US cents)

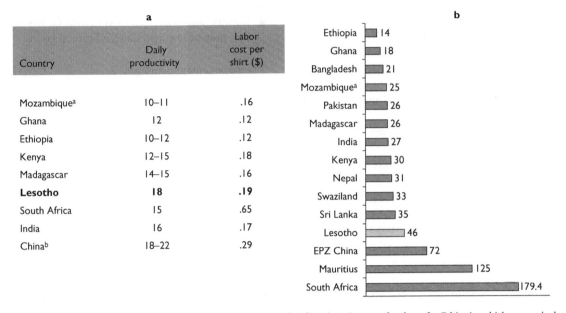

	a	
Country	Daily productivity	Labor cost per shirt ($)
Mozambique[a]	10–11	.16
Ghana	12	.12
Ethiopia	10–12	.12
Kenya	12–15	.18
Madagascar	14–15	.16
Lesotho	**18**	**.19**
South Africa	15	.65
India	16	.17
China[b]	18–22	.29

b

Ethiopia	14
Ghana	18
Bangladesh	21
Mozambique[a]	25
Pakistan	26
Madagascar	26
India	27
Kenya	30
Nepal	31
Swaziland	33
Sri Lanka	35
Lesotho	46
EPZ China	72
Mauritius	125
South Africa	179.4

Source: Labor productivity figures and costs are from Eifert, Gelb, and Ramachandran (2005) except for those for Ethiopia, which were calculated using Global Development Solutions (2005). Hourly wages were collected from government sources.
Note: Daily productivity is the number of men's casual shirts made by a machine operator in one day.
a. Mozambique wage indicates the minimum industry wage specified under the national labor law.
b. Data for China is for export processing zones only.

effectively creating an independent authority that is representative of the government, employees, and employers.

The global labor movement has benefited the local labor movement in Lesotho. As manufacturing has shifted from developed to developing countries, there has been growing concern among developed-country consumers, as well as from activists and nongovernmental organizations (NGOs), regarding the wages and work conditions under which products are manufactured. As a result, most major multinational companies have adopted codes of conduct they require their suppliers to meet. In addition, a number of NGOs have devised codes of conduct in partnership with the multinationals: these include the U.K.-based Ethical Trading Initiative (sponsored, in part, by the Department for International Development, or DFID), the Institute of Social and Ethical Accountability, the Global Reporting Institute, the Netherlands-based Clean Clothes Campaign, the U.S.-based Fair Labor Association, the U.S.-based Worker Rights Consortium, and the EU's European Code of Conduct. A major private initiative called Social Accountability 8000 (SA8000), along with the nonprofit organization Account-Ability's AA1000, are attempting to create a benchmark for

social accountability much like the ISO9000 has done for quality. Meanwhile, several multinational apparel manufacturing companies have formed the Worldwide Responsible Accredited Production (WRAP) principles to accredit suppliers. In addition, all major multinational apparel manufacturing companies have their own codes of conduct.

The need to comply with the various codes of conduct has created a major change in most apparel factories in Lesotho. And though the inspections surrounding such codes of conduct can measure a degree of compliance, industrial relations will be smooth and sustainable in the long term only if they contribute to productivity.

LABOR PRODUCTIVITY MUST INCREASE. A typical apparel factory now works with its workers, regulators, and service providers as a group to drive down costs and improve standards. By working with providers of training and skills, factories are able to shift to new production methods that reduce costs, improve product quality, and enhance factories' commitment to their workers. Nike's shift from a normal assembly line production system to "lean manufacturing," for example, has been marked with significantly higher productivity and better labor conditions. The initiative has been followed by the incorporation of more sophisticated production planning and merchandising systems, such as "Just in Time," that aim to eliminate inefficiencies in space, time, and activity and also manage the inventory stock.

Most buyers of apparel assess their producers on four key criteria: cost, quality, timeliness, and corporate responsibility (that is, labor and environmental standards) (figure 13.8). After an initial baseline is developed, buyers regularly measure factories' performance to track delivery, quality, and prices over time. Indicators are typically expected to improve each quarter. Such proactive measures toward labor productivity are not yet under way in Lesotho, although a number of initial steps have been taken. The fact that Lesotho is at the lower end of productivity in apparel manufacturing means that it needs to develop systematic analyses to diagnose bottlenecks and then design institution measures to tackle those bottlenecks accordingly.

SUCCESSFUL SKILL DEVELOPMENT INITIATIVES. In 1999 the Lesotho Garment Center (LGC) was opened to provide necessary training for the apparel workforce. Developed with funding from the DFID, the LGC had the objective of training workers and entrepreneurs in the management of industrial apparel production in anticipation of their participation in the opportunities presented by AGOA. Although the LGC succeeded in training hundreds

of machinists, its primary aim of launching entrepreneurs into the formal garment subsector was not successful, and it was terminated in 2003. Lesotho's experience with the LGC is similar to that of several other developing countries, where the public sector has developed channels to support the private sector that turn out to be ineffective. Coordination and incentive structures have been major problems in making public sector efforts useful for the private sector.

No other training institutes have been created to fill the void left by the termination of the LGC. Several other training establishments, such as Lerotholi Polytechnic and the Institute of Development Management, offer a range of generic management and general studies, although none are tailored to the needs of the formal garment sector. Lerotholi Polytechnic offers a two-year series of courses related to the apparel industry, for example, but the focus is on design, pattern construction, and bespoke tailoring. The Commercial Training Institute offers similar courses that lead to the award of a certificate in tailoring and dressmaking. The Basotho Enterprise Development Corporation (BEDCO) also runs a series of short courses, including marketing skills and, actively seeks to identify and focus on the future needs of the garment industry. Saint Luke's Mission in Maputsoe offers a three-year course providing students with a range of apparel industry skills, including pattern construction, machine knitting, small business studies, leadership, management skills, and industrial garment production on the appropriate machinery.

Upon completion of these courses, many students are employed in the local craft industry or their own enterprises, but very few graduates from these institutes end up working on the apparel shop floors. The training institutes are seldom approached by apparel manufacturers to train managers, workers, or technicians, underscoring the need for sector-specific contents and modules in training institutes for them to be truly useful to employers. This scenario highlights a larger problem in the apparel industry in Lesotho: while existing training institutes do not cater to the apparel industry, apparel factories report that their in-house training facilities are not sufficient. For the most part, trainees in factories are taught single machine skills rather than being cross-trained.

Most apparel factories in Lesotho also acknowledge the need for trained supervisors and indicate that they are prepared to pay for it. In the factory survey, 69 percent of interviewees confirmed that they would support training programs that addressed their particular sector needs if such programs were delivered in a way that minimized employees'

Figure 13.8   Buyer's Scorecard for Assessment of Producer Competitiveness

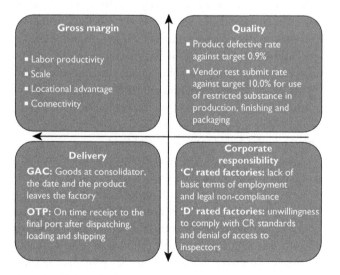

Source: World Bank 2006.

time away from the workplace. Approximately 11 percent said they might support such a facility, while 20 percent said they would not. Only one of the companies surveyed had actually developed a supervisory training course, and is using its own staff to deliver the training. The course covers a range of topics, from organization and planning to industrial relations and health and safety. The most common reasons companies gave for developing their own courses were that no such courses were available locally and that they had concerns about quality of delivery and training materials provided by third parties.

The fact that services offered by existing training institutes are not used by apparel factories while the same factories acknowledge need for more effective training indicates a coordination gap. While an initiative is under way in Lesotho to develop broader public-private coordination on skill development, it is too early to comment on its success. Among the commendable initiatives in this direction has been the development of an interactive database that would collate information on leading global and regional experts in specific areas. Depending on the interest from the private sector, selected experts would be invited to develop training modules that would feed into this interactive database. Eventually, private sector participants would be expected to use those modules to commission training at their own expense. The success of such an initiative will depend on the degree of collaboration among various stakeholders. A breakthrough in this area will be necessary for Lesotho to climb up the global apparel quality value chain.

Transport, logistics, and customs

The time and cost of transport is often an important barrier to competitiveness in the apparel industry. A smooth transport corridor supported by competent logistical service providers and punctuated by efficient border crossing mechanisms is a prerequisite for any exporting economy. Thanks to the critical mass of apparel producers that regularly use the corridor between Maseru and Johannesburg, Lesotho has made enormous strides in developing systems for transport, customs, and logistics.

The road infrastructure in Lesotho is substantially developed and is well connected to the extensive road networks of South Africa. Trucking services are provided by private operators that cater to a wide range of apparel producers. Although there is only one railhead in Lesotho, it is located in Maseru, just across the river border with South Africa. Railway lines, station buildings, and handling facilities in

Lesotho are owned and operated by Spoornet, the South African rail service.

Customs processes in Lesotho have significantly improved since AGOA took effect. The government has put in place a rigorous training and regulation system among the customs staff to meet the requirements of exports under the AGOA visa scheme and now offers duty rebates on fabrics imported in the production of apparel exports. Further, a duty credit scheme was put in place for exporters of manufactured goods that use raw materials sourced from Southern African Customs Union countries. For certain factories, customs requires closer inspection of waste and offcuts disposal before rebates on imported materials are issued, though such inspections are expedited after factories establish a good track record or after in-factory inspections are streamlined with other regulatory measures. Such multiple inspection requirements necessitate an efficient, well-trained customs team to ensure smooth implementation.

LESSONS FROM LESOTHO'S APPAREL INDUSTRY EXPERIENCE

Integration into global supply chains has been an important avenue for growth and competitiveness for Lesotho's apparel industry. Geographical advantages and disadvantages—of weather, location, and connectivity—cannot be ignored, but discovery and pursuit of new opportunities through correct formulation of policies and development of effective public-private partnerships has been the key channel through which Lesotho has achieved apparel industry success. Several key features of this success story can be identified.

First, the government of Lesotho was successful in attracting foreign investors through its policy of constructing industrial zones and serviced factory shells. Throughout this process, the government has remained cognizant of the geographical implications of such facilities, ensuring that they are not far from the public goods necessary for industrialization. Construction and effective management of the factory shells compensated for inherent inefficiencies in the land market in the form of prohibitions on private ownership and sales-based transactions of land.

Second, when AGOA-related opportunities became available, Lesotho made stronger, clearer efforts to attract FDI than other countries in Southern Africa. Lesotho not only moved quickly to administer AGOA in country but also offered generous tax and financial incentives to early investors to help develop a critical mass of apparel manufacturers that then made way for service providers and regulatory bodies to join in.

Third, Lesotho's export and investment promotion efforts would not have been effective without the LNDC, which pursued promotion measures through appropriate information dissemination models and targeted interest solicitation. Once a critical mass of apparel investors came to Lesotho, the LNDC developed an effective one-stop shop for business development, firm registration, financing, and state-industry coordination on issues such as tax management and access to state industrialization incentives.

Fourth, when labor disputes arose around the industrial transition, the government of Lesotho quickly stepped in to mediate among multiple stakeholders who were nurturing mutual antagonism.

And fifth, although it is too early to make informed verdicts, the government of Lesotho has acknowledged its past mistakes on skill development and is developing a coordinated skill development initiative in conjunction with the private sector. If successful, the initiative will compensate Lesotho for its competitive disadvantage in labor costs.

NOTES

1. As per the definition as used in AGOA, a least developed country in Sub-Saharan Africa is a country with gross national product (GNP) per capita of less than $1,500 in 1998. This provision was renewed in 2006 for the period 2007–12.

2. The Multifibre Arrangement governed textile and clothing quotas between 1974 and the end of 1994. Upon formation of the World Trade Organization in 1995, textile exports became governed by the Agreement on Textiles and Clothing.

BIBLIOGRAPHY

Edwards, L., and R. Lawrence. 2009. "Lesotho's Export Performance: An African Successful Story?" National Bureau for Economic Research, Cambridge, MA.

Eifert, B., A. Gelb, and V. Ramachandran. 2005. "Business Environment and Comparative Advantage in Africa: Evidence from the Investment Climate Data." Working Paper, Center for Global Development, Washington, DC.

DFID. 2006. "Lesotho Garment Industry Subsector Study" conducted for the government of Lesotho.

EIU (Economist Intelligence Unit). 2007. "Country Profile: Mozambique." EIU, London.

FIAS (Foreign Investment and Advisory Services). 2006. "Market Diversification of the Lesotho Garment Industry." Discussion draft, Innernational Finance Corporation and World Bank, Washington, DC.

Global Development Solutions. 2005. "Value Chain Analysis for Strategic Sectors in Mozambique." Reston, VA.

Horton, C. 1996. "Capital Flows from South Africa into Neighboring Countries: The Case of Textiles and Clothing." Naledi papers. National Labour and Economic Development Institute, Johannesburg.

Kaplinsky, R., D. McCormick, and M. Morris. 2006. "Dangling by a Thread: How Sharp Are the Chinese Scissors?" Institute of Development Studies, University of Sussex, Brighton, United Kingdom.

Minor, P. 2005. "Survey of US Apparel Buyers: Sourching from Sub-Saharan Africa in the Post-Quota MFA." Unpublished paper, Nathan Associates Inc. Arlington, VA.

———. 2007. "Developing a Cotton Textile and Apparel Value Chain in Mozambique." Nathan Associates Inc, Arlington, VA.

Morris, M., and L. Sedowski. 2006. "Report on Government Responses to New Post-MFA Realities in Lesotho." PRISM Working Paper, Centre for Social Science Research, University of Cape Town.

World Bank. 2006. "Lesotho Country Economic Memorandum: Growth and Employment Options Study." World Bank, Washington, DC.

CHAPTER 14

The Success of Tourism in Rwanda: Gorillas and More

Hannah Nielsen and Anna Spenceley

Rwanda is well known for its mountain gorillas. First brought to international attention by the conservation efforts of Dian Fossey in the 1960s and 1970s, Rwanda's gorillas have been featured in numerous documentaries and have been visited by well-known figures such as Bill Gates, Natalie Portman, and Ted Turner, all of whom have participated in Rwanda's annual gorilla-naming ceremony.

Rwanda and Uganda are currently the only two countries in the world where mountain gorillas can be visited safely, and the number of tourists visiting the Volcanoes National Park (VNP) has increased dramatically since the end of the war. Rwanda also views gorilla tourism as a valuable conservation tool, and as such enforces strict rules for the habituation of, and trekking with, gorilla families. Tourists are willing to pay high fees for a limited number of permits, which are usually sold out. Revenues from gorilla tourism provide funds to national parks and facilitate conservation activities.

Although Rwanda is known for its violent past, international perception of the country is shifting. As of 2010 Rwanda is considered one of the safest destinations in East Africa. This rebranding goes hand in hand with the marketing of the country and, in particular, the mountain gorillas. The revival of gorilla tourism demonstrates that with the right strategy, a postconflict country can successfully focus on high-end tourism while maintaining conservation and contributing to poverty reduction through the involvement of communities.

Besides the VNP, Rwanda has two other national parks that offer a range of wildlife and biodiversity. Furthermore, the country has been particularly successful in attracting large numbers of business and conference travelers, mainly from the Democratic Republic of Congo and other neighboring countries of the East African Community (EAC).[1] This success is evidenced by the large increase in the number of hotel rooms, restaurants, and the planned construction of a convention center. Local and foreign direct investments have been substantial, accounting for 16 and 20 percent of total local and foreign direct investment, respectively, over the last 10 years. In terms of export revenue, tourism already outperforms coffee and tea by a wide margin.

Several key characteristics have contributed to the successful revival of the tourism sector in Rwanda. First and foremost, the government has shown a clear commitment to the development of tourism and has established Rwanda as a safe destination in the region. The early development of a strategy and policy demonstrated this commitment. Furthermore, the government involved the private sector from the start and has implemented policies that enhanced the business environment and promoted private sector

Hannah Nielsen is an economist in the Poverty Reduction and Economic Management Network of the Africa Region of the World Bank. Anna Spenceley, PhD, is an independent consultant based in South Africa, and formerly a senior tourism advisor at SNV in Rwanda.

investment in tourism, thereby marketing Rwanda as a destination. The business environment has improved markedly in recent years, promoting private sector involvement in tourism. In addition, Rwanda has always seen tourism as an instrument to reduce poverty, for example by directly involving local communities.

THE SUCCESS OF GORILLA TOURISM

Background: How did Rwanda start to develop gorilla tourism?

The Virunga mountain gorilla (*Gorilla beringei beringei*) is a highly endangered African ape subspecies, with a total estimated population of 380, that exists only in the Virunga Conservation Area encompassing Rwanda, the Democratic Republic of Congo, and Uganda(figure 14.1). The distribution of the Virunga mountain gorillas is limited to an approximate area of 447 square kilometers, which encompasses the Mgahinga Gorilla National Park in Uganda, the VNP in Rwanda, and the Mikeno sector of the Parc National des Virunga of the Democratic Republic of Congo (Gray et al. 2005). The VNP consists of about 160 square kilometers of montane forest. Until Rwanda's independence in 1962, the VNP was part of Africa's first national park, the Parc National Albert, which was created in 1925 with the intention of protecting the great apes (ORTPN 2004).

Tours to view wild mountain gorilla groups have been organized since 1955 (Butynaski and Kalina 1997), with the first attempts at habituation for this purpose occurring as early as 1966 (Murnyak 1981). These early tourism programs displayed an almost complete lack of structure and control. The focus was on revenue rather than conservation, and there are many anecdotal reports of large groups of tourists visiting groups of nonhabituated or semihabituated gorillas (Fawcett, Hodgkinson, and Mehlman 2004).

In 1979 the Virunga region's first official mountain gorilla tourism program was launched by Bill Webber and Amy Vedder with funding from the African Wildlife Foundation, World Wide Fund for Nature, and Fauna and Flora International (Bush 2009). It was one part of the three-part approach of the Mountain Gorilla Project, which also included antipoaching and education programs. The gorilla tourism program had a dual purpose: providing the Rwandan government and park authorities an incentive to conserve the VNP and the animals within it from the threat of proposed conversion of 5,000 hectares of the VNP for agricultural purposes; and generating local employment and tourism-related revenue (Weber 1982, 1985; Vedder and Weber 1990). The program subsequently evolved into what is now the International Gorilla Conservation Program, still organized as a coalition of the three agencies (Bush 2009).

Two wild groups of gorillas were initially habituated for tourism visitation purposes, with strictly enforced limits on the number of visitors and length of visits (box 14.1). The combination of quality control and international interest in

Figure 14.1   Area of Distribution of the Mountain Gorillas

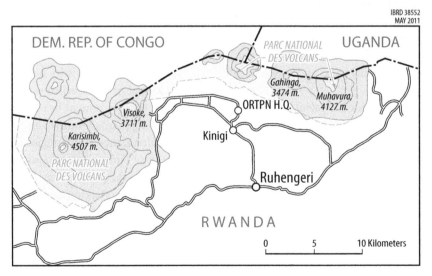

Source: Bush and Fawcett 2007.

Box 14.1   Current Rules Controlling Gorilla Tourism in Rwanda

A number of rules designed to protect both gorillas and tourists have been established, as follows:

- Maintenance of a distance of 7 meters between the tourists and the gorillas
- A maximum of eight tourists per visit
- A limit of one tourist group per day to each gorilla group
- A limit of one hour per visit
- Tourists who are visibly unwell or declare themselves to be ill may not visit

As of 1989 the number of tourists allowed in a single visit was increased to eight people (six people for smaller gorilla groups). In 1999 the required separation distance between tourists and gorillas (to reduce the risk of disease transmission) was increased from 5 to 7 meters. Other rules have been added over time:

- Minimum age of 15 years for tourists
- No flash photography

Source: Fawcett, Hodgkinson, and Mehlman 2004; Homesy 1999.

- Tourists must remain together in a tight group
- No loud noises or pointing
- Eating, drinking, and smoking are not permitted within 200 meters of the gorillas
- Tourists must turn away and cover their mouths when coughing and sneezing
- Human feces must be buried in a hole of a minimum depth of 30 centimeters
- No trash may be deposited in the park
- Tourists are not allowed to clear away vegetation to get a better view

These rules (adapted from Litchfield 1997) were designed and set to minimize behavioral disturbance and disease transmission to the gorillas from tourists. Although the welfare of the gorillas has always been the primary concern, the majority of these regulations were created based on expert opinions rather than specific research findings.

Dian Fossey's highly publicized gorilla studies resulted in steadily increased visitation throughout the 1980s, peaking around 6,900 in 1989 (ORTPN 2008b). By the mid-1980s local attitudes toward and political support for conservation increased significantly as a direct result of this program (Weber 1987). Stimulated by the attraction of gorilla tourism, Rwanda received almost 22,000 visits to its three national parks in 1990 (Bush, Hanley, and Colombo 2008), before conflict brought tourism to a halt.

Since the VNP reopened in 1999, visitation has rebounded from 417 visits that year to nearly 20,000 visits in 2008 (of which 17,000 were to see the mountain gorillas) (ORTPN 2008b). Gorilla visitation shows some amount of seasonality, with a peak in the number of permits sold between June and September (figure 14.2).

Factors contributing to the success of gorilla tourism

A number of factors have contributed to the success of gorilla tourism in Rwanda. A prerequisite is the relative ease of habituating mountain gorillas to the presence of humans, facilitated by the temperate climate and benign habitat. The only other country where mountain gorillas can currently

be visited safely is Uganda. With a broad client base[2] and a limited number of permits (around 17,000 per year), demand is higher than availability of permits. The accessibility of the gorillas is another advantage. Because of Rwanda's small size, tourists can reach the gorillas in two hours from Kigali; by comparison, it takes six hours to reach the gorillas from Kampala in Uganda. In addition, the condition of infrastructure in Rwanda, especially roads, is relatively good compared with that of its peers.

Besides viable tourism assets and relatively good infrastructure, Rwanda has shown a strong commitment to promoting the tourism sector. It has developed a clear tourism strategy, marketed the destination Rwanda successfully, involved the private sector in the policy dialogue, and generally improved the country's business environment.

OVERALL STRATEGY AND VISION. Between 1994 and 2001 the Rwandan government worked to establish a tourism-friendly environment. The first meetings with the private sector on the development of the tourism sector were held in 1999. From 2000 onward Rwanda participated in major tourism fairs, and in late 2001 the Tourism Working Group, which included the public and the private sectors, was established. The Rwanda Tourism Strategy was developed

Figure 14.2 Gorilla Trekking in Volcanoes National Park

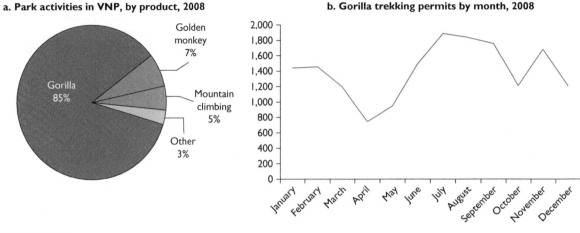

a. Park activities in VNP, by product, 2008

Gorilla 85%
Golden monkey 7%
Mountain climbing 5%
Other 3%

b. Gorilla trekking permits by month, 2008

Source: ORTPN 2008b.

and approved by the Cabinet in 2002. A revised Rwanda Tourism Strategy ("Sustaining the Momentum") was elaborated in 2007. A National Tourism Policy was put in place in 2006, a revision of which is currently under way. With support from the United Nations World Tourism Organization, the government of Rwanda has also prepared a 10-year Sustainable Tourism Development Master Plan (Republic of Rwanda 2002, 2007b, 2009a, and 2009b).

Rwanda's overall strategic vision is to focus on high-end ecotourism rather than mass tourism. In the first Rwanda Tourism Strategy, three core market segments were identified: ecotravelers, explorers, and business travelers. The targets set in that document were soon surpassed, however, mainly through the success of the gorilla product. The revised strategy in 2007 identified the primates as Rwanda's unique selling proposition but recognized the need to diversify the tourism sector and identified international conferences and birding as two additional core segments. Tourism receipts are already higher than the targets set for 2012 in the revised strategy. In the latest tourism policy, objectives are set within the framework of other national strategic documents, such as the Vision 2020 and the Economic Development and Poverty Reduction Strategy.

The Sustainable Tourism Development Master Plan for Rwanda consolidates previous strategies and policies, gives clear and detailed recommendations, and sets ambitious targets. Tourist arrivals to Rwanda are projected to increase from about 980,000 in 2008 to more than 2 million in 2020, with an expected increase in foreign exchange earnings from about $200 million to more than $600 million. Separate strategies are being developed for MICE (meetings,

incentives, conferences, and exhibitions) tourism and for birding activities (OTF Group 2008a, 2008b).

Although the different strategies have not yet been implemented completely, the Rwandan government has consistently demonstrated strong commitment to the execution of tourism-related reforms and to the overall improvement of the performance of the sector. Despite the limited number of staff in the Rwanda Office of Tourism and National Parks (ORPTN), its leadership has effectively led the advancement of reforms. Further, Rwanda has learned from the experience of other countries. Study tours have been undertaken to Kenya and Mauritius to learn from the tourism development strategies of those countries.

MARKETING. Following the passing of formal tourism plans in Rwanda, a national campaign was launched to improve the image of tourism in the country. (The word for tourism in *Kinyarwanda*, the local language, means "wandering around aimlessly" and has therefore a negative connotation.) A media campaign was launched to sensitize the population and convey that the country can benefit from tourists and should therefore welcome foreigners. Simultaneously, Rwanda has worked to improve its image on an international basis. In the late 1990s international perceptions of Rwanda were primarily associated with the genocide. Even still in 2002 market research conducted in neighboring countries showed that more than half of international visitors believed that Rwanda was an unsafe destination (Grosspietsch 2006). Despite concerns about the safety situation, however, surveys carried out in 2003 showed that the satisfaction level of visitors in terms of safety and stability was very high after they had visited the country (Grosspietsch 2006).

Specific public relations and marketing efforts pursued by Rwanda include contracting international public relations and marketing agencies in the United Kingdom and United States and launching a new Web site in 2003. In addition, Rwanda has been featured extensively in documentaries on international television channels and has received positive coverage in more than 350 credible international press publications, as well as in major travel guides. Rwanda has also represented itself well at major tourism fairs since 2000, earning first prize for the best African stand at the International Tourism Bourse in Berlin for three consecutive years, 2007–09, and at the World Travel Market in London in 2009. ORTPN's financing of travel fees for several Rwandan tour operators to these trade fairs has contributed to cooperation between the government and the private sector on issues related to tourism. To foster the interest of tour operators and travel agents in Rwanda, the government has also organized familiarization tours for international investors and tour operators, during which the Minister of Commerce and ORTPN have received the delegates to demonstrate the importance of their visit.

Rwanda's annual gorilla naming ceremony (*Kwita Izina*), launched in 2005, during which mountain gorillas born in the previous 12 months are named, has attracted a number of international celebrities. The baby gorillas have been named, among others, by the president of Rwanda and his wife, ambassadors, Hollywood stars, international conservationists, and performing artists. The ceremonies provide a good platform to promote Rwanda as a destination and the need for efforts to protect gorillas and conserve their habitat. The ceremony is now accompanied by several other events, including a cross-country cycling tour and a conservation conference. Thanks partly to the awareness of the need to protect the gorillas that the gorilla naming ceremony and gorilla tourism in general have brought about, poaching has been significantly reduced and the number of gorillas has increased steadily.

IMPROVED BUSINESS ENVIRONMENT AND INVOLVEMENT OF THE PRIVATE SECTOR. Initially, promotion of Rwanda's tourism sector was almost entirely driven and implemented by the government. The private sector lacked the capacity and funding and was not well organized. The government, however, made efforts to involve the private sector from the start with the long-term objective that the private sector would take over as the driving force for encouraging tourism in Rwanda. As a result, there is now a strong public-private dialogue surrounding tourism in Rwanda, and a tourism working group composed of private and public stakeholders in the tourism industry is now in place. The private sector is consulted in the development of new policies and strategies, such as the Sustainable Tourism Development Master Plan. In addition, the private sector federation, of which the tourism chamber is a member, is consulted before new strategies and laws are adopted.

Rwanda has implemented a number of market-based reforms to strengthen the role of the private sector in tourism. Several important laws and codes have been revised, including the investment code, company law, secure transactions law, labor law, and insolvency law. The new insolvency law facilitates the access to finance, allowing movables, such as livestock, to be used as guarantee. Customs procedures are also being simplified. A pilot, one-stop-window was successfully launched at one border crossing, and plans are in the works to replicate it at other border posts.

Rwanda's business environment has also improved substantially in recent years. A one-stop-window has been introduced to register a business, and the administrative costs of registering a business have been lowered. It is now possible to register a business within one day for a flat fee of RF 25,000 ($43). Rwanda's success in this area has been documented by a substantial improvement in the World Bank's *Doing Business* indicators: Rwanda was named the top performer in 2009. Rwanda outperforms all other countries in the EAC in the rankings and has shown a strong commitment to further improving private sector conditions, particularly in the tourism sector.

A number of tourism sector–related incentives are offered to investors. According to the investment code, tax exemptions are granted to investors who invest $100,000 or more in a facility. Airplanes imported to transport tourists are tax exempt, and specialized vehicles such as hotel shuttles are exempt from import and excise duties. An investor in the tourism and hotel industry is also exempt from payment of import duties on equipment such as bedroom fittings, swimming pools, and outdoor leisure equipment.

BENEFITS OF GORILLA TOURISM

Implications for communities

Bush, Hanley, and Colombo (2008) note that the Virunga mountain gorilla represents an isolated island population in an upland area surrounded by a sea of humanity at some of the highest densities found on the African continent (in some areas of Rwanda, population density reaches 820 people per square kilometer), and much of the land surrounding areas where gorillas live is inhabited by extremely poor people who derive their incomes from agricultural activities. Gorillas are severely threatened by anthropogenic disturbances such as agricultural conversion and illegal extraction of resources (for example, snare setting for smaller mammals that entrap young gorillas). While gorillas are no longer hunted for their meat in the Virunga range, they are the focus of illegal animal trafficking. Members of gorilla groups are killed and wounded in an effort to trap infants for the black market, sometimes leading to the disintegration of groups. This hunting pressure currently represents the greatest threat to the survival of the mountain gorillas and the integrity of their habitat. Illegal hunting is mainly motivated by meeting subsistence needs for the poorest people around the VNP (Plumptre et al. 2004).

To address local welfare needs to mitigate some of these poverty-related conservation threats, a key focus of contemporary conservation strategies is on local communities (Hulme and Murphee 2001). Combining conservation with local development through integrated conservation and development projects is now a standard approach in many developing countries (Barrett and Arcese 1995). Rwandan communities are involved in gorilla tourism in the following ways:

- **Creation of a department for community conservation** to work on local education and social infrastructure projects (Uwingeli 2009).
- **Revenue sharing:** Since 2005 ORTPN (which was absorbed into the Rwanda Development Board, or RDB, in early 2009), with the support of the government, has overseen a revenue-sharing scheme whereby 5 percent of tourism revenues from VNP fees are injected into local community projects around the national park to ensure that the local people feel some ownership of the parks (box 14.2). Although it is not known what proportion of the budget of local councils is represented by the shared revenue, it is clear that local governments must be actively involved in selecting local projects to finance.
- **Employment opportunities** are offered through national parks: guides, trackers, and antipoaching agents, for example. Some of the private tour operators also offer community-based tourism activities, such as stays with local families, village walks, banana beer production, and even volunteer opportunities in local communities.

DISBURSEMENT OF FUNDS TO COMMUNITIES. Since 2005 nearly $428,248 has been directly invested in community projects and used to empower communities. The total amount, however, equates to an investment of only $1.45 per person since the program's inception, or an average of $0.36 per person per year. Projects for which funds have been used include education, environmental protection (tree planting, soil erosion control, and fencing in protected areas to limit access by poachers), food security, basic infrastructure, and water and sanitation (figure 14.3). Specific community projects have included construction of schools, water tanks, and hospitals; basket weaving; establishment of culture centers; potato farming; tree planting; bee-keeping; milk cooler construction; goat rearing; and mushroom and pepper farming. Education projects have received the most

---

Box 14.2 Process for Disbursing Community Funds

Five percent of tourism revenues from the protected areas in Rwanda are put into a fund for community projects in administrative sectors that neighbor national parks. The Rwanda Development Board issues calls for proposals, and a project selection process is completed at the sector and district levels. Selection criteria include positive impacts on local communities and on conservation of biodiversity in protected areas. Areas that register a large number of cases of conflict between protected areas and the community, according to the results of a ranger-based monitoring system, have preferential access to funds, as do areas that are located close to the protected areas.

Sustainability of projects (gauged through the economical, social, and environmental indicators stated in the proposal and their likelihood of being achieved) and the proportion of community contribution are also considered.

Once projects are selected, contracts are signed with the district authority and the community. Contracts cover lengths of time that depend on the project complexity and can vary from 1 month to 15 months. The community is often grouped into cooperatives or direct-specific target groups when their ownership and level of organization guarantee effective implementation of the project.

Source: Tusabe and Habyalimana 2010.

Figure 14.3 Funds Disbursed to Community Projects around the VNP, by Sector, 2005–08

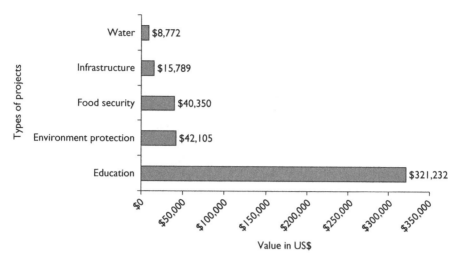

Source: Télesphore 2009.

funds because of the high priority education is given within the sectors in the Musanze district, near the VNP. The annual amount disbursed is directly correlated to tourism revenues collected in the previous year. The amount of funds disbursed to communities in each year between 2005 and 2008 is shown in figure 14.4.

By 2008 seven districts bordering parks in Rwanda with a population of almost 300,000 people had been reached by the community project financing scheme (Bush 2009). Although no formal study has yet been carried out to assess the impact of the scheme on the livelihoods of people living near the VNP, the RDB and local authorities indicate that the scheme has contributed to an increased awareness of tourism benefits to the community and to the need to protect biodiversity in the VNP (Spenceley et al. 2010).

One specific project that has benefited from community fund financing is the high-end Sabyinyo Silverback Lodge. The eight-room lodge located at the periphery of the VNP is a joint venture of the local Kinigi and Nyange communities (represented by the Sabyinyo Community Livelihoods Association, or SACOLA); the private sector (Governors Camps Ltd); international NGOs, in particular, the International Gorilla Conservation Program (IGCP) and the African Wildlife Foundation (AWF); and the RDB. Planning for the lodge began in 2004, and the first tourists began to arrive in August 2007 (Makambo 2009). Some initial funding was obtained from the U.S. Agency for International Development (Verdugo 2009). The joint venture agreement includes a 15-year lease agreement between Governors Camps Ltd and SACOLA. The private sector operator built

Figure 14.4 Funds Disbursed to Community Projects around the VNP, 2005–08

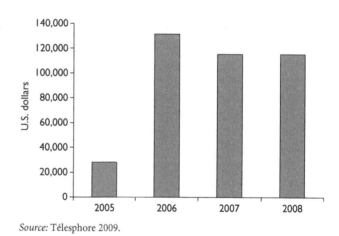

Source: Télesphore 2009.

and operates the lodge, and pays the communities a $50 occupied bed night fee and also 7.5 percent of net sales (Makambo 2009).

This joint venture operation allows people who live close to the VNP to benefit from tourism in four main ways: equity in a tourism business, employment opportunities at the lodge, the supply of goods and services, and dividends from profits. The lodge employs 45 local people, who receive training and experience in hospitality and tourism. Local agricultural produce is purchased for use by the lodge, and there are plans to establish traditional dancing, a cultural center, a community walk, and handicraft sales at the lodge. In addition, there are plans under the joint venture to use funds from the lodge to finance infrastructure, such as roads, in the area (Makambo 2009). Weaknesses of the joint venture, however, include poor leadership and weak governance of SACOLA and the reliance on the private sector operator to generate revenue from tourists (Makambo 2009).

SOCIAL BENEFITS FROM GORILLA TOURISM. Since the tourism revenue-sharing scheme was initiated in 2005, a number of direct and indirect projects with social benefits of gorilla tourism for local communities living near the VNP have been implemented (Uwingeli 2009):

- **Schools:** Ten schools have been constructed, with 56 classrooms and an average of 65 pupils per classroom per rotation (morning and afternoon). The school construction has reduced the distance traveled by children to the nearest schools, allowing them to spend more time on their studies after school.
- **Water tanks:** Thirty-two water tanks have been constructed. These provide 20 liters of water per person per day, and at least 1,250 people are served by each tank.
- **Income-generating activities:** Ten community associations have been supported directly through the revenue-sharing scheme, and a number of other projects, such as bee-keeping and basket weaving, have been implemented. In all of these projects, the focus has been on training for income-generating activities.
- **New partnerships in conservation and community development** brought to the construction of the Sabyinyo community lodge, which is owned by SACOLA, but managed by a specialized ecolodge company. At least 3,000 households are members of SACOLA and benefit from the agreement with the managing company to pay SACOLA bed night fees and a percentage of monthly net income.

EMPLOYMENT FROM GORILLA TOURISM. The VNP employs at least 180 people, who work as guides, gorilla group trackers (for both tourism and research groups), and antipoaching teams deployed in the five protected sectors of the VNP (Uwingeli 2009). In addition, an estimated 800 community members around the VNP are involved in day-to-day management activities and benefit from opportunistic and temporary employment and the revenue-sharing scheme. VNP management has helped to form two umbrella associations: one for conservation activities in the VNP (*Amizero*, or hope) and another for community development activities (*Iby'Iwacu*). Several hundred volunteers work with the two organizations as crop rangers, conservationists, porters, and community awareness representatives.

The *Iby'Iwacu* cultural village has been developed in collaboration between a private sector tour operator, Rwanda Ecotours, and a group of former poachers living near the VNP. As a result of an academic research project, a participatory process began in 2005 to transform the livelihoods of poachers toward farming, and then tourism. Part of the concept was to benefit conservation, by providing alternative livelihood opportunities to illegal hunting of buffalo and other wildlife in the VNP. Meetings with poachers were held to gain their trust and insights, and study tours were undertaken to raise understanding of cultural tourism products elsewhere.

Interviews were undertaken with tourists to establish what they would be willing to pay for a cultural experience. Community members engaged in the design, construction, and operation of the cultural village. Local architectural techniques were used in the construction along with local materials such as thatching grass and wood. Tourists can stop at the Iby'Iwacu and experience local attire, practice traditional fire-making techniques, archery, drumming, and dancing; visit a traditional healer; and prepare and eat traditional food. The village generates around $14,000 per year, and community representatives identify projects in the community that they can finance (Sabuhoro 2009).

CHALLENGES. Studies show that tourists to Rwanda do not have a particular willingness to pay for community benefits. Bush, Hanley, and Colombo (2008), for example, find that the percentage of VNP revenues used to enhance local community development does not have a significant effect on tourism demand. Bush, Hanley, and Colombo also note that these findings do not imply that tourists are unwilling to take part in community-based tourism—rather, that they are not willing to sacrifice other immediate benefits of the trekking experience relative to increases in permit prices that were dedicated to revenue sharing. This represents an important departure from common ecotourism principles about social benefits. Bush (2009) suggests that tourists need to be better educated about the human dimension of conservation to emphasize the conceptual link between the needs of the local populations and biodiversity conservation.

Furthermore, Rutagarama and Martin (2006) state that there is something of a catch-22 in relation to community conservation in Rwanda. On one hand, the empowerment of local partners will be constrained when appropriate powers are not devolved to them. On the other hand, it is impossible to impose powers on those who feel neither capable nor inclined to exercise them. Rutagarama and Martin (2006) therefore suggest the need for a flexible framework that enables capacity and power to coevolve in locally appropriate ways. Developing the assets that partners need to maximize their opportunities for entering productive partnerships should be a fundamental part of plans to widen (and deepen) local participation in tourism. In some countries this has been done through a hybrid approach, and by retrofitting community-based tourism enterprises into joint-venture partnerships with private sector operators. Although the transaction costs, such as the time needed to negotiate deals, can be high, these partnerships can provide a win-win for the private sector and community members with appropriate agreements (examples are Damaraland in Namibia, Rocktail Bay and Phinda Reserve in South Africa, and Covane Fishing and Safari Lodge in Mozambique). In these situations the capacity of community members is built over time through partnerships with businesses that understand the tourism sector, how to operate a business, and how to establish market linkages.

Implications for conservation

Mountain gorilla tourism in Rwanda has long been viewed as a valuable conservation tool. An economic incentive to conserve the mountain gorilla is provided by international tourists paying relatively large sums of money to spend a short amount of time with the gorillas. Since its conception, organized gorilla tourism has provided funds to VNP authorities to assist with conservation activities. Nature-based tourism has thus been enthusiastically accepted and supported by governments, conservationists, and tourists alike and, in Rwanda, has been acknowledged as playing a crucial role in the success of mountain gorilla conservation in the VNP (Bush, Hanley, and Colombo 2008).

The number of mountain gorillas left in the world is estimated to be approximately 700. As of 2003, 380 gorillas lived in the Virunga volcanoes range, while 320 lived in Bwindi Impenetrable National Park in Uganda as of 2006 (Uwingeli 2009). Research indicates that the gorilla populations in areas frequented by tourists are increasing, with an overall growth in the population of 1.1 percent between 1989 and 2003 (Fawcett 2009) (box 14.3). Gorilla groups in the Democratic Republic of Congo are doing less well in terms of population growth, which may be due to the lower presence of patrols, researchers, and tourist visits there compared with Rwanda and Uganda (Fawcett 2009).

Box 14.3   Growth in Gorilla Conservation Efforts

Mountain gorillas in the Virunga region of Rwanda, Uganda, and the Democratic Republic of Congo were censused five times between 1970 and 1989, when the population was estimated at 324 gorillas. War and political unrest in the region since 1990 meant that no census was conducted over the next decade, and in 2000, the observation of 32 groups provided an estimate of between 359 and 395 gorillas. This represents a 0.9 percent to 1.8 percent annual growth rate over 10 years and a 1.0 percent to 1.3 percent annual growth rate between 1972 and 2000.

Source: Kalpers et al. 2003.

Biological research on mountain gorillas by teams of researchers in the Karisoke Research Centre in Rwanda provides important information on trends in sound tourism management. Of the estimated 380 gorillas in the Virunga Volcanoes Range, at least 260 are habituated and regularly monitored in Rwanda (Uwingeli 2009): These gorillas are checked on a daily basis; health reports are shared, and actions taken when necessary. The habitat is patrolled daily to detect illegal activities and discourage attempts to set snares. The use of information technology allows the habitat of the mountain gorillas to be mapped—in particular, to show where gorilla groups are moving and what illegal activities are occurring and to plan ranger patrol activities accordingly.

Over the years, the Rwandan government has become more supportive of gorilla conservation, including allocating more land around the VNP for cultivation to reduce pressure on the park for agriculture and natural resource use (Uwingeli 2009). A consultation exercise is currently under way to assess the feasibility of a VNP expansion program (Bush 2009). Although the number of snares found in the VNP have increased over time (Fawcett 2009), some former poachers have begun working on conservation efforts, and there is even an "ex-poachers association" consisting of about 400 local community members, who patrol with ORTPN staff and also help with local education, collecting information, and addressing human-wildlife conflict (for example, crop raiding) (Uwingeli 2009).

Although no systematic method currently exists for registering or training guides in Rwanda, VNP staff have benefited from capacity-building programs by the RDB (and previously, by ORTPN) and their partners in guiding, gorilla health monitoring, and general biodiversity conservation. Also, with the support of IGCP and the Karisoke Research Centre, additional training has been provided for gorilla trekking guides on how to work with visitors and how to minimize adverse impacts on the gorillas (Kalpers et al. 2003; Fawcett 2009).

Revenues from Rwanda's national parks are primarily used to fund conservation efforts in the parks and worldwide tourism marketing activities. Salaries for all of the staff are paid out of national park fees. VNP park management is cofunded through the research activities of the Karisoke Research Centre, which provides basic park management functions such as monitoring and antipoaching patrols for gorillas. Further conservation funds are contributed by NGOs such as the IGCP and CARE. These additional funds and support have contributed enormously to gorilla conservation successes in Rwanda (Bush 2009).

Willingness to pay for conservation

Research by Bush, Hanley, and Colombo (2008) finds that gorilla trekking tourists are willing to pay for biodiversity conservation, for both gorillas and other wildlife. The authors also find that tourists prefer to be in small

groups[3] and prefer the length of their trek to be between one and three hours. These two findings could be interpreted as showing that tourists support the ecotourism principle of minimizing ecological impact, since more people taking longer trips would increase adverse ecological impacts.

However, price increases in gorilla permits appear to affect tourism visitation, at least in the short term. Research by Bush and Fawcett (2007) reveals that the price increase in June 2007 from $375 to $475 had a marked impact on the demographics of visitors to the mountain gorillas (figure 14.5). In particular, the percentage of visits by people in the highest income group increased significantly, while visits by all but one of the other income groups decreased. The length of the stay also decreased significantly, from a mean number of 4.2 nights to 3.6 nights.

The proportion of visitors going to the other national parks in Rwanda was also significantly lower after the price increase, as was the proportion of visitors to the genocide memorial and taking the Kigali city tour. The proportion of visitors participating in alternative activities within the VNP increased, however: hikes on the Karisimbi and Bisoke volcanoes, viewing golden monkeys, visits to Dian Fossey's tomb, and nature walks.

Figure 14.5   Impact of the 2007 Gorilla Permit Price Increase on Visitation

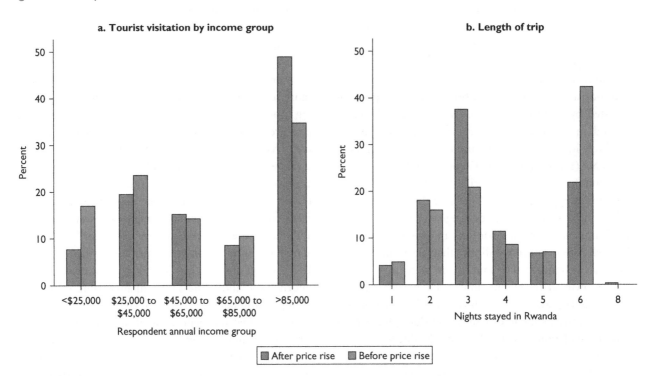

Source: Bush and Fawcett 2007.

The reduction in visitors' length of stay and in the frequency of other activities caused by the price increase in gorilla tourism has implications for the overall economic impact of international tourism in Rwanda. However, Bush (2009) notes that it is probably time to repeat the study and establish whether the changes in demographics and consumption were temporary or lasting. This study would also provide guidance for decision making about further price changes. A study of tourism satisfaction and pricing for alternative products to ensure value for money is also needed in order to increase the number of bed nights and overall trip spending (Bush 2009).

Remaining constraints and lessons learned

There are a number of constraints to the further development of gorilla tourism in Rwanda:

- Gorilla tourism can present a threat to gorilla conservation, affecting, for example, the health and behavior of gorillas (box 14.4), and needs to be well managed.

- Although the number of tourist accommodation facilities is growing, the facilities are not sufficient at key tourism sites, including the VNP. Additionally, the quality of accommodations is not standardized, and prices are high relative to accommodations of equivalent quality in other East African countries.

- The quality of customer service is inconsistent and generally poor compared with that in neighboring countries. Also the focus on high-end consumers implies demand for higher quality. Bush found that after the increase of the permit price respondents registered significantly lower levels of satisfaction with their trekking experience (Bush 2009).

- Public and private sector collaboration is improving through the Joint Action Development Forum and Steering Committees, though it is still weak.

- Although the road distance between Kigali and Musanze is short, the quality of the road could be improved.

- While regional collaboration is of interest to government authorities of the Democratic Republic of Congo, Rwanda, and Uganda, regional instability has made it difficult to harmonize tourism and conservation in

---

Box 14.4   Threats to Gorilla Conservation from Tourism

All six great apes—gorillas *Gorilla gorilla* and *Gorilla beringei*, chimpanzees *Pan troglodytes* and *Pan paniscus*, and orangutans *Pongo pygmaeus* and *Pongo abelii*—are categorized as endangered on the International Union for Conservation of Nature's 2000 Red List. Threats to these species include loss of habitat to settlement, logging, and agriculture; illegal hunting for bushmeat and traditional medicine; the live ape trade; civil unrest; and infectious diseases. The great apes are highly susceptible to many human diseases, some of which can be fatal. If protective measures are not improved, ape populations that are frequently in close contact with people will eventually be affected by the inadvertent transmission of human diseases. Regulations that protect habituated apes from the transmission of disease from people are often poorly enforced. Enforcement of existing regulations governing ape-based tourism, and the risk of disease transmission between humans and the great apes minimized (Woodford, Mutynsky, and Karesh 2002).

Tourism might also be changing gorilla behavior in negative ways. In one research study, Fawcett, Hodgkinson, and Mehlman (2004) assessed more than 10 months of behavioral data collected from three gorilla groups during one-hour observation sessions before, during, and following tourist visits. Results from these data show clearly that the current tourism program is having a significant impact on gorilla behavior. All three gorilla groups were found to spend significantly less time feeding and more time moving during tourist visits. In addition, the frequency of certain aggressive behaviors, many directed at humans, increased in all three groups during tourist visits, and the gorillas increased their proximity to the silverback members (adult male gorillas usually more than 12 years of age).

Some gorilla behaviors observed during the study were correlated with the distance maintained between the gorillas and the tourists and the number of tourists in the gorilla group. Reducing this impact on gorilla behavior may be a simple matter of better training guides to maintain the 7-meter distance rule between tourists and gorillas. Many of these changes in gorilla behavior during tourist visits are believed to indicate higher levels of stress in gorillas (Fawcett, Hodgkinson, and Mehlman 2004).

accordance with the Virunga Massif Transboundary Plan (Uwingeli 2009; Mehta and Katee 2005).

- There is widespread poverty around the VNP and increasing pressure for more agricultural land by a growing rural population.
- Benefits accruing from the VNP should be in relation to the needs of people living close to the park. Local people desire individual benefits (such as money), and not only collective infrastructure that is used by the whole population, such as water tanks or clinics (Uwingeli 2009).

Several tourism-related lessons learned at the VNP have the potential to improve other protected areas in Rwanda:

- Because of the limited number of available gorilla permits, product diversification and promotion is required to encourage visitors (particularly repeat visitors) to stay longer, spend more money, and visit other destinations in the country.
- Gorilla conservation needs to be balanced with research visits and tourism trips to ensure that the health of the gorillas and the integrity of their habitat are maintained.
- Conservation efforts focused on the key species is important, but the contribution to the habitat/ecosystem conservation must also be ensured. Long-term dedication and partnerships in conservation (research, protection, and tourism) are essential.
- Sustainability of gorilla tourism can be achieved only if regional collaboration is established to conserve transboundary protected areas and cross-border resources.
- Standardized and high-quality training for guides is needed, for those working both within and outside protected areas.
- A more diverse range of accommodation and restaurant facilities is required, with higher quality and better value for money.

TOURISM IN RWANDA: THE BIGGER PICTURE

Besides the mountain gorillas in the VNP, Rwanda has other excellent tourism assets that create a wider foundation for the tourism sector. Rwanda has three national parks that cover about 10 percent of the country's area, one of which is the VNP. The Akagera National Park offers a range of wildlife including elephants, hippopotamuses, giraffes, and zebras. The Nyungwe Forest National Park has a large tract of mountain forest and is rich in biodiversity. Guided walks and chimpanzee tracking is offered. Lake Kivu has recreational facilities as well, but there is still potential for significant

tourism development. Rwanda also offers business opportunities, mainly for travelers from the eastern part of the Democratic Republic of Congo and other neighboring countries. Rwanda has also been successful in attracting national, regional, and international conferences.

Development and structure of the tourism sector

In the 1970s and early 1980s only a small number of international tourists visited Rwanda. Most tourists visited Akagera National Park, a government-owned, high-end destination used mostly for hunting. Only a very limited number of tourists visited the gorillas. Tourism was not a national priority and was not viewed as a tool to reduce poverty. The first hotel, the Mille Collines, was built in 1973 and the ORTPN was created in 1974. No tour operators existed in the 1970s and 1980s, and the sector was dominated by the government, which owned all hotels except the Mille Collines.

Tourist arrivals started to increase notably in the 1980s (figure 14.6). Most tourists still visited only Akagera National Park at that point, but the first official mountain gorilla tourism program was launched in 1979, leading to continuously increasing visitor numbers in the VNP, peaking at 6,900 in 1989 (ORTPN 2008b). This trend was brought to an abrupt end with the outbreak of the war in mid-1990s, however. Visits to the VNP, which provided most of the tourism revenue by the mid-1990s, dropped in 1994 due to the genocide and again between 1997 and 1999, when the VNP had to be closed for some time due to an insurgency. Visits increased in the years following, however. In 2008 about 17,000 people visited the VNP to see the gorillas, a dramatic increase from the late 1980s and an impressive recovery from only 417 tourists in 1999 after the reopening of the VNP following the war. Total visits to all Rwanda's national parks reached more than 43,000 visitors in 2008. Today, the majority of visitors to the VNP are foreigners, while Akagera National Park is visited by a more equal mix of Rwandan and foreign residents.

Reliable tourist arrival statistics for Rwanda as a whole are available only for 2007 onward, when entry cards were introduced. This innovation led to a substantive upward revision of tourism revenue. The use of statistics on park visits alone led to a significant underestimation of the total number of tourists. Most important, the large number of business and conference tourists had not been taken into account. Although data are still not collected electronically and the quality of data is not high, there is little doubt that the recovery of the tourism sector in Rwanda has been successful.

Figure 14.6   Visits to Rwanda's National Parks, 1974–2008

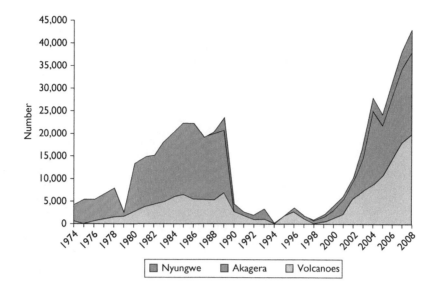

Source: ORTPN.

Table 14.1   Tourist Arrivals to Rwanda by Purpose of Visit, 2007–09
Thousands

Year	Holiday/vacation		Visiting friends and relatives		Conference/ business		Transit		Other		Total
	Number	Share (%)	Number	Share (&)	Number	Share (%)	Number	Share (%)	Number	Share (%)	
2007	21.5	2.6	332.0	40.2	275.8	33.4	150.1	18.2	47.0	5.7	826.4
2008	59.4	6.1	248.3	25.3	345.9	35.3	307.8	31.4	19.1	1.9	980.6
2009 (Jan - Jun)	21.4	4.9	112.2	25.6	187.9	42.8	83.3	19.0	34.1	7.8	439.0

Source: ORTPN.

A total of 980,577 international arrivals were recorded in 2008, up from 826,374 in 2007 (table 14.1). The main characteristics of international tourists entering Rwanda are:

- Most visitors came for business and conferences (35 percent in 2008). This had already been indicated in a hotel market study, which found that 75 percent of all tourists in the country in 2006 were business travelers (IFC 2007).
- The share of tourists arriving in Rwanda for vacation is relatively small, but increased from 3 percent in 2007 to 6 percent in 2008.
- The large number of international arrivals includes transit passengers, thereby reducing the overall number of arrivals that can be counted as tourists entering Rwanda.

The tourist entry cards offer more details about travelers entering Rwanda. Overall, 88 percent of total international arrivals came from Africa. The country or region of origin, however, varies considerably by the purpose of the visit. Most of the tourists on vacation came from Europe and the United States (figure 14.7a). The majority of business and conference travelers came from the Democratic Republic of Congo and the other EAC member states (figure 14.7b). Most international tourists visiting friends and relatives in 2008 came from the EAC and Congo Republic (figure 14.7c). According to estimates by ORTPN and the Ministry of Economy and Finance, non-African tourists coming to Rwanda for leisure or conference and business purposes spent the most money among the various categories of tourists (table 14.2).

Most leisure tourists visit the region as part of a multi-country itinerary and do not yet consider Rwanda as a stand-alone destination. A recent survey of tourists, tour operators, and accommodation providers in Rwanda (SNV and RDB 2009) finds that the most common length of stay for

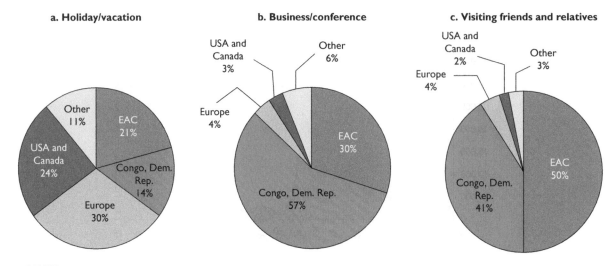

Source: ORTPN.

Table 14.2 Average Spending by Tourists in Rwanda, by Purpose of Visit, 2009

Purpose of visit	Average amount spent per visit (US$)	
	Non-African visitors	African visitors
Leisure	1,623	1,136
Conference and business	1,623	108
Visiting friends and relatives	120	84
Transit/other	119	83

Source: RDB/ORTPN/MINECOFIN, based on visitor expenditure survey from 2006, adjusted for inflation.

Table 14.3 Growth in Hotel Rooms, Restaurants, Tour Operators, and Travel Agencies in Rwanda

Service	2003	2009	Average annual growth rate (%)
Hotel rooms	650	4,256	37
Restaurants	50[a]	94	17
Tour operator companies	12	26	14
Travel agencies	5	24	30

Source: RDB/ORTPN.
a. Data from 2005.

domestic tourists was two days, while the most frequently cited length of stay by international tourists was four days.

The number of hotel rooms and tour operators in Rwanda has increased significantly in recent years, underscoring the successful recovery of the tourism sector. Data available from RDB and ORPTN show that the number of hotel rooms increased from 650 in 2003 to 4,256 in 2009, more than 500 percent overall and 37 percent annually on average (table 14.3). Information on occupancy rates, however, is very limited. The only available information spans January to March 2008 and indicates an average room occupancy rate of 36 percent. There was a large difference in the occupancy rates by the grade of accommodation. Room occupancy rates for upper-grade accommodation (a total of 453 rooms) were more than 70 percent on average, whereas

rates for lower-grade accommodation (2,264 rooms) were only 28.5 percent (ORTPN 2008c, 2008d).

A total of 26 tour operators were active in Rwanda as of 2009, compared to none in the 1980s. The number of restaurants and travel agencies has grown as well. Most Rwandan tour operators started out with little available finance, which limited their possibilities. They could, for example, not afford to buy a car, but had instead to rent cars as they needed them. Most of those tour operators have successfully expanded their businesses by now, though, and some regional operators have also opened offices in Kigali.

The tourism sector has also experienced a significant amount of privatization. The situation is much different from the 1980s, when all hotels except one were government owned. Although the government still held a share in two hotels in 2010, it was not involved in their management, leaving the tourism sector almost entirely in the hands of the private sector. The government still owns and runs the national parks, although in 2009 a concession was awarded to the private company African Parks to manage Akagera National Park.

Tourism income, as recorded by ORPTN, has increased in recent years. The majority of revenue is derived from VNP entrance and gorilla permit fees. Other income is raised through the gorilla naming ceremony, partners and donors, and interest from treasury bills and other income. Most of the revenue is spent on operating expenditures, whereas capital expenditures paid out of the budget of ORPTN are limited. Large investments are funded by the overall central government budget. Revenue shared with communities has increased since 2005, representing 8 percent of total operating expenditure in 2008, up from 6 percent in 2006.

Foreign investment in Rwanda's tourism sector is substantial. Between 2000 and 2009, foreign direct investment of RF 258 billion went into hotels and leisure, accounting for 20 percent of total FDI inflows into the country (figure 14.8). Local investment in hotels, restaurants, and other tourism activities amounted to RF 140 billion between 1999 and 2009, representing 16 percent of total local investment over that period.

Although the amount of foreign investment exceeded the amount of local investment, it has been concentrated on a small number of projects. Local investors play an important

role in the development of the tourism sector in Rwanda. Eighty-six percent of all new projects since 1999 that are operational were financed by local investors. Moreover, a group of private investors has established the Rwanda Investment Group (RIG) to pool resources. Several sub-RIGs have also been created, one of which is currently planning the construction of a convention center intended to hold up to 2,000 participants, which would increase Rwanda's chance of attracting large conferences.[4]

Finally, the structure and organization of the tourism sector has been reformed to assign clear responsibilities. The Ministry of Commerce, Industry, Investment Promotion, Tourism, and Cooperatives (MINICOM) holds overall responsibility for tourism. The private sector is represented by the tourism chamber, which consists of four industry associations: accommodation, tour operators, transport, and private education establishments. The tourism chamber is, however, still supported by the government because of insufficient resources. It is part of the private sector federation, the equivalent of a chamber of commerce and industry.

Contribution of tourism to the economy

Rwanda has made remarkable progress in terms of economic growth since the genocide in 1994 (figure 14.9). Growth averaged 15.6 percent in the five years after the genocide in 1994, declined to an average of 6.6 percent between 2000 and 2004, and increased again to an average of 8.4 percent between 2005 and 2008. A significant increase in GDP per capita has been recorded along the way, from $142 in 1994 to $313 in 2008 (both in 2000 prices).

While the contribution of tourism to GDP remains small, the sector has become Rwanda's main source of export revenue. The category "restaurants and hotels" has contributed less than 2 percent to overall GDP and 4 percent to the services sector on average since 1999, but value added from restaurants and hotels (at constant prices) has recorded a steady increase of 21 percent on average.[5] The main increase in the services sector came from wholesale and retail trade and other services (education, health, finance and insurance, and real estate). The measurement of tourism's contribution to GDP, however, is difficult, because transport services, for example, constitute a large share of tourism revenues but are not included in the "hotel and restaurants" category.

Overall, exports of nonfactor services from Rwanda have outperformed exports of goods (such as coffee and tea) as Rwanda's main foreign exchange earner (figure 14.10). Travel is the largest component of exports of nonfactor

Figure 14.8   FDI to Rwanda, by Sector, 2000–2009

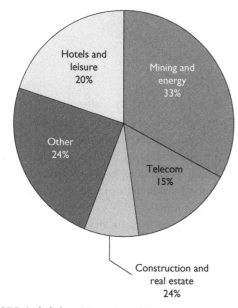

Source: RDB; included are RDB registered investments.

Figure 14.9   Growth in Real GDP and GDP per Capita, 1993–2008

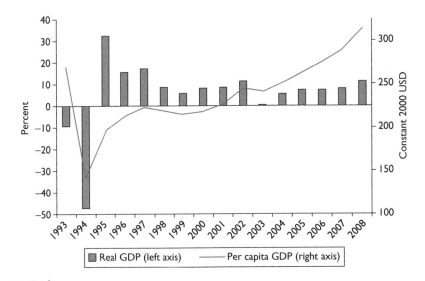

Source: International Monetary Fund.

Figure 14.10   Comparison of Composition of Export of Goods and Nonfactor Services
(*Averages*)

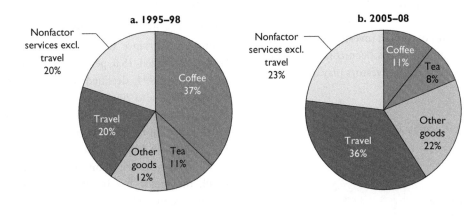

Source: IMF.

services; other categories include other transportation and freight and insurance. After a decline from $19 million in 1993 to only $6 million in 1995, revenue from tourism increased tremendously to $202 million in 2008 (figure 14.11). A comparison with the preconflict period is difficult, because data on tourism revenue are available only for 1992 onward.

Rwanda has identified tourism in its Economic Development and Poverty Reduction Strategy as a national priority sector to eradicate poverty (Republic of Rwanda 2007). According to rough estimates, each of the three big business hotels in Kigali[6] generates about $500,000 per year in income for semiskilled and unskilled workers, food pro-

ducers, and artisans. Tourists visiting the VNP and the Musanze area generate around $1 million in income for poor workers and producers. In addition, the area receives large amounts of donations and grants[7] (SNV and ODI 2008). As much as possible, hotels source their supplies (particularly food products) from the local market to contribute to the economy.

Estimates for 2009 indicate that the tourism industry directly employs 33,800 people in Rwanda, whereas indirect employment accounts for another 40,500 jobs, resulting in total travel and tourism–related employment of 74,300 jobs. Tourism thus represents 4.0 percent of total employment in Rwanda, only slightly below the Sub-Saharan African

Figure 14.11   Tourism Revenue, 1992–2008

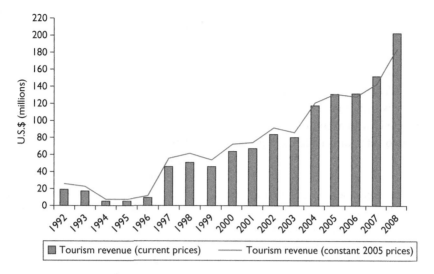

Source: IMF and World Bank, World Development Indicators database.

average of 4.6 percent, and well below the amount in Kenya (7.1 percent), Tanzania (7.1 percent), and Uganda (6.6 percent). Employment in the tourism industry (direct and indirect) has grown by 2.8 percent on average in Rwanda over the past 10 years, compared with 3.4 percent in Kenya, 2.5 percent in Tanzania, and 2.4 percent in Uganda (World Travel and Tourism Council 2009).

REMAINING CONSTRAINTS AND EMERGING POSSIBILITIES FOR TOURISM

Despite the good performance of the tourism sector in Rwanda, several challenges remain. The main impediment cited by almost all actors in the sector is the large skill deficit. This deficit applies to all areas of tourism, including guides, chefs, and hotel service personnel and technicians. Hotels and tour operators either train their staff in house or send them to neighboring countries to be trained, although recently some tourism schools have been opened by the private sector. The emphasis of the curriculum is on managerial rather than technical skills, meaning that the demands of the sector are not taken into account adequately. To accomplish the goal of turning Rwanda into a service-oriented economy, skill development is of utmost importance.

Several other challenges confront the tourism sector:

- There is an overreliance on gorilla tourism. The number of permits cannot be easily increased, and the existing permits are typically sold out. Tourism needs to be

diversified and other attractions promoted, such as birding and primates in Nyungwe, visits to Lake Kivu, and conference tourism. Diversity is particularly important in establishing Rwanda as a stand-alone destination.

- Access to finance is still an impediment for the development of the sector. Banks seem reluctant to finance tourism projects because they are within a service-oriented sector rather than attached to a sector producing tangible goods. Stakeholders in the tourism sector have proposed the establishment of a guarantee fund by the government.

- Other sectors need to be further promoted through the tourism sector in order to reduce poverty. Pro-poor links that can be exploited further include the food supply chain to hotels, lodges, and restaurants; assistance to poor households to access training, employment, and promotion in hospitality; practical initiatives to help businesses enhance their own business models; and partnerships with more domestic and regional tour operators, hotels, and lodges to promote community activities such as cultural events and the sale of handicrafts (SNV and ODI 2008).

- Rwanda needs to comply with international standards. Currently, hotels are being classified according to the EAC standard. While this is an important step, it poses challenges to a number of hotels. Once Rwanda shifts to an international system of standards and classifies hotels accordingly, the pricing structure might have to be revised to remain competitive with the neighboring countries.

- RDB and MINICOM do not have sufficient staff. In MINICOM, only one part-time person is responsible for tourism. RDB, as well, has only a limited number of staff. Given the very ambitious agenda for the tourism agenda, sufficient staffing should be in place.
- Infrastructure needs improvement. Although roads in Rwanda are broadly adequate, the air transport connection to the country is still limited. A new airport is currently being planned, which could attract more international carriers to offer direct flights, especially from Europe.

In the face of the challenges, several possibilities are emerging to diversify the tourism sector and increase its contribution to the economy. Regarding leisure tourists, primate tours, and birding in the Nyungwe Forest are the most promising areas of diversification. New experiences would extend the length of stay of tourists and eventually establish Rwanda as a stand-alone destination. Lessons learned from gorilla tourism regarding conservation, however, should be taken into account when developing tourism attractions in other national parks. The development concept of Rwanda's Destination Management Areas is identified in the Sustainable Tourism Development Master Plan (Republic of Rwanda 2009b). Conference tourism could also be of great benefit to Rwanda. In this regard, the construction of a conference center that will accommodate up to 2,000 people is under way. Further, a draft action plan for the development of MICE (meetings, incentives, conferences, and exhibitions) tourism has been prepared by the Tourism Working Group.

NOTES

1. EAC member countries are Burundi, Kenya, Rwanda, Tanzania, and Uganda.

2. The gorillas are visited by independent travelers, overlanders, and high-end tours (ORTPN 2004).

3. The optimum group size, according to tourists, is six people; tourists are not willing to pay more to reduce group size beyond this (Fawcett 2009; Weber 1993).

4. The currently available conference facilities can host a maximum of 500 and 1,000 participants.

5. The share of hotels and restaurants is not available for years before 1999.

6. Serena Hotel Kigali, Hotel de Mille Collines, and Laico Umubano Kigali Hotel (former Novotel Kigali).

7. Including contributions to community development from ORTPN's revenue-sharing program and donations by tourists.

BIBLIOGRAPHY

Barrett, C., and P. Arcese. 1995. "Are Integrated Conservation-Development Projects Sustainable?" *World Development* 23 (supplement 7): 1073–84.

Bush, G. 2009. Personal Communication, Woods Hole Research Center, November 30.

Bush, G., and K. Fawcett. 2007. "An Economic Study of Mountain Gorilla Tourism in the Virunga Volcanoes Conservation Area." U.S. Fish and Wildlife Service, Dian Fossey Gorilla Fund International, Ruhengeri, Rwanda.

Bush, G., N. Hanley, and S. Colombo. 2008. "Measuring the Demand for Nature-based Tourism in Africa: A Choice Experiment Using the 'Cut-off' Approach." Discussion Paper 2008-06, Stirling Economics, University of Stirling, Stirling, U.K.

Butynaski, T. M., and J. Kalina. 1997. "Gorilla Tourism: A Critical Look." Africa Biodiversity Conservation Program, Nairobi.

Fawcett, K. 2009. Personal Communication, Director, Karisoke Research Centre, September 16.

Fawcett, K., C. Hodgkinson, and P. Mehlman. 2004. "An Assessment of the Impact of Tourism on the Virunga Mountain Gorillas: Phase I—Analyzing the Behavioral Data from Gorilla Groups Designated for Tourism." Dian Fossey Gorilla Fund International, Atlanta, GA.

Gray, M., et al. 2005. "Virunga Volcanoes Range and Census, 2003." Joint organizers report, Uganda Wildlife Authority/ORTPN/Institut Colombaise pour la Conservation du Nature.

Grosspietsch, M. 2006. "Perceived and Projected Images of Rwanda: Visitor and International Tour Operator Perspectives." *Tourism Management* 27: 225–34.

Homesy, J. 1999. "Ape Tourism and Human Diseases; How Close Should We Get?" Technical Report, International Gorilla Conservation Program, Nairobi.

Hulme, D., and M. Murphee. 2001. "Community Conservation in Africa." In *African Wildlife and Livelihoods: The Promise and Performance of Community Conservation*, ed. D. Hulme and M. Murphee. Oxford, U.K.: James Curry Ltd.

IFC (International Finance Corporation). 2007. "Rwanda Hotel Market Study." Washington, DC.

Kalpers, J., et al. 2003. "Gorillas in the Crossfire: Population Dynamics of the Virunga Mountain Gorillas over the Past Three Decades." *Oryx* 37 (3): 326–37.

Litchfield, C. A. 1997. "Treading Lightly: Responsible Tourism with the African Great Apes," Travellers' Medical and Vaccination Centre, Adelaide. Cited in Fawcett, Hodgkinson, and Mehlman (2004).

Makambo, W. 2009. "Sabyinyo Silverback Lodge: A Community Partnership for Conservation." Presentation from RDB-TC tourism forum, International Gorilla Conservation Program, Nairobi.

Mehta, H., and C. Katee. 2005. Viriunga Massif Sustainable Tourism Development Plan, DR Congo, Rwanda, Uganda. ECDA: Fort Lauderdale FL.

Murnyak, D. F. 1981. "Censusing the Gorillas in Kahuzi-Biega National Park." *Biological Conservation* 21: 163–76.

OTF Group. 2008a. "Building a Winning MICE Tourism Product—Target Customer Needs." Rwanda Tourism Workgroup.

———. 2008b. "Building a Winning Bird Product—Target Customers and Channel Partner Needs." Rwanda Tourism Workgroup.

ORTPN (Office Rwandaise du Tourisme et des Parcs Nationaux). 2004. "Strategic Plan 2004–2008." Draft version 2, Kigali.

———. 2008a. "Highlights on National Parks Visitation in Rwanda—2008." Vol. l.1, Kigali.

———. 2008b. "Highlights of International Visitor Arrivals in Rwanda—2008." Kigali.

———. 2008c. "Highlights on Accommodation Statistics in Rwanda—January 2008." Vol. I., Kigali.

———. 2008d. "Highlights on Accommodation Statistics in Rwanda—March 2008." Vol. I.2, Kigali.

Plumptre, A. et al. 2004. "The Socio-economic Status of People Living Near Protected Areas in the Central Albertine Rift." Albertine Rift Technical Reports 4, Albertine Rift, Program, Wildlife Conservation Society, New York.

Republic of Rwanda. 2002. "A Plan to Unleash Rwanda's Tourism Potential." Kigali.

———. 2007a. "Economic Development and Poverty Reduction Strategy, 2008s–2012." Ministry of Finance and Economic Planning, Kigali.

———. 2007b. "A Revised Tourism Strategy for Rwanda—Sustaining the Momentum." Ministry of Commerce, Industries, Investment Promotion, Tourism and Cooperatives, Kigali.

———. 2009a. "Rwanda Tourism Policy." Ministry of Trade and Industry, Kigali.

———. 2009b. "Sustainable Tourism Development Master Plan for Rwanda—Final Report." Project of the Republic of Rwanda and the United Nations World Tourism Organization.

Rutagarama, E., and A. Martin. 2006. "Partnerships for Protected Area Conservation in Rwanda." *Geographical Journal* 172 (4): 291–305.

Sabuhoro, E. 2009. "Contribution of Tourism to Poverty Reduction in Rwanda: A Tour Operator's Perspective." Presentation at the Delphe/EPA Workshop, July 6–7.

SNV Rwanda and ODI. 2008. "Creating Pro-poor Linkages around Rwanda Tourism." Kigali.

SNV Rwanda and RDB. 2009. "Tourism Market Research for Rwanda 2009: A Survey of Tourists, Tour Operators and Accommodation—Final Report." Kigali.

Spenceley, A., S. Habyalimana, R. Tusabe, and D. Mariza. 2010. "Benefits to the Poor from Gorilla Tourism in Rwanda." *Development Southern Africa,* 27 (5): 647–62.

Télesphore, Ngoga. 2009. Interview. September. RDB, Kigali.

Townsend, C. Forthcoming. "Guidelines for Community-based Tourism in Rwanda." ORTPN / UNWTO ST-EP. (Sustainable Tourism–Eliminating Poverty).

Tusabe, R., and S. Habyalimana. 2010. "From Poachers to Park Wardens: Revenue Sharing Scheme as an Incentive for Environment Protection in Rwanda." *Mountain Forum Bulletin* (10) 1.

Uwingeli, P. 2009. Personal Communication, Chief Park Warden, Volcanoes National Park, November 3.

Vedder, A., and B. Weber. 1990. "The Mountain Gorilla Project." In *Living With Wildlife: Wildlife Resource Management with Local Participation in Africa,* ed. A. Kiss. Washington, DC: World Bank.

Verdugo, D. 2009. "Challenges for Developing Community Understanding of Tourism in an Emerging Destination." Unpublished paper cited in Spenceley, A. et al. (2010).

Weber, B. 1982. "People, Gorillas...or Both?" London: Earthscan.

———. 1985. "Le Parc National des Volcans Biosphere Reserve, Rwanda: The Role of Development in Conservation." *Parks* 10 (3): 19–21.

———. 1987. "Socioecologic Factors in the Conservation of Afromontane Forest Reserves." In *Primate Conservation in the Tropical Rainforest,* ed. C. Marsh and R. Mittermeier, 205–29. New York: Alan R. Liss, Inc.

———. 1993. "Ecotourism and Primate Conservation in African Rain Forests." In *The Conservation of Genetic Resources,* ed. C. Potter, 129–50. Washington, DC: AAAS Press.

Woodford, M., T. Mutynsky, and W. Karesh. 2002. "Habituating the Great Apes: The Disease Risks." *Oryx* 36 (2): 153–60.

World Bank. 2008. "Country Assistance Strategy for the Republic of Rwanda for the Period FY09-FY12." Report No. 44938-RW, Washington, DC.

World Travel and Tourism Council.s 2009. "Travel and Tourism Economic Impact—Rwanda 2009." London.

PART IV

Boosting Agricultural Efficiency and Output through Targeted Interventions

Increasing Rice Productivity and Strengthening Food Security through New Rice for Africa (NERICA)

Aliou Diagne, Soul-Kifouly Gnonna Midingoyi, Marco Wopereis, and Inoussa Akintayo

Despite Africa's potentially rich land and water resources, its farmers are among the poorest in the world. Because the vast majority of people in Africa derive their livelihoods from agriculture, the weak state of the sector has profound implications for poverty.[1] Agricultural innovation in Africa needs to internalize the region's biophysical, institutional, and socioeconomic constraints and establish efficient value chains to support sustainable growth and reduce poverty.

Agricultural research can catalyze agricultural innovation and the development of the value chain. A prime example is the New Rice for Africa (NERICA) varieties developed by the Africa Rice Center (AfricaRice[2]) and partners, which gained popularity among Africa's rice farmers in a relatively short period of time.[3] NERICA varieties were developed from crosses between the African species *Oryza glaberrima Steud.* and the Asian species *O. sativa L.*, using conventional biotechnology to overcome the sterility barrier between the two species. This chapter describes the history, development, and impact of NERICA and makes recommendations about its expansion.

THE IMPORTANCE OF RICE AND THE DEVELOPMENT OF NERICA VARIETIES

Rice has long been the food staple in many traditional rice-growing communities and in major cities in West Africa.[4] It is now the fastest-growing food staple in Africa. Annual per capita rice consumption in West Africa increased from 14 kilograms in the 1970s to 22 kilograms in the 1980s and more than 39 kilograms in 2009. For Africa as whole, annual per capita rice consumption increased from 11 kilograms in the 1970s to 21 kilograms in 2009 (figure 15.1). Since the early 1970s rice has been the number one source of caloric intake in West Africa and the third most important source of calories (after maize and cassava) for the continent as a whole (figure 15.2).

Domestic rice production grew at the rate of 6 percent a year between 2001 and 2005.[5] But production still falls far short of demand. As a result, Africa imports up to 40 percent of its rice consumption. The continent as a whole imports 30 percent of world rice imports, a potentially very risky and unsustainable situation, as shown during the food crisis in 2008. Rice imports cost Africa almost $4 billion in 2009 (Seck et al. 2010)—money that could have been invested in developing the domestic rice sector.

Until the early 1990s, rice breeding programs in Africa worked almost exclusively on improving *O. sativa* lines for Africa's diverse rice growth environments. Some breeders even voted to accelerate the disappearance of *glaberrima* (IRAT 1967), even though *sativa* varieties are generally much more vulnerable than *glaberrima* to the numerous biotic stresses (rice diseases, insect attacks, weeds, and so forth) and abiotic stresses (soil acidity, drought, salinity, iron toxicity, and so forth) of the African environment.

Figure 15.1 Annual per Capita Rice Consumption in Africa and West Africa, 1961–2009

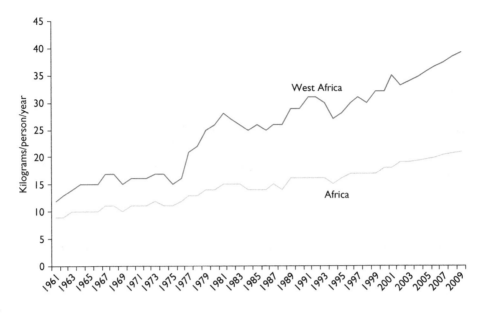

Source: FAO 2009.

Figure 15.2 Share of Calories in African Diet Provided by Various Sources, 1961–2007

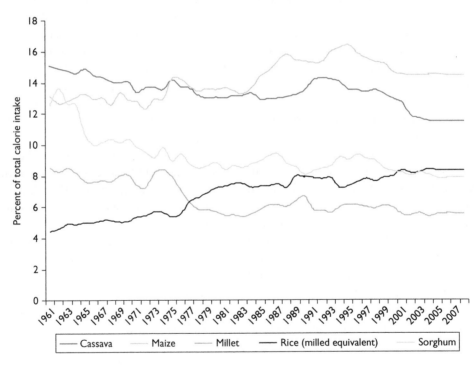

| —— Cassava | —— Maize | —— Millet | —— Rice (milled equivalent) | —— Sorghum |

Source: FAO 2009.

Some visionary breeders thought about combining the favorable characteristics of *O. sativa* with those of *O. glaberrima*. Crossing was difficult, however, because of the sterility barrier between the two species. A few breeders, includ-

ing breeders from the Institut de Recherche Agronomique Tropicale (IRAT) and the Institute of Savannah (IDESSA) Bouaké, in Côte d'Ivoire, worked on the problem during the 1970s and 1980s (Diagne 2006). Their work did not produce good results, with the crosses resulting in either sterile offspring or offspring that had some of the undesirable characteristics of the *glaberrima* parent (lodging, shattering, low yield).[6]

Development of the NERICA varieties began in 1991, when AfricaRice initiated an interspecific breeding program for the upland ecosystem. This long-term investment paid off, when breeders eventually overcame the obstacles encountered earlier, through perseverance and the use of biotechnology tools such as anther culture and embryo rescue techniques. In 1994 the first interspecific line with promising agronomic performance was obtained (Wopereis et al. 2008; Jones et al. 1997a, b).[7] Several hundred interspecific progenies were generated, opening new gene pools and increasing the biodiversity of rice.

The main objective of the breeding work that led to the NERICAs was to combine the high-yielding attribute of *O. sativa* with the resistance of the indigenous *O. glaberrima* to the African environment. Another long-sought attribute for a good upland variety is the ability to provide acceptable yields under the low-input use conditions typical of upland rice farming in Africa. Both objectives have been largely met, as evidenced by the experimental trials data summarized in

table 15.A1 and figure 15.A1 in annex 15.A1, which compare the performance of NERICA progenies with that of their *sativa* and *glaberrima* parents and other *sativa* checks under high and low input conditions and under major stresses in upland rice ecologies in AfricaRice's key research sites in Cote d'Ivoire.[8]

Indeed, the agronomic trials data show that the NERICA varieties bring to upland farmers the high yield potential of the *sativa* varieties under both low and high input conditions (see figure 15.A1), with what is in essence insurance against the risk of significant yield losses in the face of major upland biotic and abiotic stresses. Given that the *sativa* and *glaberrima* parents of these first-generation NERICAs are not the best-performing varieties within the two species, there is reason to expect that the performance of the next generations of NERICAs will be much higher.[9]

Through participatory varietal selection (box 15.1), farmers all over Africa have evaluated interspecific lines. The most successful lines have been named NERICA varieties. There are currently 18 varieties suited for upland growth conditions (NERICA1 to NERICA18) and 60 varieties suited for lowland growth conditions (NERICA-L1 to

---

Box 15.1 The Participatory Varietal Selection Methodology

Participatory varietal selection (PVS) aims to improve rice production through direct involvement of farmers, who play an active role in varietal selection, development, and dissemination. PVS is an adjunct to conventional breeding that markedly reduces the time taken for new varieties to reach farmers. In conventional breeding schemes, selection and testing procedures involve a series of multilocation trials over 8 to 12 years using a diminishing number of varieties. Through PVS, a large number of potentially interesting varieties reach farmers for evaluation in 5 years, and farmers have a major input into the selection of varieties to be released. By involving farmers in the varietal selection process, PVS aims to meet a diversity of demands for varieties, taking account of site-specificity for agronomic adaptation and selection criteria.

AfricaRice's approach to PVS research involves a three-year program. In the first year, breeders identify centralized fields near villages and plant a rice garden trial of up to 60 upland varieties. The varieties range from traditional and popular *O. sativas* to NERICAs,

African *O. glaberrimas*, and local varieties as checks. Male and female farmers are invited to visit the plot informally as often as possible. Groups of farmers formally evaluate the varieties at three key stages: maximum tillering (development of the plant leaves), maturity, and postharvest. At the first two stages, farmers compare agronomic traits. Each farmer's varietal selection and the criteria for selection are recorded and later analyzed.

In the second year, each farmer receives as many as six of the varieties he or she selected in the first year to grow. PVS observers, including breeders and technicians from nongovernmental organizations and extension services, visit participating farmers' fields to record seed performance and farmer evaluations of the selected varieties. At the end of the year, farmers evaluate threshability and palatability to provide an overall view of the strengths and weaknesses of the selected varieties. In the third year, farmers are asked to pay for seeds of the varieties they select. Willingness to pay provides evidence of the value farmers place on the seeds.

Source: Gridley and Sié 2008.

NERICA-L60). Agronomic characteristics of these varieties vary widely, but they are generally high yielding and early maturing (a trait much appreciated by farmers), do not lodge or shatter, yield good grain quality, and are relatively resistant to the biotic and abiotic stresses of the continents harsh growth environment. Weed resistance of the NERICAs, especially the upland NERICAs, still needs improvement. (For details on the development and the characteristics of different NERICA varieties, see Somado, Guei, and Keya 2008; Wopereis and others 2008; and Kaneda 2007a, b, c, and d.)

ADOPTION AND IMPACT OF NERICA VARIETIES IN SUB-SAHARAN AFRICA

The first generation of interspecific progenies was introduced through participatory varietal selection trials in Côte d'Ivoire in 1996 and in other member countries of AfricaRice in 1997. NERICA1 and NERICA2 were officially released in 2001 in Côte d'Ivoire (Diagne 2006; Science Council 2007). NERICA varieties have now been introduced in more than 30 countries in Sub-Saharan Africa using PVS approaches, mostly thanks to the African Rice Initiative (ARI).[10] By 2007, 17 upland NERICA varieties and 11 lowland NERICA varieties had been adopted. Where needed, ARI produced foundation seed to stimulate uptake of NERICA and other improved varieties. Seed production by ARI has increased steadily, from 2,733 tons in 2005 to 7,238 tons in 2007 and 13,108 tons in 2008 (Akintayo et al. 2009).

About 700,000 hectares in Sub-Saharan Africa were estimated to be under NERICA varieties as of 2009, covering an estimated 5 percent of the continent's upland rice-growing areas. This level of penetration is impressive 8–10 years after release of the first varieties. The studies reviewed in this section describe the areas under NERICA varieties in selected countries, actual and potential rates of adoption among farmers, and the impact of NERICA varieties on rice productivity and the livelihoods of family farmers.

Estimated area under NERICA

Surveys conducted by national agricultural research systems provide estimates of the total area under NERICA varieties in different countries. Diagne et al. (2006) and Adegbola et al. (2006) estimate the total area under NERICA varieties at 51,000 hectares in Guinea in 2004 and 5,000 hectares in Benin in 2003. Based on its estimates of the quantities of seed produced and distributed to farmers, the National Food Reserve Agency (NFRA) of Nigeria reports 186,000 hectares under NERICA1 in Nigeria in 2007 (ARI 2008). The Uganda National Research Institute, citing a report of the Statistics Office of the Ministry of Agriculture in Uganda, estimates that 35,000 hectares were under NERICA4 in 2007 (ARI 2008).

Except in Guinea and Benin, where surveys were conducted (in 2003 in Guinea and in 2005 in Benin), the estimated areas under NERICA reported above by national agricultural research systems are based on quantities of seed produced and distributed to farmers. To meet the need to quantify uptake of NERICA and other improved varieties in a much more reliable manner, AfricaRice and partners are currently conducting surveys in many countries where NERICA is cultivated. Surveys conducted in 2009 by national agricultural research systems and national agricultural statistical services in 21 Sub-Saharan African countries provide more recent estimates for some countries (AfricaRice 2010). According to these data, the area under NERICA was about142,391 hectares in Guinea and 244,293 hectares in Nigeria in 2009.[11]

Adoption of NERICA varieties

A 2009 study on adoption in Sub-Saharan African countries estimates actual rates of adoption of NERICA varieties (table 15.1).[12] These rates illustrate a largely unrealized potential adoption rate if the full rice farming population of these countries could be exposed to NERICA varieties and provided access to seed.

Uptake of NERICA varieties was reportedly high in the Kaduna and Ekiti states of Nigeria (Spencer et al. 2006). About 30 percent of farmers in Ekiti cultivated NERICA1 in 2005; 42 percent of farmers in PVS villages and 19 percent in near–PVS villages did so in Kaduna.[13] Adoption of NERICA1 appears to have continued during 2004 and 2005, despite the scaling down of PVS activities. About 35 percent

Table 15.1 Estimated Actual and Potential Rates of Adoption of NERICA Varieties in Selected African Countries (*percent*)

Country (year)	Rate of adoption	Potential rate of adoption
Benin (2004)	19	47
Côte d'Ivoire (2000)	4	24
Guinea (2001)	20	61
The Gambia (2006)	40	87

Source: Diagne 2009.

of farmers in near–PVS villages in Ekiti and Kaduna had not heard about NERICA1, showing the potential for increase in adoption rates (Spencer et al. 2006). In 2005 an estimated 14 percent of farmers in PVS villages in Kaduna and 9 percent of farmers in near–PVS villages had adopted NERICA2.

The percentage of households that grew NERICA varieties in Uganda increased from 0.9 percent in 2002 to 2.9 percent in 2003 and 16.5 percent in 2004, according to Kijima, Otsuka, and Sserunkuuma (2008). They find that membership in a farmers group, formal education of the head of household, and the number of household members significantly increased the probability of adopting NERICA varieties as well as the scale of area planted to NERICA varieties. Land size per person had a negative effect on the share of land planted to NERICA varieties, suggesting that land-poor households tend to allocate a larger proportion of land to cultivation of NERICA varieties. This pattern is also observed among households headed by women, who are likely to be poorer. Poorer households in Uganda thus tend to allocate a larger proportion of their land to NERICA varieties, which may suggest that the adoption of NERICA has the potential to reduce poverty and improve income distribution as it increases rice yields.

Impact of NERICA varieties on productivity and livelihoods of farmers

NERICA rice varieties were developed with the aims of improving rice productivity, raising income, and reducing food insecurity of poor upland rice farmers (mostly women), who rarely use fertilizer, which they say they cannot afford. Empirical evidence from impact assessment studies conducted in West Africa points to a heterogeneous impact of NERICA adoption across and within countries (table 15.2). Impacts have been significantly positive in Benin and Gambia. In almost all countries, the impacts have generally been higher for women than for men (Diagne, Midingoyi, and Kinkingninhoun 2009).

In Benin farmers adopting NERICA enjoyed an additional yield gain of about 1 metric ton per hectare. The impact at the national level was very limited, however, because of the low diffusion of NERICA varieties in Benin (Adegbola et al. 2006).

Results from another analysis based on data from the 2004 season show that the impact of NERICA adoption is higher for women than for men (Agboh-Noameshie, Kinkingninhoun-Medagbe, and Diagne 2007). Female potential adopters have a surplus of production of 850 kilograms of paddy per hectare, compared with 517 kilograms of paddy

Table 15.2 Yields and per Capita Income in Selected African Countries, by Gender

Country (year)	Yield (tons/hectare)	Income ($)
Benin (2004)		
Men	0.26***	22***
Women	0.97***	38***
All	0.71***	25***
Côte d'Ivoire (2000)		
Men	0.44	—
Women	−0.45	—
All	^0.44	—
The Gambia (2006)		
Men	0.18	4.6
Women	0.142***	10.6**
All	0.146***	10.2**

Source: Authors compilation, based on data from Agboh-Noameshie, Kinkingninhoun-Medagbe, and Diagne (2007) for Benin, Diagne; Midingoyi, and Kinkingninhoun (2009) for Côte d'Ivoire; Dibba et al. (2008a, b) for The Gambia; Dontsop et al. (2010) for Nigeria; and Kijima, Otsuka, and Sserunkuuma (2008) for Uganda.
— = Not available.
*** Significant at the 1 percent level; ** significant at the 5 percent level.

per hectare for men; the potential net income gain from adopting NERICA is estimated at about $337 per hectare for women and $277 for men. Results in The Gambia indicate that an additional yield gain of 0.14 ton per hectare was achieved by rice farmers, most of them women, adopting NERICA varieties (Dibba 2010).[14] Results from Côte d'Ivoire show that the impact is heterogeneous, with a sizable and statistically significant impact found for female farmers (0.7 ton per hectare) and a nonstatistically significant impact found for male farmers (Diagne 2006; Diagne, Midingoyi, and Kinkingninhoun 2009).

In Uganda NERICA had positive effects on productivity and allowed farmers to improve their yields (Kijima, Sserunkuuma, and Otsuka 2006; Kijima, Otsuka, and. Sserunkuuma 2008; Bergman-Lodin 2005). According to Kijima, Sserunkuuma, and Otsuka (2006), the average yield of NERICA in Uganda was 2.2 tons per hectare—twice the average rice yield in Sub-Saharan Africa. They find large differences in yields between experienced (2.46 tons per hectare) and inexperienced (1.72 tons per hectare) households, indicating that experience matters in achieving high yields. Other yield determinants were rainfall and cropping patterns.

A few studies document the impact of adoption of NERICA varieties on household income and poverty. Most find that adoption increases household income and improves income distribution within households. In Uganda, for example, adoption of NERICA varieties has the potential to increase annual per capita income by $20 (12 percent of actual per capita income) and to reduce the incidence of poverty, measured by the headcount ratio, by 5 percentage points (from 54.3 percent to 49.1 percent) (Kijima, Otsuka, and Sserunkuuma 2008). The poverty gap index and the squared poverty gap index also declined following the introduction of NERICA, suggesting that adoption can increase incomes among the absolute poor in Uganda.

NERICA adoption has had a positive impact on household rice and total incomes in The Gambia (Glove 2009; Dibba 2010). Dibba (2010) finds that adoption of NERICA increases rice farmers' daily income by about $0.34 on average (about 30 percent of the average daily income of adopters). Sogbossi (2008) identifies NERICA adoption as a key determinant in poverty reduction in Benin, where it reduced the probability of being poor by 13 percent.[15] The impact of NERICA adoption was higher for women farmers (reduction in probability of being poor was 19 percent) than for men (reduction in probability of being poor was 6 percent). Findings from a study conducted in Nigeria indicate that adoption of NERICA increased total farm household gross income from rice by about $555 (about 46 percent of average gross income from rice), increasing farmer's probability of escaping poverty (Dontsop et al. 2010).

These results suggest that NERICA can bring hope to millions of poor, small-scale farmers in Africa by reducing poverty and income inequality. Realization of this hope requires wider dissemination of NERICA, however, which can take place only if the seed bottlenecks and other production constraints examined in the next section are addressed.

LESSONS LEARNED

The use of the PVS approach allowed farmers to evaluate the new varieties in comparison with their own material. It enhanced capacity building and ownership of the NERICA varieties among farmers and national research and extension communities. PVS also reduced the time involved in the varietal release process in many countries.

Different partnerships and approaches were essential for NERICA adoption and seed production (box 15.2). In many countries the active involvement of government authorities at the highest level helped stimulate uptake. Major government initiatives on rice in Guinea, Mali, Nigeria, and Uganda focused on NERICA varieties. In Benin a private

---

Box 15.2 Successfully Disseminating NERICA Varieties in Burkina Faso, The Gambia, Guinea, and Uganda

Partnerships with the National Agricultural Research Extension Systems, nongovernmental organizations, and farmer organizations, with support from donors and development partners, were key ingredients in scaling up the dissemination of NERICA varieties throughout Sub-Saharan Africa.[a] Governments across the region also supported the dissemination of NERICA varieties through major rice development initiatives well before the 2008 food crisis.

Burkina Faso

Domestic rice production in Burkina Faso increased by an astonishing 241 percent in 2008 (Solidarité et Progres 2008), partly as a result of the adoption of NERICA varieties. This remarkable achievement reflected the government's response to the world food crisis in 2008. Emergency support facilitated farmers' access to mineral

fertilizer and quality seed of high-yielding rice varieties, including NERICA varieties.

The Gambia

NERICA varieties were introduced into The Gambia through PVS trials in 1998, initially in three villages and later more widely through farmers' own channels and efforts by the National Agricultural Research Institute and the Department of Agricultural Services. The uptake of NERICA varieties continued through the African Rice Institute and NERICA dissemination project funded by the African Development Bank in 2004. Even the head of state was growing NERICA varieties on his own land and encouraging farmers to grow these varieties. According to FAO data, from 2001 to 2007, the rice-growing area was relatively constant, at about 17,000 hectares. A doubling to 34,000 hectares occurred

(continued next page)

Box 15.2 *(continued)*

in 2008, partly as a result of the enthusiasm generated by NERICA varieties, the support of the government, and the efforts of researchers and technicians. NERICA varieties are now cultivated in all six agricultural regions of the country. Introduction of the varieties has brought hope for increased rice productivity and poverty reduction.

Guinea

The first interspecific lines were introduced in Guinea in 1997 by the Institut de Recherche Agronomique de Guinée (IRAG) and the Service National de la Promotion Rurale et de la Vulgarisation (SNPRV) through an intensive program to introduce new upland rice varieties. NERICA varieties subsequently experienced a very rapid spread in the regions of Upper Guinea and Forest Guinea after only two years of experimental testing and PVS (Camara et al. 2002; Diagne 2006). A study by researchers from AfricaRice, IRAG, and SNPRV in the four regions of Guinea estimates the area under NERICA varieties at 51,000 hectares in 2003, slightly less than 10 percent of the 525,000 hectares used for rice production according to Food and Agriculture Organization (FAO) statistics (FAOSTAT 2010)—a remarkable achievement in a relatively short time. In 2007 the area under NERICA varieties in Guinea was estimated at 82,930 hectares, 12 percent of the total rice area (ARI 2008). Estimates from the nationwide survey show that the area under NERICA has grown significantly since 2007 to 142,391 hectares, representing about 18 percent of the total rice area in Guinea (AfricaRice 2010).

Several factors explain the success of NERICA varieties in Guinea. First, NERICA varieties appeared when Guinea was experiencing a period of prolonged drought that had pushed the Guinean government to seek assistance from AfricaRice to put at farmers' disposal short-season varieties that could better cope with drought (Diagne 2006). NERICA varieties corresponded well to what was needed. Second, Guinean farmers were very receptive to experimenting with new varieties in their fields. Third, an effective partnership between national and international institutions greatly contributed to the rapid adoption of the new rice varieties. The World Bank funded the program through its Special Program for Agricultural Research in Africa (SPAAR). IRAG and SNPRV worked together to select the most appropriate testing sites and methods of introduction, joining hands with an international nongovernmental organization, Sasakawa Global 2000. This cooperation facilitated access to inputs for farmers involved in the trials. AfricaRice staff provided training to IRAG and SNPRV scientists and technicians in the conduct of the PVS trials and seed production throughout the duration of the program (Kaneda 2007d; Diagne 2006).

Uganda

Rice farming is relatively marginal in East Africa, especially in Uganda. Before 2002 rice farming was practiced mostly as a cash crop by only a few farmers on a very small upland area and in very few small irrigated schemes. Research support had been abandoned in the 1970s, and rice yields had gradually declined to about 0.4 ton per hectare in 2002. The introduction of NERICA varieties enabled farmers to attain yields of up to 3 tons per hectare on fertile land in Uganda.

By 2002 NERICA varieties were being cultivated in many parts of Uganda. Rice acreage increased sixfold in the six years following the release of the new varieties, from 6,000 hectares in 2002 to 40,000 hectares in 2008, and the number of rice growers rose from 4,000 in 2004 to 35,000 in 2007 (Akintayo et al. 2009). Uganda reduced its rice importation from 60,000 tons in 2005 to 35,000 tons in 2007—an almost 50 percent reduction in rice imports, leading to savings of about $30 million (Akintayo and others 2009). Several factors explain the rapid uptake in Uganda. The great interest shown by the National Institute of Agricultural Research for the new varieties at the time of revitalizing its rice program and the dynamism of Sasakawa Global 2000 played very important roles in the introduction and diffusion of NERICA varieties. The interest and dynamism of the private sector was essential in producing and marketing seed of NERICA varieties, as was the active involvement of the highest political authorities of the country, particularly Uganda's vice president (Akintayo et al. 2009).

a. Donors included the African Development Bank, the Food and Agricultural Organization, the Government of Japan, the International Development Research Centre, the International Fund for Agricultural Development, the Rockefeller Foundation, the United Nations Development Programme, the U.S. Agency for International Development, and the World Bank.

entrepreneur was instrumental in the diffusion of NERICA varieties, paying for demonstration plots across the country and promoting seed production (Akintayo et al. 2009).

The ARI–coordinated NERICA dissemination project funded by the African Development Bank and numerous smaller projects run by the Japan International Cooperation Agency, FAO, and many nongovernmental organizations (NGOs) greatly accelerated the uptake of NERICA varieties across Sub-Saharan Africa (map 15.1). Despite these efforts, seed production remains a major bottleneck, especially in West and Central Africa, where many farmers lack access to improved rice varieties. In many countries, national seed regulatory bodies do not exist or are dysfunctional. Functioning bodies are essential to estimate and meet the demand for rice seed for different ecosystems and consumer preferences. Incentives should be provided to small-scale enterprises to develop viable seed businesses.

The data on potential adoption rates of NERICA varieties illustrate its tremendous potential to reach still more farmers. The constraints to doing so are numerous and vary from country to country. One major factor is the desperate lack of capacity at all levels in the rice value chain, especially the neglect of Africa's rice research capacity. Only about 250–275 researchers (including only about 15 women) are involved to some extent in rice research in AfricaRice member states, according to a 2008 survey—and most of them work on many other crops and spend only a fraction of their time on rice. Egypt alone accounts for the lion's share of this research pool, with 50 highly qualified researchers working full time on rice, including 12 rice breeders. In comparison, Nigeria has only 2 rice breeders.

Other issues include lack of access to seed, fertilizer, and credit and inadequate rice production, processing, distribution, and marketing infrastructure. These factors need to be identified, and relevant actions taken to develop the rice sector. An integrated approach from seed to plate is needed.

Africa has tremendous potential to expand the area under rice cropping, especially in the rainfed lowland ecosystem. It has been estimated that 200 million hectares of rainfed lowland area could be developed for rice across the continent. If just 1 percent of this land were allocated to growing rice and the average yield was just 3 tons per hectare, Africa would produce another 6 million tons of rice a year, making a major dent in the 10 million tons of rice it imports. The lowlands offer great potential for the sustainable expansion, intensification, and diversification of rice-based systems. Given this potential, the lowland NERICA varieties and their successors are expected to have an even greater impact than the upland NERICA varieties.

Map 15.1   Areas of Sub-Saharan Africa Producing NERICA Varieties, 2005 and 2006

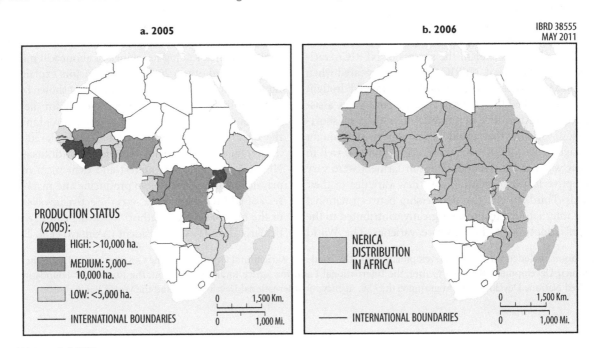

Source: Akintayo et al. 2009.

CHAPTER 15: INCREASING RICE PRODUCTIVITY AND STRENGTHENING FOOD SECURITY THROUGH NEW RICE FOR AFRICA (NERICA)

CONCLUSIONS

As a result of the increase in rice consumption across Sub-Saharan Africa, the continent accounted for 30 percent of world rice imports in 2009, costing African economies an estimated $4 billion. Relying on the world market to feed Africa's rice consumers is a risky and unsustainable strategy. Encouraging the development of Africa's rice sector is crucial for food security. The sector could also serve as an engine for economic growth (IFPRI 2006).

Development of Africa's rice sector will require an integrated seed to plate value chain approach. Much work is still needed to identify the varieties that respond to consumer demand and grow well in the various ecosystems in which rice is grown in Africa, under both current and future climate scenarios. Much greater input in varietal development is needed at the national level, and greater capacity in rice breeding is needed across the continent.

NERICA varieties have shown great potential in both upland and lowland ecosystems in Africa, where they currently cover more than 700,000 hectares. Women farmers in particular have profited from NERICA varieties. More effort is needed to ensure that larger numbers of rice farmers, including farmers who have never seen a new rice variety, can profit from these new varieties, especially in rainfed ecologies.

AfricaRice is already working on new varieties that will replace the first generation of NERICA varieties, in close collaboration with national agricultural research institutes, the International Rice Research Institute, and other international research institutes in Japan, Europe, and the United States. These efforts, together with a better definition of farmers' needs and consumer demands, are expected to lead to the development of varieties that will eventually outperform the current generation of NERICA varieties.

AfricaRice is an active member of the Coalition of African Rice Development, an initiative of the Japan International Cooperation Agency and the Alliance for a Green Revolution in Africa, which aims to double rice production in Sub-Saharan Africa between 2008 and 2018. Such partnerships and commitment at the national and regional level to hire, train, and retain new staff in rice research and invest in rice production, storage, processing, and distribution capacity will be instrumental in boosting Africa's rice sector.

Table 15.A1   Performance of NERICA Progenies and Their Parents under Various Conditions

Item	Yield under high- and low-input conditions[a]		Yield under drought- and nondrought-prone sites		Yield under acid and nonacid soil sites		Susceptibility to gall midge attack
	Low input	High input	Drought	Nondrought	Acid	Non-acid	
NERICA progeny line							
Sample size	19	19	16	16	25	25	100
Mean (across replications and lines)	1.16	3.07	1.62	2.05	1.99	3.19	40.72
Standard deviation (across lines)	0.16	0.50	0.39	0.36	0.27	0.40	8.95
Minimum	0.91	1.70	1.08	1.49	1.57	2.15	8.76
Maximum	1.47	3.86	2.27	2.66	2.63	3.96	58.69
Sativa parent (WAB56-104)							
Mean value (across replications)	0.90	3.26	1.19	1.96	1.35	3.26	52.77
T-test for equality with mean of NERICA lines							
p-value	0.00	0.12	0.00	0.33	0.00	0.36	0.00
Glaberrima parent (CG14)							
Mean value (across replications)	0.64	1.00	1.24	0.86	1.23	1.00	
T-test for equality with mean of NERICA lines							
p-value	0.00	0.00	0.00	0.00	0.00	0.00	
Sativa tolerant check[b]							
Mean value (across replications)			1.51	1.96			12.07
T-test for equality with mean of NERICA lines							
p-value			0.25	0.33			0.00
Sativa susceptible check[c]							
Mean value (across replications)			0.49	1.12			38.36
T-test for equality with mean of NERICA lines							
p-value			0.00	0.00			0.01

Source: Authors, based on data from experiment in 1999 at AfricaRice headquarters (in M'bé) and at two of its on-farm research sites (in Man and Korhogo). The trials used a randomized complete block design with three replicates at each site: the NERICA progenies, their two *sativa* and *glaberrima* parents (WAB56 104 and CG14), and a select set of *sativa* checks, which varied across the trials. The set of NERICA progenies also differed across trials.

a. Yield data are mean values for two sites (M'bé and Man) from a 1999 randomized complete block design trial with three replicates at each site.

b. *Moroberekan*, a local *sativa* variety commonly used as check for drought.

c. IR20, an improved *sativa* variety used as check for drought.

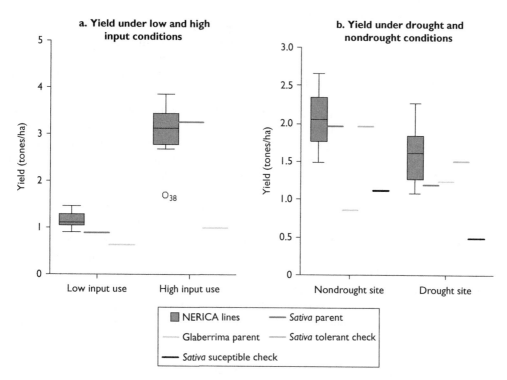

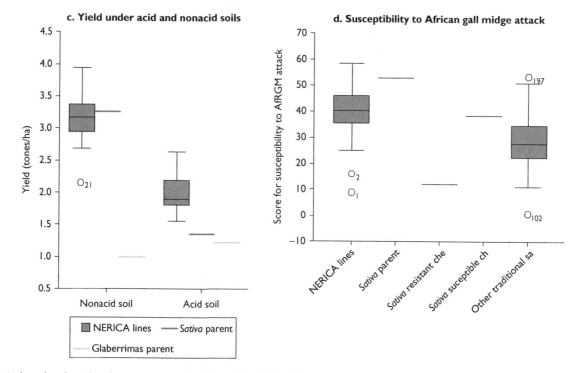

Source: Authors, based on data from experiment in 1999 at AfricaRice headquarters (in M'bé) and at two of its on-farm research sites (in Man and Korhogo). The trials used a randomized complete block design with three replicates at each site: the NERICA progenies, their two *sativa* and *glaberrima* parents (WAB56 104 and CG14), and a select set of *sativa* checks, which varied across the trials. The set of NERICA progenies also differed across trials.
Note: Sample sizes are 19 for panel a, 16 for panel b, 25 for panel c, and 100 for panel d.

1. The role of technological innovation in raising agricultural productivity and fostering overall agricultural development is documented in the World Bank's 2008 *World Development Report*.

2. The Africa Rice Center—AfricaRice for short—is the new official name, adopted in September 2009, for the organization previously known as the West Africa Rice Development Association (WARDA). This intergovernmental association of African countries is one of the 15 international agricultural research centers supported by the Consultative Group on International Agricultural Research (CGIAR). The center was created in 1971 by 11 African countries. With the continuing expansion of its activities into Central, East, and North Africa, the Council of Ministers passed a resolution at their 27th meeting, held in LomÈ, Togo, in September 2009, to change its name from WARDA to AfricaRice. Today its membership comprises 24 countries: Benin, Burkina Faso, Cameroon, Central African Republic, Chad, Côte d'Ivoire, Democratic Republic of Congo, Arab Republic of Egypt, Gabon, The Gambia, Ghana, Guinea, Guinea-Bissau, Liberia, Madagascar, Mali, Mauritania, Niger, Nigeria, Republic of Congo, Senegal, Sierra Leone, Togo, and Uganda.

3. The importance of the development of NERICA varieties has been widely recognized. The Consultative Group on International Agricultural Research (CGIAR) presented the King Baudouin Award to the Africa Rice Center (then WARDA) in 2000 for the development of NERICA varieties. In 2004 the center's Dr. Monty Jones became the first African to receive the World Food Prize, for his contribution to the development of the family of NERICA rice varieties suitable for upland growth conditions. Dr. Moussa SiÈ, a senior rice breeder at AfricaRice, was awarded the prestigious International Koshihikari Rice Prize of Japan, in recognition of his leadership in developing the family of NERICA rice varieties suitable for lowland growth conditions.

4. Rice is generally associated with Asia, but it is also an integral part of the history and culture of Africa, where it has been grown for more than 3,000 years. *Oryza glaberrima* was grown largely in the central delta of the Niger River and in the Higher Gambia and the Casamance region of what is now Senegal (Carney 1998; Poteres 1962, cited in Linares 2002). *Oryza glaberrima* was the only rice species grown in West Africa until the 16th century, when the Portuguese introduced the Asian species *Oryza sativa* in the West African coastal regions (Linares 2002). Over the years, *O. sativa* gradually replaced *O. glaberrima*, which has some unfavorable characteristics. Farmers who still grow *O. glaberrima* do so mostly for social or religious reasons, for its culinary and nutritional qualities, or because it is better adapted to their agroclimatic environments.

5. Seventy percent of the production increase came from land expansion, with just 30 percent attributable to productivity enhancement.

6. Lodging is the process in which rice plants fall over at, or just before, maturity; shattering is the process in which plants' panicles scatter their seeds on the ground at maturity.

7. NERICA rice varieties are interspecific but not genetically modified.

8. AfricaRice has five on-farm research sites in Côte d'Ivoire, known as "key sites." The sites—selected in the early 1990s, when AfricaRice moved its headquarters to Côte d'Ivoire from Liberia—were chosen to cover all nine rice ecologies and the main rice-producing regions in the forest and savanna agroecological zones of Côte d'Ivoire and to be representative of almost all of the rice- growing ecologies in West Africa.

9. NERICA varieties have retained only about 5–10 percent of the genome of the African parent, because of backcrosses to the *O. sativa* parent. They are also based on crosses between only a handful of *O. sativa* and *O. glaberrima* accessions. AfricaRice breeders have since developed "bridge varieties" that show full fertility when crossed with *O. glaberrima*, potentially allowing the full exploitation of all 2,300 accessions of the *O. glaberrima* species in the gene bank of AfricaRice and a much greater retention of the *O. glaberrima* genome. Molecular assisted breeding is also becoming a routine tool, accelerating varietal development.

10. ARI was established in 2002 by AfricaRice and key donor partners, including the African Development Bank, the government of Japan, the Rockefeller Foundation, and the United Nations Development Programme, in order to facilitate the dissemination of NERICA varieties and other improved varieties in Sub-Saharan Africa. This network of rice research and extension organizations and private sector partners plays an important role in making quality rice seed available. This role is crucial, as seed availability is one of the weakest links in the rice value chain in Africa.

11. Data from these national surveys, which are still being processed, are expected to provide more accurate estimates of the total area under NERICA in Sub-Saharan Africa. Preliminary figures from these surveys and other secondary sources suggest that about 700,000 hectares was under NERICA in Sub-Saharan Africa in 2009.

12. The potential adoption rate estimated here is the adoption rate when the entire population of rice farmers is made aware of the existence of the NERICA varieties (Diagne and Demont 2007). Observed adoption rates are lower than these estimated potential adoption rates because many farmers simply lack awareness of the NERICA's existence.

13. PVS villages are villages in which NERICA varieties were tested and evaluated by farmers through participatory varietal selection (PVS) trials. The nearby villages are villages

not hosting PVS trials but within 2–5 kilometers radius of the selected PVS-hosting villages.

14. With women making up 93 percent of sample farmers in The Gambia (sample includes 39 men and 532 women), it is not surprising that the average for the whole sample and the sample for women are almost the same. The average gain for men is not significant. Although seemingly small, the 0.14 ton per hectare average gain from NERICA adoption is statistically significant and represents about 15 percent of the average rice yield obtained by farmers (just under 1 ton per hectare).

15. The poor are defined using the income poverty line in Benin, estimated at CFA 51,413 a year (about $100) in rural areas and CFA 91,709 a year (about $180) in urban areas (Sogbossi 2008).

REFERENCES

Adégbola, P. Y., A. Arouna, A. Diagne, and A. A. Souléïmane. 2006. "Evaluation de l'impact économique des nouvelles variétés de riz NERICA au Bénin: évidence avec les modèles basés sur l'approche contre factuel." Paper presented at the First Africa Rice Congress, Dar es Salaam, July 31–August 4.

Adékambi, A. S., A. Diagne, F. Kinkingninhoun-Medagbe, and G. Biaou. 2009. "The Impact of Agricultural Technology Adoption on Poverty: A Case Study of NERICA Varieties in Benin." Paper presented at the meetings of the International Association of Agricultural Economists, Beijing, August 16–22.

AfricaRice. 2010. *Rice Data Systems for Sub-Saharan Africa: Contribution to the Japan–AfricaRice Emergency Rice Project.* Updated synthesis report submitted to the government of Japan, September 30, Cotonou.

Afriquenligne 2009. "Le riz NERICA pour assurer la sécurité alimentaire." In *Actualités africaine en ligne.* http://www.afriquenligne.fr/actualites/economie/le-riz-nerica-pour-assurer-la-securite-alimentaire-200804252475.html.

Agboh-Noameshie, A. R., F. M. Kinkingninhoun-Medagbe, and A. Diagne. 2007. "Gendered Impact of NERICA Adoption on Farmers' Production and Income in Central Benin." Paper presented at the meetings of the African Association of Agricultural Economists, August 20–22, Accra.

Akintayo, I., O. Ajayi, R. A. Agboh-Noameshie, and B. Cissé. 2009. *Report of the Seventh African Rice Initiative Steering Committee/Experts Meeting,* May 4–6, Cotonou.

ARI (African Rice Institute). 2008: *Initiative africaine sur le riz: rapport annuel 2008.* Centre du Riz pour l'Afrique ADRAO, Cotonou.

Bentley, J., C. Almekinders, D. Yawovi, and D. Dalohoun. 2008. *Center Commissioned External Review of the African Rice Initiative.* AfricaRice, Cotonou.

Bergman-Lodin, J. 2005. "The NERICA Conundrum: From Rice to Riches." Lund University, Department of Economic and Social Geography, Lund, Sweden.

Camara, B., A. Conde, M. S. Diallo, M. B. Barry, B. Sekou, and T. Berhe. 2002. *NERICA, the Guinea Experience.* Report of the Departments of National Research, Extension and Rural Development and Sasakawa Global 2000/Guinea Agricultural Project, Conakry.

Carney, J. A. 1998. "The Role of African Rice and Slaves in the History of Rice Cultivation in the Americas." *Human Ecology* 26 (4): 525–45.

Dalton, Timothy. J. 2004. "A Household Hedonic Model of Rice Traits: Economic Values from Farmers in West Africa." *Agricultural Economics* 31: 149–59.

Diagne, A. 2006. "Le NERICA: mythe et réalités?" *Grain de sel, la revue de l'inter-réseaux* (March–August): 34–37.

———. 2009. "Technological Change in Smallholder Agriculture: Bridging the Adoption Gap by Understanding Its Source." Paper presented at the conference on Agriculture for Development sponsored by the African Economic Research Consortium, Mombasa, May 28–29.

Diagne, A., and M. Demont. 2007. "Taking a New Look at Empirical Models of Adoption: Average Treatment Effect Estimation of Adoption Rates and Their Determinants." *Agricultural Economics* 37 (2–3): 201–10.

Diagne, A., G. S. Midingoyi, and F. Kinkingninhoun. 2009. "The Impact of NERICA Adoption on Rice Yield in West Africa: Evidence from Four Countries." Paper presented at the meetings of the International Association of Agricultural Economists Conference, Beijing, August 16–22.

Diagne A., M. J. Sogbossi, S. Diawara, and Camara, A. 2006. *L'étendu du succès de la dissémination des variétés NERICA en Guinée: estimation des superficies emblavées.* West Africa Rice Development Association, Cotonou.

Dibba, L. 2010. "Estimation of NERICA Adoption Rates and Impact on Productivity and Poverty of Small-Scale Rice Farmers in The Gambia." M.Phil. thesis, Kwame Nkrumah University, Faculty of Agriculture, Department of Agricultural Economics, Agri-business and Extension, Kumassi, Ghana.

Dibba, L., A. Diagne, and S. Fialor. 2010. "Impact of NERICA Adoption on Productivity and Poverty of the Small-Scale Rice Farmers in The Gambia." Kwami Nkrumah University of Science and Technology Kumasi Ghana and Africa Rice Center, Cotonou.

Dibba, L, A. Diagne, F. Simtowe, M.J. Sogbossi and M. Mendy. 2008a. "Diffusion and Adoption of NERICA in Gambia." Africa Rice Center, Cotonou.

———. 2008b "The Impact of NERICA Adoption on Yield in Gambia. Africa Rice Center Cotonou.

Dontsop, P., A. Diagne, V. O. Okuruwa, and V. Ojehomon. 2010. "Impact of Improved Rice Technology on Income and Poverty among Rice Farmers in Nigeria: The Case of NERICA Varieties." University of Ibadan Nigeria and Africa Rice Center, Ibadan.

FAO (Food and Agriculture Organization). 2009. "The Special Challenges for Sub-Saharan Africa." High-Level Experts' Forum, Rome, October 12–13.

———. 2010. Food and Agricultural Organization statistics. http://www.fao.org/corp/statistics/en/.

Glove, S. 2009. "Agricultural Technology Dissemination in West Africa: A Quantitative Analysis of NERICA Adoption and Its Impact in Guinea and The Gambia." MSc. thesis, University of London, Department of Development Economics, the School of Oriental and African Studies.

Gridley, H., and M. Sié. 2008. "The Role of PVS: Farmer in the Driving Seat." In NERICA: New Rice for Africa. A Compendium, ed. E. Somado, R. Guei, and S. O. Keya. AfricaRice, Cotonou.

IFPRI (International Food Policy Research Institute), in collaboration with IITA (International Institute of Tropical Agriculture), CORAF/WECARD (Conseil Ouest et Centre Africain pour la Recherche et le Développement Agricoles/West and Central African Council for Agricultural Research and Development), and ECOWAS (Economic Community Of West African States). 2006. Regional Strategic Alternatives for Agriculture-Led Growth and Poverty Reduction in West Africa. Final Draft Report. Washington, DC.

IRAT (Institut de Recherche Agronomique Tropicale). 1967. "Les variétés de riz au cercle de Banfora. IRAT/Haute Volta." L'Agronomie Tropical 24: 691–707.

Johnson, D. E 1997. Weeds of Rice in West Africa. West Africa Rice Development Association (WARDA). Bouaké, Côte d'Ivoire.

Jones, M. P., M. Dingkuhn, G. K. Aluko, and M. Semon. 1997. "Interspecific Oryza sativa × O. glaberrima Steud. Progenies in Upland Rice Improvement." Euphytica 92: 237–46.

Kaneda, C. 2007a. "Breeding and Disseminating Efforts of NERICA: Breeding of Upland Rice." Journal of Japanese Tropical Agriculture 51 (1): 1–4.

———. 2007b. "Breeding and Disseminating Efforts of NERICA: Evaluation of Important Characteristics." Journal of Japanese Tropical Agriculture 51 (2): 41–45.

———. 2007c. "Breeding and Disseminating Efforts of NERICA: Important Characteristics of Lowland Rice." Journal of Japanese Tropical Agriculture 51 (3): 79–83.

———. 2007d. "Breeding and Disseminating Efforts of NERICA: Efforts for Dissemination of NERICA in Africa." Journal of Japanese Tropical Agriculture (51): 4: 145–51.

Kijima, Y., K. Otsuka, and D. Sserunkuuma. 2008. "Assessing the Impact of NERICA on Income and Poverty in Central and Western Uganda." Agricultural Economics 38: 327–337.

———. 2009. "Determinants of Changing Behaviors of NERICA Adoption: An Analysis of Panel Data from Uganda." University of Tsukuba, Graduate School of Systems and Information Engineering, Tsukuba, Ibaraki, Japan.

Kijima, Y., D. Sserunkuuma, and K. Otsuka. 2006. "How Revolutionary Is the 'NERICA Revolution'? Evidence from Uganda." Developing Economies 44 (2): 252–67.

Linares, O. F. 2002. African Rice Oryza Glaberrima: History and Future Potential. Smithsonian Tropical Research Institute, Balboa-Ancon, Panama.

Ndjiondjop, M-N., K. Semagn, M. Cissoko, M. P. Jones, and S. McCouch. 2008. "Molecular Characterization of NERICA Lines." In NERICA: New Rice for Africa. A Compendium, ed. E. Somado, R. Guei, and S. O. Keya. Cotonou: AfricaRice.

Porteres, R. 1962. "Berceaux agricoles primaires sur le continent africain." Journal of African History 3 (2): 195–210.

Science Council. 2007. Report of the Fifth External Program and Management (EPMR) of the Africa Rice Center (WARDA). Consultative Group on International Agricultural Research (CGIAR), Science Council Secretariat, Rome.

Seck P. A., E. Tollens, M. C. S. Wopereis, A. Diagne, and I. Bamba. 2010. "Rising Trends and Variability of Rice Prices: Threats and Opportunities for Sub-Saharan Africa." Food Policy 35 (5): 403–11.

Sogbossi, M-J. 2008. "Riziculture et réduction de la pauvreté au Bénin: impact de l'adoption des nouvelles variétés rizicoles sur la pauvreté et l'inégalité du revenu dans le Département des Collines Bénin." Master's thesis, University of Abomey-Calavi, Département d'Economie Socio-anthropologie et Communication, Abomey-Calavi, Benin.

Solidarité et Progrès. 2008. "Mauvais temps pour les malthusiens! La production de riz explose en Afrique." http://www.solidariteetprogres.org/article5783.html.

Somado, E., R. Guei, and S. O. Keya. 2008. NERICA: New Rice for Africa. A Compendium. Cotonou: AfricaRice.

Spencer, D., A. Dorward , G. Abalu, D. Philip, and D. Ogungbile. 2006. Evaluation of Adoption of NERICA and Other

Improved Upland Rice Varieties Following Varietal Promotion Activities in Nigeria. Reported prepared for the Gatsby and Rockefeller Foundations, New York.

Wopereis, M. C. S., A. Diagne, J. Rodenburg, M. Sié, and E. A. Somado. 2008. "Why NERICA Is a Successful Innovation for African Farmers: A Response to Orr et al. from the Africa Rice Center." *Outlook on Agriculture* 37 (3): 169–76.

World Bank. 2008. *World Development Report 2008: Agriculture for Development.* Washington, DC: World Bank.

CHAPTER 16

Fertilizer in Kenya: Factors Driving the Increase in Usage by Smallholder Farmers

Joshua Ariga and T. S. Jayne

ertilizer use is notably lower in most of Sub-Saharan Africa than in other developing regions. Too little irrigation and varieties unresponsive to fertilizer may explain this low use to some degree. But more often, the causes are lack of credit, long distances between farmers and the nearest fertilizer retailer, weak market infrastructure, and lack of government support. Indeed, in many countries, the withdrawal of state input delivery systems has led to a reduction in fertilizer use as commercial distribution systems compete with subsidized government programs.

Kenya, however, stands as a notable departure from this common Sub-Saharan African narrative. In the early 1990s fertilizer markets were liberalized, government price controls and import licensing quotas were eliminated, and fertilizer donations by external donor agencies were phased out. Fertilizer use then almost doubled over the 15-year period from 1992 to 2007, with much of the increase attributable to smallholder farmers. In the productive farming areas of western Kenya, rates of fertilizer application on maize are comparable with rates in Asia and Latin America.

Kenya's economy is predominantly agrarian, with more than 70 percent of its people dependent on agriculture-related farm and off-farm activities for their livelihoods (Ministry of Agriculture 2004). Food security is a concern for the 60 percent of the population living below the $1-a-day poverty line. While increasing the available supply of food is an important goal, the problem of access to food is perhaps the primary cause of food insecurity in Kenya. Ensuring access to food requires that the poor are able either to produce or to buy enough food for a healthy diet.

Because of unpredictable weather and poor infrastructure, producers and consumers of agricultural products in Kenya face volatile market prices, with periods of surplus production providing a boon for consumers and periods of deficit benefiting a relatively few producers who are net sellers and hurting the majority of consumers. The justification for state participation in the market for agricultural products in Kenya has been to maintain prices at levels that both provide incentives to raise farm incomes for producers and ensure that consumers can access food, the classic "food price dilemma."

Before 1990 Kenya addressed this dilemma through direct participation in input and output markets for national "strategic" crops through either state-run agencies that set prices at panterritorial levels or ostensible farmer organizations that were managed by state-connected political agents or their surrogates. For example, in the coffee sector, the government helped enact laws that created the Coffee Board of Kenya and Kenya Planters Cooperative Union; for pyrethrum (chrysanthemums), it encouraged the creation of the Pyrethrum Board of Kenya; and for milk, tea, and maize, the government helped create the Kenya Cooperative

Joshua Ariga is a senior research fellow with the Tegemeo Institute of Agricultural Policy and Development, Egerton University, and a research specialist at Michigan State University. T. S. Jayne is Professor, International Development, Michigan State University.

Creameries, the Kenya Tea Development Agency, and the National Cereals and Produce Board (NCPB). In its heyday, the NCPB generally bought maize grain from farmers at higher-than-market prices and sold it to industrial maize millers at below-market prices. On the input side, the 1970s and 1980s brought the formation of the state-run Kenya National Trading Corporation (KNTC) and the Kenya Grain Growers Cooperative Union (KGGCU), later the Kenya Farmers Association (KFA), which worked with the output organizations.

Of all the crops mentioned in the previous paragraph, policy makers in Kenya—and indeed, throughout East Africa—have been most concerned with increasing fertilizer use on maize, the main food security crop in the region. For a number of reasons, however, state efforts in the 1980s to improve food security through increased production and incomes did not produce desired results. As a result, several reform measures were implemented that sought to achieve food security objectives in a more efficient way, in the lines of a laissez faire or competitive markets dogma.

Fertilizer and maize market reforms

The period before market reforms in Kenya was characterized by a predictable pattern involving the participation of state-run agencies or private farmer organizations (with heavy state intervention in their management) in input and output markets for import and export, distribution, and retailing. Although these state agencies continually reinvented themselves under different names, particularly when they came under scrutiny for corruption and unsustainable budgets, their reincarnation followed the same general modus operandi, and all eventually failed to achieve their goal of improving the livelihoods of smallholder farmers.

To put the reform process into perspective, it is important to recognize that agricultural policy in Kenya has also gone through a number of key phases characterized by an unpredictable shelf life. In the immediate postindependence period (late 1960s), agricultural policy was concerned with supporting a smooth transfer of prime land from white settlers to indigenous Kenyans with help from state-supported agencies in the production and marketing of produce (such as NCPB for maize). Agricultural inputs were marketed through the farmers' union, KFA, and credit was provided through the Agricultural Finance Corporation (AFC).

In the 1960s KFA could, for instance, offer inputs on credit (through AFC) to select farmers, who repaid the union after harvesting the crop and delivering it to relevant

marketing agencies such as the NCPB (which deducted the cost of the loans on behalf of the KFA and AFC). To deal with high prices and a weak distribution network for smallholder farmers, fertilizer subsidies were also introduced through these agencies (Ariga, Jayne, and Nyoro 2006). This conflict of interest across interlinked agencies generated widespread corruption and bureaucratic costs that led to a policy change in 1972 in favor of introducing another agency (KNTC), which was tasked with importing fertilizer, while the KFA was to be the distributor. This shift was intended to increase competition within Kenya's market for fertilizer, but it did not succeed in keeping fertilizer prices at low levels, and the agencies, influenced by the state, fell into the same patterns of bureaucracy and corruption as before. On the output side, the NCPB controlled maize prices at all levels of the market chain (Nyoro, Kiiru, and Jayne 1999). By setting fixed panterritorial prices and removing arbitrage opportunities for all market participants, these entities stifled private trade. Requirements that private traders apply for permits to transport grain across district boundaries made the situation more difficult.

In the 1980s the government started relaxing its monopoly, allowing the private sector to compete with state agencies, albeit under state rules. Fertilizer traders were to adhere to official prices, and the state influenced competition through strict trade licensing requirements and control of the allocation of scarce foreign exchange to importers (Argwings-Kodhek 1996). Licensing and allocation of foreign exchange provided rent-seeking opportunities for public sector officials (Kimuyu 1994). While the controlled pricing structure was designed to improve farmers' access to fertilizer, it had the opposite effect in geographically remote areas, where the controlled prices were too low for fertilizer retailers to recoup the costs of transporting fertilizer from district towns to remote areas. Hence, retailers in remote locations were less likely to stock fertilizer than those in more urbanized areas, leaving the average distance traveled by farmers to procure fertilizer relatively high in the 1980s and early 1990s.

In addition to the market inefficiencies they created, state agencies also imposed a heavy burden on public resources in Kenya, contributing to deficits and inflation in the 1980s. A decline in budgetary support to the agricultural sector by late 1980s probably contributed to the subsequent decline in agricultural growth, as did the mismanagement of agricultural institutions, the ad hoc reform agenda, withholding of donor funds over disagreements about democracy and governance, and depreciation of the Kenyan shilling, the last of which raised input prices (Argwings-Kodhek 2004). In the late 1980s and early 1990s, however, Kenya began easing trade restrictions in the fertilizer and maize markets. The government started removing some import quota restrictions, for example, in January 1990 and abolished licensing requirements for fertilizer imports in 1992.

In a major policy change, the government liberalized the fertilizer subsector specifically in 1993 to allow the participation of the private sector in importing, local trading, and distribution of fertilizer. Coupled with the liberalization of the foreign exchange regime in 1992, these changes in the policy environment led to the entry of a significant number of private sector firms in importing, wholesaling, distribution, and retailing of fertilizer (Wanzala 2001). Government price controls and import licensing quotas were ultimately eliminated, and fertilizer donations by external donor agencies were phased out. Maize trading controls were relaxed in the early 1990s to allow private traders to transport a few bags across districts with permission from government officials, a situation that led to rent-seeking behavior and increased costs for businesses (Kimuyu 1994). The NCPB, however, helped stabilize prices for producers and consumers by continuing to buy maize (mostly from large producers) at above-market prices and, during shortages, selling it to consumers at subsidized prices (Jayne, Myers, and Nyoro 2008).

With the participation of stakeholders from all facets of society in the 1990s and 2000s, a number of government policy papers emphasized a multisectoral approach to rural development in Kenya, including private-public synergies in development. By 1996, 12 major importers, 500 wholesalers, and roughly 5,000 retailers were distributing fertilizer in Kenya (Allgood and Kilungo 1996), and by 2000 the number of retailers was estimated to have risen to between 7,000 and 8,000 (IFDC 2001). (These are estimates because there is no comprehensive business registry or database covering all types of businesses in Kenya.) Even with the easing of trade restrictions, the high costs of upland transportation and logistical problems at the port of Mombasa continued to inflate the cost of fertilizer and reduce effective demand (Wanzala 2001; Ariga and Jayne 2008). Although markups are less than 11 percent of the farm gate price of fertilizer in western Kenya, in a number of farming areas no fertilizer is applied because of the risk from markets, poor rainfall, and agricultural conditions. But in other areas, application rates rival those of Asia, and selling fertilizer is clearly profitable. The overall trend in national consumption of fertilizer has followed a steady growth path since 1990, with government imports declining and the role of the private sector increasing (figure 16.1).

Since 2007 a major escalation in the world price of fertilizer has led to increased government involvement in fertilizer marketing. The post-2007 period, which has been marked by uncertain policy regimes, follows a fairly stable and transparent period since 1993. In Kenya, in a move to

Figure 16.1   Trends in Consumption, Commercial Imports, and Donor Imports of Fertilizer in Kenya, 1990/91–2010/11

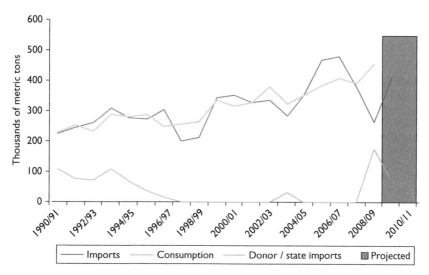

Source: Estimated from Kenya Ministry of Agriculture data by the authors.
Note: In 2004 and 2008, respectively, NCPB imported approximately one-third and 40 percent of national fertilizer needs. The estimate given for 2010/11 is a projection that includes private and government imports. The shaded years cover the time period after 2006/07, when government imports/subsidies were reinstated partly as a reaction to deficits in maize production and postelection disruptions of agricultural activities.

bolster agricultural production after postelection violence led to disruption of farm activities, NCPB imported fertilizer in 2008 but delivered it to farmers late, which contributed to the low levels of maize production that year. This situation, in turn, created pressure from some farmer lobby groups and activists for increased subsidization of inputs (fertilizer and seed) to raise productivity of maize to counter an expected increase in hunger in 2009. In 2009 the government of Kenya imported substantial amounts of fertilizer through NCPB to be distributed through its branches and select private retailers at prices that included a 40 percent subsidy. In early 2010 news reports indicated that the government planned to import 1.5 million bags (75,000 tons) of fertilizer.[1] Table 16.1 details key points in the liberalization of the maize sector, especially the role played by NCPB, the main grain-marketing state agency.

Although the increased participation of the Kenyan government in the agricultural market was expected to be short-lived and not significant enough to disrupt private sector investments, unforeseen events (such as poor rains in recent years) may mean that occasional state subsidies will be implemented over the upcoming few years in an attempt to meet national food requirements, particularly as political pressure for such measures increases. If recent indications are reliable, the incidence of government subsidies will probably decline after a few years as they become unsustainable unless international partners shoulder some of the responsibility.

Table 16.1   Evolution of Maize and Fertilizer Market Policy Reforms in Kenya, 1988–2010

State marketing agency	Maize market policy	Fertilizer market policy
1988: NCPB faces deficits and is financially restructured. NCPB depots are phased out. NCPB debts are written off; crop purchase fund is established but not replenished.	**1988:** Cereal Sector Reform Program envisages widening of NCPB price margin. In fact, margin narrows. Proportion of grain that millers are obliged to buy from NCPB declines. Limited unlicensed maize trade is allowed. State sets all prices for maize grain and flour.	**Pre-1990:** KGGCU / KFA and KNTC are main input agencies. Mismanagement and deficits are common. Government control of the fertilizer industry is heavy. Imports are poorly coordinated, leading to surplus/deficits. Licensing of private trade in the late 1980s is controlled but under panterritorial pricing. State agencies are financially weak.
Early 1990s: NCPB narrows its margins. Private sector finds it unprofitable to reach remote areas.	**1991:** Local and international pressure for reforms builds up. Interdistrict trade is further relaxed.	
	1992: Kenya moves from a one-party political system to a multiparty system. Restrictions on maize trade across districts are reimposed. NCPB is unable to defend ceiling prices. **1993:** Maize and maize meal prices deregulated. Import tariffs are abolished. No subsidies are provided to registered millers.	**1992:** Foreign exchange regime is liberalized. Fertilizer import restrictions are relaxed. **1993:** Fertilizer market is liberalized. Private traders are allowed to import and distribute. State and donor imports decline dramatically. **1994:** Custom duty and value added tax (VAT) are removed.
1995: Donor pressure leads to NCPB being restricted to the role of buyer and seller of last resort. NCPB market share declines to 10–20 percent of marketed maize trade. NCPB operations are confined mainly to high-potential areas of western Kenya.	**1995:** Internal maize and maize meal trade is fully liberalized. Maize import tariff of 30 percent is reimposed. **1996:** Export ban is imposed after poor harvest. **1997:** Import tariff is imposed after poor harvest.	**1996:** Number of market entrants is estimated at 12 major importers, 500 wholesalers, and roughly 5,000 retailers (Allgood and Kilungo 1996)
2000 onward: NCPB is provided with funds to purchase a greater volume of maize. NCPB's share of total maize trade rises to 25–35 percent of total marketed maize.	**1997–2005:** External trade and tariff rate levels change frequently and become difficult to predict. NCPB producer prices are normally set above import parity levels	
	2005 onward: The government withdraws the import tariff on maize entering Kenya from East African Community member countries. An official 2.75 percent duty is still assessed, and a variable import duty is still assessed on maize entering Kenya through the Mombasa port.	

(continued next page)

Table 16.1   (continued)

State marketing agency	Maize market policy	Fertilizer market policy
2008: World food prices are high. NCPB is asked to sell subsidized grain to millers, who in turn could lower prices for consumers. State has difficulty enforcing and monitoring at millers' end because of unknown milling costs. Allegations of corruption emerge.	**2008:** Postelection violence erupts. African Centre for Open Governance estimates that 3.5 million bags of maize are destroyed. NCPB begins importing maize from United States and South Africa in late 2008. An estimated 5 million bags arrive, according to the center.	**2008:** High world prices for fertilizer exacerbate food crisis effects from postelection violence. Prices more than double. Petrol and transport costs also go up.
2009: Briefcase firms and NCPB employees take advantage of crisis and subsidy arrangements to favor some firms in return for kickbacks. Weaknesses in disaster preparedness, institutions, and food policy are revealed. Top management of NCPB and some Ministry of Agriculture officials are fired for corruption during the crisis.	**2009:** Imports continue, but domestic maize production is greater than expected. Claims of monopoly at Mombasa port involving grain handling (particularly related to one large grain handler, Grain Bulk Handlers Limited) and milling arise but are not substantiated.	**2009:** NCPB imports state-subsidized fertilizer to aid in recovery from postelection violence. Fertilizer is distributed through private trade networks.
2010: NCPB allocates funds to buy maize produced in eastern Kenya during short rainy season.	**2010:** Short rainy season results in large amount of maize production, but farmers report poor prices from private traders.	**2010:** State imports more than 30,000 tons of fertilizer and distributes to vulnerable farmers. Distribution is managed by NGOs.

Source: Authors, adapted from Ariga and Jayne (2008).

THE EFFECT OF REFORMS IN FERTILIZER AND MAIZE MARKETS

Data collected in household surveys and found in secondary sources can be used to analyze the effects of policy reforms on fertilizer and maize markets in Kenya during the 1980s, 1990s, and 2000s. The panel data consist of nationwide rural household panel survey data covering the 1996/97, 1999/2000, 2003/04, and 2006/07 crop seasons. The panel household survey was designed and implemented under the Tegemeo Agricultural Monitoring and Policy Analysis Project (TAMPA), implemented by Egerton University/Tegemeo Institute with support from Michigan State University. Out of the national sample of 1,260 households, a balanced panel of 899 households was interviewed in all four periods. Other data, such as monthly maize price levels and NCPB maize purchases and sales, were obtained from various Kenyan government ministries.

For analytical convenience, the survey sample has been classified into zones based on agro-ecological characteristics, districts, and agricultural production potential. Each of these agro-ecological zones has been split into two broader categories—high-potential and low-potential regions—based on soil quality, rainfall, yield potential, and fertilizer use.[2]

Processes leading to growth in smallholder fertilizer use and maize yields

Figure 16.2 provides a schematic description of how public investments in market infrastructure and policy reform within fertilizer and maize markets generated specific responses from the private sector and smallholder farmers. The basic story is one of synergies between liberalization of input and maize markets and public investments in support of smallholder agriculture that led to substantial private sector investment in fertilizer retailing and maize marketing, which in turn resulted in an impressive increase in the use of fertilizer by smallholder farmers and in the maize yields of smallholder farms over 1997–2007.

Distance from farm to fertilizer seller

One indicator of how reforms have contributed to fertilizer availability in Kenya is the distance farmers now have to travel to buy fertilizer compared with the distance in the prereform period (figure 16.3). This variable is a measure of increased private sector competition leading to more investment in locating retail services closer to producers, with retailers opening stores in new catchment areas that were hitherto not serviced by the government-run input system and opening additional stores in already-served areas to capture more business.

In general, distances in the low-potential region are longer than those in the high-potential region, which is one reason why the sample is split into two broad groups in the analysis presented here. The private sector investment in fertilizer trade has expanded rapidly after the state allowed competition and removed trade restrictions. Although absolute distances are generally higher for the

Figure 16.2   Synergies Increasing Fertilizer Use and Maize Yields by Smallholder Farmers

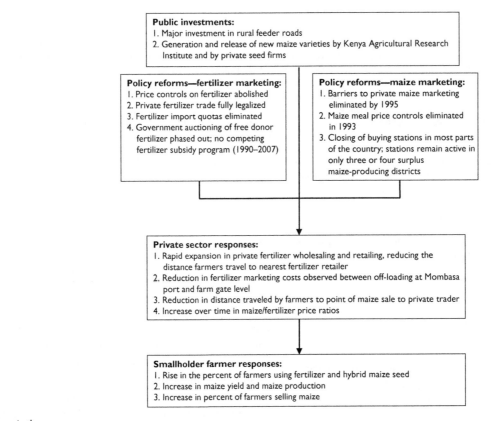

Public investments:
1. Major investment in rural feeder roads
2. Generation and release of new maize varieties by Kenya Agricultural Research Institute and by private seed firms

Policy reforms—fertilizer marketing:
1. Price controls on fertilizer abolished
2. Private fertilizer trade fully legalized
3. Fertilizer import quotas eliminated
4. Government auctioning of free donor fertilizer phased out; no competing fertilizer subsidy program (1990–2007)

Policy reforms—maize marketing:
1. Barriers to private maize marketing eliminated by 1995
2. Maize meal price controls eliminated in 1993
3. Closing of buying stations in most parts of the country; stations remain active in only three or four surplus maize-producing districts

Private sector responses:
1. Rapid expansion in private fertilizer wholesaling and retailing, reducing the distance farmers travel to nearest fertilizer retailer
2. Reduction in fertilizer marketing costs observed between off-loading at Mombasa port and farm gate level
3. Reduction in distance traveled by farmers to point of maize sale to private trader
4. Increase over time in maize/fertilizer price ratios

Smallholder farmer responses:
1. Rise in the percent of farmers using fertilizer and hybrid maize seed
2. Increase in maize yield and maize production
3. Increase in percent of farmers selling maize

Source: Authors.

Figure 16.3   Average Distance from Farm to Fertilizer Seller

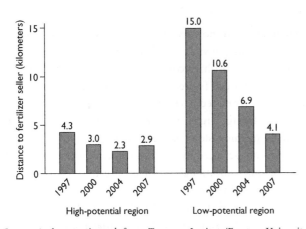

Source: Authors, estimated from Tegemeo Institute/Egerton University household surveys, 1997, 2000, 2004, and 2007.
Note: The high-potential region includes the districts of Bomet, Bungoma, Gishu, Kakamega, Kisii, Meru, Muranga, Narok, Nakuru, Nyeri, Trans Nzoia, Uasin, and Vihiga. The low-potential region includes the districts of Kilifi, Kisumu, Kitui, Kwale, Machakos, Makueni, Mwingi, Siaya, Taita, and Taveta.

low-potential region, the rate at which distances have declined is generally higher than in the high-potential region. The consumption of fertilizer has not followed the same regional pattern, however, implying the presence of other constraints.

Increasing proportion of households using fertilizer

Data from a balanced panel of households in Kenya show that the percentage of households using fertilizer on at least one farm plot rose from 59 percent in 1997 to 72 percent in 2007 for the national sample (table 16.2). However, there are differences in growth across agro-ecological zones and the two broad regions of interest. For the high-potential region, which began with a much higher proportion of fertilizer users, use increased from 77 percent to 91 percent of households between 1997 and 2007. Use in the low-potential region more than doubled during the same period, increasing from 12 percent in 1997 to 26 percent in 2007, but the proportion of households using fertilizer remained relatively small.

Region and zone	1997	2000	2004	2007
High-potential region				
Western transitional	41	65	71	81
High-potential maize zone	84	89	89	92
Western highlands	78	90	91	95
Central highlands	90	91	91	93
Subtotal	*77*	*85*	*86*	*91*
Low-potential region				
Coastal lowland	4	4	5	11
Eastern lowland	26	27	47	48
Western lowland	2	5	7	13
Subtotal	*12*	*14*	*23*	*26*
Grand total	**59**	**65**	**68**	**72**

Source: Authors, estimated from Tegemeo Institute/Egerton University household surveys, 1997, 2000, 2004, and 2007.
Note: This sample consists of a balanced panel of 899 households interviewed in all four periods.

Dynamics of fertilizer application rates

By examining fertilizer application rates for households using fertilizer and for the whole sample of households surveyed, including nonusers, one can observe a trend in the intensity of fertilizer use (kilogram per acre of maize) since the inception of fertilizer reforms in the 1990s. For comparison at the household level, plot-level application rates using plot area (acres) as weights are aggregated.[3] First, for each region, the differences between the weighted mean household application rates (kilograms per acre) for the years 2000, 2004, and 2007 are compared with the rates for 1997, revealing whether application rates increased, decreased or remained the same in subsequent years compared with the base period of 1997. Figure 16.4 shows the trend in this indicator using the base year 1997.

Clearly, weighted mean household application rates have increased relative to those in 1997 (and also from one year to the next) for each region. It is also obvious that in absolute terms, the differences are much smaller in the low-potential region, probably as a result of lower application rates and the lower proportion of fertilizer users (the latter shown in table 16.2). Table 16.3 supplies information on fertilizer application rates (kilograms per acre) for two sets of households: the whole sample of households surveyed (the sum of fertilizer users and nonusers), and a subset consisting of households that used fertilizer (only users).

As shown in table 16.3, fertilizer application rates have increased from their 1997 levels for all regions and agrozones, although intensities differ across regions and agrozones. The high- potential maize zone (HPMZ), which

Figure 16.4 Average Difference in Mean Household Fertilizer Application Rates from 1997 Levels, by Region

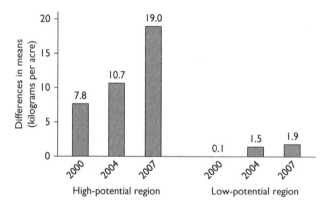

Source: Authors, estimated from Tegemeo Institute/Egerton University household surveys, 1997, 2000, 2004, and 2007.

includes Trans Nzoia and Uasin Gishu, and the Central Highland zone have some of the highest application rates in the sample. For example, the HPMZ's rates for fertilizer users only in 1997 and 2007 are 157.3 and 181.1 kilograms per hectare, similar to rates in Asia, which benefited from the green revolution and now has one of the highest fertilizer application rates in the world.

Trend in maize yields for unfertilized plots and different seed technologies

As shown in figure 16.4 and table 16.3, fertilizer application has increased significantly since the reforms of the 1990s,

Table 16.3 Fertilizer Application Rates for Maize-Growing Households in Kenya, by Region and Zone *(kilograms per acre)*

Region/zone	Sum of fertilizer users and nonusers				Fertilizer users only			
	1997	2000	2004	2007	1997	2000	2004	2007
High-potential region								
Western transitional	23.0	47.1	46.5	57.3	57.5	73.0	63.8	71.8
High-potential maize zone	53.1	58.5	60.9	65.4	63.7	66.5	70.4	73.3
Western highlands	26.9	40.6	49.6	48.4	36.3	45.4	54.0	51.7
Central highlands	62.2	68.4	73.4	67.2	68.8	77.9	84.2	74.1
Subsample	*46.3*	*56.1*	*59.5*	*61.6*	*60.6*	*66.7*	*70.0*	*69.6*
Low-potential region								
Coastal lowland	0.4	0.8	0.1	1.6	10.4	19.6	2.1	13.9
Eastern lowland	3.1	5.7	8.3	9.6	12.1	24.8	19.7	23.9
Western lowland	0.4	0.5	0.9	2.3	21.3	16.4	19.4	18.6
Subsample	*1.4*	*2.8*	*4.0*	*5.3*	*12.7*	*23.6*	*19.1*	*22.0*
Grand total	*33.3*	*38.0*	*43.1*	*45.0*	*58.0*	*63.8*	*65.2*	*64.7*

Source: Authors, estimated from Tegemeo Institute/Egerton University household surveys, 1997, 2000, 2004, and 2007.

Note: When estimating rates for the whole set of households, "zeros" are used for households not using fertilizer, making these rates lower or equal to rates calculated for the group including fertilizer users only (depending on presence of nonusers).

when markets were opened up to competition. But have the reforms and the rise in consumption of fertilizer, had an effect on maize production? Looking at the dynamics of maize yields for plots that received fertilizer and those that did not across the survey years and for different seed types provides information on this question.

First, as shown in figure 16.5, yields from fertilized and unfertilized plots generally increased between 1997 and 2007. Second, irrespective of fertilization, yields for hybrid seed plots are higher than those for nonhybrid plots. Third, for each seed technology, yields for fertilized fields are higher than those for unfertilized fields. And finally, yields for plots that receive fertilizer and use hybrid seeds are the highest for each of the four survey years.[4]

Although yields generally increased between each survey year and the next, the increase was particularly significant between 1997 and 2000. This may partly be explained by the favorable prices for maize following a poor maize crop in the 1998/99 season; as a result, the fertilizer-to-maize price ratio was lower at the start of the planting season for year 2000, an incentive to farmers to increase their fertilizer use during that season (using naive price expectations based on recent output prices). Figure 16.6 shows the existence of regional differences in the yield-fertilizer nexus for the period covered by the household surveys.

Figure 16.6 shows clear differences in the potential for maize production in the two regions. Even without fertilization, yields for unfertilized plots in the high-potential region are generally higher than those from fertilized plots

in the low- potential region, indicating that the effects of fertilizer use vary according to other factors.

Table 16.4, which expresses yields in metric tons per acre, can be used to show why the maize yield estimates reported by the Ministry of Agriculture are different from the composite yield measure used in this paper. The Ministry of Agriculture estimates are generally lower than the composite yield (that is, the sum of the yields for maize and other crops in the same plot converted to an index using price ratio of each crop to that of maize), and they do not reflect the true returns to inputs applied to the plot or field. The composite yield measure increased from 0.9 ton in 1997 to 1.4 tons in 2007, whereas the standard measure by the Ministry of Agriculture, increased from 0.6 to 1.0 ton per acre over the same years.

Trends in wholesale price margins

Price margins can indicate the state of competition and innovations that reduce marketing costs between two points of interest by improving market efficiency. As shown in figure 16.7, the margin between the wholesale world price of fertilizer, as measured by the cost, insurance, and freight (CIF) of fertilizer arriving in the port of Mombasa on the east coast of Kenya, and prices in the hinterland town of Nakuru has declined dramatically in the years between 1990 and 2008.

The world price of fertilizer remained fairly constant from 1990 to 2007, when it rose sharply (see figure 16.7). During this period the wholesale cost of fertilizer in Nakuru steadily

CHAPTER 16: FERTILIZER IN KENYA: FACTORS DRIVING THE INCREASE IN USAGE BY SMALLHOLDER FARMERS

Figure 16.5 Trend in Maize Yields in Fertilized and Unfertilized Plots in Kenya for Different Seed Technologies

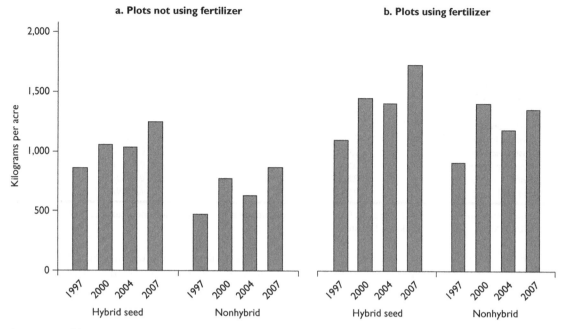

Source: Authors, estimated from Tegemeo Institute/Egerton University household surveys, 1997, 2000, 2004, and 2007.

Figure 16.6 Trend in Maize Yields for Fertilized and Unfertilized Plots in Kenya, by Region

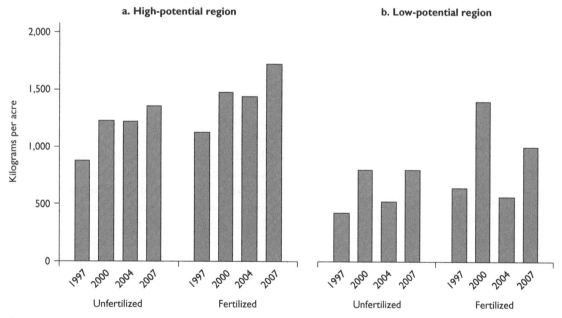

Source: Authors, estimated from Tegemeo Institute/Egerton University household surveys, 1997, 2000, 2004, and 2007.

declined, implying that the costs of marketing fertilizer there had declined, leading to lower prices at Nakuru. Studies (Kimuyu 1994; Wanzala, Jayne, and Staatz 2002; Allgood and Kilungo 1996; IFDC 2001), based on interviews with stake-holders suggest this reduction is a result of increased competition after reforms in the 1990s, economies of scope resulting from mergers, and access to competitive credit from international sources.

Table 16.4   Trend in Composite and "Standard" Maize Yields in Kenya, by Region and Zone
(tons per acre)

	1997	2000	2004	2007
High-potential region				
Western transitional	0.7(0.5)	1.2(0.8)	1.0(1.0)	1.6(1.2)
High-potential maize zone	1.3(1.1)	1.3(1.0)	1.6(1.4)	1.6(1.3)
Western highlands	0.7(0.5)	1.7(0.9)	0.9(0.8)	1.4(0.9)
Central highlands	1.2(0.6)	1.8(1.1)	1.7(1.0)	2.3(1.3)
Subtotal	*1.1(0.8)*	*1.4(1.0)*	*1.4(1.1)*	*1.7(1.2)*
Low-potential region				
Coastal lowland	0.5(0.2)	1.0(0.6)	0.5(0.3)	0.8(0.5)
Eastern lowland	0.4(0.2)	1.0(0.5)	0.6(0.4)	0.8(0.5)
Western lowland	0.5(0.3)	0.7(0.4)	0.5(0.3)	0.9(0.7)
Subtotal	*0.5(0.2)*	*0.9(0.5)*	*0.5(0.3)*	*0.9(0.6)*
Grand total	*0.9(0.6)*	*1.3(0.8)*	*1.2(0.9)*	*1.4(1.0)*

Source: Composite yield estimated by authors from Tegemeo Institute/Egerton University household surveys, 1997, 2000, 2004, and 2007. Maize-only yield from Kenya Ministry of Agriculture.

Figure 16.7   Price of Diammonium Phosphate in Mombasa and Nakuru

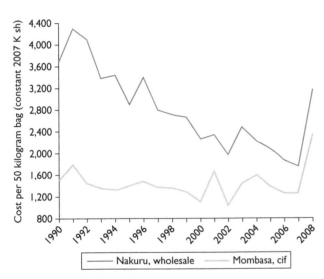

Source: Kenya Ministry of Agriculture.

HOUSEHOLD AND OTHER DETERMINANTS OF FERTILIZER DEMAND

Using variables including education, value of assets, land size, land preparation technology, gender of the household head, as well as geographic factors such as distance to fertilizer seller, agro-ecological conditions, soil types, and market conditions, it is possible to conduct a regression analysis of fertilizer demand in the high-potential and low-potential regions of Kenya. This analysis will provide a measure of diversity or heterogeneity in demand across the country and between different households that face varied surroundings, knowledge that is important in setting appropriate policy geared to achieving food security for smallholders.

The analysis conducted for this paper used regression methods including random effects (RE), fixed effects (FE), and correlated random effects (CRE) to model fertilizer demand (application rate per acre). The RE approach assumes strict exogeneity between explanatory variables and composite error term, which includes unobserved household-specific heterogeneity. On the other hand, FE does not assume strict exogeneity but takes the unobserved effects as constant over time and uses a differencing approach to remove these effects to generate consistent estimates. Unlike FE, the CRE method extends the RE analysis by modeling unobserved heterogeneity using the household means of time-varying variables. Therefore, with CRE, it is possible to test whether the model captures unobserved effects and to use estimates of these effects to classify households or explain differences between households (Wooldridge 2002). An additional benefit of CRE is that the estimates on the time-varying variables are the same as those in the FE estimation, and unlike in the FE approach, the effect of time-constant factors (such as gender and location dummies) are estimated as well (not differenced away as in FE).

Using CRE, it is possible to reject the null hypothesis of nonexistence of unobserved heterogeneity, implying that the FE approach is more appropriate than RE, which assumes exogeneity. However, CRE regression offers the benefit of producing the same estimates as FE regression for time-varying variables, while at the same time providing a way to model heterogeneity so as to explain differences across households based on skills and other factors that cannot be observed or for which data cannot be obtained. For these reasons, the results of only the CRE method are discussed here, using a double-hurdle approach.

Table 16.5, presents the results of the CRE regressions for the high- and low-potential regions for fertilizer market participation and consumption or use decisions. For the double-hurdle model, the same variable can have different sign and magnitude in the market participation and demand equations, unlike the Tobit model, which assumes the same effect and magnitude in both equations.

Table 16.5 Fertilizer Market Participation and Demand Using Correlated Random Effects to Model Household Heterogeneity

Variables	High-potential region		Low-potential region	
	Market participation	Consumption (kilograms/acre)	Market participation	Consumption (kilograms/acre)
Dependent variable (units)	(0/1)	(kilograms/acre)	(0/1)	(kilograms/acre)
Price for nitrogen (K Sh/kilogram)	0.015	−0.831*	−0.009	−0.175**
	(0.005)	(0.439)	(0.009)	(0.081)
Price for maize grain (K Sh/kilogram)	−0.003	0.313	−0.003	−0.016
	(0.003)	(0.218)	(0.004)	(0.026)
Age of household head (years)	−0.002**		−0.001	
	(0.001)		(0.001)	
Quintiles for value of household assets:				
2	0.012	0.853	−0.047	0.359*
	(0.016)	(1.421)	(0.029)	(0.206)
3	0.001	1.108	0.016	0.571***
	(0.019)	(1.554)	(0.031)	(0.219)
4	−0.017	−0.101	−0.001	0.401*
	(0.022)	(1.704)	(0.032)	(0.241)
5	−0.012	2.454	0.021	0.897***
	(0.024)	(1.849)	(0.036)	(0.261)
Quintiles for total cropped land:				
2	0.021	−3.767***	0.007	0.130
	(0.019)	(1.394)	(0.026)	(0.202)
3	0.038*	−4.270***	−0.006	−0.326
	(0.021)	(1.505)	(0.027)	(0.216)
4	0.068***	−3.995**	−0.007	0.058
	(0.022)	(1.680)	(0.028)	(0.235)
5	0.069***	−1.594	0.006	−0.261
	(0.025)	(1.926)	(0.032)	(0.264)
Categories for education of head of household:				
2 1–4 years	−0.018	1.475	−0.066	−0.305
	(0.022)	(2.696)	(0.035)	(0.338)
3 5–8 years	−0.017	0.546	−0.036	−0.155
	(0.022)	(2.640)	(0.034)	(0.289)
4 9–12 years	0.001	5.605*	0.043	0.379
	(0.024)	(2.897)	(0.044)	(0.357)
5 > 12 years	0.032	6.416*	0.100	0.133
	(0.029)	(3.698)	(0.067)	(0.537)
Categories for land preparation technology:				
2 Oxen	0.101***	4.330**	−0.016	0.011
	(0.021)	(1.768)	(0.027)	(0.200)
3 Tractor	0.147***	5.670***	−0.030	0.056
	(0.020)	(1.701)	(0.040)	(0.293)
Categories for land tenure:				
2 Own land without title	0.005	−0.088	0.027	0.068
	(0.014)	(1.069)	(0.018)	(0.142)
3 Renting land	0.054***	−1.047	0.030	−0.299
	(0.018)	(1.508)	(0.036)	(0.303)
Dummy (1= female head of household)	−0.023	−0.647	−0.060***	−0.281*
	(0.018)	(1.669)	(0.020)	(0.197)
Categories of soil types:				
2	0.007	−1.595	−0.162**	−0.479
	(0.040)	(4.346)	(0.079)	(0.872)

(continued next page)

Table 16.5 (continued)

Variables	High-potential region		Low-potential region	
	Market participation	Consumption (kilograms/acre)	Market participation	Consumption (kilograms/acre)
3	0.020	−1.643		
	(0.028)	(2.903)		
4	0.009	−1.708	−0.008	−0.143
	(0.024)	(2.577)	(0.075)	(0.578)
5	−0.094*	−7.913*	−0.083	−0.377
	(0.054)	(4.362)	(0.103)	(0.907)
Agro-zone dummies (central lowland and west transitional dropped):				
3 Eastern lowlands			−0.036	−0.195
			(0.064)	(0.710)
4 Western lowlands			0.389***	2.324**
			(0.110)	(1.133)
6 High-potential maize	0.398***	−0.435		
	(0.050)	(3.891)		
7 West highlands	0.263***	−2.239		
	(0.059)	(4.134)		
8 Central highlands	0.423***	19.053***		
	(0.058)	(6.189)		
Dummy (1= single crop in plot)	−0.061***	−0.307	−0.001	−0.042
	(0.016)	(1.084)	(0.018)	(0.161)
Mundlak–Chamberlain device:				
Price for nitrogen (K Sh / kilogram)	−0.064**	−1.246	−0.062	0.525
	(0.025)	(2.880)	(0.061)	(0.576)
Price for maize grain (K Sh/kilogram)	0.053***	−1.669	0.030***	0.098
	(0.011)	(1.075)	(0.010)	(0.092)
Dependency ratio (dependants to productive members)	−0.001	−0.359	0.002	−0.005
	(0.002)	(0.287)	(0.004)	(0.039)
Distance to fertilizer seller	−0.023***	0.641	−0.009***	−0.012
	(0.005)	(0.629)	(0.003)	(0.025)
Duration as head of household (years)	0.004**		0.001	
	(0.002)		(0.002)	
Quintiles for value of household assets:				
2	0.015	4.074	0.096	−0.495
	(0.036)	(4.228)	(0.065)	(0.561)
3	0.088**	−3.910	0.046	−0.396
	(0.038)	(4.261)	(0.061)	(0.537)
4	0.111***	0.454	0.058	0.218
	(0.040)	(4.353)	(0.062)	(0.567)
5	0.103**	−1.483	0.057	−0.064
	(0.044)	(4.683)	(0.064)	(0.593)
Quintiles for total cropped land:				
2	−0.046	−2.737	0.190***	−1.039
	(0.037)	(4.147)	(0.068)	(0.548)
3	−0.002	4.387	0.238***	−0.278
	(0.038)	(4.129)	(0.065)	(0.529)
4	−0.067*	0.031	0.173***	−0.489
	(0.038)	(4.117)	(0.064)	(0.562)
5	−0.007	2.099	0.178***	−0.657
	(0.043)	(4.483)	(0.068)	(0.585)
Fractions of 20-day periods with < 40 millimeters of rain in season	−0.185***	−26.845**	0.100	6.206
	(0.124)	(12.346)	(0.254)	(2.479)
Observations (plots)	4,051	4,051	1,782	1,782

Source: Authors.

Note: Quintiles range from lowest (1) to highest (5) for asset values and land sizes (estimates shown in the table are compared with lowest quintile, which is dropped). Estimates for the remainder of categories (land preparation, zones, tenure, and others) should be interpreted in relation to the omitted category (category 1). Standard errors are in parentheses; *** $p < 0.01$, ** $p < 0.05$, * $p < 0.1$.

Effect of fertilizer and maize prices on demand for fertilizer

Results of the regression analysis presented in table 16.5 show that when fertilizer prices increase by approximately 278 shillings per 50 kilogram bag, household fertilizer application rates (kilograms per acre) decline by 4.4 kilograms (high-potential region) and 1.1 kilograms (low-potential region). For the high-potential region, this translates to a response elasticity of 0.52 (that is, a 10 percent increase in fertilizer price leads to a 5.2 percent decline in application rates per acre). The elasticity for low-potential region is 0.32.

From the Mundlak-Chamberlain device (Wooldridge 2002), it is evident that households facing higher fertilizer prices have lower probability of participation, while those facing higher maize output prices have higher probability of participation in fertilizer markets. There is a reduction in probability of market participation of 0.64 points for households facing a 10 K Sh-per-kilogram higher fertilizer price (or K Sh 500 per 50-kilogram bag), while the probability of participation by households facing a similar higher maize output price is higher by 0.53 points for the high-potential region (0.30 in low-potential region)—that is, households facing higher fertilizer prices have lower probability of market participation, while those facing higher output prices have higher probability. However, the effect of prices on the decision about how many kilograms of fertilizer to apply per acre is not significantly different across households. This finding implies that price signals are important in determining farmers' decision to participate in fertilizer markets.

Effect of household resource endowments on demand for fertilizer

The analysis also takes into account the effect of some measures of resource endowment (asset values and land size) on fertilizer demand. Although the probability of market participation for the low-potential region does not change with value of assets, the application rate rises with assets. Raising a household's assets from the lowest quintile to the third quintile or the fifth quintile, for example, raises the application rates by 0.571 and 0.897 kilogram per acre, respectively. But when contrasting different households in the high-potential region, it is evident that households with assets of a higher value have a greater probability of participating in the fertilizer market.

A related measure of resources is the amount of land under crops during the season (because data used for this analysis do not include total land owned for the year 2000, land under crops is used as a proxy for this variable). Although the probability of market participation rises with an increase in the size of land for households in the high-potential region, the amount applied per acre decreases with land size. Households with more land under crops in the low-potential region have a higher probability of market participation, although the rates per acre are not significantly different from those with less land under crops.

Effect of land tenure, gender, land preparation technology, and mixed cropping on demand for fertilizer

Households that rent land have a higher probability of fertilizer market participation (by 0.05 points) than those that have title to their land, but differences in application rates across land tenure categories are not significant. Female-headed households have a lower probability of market participation (0.06) and intensity per acre (0.28) compared with male-headed households in the low-potential region. Although signs of estimates are the same as those in the high-potential region, gender estimates for the high-potential region are not significant. The authors find no plausible explanation why the low-potential region has a gender effect while the high-potential region does not.

In terms of agro-ecological zones, households in the central highlands have a 0.4-point higher probability of participating in fertilizer markets than those in the western transitional zone and apply 5.95 kilograms more fertilizer per acre. On land preparation technology, there is a higher probability of market participation for households using animal draught (0.1) or tractors (0.14) compared with manual hoeing; fertilizer application per acre for these households also increases by 4.4 and 5.6 kilograms, respectively, over manual technologies. Households that do intercrop or mix cropping (that is, plant maize with one or more other crops in the same plot) have a higher probability of fertilizer market involvement than those growing only maize. However, application rates do not significantly differ with intensity of mixed cropping.

Effect of distance to fertilizer seller, education, and experience on demand for fertilizer

Households that are further away from fertilizer sellers have lower probability of participating in the market (0.023 points per kilometer for the high-potential region and 0.01 points for low-potential region). In other words, households in the high-potential region that are located 10 kilometers away from fertilizer retailers have a 0.23-point lower probability of participating in fertilizer markets, but application rates per acre do not differ significantly. Households with head who have more years of schooling have a positive but insignificant probability of participating in the market than those who do not. The intensity of application per acre is positive with years of education (and significant for high-potential region). Age of household head in the high-potential region has a negative relationship with probability of participation but not the intensity of application. The number of years or duration as the head of household has a positive effect on probability of participation in the market in the high-potential region; experience as head of household raises chances of market participation.

LESSONS LEARNED, SUSTAINABILITY, AND POTENTIAL FOR REPLICABILITY

When examining the factors driving growth in fertilizer use and maize productivity in Kenya from the early 1990s to 2007, the basic story is one of synergies between the liberalization of input and maize markets on one hand and public investments in support of smallholder agriculture on the other, a situation that has led to tangible private sector investment in fertilizer retailing and maize marketing, which in turn has encouraged an impressive rise in fertilizer use and maize yields on smallholder farms over the period 1997–2007. This narrative is complicated, however, by the many changes that Kenya's economy and business environment has experienced during this period, both positive and negative, which have also undoubtedly affected the incentives of farmers, consumers, and private marketing agents. These factors may not be directly linked to the fertilizer and maize markets, but their influence on observed indicators cannot be analytically separated from those of the reforms highlighted in this paper. However, it is reasonable to assume that these influences outside the agricultural sector are of second-order magnitude, compared with the more direct agricultural policy reforms and investments, in explaining the behavioral responses of farmers and fertilizer and maize marketing agents.

There are several pathways through which government actions in fertilizer and maize markets has positively affected the agricultural sector and rural and urban living standards in Kenya in recent years. As shown in figure 16.2, the government of Kenya implemented a number of policy reforms affecting the incentives for investment by private fertilizer distribution firms. The government also legalized domestic and regional maize trade, although other actions during the 1990s partially eroded the potential response by the private sector. Despite the mixed government stance toward maize market liberalization during the 1990s and early 2000s, evidence of increased private sector investment is tangible. Traders buying maize directly from farmers have penetrated more deeply into smallholder areas. Increased competition and efficiency in maize milling and retailing is also evident in the significant decline in maize marketing margins. There is also strong evidence of increased state investment in public goods supportive of private sector investment, especially since the creation of the Constituency Development Fund (CDF) in 2003. The combination of supportive policy changes in the fertilizer, foreign exchange, and maize markets, coupled with improved access to markets and services made possible by public good investments, appears to have stimulated investment by the private sector in both maize and fertilizer marketing. These factors have worked synergistically to bring about important gains in maize productivity and benefits to smallholder farmers and consumers in Kenya.

Evidence of increased smallholder fertilizer use and maize yields is drawn from nationwide household panel data from four surveys conducted by Egerton University's Tegemeo Institute between 1997 and 2007. Because the data constitute a balanced nationwide panel of 1,260 households,[5] the results provide a fairly reliable indicator of the changes in fertilizer use patterns over time, although the surveys are not strictly nationally representative. The main findings of the surveys are as follows:

- The percentage of sampled smallholders using fertilizer on maize increased from 56 percent in 1996 to 70 percent in 2007.
- Fertilizer application rates (for all maize fields including unfertilized fields) rose from 34 kilograms an acre in 1997 to 45 kilograms an acre in 2007, a 32 percent increase.
- There are wide regional variations in fertilizer use. More than 90 percent of smallholder farmers use fertilizer on maize in three of the broad zones surveyed: the high-potential maize zone, western highlands, and central highlands. Fertilizer use is low and barely rising in most of the semiarid regions (coastal and western lowlands, and the marginal rain shadow). However, fertilizer use has risen impressively in the medium-potential eastern lowlands and Western Transitional zones, where the percentage of households using fertilizer on maize rose from 21 and 39 percent, respectively, in 1997 to 43 and 81 percent in 2007.

- While the total area under maize in Kenya remained largely constant over 1997–2007, maize yields increased by roughly 18 percent during the same period. This yield improvement is not borne out in official government maize production statistics, however, which do not take into account the shift over time in the proportion of maize area grown under intercropped cultivation or the shift over time in the proportion of maize area grown in relatively semiarid regions, which has been facilitated by the release of improved maize cultivars well suited to mid- and low-altitude areas of the country. To assess changes in maize yield, it is important to account for the gradual shift in the proportion of maize area under monocropped versus intercropped cultivation as well as the expansion of maize production in the more semiarid parts of the country. After stratifying between hybrid and nonhybrid users and between intercropped and monocropped maize fields, the household survey data show that maize yields on all types of fields have increased over time, reflecting the influence of many factors in addition to fertilizer use. Fertilizer use and maize yields have increased especially rapidly on the intercropped fields, less so on monocropped fields.

- Fertilizer marketing costs declined substantially in constant K Sh between the mid-1990s and 2007. Interviews with key informants in Kenya's fertilizer sector identified four factors responsible for the declining fertilizer marketing costs observed in Kenya: the potential for cheaper backhaul transportation has been exploited by making more use of trucks transporting cargo from Rwanda and Democratic Republic of Congo to the port of Mombasa; private importers are increasingly using international connections to obtain credit at lower interest rates and financing costs than are available in the domestic economy; local and international firms have merged, enabling shared knowledge and economies of scope that save local distribution costs; and increased competition among local importers and wholesalers has expanded the number of firms engaged in fertilizer marketing since the early 1990s. It is likely that the fourth factor—increased competition—has to some extent stimulated firms to exploit the other cost-reducing innovations identified in order to maintain their market position.

To assess the robustness of the Tegemeo Institute's survey findings, the proportion of smallholder households purchasing fertilizer according to the survey results was compared with estimates based on three other analyses covering a subset of the same districts during the same general time period. The Tegemeo survey estimates are comparable and in some cases lower than other estimates of fertilizer purchases and dose rates. The rise in smallholder use of fertilizer in the Tegemeo survey data is also consistent with official Ministry of Agriculture figures (shown in figure 16.1), which indicate that total fertilizer consumption in Kenya rose 65 percent between 1997 and 2007.

The rise in fertilizer use in Kenya has not been uniform across regions, however. Use rates are much higher in areas where the main-season rainfall is relatively high and stable than they are in the drier areas. Fertilizer use is highly risky in many of the semiarid regions, where environmental factors are likely to limit the role of fertilizer in contributing to poverty alleviation and food security unless it is accompanied by actions to improve soil organic matter and moisture (Marenya and Barrett 2008). Within a given agro-ecological zone, it is evident that the decision of households to purchase fertilizer is only slightly related to farm size and unrelated to household wealth. In relatively productive areas, the proportion of poorer and wealthier households applying fertilizer on maize is similar. In risky environments, only a small proportion of either poor or wealthy households use fertilizer on maize.

These gains in smallholder fertilizer use and maize yields have been encouraged by Kenya's decision to liberalize input and maize markets in the early 1990s. New entries and investment in fertilizer wholesaling and retailing have been massive since the early 1990s. The International Fertilizer Development Center (IFDC) estimates that more than 500 wholesalers and 7,000 retailers are operating in the country. This has led to a denser network of rural retailers and a major reduction in the distance between farms and fertilizer sellers, which has contributed to the impressive growth in fertilizer use by Kenyan smallholders from the early 1990s to 2007. The Tegemeo Institute survey data also indicate that the mean distance traveled by farmers to sell their maize to private traders declined over 1997–2007; the median distance as of 2007 was zero, indicating that assembly traders tend to purchase maize right from farmers' fields. Analysis of wholesale maize grain prices and retail maize meal prices indicate that the miller-retail marketing margin has declined significantly over time, conferring benefits mainly to consumers. More than 50 percent of rural farm households are either buyers or net buyers of maize, while virtually all urban households purchase maize meal each year (Mukumbu and Jayne 1994; Jayne and Argwings-Kodhek 1997).

Other signs of improvement in maize markets in Kenya include farmers' level of satisfaction with the performance of maize markets from their subjective perspective. More than 65 percent of farmers surveyed in the nationwide Tegemeo Institute rural surveys indicated that they prefer the current liberalized maize marketing system to the former controlled marketing system, primarily because grain is easier to sell, farmers are paid in cash at the time of sale, and maize is more reliably available for purchase.

In 2008, however, the positive trends in Kenya's maize and fertilizer markets were reversed by civil disruption, drought, and the unprecedented surge in world fertilizer prices. The civil unrest led to the destruction of much physical infrastructure in western Kenya, such as petrol stations and grain storage, as well as to the closing of many input supply stores, in early 2008. Moreover, incentives to use fertilizer in Kenya have been adversely affected both by drought and world events as maize/fertilizer price ratios plunged to their lowest level in at least 18 years. Figure 16.8 plots monthly wholesale maize to wholesale fertilizer price ratios per ton in Nakuru. The higher the ratio, the more profitable the maize, and therefore the greater the incentive to apply fertilizer on maize. While this ratio has historically ranged between 0.4 and 0.6 at the time of planting, in 2008 it plunged to below 0.25 because of the increase in world fertilizer prices. The price of maize in Kenya has not risen nearly as dramatically as fertilizer.

These findings have implications for policy options. The main general lesson is the need for a public-private relationship that encourages investment in input and output marketing services for smallholder farmers. In Kenya's case, this relationship was achieved through a combination of investments in public goods and institutional reforms supportive of liberalized marketing, even though the maize marketing reforms were at times subject to reversals. Considerable additional gains could be made in smallholder and consumer welfare if progress could also be made in the following areas:

CONSIDER CHANGES IN GOVERNMENT ACTIONS IN THE TRANSPORT SECTOR THAT COULD REDUCE FERTILIZER AND GRAIN DISTRIBUTION COSTS. For example, because of frequent delays in off-loading of commodities at the port of Mombasa and because of the erosion of the regional railway system, it is difficult to arrange for upcountry transport of a full shipload of fertilizer. Because of this coordination problem, fertilizer importers have invested in storage facilities near the port where fertilizer can be temporarily stored until trucks arrive for loading and upcountry distribution. These investments make sense if upland transport constraints and the delays and inefficiency at the Port of Mombasa are taken as given. However, if procedures for streamlining the efficiency of off-loading at the port could be achieved (for example, by privatizing stevedore services and issuing performance contracts or by devolving wider management of port operations to professional firms), thus reducing off-loading time and the storage costs incurred at Mombasa for lack of sufficient transport, then fertilizer importing firms could avoid these extra charges. In a competitive marketing environment, these reductions in fertilizer marketing costs would then be passed along in the form of lower farm gate prices.[6]

REDUCE TRANSACTION COSTS ASSOCIATED WITH VAT AND PORT OPERATIONS. Currently fertilizer, as well as most other farm inputs, is zero-rated with respect to import duties. This means that no duty is charged on fertilizers, although at least until 2007, a VAT on related services was still levied. A VAT is charged, for example, on transport and services such as bagging at the port of Mombasa. Although the VAT is supposed to be refunded, the process is lengthy and is a source of continuing frustration for market participants. In addition, port handling charges, Kenya Bureau of Standards charges, and other taxes account for 17 percent of CIF (Gitonga 2004). Port fees, levies, and accessorial charges need to be rationalized and aggregated. In addition, the numerous documentation procedures need to be reduced and, if possible, provided through electronic means.

Figure 16.8 Maize/Fertilizer Price Ratios, Nakuru, Kenya, 1994–2008

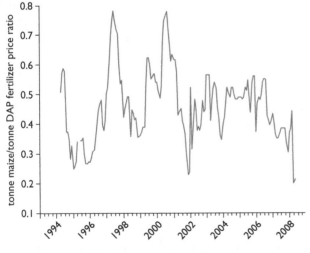

Source: Kenya Ministry of Agriculture, Market Information Bureau.
Note: Price ratio is defined as the wholesale market price per ton of maize in Nakuru divided by the cost of diammonium phosphate (CIF) in Nakuru per ton, in nominal Kenyan shillings.

Interviews with key informants in the fertilizer industry have identified numerous other potential sources of cost savings, many of which require action on the part of government to improve efficiency.

INVEST IN REHABILITATING THE ERODED RAIL, ROAD, AND PORT INFRASTRUCTURE, WHICH WOULD REDUCE DISTRIBUTION COSTS. The farm gate price of fertilizer in western Kenya is roughly twice as high as the landed cost at Mombasa, and transport costs are the major component of this cost difference. High farm gate prices of fertilizer restrict demand for its use and depress agricultural productivity. Hence, efforts to improve the efficiency of port costs and upland shipping would bring major economywide benefits. In particular, rail transport could reduce these costs substantially and also save government spending on repairing roads damaged by heavy truck traffic.

TAILOR FERTILIZER PACKAGES TO LOCAL DEMAND CONDITIONS. This action would increase demand from smaller farmers who require and are able to purchase only small packets. Repackaging of fertilizers from 50 kilogram packets into packets of 25, 10, 2, and 1 kilograms is increasingly taking place, but the process is sometimes associated with fertilizer adulteration and counterfeit products. (That said, adulteration and sales of counterfeit products are often isolated events rather than a well-organized activities, according to Global Development Solutions.)[7] Part of the wide fluctuation in the nitrogen and phosphorous concentration in fertilizers can be attributed to the absence of effective measurement and calibration facilities. In this context, the Kenya Plant Health Inspectorate Service and the Kenya Pesticide Board should become more effective in monitoring and controlling adulteration and counterfeit products, as well as in intensifying farmer and retailer awareness programs to help protect farmers from substandard products.

RAISE FERTILIZER RESPONSE RATES THROUGH AGRONOMIC TRAINING OF FARMERS. The profitability of fertilizer use could be enhanced by improving the aggregate crop yield response rates to fertilizer application. This requires making complementary investments in training for farmers on agronomic practices, soil fertility, water management, and efficient use of fertilizer and investing in crop science to generate more fertilizer-responsive seeds.[8] Emerging problems of soil acidity in the maize belt of western Kenya indicate that soil pH levels may need to be raised to ensure profitable use of fertilizer in these areas. Survey data commonly indicate that the contribution of fertilizer to food grain yields varies tremendously across farms even within the same villages. Simply bringing fertilizer response rates among the bottom half of the distribution up to the mean would result in substantial improvements in household and national food security (Nyoro, Kirimi, and Jayne 2004).

PRODUCER ORGANIZATIONS, DESPITE THEIR POOR TRACK RECORD, WILL BE INCREASINGLY IMPORTANT FOR RURAL INCOME GROWTH. Assuming that the management problems and politicization of producer organizations and cooperatives could be minimized, they might afford an important pathway for smallholders to achieve higher levels of input use and to adopt better production and marketing practices than the current separate and uncoordinated stages in the supply value chains. The role of independent producer groups would be to reduce the transaction costs and risks of private marketing firms dealing with farmers and to develop a production base through the transfer of credit, inputs, and know-how. The Farm Inputs Promotions and the Kenya Market Development Program/Cereal Growers Association farmer training programs are examples of successful attempts by the government, development partners, and NGOs to assist and train groups and to utilize farm extension knowledge, supply chain development, and fertilizer technologies.

While all of these measures can contribute to increased fertilizer use, none is likely to prove effective on its own. Policy makers should, therefore, select strategic combinations of supply- and demand-side measures to allow supply and demand to grow in parallel—strengthening the basis for viable private sector-led commercial fertilizer markets.

The final question is about the role of fertilizer subsidies. The greatest scope for subsidies to promote fertilizer use is in areas where fertilizer use is far below its optimal levels after taking into account the maize yield response to fertilizer and the riskiness of applying fertilizer, especially in semiarid regions where crop failure is not unusual. Recent evidence indicates that crop response to fertilizer application varies widely among smallholder farmers even within the same villages because of differences in management practices, soil quality, timeliness of application, and so forth. The evidence also shows substantial scope for raising the efficiency of fertilizer use, at least for farmers who are currently getting lower response rates from fertilizer application than their more efficient neighbors (Marenya and Barrett 2009; Xu et al. 2009). Moreover, there is little empirical evidence to determine how prevailing levels of fertilizer application compare with optimal levels when taking these factors into account. Fertilizer use rates are clearly low in the semiarid areas of Kenya, and fertilizer subsidies in these areas would likely raise fertilizer use, but the contribution to yields and smallholder incomes may be quite limited because of the environmental riskiness and low response rates in such areas. A major question for semiarid areas, therefore, is whether poverty reduction and food security objectives can be best achieved through fertilizer subsidies or other types of public programs and investments. Given that resources are scarce, efforts should be made to identify the types of agricultural expenditures that will generate the greatest payoffs.

In the high-potential areas, a large majority of farmers is already purchasing fertilizer. Although use rates were quite high in 2007, they are likely to have fallen given the ensuing adverse conditions since then. Fertilizer subsidies are politically attractive in that they promise increased fertilizer use and food production, but these outcomes are by no means assured. In 2009 Kenya faced its lowest maize production level in recent history after having initiated a major fertilizer subsidy program; poor rains in 2009 rendered the fertilizer subsidy program relatively ineffective, leading the country to import more than 1 million tons of maize in 2009. Moreover, providing subsidized fertilizer in areas of high commercial demand will almost certainly result in a partial crowding out of commercial sales, as shown by the findings of studies conducted in Zambia and Malawi, where commercial demand for fertilizer is considerably lower than in Kenya (see Xu et al 2009; Dorward et al. 2008). Where purchase of commercial fertilizer is high, then a ton of subsidized fertilizer distributed by government is unlikely to result in an additional ton of fertilizer being applied on farmers' fields, because the farmers previously purchasing fertilizer are no longer likely to buy it if they can acquire the same amount more cheaply from a government program.

In the current high price environment, the availability of seasonal loans for input purchases takes on heightened importance for maintaining farmers' effective commercial demand for fertilizer. Many Kenyan farmers have been able to finance fertilizer through the credit offered in the integrated input-output chains for crops such as tea, sugar, and coffee. These integrated marketing arrangements have also provided the means for farmers to obtain fertilizer for their food crops, since the companies can recoup their loans for other crops as well when the farmers sell their cash crop back to the company. But in areas where fertilizer use on a particular crop is profitable, such as maize in western Kenya and horticulture throughout the country, most farmers have achieved reasonable levels of fertilizer use without credit. Support for the development of viable credit programs may also help smallholder farmers maintain their access to fertilizer use despite current high prices for households in which liquidity constraints are the main problem.

The experience of Kenya demonstrates the role of a supportive policy environment that attracts local and foreign direct investment in improving smallholder farmers' access to input and commodity markets. In Kenya's case, a stable input marketing policy environment has fostered a private sector response that supports smallholder agricultural productivity and poverty alleviation. These goals remain elusive in countries lacking a sustained commitment to the development of viable commercial input delivery systems. While the government's policy stance toward maize marketing has been prone to vacillation, the operations of the NCPB and the elimination of regional trade barriers since the inception of the East Africa Community Custom Union in January 2005 have both promoted maize price stability (Jayne, Myers, and Nyoro 2008; Chapoto and Jayne 2009). Complementary programs to support small farmer productivity, such as the Farm Inputs Promotion program, the agro-dealer training and credit program, and the organization of farmers into groups to facilitate their access to extension and credit services under the Kenya Market Development Program have also been important factors in raising fertilizer use in Kenya.

Because mean household incomes are higher and infrastructure relatively better in Kenya than in many other African countries, the market-led growth in smallholder fertilizer use in Kenya may not be easily transferable to countries where effective demand is highly constrained. Kenya's success in increasing fertilizer usage among smallholder farmers is also tenuous. Sustaining the momentum will depend on continued public investment, good policy choices, favorable weather conditions, and avoidance of international events detrimental to Kenya. Governance problems and civil disruption are jeopardizing the sustainability of the commercially driven input distribution system and rural development more generally. Continued access to input credit for small farmers in many parts of the country will require government commitment to limit the potential for politicization and interference in the management of the interlinked crop marketing systems for sugarcane, tea, and coffee, which have provided a means for farmers to acquire additional fertilizer on credit for use on food crops. Also, new investment is needed in Kenya's eroded rail, road, and port infrastructure if Kenya is to maintain its competitiveness. Last, effective systems to improve smallholders' crop husbandry and management practices are needed to provide incentives for continued expansion of fertilizer use and productivity growth in areas where fertilizer is only marginally profitable at present.

NOTES

1. "Kenya to Import 1.5 Million Bags of Cheap Fertilizer," *Daily Nation*, June 23, 2009, p. 33. Throughout this chapter, "tons" are metric tons.

2. The high-potential region has higher productive potential and covers the agro-zones of Western and Central Highlands, High Maize Potential, and Western transition areas, which include the districts of Bomet, Bungoma, Gishu, Kakamega, Kisii, Meru, Muranga, Narok, Nakuru, Nyeri, Trans Nzoia, Uasin, and Vihiga. The low-potential region consists of the lowland zones in the coast, east, and west of the country (which are generally drier and have poorer-quality soil). The low-potential region includes the districts of Kilifi, Kisumu, Kitui, Kwale, Machakos, Makueni, Mwingi, Siaya, Taita, and Taveta.

3. The sum of the product of plot fertilizer application rates and ratio of plot size (acres) to total acres is calculated for all plots in the household. This procedure gives more weight to application rates in bigger plots indetermining aggregate household application rates. Rate = Σ (plot rate * plot area / total household area).

4. Note that "hybrid" stands for purchased hybrid seed and open pollinated varieties and "nonhybrid" consists of recycled or replanted hybrids and some "traditional" seed types of unknown source.

5. In other Tegemeo papers, the balanced panel consists of 1,275 households, but 15 households did not have complete information on all variables used in this study, hence the 1,260 sample size.

6. Some efficiency improvements in Mombasa port operations have been recently implemented, and more comprehensive reforms are currently under consideration.

7. According to Global Development Solutions (2005), nearly 3–5 percent of repackaged fertilizers are sold using counterfeit labels and packages. Specifically, fake brand name labels are used to sell inferior quality fertilizers.

8. Research indicates that the highest crop yield response is obtained when improved seed, fertilizer, and agronomic practices to raise soil organic matter are combined (Marenya and Barrett 2008; Kelly 2006). In some areas, improved management practices may have greater impact on yields than use of fertilizer alone (Haggblade, Tembo, and Donovan 2004).

REFERENCES

Allgood, J. H., and J. Kilungo. 1996. "An Appraisal of the Fertilizer Market in Kenya and Recommendations for Improving Fertilizer Use Practices by Smallholder Farmers: A Field Report." International Fertilizer Development Center (IFDC), Muscle Shoals, AL.

Ariga, J. M., and T. S. Jayne. 2008. "Maize Trade and Marketing Policy Interventions in Kenya." Paper presented at the Conference on Food Marketing and Trade Policies in Eastern and Southern Africa. EST Division, Food and Agriculture Organization (FAO), Rome, March 1.

Ariga, J. M., T. S. Jayne, and J. Nyoro. 2006. "Factors Driving the Growth in Fertilizer Consumption in Kenya, 1990–2005: Sustaining the Momentum in Kenya and Lessons for Broader Replicability in Sub-Saharan Africa." Working Paper 24, Tegemeo Institute, Egerton University, Nairobi.

Argwings-Kodhek, G. 1996. "The Impacts of Fertilizer Market Liberalization in Kenya."

Policy Analysis Matrix Project of the Kenya Marketing Development Programme. Nairobi.

———. 2004. "Kenya Agriculture Sector Brief." FAO, Rome.

Chapoto, A., and T. S. Jayne. 2009. *Open versus Closed Maize Border Policy: A Comparison of Maize Price Instability in East and Southern Africa.* International Development Working Paper. Department of Agricultural, Food, and Resource Economics, Michigan State University, East Lansing, MI.

Dorward, A., E. Chirwa, V. Kelly, T. Jayne, R. Slater, and D. Boughton. 2008. "Evaluation of the 2006/7 Agricultural Input Supply Programme, Malawi." Final Report of the School of Oriental and African Studies, Wadonda Consult, Michigan State University, and Overseas Development Institute, undertaken for the Ministry of Agriculture and Food Security, Government of Malawi, Lilongwe.

Global Development Solutions. 2005. "From Laboratory to the Dining Table: Tracing the Value Chain of Kenyan Maize." Report prepared for the World Bank. Reston, VA.

Gitonga. K. T. 2004. "Study on Rationalization and Harmonization of Policies, Regulations, Procedures, Grades, and Standards in the Fertilizer Sub-sector in Eastern Africa." Kenya Report. Kampala: Eastern and Central Africa Program for Agricultural Policy Analysis.

Haggblade, S., G. Tembo, and C. Donovan. 2004. "Household Level Financial Incentives to Adoption of Conservation Agricultural Technologies in Africa." Working Paper 9. Food Security Research Project, Lusaka.

IFDC (International Center for Soil Fertility and Agricultural Development). 2001. "An Assessment of Fertilizer Prices in Kenya and Uganda: Domestic Prices vis-à-vis International Market Prices." IFDC, Muscle Shoals, AL.

Jayne, T. S., and G. Argwings-Kodhek. 1997. "Consumer Response to Maize Market Liberalization." *Food Policy* 22 (5): 447–58.

Jayne, T. S., R. J. Myers, and J. Nyoro. 2008. "The Effects of Government Maize Marketing Policies on Maize Prices in Kenya." *Agricultural Economics* 38 (3): 313–25.

Kelly, V. 2006. "Factors Affecting Demand for Fertilizer in Sub-Saharan Africa." Agriculture and Rural Development Discussion Paper 23, World Bank, Washington, DC.

Kimuyu, P. 1994. "Evaluation of the USAID/Kenya Fertilizer Pricing and Marketing Reform Program." U.S. Agency for International Development, Nairobi.

Marenya, P. P., and C. B. Barrett. 2008. *Soil Quality and Fertilizer Use Rates among Smallholder Farmers in Western Kenya.* Ithaca, N.Y: Cornell University.

Ministry of Agriculture, Kenya. 2004. "Strategy for Revitalizing Agriculture: 2004–2014." Nairobi.

———. 2008. "Economic Review of Agriculture: 2008." Central Planning and Project Monitoring Unit, Nairobi.

Mukumbu, M., and T. S. Jayne. 1994. "Urban Maize Meal Consumption Patterns: Strategies for Improving Food Access for Vulnerable Urban Households in Kenya." Paper presented at the Symposium on Agricultural Policies and Food Security in Eastern Africa, Egerton University, Tegemeo Institute, Nairobi, May 19–20.

Nyoro, J., M., W. Kiiru, and T. S. Jayne. 1999. "Evolution of Kenya's Maize Marketing Systems in the Post Liberalization Era." Working Paper 2, Tegemeo Institute, Egerton University, Nairobi.

Nyoro, J., L. Kirimi, and T. Jayne. 2004. "Competitiveness of Kenya and Ugandan Maize Production: Challenges for the Future." Working Paper 10, Tegemeo Institute, Egerton University, Nairobi.

Tegemeo Institute. 2007. "Enhancing Market Access and Technology Adoption among Smallholders: A Baseline Report for Evaluating Agricultural Interventions Funded by the Rockefeller Foundation in Western Kenya." Report prepared for the Rockefeller Foundation, Egerton University, Nairobi.

Wanzala, M., T. S. Jayne, and J. Staatz. 2002. "Fertilizer Markets and Agricultural Production Incentives: Insights from Kenya." Working Paper 4, Tegemeo Institute, Egerton University, Nairobi.

Wooldridge, J. 2002. *Econometric Analysis of Cross Section and Panel Data.* Cambridge, MA: MIT Press.

Xu, Z., B. Burke, T. S. Jayne, and J. Govereh. 2009. "Do Input Subsidy Programs "Crowd In" or "Crowd Out" Commercial Market Development? Modeling Fertilizer Demand in a Two-Channel Marketing System." *Agricultural Economics* 40 (1): 79–94.

CHAPTER 17

Malawi's Agricultural Input Subsidy Program Experience over 2005–09

Andrew Dorward, Ephraim Chirwa, and T. S. Jayne

The implementation in Malawi of a large-scale agricultural input subsidy program in the 2005/06 agricultural season and in subsequent years has attracted significant international interest.[1] While much of this attention has applauded reported growth in maize production and food security in the country, there have also been significant criticisms and questions. These have focused on the effectiveness and efficiency of the program in raising maize productivity, its impacts on the development of sustainable commercial input markets (Ricker-Gilbert, Jayne, and Chirwa 2011), its high and (from 2005/06 to 2008/09) dramatically rising fiscal and macroeconomic costs, its opportunity costs (in terms of crowding out of other investments), its overall return on investment, and its sustainability (SOAS et al. 2008; Dorward and Chirwa 2009a, 2009b, 2010; Dorward, Chirwa, and Slater 2010a, 2010b; Kelly, Boughton, and Lenski 2010).

The importance of agriculture—specifically, maize—to the Malawian economy and to the livelihoods of most Malawian people is the critical backdrop to the agricultural input subsidy program (AISP), together with low agricultural and maize productivity and associated high national, individual, and household food insecurity.[2] Large numbers of very poor people in Malawi work on very small areas of land that are predominantly planted to maize (see table 17.1 for some key indicators). Continual cultivation of maize on the same land without addition of organic or inorganic fertilizers leads to low yields. Low yields then lead to inability to afford the purchase of inputs. Purchase of inputs on credit is also not possible for most farmers because rural credit markets are underdeveloped and the costs of credit administration are too high, as are risks for both borrowers and lenders. Low volumes of input demand, poor infrastructure, and high transport costs lead to high input costs and inhibit the development of input supply systems in less accessible areas, while highly variable maize prices (discussed below) add to the risks of input use (whether purchased with cash or credit).

Increasing maize productivity is difficult for several reasons. Only 10 percent of Malawian maize producers are net sellers of maize, while 60 percent are net buyers of maize (SOAS et al. 2008), and hence most (particularly poorer) people's livelihoods and food security are damaged by high maize prices. Increased maize productivity from the use of purchased inputs requires, however, that the use of the inputs is profitable for farmers, and that requires sufficiently high maize prices and yield responses to cover the costs of inputs. Unless substantial improvements can be made in

Andrew Dorward is Professor of Development Economics at the School of Oriental and African Studies, University of London; Ephraim Chirwa is Professor of Economics at Chancellor College, University of Malawi; and T. S. Jayne is Professor of International Development at Michigan State University.

Table 17.1   Key Data on Smallholder Agriculture in Malawi, 2004/05

Indicator	North	Center	South	National
Rural population (percent of total population)	10	38	40	88
Income and poverty				
Median expenditure/capita (MK thousands)	17	20.9	16.9	17.5
Poor households (percent of rural population)	56	47	64	52
Nutrition and food security				
Mean rural daily per capita consumption (kilocalories) for people living below the poverty line	1,738	1,811	1,703	1,746
Incidence of stunting in children 6 months–5 years (percent)	39.6	47.9	40.8	43.7
Incidence of underweight children 6 months–5 years (percent)	16.1	20	17.2	18.3
Share of calories from own production	0.53	0.58	0.47	0.52
Median month after 2004/05 harvest own food crop exhausted (actual)*	—	—	—	4
Suffered large rise in food prices in past 5 years (percent)	—	—	—	79.2
Smallholder agriculture				
Landholding:				
Less than 0.5 hectare/household (percent)	12.1	15.4	25.4	19.9
Less than 1.0 hectare/household (percent)	31.4	40.6	54.1	46.2
Suffered crop yield loss in past 5 years (percent)	—	—	—	68.8
Maize growers (percent)	93	97	99	97
Access to credit for food crop inputs (percent)	2.5	4.2	3.0	3.4
Percentage of smallholder farmers purchasing fertilizer (percent)	37	44	39	43
Fertilizer applied on all fields (kilograms)[a]	32	45	24	34
Fertilizer applied on *fertilized* maize fields (kilograms/hectare)	139	111	77	101

Source: SOAS et al. (2008) using data from NSO (2005) except * (authors' calculations from NSO 2006).

Note: — = not available. $1 = MK 140 for most of the years covered in this paper.

a. Fertilizer rates on tobacco plots are roughly double rates across all plots.

yield responses, there is a significant dilemma between the need for low maize prices for a large numbers of poor maize buyers (who are also significant maize producers) and the need for higher maize prices to allow increased returns from input use to reliably cover the purchase costs. Further difficulties arise from high maize price variability, which damages both producers and consumers—low prices present risks to investments in inputs by producers who aim to have a marketable surplus, while high prices present risks to consumers (including the majority of smallholder farmers). Poor access to international and domestic markets (caused in large part by historically low public investment in transport infrastructure), seasonal scarcities, and poor local market development (resulting from low and uncertain volumes, high costs of transport, and uncertain government intervention) have led in the past to high intra- and interseasonal maize price variation (as well as higher farm gate input prices and lower farm gate produce prices), further depressing market development. Risks of high maize prices encourage poor consumers to grow as much of their own staple food as possible, even at very low levels of productivity. At the same time, there are limited higher-earning opportunities within or outside agriculture. The result is a lock-in to low-productivity maize cultivation.

Productivity and investment in productive activities are further constrained by poverty and by vulnerability to a wide variety of (often related) shocks, particularly low crop yields, sickness affecting household members, high food prices, and losses of employment or remittance income. Women, who play a key role in agricultural production and rural livelihoods, tend to be particularly vulnerable to these shocks. Macroeconomic conditions before 2005—namely, high real interest rates, high inflation, and significant devaluation of the kwacha (MK)—also inhibited growth. However, macroeconomic management has improved dramatically since 2004.

Agricultural, rural, and national economic development in Malawi are therefore constrained by a number of interacting household, local, and national vulnerability, poverty and productivity traps, as illustrated in figure 17.1. These traps constrain input and maize market development, investments in maize intensification, diversification out of maize into other agricultural and nonagricultural activities, the ability of rural people (particularly the poor) to protect themselves from shocks, and wider local and national economic development. The result is a vicious circle of unstable maize prices inhibiting net producers' investment in maize production, net consumers' reliance on the market

Figure 17.1   Vicious Circle of the Low Maize Productivity Trap

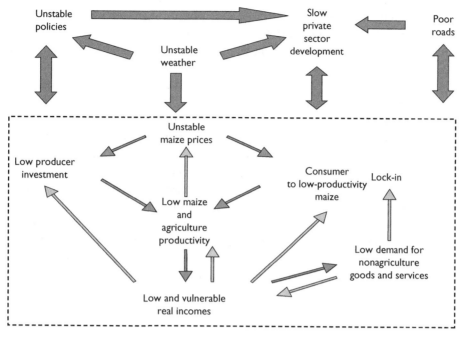

Source: Authors.
Note: Light green arrows represent feedback effect.

for maize purchases, and poor consumers' escape from low-productivity maize cultivation. These in turn inhibit the growth of the nonfarm economy. Sustained improvements in maize productivity with low and stable prices are required to drive diversification out of low productivity maize into a more diversified and productive economy that benefits all Malawians, particularly those who are currently poor and food insecure.[3]

Input subsidy and maize market intervention policies have been a long-standing, major, though often contentious, feature of strategies of both the government of Malawi and varied donors' to promote agriculture and food security. From the mid-1970s to the early 1990s, the government financed a universal fertilizer subsidy, subsidized smallholder credit, and controlled maize prices. The system began to break down in the late 1980s and early 1990s, however, with cash flow difficulties, rising treasury deficits, partial market liberalization and increasing importance of parallel grain markets. The state system of subsidized input loans, with loan recovery through farmers' delivery of grain to the Agricultural Development and Marketing Corporation (ADMARC), collapsed in the mid-1990s as a result of the coincidence of widespread harvest failure, multiparty elections, credit default, the rise of parallel grain markets, partial implementation of liberalization and structural

adjustment policies, and substantial devaluation (raising local fertilizer prices). With other policy changes drawing more productive smallholders away from surplus maize production and into tobacco production, there was a widespread perception in Malawi in the mid-1990s that falling fertilizer support was leading to diminished maize production and a food and political crisis. From 1998/99 the government, with mixed donor support, reinstated a variety of interventions subsidizing maize fertilizer and seed access, with intermittent interventions in maize markets. Seed and fertilizer subsidies shifted from universal price subsidies to free provision of small "starter packs" initially provided to all households in 1998/99 and 1999/2000, and then to a more limited (but varying) number of targeted households in 2001/02 to 2004/05 (see, for example, Harrigan 2003).

Analysis of smallholder agricultural performance since the late 1990s is complicated by difficulties with data and in separating out the effects of poor rainfall and of policy changes responding to perceptions of an impending food crisis. In contrast to the widespread perception that maize production fell during the 1990s and 2000s, official maize production and overall food production estimates show a strong rising trend through the 1990s to 2006, together with a modest rising trend during the same period in per capita food production (including sometimes disputed estimates of increasing cassava production). There were two years of very poor rainfall in 1991/92 and 1992/93, two years of good rainfall with universal distribution of small free fertilizer packs in 1998/99 and 1999/2000, poor rainfall and lower fertilizer subsidies and production with widespread hunger in 2000/01, 2001/02, and 2004/05, and good rainfall and a large fertilizer subsidy in 2005/06.

Fertilizer use also rose impressively through the 1990s, with an annual average of 6 percent growth in fertilizer use on all crops and commercial and smallholder farms between 1984/85 and 2004/05 (SOAS et al. 2008). Starting in the mid-1990s, private input suppliers took over an increasing share of the fertilizer market from ADMARC and the Smallholder Farmers Fertiliser Revolving Fund (SFFRFM), both parastatals responsible for importing and distributing fertilizers to smallholder farmers. By the end of the 1990s private input suppliers were responsible for more than 70 percent of national fertilizer imports and for a large proportion of sales to smallholders (SOAS et al. 2008). During the 2002/03 and 2003/04 crop seasons, 43 percent of smallholders surveyed in a nationally representative survey purchased some fertilizer (see table 17.1). Smallholders *using* fertilizer on maize applied an average of 101 kilograms per hectare (see table 17.1). Major parastatal involvement in fertilizer imports for subsidized fertilizer sales has, however, affected private sector sales and confidence in investment in imports and retail systems by varying, and debated, amounts.

Widespread fertilizer use on maize produced by smallholder farmers is constrained by two problems: profitability and affordability. Unsubsidized fertilizer was not generally profitable on maize produced for sale in Malawi from the mid-1990s to the mid-2000s.[4] It was, however, more profitable on maize grown for households' own consumption, with a higher subjective valuation stemming from farmers' fears of the effects of a bad year on maize purchase prices. For poorer farmers with this higher subjective valuation, however, affordability of fertilizer becomes a major problem. Liquidity presents substantial difficulties for poor farm households, who on the one hand face a "hungry gap" during the cropping period (when farmers need to invest labor, seed, and other inputs in crop production while food stocks from the previous season are running low, and children are particularly susceptible to sickness) and on the other very high borrowing costs and an absence of low-cost financing services for inputs. Hungry-gap problems at the livelihood level are exacerbated by rural economy market effects (which depress wage rates and asset prices and raise food prices). These problems are widely recognized as very severe for poor rural households

in Malawi, causing major production and welfare problems in rural areas.[5]

Improving the profitability of fertilizer use in maize production requires lower fertilizer prices (as a result of greater efficiency in fertilizer supply and reduction in transport costs for importation or distribution of a subsidy, or both), higher maize prices, or greater efficiency in the use of fertilizer (raising the grain output to nitrogen ratio).[6] Changes to maize prices and improved efficiency of fertilizer use will not, however, improve the affordability of fertilizer for large numbers of poor rural households in Malawi. Making fertilizer more affordable requires very substantial reductions in fertilizer prices, the development of low-cost and accessible financial services, or both. Development of such financial services, however, requires that maize be profitable, that smallholders have other sources of cash income that can be used to repay fertilizer loans when the majority of the maize they produce is for home consumption, and that very low-cost systems be used for loan disbursement and recovery. All these requirements are difficult to achieve in Malawi.

REVIEW OF INPUT SUBSIDIES

To understand the implementation, impacts, strengths, and weaknesses of the Malawi Agricultural Input Subsidy Program, it is helpful to examine broader historical and theoretical lessons on input subsidies' implementation, performance, and impacts.[7]

Wider experience with agricultural input subsidies

Large-scale (so-called universal) agricultural input subsidies were a common and prominent feature of agricultural development policies in poor rural economies from the 1960s to the 1980s. They were subsequently criticized, however, as a major element in fiscally and economically unsustainable policies that were inefficient, ineffective, and expensive in Africa (see, for example, World Bank 1981). These policies distorted market incentives, blunted competitiveness and farmer incentives, and undermined the growth of private sector agricultural services. While subsidized input systems may have seemed attractive to farmers (in regard to the services that were supposed to be provided), theoretical difficulties with subsidy benefits (see below) were compounded by diversion and inefficiency, which often limited actual benefits to farmers.

Evaluations of the rate of return to alternative public investments in Asia tend to rank input subsidies as fourth or fifth, after investments in road infrastructure, agricultural research and development, education, and often other types of public investments (see, for example, Fan, Thorat, and Rao 2004; Economist Intelligence Unit 2008). There are also arguments, however, that while returns to agricultural input subsidies were often low, they did yield substantial benefits in some countries at certain times. Such arguments stress the importance of differences between subsidies benefiting fertilizer suppliers and those benefiting (poorer) farmers, falling returns over time where subsidies are effective, and the need for judicious (and changing) decisions on the scale of different investments, recognizing trade-offs, complementarities, differences in the timing of returns, and potential diminishing (and sometimes increasing) marginal returns across different investments (see Dorward et al. 2004; Djurfeldt et al. 2005; Timmer 1989, for Indonesia; Fan, Gulati, and Thorat 2007, for India; and Dorward 2009).

Information on the performance of most of the recent input subsidy programs in Africa is limited despite the very substantial investments of public funds in these programs. However, recent empirical evidence from Malawi and Zambia shows that subsidies tend to be targeted disproportionately to better-off farmers compared with poor and female-headed households, where affordability constraints are most severe (Govereh et al. 2006; SOAS et al. 2008); input subsidies have partially displaced commercial fertilizer demand, which has hindered policy objectives to promote sustainable development of commercial input distribution systems (Xu et al. 2009; Ricker-Gilbert, Jayne, and Chirwa 2011); and the high costs of large-scale input subsidies means that there are very substantial opportunity costs in terms of forgone public investments, investments that, as shown by the Asian experience discussed earlier, may have greater long-term impacts on poverty reduction and agricultural growth. Moreover, Kenya has achieved impressive growth in fertilizer use on food crops based on strong commercial demand for inputs after the liberalization of input marketing and foreign exchange controls, without the use of subsidies (chapter 17; Ariga et al. 2008; Ariga and Jayne 2009). The potential applicability of the Kenyan model, or parts of it, to other Sub-Saharan African countries needs to be considered, taking account of particular features of the Kenyan situation and experience.

Dorward (2009), in a review of a number of input subsidy programs across Africa, also notes apparent tendencies for these programs to focus on production objectives and producer welfare (largely ignoring potential benefits for consumers and for wider pro-poor economic growth); for poor integration of many programs with complementary investments; and in some programs, for an unfortunate lack

of interest in improving effectiveness and efficiency. Two further commonalities are a limited focus on replenishing soil fertility and a strong prevalence of heavy subsidies (50 percent to 100 percent subsidy rates) on rationed inputs (Dorward 2009).

Theoretical benefits and costs of agricultural input subsidies

Conventional arguments for subsidies in agricultural development have focused on the promotion of increased agricultural productivity through the adoption of new technologies (Ellis 1992). Reduced costs of subsidized inputs increase the profitability of these technologies and reduce the risks perceived by farmers in adopting them. Together with credit and extension services, input subsidies were supposed to help farmers implement, benefit from, and then, with the withdrawal of the subsidy, fully fund efficient input purchases and use themselves.

Supply and demand analysis of input subsidies shows that because of deadweight losses, a subsidy can generate a positive net economic return to a country only if it addresses some market failure (Siamwalla and Valdes 1986). This may occur when:

- farmers' private costs of working capital for input purchase are greater than the social cost of capital,
- farmers' lack of knowledge about the benefits of inputs means that their expectation of the production benefits from input use are less than the benefits they will gain,
- there are learning costs with input use, meaning that initial farmer returns are low but will increase with experience (Ellis 1992; Crawford, Jayne, and Kelly 2006; Morris et al. 2007), and
- farmers' risk assessment and aversion to investing working capital in input purchase and use are higher than society's risk assessment and aversion.

The size of the deadweight loss and the distribution of benefits between consumers and producers also depend on the elasticity of supply and demand. Demand or supply inelasticity tends to be associated with smaller deadweight losses. Inelastic demand is associated with larger shares of consumer surplus benefits, while inelastic supply is associated with larger shares of producer benefits (Dorward 2009). Staple food markets in landlocked countries tend to be associated with more inelastic demand by poor consumers (where prices lie between export and import parity prices). Demand tends to be more elastic for cash crops, particularly for cash crops that are exported.[8]

Subsidy inefficiencies also arise when part of the cost of the subsidy goes to reducing the cost of production for produce that would be produced anyway; when subsidies bid up demand and prices for land, labor, or inputs, and are passed back to suppliers of these inputs,[9] and when rationing leads to opportunities for those controlling subsidized inputs to demand payments for provision of subsidized inputs. Another major concern with input subsides is the extent of leakage and diversion away from their intended use as a result of diversion between products, diversion from intended beneficiaries to others within the country, and cross-border leakage.

A final, crucial point is that the technical efficiency of input use in generating additional agricultural production is critical in determining deadweight losses, distribution of benefits between producers and consumers, and wider economic gains. This efficiency depends upon the quality and appropriateness of the inputs to the product on which they are used, the timing of the delivery of inputs to farmers, the availability of complementary resources (for example, seed and fertilizer together), agro-ecological conditions, and farmers' technical skill or competence in using the inputs.

This analysis suggests that large-scale input subsidies should be focused on:

- producers who are not using inputs because of market failure,
- crops and geographical areas for which increased input use can induce a large supply shift (this may also require complementary infrastructure and services for input delivery, extension, and output markets), and
- stimulating products with inelastic demand and supply, particularly inelastic demand, among poor producers and consumers (staple grain production tends to have these characteristics in poor large or landlocked countries).

The analysis also suggests the importance of consumer benefits in addition to (or rather than) producer benefits for achieving economic and welfare gains from subsidies; subsidy implementation that reduces deadweight losses and rents from straight transfers, leakages, and high administrative costs; and comparing distributional impacts and multipliers from expenditure on input subsidies with alternative (tax, subsidy, or other transfer) instruments for changing income distribution and for stimulating growth.

The conclusions from this neoclassical supply and demand analysis influenced conventional wisdom on a number of difficulties with input subsidy programs: in controlling costs, in achieving "exit strategies" after subsidy programs have become entrenched, in effective targeting of input subsidies to particular farmer types, in ensuring inputs are not overused, in controlling regressive benefits that favor larger farmers who can access subsidized inputs, and in preventing market distortions where parastatal involvement crowds out private sector investment in input supply systems and provides opportunities for corruption.

In recent years, however, some scholars and many government policy makers have departed from orthodox neoclassical thinking on input (particularly fertilizer) subsidies. Factors giving rise to this rethinking in Sub-Saharan Africa include perceptions by some that liberalization policies have failed to support sustainable intensification of staple food crop production; political demands for fertilizer subsidies; tensions among donors facing such demands; concerns about declining soil fertility; and interest in using input subsidies as an instrument for social protection policies and as a means of promoting input market development.

On the basis of this analysis, Dorward (2009) suggests that the following design and implementation features are important if subsidy programs are to be effective and efficient in stimulating increased productivity and broad-based growth:

- Large unit (or percent) subsidies on rationed supplies targeted to credit constrained farmers to reduce *input affordability* problems.
- *Targeting* access to subsidized inputs for specific household types where input use is constrained by the market failures that the program effectively addresses; where these inputs can be used effectively and efficiently;[10] and where substantial political, economic, welfare, equity, and administrative challenges in effective and low-cost targeting can be overcome.
- *Rationing* to control the costs of input subsidies with large per unit or percent subsidies and limited secondary markets in which recipients sell subsidized inputs to others.
- Encouragement of *private sector input supply* systems' efficiency and investments by economies of scale and by competition in the sale of large volumes of inputs (especially in remote and previously poorer and less productive areas and producers), with measures to limit uncertainty and the diversion of suppliers' focus to capturing subsidized sales without developing retail systems.
- Promotion of *dynamic effects on pro-poor growth* through higher land and labor productivity in staple food production, lower food prices, and higher producer incomes

that facilitate wider nonagricultural development, market thickening, and reduced coordination and transaction costs and risks in poor rural economies.

■ Effective and efficient *entitlement and distribution systems* supporting targeting, rationing, supply system development, control of secondary markets and leakages, and cost control. A combination of paper vouchers (or coupons),[11] scratch cards, and electronic systems (involving bank cards, electronic "smart" cards, mobile phones, or some combination of the three) may be used as evidence of entitlement. Different systems offer different potential benefits and political, technical, administrative, and social challenges within communities and households. Entitlements may be input specific or flexible with regard to inputs allowed and may have a fixed value (with a variable top-up at redemption) or a variable value (with a fixed top-up). There are also important interactions between entitlement systems, secondary markets, recipient choice (of inputs and suppliers), control of fraud and program costs, and gendered access to and control of subsidized inputs within households.

■ *Complementary investments, policies, and instruments* critical for subsidy effectiveness and efficiency, with balanced investments in the subsidy program itself, research and extension support, transport and communications infrastructure, and efficient and stable output markets.[12]

■ Matching of *political interests* with more technical and bureaucratic needs for cost control, limited leakages, targeting, rationing, and private sector development.

Given the experience with subsidies in Africa discussed earlier, implementing some of these features is a major challenge.

Issues to consider in evaluating agricultural input subsidies

The success of an input subsidy program has to be judged against its objectives, and input subsidy programs can have a wide range of possible objectives: wider (pro-poor) economic growth, benefits for poor consumers from lower output prices, national (or household) food self-sufficiency or security, increased input adoption, increased efficiency of input use, benefits for poor producers, input supply system development, soil fertility replenishment, and political benefits. Most, but not all, of these objectives can be mutually complementary, depending on how a program is implemented. The balance of program objectives, and their context, should then determine the key design and implementation

elements of input subsidy programs as discussed earlier. Figure 17.2 provides a conceptual framework that identifies key variables and relationships affecting input subsidy program impacts and guides this discussion of the Malawi Agricultural Input Subsidy Program.

MALAWI'S 2005/06 TO 2008/09 EXPERIENCE WITH AGRICULTURAL INPUT SUBSIDIES

Following severe food security difficulties in the early 2000s and in line with election commitments, the government of Malawi decided to implement a large national input subsidy program for the 2005/06 growing season.[13] The popular program has been repeated and expanded in subsequent seasons, building on core experience but also incorporating modifications in components and implementation systems from year to year. Core elements of the program common to the different years have been its use of vouchers targeting roughly 50 percent of farmers across the country for the receipt of fertilizers for maize production, with further vouchers for improved maize seeds and for fertilizers for tobacco. The core objective of the program, which has been refined over time, has been twofold: to increase resource-poor smallholder farmers' access to improved agricultural inputs in order to achieve food self-sufficiency, and to raise these farmers' incomes through increased food and cash crop production. The main features of the program across the four years are summarized in table 17.2, and details of its design, implementation and various achievements are detailed in the following sections.

Program design and implementation

The 2005/06 program provided the foundation on which subsequent input subsidy programs in Malawi have been built. We therefore describe this program in more detail before considering changes made in subsequent programs. The objective of the program was to promote access to and use of fertilizers in maize and tobacco production in order to increase agricultural productivity and food security. Fertilizer coupons were distributed to districts and within districts to extension planning areas in two rounds. In the first round, allocation was broadly in proportion to cropped maize and tobacco areas. Coupons were distributed to districts and Traditional Authorities (TAs) by the Ministry of Agriculture and Food Security (MoAFS). TAs were supposed to allocate coupons to Village Development Committees (VDCs), which were then supposed to identify recipients to receive two coupons that they could redeem, at

Figure 17.2 Conceptual Framework for Investigating Agricultural Input Subsidy Impacts

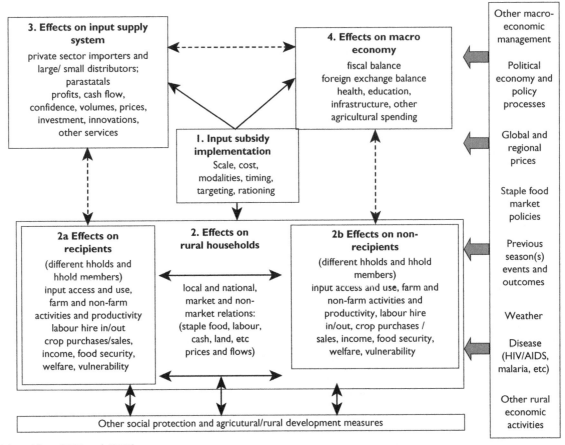

Source: Adapted from SOAS et al. (2008).
Note: hholds = households.

Table 17.2 Summary of Malawian Agricultural Input Subsidy Programs, 2005/06 to 2008/09

Indicator		2005/06	2006/07	2007/08	2008/09
Fertilizer voucher distribution (mt equivalent)		166,156	200,128	216,000	195,369
Households receiving one or more fertilizer coupons (percent)		—	54	59	65
Subsidized fertilizer (mt For maize)		108,986	152,989	192,976	182,309
For tobacco		22,402	21,699	23,578	19,969
Total subsidized	Planned	137,006	150,000	170,000	170,000
fertilizer sales	Actual	131,388	174,688	216,553	202,278
Redemption price (MK/50-kilogram bag)		950[a]	950	900	800
Approximate voucher value, (MK/bag)		1,750	2,480	3,299	7,951
Approximate subsidy (%)		64	72	79	91
Subsidized maize seed (mt)		—	4,524	5,541	5,365
Hybrid seed (%)		0	61	53	84
Cotton seed (mt)		0	0	390	435
Legume seed (mt)		0	0	24	—
Cotton chemical vouchers		0	0	131,848	—
Total program	Planned	5,100	7,500	11,500	19,480
cost (MK millions)	Actual	7,200	12,729	16,346	39,847

Sources: Logistics Unit reports; Nakhumwa 2006; SOAS et al. 2008; MoAFS 2008; Dorward and Chirwa 2009a; MoAFS implementation guidelines; government of Malawi budget statistics; Dorward, Chirwa, and Slater 2010b; key informants.
Note: — = not available; mt = metric tons.
a. seed or fertilizer coupon (NSO 2008).

CHAPTER 17: MALAWI'S AGRICULTURAL INPUT SUBSIDY PROGRAM EXPERIENCE OVER 2005–09

a reduced cash price, for any of four types of fertilizer. There was considerable variation within areas in the criteria determining prioritization and selection of beneficiaries, in numbers of people receiving coupons, and in numbers of coupons received per recipient household. A second, supplementary round of coupon allocation and distribution was made later in the season. Under the program, 6,000 metric tons of open pollinated variety (OPV) maize seed was also offered for sale without coupons, at a subsidized price of MK 150 for a 3-kilogram bag, compared with the market price of MK 500. Although the parastatals ADMARC and SFFRFM were responsible for distributing subsidized inputs, 48 percent of subsided fertilizer was supplied by private sector importers.

Holders of coupons were entitled to redeem coupons for fertilizer at the rate of one coupon and MK 950 for one 50-kilogram bag of 23:21:0 +4S or urea ("maize fertilizers"), and at one coupon plus MK 1,450 per bag of Compound D or CAN ("tobacco fertilizers"). These prices represented, on average, a two-thirds subsidy to farmers on the market cost of inputs. Coupons intended for different types of fertilizer were not marked as such, and many coupons allocated for "tobacco fertilizer" may have been used to buy "maize fertilizer" instead. Sales continued into January 2005, and in various areas were limited either by a shortage of fertilizer stock or a shortage of coupons. In the latter case, supplementary coupons were used in some areas, but unavailability of fertilizer in time for it to be agronomically useful meant that

significant numbers of coupons were not used. ADMARC/SFFRFM reported total sales of 131,803 metric tons of subsidized fertilizer (representing 2.62 million coupons).[14]

Malawi's 2005/06 agricultural input subsidy program is reported to have cost MK 7.2 billion, against a budget of MK 5.1 billion (SOAS et al. 2008). The reported program cost excludes overhead costs for ADMARC and SFFRFM and likely allows for only partial deduction of farmer payments to ADMARC and SFFRFM for coupon redemption: these payments amounted to a total of MK 2.7 billion.

Following the popularity of the 2005/06 program and the perception of its success, the government decided to implement the program in 2006/07 with a number of modifications (table 17.3). These included an increase in the overall amount of maize fertilizers to be subsidized, a standard redemption price of MK 950 per bag for all fertilizer types, improved coupon security (with differentiation by fertilizer type), involvement of the Logistics Unit (a unit largely funded by the U.K. Department for International Development, which had played a major role in the logistics of the nationwide starter pack and targeted input programs from 1998/99 to 2004/05), involvement of several large input supply companies in retail sales of subsidized fertilizer, and use of maize seed vouchers that could be exchanged at a wider range of outlets (including agro-dealers) for different quantities of OPV or hybrid seeds.[15] The seed component, a portion of the Logistic Unit's costs, and an independent

Table 17.3 Principal Changes in Subsidy Program Design and Implementation, 2005/06 to 2008/09

Year	Subsidized inputs	Voucher distribution system	Voucher redemption systems	Other system innovations
2005/06	Maize and tobacco fertilizers, maize seed (OPV)	District allocation by maize areas, distribution through TAs	Only through SFFRFM and ADMARC	None
2006/07	Maize and tobacco fertilizers, maize seed (hybrid and OPV)	District allocation by maize areas, distribution varied, through local government, TAs, VDCs, MoAFS	Fertilizers also through major retailers; flexible maize seed vouchers through wide range of seed retailers	Coupons specific to fertilizer type; fertilizer buy-back system; involvement of Logistics Unit
2007/08	Maize, tobacco, coffee, and tea fertilizers; maize seed (hybrid and OPV); legume seed (limited); cotton seed and chemicals	District allocation by farm households and areas, distribution through MoAFS and VDCs	Fertilizers also through major retailers; flexible maize and legume seed vouchers through wide range of seed retailers; cotton inputs through ADDs	Reduced copies of coupons; remote EPA premium; fertilizer buy-back system
2008/09	Maize and tobacco fertilizers; maize seed (hybrid and OPV); legume seed, cotton seed, and chemicals; maize storage chemicals	District allocation by farm households and areas; use of farm household register; open meetings for allocation and disbursement led by MoAFS	Fertilizers only through ADMARC and SFFRFM; flexible maize and seed vouchers through wide range of seed retailers; cotton inputs through ADDs	Extra coupon security features and market monitoring; no remote EPA premium; ADMARC computers for voucher processing

Sources: Logistics Unit; Nakhumwa (2006); SOAS et al. (2008); MoAFS (2008); key informants; Dorward and Chirwa (2009a); MoAFS Implementation guidelines; NSO (2008).
Note: EPA = Extension Planning Area.

program evaluation were funded by donors, who had not directly financed any part of the 2005/06 program (other than through budget support). Donors also funded a buyback scheme, which reduced the risks to government of holding unsold stocks at the end of the year if private sales led to lower-than-expected sales by ADMARC and SFFRFM.

Planned and achieved subsidy sales and costs in 2006/07 (and other years) are shown in table 17.2. Supplementary fertilizer voucher issues and the availability of fertilizer for sales by private companies (which sold just under 30 percent of subsidized sales) together led to higher sales volumes than budgeted. These, together with higher prices than budgeted, led to significant budget overruns. These problems were not faced in seed sales, where no extra coupons were issued.

Growing experience with the program led to consolidation in 2007/08 of many of the changes made in 2006/07, together with further changes to extend the scope of the program. Program objectives and beneficiary targeting criteria were amended to give greater emphasis to concerns for vulnerable households. Targeted quantities of subsidized maize fertilizer and seed were again increased, to roughly equal disbursements to the previous year. Changes were made to coupon allocation systems between districts to provide greater weight to the number of farming households (and less weight to crop areas), leading to an increasing proportion of coupons allocated to the more densely populated southern region, where levels of poverty and poverty incidence are greatest.

Following problems in some areas in 2006/07, systems for allocating and distributing coupons within districts were also modified in 2007/08 to give less power to TAs and more responsibility to MoAFS staff. In addition to the maize seed vouchers provided with maize fertilizer coupons, extra "flexible vouchers" allowed farmers to choose maize or legume seeds (although legume seed supplies were very limited). A "remote area premium" was also introduced to provide incentives to private retailers to extend their networks into areas with low coverage by private retailers; a premium was provided on the subsidy paid to private sector retailers for sales of subsidized fertilizers against identifiable vouchers issued to beneficiaries in designated "remote areas" with higher transport and distribution costs (with the vouchers identifiable by their location code). Coupons for cotton seed and chemicals were distributed through the MoAFS Divisional Offices (ADDs).

Subsidized fertilizer volumes were again significantly over budget in 2007/08; with higher-than-budgeted input

prices, program costs were 29 percent above the budget, compared with 18 percent the previous year. However, private sector subsidy sales were roughly the same as the previous year (increasing by only 6 percent, from 49,000 metric tons to 52,000 metric tons), whereas parastatal sales increased by approximately 30 percent, from 125,000 to 165,000 metric tons.

A number of further changes were made to the 2008/09 subsidy program. A farm household register compiled the previous year was updated and used to list coupon allocations to individual beneficiaries in open village meetings led by teams involving MoAFS and local government staff. An attempt to print coupons in the government printer was followed by a significant security breach, and vouchers for the central and northern regions were then printed outside the country with extra security features. The flexible maize and legume seed voucher and cotton input systems were continued. Grain pesticides were also subsidized, and some subsidized fertilizers were issued to tea and coffee farmers. Although private retailers were initially involved in the sale of subsidized fertilizers, this practice was discontinued at a very late stage in the season. The program went massively over budget, however, largely as a result of soaring international fertilizer costs, but there was also an approximate 15 percent overrun in quantities of inputs subsidized.

Implementation achievements

Three aspects of Malawi's achievements in implementing its agricultural input subsidies are considered: program scale, innovation and adaptation, and implementation performance.

PROGRAM SCALE. Malawi's agricultural input subsidy program has grown each year since its creation and involves complex and very significant logistical and organizational challenges to tight deadlines. The major tasks of the program are shown in figure 17.3. This summary is highly simplified, however, and in practice a complex set of interactions between various stakeholders is needed to complete each task. In 2008/09 this process involved the selection of more than 1.5 million fertilizer coupon beneficiaries from more than 2.5 million farm households, printing and distribution of 5.9 million coupons, and purchase and distribution of more than 3.4 million bags of fertilizer—all within tight deadlines. Further challenges arise because farmers served by the program are widely dispersed across the country (with a significant number being illiterate or semiliterate and living in remote and poorly accessible areas), and

Figure 17.3   Major Tasks in Implementing Malawi's Agricultural Input Subsidy Program

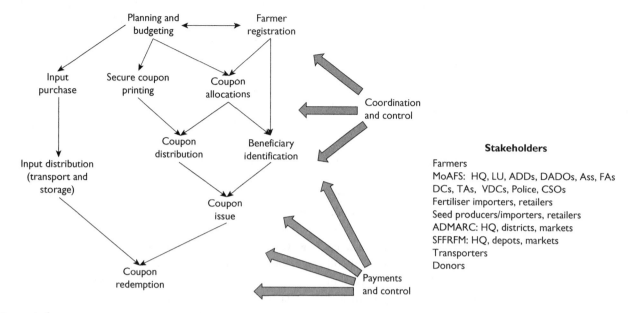

Source: Authors.

because there is a constant threat of fraud or theft of program commodities worth a total of approximately $220 million, with each fertilizer coupon worth more than 10 percent of annual household income for the more than 40 percent of the population below the poverty line.

The implementation challenges should not be underestimated, and it is significant that Malawi has been implementing such activities at varying scales annually since the inception of the starter pack program in 1998 (see below) and has therefore built up both systems and considerable expertise in these tasks.

INNOVATION AND ADAPTATION. The 2005/06 subsidy program built on Malawi's innovative experience in implementing the starter pack and targeted input programs (TIP). These programs involved large-scale registration and targeting across the country; development of systems using vouchers; coordination across different government, parastatal, private sector, donor, and community stakeholders; and substantial logistical challenges. The 2005/06 subsidy program, however, involved a change in objectives (from an emphasis on social protection and food security for vulnerable households in the TIP to national food production and self-sufficiency), an increase in the scale of subsidized inputs (from approximately 50,000 metric tons of fertilizer in 2004/05 to 130,000 in 2005/06), and the addition of tobacco inputs and cash redemption of vouchers.

Following the experience of 2005/06, the government has, with other stakeholders, implemented further innovations to improve performance of the program and broaden its impact. These changes emerged from formal and informal management and evaluation reviews and lesson learning within the government (formal internal evaluations were conducted in 2006/07 and 2007/08); from discussions with other stakeholders (donors, private sector fertilizer importers, seed and fertilizer suppliers, a parliamentary committee on agriculture, and civil society); from external evaluations (commissioned by CISANet for 2005/06 and by the government, DFID, and USAID for 2006/07 and by the government and DFID for 2008/09); and shifts in policy within a changing economic and political environment.

The major program modifications in 2006/07, 2007/08, and 2008/09, summarized in table 17.3, concerned:

■ the extent and modalities of private sector involvement in fertilizer imports, fertilizer sales, and seed sales, with a buy-back scheme to reduce government stockholding risks, a premium to stimulate private retail network development in more remote areas in 2007/08, and exclusion of the private sector from fertilizer sales in 2008/09;

■ recognition of the importance of including vulnerable households among targeted beneficiaries, with an increasing volume of inputs for maize production and modified district/EPA allocation systems;

- trialing of flexible vouchers for seed inputs and addition of cotton inputs and grain storage pesticides;
- introduction of beneficiary registration and more open and more tightly managed beneficiary selection, voucher distribution, and market monitoring systems;
- coupon design, printing, security, and farmer redemption prices; and
- sharing of the costs of some program components with donors.

IMPLEMENTATION PERFORMANCE. Effectiveness and efficiency of implementation can be assessed in terms of volume of subsidized inputs disbursed, timing of subsidy sales and supplier payments, targeted beneficiary access to inputs, and cost. As shown in table 17.2, both planned and disbursed volumes of subsidized inputs increased steadily between 2005/06 and 2008/09. Although fertilizer disbursement and sales targets were not met in 2005/06, they were exceeded in 2006/07, 2007/08, and 2008/09 by 16 percent, 27 percent, and 19 percent, respectively. Exceeding these targets demonstrates considerable success in meeting demand, but also suggests difficulties in controlling disbursement and cost overruns.

Timing of subsidy sales is determined by the timing of availability of inputs in markets and the issue of vouchers to beneficiaries. Timing is critical for the effective use of seed and fertilizer at the start of the agricultural season. For fertilizer, the timing of input availability depends upon timing of tendering of input purchases and supplier deliveries to depots, the staffing and stocking of input markets (for parastatal sales), and subsidy redemption contracts with retailers and their stocking and staffing of input sales points for private sector sales. The timing of voucher issue depends on the timing of beneficiary registration, voucher allocations, voucher printing, voucher distribution to districts, and district distribution payments. Information on some of these variables is given in table 17.4. In general, performance regarding earlier award of seed and fertilizer contracts and earlier fertilizer deliveries to depots and uplifts has improved over time. Information on the timing of fertilizer sales is incomplete, but it appears that despite some evidence of improvement between 2005/06 and 2006/07 (not shown in table 17.4), there has been little improvement since then. It is particularly important to increase sales by the end of November. These sales were highest in 2008/09 but still only 30 percent of the total. Receipt of seed vouchers by the Logistics Unit is determined by the timing of sales and the speed of voucher processing by seed suppliers; both were problematic in 2007/08.

Targeted beneficiary access to inputs is determined by coupon allocation and issue and by the use of coupons, which may be affected by the availability of subsidy inputs in accessible markets and by any "tip" needed to redeem coupons. Household surveys provide the only systematic information available on these areas. Results from focus group discussions and household surveys examining the 2006/07 and 2008/09 programs (SOAS et al. 2008; Dorward, Chirwa, and Slater 2010a) suggest the following:

- In 2008/09, 65 percent of farm households received one or more fertilizer coupons, with an average of 1.5 coupons per household receiving coupons and of 1.1 coupons per household across all households (figures for 2006/07 were 54 percent, 1.7, and 1.0, respectively);
- Targeting criteria were highly variable across different administrative areas;[16]
- Overall targeting recommendations were followed to some extent in that there was a tendency for targeting to reach households that are productive full-time farmers. However, household survey data for the of 2006/07 and 2008/09 seasons indicate that coupons were disproportionately targeted to households with relatively large amounts of land or other assets, and (in 2006/07 but not in 2008/09) to male-headed households. Smaller proportions of fertilizer coupons were given to households in the bottom half of the wealth and income distribution;
- In some areas, particularly the south and center, coupon allocations were modified so that in 2008/09 just under 40 percent of households in these regions and 36 percent nationally received one fertilizer coupon (rather than fewer households receiving two coupons);
- Open meetings for coupon allocation were introduced in 2008/09 and appear to have succeeded to some extent in increasing the proportion of coupons and subsidized fertilizer going to poorer households (Chirwa, Matita, and Dorward 2010);
- Key informants tended to underestimate the proportion of households receiving subsidized inputs compared with estimates provided in interviews with households;
- In 2006/07, 75 percent of ADMARC and private supplier outlets and 100 percent of SFFRFM outlets were reported to have suffered from frequent major queues; a similar figure of 75 percent was reported across ADMARC and SFFRFM outlets in 2008/09;
- In both 2006/07 and 2008/09, household surveys indicated that 5 percent of coupons were reported to be accessed with some payment, with a median price of MK 1,000 in 2006/07 and of MK 2,000 in 2008/09.

Table 17.4   Implementation Performance Indicators 2006/07–2008/09

Indicator	2006/07		2007/08		2008/09	
Fertilizers						
Tender awards for parastatal supplies	Late August		Mid-August		End-July	
Depot receipts end October (% of parastatal total sales)		32		58		53
Depot receipts, end November (% of parastatal total sales)		77		76		71
Outstanding payments, end Nov (% and MK millions)	28	1,216	22	1,595	16	3,500
Outstanding payments, end Dec (% and MK millions)	46	4,303	13	1,192	13	3,690
Outstanding payments, end Jan (% and MK millions)	14	1,406	21	2,620	—	7,707
Uplifts dispatched as of end November (% of parastatal total sales)		64		70		75
Total relocation transport costs (MK millions)		—		68.4		42.0
Finalization of retail fertilizer contracts	Early Nov		Mid/late Nov		—	
District voucher allocations	Early Sept		Oct 9		Sept 12	
Voucher printing	End Sept		End Oct		SR early Oct	CR/NR early Nov
Voucher and list distribution to districts completed	Nov 7		Nov 3		Nov18	
Sales end Nov (% of total season sales)		8		—		30
Sales end Dec (% of total season sales		74		—		68
SFFRFM/ADMARC voucher returns end Dec (thousands)		0		101		175
SFFRFM/ADMARC voucher returns end Jan (thousands)		111		720		1,057
Finalization of seed supply contracts	Mid/late Nov			Mid/late Nov	Early Nov	
Seed coupons in LU end Dec (% of season sales)		27		4		6
Seed coupons in LU end Jan (% of season sales)		74		18		22

Sources: Logistics Unit reports; Nakhumwa (2006); SOAS et al. (2008); MoAFS (2008); key informants.

Note: Data are not available for 2005/06. LU = Logistics Unit. — = not available.

- In 2006/07 a "tip" was paid to retail market staff for redemption of about 20 percent of fertilizer coupons, with a mean price per bag of just over MK 1,000 (compared with the official price of MK 950) and with no significant overall differences between parastatal and private sector suppliers. In 2008/09, 14 percent of fertilizer coupons were reported to require a "tip" for redemption, with a median "tip" of 200 MK, again giving a price of MK 1,000 per bag.

There are considerable difficulties in determining the extent to which fraud affects Malawi's agricultural input subsidy program. Fraud can arise in a number of ways—through allocation of vouchers to nonexistent beneficiaries (and their diversion to government staff, traditional leaders, or politicians), direct allocation of vouchers to people who do not satisfy beneficiary criteria, printing of extra or counterfeit vouchers, and payment of "tips."

Determining the extent of the fraud is rendered difficult by the lack of formal and transparent audit systems covering the whole program and by discrepancies between MoAFS and NSO estimates of the total number of farm households in Malawi (MoAFS estimates of farm households were 33 percent above NSO estimates in 2006/07 and 47 percent above NSO estimates in 2008/09). SOAS et al. (2008) concluded that there is insufficient evidence to suggest widespread fraud, and that household survey estimates of subsidized fertilizer access were broadly compatible with the MoAFS farm household estimates, but there are numerous anecdotal reports of fraud within the system. Although Dorward, Chirwa, and Slater (2010b) suggest that NSO may well underestimate the number of farm households in Malawi, it seems unlikely that underestimate could be off by a third, and there are risks (and anecdotal reports) of increasing numbers of villages and of some "ghost villages," suggesting significant diversion of subsidized inputs away from the intended beneficiaries. The discrepancy between NSO and MoAFS estimates of the number of farm families is being jointly examined by the NSO and MoAFS to resolve this issue.

Regarding the extent to which counterfeit or nonstandard vouchers (those with serial numbers outside the ranges recorded by the Logistics Unit) have been accepted by different outlets, records for 2007/08 show that these (and sales without vouchers) accounted for 27 percent of ADMARC/SFFRFM sales and 3 percent of private retailer sales (LU 2009). Rapid return of vouchers to the Logistics Unit is important for early identification of markets accepting counterfeit or nonstandard vouchers. Private retailers generally return coupons quickly in order to receive payment, but ADMARC and SFFRFM have been much slower at this task although their voucher returns have improved over the three years for which records are available (see table 17.4). A major security breach in the printing of vouchers in 2008/09 led to reprinting of more secure vouchers for issue in two regions.

Overall, the costs of Malawi's subsidy program were over budget and increasing from 2005/6 to 2008/9 (table 17.5), due to a combination of increasing subsidy volumes and large increases in fertilizer prices. Program costs were just over 40 percent above the budget for 2005/06 and 2006/07, nearly 50 percent over budget in 2007/08, and 90 percent

over budget in 2008/09. Program costs rose from just over 60 percent of the MoAFS budget in 2006/07 and 2007/08, rising to 74 percent in 2008/09, when the program accounted for over 15 percent of the total national budget. It is, however, important to note that for the 2009/10 program, actual costs were 21 percent below budget and costs fell back sharply, by 41 percent, because of both a halving of fertilizer prices and a 20 percent reduction in the amount of fertilizer disbursed, which was almost exactly on budget. As a result program costs fell back to 7 percent of the total national budget.

Data on estimated per unit fertilizer costs and on total program costs, excluding ADMARC overhead costs, are also given in table 17.5. As shown in the table, fertilizer prices and transport costs rose from 2005/06 to 2008/09. The estimated per unit fertilizer cost increases from 2005/06 to 2006/07 in Malawi (25 percent) are higher than would be expected given that international prices were static over the same period, but from 2006/07 to 2007/08 the price increase (22 percent) was markedly lower than the increase in international prices, which rose by around 50 percent or more, so the overall cost increase in Malawi over 2005/06 to 2007/08 was in line with international price increases. Fertilizer cost increases from 2007/08 to 2008/09 also appear to have been roughly in line with increases in international price increases over the same period (about 125 percent).

Table 17.5 Fertilizer and Program Costs in Malawi 2005/06–2009/10

| | 2005/06 | | 2006/07 | | 2007/08 | | 2008/09 | | 2009/10 |
	Planned	Actual	Planned	Actual	Planned	Actual	Planned	Actual	Actual
Fertilizer cost ($/mt):									
Parastatal: delivered at depots	—	—	—	454	—	555[a]	—	1,204[b]	575
Parastatal: transport, etc.	—	—	—	36	—	45	—	46	39
Parastatal: total	—	393	—	490	—	600	—	1,250	614
Private retailers: total	—	...	—	490	—	612	—	...	...
Average all suppliers	—	393	—	490	—	590	—	1,250	614
Program costs:									
Malawi government	36.4	51.4	51.4	81.4	73.6	109.6	127	227.7	137.6
Donors ($ millions)	0	0	12.5	9.5	5.7	7.1	12.1	37.8	17.5
Total ($ millions)	36.4	51.4	63.9	90.9	79.3	116.8	139.1	265.4	155.1
Net of farmer payments	—	32	—	73.9	—	95.4	—	242.3	143.7
Total as % MoAFS budget	—	—	43	61	51	61	61	74	—
Total as % national budget	4.3	5.6	5.4	8.4	6.7	8.9	8.5	16.2	6.7
Total as % of GDP	—	2.1		3.1	—	3.4	—	6.6	—

Sources: Logistics Unit; Nakhumwa (2006); SOAS et al. (2008); MoAFS (2008); Dorward and Chirwa (2009a); Government of Malawi budget statistics; key informants.

Note: The 2005/06 fertilizer costs may also include some seed and coupon production/distribution costs. Parastatal transport etc., costs exclude ADMARC overheads. Program costs exclude buy-back carried forward. — = not available. ... = not applicable.

a. Excluding costs of buy-back brought forward.

b. Including costs of buy-back brought forward.

CHAPTER 17: MALAWI'S AGRICULTURAL INPUT SUBSIDY PROGRAM EXPERIENCE OVER 2005–09

Marked monthly variation in international fuel prices from mid- to late 2006 and 2007 makes it difficult to calculate equivalent figures for transport costs.

Aside from the problems of high fertilizer prices in 2008/09, the 2006/07 to 2008/09 programs faced major challenges in controlling the volume of subsidized fertilizer disbursed. Three alternative (and complementary) approaches to limiting the volume may be used: controlling the number of coupons issued, controlling the physical stock of fertilizer available, and controlling sales of fertilizer by closing further sales once the total budget quantity has been sold. In principle, the first option is the best approach, although it is undermined by counterfeit coupons and by any high-level political pressure that may demand extra coupon issues. Control of physical stock of fertilizer (the method used in 2009/10) is difficult if the private sector is involved in retail subsidy, and may result in genuine beneficiaries being denied the opportunity to redeem genuine coupons. Closure of the program once target sales have been achieved suffers from the latter disadvantage, and in addition requires timely reporting and monitoring of sales.

The rising costs of the subsidy program over the period were met by increasing budgetary allocations to the MoAFS, and did not crowd out other MoAFS activities in terms of actually cutting budgetary allocations to them. However, the opportunity cost of the program is an issue in terms of forgone investments that could have been achieved with those funds. The program also consumes very large amounts of staff time and other resources, for people must be diverted from other activities to manage and implement the subsidy program in the critical time before and at the start of the cropping season. Similarly, while financial resources allocated to the subsidy program have grown dramatically since the start of the program, financial resources allocated to other activities have remained largely static or shown only small increases, posing severe challenges to other essential research and extension activities of the Ministry.

Input supply impacts

Malawi's subsidy program has had major, and mixed, impacts on private sector input suppliers. These effects have to be considered separately for fertilizer importers, fertilizer retailers, seed suppliers, and seed retailers. For retailers of seed and fertilizer, it is important to distinguish between small independent agro-dealers on one hand and retail outlets of larger companies involved in importation and both wholesale and retail sales on the other.

Fertilizer importers have been responsible for generally increasing proportions and volumes of government subsidy sales, with particularly large volumes in 2008/09 (table 17.6). Importers have clearly benefited from their growing share in imports, although they have faced some difficulties from exposure to foreign exchange losses caused by delays in payments in local currency. Insofar as currency risks are factored into tender margins, these raise fertilizer costs for government. Some importers have expressed concerns about increasing competition in import tenders from new players without proper qualification criteria, leading to the award of some tenders to suppliers who are unable to deliver. If the award of such tenders leads to late cancellation and reordering at short notice, they may also raise fertilizer costs for the government.

Maize seed suppliers have also benefited from significant growth in sales over the life of the program (see table 17.2). Government and the seed suppliers association negotiate prices, which involves a difficult balance between competition and coordination in supply. The subsidy program affects retail sales through three processes, each of which has a different effect on whether retail outlets sell subsidized inputs. These are set out in table 17.7.

Displacement of commercial sales occurs when a farmer chooses not to buy an input received on subsidy when he or she would have bought it commercially if the subsidy had not been available. This affects private retail outlets irrespective of their participation as subsidy retailers. Displacement is difficult to estimate because even without subsidies, farmers' commercial purchases change from year to year with changes in input prices, output prices, and their access to seasonal finance. Input suppliers appear to be very concerned about losses of fertilizer sales through displacement if these are not counteracted by gains in subsidized sales and customers from participation in the subsidy scheme. Displacement rates have been estimated from examination of changes in aggregate sales (SOAS et al. 2008)

Table 17.6 Private Sector Involvement in Subsidized Fertilizer Sales

Private sector involvement	2005/06	2006/07	2007/08	2008/09
Subsidized tender deliveries (mt)	70,000	99,386	97,845	162,840
Subsidized tender deliveries (%)	48	72	71	88
Retail sales (%)	0	28	24	0

Source: Logistics Unit; SOAS et al. 2008; Dorward and Chirwa 2009a.

Table 17.7 Impacts of Subsidy Program on Seed and Fertilizer Private Retail Outlets

Processes by which the subsidy program affects retail sales	Participating retail outlets	Excluded retail outlets
Displacement of commercial sales by subsidy sales	Loss of sales	Loss of sales
Sales of subsidized inputs	Gain in sales	No effect
Gain/loss of customers going to outlets to redeem their subsidy vouchers	Gain in sales	Loss of sales
General increases in demand as a result of program-induced growth and income/cash gains in previous season	Gain in sales	Gain in sales
Private fertilizer retailers	Retail chains in 2006/07 and 2007/08	Agro-dealers in all years, retail chains in 2005/06 and 2008/09
Private seeds retailers	Agro-dealers and retail chains from 2006/07 to 2008/09	Agro-dealers and retail chains in 2005/06 only

Source: Authors.

and from panel data analysis of farmer purchases (Ricker-Gilbert, Jayne, and Chirwa 2011).

Displacement estimates from examination of changes in aggregate sales were 20–30 percent in 2005/06 and 30–40 percent in 2006/07, with displacement for tobacco fertilizers higher than that for maize fertilizers (SOAS et al. 2008). Displacement estimated from panel data analysis of farmer purchases was 23 percent for 2006/07 (Ricker-Gilbert, Jayne, and Chirwa 2011) and 3 percent for 2008/09 (Ricker-Gilbert and Jayne 2010), but in all years some further displacement may be expected if some subsidized fertilizers are not received by smallholders. Estimating displacement from aggregate fertilizer sales for 2007/08 and 2008/09 has not been possible due to lack of data on aggregate commercial sales. Table 17.8 shows incremental fertilizer use estimates for 2005/06 and 2006/07 and predictions for 2007/08 and 2008/09, assuming similar implementation in these years.[17] Displacement of maize seed sales appears to be much lower, with strong growth in commercial seed sales in 2006/07.

As table 17.7 shows, however, overall impacts of the subsidy program on input sales depend not only on displacement effects but also on the impact of participation or exclusion in the program on subsidy sales and on customers visiting the outlet. The last two lines of the table identify the status of agro-dealers and retail outlets for larger companies with regard to subsidized fertilizer and seed sales. Notably, both reported a significant increase in sales in 2006/07 when they were able to participate in subsidized seed sales and in subsidized fertilizer sales (only retail outlets for larger companies) (Kelly, Boughton, and Lenski 2010). Conversely, the exclusion of the private sector from all retail subsidy sales in 2005/06 led to a substantial drop in reported fertilizer sales from all retail outlets. Sales recovered in 2006/07 and

2007/08 for the larger importers with retail outlets with their inclusion in retail subsidy sales, but they again reported declines in retail outlet fertilizer sales when they were excluded from the program in 2008/09 (Kelly, Boughton, and Lenski 2010). Small agro-dealers had been excluded from retail sales of fertilizer subsidies during all four seasons of the program.

Maize market impacts

The input subsidy program may affect maize markets in a number of ways. We identify four potential impacts:

- Direct impact through increased supply of maize for sale and reduced demand for purchases by net surplus and deficit farmers;
- Indirect impacts as a result of policy changes influenced by the subsidy;
- In the longer term, if the subsidy program leads to rising incomes, demand for maize should increase as a result of consumption by both humans and livestock;
- Finally, if the net effect of these impacts is to lower (or raise) maize prices, then a supply response to increase (or reduce) resources allocated to maize production should be expected.

These impacts arise in the context of wider changes in production (as a result of seasonal weather), in policies, in regional and national maize markets, and in urban and rural incomes (as a result of other processes of livelihood change and growth). Although data and analytical limitations make it difficult to tease out these different influences, Malawi does have good information on maize prices. As

Indicator		2005/06	2006/07	2007/08	2008/09
Incremental fertilizer sales as % of subsidy sales		70–80	60–70	60–70	90
Incremental fertilizer use (mt)		98,541	113,547	140,760	181,800
Incremental seed use (mt)	OPV	3,000	1,764	2,604	833
	Hybrid	0	2,760	2,937	4,532
Yield response as % of 2008/09 estimate		80	100	70	100
Subsidy program incremental maize production estimates (mt)	Medium estimate	406,348	647,474	566,235	968,900
	Above 2002/03 and 2003/04	273,609	514,735	433,496	836,161
	High estimate: +20 percent	487,618	776,969	679,482	1,162,800
	Above 2002/03 and 2003/04	328,332	617,683	520,196	1,003,514
	Low estimate: –20 percent	325,078	517,979	452,988	775,200
	Above 2002/03 and 2003/04	218,887	411,788	346,797	669,009
National crop production estimates	Increment above 2002/03 and 2003/04 (mt)	975,262	1,698,956	1,031,938	2,031,816
Net maize exports in following year (exports minus imports, mt)		–78,491	224,972	–101,027	–50,398

Source: Incremental fertilizer and seed sales figures are from Dorward and Chirwa (2009a). Figures for yield response and incremental seed impact for 2008/09 are from Dorward and Chirwa (2010). National crop estimates are from MoAFS. Net maize exports are from Jayne et al. (2010).
Note: Production seasons 2002/03 and 2003/04 are considered nondrought years for presubsidy comparisons, although targeted input subsidies of 35,000 and 22,000 metric tons of fertilizer were provided in these years, and a 10 percent displacement is assumed for these years. OPV sales for 2005/06 are estimated to be 50 percent of budgeted sales.

noted earlier, prices have varied widely in the past, and, as shown in figure 17.4, variability has continued in the period of subsidy implementation—indeed, maize prices reached historic highs in early 2009.

High maize prices would not be expected given the large maize production estimates in each subsidy year—rather, low prices would be expected.[18] Low prices were observed in the 2006/07 marketing season (following the 2005/06 subsidy) and initially in 2007/08 (following the 2006/07 subsidy). In the latter year, however, prices rose toward the end of the season, so that the maximum monthly price within the year was high, although substantially larger estimated production as compared with the previous year should have led to lower prices. Prices following the 2007/08 subsidy were even higher, with average annual prices exceeding those of the 2001/02 and 2005/06 famine years,[19] but these high prices did not lead to any reports of widespread suffering and distress such as those experienced in previous years with equivalent prices. Prices in the first half of the 2009/10 season (following the 2008/09 subsidy) were considerably lower than in the previous year, although the estimated production was still very high by historical standards (figure 17.5).

A number of explanations for this pattern of prices and estimated production may be put forward:

- In 2007/08, roughly 330,000 metric tons of maize were exported. In 2009/10, 130,000 tons were purchased by government for the strategic grain reserve (SGR), and a further 100,000 tons are estimated to have been bought and held in storage by private traders (FEWSNet 2009).

Exports and purchases of stocks to carry over to the following season would reduce maize volumes (this would not be the case for 2009/10 SGR and other stock purchases subsequently sold later in the 2009/10 season). The effect of this on figure 17.5 would be to shift the 2006/07 and 2008/09 subsidy figures to the left by around 300,000 and 100,000 metric tons, respectively.[20] This does not, however, bring the three later subsidy years anywhere near the pattern of the 1993/94, 1995/96 to 2004/05, and 2006/07 seasons. Indeed, there were reports of maize imports of roughly 50,000 tons from Mozambique and 36,000 tons from South Africa during the 2008/09 season (FEWSNet 2009; South African Revenue Service 2009).

- Rising real incomes alongside falling poverty rates and rising population may lead to rising national demand, which would cause the 1995/96 to 2004/05 demand to increase over time—but not as suddenly and dramatically as shown in figure 17.5. Such a trend is compatible with the lack of distress in later years despite high prices.

- Storage losses may be rising as a result of increasing production of hybrid maize promoted by the 2006/07 and subsequent subsidy programs. However, 2009 household survey results suggest that storage losses are not particularly high, with 50 percent of respondents reporting no losses in the 2007/08 and 2008/09 storage years and only a little over 20 percent reporting high losses (Dorward and Chirwa 2009b). Mangisoni (2010) also reports relatively low storage losses, in the range of 12 percent over a 10-month period.

Figure 17.4 Mean Annual Maize Price in Malawi, by Marketing Season

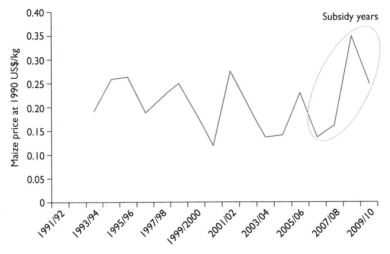

Source: MoAFS.
Note: Maize prices are simple averages across all markets obtained from weekly surveys, all deflated to 1990 prices.

Figure 17.5 Peak Monthly Maize Prices in Malawi by Estimated Maize Supply per Capita, by Season

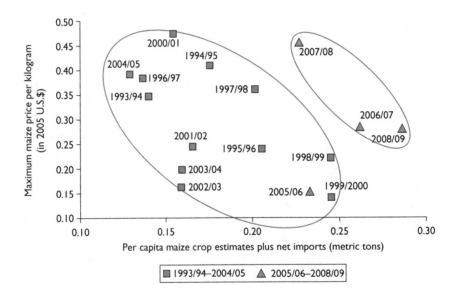

Source: Calculated from MoAFS annual crop production estimates and weekly maize price data with export-import data from Jayne et al. 2010, Minot 2009, and FAO 2009.
Note: Estimated maize supply = crop estimate plus exports – imports. Labels show production season.

- Higher welfare and real incomes following the 2005/06 harvest and low maize prices led to greater retention and consumption of the 2006/07 harvest and hence a thinner and tighter market.
- Changes in informal cross-border flows could also have occurred (Jayne et al. 2010).

- Finally, national maize production following the implementation of the subsidy program could have been over-estimated. Although there are no clear changes in methodology in the last few years, the method appears to rely substantially on field workers' subjective estimates of crop area and yield, which may be affected by the very substantial involvement of field workers in the subsidy program. Production impacts of the subsidy program are discussed in more detail below.

None of these explanations (except possibly the last) can fully explain the high prices despite the high estimated production following the 2006/07, 2007/08, and 2008/09 subsidy programs. To illustrate this, figure 17.5 plots maximum monthly price against estimated per capita net maize supply. From the 1993/94 to 2004/05 production seasons, there was a roughly downward sloping relationship, with high prices following years of low supply and low prices in years following high supply (although the 2002/03 and 2003/04 seasons do not fit this relationship). Prices following the first (2005/06) subsidy fit this pattern. The three subsequent seasons, however, when prices were high despite high estimates of production, do not fit this pattern.

Two clear and important conclusions emerge from this analysis. First, in three out of four years, the subsidy program did not lead to lower market prices for maize. Second, the subsidy program has not led to increases in maize supply as large as those suggested by increases in maize crop estimates from 2006/07 onward, particularly in 2007/08 and 2008/09, when prices appeared to be very high compared with estimated supplies. We therefore consider estimates of the subsidy programs impacts on production.

Production impacts

The major stated objectives of Malawi's subsidy program have been to achieve food self-sufficiency and to increase the incomes of resource-poor households through increased food and cash crop production. Increased production is therefore critical to achievement of program objectives. This results from incremental use of inputs (mainly fertilizers and seeds) leading to increased yields, with yield responses to these inputs dependent upon the weather and the efficiency of input use and of crop production. Estimated incremental fertilizer sales were discussed earlier in terms of the effects of displacement on input supply markets. Incremental fertilizer sales are also important for estimating the incremental production effects of the program, with responses to fertilizer depending upon rainfall, crop variety, and management (including timing of planting, weeding, and timing and methods of fertilizer application), and soil fertility.

SOAS et al. (2008) and Dorward and Chirwa (2009a) calculate estimated incremental production for 2005/06 to 2007/08 using a range of 12 to 18 kilograms of grain per

kilogram of nitrogen. Results from crop-cutting survey estimates in the 2008/09 crop year demonstrate that substantial problems in obtaining precise estimates of crop responses[21] make it difficult to obtain precise estimates of incremental production from the subsidy program. They do, however, support the broad response of 12 to 18 kilograms of grain per kilogram of fertilizer, with 15 kilograms per hectare a reasonable "medium expectation." Using different estimates of incremental fertilizer use and of yield responses gives different estimates of incremental production as a result of the input subsidy program. Table 17.8 sets out such estimates by year of implementation.

For each year estimated, incremental fertilizer use is multiplied by a grain-to-nitrogen response ratio adjusted to reflect differing conditions in subsidy implementation between years (good weather but very little hybrid seed in 2005/06 compared with 2008/09; similar conditions in 2006/07 but a bit less hybrid seed; late fertilizer delivery in the southern region and only slightly more hybrid seed in 2007/08). This is added to a yield gain from subsidized hybrid seed separate from fertilizer to arrive at an estimate of total incremental maize production from the subsidy.[22] High and low estimates are, respectively, 20 percent above and below the 2008/09 medium estimate (which averaged 15 kilograms of grain per kilogram of fertilizer across hybrid and local seed plots).

While the estimates in table 17.8 are necessarily approximate, indeed indicative, as noted above, they nevertheless demonstrate several important points:

■ Incremental production is very sensitive to yield responses to inputs (hybrid seed and fertilizers) and the potential is therefore considerable for raising yields and yield responses with good subsidy program and crop management—with early subsidy sales, planting and fertilizer application, high plant populations, and greater use of organic matter, for example.

■ Not explicitly shown in table 17.8 is the importance of hybrid seed in raising yield responses to fertilizer. Increasing hybrid seed sales (subsidized or unsubsidized) is therefore another potential way of increasing subsidy impacts on incremental production.[23]

■ Incremental production estimates are considerable, and they grow over the life of the program as a result of the increasing volume of incremental fertilizer use and increasing supply of hybrid seed.

■ Incremental production estimates are, however, considerably less than the production increases estimated in the national crop estimates for maize production since the start of the subsidy program, and these differences are too large to be explained by upward revision of the yield response to fertilizer.[24]

- Differences in production between presubsidy and subsidy years as estimated above are more compatible with price differences between these years as shown in figure 17.5 (for example the export of 330,000 metric tons following the 2006/07 harvest would more than cancel out the increased subsidy impact that year, compared with 2005/06). The very high prices in 2007/08 remain a puzzle but may be explained by the subsidy program's incremental production being insufficient to counteract production losses from adverse conditions affecting all maize in some parts of the country (late subsidized input delivery and local events such as flooding and drought spells).

Macroeconomic impacts

The large size of Malawi's subsidy program could be expected to have macroeconomic impacts. As a proportion of total government expenditure, the subsidy increased from 5.6 percent in 2005/06 to 8.4 percent in 2006/07 to 8.9 percent in 2007/08. With very large increases in fertilizer prices and costs for 2008/09, actual expenditure on the subsidy rose to 16.2 percent of total government expenditure (see table 17.5). As a proportion of gross domestic product (GDP), subsidy program costs rose from 2.1 percent in 2005/06 to 3.4 percent in 2007/08 and to 6.6 percent in 2008/09 (excluding remittance by ADMARC and SFFRFM of the farmer's redemption price to government). (As noted earlier and shown in table 17.5, program costs have subsequently fallen back markedly.)

On the positive side, estimates of GDP growth have been significantly affected by large increases in estimated maize production since the implementation of the subsidy program. Estimates of incremental production attributable to the subsidy program are not as high but are nevertheless very large, and incremental maize production and increases in land and labor productivity in maize production attributable to the program should have had a significant positive impact on GDP growth.

No evidence of negative macroeconomic impacts was found in the subsidy's first two years (SOAS et al. 2008). Important contributors to GDP were sound macroeconomic management; improving macroeconomic indicators including growth, inflation, and government deficit (table 17.9); and increased growth across the economy at that time; and the subsidy program itself was a contributor to that growth (good tobacco prices, good weather for agricultural

Table 17.9 Trends in Macroeconomic Performance Indicators, 2005–09 (*percent*)

Indicator	2005	2006	2007	2008	2009
Real GDP growth	3.3	6.7	8.6	9.7	6.9
Inflation	15.4	13.9	8.0	8.7	10.1
Deficit/GDP ratio (budget)	2.6	1.5	1.8	1.9	3.7
Deficit/GDP ratio (actual)	0.4	1.4	4.0	6.3	8.0

Source: Reserve Bank of Malawi 2010.

production, and improved macroeconomic management and conditions were other important contributors). Improved macroeconomic management, together with budgetary support from donors, was also undoubtedly important in enabling the government to finance such a large program.

The situation was, changing, however, as increasing volumes and increasing prices in subsequent years led to very high cost overruns. At the same time, Malawi's economy was facing a number of internal and external pressures that led to adverse changes in macroeconomic indicators. The subsidy program both contributed to and was affected by these macroeconomic changes, this time adversely (other macroeconomic pressures were very high government expenditure and import costs for the subsidy program with high fuel costs, high maize prices, other government expenditures, and lower tobacco prices), although the incremental maize production from the subsidy program should have exerted a downward influence on maize prices. In a fixed exchange rate environment, these pressures contributed to a foreign exchange crisis in Malawi in November and December 2009.

Very high budgetary and foreign exchange allocations to the subsidy program also reduced funding available to activities such as health, education, and infrastructure development. It is clear that the 2008/9 level of spending on the program was not sustainable, and as noted earlier the government is addressing this: although the very high fertilizer prices in the 2008/09 season were a temporary phenomenon, the government has committed itself to controlling costs by limiting the volume of subsidized fertilizers in future years. It has also restricted the subsidy to inputs for the production of only maize.

Economic returns

Economic returns to Malawi's subsidy program depend upon the economic price of maize, the price of inputs, and production responses to increased input use. Producer benefit-cost ratios estimated for the 2006/07 program showed that the net economic return to the project is very sensitive to maize prices and the production response, and, with reasonable variation in assumptions, these ratios range from 0.81 to 1.30, with a mid estimate of 1.06 (table 17.10). Adjustments to this analysis using estimated maize and fertilizer prices for other program years suggest that both the 2005/06 and 2007/08 programs should have yielded equivalent or higher returns. However, the very high fertilizer prices that prevailed when fertilizers were being purchased for the 2008/09 program adversely affected returns in 2008/09, despite good weather and yields and high maize prices (although these did offset the effects of high fertilizer prices to some extent).

Fiscal efficiency estimates (net economic benefit per unit of fiscal investment) show a similar pattern to economic returns, but in addition these are (negatively) affected by high rates of displacement of unsubsidized sales by subsidized sales (displacement lowers the net benefit of subsidized sales). Key conclusions from the benefit-to-cost and fiscal efficiency analyses are that economic returns are highly sensitive to the yield response to fertilizer (as discussed earlier under production impacts); fiscal returns are highly sensitive to displacement rates; and with good program implementation and good (but achievable) yield responses to fertilizer, the program can be a very good investment. It is therefore critical that the program design and implementation deliver low displacement and high responses to inputs.

Growth and poverty reduction impacts

While the producer benefit-cost and fiscal efficiency analyses can yield valuable information about the efficiency of the subsidy program, they can be misleading when examining the contributions of the program to poverty reduction, economic growth, and food security. Understanding the full economic benefits of the program requires consideration of the direct effects of the program on subsidy recipients and of the different ways that these effects subsequently work through their own and others' livelihoods and the rural economy. Because the program is large, it is very important for the wider market effects of the intervention to be properly recognized.

Figure 17.6 shows three possible uses of the subsidy by subsidy recipients: reselling of coupons or of subsidized inputs, incremental use of the inputs in production, or use of the inputs with displacement of purchase of unsubsidized inputs. These should lead to two main types of direct benefit for recipients: immediate income transfers (from reselling of coupons or subsidized inputs or from reduced expenditure on inputs as a result of displacement of unsubsidized purchases by cheaper, subsidized purchases), or incremental production at harvest if the inputs are used on farm. If poorer households sell their coupon(s), then immediate income and welfare gains should also be accompanied by an easing of short-term seasonal cash constraints. This easing may reduce the extent to which they have to hire out their own labor (as casual *ganyu* labor) to obtain food, thus allowing them to work more on their own farms, both increasing end-of-season yields and reducing the supply of labor into the local labor market. At the same time, if less poor households obtain cheaper inputs directly from the program or buy those inputs from subsidy recipients, then this increase in income should increase their demand for hired-on farm labor or for local goods and services. The result should be a tightening of both demand and supply in the local labor market, and a consequent rise in wages, to the benefit of poorer households.

Further direct and indirect benefits may also accrue in subsequent seasons. At the end of the season, higher maize production should result from incremental fertilizer use and increased crop labor inputs, increasing households' incomes. Higher production should also depress maize prices. Higher household maize stocks and lower maize prices carried forward into the following season should again benefit poorer households, reducing their seasonal cash flow constraints and their need to hire out their labor, so that they can again work more on their own farms. This will again tighten the labor market. Higher incomes from higher wages should stimulate demand for nonfarm goods and services, with spin-off benefits and multipliers in the local economy.

There is considerable empirical support from Asia and from Africa for the importance of some of these processes and of indirect effects of agricultural growth on wider economic growth. Hazell and Rosegrant (2000) show that the indirect effects of increased agricultural production in the green revolution in Asia were the major process driving pro-poor growth in the second half of the 20th century. There is also a large body of literature on agricultural growth "multipliers" in Africa, with estimates that vary from around 1.5 to over 2.0 (a multiplier of 1.5 indicates that $1.00 of extra income from agricultural production results in further income growth of $0.50) (Hazell and Hojjati 1995; Reardon 1998; Delgado, Hopkins, and Kelly 1998). Studies of countries across Africa and Asia also generally show that consumption

Table 17.10 Estimated Economic Impacts of Subsidy Programs in Malawi

Economic impact	2005/06		2006/07		2007/08		2008/09	
	May–Oct 2006	Nov 2006–Apr 2007	May–Oct 2007	Nov 2007–Apr 2008	May–Oct 2008	Nov 2008–Apr 2009	May–Oct 2009	Nov 2009–Apr 2010
Domestic maize prices ($/mt)	139.5	142.7	119.3	243.8	336.6	434.6	271.4	307.1
Maize price in benefit-cost and fiscal efficiency analysis ($/mt)	143		154		250		280	
Fertilizer price in analysis ($/mt)	393		490		590		1,250	
Benefit-cost ratio, high response	1.38		1.30		1.90		1.08	
Benefit-cost ratio, moderate response	1.12		1.06		1.54		0.90	
Benefit-cost ratio, low response	0.86		0.81		1.18		0.72	
Fiscal efficiency, high response	0.76		0.44		1.13		0.09	
Fiscal efficiency, moderate response	0.24		0.09		0.68		negative	
Fiscal efficiency, low response	negative		negative		0.23		negative	
	2005		2006		2007		2008	
Poverty incidence	50%		45%		40%		40%	
Meals per day	2.0		2.2		2.3		2.3	

Sources: SOAS et al. 2008; Dorward, Chirwa, and Slater 2010b; Food and Nutrition Security Program 2008; NSO 2006, 2009.

Note: The benefit-cost ratio and fiscal efficiencies were calculated with high, medium, and low fertilizer responses of 18, 15, and 12 kilograms of grain per kilogram of fertilizer, respectively. The benefit-cost ratio is calculated as the gross incremental benefits divided by the gross incremental cost, valued at social prices. Fiscal efficiency is calculated as the net economic benefit divided by fiscal cost.

Figure 17.6 Tracing Direct and Indirect Subsidy Impacts

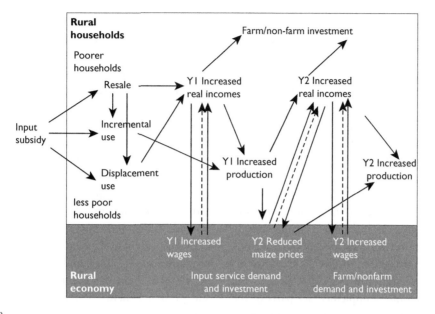

Source: SOAS et al 2008.
Note: Solid lines indicate positive impacts for poorer, food-deficit producers and sellers of labor; dashed lines indicate negative impacts for the less poor, maize surplus producers, and buyers of labor.

linkages are more important than production linkages, accounting for between 50 percent (in Senegal) and 98 percent (in Zambia) of overall multipliers calculated (Delgado, Hopkins, and Kelly 1998). These studies do not, however, explicitly consider the further effects of transfers and growth on seasonal capital constraints, or the knock-on effects of relaxing these constraints.

The extent of these effects and of direct and indirect increases in wages and benefits to poorer households as a result of implementation of the subsidy program is, however, an empirical question, as is the extent to which productivity and welfare benefits are carried forward from one year to the next. Focus group discussions in 2007, reporting on the effects of the 2005/06 subsidy, clearly (and independently) articulated processes of easing of seasonal cash constraints in the hungry gap and tightening of labor markets, with higher wages and low maize prices throughout the season (SOAS et al. 2008). Similar focus group discussions conducted in 2009 reported income benefits from higher wages and increased maize availability, though they were also concerned about the adverse effects of high maize prices—and the high maize prices experienced after 2006/07 would be expected to undermine these processes.

Livelihood and rural economy models have also been used to investigate and describe this process in 2006/07 (see

SOAS et al. 2008) and for 2008/09 (Dorward 2010). These studies provide results consistent with those of the focus group discussion reports, finding that the subsidy contributes to higher wages but had lower wage effects in 2008/09 and that subsidy benefits have become more concentrated among beneficiaries (because the value of direct production benefits to subsidy recipients is increased with higher maize prices, but the benefits of lower maize prices and higher wages to poor nonbeneficiaries are absent or reduced). Fragmented information on wage rates over the period 2005/06 to 2008/09 suggests that wage rate increases over the period were higher than maize price increases over the same period, representing real increase in wage rates.

Further empirical work is required to investigate the scale of the indirect benefits through wage effects, because they depend heavily upon the scale of growth multipliers (consumption multipliers of slightly more than 1.5 embedded in the livelihood and rural economy models are derived from historical expenditure patterns in Malawi, which are augmented by savings multipliers in the model). Without these multipliers, wage impacts would be very low—analysis of 2006/07 and 2008/09 household survey data suggests that agricultural wage labor constitutes less than 20 percent of household income even among the poorest 20 percent of rural households in Malawi, although observed rises in agricultural wages suggest that unskilled, nonagricultural wages have also risen, unless these two labor markets are completely separated, an unlikely scenario.

The overall increase in real wages over the period is supported by anecdotal reports of rising rural wages and is consistent with the limited political and social impact of and response to high nominal maize prices in early 2009. It is also consistent with reports of falling poverty rates and decreased wasting among children under the age of five. The subsidy program is not the only contributor to these improvements. Over the same period, there were good rains, a marked improvement in macroeconomic management, and relatively high tobacco prices. These factors will have made direct contributions to economic growth, and also facilitated the implementation and impact of the subsidy program (the tobacco prices and macroeconomic management contribute to the availability of foreign exchange for fertilizer imports, reduce the crowding-out effects of the program, and stimulate other complementary parts of the economy; good rains promote good yield responses to fertilizers).

While attribution of these changes to the program is difficult, there are reasons to believe that the stimulus to maize production from the subsidy and the good rains has been a critical element in rural economic growth and poverty reduction, as compared with the effects of good tobacco prices alone. Limited evidence from elsewhere in Africa and the world suggests that even labor-demanding smallholder cash crops can drive pro-poor growth in such a broad way. Further empirical work is also needed to establish the extent to which productivity and welfare gains in one year are carried forward to subsequent years, the conditions under which these gains can be maximized, and the implications for subsidy program design and implementation and questions about graduation.

CONCLUSIONS AND LESSONS

This chapter suggests that the Malawi agricultural input subsidy program has achieved substantial benefits and successes, although these are more nuanced than some press reports on the program suggest. The measured producer benefits of the program relative to its costs have been relatively modest; however, our benefit-cost analysis does not capture all the benefits of the program, nor all of its costs. Moreover, there is scope for considerable improvement in the program's effectiveness and efficiency, although there are also practical and political difficulties regarding the implementation of some of these and questions about their effects.

Other African countries considering the introduction of agricultural input subsidies can learn important lessons from Malawi's experience. The program is a bold, large-scale initiative that has achieved substantial increases in maize production. The implementation of such a program represents a very considerable logistical achievement, and the government is to be commended for this and for its continuing and often imaginative attempts to improve the program. Nevertheless, higher maize prices and calculation of the agronomic yield effects of incremental fertilizer and seed suggest the production increases resulting from the program are not as large as might appear from the post-2005/06 national maize production increases reported by MoAFS. The benefits of the program also have to be weighed against its very considerable costs (with an average of over 9 percent of the national budget going to the subsidy program since 2005/06) and the loss of benefits from alternative investment of these funds. While the food security and growth benefits of the program have been partially undermined by high maize prices, there have still been significant improvements in productivity and welfare from 2005/06 associated with greater maize availability and with increases in real wages.

Ongoing implementation challenges that the government is working on include controlling costs, timing of input deliveries, effective targeting of subsidized inputs, reducing diversion and fraud, improving agronomic and market returns with complementary investments (for example, in extension, research, organic soil fertility improvement, and roads), and using the subsidy program to extend private sector input delivery systems. Success in addressing these challenges will lead to new challenges because increasing success will lead to changes in the need for such a large-scale program with these objectives—and continuing political, strategic, economic, technical, and logistical system innovations will be needed to respond to these changes.

Malawi's experience with its large-scale agricultural input subsidy program offers a number of important lessons to other countries in Africa considering the introduction of agricultural input subsidies.

First, any growth and development strategy that involves agricultural input subsidies must be rooted in the opportunities for and constraints to growth and development facing a country and particular groups within it. This chapter has set out in some detail specific difficulties that constrain broad-based growth in Malawi, highlighting the reliance on low-productivity maize and the difficulties and limited options faced by very large numbers of poor, food-deficit farmers, and indeed by the Malawian economy as a whole, in breaking out of the low-maize-productivity and poverty traps.

This low-productivity trap arises as a result of severe seasonal credit constraints affecting very large numbers of poor, food-deficit farming families, together with thin and high-risk, high-margin input and maize markets. Malawi's key achievements with its subsidy program have been the ability to raise land and labor productivity and improve food security for large numbers of poor households by relieving both profitability and affordability constraints on the use of inputs needed to increase staple crop productivity, leading to some combination of increased real wages and reduced food prices. The Malawian model thus applies to other countries only if there are large numbers of people facing similar staple-food-productivity constraints alongside increased input use constrained by thin input markets, poorly developed input supply systems, and widespread profitability and affordability problems.

Malawi's experience also shows that, in the right context, large-scale agricultural input subsidy programs have the potential to yield substantial benefits to people and their governments with good design and implementation. The chapter has also shown the very substantial costs and resources required for such programs, and the difficulties and challenges that must be overcome for effective, efficient, and sustainable delivery of program benefits. Several issues from Malawi's experience are relevant to other countries considering similar subsidy programs:

- *Focus*: subsidies should be provided for inputs whose use for important staple crops is constrained by affordability difficulties despite high potential responses to input use.
- *Consumer gains*: strong emphasis should be put on wider contributions to economic growth and poverty reduction through consumer as well as producer gains.
- *Scale*: the subsidy should affect staple crop prices, labor markets, or both, requiring sufficient local or national scale to affect markets, but strict limits on scale and the control of costs are needed to limit displacement of existing purchases, crowding out of critical complementary investments, and adverse macroeconomic impacts.
- *Logistical systems* face major challenges in delivering timely, targeted subsidies to large numbers of widely dispersed farmers, and the establishment of such logistical systems requires time and major investments.
- *Performance monitoring, information, and auditing systems* are needed to develop trust, control fraud, and promote efficiency and effectiveness. Debates on crop production

estimates and the number of farm families in Malawi also demonstrate the importance of reliable information for issues beyond specific matters related to the implementation of the subsidy program and assessments of its impacts.

- *Effective targeting and rationing systems* are needed to limit scale and increase subsidy impacts on productivity, but different (geographical or household) approaches face different costs and difficulties (Dorward 2009), and in some situations strict rationing of universal provision may be a practicable alternative.
- *Entitlement systems* are needed for targeting and rationing, and these need to be robust against inevitable counterfeiting and diversion.
- *Input supply system development* requires close attention to the complementary and changing roles and interests of different public sector and commercial stakeholders, but improved farmer access to input services should be a major objective and outcome of agricultural input subsidy programs.
- *Complementary policies and investments*: if a subsidy program is seen as part of a broad, long-term strategy for poverty reduction and economic development, then investments in complementary activities must be made in areas such as extension, research, organic soil fertility improvement, health, education, markets, transport and communication infrastructure, and services. Consideration of the different roles of these complementary investments should also guide decisions on the nature, scale, and implementation of the input subsidy, as well as of other investments, in order to achieve positive interactions among investments.
- *Macroeconomic management* to promote favorable growth conditions and provide budgetary resources needed for such a program is also important.
- *Political commitment* is required for sustained mobilization of program resources, but there may also be potential conflicts between the need for political support on the one hand and targeting, rationing, cost control, and performance monitoring needed for efficient and sustainable implementation on the other.
- *Sustainability* of program implementation should be addressed by attention to cost control, scale, and logistical and performance monitoring and audit systems. There is also need for investigation of sustainability of impacts, with examination of the extent to which productivity and welfare gains carry forward from one year to the next and the implications of this analysis for program design and implementation and for questions about graduation.

An innate dilemma in the design and implementation of large-scale subsidy programs is that such programs require both stability and flexibility, with innovation. Stability is needed to provide stakeholders with confidence and security that will justify long-term financial and other investments associated with the program's implementation. Stability can be undermined, however, by the need for flexibility to adjust to changing conditions (for example in the weather, in international and national markets and economies, or in politics), and some of these changes may be anticipated or unanticipated results of the program. Alongside flexibility is the need for innovation (in technology, systems, and prices) to take advantage of learning and change during program implementation. Although flexibility and innovation can undermine stability, lack of flexibility and innovation may also undermine stability if conditions, such as increasing incidence of fraud, make the system unsustainable and ineffective in its initial form. To achieve mutually supportive stability, flexibility, and innovation, trust and stable principles must govern both the long-term objectives of and relations between different stakeholders on one hand and the processes for successful learning, flexibility, and innovation on the other.

NOTES

1. This section draws heavily on material from SOAS (2008).

2. Reasons for the high dependency on maize as opposed to other food crops include dietary preferences, different crops' relative calorific yields per hectare in different agro-ecologies, farmers' familiarity with the crop, and long-standing strong government policies aimed at promoting maize production and input and crop marketing subsidies focused on maize.

3. Understanding of the nature, causes, and relative importance of these problems varies (indeed, elements of the analysis presented here are not universally accepted, nor is this paper a comprehensive account of the complex issues involved).

4. The postharvest value-to-cost ratio has generally been less than 2, widely considered to be the minimum required to make fertilizer use profitable in moderately but not highly risky situations (Morris et al. 2007). Even for higher preharvest maize prices, the ratio typically has been around or below 2 (SOAS 2008), depending on the yield response achieved. With high yield responses, the value-to-cost ratio has been above 2 in some years (Maize Productivity Task Force 1997).

5. Table 17.1 shows, for example, that the median for maize stocks running out each year is between four and six

months after harvest, and that in 2003/04 one bag of fertilizer represented approximately 10 percent of rural households' median per capita annual expenditure (and more than 20 percent of median per capita expenditure of the lowest expenditure quintile).

6. A ratio of 15 was used in the calculations cited above based on what are believed to represent mean grain-to-nitrogen response rates to fertilizer application on farmers' fields. Improved management and uptake of hybrid seed provide the potential for higher ratios (in the range of 22 to 28 kilograms of maize per kilogram of fertilizer applied). Hence, improved farm management practices have the potential to make fertilizer use on maize profitable even without subsidy, although the affordability constraint remains.

7. This section draws heavily on Dorward (2009).

8. This analysis applies only to subsidies implemented on a scale large enough to affect output prices. Small-scale subsidies that do not significantly affect product prices are equivalent to highly elastic product demand: subsidy benefits are largely captured by suppliers and producers, and deadweight costs depend upon the elasticity of supply.

9. This is not a problem in situations in which the providers of land and labor are poor. Indeed, subsidies can promote pro-poor growth in such situations.

10. For this, complementary constraints to effective use of inputs by targeted beneficiaries must be addressed.

11. The terms "coupon" and "voucher" are used interchangeably in wider discussions of the Malawi Agricultural Input Subsidy program and in this paper.

12. Efficient and stable output markets may require less government intervention in direct market operations but more focused investment in market insurance and in facilitating infrastructure and institutions.

13. This section draws heavily on SOAS (2008) and on Dorward and Chirwa 2009a.

14. No information is available on seed sales.

15. A standard maize subsidy pack in 2005/06 consisted of one voucher for a 50 kilogram bag of 23:21:0+4S, one voucher for a 50 kilogram bag of 23:21:0+4S, and one voucher for improved maize seed. A standard tobacco subsidy pack consisted of one voucher each for a 50 kilogram bag of calcium ammonium nitrate (CAN) and a 50 kilogram bag of D Compound. The fertilizer vouchers were redeemable for MK 950. The seed voucher required no top-up and could be used to purchase 2 kilograms of hybrid seed or 3 to 4 kilograms of OPV seed, depending on the price set by the seed supply company.

16. These variations in targeting stem from vagueness in the definition of target beneficiaries in the guidelines and differences in the way communities dealt with problems of

shortages. Variations meant that those that were targeting beneficiaries placed different emphasis on different criteria and processes.

17. Displacement for 2007/08 is assumed to be similar to that for 2006/07 (higher subsidy sales may increase displacement, but greater farmer familiarity and higher fertilizer prices would be expected to reduce displacement). A lower displacement is assumed for 2008/09 as a result of much higher fertilizer prices and earlier (separate) beneficiary registration.

18. Low average prices in some years in the early 1990s were brought about by large-scale imports, and at the turn of the century by the starter pack subsidy program (with good weather).

19. Although the annual average price in 2008/09 was very high, peak prices were equivalent to those in 2001/02 and 2005/06 because prices rose much earlier in the season in 2008/09 but then flattened out.

20. The latter may be higher if there are significant exports or commercial carryover stocks at the end of the season.

21. These include inherent and difficult-to-quantify biases in different methods of collecting yield data, multicollinearity between input use and other management variables, high variability in smallholder agriculture, and variation of response rates with average rates of subsidized fertilizer use.

22. This calculation considers only maize production. Provision of the fertilizer subsidy for tobacco leads to a much higher displacement than for maize; thus, assuming that all incremental fertilizer is used on maize is not unreasonable. Fertilizer impacts on crops mixed with maize are ignored here.

23. It is important to note that increased hybrid seed subsidies may not be required if farmers are able and willing to purchase unsubsidized seed—improved access to seed, increased distributors, and effective extension *may* be more effective in increasing hybrid seed use.

24. For 2007/08, however, low crop output resulting from local droughts and floods affected total production, not just incremental production from the subsidy.

REFERENCES

Ariga, J., and T. Jayne. 2009. "Private Sector Responses to Public Investments and Policy Reforms. The Case of Fertilizer and Maize Market Development in Kenya." Discussion Paper 00921. International Food Policy Research Institute (IFPRI), Washington, DC.

Ariga, J., T. Jayne, B. Kibaara, and J. K. Nyoro. 2008. "Trends and Patterns in Fertilizer Use by Smallholder Farmers in Kenya, 1997–2007." KeWP 28, Tegemeo Institute, Nairobi.

Chapoto, A., and T. S. Jayne. 2010. "Maize Price Instability in Eastern and Southern Africa: The Impact of Trade Barriers and Market Interventions." Prepared for the COMESA policy seminar "Variation in Staple Food Prices: Causes, Consequence, and Policy Options." Maputo, Mozambique, 25-26 January 2010 under the Comesa-MSU-IFPRI African Agricultural Markets Project.

Chirwa, E., M. Matita, and A. Dorward. 2010. "Factors Influencing Access to Agricultural Input Subsidy Coupons in Malawi." Future Agricultures Consortium, Brighton, U.K.

Crawford, E. W., T. S. Jayne, and V. A. Kelly. 2006. "Alternative Approaches for Promoting Fertilizer Use in Africa." Agriculture and Rural Development Discussion Paper 22, World Bank, Washington, DC.

Delgado, L. C., J. Hopkins, and V. A. Kelly. 1998. "Agricultural Growth Linkages in Sub-Saharan Africa." IFPRI Research Report. IFPRI, Washington, DC.

Djurfeldt, G., H. Holmen, M. Jirstrom, and R. Larsson, eds. 2005. *The African Food Crisis: Lessons from the Asian Green Revolution.* Wallingford, U.K.: CABI Publishing.

Dorward, A. R. 2006. "Markets and Pro-poor Agricultural Growth: Insights from Livelihood and Informal Rural Economy Models in Malawi." *Agricultural Economics* 35 (2): 157–69.

———. 2009. "Rethinking Agricultural Input Subsidy Programs in Developing Countries." *Non-Distorting Farm Support to Enhance Global Good Production,* ed. A. Elbehri and A. Sarris, pp. 311-74. Rome: Food and Agriculture Organization. Also available at http://www.fao.org/es/esc/common/ecg/586/en/Dorward_FAO_Subsidy_Paper_FINAL.pdf.

———. 2010. "Informal Rural Economy Modelling of Subsidy Impacts." Unpublished paper, SOAS (School of Oriental and African Studies), London.

Dorward, A. R., and E. Chirwa. 2009a. "The Agricultural Input Subsidy Program 2005 to 2008: Achievements and Challenges." School of Oriental and African Studies, London.

———. 2009b. "The Malawi Agricultural Input Subsidy Programme: 2009 Fieldwork Preliminary Report." School of Oriental and African Studies, London.

———. 2010. "Evaluation of the 2008/09 Agricultural Input Subsidy Malawi: Maize Production Impacts." School of Oriental and African Studies, London.

Dorward, A., E. Chirwa, and R. Slater. 2010a. "Evaluation of the 2008/09 Agricultural Input Subsidy Malawi: Preliminary Report on Program Impact." School of Oriental and African Studies, London.

———. 2010b. "Evaluation of the 2008/09 Agricultural Input Subsidy Malawi: Report on Program Implementation." School of Oriental and African Studies, London.

Dorward, A. R., J. G. Kydd, J. A. Morrison, and I. Urey. 2004. "A Policy Agenda for Pro-Poor Agricultural Growth." *World Development* 32 (1): 73–89.

Economist Intelligence Unit. 2008. "Lifting African and Asian Farmers Out of Poverty: Assessing the Investment Needs." Custom research project for the Bill and Melinda Gates Foundation, New York.

Ellis, F. 1992. *Agricultural Policies in Developing* Countries. Cambridge, U.K.: Cambridge University Press.

Fan, S., A. Gulati, and S. Thorat. 2007. "Investment, Subsidies, and Pro-Poor Growth in Rural India." Discussion Paper 716, IFPRI, Washington, DC.

Fan, S., S. Thorat, and N. Rao. 2004. "Investment, Subsidies, and Pro-Poor Growth in Rural India: Institutions and Economic Policies for Pro-poor Agricultural Growth." IFPRI discussion paper, IFPRI, Washington, DC.

FAO (Food and Agriculture Organization). 2009. FAO Agricultural production data. Rome.

FEWS NET. 2009. "Malawi Food Security Outlook, October 2009–March 2010." Lilongwe.

Food and Nutrition Security Program. 2008. "Monitoring and Evaluation, 6th Report," (draft). Lilongwe.

Govereh, J., J. Shawa, E. Malawo, and T. S. Jayne. 2006. "Raising the Productivity of Public Investments in Zambia's Agricultural Sector." Working Paper 20, Food Security Research Project, Lusaka.

Harrigan, J. 2003. "U-Turns and Full Circles: Two Decades of Agricultural Reform in Malawi 1981–2000." *World Development* 31 (5): 847–63.

Hazell, P., and B. Hojjati. 1995. "Farm/Non-Farm Growth Linkages in Zambia." *Journal of African Economies* 4 (3): 406–35.

Hazell, P., and M. Rosegrant. 2000. *Rural Asia: Beyond the Green Revolution*. Manila: Asian Development Bank.

Jayne, T. S., J. Mangisoni, N. Sitko, and J. Ricker-Gilbert. 2010. "Malawi's Maize Marketing System." Report commissioned by the World Bank and Ministry of Agriculture of the Government of Malawi, Lilongwe.

Kelly, V. A., D. Boughton, and N. Lenski. 2010. "Malawi Agricultural Inputs Subsidy Program: Evaluation of the 2007/08 and 2008/09 Input Supply Sector Analysis." Michigan State University, East Lansing, MI.

Levy, S., ed. 2005. *Starter Packs: A Strategy to Fight Hunger in Developing and Transition Countries? Lessons from the Malawi Experience, 1998–2003*. Wallingford, U.K.: CABI.

Logistics Unit. 2009. "Final Report: Implementation of Agricultural Inputs Subsidy Program 2008/09." Lilongwe.

Maize Productivity Task Force, Ministry of Agriculture of Malawi. 1997. "Area-specific Recommendations for Hybrid Maize Grown by Malawian Smallholders: A Manual for Extension Field Assistants." Lilongwe.

Mangisoni, J. 2010. "Defects and Storage Loss Analysis of Maize Grain in Malawi." Unpublished paper, Bunda College, University of Malawi.

MoAFS (Ministry of Agriculture and Food Security of Malawi). 2008. "The 2007/2008 Inputs Subsidy Program Review Report: An Internal Review." Department of Agricultural Planning Services, Lilongwe.

Minot, N. 2009. "Staple Food Prices in Malawi." Prepared for the COMESA policy seminar "Variation in Staple Food Prices: Causes, Consequences, and Policy Options." Maputo, 25–26 January 2010 under the African Agricultural Marketing Project, IFPRI.

Morris, M., V. A. Kelly, R. Kopicki, and D. Byerlee. 2007. "Fertilizer Use in African Agriculture." World Bank, Washington, DC.

Munthali, M. W. 2007. "Integrated Soil Fertility Management Technologies: A Counteract to Existing Milestone in Obtaining Achievable Economical Crop Yields in Cultivated Lands of Poor Smallholder Farmers in Malawi." In *Advances in Integrated Soil Fertility Management in Sub-Saharan Africa*, ed. A. Bationo, B. Waswa, J. Kihara, and J. Kimetu, pp. 533–536. Dordrecht, The Netherlands: Springer.

Nakhumwa, T. O. 2006. "Rapid Evaluation of the 2005 Fertilizer Subsidy Program in Malawi." Policy Paper No 10, CISANET, Lilongwe.

NSO (National Statistical Office of Malawi). 2005. "Integrated Household Survey 2004 –2005." Zomba.

———. 2006. "Welfare Monitoring Survey 2005." Zomba.

———. 2008. "Welfare Monitoring Survey 2008." Zomba.

———. 2009a. "2008 Population and Housing Census: Preliminary Report." Zomba.

———. 2009b. "Welfare Monitoring Survey 2008." Zomba.

Reardon, T. 1998. *Rural Non-farm Income in Developing Countries: The State of Food and Agriculture 1998*. Rome: Food and Agriculture Organization.

Reserve Bank of Malawi. 2010. "Financial and Economic Review 2009." Lilongwe.

Ricker-Gilbert, J., and T. Jayne. 2010. "The Impact of Fertilizer Subsidies on Displacement and Total Fertilizer Use." Unpublished presentation, Lilongwe.

Ricker-Gilbert, J., T. S. Jayne, and E. Chirwa. 2011. "Subsidies and Crowding Out: A Double-Hurdle Model of Fertilizer Demand in Malawi." *American Journal of Agricultural Economics* 93 (February): 26–42.

SOAS (School of Oriental and African Studies), Wadonda Consult, Overseas Development Institute, and Michigan State University. 2008. "Evaluation of the 2006/07 Agricultural Input Supply Program Malawi: Final Report." SOAS, London.

South African Revenue Service. 2009. Monthly maize quantities exported to Malawi. SARS database. Pretoria.

Siamwalla, A., and A. Valdes. 1986. "Should Crop Insurance Be Subsidized?" In *Crop Insurance for Agricultural Development: Issues and Experience*, ed. P. Hazell, C. Pomareda, and A. Valdes, pp. 117–25. Baltimore: IFPRI and John Hopkins University Press.

Timmer, C. P. 1989. "Indonesia: Transition from Food Importer to Food Exporter." In *Food Price Policy in Asia*, ed. T. Sicular, pp. 22–64. Ithaca, NY: Cornell University Press.

World Bank. 1981. "Accelerated Development in Sub-Saharan Africa: An Agenda for Action." World Bank, Washington, DC.

Xu, Z., W. A. Burke, T. S. Jayne, and J. Govereh. 2009. "Do Input Subsidy Programs 'Crowd In' or 'Crowd Out' Commercial Market Development? Modeling Fertilizer Demand in a Two-Channel Marketing System." *Agricultural Economics* 40 (1).

CHAPTER 18

MoneyMaker Pumps: Creating Wealth in Sub-Saharan Africa

I. V. Sijali and M. G. Mwago

The first of the Millennium Development Goals (MDGs) is to eradicate extreme poverty and hunger, with the target of halving the proportion of people whose income is less than $1 a day between 2000 and 2015. In Sub-Saharan Africa, rural poverty accounts for 83 percent of total extreme poverty, with 85 percent of the poor depending partly on agriculture for their livelihoods (World Bank 2000). Considering that agriculture can have the greatest impact on poverty and food security if the benefits of its development are reaped by the poor, priority should be given to the development of small-scale irrigation (Kidane, Maetz, and Dardel 2006). Agricultural growth is therefore a key to the realization of the first MDG.

Stimulating agricultural growth is critical to reducing poverty in Africa. Commercial agriculture, potentially a powerful driver of agricultural growth, can develop along a number of pathways. But agricultural productivity in Sub-Saharan Africa is the lowest in the world, with per capita output only 56 percent of the world average (FAO 2005), and agricultural output in Sub-Saharan Africa has not kept pace with population increase (Msangi and Rosegrant 2005). More than 80 percent of output growth in Sub-Saharan Africa since 1980 has come from expansion of the cropped area, compared with less than 20 percent for all other regions. Food self-sufficiency among Sub-Saharan Africans declined from 97 percent in the mid-1960s to 82 percent in 1997–99, without a substantial increase in household incomes that would allow people to afford food

purchases. Agricultural families have remained locked in a low-input, low-income system, with low and stagnating agricultural yields.

Agricultural intensification has become the main avenue of growth in crop production, with agricultural water management (water harvesting and irrigation) the focus of this intensification in Sub-Saharan Africa. More reliable access to water for irrigation would stabilize yield, reduce the risk of harvest failure, and increase productivity and agricultural growth. Successful investment in agricultural water management technologies therefore presents an important opportunity for poverty reduction and economic growth. However, major constraints to using irrigation—including lack of surface storage structures, appropriate irrigation technologies, capacity to exploit underground water, community skills for irrigation, information on appropriate irrigation technologies, and investment in irrigation—must be addressed.

In some parts of Sub-Saharan Africa, investment in irrigation development at the community level is already bearing fruits. In Tanzania the Participatory Irrigation Development Project has had striking impacts, increasing farm income by 86 percent and enabling irrigator households to enjoy better-quality housing, acquire agricultural and household assets, access health services, and finance children's education (IFAD 2005). In four representative subproject areas, ownership of oxcarts and cattle increased considerably, the total number of grinding mills increased from 2 to 12, and the number of shops increased from 2 to 74. Similarly, in Zimbabwe, irrigator households in the European Union-funded *Maunganidze* Irrigation Scheme reported an increase in income of more than 200 percent and turned a food deficit into a surplus. Investment in new housing and in water and sanitation was the most obvious sign of improved livelihoods, with a number of modern two- and three-room houses with ventilated pit latrines and in several cases protected water wells. IFAD concluded that these impacts were the result of investment in irrigation, because there were no other sources of income in the area.

Studies have shown that small-scale irrigation offers opportunities to improve livelihoods in Africa. However, there has been little technology-driven jump in productivity for the majority of resource-poor African farmers. IFAD (2005) estimates that of the potentially irrigable 39.4 million hectares in Africa, only 7.1 million hectares, or 18 percent of the total, have been equipped for irrigation. Expansion of irrigation has been slow. Over the past forty years, only 4 million hectares have become irrigated in Africa, by far the smallest expansion of any world region. The area developed for irrigation as a fraction of the irrigation potential for African countries is shown in map 18.1. A majority of African countries have exploited less than 50 percent of their potentially irrigable land, with 10 countries at less than 10 percent, 8 countries at 10 to 25 percent, and 6 countries at 26 to 50 percent. Eleven countries have exploited 50–75 percent, while only 2 countries have exploited more than 75 percent of their potential (FAO 2005).

The lack of exploitation of irrigation potential in Sub-Saharan Africa can be attributed to lack of access to appropriate and affordable irrigation technologies by the majority of farmers in these countries. The cost per hectare of developing land for irrigation in Sub-Saharan Africa ranges from $2,000 to $4,000 for small-scale irrigation and from $9,000 to $15,000 for large-scale irrigation, making it out of reach for most families and communities (Kidane, Maetz, and Dardel 2006). In India, the comparable cost for large-scale irrigation ranges from $1,500 to $2,000 per hectare.

In recent years, however, the development of appropriate and affordable irrigation technologies for poor Sub-Saharan Africa farmers and communities has been remarkable. One of these technologies is the human-powered irrigation pumps developed by KickStart International, which have been used by dynamic farmers and entrepreneurs to establish and run profitable small-scale agribusinesses.

KICKSTART INTERNATIONAL

KickStart International is a nonprofit social enterprise organization founded in Kenya in 1991. It now operates in Burkina Faso, Kenya, Mali, and Tanzania. KickStart's mission is to promote economic growth and employment creation in Africa by developing and promoting technologies that entrepreneurs can use to establish and run profitable small-scale businesses. The entrepreneurs raise small amounts of capital ($100–$1,000) to start a new enterprise, and KickStart helps them to identify viable business opportunities and obtain the appropriate technologies required.

KickStart addresses poverty alleviation through development of appropriate technologies and innovations to enhance production, value addition, and income generation. These include, among others, irrigation pumps, an oil press, and a brick press. KickStart's irrigation pumps enable smallholder farmers to enhance productivity and improve household incomes and thus contribute to sustainable poverty reduction. KickStart has developed several human-powered pumps. These pumps have the distinct advantage of being operable without fossil fuels or electricity, which is not always available in remote areas.

The business model

KickStart's business model is a fivefold strategy:

- *Market research for business opportunities.* KickStart identifies business opportunities through market research and feasibility studies that are aimed at assisting the rural poor.
- *Research and development.* KickStart designs tools to end poverty that can be used by small-scale entrepreneurs to start their own profitable businesses.
- *Private manufacturing.* After developing the tools, private manufacturers are contracted to produce the products in a way that ensures high-quality standards and optimal pricing for customers. KickStart's manufacturers are located in China, Kenya, and Tanzania, with the bulk of the products originating from China and, to a lesser extent, from Kenya. As of 2010, the manufacturer in Tanzania is capable of supplying only a portion of the Tanzania demand.
- *Marketing and distribution.* KickStart's products are introduced to the market through its own marketing and promotional activities, and the private sector supply chain is used to distribute the products locally. KickStart has more than 160 distributors in Kenya, more than 150 in Tanzania, more than 80 in Mali, and a few in

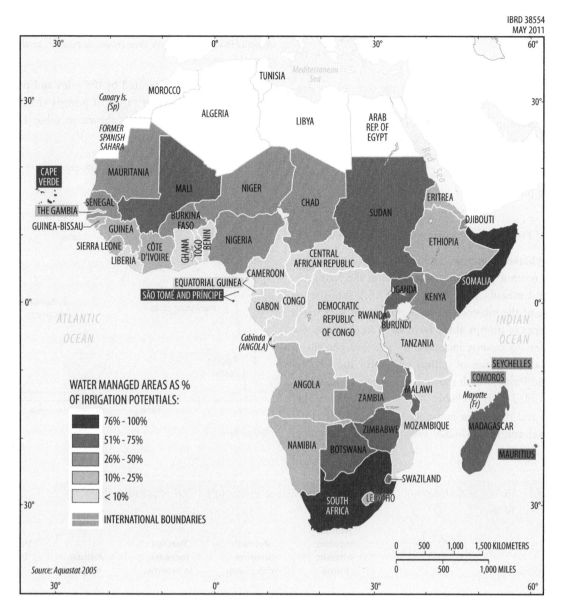

IBRD 38554
MAY 2011

WATER MANAGED AREAS AS %
OF IRRIGATION POTENTIALS:

76% - 100%

51% - 75%

26% - 50%

10% - 25%

< 10%

INTERNATIONAL BOUNDARIES

Source: Aquastat 2005

Source: FAO 2005.

Burkina Faso. In countries in which KickStart does not have a marketing program, distributors have been hired. KickStart also liaises with local and international nongovernmental organizations (NGOs) and with United Nations agencies to serve those organizations' beneficiaries and programs.

■ *Impact assessment.* KickStart conducts socioeconomic impact assessments on the incremental benefits resulting from its products. Information gleaned from these

assessments is used to make improvements to the technology and to generate ideas for future innovation.

Very often, KickStart is asked whether it would be better or more effective to simply give the pumps away. In both cases, the answer cases is no. The KickStart model of selling pumps through a profitable supply chain has been shown to be both profitable and sustainable in many African countries, creating employment opportunities and new sources of income. Analysis has shown that the KickStart model increases the livelihood of farmers and their families more cost effectively than giving the pumps away would. Annex 18.1 provides further details on this topic.

KickStart uses a tipping-point concept to mark the beginning of sustainable technology infusion. The tipping point is where the volume of sales of the technology dramatically rises or increases, decreasing the marketing costs to a minimum, as illustrated in figure 18.1. KickStart estimates that the tipping point is achieved when 15 to 20 percent of the market potential in terms of sales is achieved. In Kenya, for example, KickStart aims to surpass the tipping point by 2014.

Impacts of MoneyMaker pumps at the farm level

The MoneyMaker pump technology has had a significant impact on revenue generation and wages at the farm, distributor, and manufacturer levels. Table 18.1 summarizes survey data of the income and wage impacts of KickStart's different types of pumps at the farm level. As shown in the table, household income increased by 191–200 percent in Kenya for all categories of pumps except for the Money-Maker Hand Pump, which showed no change. In Tanzania, income doubled for households that used the MoneyMaker Hip Pump and tripled for households that used the Super MoneyMaker and MoneyMaker Plus pumps. For countries

other than Kenya and Tanzania, the revenue data show an increase of 440 percent for the MoneyMaker pump.

Impacts of pumps at the manufacturer and retailer levels

Profits have been generated by the sales and manufacturing of the MoneyMaker range of pumps at the manufacturer and retailer levels, as shown in table 18.2. Skilled

Figure 18.1   The Tipping Point Concept

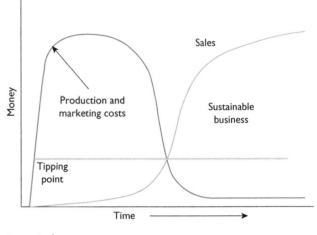

Source: Authors.

Table 18.1   Farm-Level Household Revenues and Wages per Pump, July 1991–November 2009 (*dollars*)

Pump	Annual income without pump	Annual income with pump	Percent increase in income	Annual wages	Wages over lifespan of pump[a]
Kenya					
MoneyMaker	628	1,885	200	126	379
Super MoneyMaker and Super MoneyMaker Plus	1,148	3,443	200	71	214
MoneyMaker Plus	248	744	200	21	63
MoneyMaker Hand	93	279	200	4	12
MoneyMaker Hip	832	2,423	191	60	174
Tanzania					
Super MoneyMaker and MoneyMaker Plus	493	1,478	200	41	123
MoneyMaker Hip	826	1,651	100	3	6
Other countries[b]					
MoneyMaker pump	183	995	444	18	54
Super MoneyMaker and Super MoneyMaker Plus	345	1,034	200	29	86
MoneyMaker Hand	38	—	—	2	6
MoneyMaker Hip	578	1,156	100	3	9

Source: KickStart International.

a. Wages over lifespan of pump = annual wages x lifespan of pump.

b. Burundi, Democratic Republic of Congo, Malawi, Mali/Burkina Faso, Mozambique, Rwanda, Sudan, Uganda and Zambia.

— = Data not available.

Table 18.2   Manufacturer and Retailer Profits and Manufacturer Skilled Jobs, July 1991 to November 2009

Technology	Manufacturing		Retailing
	Pretax profit ($)	Skilled man days	Pretax profit ($)
Kenya			
MoneyMaker	310,694	1,738	20,918
Super MoneyMaker	61,378	10,391	155,882
Super MoneyMaker Plus	75,604	12,799	215,000
MoneyMaker Plus	33,999	3,837	58,284
MoneyMaker Hand Pump	27,712	1,564	6,455
MoneyMaker Hip Pump	33,197	2,997	37,844
Total	**542,584**	**33,325**	**494,382**
Tanzania			
MoneyMaker	26,874	219	2,239
Super MoneyMaker	38,248	2,878	35,306
Super MoneyMaker Plus	269,024	20,241	292,034
MoneyMaker Plus	985	132	985
Money maker Hand Pump	925	108	1,013
MoneyMaker Hip Pump	a	a	17,332
Total	**311,870**	**23,578**	**348,910**

Source: KickStart.

a. Not manufactured in the country.

manpower jobs have also been created in the manufacturing of the pumps. Between July 1991 and November 2009, retailers' profits from MoneyMaker pumps totalled $494,382 in Kenya and $348,910 in Tanzania. At the manufacturer level, profits over the same period amounted to $542,584 in Kenya and $311,870 in Tanzania. The manufacturing of the pumps involved more than 33,000 and nearly 24,000 skilled man days in Kenya and Tanzania, respectively.

MONEYMAKER PUMPS PRODUCT LINE

Criteria for pump creation

KickStart is guided by a unique set of criteria in designing its products: income generation, return on investment, affordability, energy efficiency, portability, ease of use and installation, strength and durability, design for manufacturing, and cultural acceptability. These criteria are defined as follows:

- *Income generation.* Every pump model developed and marketed must have a business model that clearly predicts profitability and can be supplied to entrepreneurs.
- *Return on investment.* A purchaser of a MoneyMaker pump should be able to fully recoup his or her investment within six months.
- *Affordability.* Because the target purchasers of the pumps are some of the world's poorest people, designs

and manufacturing must ensure that retail prices are affordable, ideally less than $150.
- *Energy efficiency.* All pumps are human powered and thus must be extremely efficient at converting human power to mechanical power
- *Ergonomics and safety.* The pumps must be safe to use for long periods of time without stress or injury.
- *Portability.* Pumps must be small and light enough to carry home from the point of purchase on foot, by bike, or by minibus.
- *Ease of installation and use.* All pumps must be easy to set up and use, without additional training or tools, not even a hammer or screwdriver.
- *Strength and durability.* The pumps are designed and built to withstand heavy use. The pumps carry a one-year guarantee upon purchase.
- *Design for manufacturing.* For manufacturing to be truly effective, pumps must be produced in large quantities, but in the developing world manufacturing capacity is limited. The design of pumps must be such that the pumps can be manufactured within the capacity of the local manufacturing industry.
- *Cultural acceptability.* The pumps must be adapted to the culture in the countries where they are sold.

A team of engineers, designers, and technicians develop and test prototype pumps to ensure their performance, cultural acceptability, and durability. In addition to design and development, KickStart creates marketing awareness and assembles sales teams to sell the pumps. Importantly, Kick-Start employs innovative marketing techniques that are accessible to potential customers in remote villages without fossil fuels and electricity, including community pumping competitions during market days and demonstrations at retail shops and individual farms.

Types of pumps

ORIGINAL MONEYMAKER PUMP. KickStart's debut pump, the original MoneyMaker, was introduced in September 1996. This small, treadle-operated pump could pull water from as deep as 7 meters and be used to furrow irrigate up to 0.8 hectares of land. The pumps demonstrate the potential poverty reduction effects of micro-irrigation: more than 4,050 original MoneyMaker pumps were sold between 1996 and 1999, generating more than $3.9 million annually among user households in East Africa. User feedback, however, indicated that farmers needed a pump that could lift and push water through a hosepipe or sprinklers. In response, KickStart introduced the new Super MoneyMaker pump in October 1998. The new suction and pressure pump superseded the original MoneyMaker, which was taken off the market in February 1999.

SUPER MONEYMAKER PUMP. The Super MoneyMaker pump is used to pump water from hand-dug wells, rivers, streams, lakes, and ponds. A twin-cylinder pump, it is ideal for sprinkler and drip irrigation, for filling overhead water tanks, and for use with nozzles and sprays attached to the end of the delivery hose. The pump can draw water from a depth of 7 meters and pump it 14 meters above the ground. It can be used to irrigate up to 0.8 hectares of land. The design and operation of the Super MoneyMaker pump is shown in figure 18.2. An improved, easier-to-use design of the Super MoneyMaker pump, Super Money-Maker Plus, was subsequently introduced.

MONEYMAKER PLUS PUMP. Responding to demand for a lower-cost pressure irrigation pump, KickStart designed and launched the MoneyMaker Plus pump in July 2001. This small, leg-operated pump has one piston and one cylinder but can still pull water from 7 meters deep and push it more than 14 meters above the ground. It can be used to irrigate up to 0.4 hectares of land. The design and operation of the MoneyMaker Plus pump is shown in figure 18.3.

Figure 18.2   Design Diagram and Field Operation of the Super MoneyMaker Pump

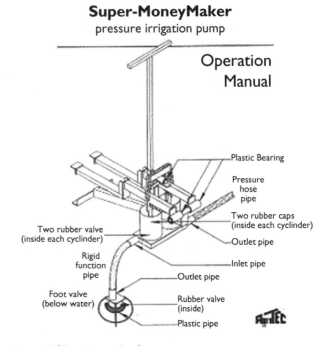

Source: KickStart International.

Figure 18.3   Design Diagram and Field Operation of MoneyMaker Plus Pump

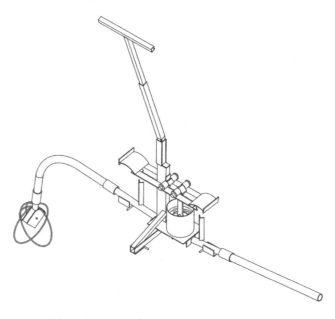

Source: KickStart International.

MONEYMAKER HIP PUMP. The MoneyMaker Hip Pump is a unique pump developed to meet the needs of the very poor people who cannot afford the twin-cylinder Super MoneyMaker pump or the single-cylinder MoneyMaker Plus. The MoneyMaker Hip Pump debuted in stores in 2006, however, sales and marketing efforts began in 2008. The pump weighs only 4.5 kilograms, and can irrigate up to 0.4 hectares of land.

The design of the MoneyMaker Hip Pump includes a super-efficient valve box and a simple pivot hinge. By attaching a hand pump to a hinged platform, the mechanics of the pump were changed to allow operators to use their legs, body weight, and momentum, rather than the few muscles of the upper back and shoulders. This makes the pump more energy efficient, and it is capable of irrigating at least 0.4 hectares. Like the Super MoneyMaker, the MoneyMaker Hip Pump can draw water from 7 meters and pump up to 14 meters above the ground.

These pumps retail for $35 to $100. Between July 1991 and November 1999, more than 137,000 MoneyMaker pumps of all types were sold, with a vast majority of them purchased by residents of African countries. Kenya, Tanzania, and Malawi are the countries in which the greatest number of pumps have been sold, and the Super MoneyMaker Plus is by far the most commonly sold MoneyMaker pump (annex 18.2). Figure 18.4 details the number of pumps that have been sold across the continent.

MoneyMaker pumps are developed through design criteria consideration to meet the needs of the target market. Final prototypes are field tested for long periods of time (six months or more) with all feedback incorporated into the final design. The first batch of pumps was field tested through the private sector supply chain that stocked the products and retailed them to the end users. Because KickStart's mission includes poverty reduction, an assessment of the pumps' impact is carried out at "zero age," and again in the 9th and 18th month after procurement. The zero age survey provides the baseline data on which comparison is made for the subsequent 9th-month and 18th-month surveys. Manufacturing begins after the successful testing of the pumps. Manufacturers are trained and provided with parts produced by KickStart to ensure quality standards for all the pumps. The pumps are supplied through distributors and retailers for eventual sale to farmers.

KickStart embarks on intensive promotion and marketing campaigns to create awareness about and generate demand for its products. Marketing and promotion of high-quality products to poor people requires substantial resources. For KickStart, this is possible through donor and government support. Until a critical mass is reached (15 to 20 percent of the market share), the tipping point is not realized. However, once the tipping point is achieved, operation costs are substantially reduced and the business becomes sustainable and profitable and many more distributors start selling the product.

MoneyMaker pumps are designed to last for three years but some have, with good maintenance, operated for more than six years. Critical in this good maintenance is the replacement of piston cups every 3–12 months (depending on hours of usage and the quality of water used).

Figure 18.4   Number of MoneyMaker Pumps in Various Countries, 1996–June 2009

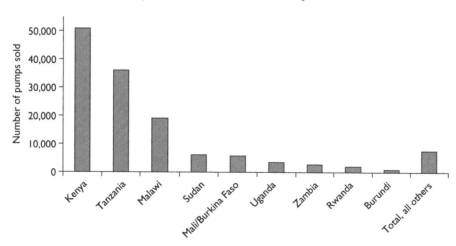

Source: KickStart sales data 1996–2009.

Figure 18.5   MoneyMaker Pump Supply Chain

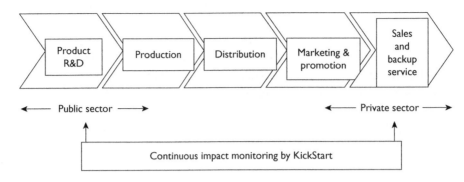

Source: KickStart International.

Table 18.3 Costs of Various Steps in the MoneyMaker Pump Supply Chain	
Supply Chain Step	**Cost ($)**
Manufacturer	65
KickStart	72
Wholesaler	100
Retailer	115

Source: KickStart International.

MoneyMaker pumps supply chain

The MoneyMaker supply chain is a five-phase process including research and development (R&D), production, distribution, marketing and promotion, and sales and backup services, as shown in figure 18.5. KickStart carries out R&D and marketing and promotion directly. The other phases are executed by the private sector with monitoring by KickStart. Donor participation is very crucial to carrying out product R&D and creating product awareness because it enhances demand and consequently creates an attractive business opportunity for the private sector.

Production, distribution and retailing costs, and profits amount to $115 per pump for the Super Moneymaker pump (table 18.3) and are borne by the farmers who purchase the pumps. Other costs amounting to $264 a pump, incurred during technology development, promotion, sales, and impact monitoring, are currently borne by donors.

All the design work behind KickStart's products is carried out at Nairobi, while products are manufactured in either Thika, Kenya; Arusha, Tanzania; or in China. KickStart recruits and trains a network of distributors and dealers (more than 150 dealers in Kenya alone) in cities, towns, and small market centers. The pumps are sold, with a markup of 7 percent to KickStart, to distributors in the private sector through KickStart's coordination, which maintains business accounts with each distributor or dealer. Most of KickStart distributors are Agrovets shops (sellers of agrochemicals and veterinary products) frequently visited by farmers. Initially, KickStart provided distributors with credit terms that required them to pay KickStart once the consignment was sold. As demand for KickStart products grew, the credit period was reduced to 30 days after receipt of consignment. KickStart also requires that distributors be willing to demonstrate and market the pumps.

KickStart identifies different marketing and promotion strategies to create awareness among potential end users of its products. These include above-the-line (those using mass media) and below-the-line (nonmedia) promotions to close sales. In Kenya, Tanzania, Mali, and Burkina Faso, sales teams are trained to communicate the benefits of the MoneyMaker pumps and promotion of farming as a business to potential customers.

IMPACT OF MONEYMAKER PUMPS ON DEVELOPMENT

Impact assessment methodology

Through its monitoring teams, KickStart assesses key indicators of the impacts of the MoneyMaker range of pumps. A range of data is collected to carry out this monitoring process: the number of pumps manufactured and sold is logged, purchasers' details are recorded in a database, and training recipients' details are recorded. Later, KickStart's monitoring staff visit a random selection of distributers, retailers, and purchasers to interview, administer questionnaires, and gather statistical data for technology impact analysis. These socioeconomic surveys are conducted at three points in time: at "zero age" (before use of the pumps) and during the 9th and 18th month of usage. The parameters monitored include pump ownership; pump management; and impact of the pumps on incomes, food security, livelihoods, and investment.

Pump ownership and management

KickStart's impact assessments (KickStart 2008) show that 88 percent of the people who purchase pumps are male. Management of the pumps, however, is not carried out strictly by pump owners; rather, it changes with time. At zero age, 81 percent of the pumps are managed by the owners, a figure that fell to 46 percent at 18 months. On the basis of gender, the surveys show that at zero age, 23 percent of pumps are managed by females, a figure that increased to 60 percent at 18 months. This is not surprising since, as time passes, women's interest in the pump grows because it provides a means of increasing income for families' daily needs. Men, on the other hand, look at other long-term high-capital investments that subsequently generate higher returns. For example, farmer Samuel Ndungu (one of the four profiled below) opted to leave his treadle pump to his wife while expanding his irrigated enterprise with a motorized pump. This change in management shows how women have been empowered to improve their livelihoods with MoneyMaker pumps.

Impact on irrigated area

The area under irrigation using the pumps sold in Sub-Saharan Africa between 1991 and 2009 is estimated to be more than 31,000 hectares (table 18.4).

Table 18.4	Area under Irrigation Using the Pumps, and Crops Grown in those Areas in Various Sub-Saharan Africa Countries, 1991–2009	
Country	Area being irrigated[a]	Crops
Kenya	12,326	Horticultural crops
Tanzania	8,785	Horticultural crops
Malawi	4,665	Maize, horticultural crops
Sudan	1,531	Horticultural crops
Mali/Burkina Faso	1,433	Horticultural crops
Uganda	896	Horticultural crops
Zambia	679	horticultural crops
Rwanda	540	Horticultural crops
Burundi	284	Horticultural crops
Total	**31,138**	

Source: Generated with KickStart sales data 1991–2009.

a. Area irrigated is generated using a conversion figure of 0.3 hectares per pump at 80 percent pump utilization.

In Kenya, socioeconomic surveys have shown a substantial increase in the area under irrigation at the household level following the purchase of a MoneyMaker pump. At the zero age survey an average of 0.02 hectares per household was under irrigation (typically bucket irrigation) but rose to 0.2 hectares under hip pump irrigation, a nine-fold average increase.

Impact on households

Although rural farmers are risk averse and have very little cash to spare, demand for MoneyMaker pumps has increased steadily over the years, a trend that may arise from the change in lifestyles after purchasing the MoneyMaker pumps, as indicated by the profiles of four typical "farmer-preneurs" shown in table 18.5.

According to KickStart survey data, incomes in households using MoneyMaker pumps have risen from as little as $100 to more than $10,000 annually, in addition to extending food availability periods from 3 months to 12 months, thus eliminating food insecurity. The change in livelihood of the irrigating households is manifested in investment of the extra income in purchase of assets such as bicycles, motorized pumps, dairy cows, modern houses, and land. Some irrigating households have also expanded their enterprises to include dairy, poultry, small-scale maize milling, and transport. With the increased incomes, payment of school fees for their children has eased, and the number of people employed on such farms has also increased. In addition, the MoneyMaker technology has encouraged the introduction of high-value crops, with their attendant improved agronomic practices. And the technology has been frequently adopted by neighboring farms, whose owners and workers have received on-farm training nearby.

Job Creation. Investment in agricultural water management through small-scale irrigation creates jobs both for the families who own the pumps and the labor they hire, because irrigation increases farm output and requires more workers, especially where high-value crops are grown. Statistical analysis by KickStart (1991–2009), for some Sub-Saharan countries, has shown that, on average, when families started bucket irrigation, 0.17 jobs were created; after the acquisition of a MoneyMaker pump, the number of jobs created rose to 0.55 per household.[1] Of that 0.55, family members represented 0.51 and waged labor represented 0.04, while distribution on gender basis was 0.32 and 0.22 for men and women, respectively. The jobs created included pump operation, land preparation,

Table 18.5 Farmerpreneur Profiles before and after Investing in MoneyMaker Pumps

Name	Samuel Mburu Ndungu		Felix Muiruri		Catherine Gwambie		Mahamoud Guindo	
Country	Kenya		Kenya		Tanzania		Mali	
Age	45		34		40		48	
Gender	Male		Male		Female		Male	
	Before	After	Before	After	Before	After	Before	After
Farm enterprise	Bucket irrigation	Super MoneyMaker and petrol pump	Bucket irrigation	MoneyMaker Hip Pump	Rainfed and bucket irrigation	Super MoneyMaker	Bucket irrigation	Super MoneyMaker
Income ($/year)	$100	$1,000–$2,000	$480	$10,440	—	—	$400	$700
Food availability (months)	3	12	3	12	3	12	3	12
Assets (house, bicycle, farm animals, etc.)	1 house, 1 cow, 1 goat	2 houses, 2 cows, 7 goats, 3 bicycles, one motorized pump	—	—	Chickens	1 modern house, 2 businesses, chickens	—	—
Land size (number of hectares)	0.6	1.0 (0.4 being purchased as of time of survey)	0	0	0.8	1.2	0	0
Land irrigated (hectares)	0.4	MoneyMaker: 0.8 hectares (0.4 rented); motorized pump: 2 hectares	0.2 (rented)	0.8 (rented)	0.8	1.2	150 square meters	300 square meters
Family size	8		5		5		6	
Number of employees on the farm	None	Workforce has grown fivefold	None	Workforce has doubled	0	2	None	None
Crops	French beans	French beans, tomatoes	French beans	French beans, tomatoes, baby corn, green maize	Maize, beans	Vegetables	Vegetables	Vegetables and fruits
Ease of facilitating children's education	Difficult	Easy	Difficult	Easy	Difficult	Easy	Difficult	Easy

Source: KickStart International.

— = Unavailable.

weeding, and harvesting. Pump operation represented the largest proportion of the jobs created, with 33 percent of the pumps being lent out to neighbors, generating 0.03 jobs at no cost. The Kickstart analysis also shows that MoneyMaker pumps increased the number of jobs created by more than 220 percent. In most countries, where many youths are not currently engaged in productive activities, irrigation provides an opportunity for a net increase in the jobs created.

INCOME. In addition to job creation, MoneyMaker pumps have a positive impact on farm incomes generated through irrigation, as shown in table 18.2.

POVERTY. Data (1991–2009) from Kenya, Tanzania, Mali, Burkina Faso, and other countries show that 439,839 people have been moved out of poverty (table 18.6). The poverty reduction to pump ratio (number of people moved from poverty per pump unit) varies but is clearly higher in Kenya, Tanzania, Mali, and Burkina Faso than in other countries in which the pumps are sold. This implies a higher efficiency of pump utilization in the above four countries and is commensurate with the level of technology promotion and demonstration of on-farm profitability. These last two factors are essential ingredients in high pump utilization efficiency and need to be replicated in other Sub-Saharan Africa countries to achieve similar success levels in those locations.

IMPACT ON SUB-SAHARAN AFRICA

The impact of a technology depends on its adoption rate, which is largely determined by the awareness created. Marketing of the MoneyMaker technology requires a huge financial investment that is not possible for many African countries. Financial resources are particularly limited in Mali and Burkina Faso, leading to low awareness levels and hence low levels of impact compared with Kenya and Tanzania.

Despite the financial constraints, KickStart estimates that between 1991 and 2009, more than 87,000 small-scale agricultural enterprises were created using the MoneyMaker range of pumps. These businesses generated new profits totalling over $77.2 million annually and employing more than 100,000 people. Each pump is used to irrigate 0.3 hectares of land (on average), and generates an average net annual income of $1,100 a year for its owner, representing a 100–450 percent increase in the incomes that poor rural people made from sale of crops before the adopting the MoneyMaker technology. In Kenya by 2009 more than 12,000 hectares of land were estimated to be irrigated using KickStart irrigation pumps. Irrigation investment costs less than $60 per hectare annually compared with the conventional sprinkler systems, which cost more than $600 per hectare annually. In short, MoneyMaker pumps remove the obstacle of huge initial capital investment for demand-driven, small-scale irrigation development.

Kenya's experience with MoneyMaker pumps

Thousands of entrepreneurial farmers in Kenya are now irrigating with KickStart's range of MoneyMaker pumps, changing their small subsistence farms into vibrant commercial enterprises. The average size of plots held by smallholder farmers is between 0.2 and 1.0 hectare and generates about 25–80 percent of total family income annually (IPTRID 2005). When they use irrigation, farmers are typically able to grow and sell three to four high-value crops annually. These "farmerpreneurs" in Kenya over 2007–09, have increased their incomes ten-fold on average, and some have made annual profits of up to $5,400.

Table 18.6 Number of People Using Kickstart Pumps Who Have Moved Out of Poverty in Select Sub-Saharan Africa Countries, 1991–2009

Country	Pumps sold	Enterprises created or transformed	People moved out of poverty	Poverty reduction to pump ratio
Kenya	51,357	40,720	203,600	3.96
Tanzania	36,603	29,495	147,475	4.03
Mali and Burkina Faso	5,970	4,673	23,365	3.91
Other countries[a]	43,676	13,079	65,399	1.50
Total	**137,606**	**87,967**	**439,839**	**3.20**

Source: KickStart 2008.

Note: Here, poverty is defined as an income of less than $1 a day.

a. Burundi, Democratic Republic of Congo, Malawi, Mozambique, Rwanda, Sudan, Uganda, and Zambia.

DISTRIBUTION AND UTILIZATION. The distribution of the MoneyMaker range of pumps in various regions of Kenya is shown in figure 18.6. This distribution reflects the agricultural potential in the region, the ability of farmerpreneurs to purchase the pumps, and the availability of surface and shallow groundwater sources.

WEALTH CREATION. According to KickStart data, the average net annual income per family using the MoneyMaker pumps in Kenya ranges from $800 to $10,440. As of December 2005 about 33,000 pumps had been purchased by farmers and were generating household income totalling $31.4 million (K Sh 2.2 billion) annually. Impact monitoring survey data showed that 91 percent of the purchased pumps generated total income of $93.8 million (K Sh 6.7 billion) during their life span of three years. The other 9 percent are pumps that were not used for various reasons such as water source being too deep for the pump

to reach. Table 18.7 shows the income generated by each type of MoneyMaker pump.

INCOME AND EMPLOYMENT CREATION. In most parts of rural Kenya, as elsewhere in Sub-Saharan Africa, time is an available resource that is very often underutilized because opportunities for productive employment activities are lacking. KickStart's ranges of MoneyMaker pumps are designed to create opportunities for rural people to more fully use their available time on productive activities. In Kenya, the average annual household income rose from $3,465 (K Sh 242,529) before the pump to $4,700 (K Sh 328,973) after acquisition of the pump (KickStart sales data 1991–2009). Although total household income rose from several sources, including farming, employment, pension, remittances, businesses, and collection of rent, income from irrigation contributed the highest proportion of the total, at 47 percent. KickStart's monitoring

Figure 18.6   Regional Distribution of MoneyMaker Pumps Sold in Kenya, 2007–09

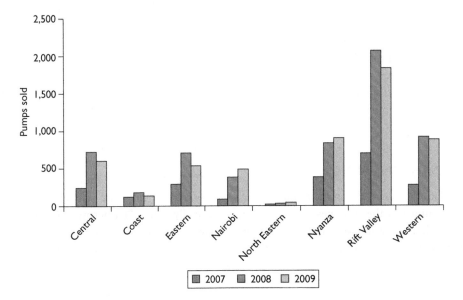

Source: KickStart.

Table 18.7   Wealth Creation with MoneyMaker Pumps in Kenya

Irrigation technology	Pumps purchased 1996 through 2005	Annual income ($ millions)	Cumulative income over three years ($ millions)
MoneyMaker Suction Pump	3,305	2.31	6.93
Super MoneyMaker	13,657	17.44	52.31
Super MoneyMaker plus	7,401	9.45	28.35
MoneyMaker Plus	6,639	2.00	6.00
Hand Pump	2,221	0.23	0.23
Total	33,223	31.27	93.82

Source: IPTRID 2005.

surveys (2008) also show that Super MoneyMaker pump irrigation over an 18-month period on average increased pumping and watering jobs by 465 percent in Kenyan farms. This is in addition to increased jobs in other crop production activities. Based on the number of pumps sold, the area irrigated and hence the number of jobs created, Kenya has made the largest gains of all the countries in which MoneyMaker pumps have been sold.

ASSETS, HOUSING, AND INVESTMENT. KickStart surveys show that in Kenyan households using MoneyMaker pumps, the number of local cattle owned declined by 31 percent, whereas the number of the more expensive dairy cows increased by 7 percent, indicating availability of surplus resources available to purchase them. Dairy cows produce more milk than the local cattle, thus increasing family income. There was also more fodder available to feed the dairy cows, which demand more fodder than local cows. Similarly, there was an increase in the number of donkeys and carts in households using MoneyMaker pumps, indicating the demand for extra transport with the use of MoneyMaker technology. In addition, households increased their investments in businesses (shops, transport, poultry, and dairy) by 32 percent. KickStart surveys also show improvement in housing among households in Kenya after they started MoneyMaker pumps. In 2008, the incidence of "improved" houses—those constructed from stone and timber—increased by 38 percent and 10 percent, respectively, demonstrating investment in better housing and therefore improved livelihoods.

FOOD SECURITY. Food security exists when people have physical and economic access to food that is sufficient and nutritious enough to meet their dietary needs and preferences for an active and healthy life. Food security can be achieved through producing one's own food (self-sufficiency), having sufficient income to purchase food, or a combination of both. KickStart surveys (2008) show that households using the Super MoneyMaker pump increased their food surplus by 35 percent in the 18 months following the adoption of the technology.

DRIVERS OF SUCCESS

MoneyMaker success stories are numerous. Three such stories from Kenya, Tanzania, and Burkina Faso are presented in box 18.1.

In developing its irrigation pumps, it is KickStart's policy to ensure four main outcomes: achieving the highest impact in the shortest time possible; achieving a

---

Box 18.1   Money Maker Success Stories

Daniel Karanja Njenga and Nancy Gathoni in Kenya

While living in an internally displaced person camp after their home and farm were looted during Kenya's postelection violence in March 2008, Daniel Karanja Njenga and his wife Nancy Gathoni participated in a promotional demonstration of the MoneyMaker Hip Pump. "When I saw the . . . demonstration and heard about it on the radio," Daniel said, "I knew it was the answer to how we could earn an income quickly and get back to farming."

Daniel's first purchase with the relief funds provided to him by the Kenyan government ($130) was the MoneyMaker Hip Pump and hoses. The manually operated pump is lightweight, costs less than other pumps, and is easy to use. It does not require electricity or fuel. With it, Daniel was able to irrigate his small 1/8th-acre plot and grow crops during the dry season when most farms are bare. Daniel and Nancy now earn a decent living selling their *sukuma wiki* (kale), a staple food for Kenyans. They

are also helping hungry neighbors and friends struggling to get back on their feet after the violence. Daniel has plans to expand his plot to grow cabbages and tomatoes and purchase a dairy cow.

Daniel and Nancy are two of many other farmers in Kenya who are becoming successful businessmen and women able to feed their families, pay school fees, and medical expenses. According to KickStart's research, an average farmer can make about $120 a month selling crops produced using the MoneyMaker pump.

In Kenya MoneyMaker pumps are also providing hope to people facing a tough combination of challenges in recent years: postelection violence, escalating food prices, a difficult economic situation, and continued high levels of poverty.

Catherine Gwambie in Tanzania

Catherine Gwambie and her husband, Hawzi Mwami, are an entrepreneurial couple from Tanzania who had dreams of becoming successful shop owners in Dar es

---

Box 18.1 (continued)

Salaam. They farmed in their native Kigoma, growing and selling maize and beans to save enough to open a shop selling household supplies.

Although the shop was reasonably successful, it did not generate as much income as the couple needed to support their family. Hawzi decided to buy land on which he could raise chickens and Catherine could start growing vegetables for sale. It was a good business, but bucket irrigation on the land took a lot of effort.

In early 2007 Catherine heard an advertisement for the Super MoneyMaker pump on the radio. She excitedly told her husband about this new pump that was affordable and made irrigation easier and quicker. Hawzi was not convinced. Catherine, however, insisted that the pump would make her life easier and decided to use her own money to purchase it. Together, the Mwamis went to the Kariakoo market in Dar es Salaam to buy a Super MoneyMaker.

The pump increased Catherine's productivity so much that she expanded to another plot and now employs her daughter and young sister. With the extra income they are now earning, the Mwamis have plans to send three of their young children to good secondary schools and to build a nicer house for their family.

Source: Authors.

Hawzi now freely admits that his wife was right about the pump, and between their two businesses, they see a bright future for their family.

Mahmoud Guindo in Mali

Mahmoud Guindo, a 48-year-old farmer with a wife and four children, had long struggled to make ends meet on credit. He moved from his home in Dogon County to Bamako, where he was employed as a security guard earning $400 annually. In an effort to boost his income, he began farming a 150-square-meter plot, which was still inadequate to meet his family's needs.

To increase his annual income, Mahmoud wanted to build a bigger garden, but he was sceptical about how he would water a larger plot of land. After seeing an advertisement for KickStart's MoneyMaker pump on television in 2008, Mahmoud wanted to buy it. He did not have enough money, however, so he approached his boss for a loan. Both men agreed it was a tangible asset that would provide a profitable and quick return on investment.

Since buying the pump in October 2008, Mahmoud has almost doubled his annual income, from $400 to $700, by selling fruits and vegetables. The additional cash flow is allowing him to pay off some debts while simultaneously providing sufficient food for his family.

---

cost-effective program; ensuring that the income-generating process is self-sustainable, and ensuring that the process if scalable and replicable in other areas.

KickStart employs six approaches to achieve its development goals, as described below. In addition, KickStart's success has been driven by the desire of farmer to produce on-farm profits and get out of poverty through adoption of appropriate and affordable technology

MARKET RESEARCH. KickStart's technological gap studies identify profitable small enterprises that can be established by local entrepreneurs with limited capital investment and determine the technological and socioeconomic requirements of those opportunities. The studies evaluate raw materials, competing products, potential market demands, and constraints and opportunities for small enterprises.

DESIGNING NEW TECHNOLOGIES AND BUSINESS PACKAGES. KickStart designs and develops the tools, equipment, manuals, and business plans required for establishing small enterprises. It also designs the production protocols and quality control procedures required for manufacturing new pumps.

TRAINING MANUFACTURERS TO PRODUCE MONEYMAKER PUMPS. KickStart trains private manufacturers to set up assembly lines and quality control mechanisms to mass-produce its machines and tools.

PROMOTION OF MONEYMAKER PUMPS. KickStart promotes the MoneyMaker and works with the private sector to ensure that pumps are well known and easily available to small-scale investors, reducing product risk for entrepreneurs. The risk to entrepreneurs is further reduced by the fact that the pumps are guaranteed for a period of one year following purchase. Farmers have the right return their pumps if their wells are too deep for the operation of the pump or if the pumps break down due any manufacturing fault.

ON-FARM PROFITABILITY. The enhanced water utilization that has come with the MoneyMaker range of pumps has increased farm incomes, a major incentive for practicing and potential farmers.

FARMERS' NEED TO GET OUT OF POVERTY. Despite being hardworking and dedicated, farmers in Sub-Saharan Africa have long been seeking a means to escape poverty. The MoneyMaker technology has accorded them an affordable opportunity to do just that.

PARTNERSHIP WITH DONORS. KickStart raises funds for research and development, marketing, and awareness promotion of MoneyMaker technologies and associated business plans. KickStart's donors include a large number of public and private donors such as the Bill and Melinda Gates Foundation, the Rockefeller Foundation, and the David and Lucille Packard Foundation.

SCALABILITY AND TRANSFERABILITY OF THE SUCCESS

The scalability and transferability of KickStart depends crucially on the existence of three things: a sustainable supply chain involving manufacturers, distributors, and retailers; use of appropriate marketing technologies until the tipping point is reached; thereafter, the technology is self-propagating; and policy changes to encourage entrepreneurship and removal of handouts of technologies.

Maximization of the use of the technology is essential. For example, the Super MoneyMaker is currently used to irrigate an average 0.3 hectares, despite being designed to irrigate 0.8 hectares. This limitation is attributed to the limited land available to the farmer. Participatory usage, in which farmers share a single pump, can also increase the use of the pumps and the amount of land area being irrigated. Additionally, expansion of the pump's utility from sprinkler irrigation to include drip irrigation would enhance the water and energy use efficiencies and therefore increase the land coverage. In Naro Moru, Kenya, for example, MoneyMaker pumps are used to pump water from shallow wells into raised storage tanks that feed into drip irrigation systems. This arrangement has the effect of increasing the area under irrigation.

If each family in Kenya with access to water from underground storage, rivers, streams, ponds, or dams used a treadle pump and irrigated 0.3 hectares of land, for example, that country would not be experiencing the food shortages and hunger it has recently. Assuming water accessibility, an irrigation potential of 540,000 hectares, and a 20 percent share of this irrigation potential for the MoneyMaker technology, Kenya would need about 360,000 of the MoneyMaker range of pumps. Based on KickStart's sales figures, as of 2005, only 9.2 percent of the potential number of pumps had been sold, and 14.2 percent by October 2009 (KickStart sales data 1991–2009). Additionally, KickStart aims to increase access to 20 percent of the potential irrigation market in Kenya, after which the technology will be self-propagating. After the tipping point is reached and assuming 80 percent pump utilization efficiency, 17,280 hectares would be under irrigation through the MoneyMaker range of pumps.

In Sub-Saharan Africa, more than 87,967 small agricultural enterprises had been created by 2009 using Money-Maker pumps. These businesses generate $81 million each year and offer 93,462 new jobs annually. This new wealth has helped move 439,839 people out of poverty. A further indication of the benefits of irrigation is the establishment of small-scale businesses within the vicinity of nearby village markets, thus creating indirect employment. This has led to improved access to nutrition, education, health, housing, and welfare services for farming communities.

KickStart's systematic, replicable method of measuring the impacts of its products is an aspect of the organization's success that could be replicated by other organizations. Every product comes with a one-year guarantee, and every buyer fills out a guarantee form when the product is purchased. The guarantee reduces the perceived risk of buying the product, and the forms give KickStart a database of all pump owners.

Scaling up the MoneyMaker technology success in Sub-Saharan Africa should involve technology promotion, demonstration of on-farm profitability and a sustainable supply chain, and high levels of efficient pump use. The still-low pump utilization needs to be addressed through on-farm pump utilization research that looks at, for example, shifting from direct irrigation pumping to indirect through storage tanks, or changing the application method from sprinkler to drip. All these require enhanced budget levels similar to or greater than the current promotional budgets in Kenya and other African countries. In addition to the aforementioned interventions, government policies should shift to favor accessible small-scale irrigation technologies.

LESSONS LEARNED FROM MONEYMAKER PUMPS

Prospects

In Sub-Saharan Africa, intensification, rather than expansion, of cropped areas, is key to agricultural growth and poverty reduction. One way of achieving this is introduction of simple innovative technologies such as Money-Maker pumps for agricultural water management. Through irrigation, farmers can diversify into high-value horticultural crops and fodder crops.

The concept of farmer entrepreneurs, in which agricultural enterprises are run as viable businesses, is now fully integrated as policy in Kenya and needs to be introduced in other African countries. As KickStart's products have shown, when poor people have access to technology to generate wealth, they use that technology quite effectively to move themselves out of poverty. Technology acceptance by farmers and a sustainable supply chain is assured through the KickStart model. A study (IPTRID 2006) on the experience with treadle pumps, introduced in West Africa by an international NGO, Enterprise Works, found the need for improved after-sales service and a coordinating agency with a longer-term program, such as the sort KickStart provides in East Africa. The study recommended the adoption of the KickStart model to ensure the sustainability of the West African program.

Technology infusion

The participatory approaches to technology infusion employed in the KickStart model involve marketing through demonstration and competitions. Marketing of technology is important in creating and enhancing adoption of technology. Creation of organized marketing groups and structures is important in poverty reduction. Cultural and gender sensitivity in technology development and infusion is an important consideration in technology. Technology evolution changes are driven by users of the technology. For example, in response to user demands, the Super MoneyMaker pressure pump, which facilitated sprinkler irrigation, was developed to replace the original suction-only pump and was quickly adopted by farmers.

Challenges

Despite its efforts and success, KickStart has not been able to design the ideal pump that combines high performance without maintenance irrespective of the intensity of use, terrain in which it is operated, and water quality.

The low pump utilization efficiency, irrigating on 0.3 hectares of the possible 0.8 hectares, could be attributed to direct irrigation pumping, which causes fluctuating sprays. It may be possible, however, to improve pump utilization efficiency through indirect irrigation pumping through storage tanks or using the pumps in combination with more efficient water application methods.

Annex 18.1 Economic Analysis of Pumps Given Away versus Sold

Item	Giveaway model	KickStart selling model	Remarks
Donor funds	$2 million	$2 million	Start with the same amount of funds.
Costs per pump	$290	$257	Each pump is $33 cheaper to sell than to give away.
Manufacturing	*65*	*65*	Why? It costs $65 to manufacture each pump; they are then sold to a wholesaler at
Revenue	*0*	*$–72*	$72, giving revenue of $7 per unit. This earned income helps support the
Distribution	*$85*	*0*	organization.
Promotion and sales	*0*	*$124*	Costs of administration, fundraising, technology development, and impact monitoring
Admin, technology development, impact monitoring, fundraising	*$140*	*$140*	are the same in either model. The giveaway would not require marketing and promotion but would incur costs to distribute the pumps. Staff would be needed to coordinate, and vehicles and fuel would be needed to transport the pumps. KickStart would also need to provide hoses or the pumps would be useless. In the KickStart model, distribution costs are handled by the wholesaler.
Total units distributed	6,897	7,782	Donor funds divided by cost per pump. The KickStart model puts nearly 900 more pumps in the field.
Percent used in enterprise	30%	80%	KickStart's goal is not to distribute pumps. Rather, it is to help people create small enterprises. It is here where the difference in the two approaches becomes
Number used in enterprise	2,069	6,226	apparent. When a person makes an investment, he or she is committed to making a better future. Impact monitoring data indicates that 80 percent or more of pumps bought are used to create jobs and income. The same research shows less than 30 percent of pumps given away are used to create a business. The KickStart model creates three times more small businesses than the giveaway model.
Average new profits and wages	$1,100	$1,100	These businesses will generate an average of $1,100 in new profits and wages each year.
Net present worth over 4 years	$9,103,600	$27,394,400	Here is an estimate of the new profits and wages these new businesses will create in four years. The KickStart model leverages $2 million in donor funds into more than $27 million in profits and wages for these families—three times more than the giveaway model. This is money that is spent locally, supporting other business and stimulating the local economy.
Number of people moved out of poverty	10,345	31,130	KickStart estimates that each enterprise supports a family of five. The KickStart Model moves more than 20,000 more people out of poverty, and it does it at
Cost to move one person out of poverty	$193	$64	one-third the cost per person of the giveaway model.

Source: KickStart International.

Annex 18.2 Number and Type of Pumps Sold in Various Countries, July 1991–November 2009

Pump type	Kenya	Tanzania	Malawi	Sudan	Mali/ Burkina Faso	Uganda	Zambia	Other countries
MoneyMaker	3,305	438	0	0	0	212	0	95
Super MoneyMaker	13,683	3,837	0	80	0	539	1	857
Super MoneyMaker Plus	16,985	26,988	18,503	6,138	5,609	2,885	2,368	7,709
MoneyMaker Plus	7,674	264	0	141	0	0	0	30
MoneyMaker Hand Pump	2,217	431	30	0	0	0	0	50
MoneyMaker Hip Pump	7,493	4,645	905	120	361	97	462	2,454
Total	**51,357**	**36,603**	**19,438**	**6,379**	**5,970**	**3,733**	**2,831**	**11,295**
Grand total 137,606								

Source: KickStart International.

NOTE

1. The analysis defines a job as an economic activity that occupies an individual for five hours daily for 150 days annually.

BIBLIOGRAPHY

Aquastat. http://www.fao.org/nr/water/aquastat/main/index.stm.

Arbache, J., and J. Page. 2008. "Hunting for Leopards: Long-Run Country Income Dynamics in Africa." Policy Research Paper 4715, World Bank, Washington, DC.

Brookings Institution. 2007. "Panel 5: Africa's Economic Successes: What's Worked and What's Next." Brookings Blum Roundtable 2007. Brookings Institution, Washington, DC.

FAO (Food and Agriculture Organization). 2005. "Irrigation in Africa in Figures: Aquastat Survey 2005." http://www.fao.org/nr/water/aquastat/regions/africa/index.stm.

IFAD (International Fund for Agricultural Development). 2005. "Agriculture Development in Republic of Mozambique." Agriculture Support Programme Formulation Report, Working Paper 2, International Fund for Agricultural Development, Rome.

IPTRID (International Programme for Technology and Research in Irrigation and Drainage). 2005. "Kenya Impact Case Study Report." IPTRID, Rome.

IPTRID. 2006. "Treadle Pump Dissemination and Adoption in West Africa: Performance Problems and Prospects." *GRID Network* 24. Rome.

KickStart. 2008. "The Super MoneyMaker Pump: The 18-Months Impact Assessment Report."

Kidane W., M. Maetz and P. Dardel. 2006. "Food Security and Agricultural Development in Sub-Saharan Africa: Building a Case for More Public Support." Main Report. FAO Regional Office for Africa, Harare.

Morris, M., H. Binswanger-Mkhize, and D. Byerlee. 2009. *Awakening Africa's Sleeping Giant: Prospects for Commercial Agriculture in the Guinea Savannah Zone and Beyond.* Washington, DC: World Bank.

Msangi, S., and M. Rosegrant. 2005. "World Agriculture in a Dynamically Changing Environment: IFPRI's Long-Term Outlook for Food and Agriculture under Additional Demand and Constraints." Paper written for the FAO and United Nations Economic and Social Development Department Expert Meeting on "How to Feed the World in 2050." International Food Policy Research Institute, Washington, DC.

NEPAD (New Partnership for Africa's Development) and FAO (Food and Agriculture Organization). 2004. "Government of the Republic of Mozambique: National Medium Term Investment Programme." ftp://ftp.fao.org/docrep/fao/007/ae415e/ae415e00.pdf.

Rosegrant, M., and N. Perez. 1997. "Water Resources Development in Africa: A Review and Synthesis of Issues, Potentials, and Strategies for the Future." EPTD Discussion Paper 28, International Food Policy Research Institute, Washington, DC.

Tyler, G. 2009. "All-Africa Review of Experiences with Commercial Agriculture: The African Sugar Industry—A Frustrated Success Story." Background Paper for the Competitive Commercial Agriculture in Sub-Saharan Africa (CCAA) Study. World Bank and FAO, Washington, DC. http://siteresources.worldbank.org/INTAFRICA/Resources/257994-1215457178567/Ch6_Sugar.pdf.

UNIDO (United Nations Industrial Development Organization). 2009. *Industrial Development Report 2009: Breaking In and Moving Up: New Industrial Challenges for the Bottom Billion and the Middle-Income Countries.* Vienna: UNIDO.

World Bank. 2000. *Can Africa Claim the 21st Century?* Washington, DC: World Bank.

PART V

Engaging the Private Sector to Upgrade Infrastructure

CHAPTER 19

ICT in Sub-Saharan Africa: Success Stories

Kaoru Kimura, Duncan Wambogo Omole, and Mark Williams

As recently as 1998 few people in Sub-Saharan Africa had access to a telephone, and even fewer had access to computers. Since then, this situation has changed out of all recognition. Africa has experienced a continent-wide revolution in the growth of the information and communication technology (ICT) sector. Networks have expanded, services have been made available on a mass market basis, and prices have fallen. ICT is now an everyday service for many Africans, affordable to the majority rather than the privileged few. This growth continues today as companies innovate, bringing new products and services to the market.

This chapter examines the ICT sector in Africa. The first section describes the expansion of voice networks and broadband Internet. The second section identifies the key factors that have contributed to the expansion of the sector. The third section analyzes the impact of ICT on a variety of areas, including mobile banking, telemedicine, and agriculture. The last section examines the role of the World Bank Group, to date and in the future.

EXPANSION OF THE SECTOR

The telecommunications sector in Africa has expanded rapidly since 1998, with both an increase in network and services provided. At the same time, prices have fallen everywhere, bringing telecommunications within the economic reach of the majority of Africans.

Voice networks

Voice networks are expanding rapidly, and the number of people using the networks is growing. Between 1998 and 2008 the number of mobile cellular subscribers in Sub-Saharan Africa leaped from about 4 million to 259 million (figure 19.1)

Innovations in the way services are delivered have also made ICT more accessible to customers in Africa. Prepayment has allowed customers to control their expenditures and avoid regular monthly subscription payments. African operators have also led the way in selling prepay credits in very small units, making calling accessible to large numbers of people, including the poor.

A combination of new technologies and sound policy choices, including market liberalization, by governments has triggered private investment, which has laid the foundations of the connectivity revolution in Africa. The global standardization of mobile telephone network technology has created international competition in both network equipment and customer devices, pushing down costs and lowering prices. The liberalization of markets and the establishment of sound regulatory frameworks have allowed private investors into the market, driving the expansion of telecommunications networks. Between 1998 and 2008, total private sector investment in telecoms in Sub-Saharan Africa reached $49 billion (World Bank 2010a), mainly in the mobile market (figure 19.2). This investment has resulted in a rapid increase in the proportion of the population covered

Figure 19.1   Mobile Cellular Subscription in Sub-Saharan Africa, 1998–2008

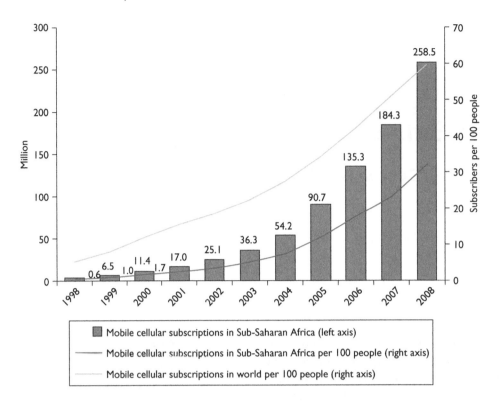

Source: World Bank 2010b.

Figure 19.2   Telecommunications Investment in
Sub-Saharan Africa, 1998–2008

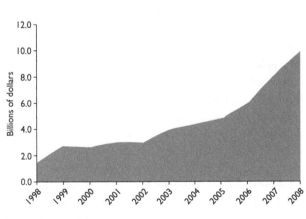

Source: World Bank 2010a.

by mobile networks, which increased from about 10 percent in 1999 to 60 percent in 2009. More than 90 percent of Sub-Saharan Africa's urban population now lives within range of a mobile signal, a remarkable transformation in only 10 years (figure 19.3).

The success of mobile communication has been very scalable, with large and small countries experiencing rapid increases in network coverage and access. Both Nigeria, a country of about 150 million people, and Rwanda, a country of about 10 million people, have experienced steady growth in network coverage (figure 19.4).

At the same time as communications networks have been expanding across Africa and the number of subscribers has risen, the price of telecommunications services has been coming down. The cost of mobile communications fell by nearly 50 percent between 2000 and 2009. By 2010 the average price of a mobile call in Africa was about $0.10 a minute (AICD forthcoming), and prices are continuing to fall as competition intensifies.

Broadband internet

Globally, broadband Internet is becoming an important part of national economies. Africa lags far behind most other parts of the world in access to broadband Internet. Broadband penetration in the region was 6.5 percent in 2008, one-quarter of the world average (ITU 2010). In 2008

Figure 19.3 Mobile Coverage in Rural and Urban Sub-Saharan Africa, 1999–2009

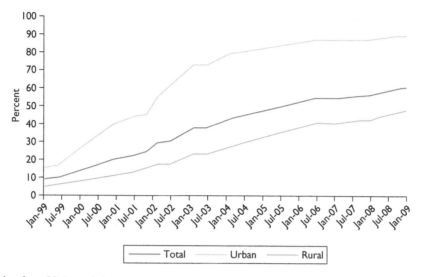

Source: Authors based on data from GSM Association.
Note: Figures show connection to GSM network.

Figure 19.4 Mobile Network Coverage in Nigeria and Rwanda, 2002–08

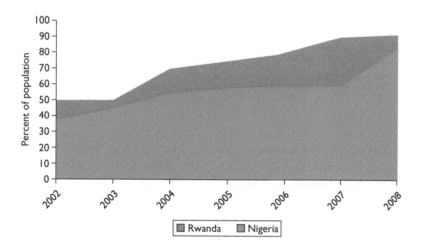

Source: ITU 2010.

fixed broadband Internet cost $100 a month in Sub-Saharan Africa, more than three times the world average of $31.40 (ITU 2010) (figure 19.5).

This situation is starting to change, as broadband Internet becomes more widely available and prices begin to fall. Nigeria, Kenya, and South Africa are leading the way in Africa, with rapidly rising numbers of broadband subscribers, mainly through wireless handsets. In most African countries, however, broadband remains beyond the reach of the majority of the population.

KEY SUCCESS FACTORS

Many factors have contributed to the success of the ICT sector in Africa. The most important of these has been the continentwide change in sector policy from one based on monopoly provision of ICT services to a privately owned, competitive market. The vast majority of countries in Africa have liberalized their telecommunications markets, and that liberalization has spurred private investment into infrastructure and created competition between operators, leading to expanded availability of services and reduced prices.

Figure 19.5 Monthly Price of Broadband Internet, by World Region, 2008

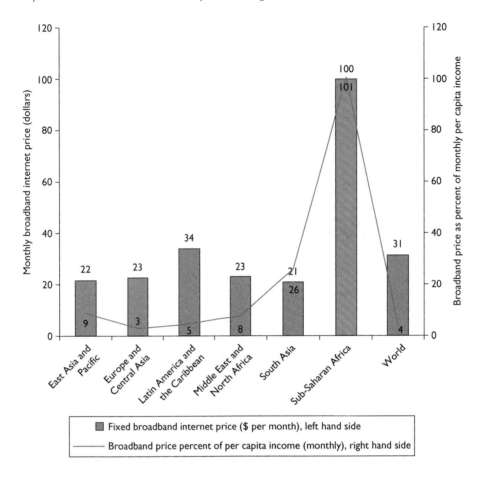

Source: ITU 2010.

Many governments have also privatized the incumbent telecommunications operator. Privatization is significant because it removes one of the main distortionary factors in the market and allows the government to carry out its main role of regulating the market without any conflict of interest.

These policies have resulted in the rapid growth of the mobile telecommunications segment of the market. Broadband Internet has been much slower to take off in part because of the inadequacy of certain segments of the broadband network infrastructure, particularly access to the international communications networks. These bottlenecks have been constraining growth of broadband Internet, limiting its availability, and making it prohibitively expensive. Recently, the growth of the submarine fiber-optic cable infrastructure has dramatically increased the availability of international bandwidth on the continent, and competition between cable providers has led to rapid declines in prices.

The success of the ICT sector in Africa is also attributable to innovation within the industry itself. Technologies and business models have been adapted to the African market, improving efficiency and tailoring services to the specific needs of customers in the region. Finally, the political economy of the telecommunications sector has affected government's willingness to undertake sector policy reforms.

Creating competitive markets

Competition in the telecommunications market was introduced in Africa in the late 1990s, when mobile networks were first established there. All but a handful of countries in Sub-Saharan Africa have introduced competition in their mobile markets, and more than half have more than two mobile operators (ACID forthcoming). This increase in competition has been one of the primary drivers of the sector growth and network expansion.

CHAPTER 19: ICT IN SUB-SAHARAN AFRICA: SUCCESS STORIES

Competition takes time to develop. Countries that reformed early have experienced better sector performance than late reformers. Performance also improves as competition intensifies. Mobile subscription penetration rates in Africa grew by less than 1 percentage point a year between the establishment of the first mobile network and the entry of the second operator. By the time a fourth operator enters the market, the subscriber penetration rate grows by 2–4 percentage points a year (AICD forthcoming).

The way in which liberalization takes place also has an impact. In Nigeria, for example, the government awarded the first three GSM (Global System for Mobile communications) licenses simultaneously, spurring a race to expand coverage and gain market share. Nigeria now has five mobile operators and is considered one of the most competitive markets in the region. With a mobile subscriber penetration rate approaching 50 percent, it is also one of the best connected countries in Africa.

Competition has been the primary driving force behind mobile network expansion and, more recently, declines in the price of calls. A recent study indicates that competition could potentially continue to drive this expansion until networks cover 90 percent of Africa's population (AICD 2010).

Privatizing state-owned enterprises

State ownership of telecommunications operators distorts markets and adversely affects competition. Governments often give state-owned operators preferential treatment by carving out areas of exclusivity for them in the market or failing to enforce regulatory rules such as interconnection payments. At the same time, these operators often find it difficult to obtain the necessary capital and skills to compete effectively with the private sector. The best long-term solution to these problems is to sell state-owned enterprises to create a level playing field for all players in the market.

Realizing this, governments across the region have privatized their state-owned telecommunications operators. By 2010, 28 African countries had gone through this process (see annex table 19A.1). Mali completed the privatization of its state-owned telecommunications operator in 2009 (box 19.1).

Overcoming infrastructure bottlenecks

Most mobile operators have built their own end-to-end networks, overcoming infrastructure bottlenecks along the way. As the focus of the ICT industry in Africa shifts toward broadband Internet, network infrastructure requirements are changing. Broadband requires networks capable of handling much higher volumes of traffic than that generated by voice services. As much of the traffic generated by broadband crosses international borders, it also requires more international network infrastructure. This type of network infrastructure has traditionally been underdeveloped in Africa. The lack of suitable infrastructure has become a significant bottleneck, contributing to the slow growth of the Internet in the region.

This situation began to change in 2009 with the development of undersea fiber-optic cables connecting Africa to the global communications networks. By 2010 Sub-Saharan Africa had 12 operational cables, and another 5 were under construction. The operational cables have a combined capacity of more than 12 terabytes per second (tbps). A total of $1.7 billion is being invested in the 5 undersea cables

---

Box 19.1   Privatization and Sector Reform in Mali

Mali's state-owned telecommunications operator, Société des Télécommunications du Mali (SOTELMA), was established in 1989 as the state-owned monopoly operator. Despite the continuous growth in the mobile market in Mali—led by the introduction of competition, in the form of a second GSM operator, Ikatel in 2003—the fixed-line market remained underserved and dominated by SOTELMA.

In 2009 SOTELMA was successfully privatized, with a 51 percent stake going to Maroc Telecom. At the same time, a new legal framework and universal access strategy were adopted. The telecommunications penetration rate rose to 40 percent, and Maroc Telecom is now focusing on revitalizing the fixed-line network and rolling out fixed broadband Internet.

This process was supported throughout by the World Bank, through a technical assistance project covering the privatization, the reform of the legal and regulatory framework, and capacity building for the government institutions. A World Bank team continues to work with the government of Mali to further liberalize the telecommunication market and improve connectivity by developing regional links to neighboring countries.

currently under construction, which will bring an additional 9 tbps of capacity to the region (figure 19.6).

The impact of this growth is already being felt. In East and Southern Africa, the SEACOM, TEAMs, and EASSy undersea cable projects were all operational by 2010. Wholesale prices for international bandwidth fell, allowing operators to provide better-quality service, usually in the form of faster download speeds or larger download caps. The arrival in 2010 of new undersea cables along the west coast of Africa (Glo-1 and MainOne) together with the expected arrival of two more cables (ACE and WACS) in 2011 and 2012 is likely to have a similar effect on markets on the other side of the continent. The international broadband infrastructure bottleneck is therefore well on its way to being overcome.

Domestic fiber-optic networks are needed to carry communications traffic both within and between countries, particularly countries that are landlocked. They are therefore as important as undersea fiber-optic networks for the

development of the Internet in Africa. Development of these networks has been much slower, although the recent upsurge of interest by African telecommunications companies in broadband has prompted new investment in domestic fiber-optic networks. For the foreseeable future, this interest is likely to focus on servicing the profitable intercity routes rather than connecting smaller towns and rural areas. A broadband infrastructure bottleneck is therefore likely to remain in these areas for some time to come (Williams 2010).

Fostering innovation

The expansion of communications services creates new business opportunities and innovative ways of delivering services. The African telecommunications industry itself has also been a source of business innovation. African operators have had to work hard to find ways of rolling out networks in difficult physical environments and creating

Figure 19.6   Undersea Fiber-Optic Cables in Africa, 2010

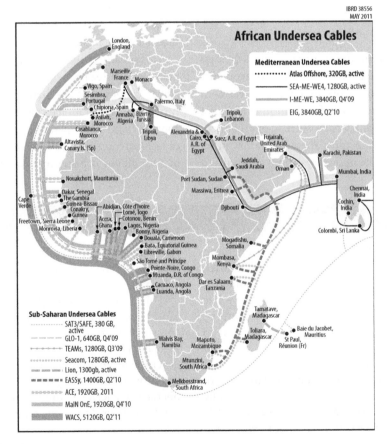

Source: http://manypossibilities.net.

commercially viable business models based on a customer base that was once considered marginal. The introduction of prepaid airtime in very small units is one example of how African operators have introduced innovations in their commercial practices to suit the African market. Zain's one-network, free regional roaming service is another innovative business model that originated in Africa (box 19.2).

Political economy of the sector

The rapid pace of policy reform in the telecommunications sector in Africa has been influenced by the political economy of the sector. Three key factors underlie this influence.

First, telecommunications has traditionally not been available to anyone other than a small elite section of the population able to afford and obtain a fixed line. But mobile phones are very popular and there is strong public demand for them, even in low-income countries. The proven ability of private companies to develop and operate mobile phone networks has therefore been less politically controversial than in other sectors.

Second, the telecommunications business, particularly mobile telephony, has been very profitable for many investors. As a result private sector interest in the sector has grown, and companies have been prepared to pay considerable sums for mobile licenses. This has provided an immediate source of revenue for governments that, combined with ongoing license-fees and tax payments, has made the telecommunications sector an important source of government revenues, which, in turn, has had an influence on government's willingness to liberalize the market and encourage private investment.

Third, the establishment of global technology standards in the telecommunications industry and the increasing level of international competition in the manufacture of telecommunications equipment have put strong downward pressure on the cost of building and operating telecommunications networks in Africa. These reduced costs have allowed many operators to maintain their profitability, even in the face of increasing competitive pressures.

IMPACT OF ICT IN AFRICA

Several studies examine the macroeconomic impact of ICT. Roller and Waverman (2001) analyze 21 advanced countries over 20 years (1970–90). They find a causal nonlinear relationship between telecommunications infrastructure investment and economic performance, where impact increases once countries pass a certain threshold of telecommunications access. Qiang and Pitt (2004) find that ICT has made a significant contribution to economic growth across a wide range of countries.

More recently, research has focused on the economic impact of broadband Internet. Qiang and Rossotto (2009) find that every 10 percentage point increase in broadband Internet penetration in developing countries results in 1.38 percentage points of additional GDP growth. Koutroumpis (2009) finds a significant and positive relationship between broadband infrastructure and local, regional, and national economic growth, including growth in small and medium-size enterprises. These findings are consistent with other research that finds that broadband is an important factor in social transformation and improved service provision, particularly in rural areas, and that mobile broadband services are particularly well suited for improving the economic

---

Box 19.2 Borderless Roaming

In late 2006 Kuwait-based mobile operator Zain (formerly Celtel) launched the world's first borderless mobile network, One Network, in the Middle East and East Africa. The service began in 4 countries in East Africa (Kenya, Sudan, Tanzania, and Uganda) and expanded to 12 other countries (Burkina Faso, Chad, the Republic of Congo, the Democratic Republic of Congo, Gabon, Ghana, Madagascar, Malawi, Niger, Nigeria, Sierra Leone, and Zambia).

Through this service, Zain's customers (both prepaid and postpaid) can make calls at local rates, roaming without incurring surcharges. They add air time with locally purchased airtime cards. In 2009 Zain added Internet access, e-mail, Multimedia Messaging Service (MMS), BlackBerry services, Short Messaging Service (SMS), international roaming, and mobile portal applications to its One Network local rate, further adding value to its African customers.

Source: Zain web site (http://www.zain.com/muse/obj/lang.default/portal.view/content/Zainpercent20World/Zainpercent20 Connect/Onepercent20Network) and Business Monitor International (BMI) database (http://www.businessmonitor.com/).

well-being of poor people (Lobo, Novobilski, and Ghosh 2008). Countries that do not develop effective broadband infrastructure may therefore be failing to capitalize on some of their economic growth potential (Gaasbeck and Kristin 2008; Tolkoff 2007).

The economic research on the impact of ICT has focused mainly on the impact at the level of the macro-economy or firms. ICT is also having a visible impact on the lives of individuals, changing the way people live and work in many different ways.

Mobile banking

Banking by cell phone in Africa is one of the most significant developments in the recent history of the continent's financial sector. The success of some of the early pioneers of cell phone banking has been replicated in other countries, through the launch of other types of financial service products delivered by cell phone.

Safaricom's M-PESA in Kenya was one of the first mobile banking applications to be launched on the continent (box 19.3 and chapter 20). MAP mobile banking in Uganda followed suit. WIZZIT, in South Africa, is another mobile-based "virtual bank," whose services can be accessed through any national mobile phone operator. In addition to providing a valuable service to customers, WIZZIT has had a positive economic effect, by employing nearly 2,000 previously unemployed "WIZZkids" as its sales force. These companies are revolutionizing the financial services sector in Africa, bringing low-cost financial services to the majority of the population, that was initially unable to access the traditional banking sector.

Telemedicine

Mobile phone operators, health service providers, health ministries, and donor organizations are working together to develop innovative ICT-based approaches to healthcare service delivery. One such application is TRACnet, which is used by the Ministry of Health in Rwanda to improve the quality of service in primary health care institutions (box 19.4).

Agriculture

Agriculture is an essential part of Africa's economy, accounting for 13 percent of GDP and employing about 194 million people (World Bank 2010b). ICT is having a positive impact on the sector in many ways (box 19.5).

IT–enabled services and business process outsourcing

In addition to being a platform for delivering services, the ICT sector has the potential to be a source of economic growth and employment itself. The IT-enabled service (ITES) sector—also known as business process outsourcing (ITES-BPO)—is becoming established around the world, including in some African countries. The sector covers a wide range of industries from applications development and services through to IT-enabled services such as call centers and other types of business process outsourcing.

The ITES-BPO industry is growing and still has considerable potential as a source of growth in Africa. Large and small companies around the world are increasingly hiring companies in Africa to help them deliver efficient, reliable, and cost-effective customer support and other key services, such as

---

Box 19.3   Serving the Banking Needs of the Poor in Kenya

M-PESA was launched in 2007 to meet the banking needs of the financially excluded. By July 2010, M-PESA had more than 11 million customers (about 30 percent of Kenya's population) and almost 20,000 agents (up from 355 at inception). Person-to-person transactions stood at more than $375 million a month (Safaricom Ltd, 2010).

There is strong demand for M-PESA's services in Kenya, which have had a positive economic impact. Use of and satisfaction with M-PESA is high. About 40 percent of households use M-PESA (63 percent of them for regular financial support), 90 percent believe their

money to be safe with M-PESA, 81 percent find it very easy to use, and 84 percent believed the service to be critical to their socioeconomic well-being (Agrawal 2010).

Morawczynski and Pickens (2009) find that incomes of rurual recipients increased 5-30 percent since they started using M-PESA.

M-PESA has succeeded mainly because it has a broad market positioning, has a built-in accountability structure, is easy and safe to use, provides 24/7 support, is affordable, is provided by the largest mobile phone network, and has a wide network of agents ensuring convenience in sending and receiving cash.

TRACnet is a mobile phone–based platform for monitoring HIV treatment in Rwanda. By 2009 it had registered more than 1,000 service providers, conducted more than 85,000 annual user sessions, and collected longitudinal data on more than 105,000 patients.

Thanks to TRACnet, Rwanda has access to robust datasets of HIV/AIDS patients located centrally and accessible from any location, allowing faster and better-informed intervention. As a result, public monitoring of HIV/AIDS transmission patterns has improved. Doctors and patients also have instantaneous access to more reliable information. Real-time monitoring of antiretroviral drug stocks leads to quicker replenishments.

The improved information exchange between remote health facilities and central actors has reinforced accountability in care and treatment of patients.

TRACnet has succeeded because it is based on simple technology using the widely available platform of the mobile phone. The centralized database is interoperable with multiple communication channels and it uses open source software giving it flexibility and scalability. It has the full support of the Rwanda government—a key to its success—and the program includes a training component that ensures that health workers are well prepared to work with the system.

Source: http://www.un.org/esa/sustdev/publications/africa_casestudies/tracnet.pdf; http://www.kiwanja.net/database/project/project_voxiva_hivaidsrelief.pdf.

Esoko leverages mobile phones to enhance productivity gains for African farmers and traders by giving them quicker access to better market information. Starting in 2007 in Ghana with only $90,000 and operating in the red by up to $21,000, Esoko had broken even by the fourth year and by the fifth year had $1.4 million in revenues and about $540,000 in profits. By 2010 Esoko had been scaled to seven other countries (Benin, Burkina Faso, Cameroon, Côte d'Ivoire, Madagascar, Mali, and Togo) and had grown to 40 full-time employees and about 9,000 users.

Esoko has led to a 6.4 percent fall in grain price market dispersion and a 3.5 percent decline in mean prices.

Transactions costs for farmers and traders have also fallen by $2–$150 per transaction by significantly reducing the role of middlemen or cutting them out altogether. It has also transformed mobile phones into a market bulletin increasing their utility beyond voice and text.

Esoko has succeeded mainly because it uses open source software, enabling it to scale up, tailor business services to local needs, use affordable mobile telephony, offer free listing of services, allow sending of and receipt of text messages in several languages, provide real-time commodity prices, and provide direct access to markets worldwide.

Source: http://www.esoko.com/; http://www.slideshare.net/slavb/s-bartlett-esoko-cirad-2010; http://www.ifc.org/ifcext/spiwebsite1.nsf/f451ebbe34a9a8ca85256a550073ff10/0e6f5be010f90329852576ba000e2dad?OpenDocument; http://www.slideshare.net/slavb/davies-esoko-cirad-2010.

data entry and document processing. A 2010 study by McKinsey and Company estimates that the addressable market for IT and ITES offshoring is $500 billion a year, of which only about 20 percent has been realized (Sudan et al. 2010).

Success in the ITES–BPO sector brings with it a number of benefits, including the following:

- *Employment of women.* Women now account for a large percentage of all professional and technical workers in the IT/ITES sector—a much higher rate of female participation than in the service sector in general (Sudan et al. 2010).

- *Increase in investment.* The IT/ITES sector helps attract foreign investment, transform the financial sector, energize local exports, and nurture ICT skills and innovation in the workforce.

- *Job creation.* It is estimated that every job created in the IT/ITES sector results in the creation of four additional jobs in ancillary sectors, such as transport, training, and catering.

Ghana and South Africa have identified ITES as one of the key sectors for enhancing economic growth. Both seek to position themselves as premier BPO destinations in Africa (box 19.6).

THE ROLE OF THE WORLD BANK GROUP

The World Bank Group has been involved in the ICT sector in Africa since 1969, when the International Development Association funded an $800,000 telecommunication project in Burkina Faso. Its work has covered investment lending, policy and regulatory reforms, privatization, and e-government and applications projects. The Bank has provided technical assistance to 27 Sub-Saharan African governments to strengthen policy and regulatory frameworks and build institutional capacity in the sector, including capacity for regulatory design and implementation.

In 2007 the World Bank Group launched an initiative to enhance broadband connectivity in Eastern and Southern Africa through the Regional Communications Infrastructure Program (RCIP). The program is currently operational in seven countries (Burundi, Kenya, Madagascar, Malawi, Mozambique, Rwanda, and Tanzania) and may be expanded to other countries in the region. Similar projects are under development in Central Africa (Cameroon, the Central African Republic, and Chad) and West Africa.

The Bank is also supporting governments in their efforts to use the ICT infrastructure to improve service delivery. In three stand-alone projects (e-Benin, e-Ghana, and e-Rwanda), it is providing funds to incorporate ICT into the delivery of public services. Implementation of the RCIP program in Kenya, Mozambique, and Tanzania also has major e-government components. ICT is also integrated throughout the broader World Bank portfolio of projects and is a major component of the Bank's research, dissemination, and policy development work in Africa. This work has included major outreach events, such as an innovations conference day held as a part of the Africa Union Summit in Ethiopia in 2010 and a seminar on "The Transformational Power of ICT for Africa" at the 2010 World Bank Group Spring Meetings.

The World Bank is also supporting African governments in their efforts to use the growing ICT infrastructure to develop the IT and ITES-BOP industry. Many of the ICT sector projects in Africa include components that support the industry through training, regulatory reforms, and, in some cases, investment in supporting infrastructure. A related initiative is the New Economy Skills for Africa Program (NESAP), a joint effort by World Bank

---

Box 19.6   Expanding Business Process Outsourcing in Ghana and South Africa

In Ghana the government's proactive policies of sector reform has created a competitive telecommunications industry with a telephone penetration of more than 60 percent. This industry is providing a platform on which an IT and IT-based services industry is growing.

One of the efforts, an $84.4 million World Bank project, is supporting is the development of a business process outsourcing center. More than 1,000 jobs were created in the industry in 2009 and 2010. Ghana estimates that it will create some 37,000 jobs by 2011, increasing the sector's contribution to GDP by about $750 million. The 2009 AT Kearney Global Services Location Index ranks Ghana 1st out of 50 countries in the world in terms of financial attractiveness and 15th in terms of location attractiveness. The partnership between the public and private sector to train some 50 training providers and 6,000 business process outsourcing agents is expected to further strengthen Ghana's position as one of the most attractive locations for ITES business in Africa.

In July 2010 Amazon.com, the world's largest Internet retailer, announced that it would open a new customer service call center in Cape Town, South Africa, where it will operate a software development center. According to the local media, this business development was brought about by the strong commitment by the central and Western Cape governments for the development of the ITES-BPO industry. It is estimated that the call center will create 1,000 new jobs (600 permanent positions and 400 seasonal positions). Servicing will be provided in English and German. Local government officials hope that the deal will boost the local economy not only by creating jobs but also by demonstrating that Cape Town has the capacity to host world-class clients.

Source: http://www.busrep.co.za/index.php?fSectionId=561andfArticleId=5554024 http://retail.bizcommunity.com/Article/196/458/49992.html.
Notes: (http://www.ites.gov.gh/IT-Industry.aspx).

NESAP–ICT is the World Bank's cross-sectoral initiative to support the development of ICT skills. Launched in 2008 in eight Sub-Saharan African countries (Ghana, Kenya, Madagascar, Mozambique, Nigeria, Rwanda, Senegal, and Tanzania), the program seeks to bridge education and industry gaps in the field, create a globally benchmarked assessment talent pool for the ITES-BPO industry, and strengthen collaboration with IT industry leaders and associations.

The initiative consists of two focus areas. Window I focuses on developing ICT skills for a new emerging ICT-based sector. Window II focuses on ICT use in education.

Implementation of Window I began in 2008. The various skills required for the IT/ITES sector were identified and segmented to meet each country's needs. Fifty-four delegates from eight countries participated in a study tour of India. Pilot projects, guided by international best practice, were launched in four countries (Ghana, Kenya, Nigeria, and Tanzania). The program established partnerships with the world's leading ICT companies (including Microsoft, Intel, Cisco, Oracle, IBM, Nokia, and EMC); with learning institutions (for example, Carnegie Mellon University); and with IT-BPO industry associations (for example, NASSCOM in India). Implementation of Window II, expected to begin in 2011, will build on the Window I accomplishments.

education, private sector development, and ICT sector units to provide skills development for the ICT industry (box 19.7).

In parallel with World Bank activities, IFC has been closely involved in the sector since the beginning of the mobile revolution in Africa. It committed a $261 million investment to 10 ICT projects in Africa during fiscal 2010. It is also investing in innovative new ICT businesses, such as WIZZIT in South Africa, which is providing mobile-based banking services, and Helios Towers Africa Ltd., which is providing tower infrastructure services to mobile operators in Nigeria.

Table 19A.1 Privatizations of Telecom Incumbents in Sub-Saharan Africa, 1995–2010

Country	Operator	Initial privatization transaction Date	sold	($millions)	Percent private 2008	Note
Burkina Faso	ONATEL	December 2006	51	295	51	Private sale to Maroc Telecom.
Cape Verde	Cabo Verde Telecom	December 1995	40	20	59	Private sale to Portugal Telecom. Subsequent distribution to employees (5 percent of total), national private investors (14 percent), and government social security system (38 percent).
Central African Rep.	Socatel	—	—	—	—	France Cable and Radio owned 40 percent of shares at one point. Current status not available.
Côte d'Ivoire	Côte d'Ivoire Telecom	January 1997	51	210	51	Private sale to France Telecom.
Equatorial Guinea	Getesa	1987	40		40	Private sale to France Telecom.
Gabon	Gabon Telecom	February 2007	51	79	51	Private sale to Maroc Telecom.
Gambia, The	GAMTEL	January 2007	50	35	50	Private sale to Spectrum Investment Holding (Lebanon).
Ghana	Ghana Telecom	December 1996	30	38	70	Original private sale to G-Com consortium headed by Telekom Malaysia. In 2002 the government of Ghana abrogated the management contract with G-Com and bought back shares. Subsequent private sale of 70 percent to Vodafone (UK) in August 2008 for $900 million.
Guinea	Sotelgui	December 1995	60	45	0	Renationalized in 2008 following private sale to Telekom Malaysia.
Guinea-Bissau	Guinée Telecom	1989	51	3	0	Renationalized following private sale to Marconi (later assumed by Portugal Telecom).
Kenya	Telkom Kenya	December 2007	51	390	51	Sale to consortium led by France Telecom (78.5 percent) with Alcazar Capital Ltd. (21.5 percent).
Lesotho	Telecom Lesotho	November 2000	70	—	70	Private sale to Mountain Communications (Econet) (Zimbabwe), Mauritius Telecom, and Eskom (South Africa). Sale price not disclosed.
Madagascar	TELMA	August 2003	34	12.6	68	Private sale to Distacom (Hong Kong, China), which also purchased France Telecom's ownership.
Malawi	Malawi Telecom (MTL)	February 2006	80	30	80	Private sale to Telecom Holdings Ltd. (THL) consisting of PCL (50.1 percent), Old Mutual (16.1 percent), NICO (5.0 percent), Detecon (Germany) (2.6 percent) and Press Trust (6.2 percent). Percentages refer to MTL ownership.
Mali	SOTELMA	July 2009	51	384	51	Private sale to Maroc Telecom.
Mauritania	Mauritel	April 2001	54	48	54	Private sale to Maroc Telecom, which subsequently engaged in a series of sales with local investors. Its ownership stood at 51 percent in 2008.
Mauritius	Mauritius Telecom	November 2000	40	261	40	Private sale to France Telecom.
Niger	SONITEL	November 2001	51	16	51	Private sale to Chinese and Libyan consortium. Government has announced intention to renationalize.

Country	Company	Date				Notes
Nigeria	NITEL	July 2006	51	500		Private sale to TransCorp (Nigeria). Government has rescinded the sale and was in process of reprivatizing in 2010.
Rwanda	Rwandatel	June 2005	99	20	80	Initial private sale to Terracom (United States), which government later repurchased. Libya Arab Portfolio later acquired an 80 percent interest for $100 million.
São Tomé and Príncipe	CST (Companhia Santomense de Telecomunicações)	1989	51	1	51	Private sale to Portugal Telecom.
Senegal	Sonatel	July 1997	33	90	73	Initial private sale to France Telecom. Subsequent additional sale to France Telecom and listing on regional stock exchanges.
Seychelles	Cable and Wireless Seychelles	1981	49	n.a.	100	Government granted the British company Cable and Wireless the right to operate the telephone network, inaugurated in 1954. Cable and Wireless was subsequently privatized by British government in three tranches (1981, 1983, and 1985).
South Africa	Telkom	May 1997	30	1,261	34	Initial private sale to Thintana Communications (SBC [United States] 60 percent) and Telekom Malaysia (40 percent). Global initial public offering in March 2003 of 47 percent. Thintana Communications sold 14.9 percent interest in Telkom to South African and international institutional investors in June 2004 and its remaining interest to the Public Investment Corporation, wholly owned by the South African Government in November 2004. Subsequent Telkom share repurchases have altered its level of private shareholding.
Sudan	Sudatel	1997	n.a.	n.a.	36	Multiple share offerings on local and regional stock exchanges.
Tanzania	TTCL (Tanzania Telecommunications Company Ltd.)	February 2001	35	65	35	Private sale to a consortium of MSI (Netherlands) and Detecon (Germany).
Uganda	Uganda Telecom	May 2000	51	34	69	Initial private sale to UCOM consortium consisting of Detecon (Germany), Telecel (Switzerland), and Orascom (Egypt). UCOM ownership subsequently purchased by Libyan Arab Portfolio (LAP), which then increased its ownership through a capital increase.
Zambia	Zamtel	June 2010	75	394	n.a.	Privatization of 75 percent stake sold to LAP Green (Libya) for $394 million in 2010.

Source: AICD 2009; Business Monitor International (BMI) database (http://www.businessmonitor.com/).

Note: n.a. = Not applicable. — = Not available.

REFERENCES

Agrawal, M. 2010. "M-Pesa: Transforming Millions of Lives – I." http://www.telecomcircle.com/2010/01/m-pesa/.

AICD (Africa Infrastructure Country Diagnostic). 2009. *Africa Infrastructure Country Diagnostic Background Paper 10. Information and Communications Technology in Sub-Saharan Africa: A Sector Review.* Washington, DC.

———. 2010. *Africa's Infrastructure: A Time for Transformation.* Washington, DC.

———. Forthcoming. *ICT Sector Volume.* Washington, DC.

Gaasbeck, V., and A. Kristin. 2008. "A Rising Tide: Measuring the Economic Effects of Broadband Use across California." *Social Science Journal* 45 (4): 691–99.

International Telecommunications Union (ITU). 2010. *World Telecommunication/ ICT indicators Database.* Geneva, Switzerland.

Koutroumpis, P. 2009. "The Economic Impact of Broadband on Growth: A Simultaneous Approach." *Telecommunications Policy* 33 (9): 471–85.

Lobo, B. J., A. Novobilski, and S. Ghosh. 2008. "The Economic Impact of Broadband: Estimates from a Regional Input-Output Model." *Journal of Applied Business Research* 24 (2): 103–14.

Morawczynski, O., and M. Pickens. 2009. *Poor People Using Mobile Financial Services: Observations on Customer Usage and Impact from M-PESA.* Consultative Group to Assist the Poor (CGAP), Washington, DC.

Qiang, C. Z-W., and A. Pitt. 2004. "Contribution of Information and Communication Technologies to Growth." World Bank Working Paper 24, Washington, DC.

Qiang, C. Z-W., and C. M. Rossotto, with K. Kimura. 2009. "Economic Impact of Broadband." In *Information and Communication for Development: Extending Reach and Increasing Impact,* 35–50. Washington, DC: World Bank.

Roller, L-H., and L. Waverman. 2001. "Telecommunications Infrastructure and Economic Development: A Simultaneous Approach." *American Economic Review* 91 (4): 909–23.

Safaricom Ltd. 2010. http://www.safaricom.co.ke/

Sudan, R., S. Ayers, P. Dongier, A. Muente-Kunigami, and C. Zhen-Wei Qiang. 2010. *The Global Opportunity in IT–Based Services: Assessing and Enhancing Country Competitiveness.* Washington, DC: World Bank.

TeleGeography CommsUpdate. 2009. July 8. http://www.telegeography.com/cu/index.php.

Tolkoff, S. 2007. "Increased Broadband Use Could Add 186,000 Jobs." *Orange County Business Journal* 30 (50): 9.

Williams, Mark D. J. 2010. *Broadband for Africa: Developing Backbone Communications Networks.* Washington, DC: World Bank.

World Bank. 2010a. *Public Private Infrastructure Indicators Database.* Washington, DC.

———. 2010b. *World Development Indicators.* Washington, DC.

CHAPTER 20

Mobile Payments Go Viral
M-PESA in Kenya

Ignacio Mas and Dan Radcliffe

M-PESA is a small-value electronic payment and store-of-value system in Kenya accessible from ordinary mobile phones. It has seen exceptional growth since its introduction in March 2007. Now in use by 9 million customers—40 percent of Kenya's adult population—the system processes more transactions domestically than Western Union does globally. M-PESA's market success is the result of the interplay of three factors: preexisting country conditions that made Kenya a conducive environment for a successful mobile money deployment; a clever service design that facilitated rapid adoption and early capturing of network effects; and a business execution strategy that helped M-PESA rapidly reach a critical mass of customers, thereby avoiding the adverse chicken-and-egg (two-sided market) problems that afflict new payment systems.

M-PESA IN A NUTSHELL

M-PESA ("M" for mobile and "PESA" for money in Swahili)was developed by mobile phone operator Vodafone and launched commercially by its Kenyan affiliate Safaricom in March 2007.[1] To access the service, customers must first register at an authorized M-PESA retail outlet. They are then assigned an individual electronic money account linked to their phone number and accessible through an application stored on the subscriber identification module (SIM) cards of their mobile phones.[2] The application has two main functions. First, it allows customers to deposit cash to and withdraw cash from their accounts by exchanging cash for electronic value at a network of retail stores. Second, it allows users to transfer funds to others, to pay bills, and to purchase mobile airtime credit. Retail stores are paid a fee by Safaricom each time they exchange cash for M-PESA credit on behalf of customers. All M-PESA transactions are authorized and recorded in real time using secure short messaging service (SMS) and are capped at $500.

M-PESA registration is free, as is making deposits into the system. Customers are charged flat fees of approximately $0.40[3] for person-to-person (P2P) transfers and bill payments, $0.33 for withdrawals (for transactions under $33) and $0.013 for balance inquiries. Individual customer accounts are maintained in a server that is owned and managed by Vodafone, but Safaricom deposits the full value of its customers' balances in the system in pooled accounts in two regulated banks. Thus, while Safaricom issues and manages the M-PESA accounts, the value of the accounts is fully backed by highly liquid deposits at commercial banks. Rather than paying customers interest on the balance in their M-PESA accounts, Safaricom sets aside a small percentage of account balances in a not-for-profit trust fund. The purpose of these funds has not yet been decided.

M-PESA's function as a retail payment platform is important because it reaches a large number of people compared with other financial services outlets in Kenya (figure 20.1).[4] There are now nearly five times as many M-PESA outlets in Kenya as there are PostBank branches, post offices, bank branches, and automated teller machines

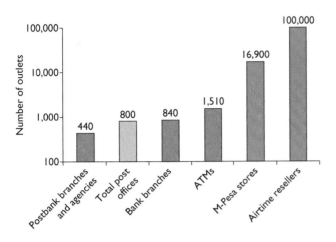

Figure 20.1 Outlets Offering Financial Services in Kenya

Sources: Central Bank of Kenya, Kenya Post Office Savings Bank, and Safaricom.

(ATMs) combined. M-PESA's presence in rural areas is particularly important, because access to financial services in such areas is limited, and the ability to use existing retail stores as M-PESA cash-in/cash-out outlets reduces deployment costs, provides greater convenience, and lowers the cost of access compared with other financial services outlets.

Importantly, both private and public actors were involved in creating and enabling M-PESA. The idea of M-PESA was conceived by a London-based team within Vodafone. This team believed that mobile phones could play a central role in lowering the cost of access to financial services for poor people. The idea was then developed by the Safaricom team in Kenya, which customized it and oversaw a very focused execution. The Central Bank of Kenya, in particular the Payments System Group, helped to enable the launch of M-PESA by allowing a mobile operator to take the lead in providing payment services to the general population. Following the first FinAccess survey in 2006, which showed very low levels of bank penetration in Kenya, the central bank was determined to explore all reasonable options for correcting the financial access imbalance. It worked in close partnership with Vodafone and Safaricom to assess the opportunities and risks involved prior to the launch of M-PESA. Conscious that premature regulation could stifle innovation, the Central Bank of Kenya chose to closely monitor and learn from early M-PESA trials and to formalize regulations later.

Finally, the United Kingdom's Department for International Development (DFID) played an instrumental role in the creation of M-PESA within Kenya, first by funding the organizations that made the FinAccess survey possible, and then by providing seed funding to Vodafone for early M-PESA trials. DFID's role in spotlighting the need for mobile payments and funding the early risk demonstrates good practice for donor funding.

A snapshot of M-PESA after three years

The speed and extent to which M-PESA has been deployed in Kenya is remarkable (figure 20.2). The number of customers hit the 9 million mark in November 2009, less than three years after the service was launched. This number of customers represents 60 percent of Safaricom's customer base, 40 percent of Kenyan adults, and 23 percent of the country's total population.[5]

By other measures, too, M-PESA has a deep reach in Kenya.[6] The number of retail stores at which M-PESA users can cash in and cash out now totals 16,900, of which nearly half are located outside urban centers. M-PESA now handles $320 million in P2P transfers per month. On an annualized basis, this is equal to roughly 10 percent of Kenya's gross domestic product (GDP).[7] An average of $650 million in cash deposit and withdrawal transactions is made at M-PESA stores every month, with an average transaction size of approximately $33. Nearly one-fifth of Safaricom airtime purchases are now conducted through M-PESA.

M-PESA's bill pay function, launched in March 2009, has been popular: 75 companies now use M-PESA to collect payments from their customers. The biggest user, the electric utility company, reports that roughly 20 percent of its 1 million customers now pay through M-PESA. At least two banks, Family Bank and Kenya Commercial Bank, are now using M-PESA as a mechanism for customers to either repay loans or withdraw funds from their banks accounts. And 27 companies are using M-PESA for bulk payment distribution.

Customer perspectives on M-PESA

A survey of 3,000 M-PESA users and nonusers conducted in late 2008 shed considerable light on the profile of M-PESA's early adopters and customer usage patterns. Compared with nonusers, the average M-PESA user is twice as likely to have a bank account (72 percent versus 36 percent) and is wealthier (65 percent higher expenditure levels), more literate, and better educated (Suri and Jack 2008). Early adopters of the service also appear to be experienced with banking services and fairly savvy with technology, which probably makes them more keenly aware of the convenience of M-PESA relative to alternative financial services.

Figure 20.3 highlights the ways customers report they use M-PESA. More than half the sample use the service primarily for sending and receiving money, a use consistent with

Figure 20.2   Growth of the M-PESA Customer Base

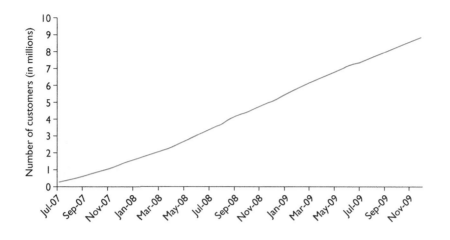

Source: Safaricom.

Figure 20.3   How M-PESA Customers Use the Service

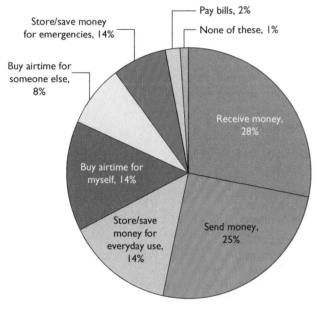

Source: Suri and Jack 2008.

M-PESA's broad market positioning. Though 21 percent report using M-PESA for storing money, the survey revealed that less than 1 percent of accounts had balances of more than K Sh 1,000 ($13), and a government audit (Okoth 2009) of M-PESA in January 2009 showed that the average balance on M-PESA accounts was only $2.70. The survey also found that 52 percent of customers use the service on only a monthly basis, suggesting that customers have yet to incorporate M-PESA into their daily lives (Suri and Jack 2008).

Ninety-eight percent of M-PESA users are happy with the service, according to the 2008 survey, and 84 percent claim that losing M-PESA would have a large, negative effect on them (Suri and Jack 2008). Figure 20.4 illustrates how customers compare M-PESA with alternative services. In all categories—speed, convenience, cost, and safety—customers reported better service with M-PESA than with other forms of financial services.

M-PESA's service evolution

M-PESA's original core offering, the P2P payment, enabled customers to send money to anyone with access to a mobile phone. Importantly, it opened up a market for transactions that previously were handled largely informally—through personal trips, friends, and public transport networks ("personal networks" in figure 20.5). Although many transactions carried out under M-PESA, such as sending a portion of salary earned at the end of the month to relatives, can be characterized as scheduled payments, others allow people to draw on a much broader network of family members, friends, and business associates to access money when required. Thus, in addition to providing a large measure of convenience for transactions that were already occurring, M-PESA also provides a basic form of financial protection for a large number of users by enabling a network for instant, on-demand payments.

In recent months, Safaricom has increasingly opened up M-PESA to institutional payments, enabling companies to pay salaries and collect bill payments. In the future, Safaricom envisions increased use of M-PESA for e-commerce and in-store purchases, a strategy represented by the downward arrow in figure 20.5.

Figure 20.4   User Ratings of M-PESA Compared with Alternatives

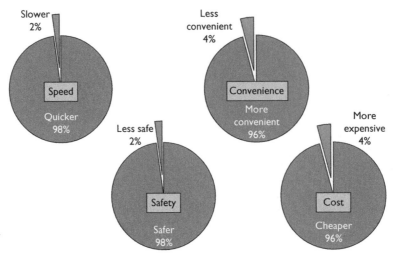

Slower
2%

Speed

Quicker
98%

Less
convenient
4%

Convenience

More
convenient
96%

Less safe
2%

Safety

Safer
98%

More
expensive
4%

Cost

Cheaper
96%

Source: Suri and Jack 2008.
Note: At the time of the survey, alternatives consisted of 876 bank branches, 1,025 Post Office branches, 1,424 ATMs and 6,104 M-PESA agents.

Figure 20.5   Potential Range of Transactions Supported by M-PESA

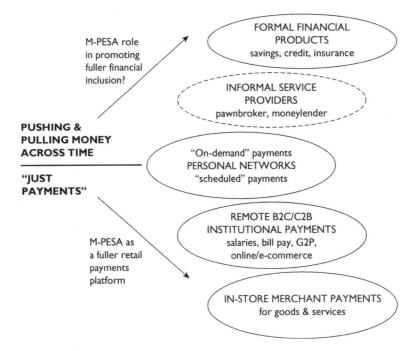

M-PESA role
in promoting
fuller financial
inclusion?

FORMAL FINANCIAL
PRODUCTS
savings, credit, insurance

INFORMAL SERVICE
PROVIDERS
pawnbroker, moneylender

**PUSHING &
PULLING MONEY
ACROSS TIME**

"On-demand" payments
PERSONAL NETWORKS
"scheduled" payments

**"JUST
PAYMENTS"**

REMOTE B2C/C2B
INSTITUTIONAL PAYMENTS
salaries, bill pay, G2P,
online/e-commerce

M-PESA as
a fuller retail
payments
platform

IN-STORE MERCHANT PAYMENTS
for goods & services

Source: Bill & Melinda Gates Foundation analysis.

As represented by the upward arrow in figure 20.5, another of M-PESA's goals is to become a vehicle for delivery of a broader range of financial services for the Kenyan population. Thus far, evidence that people are willing to use the basic M-PESA account as a store of value is limited. There is likely, however, to be a need to develop more targeted savings products that balance customers' preference for liquidity and commitment and that will connect to a broader range of financial institutions. This is the path M-PESA must take to deliver on its promise of addressing the challenge of financial inclusion in Kenya. A key precondition is regulation: the Central Bank of Kenya is in the process of finalizing regulations that will allow nonbank outlets and platforms such as M-PESA become channels for formal deposit-taking. Beyond that, Safaricom will need to develop appropriate service, commercial, and technical models under which M-PESA can interface with the systems of other financial service providers.

The broader lessons from M-PESA's success

In addition to the compelling marketing, cold business logic, and consistent execution behind M-PESA, the success of the service is also a vivid example of how great things can happen when public and private organizations rally around common challenges and innovative solutions. Three top-line lessons emerge from M-PESA's success. First, M-PESA shows the promise of leveraging mobile technology to extend financial services to a large number of unbanked poor people. Second, it demonstrates the importance of designing usage-based rather than float-based revenue models for financial services for poor customers. And third, M-PESA demonstrates the importance of building a low-cost transactional platform that enables customers to meet a broad range of payment needs.[8]

LEVERAGING TECHNOLOGY TO EXTEND FINANCIAL SERVICES TO UNBANKED POOR PEOPLE. Mobile phone technology is quickly becoming ubiquitous, even among poor segments of the Kenyan population. Mobile penetration in Africa has increased from 3 percent in 2002 to 48 percent in 2010, and is expected to reach 72 percent by 2014, according to Wireless Intelligence. The mobile device mimics some of the key ingredients needed to offer banking services. The SIM card inside GSM phones, for example, can be used to authenticate users, thereby avoiding the high costs of distributing separate bank cards to poor customers, who typically do not generate significant profits for banks. The mobile phone can also be used as a point of sale terminal to initiate financial transactions and securely communicate with the appropriate server to request transaction authorization, thus obviating the need to deploy costly dedicated devices in retail environments.

A USAGE-BASED MODEL FOR REACHING POOR CUSTOMERS WITH FINANCIAL SERVICES. Because banks make most of their profits by collecting and reinvesting deposits, they tend to distinguish between profitable and unprofitable customers based on the likely size of their account balances and their ability to absorb credit. Banks thus find it difficult to serve poor customers because the revenue from reinvesting small-value deposits is unlikely to offset the cost of serving these customers. In contrast, mobile operators in

developing countries have developed a usage-based revenue model, selling prepaid airtime to poor customers in small increments, so that each transaction is profitable on a stand-alone basis. This is the magic behind the rapid penetration of prepaid airtime into low-income markets: a card purchased is profit booked, regardless of who buys the prepaid card. This usage-based revenue model is directly aligned with the model needed to sustainably offer small-value cash-in/cash-out transactions at retail outlets and would make possible a true mass-market approach, with no incentive for providers to deny service based on minimum balances or intensity of use.

A LOW-COST TRANSACTIONAL PLATFORM THAT ENABLES CUSTOMERS TO MEET A RANGE OF PAYMENT NEEDS. Once customers are connected to an e-payment system, they can use this capability to store money in a savings account, send and receive money from friends and family, pay bills and monthly insurance premiums, receive pension or social welfare payments, or receive loan disbursements and repay them electronically. In short, when customers are connected to an e-payment system, their range of financial possibilities expands dramatically.

Putting these elements together, M-PESA has prompted a rethink on the optimal sequencing of financial inclusion strategies. Whereas most financial inclusion models have employed "credit-led" or "savings-led" approaches, the M-PESA experience suggests that there may be a third approach—focusing first on building the payment "rails" on which a broader set of financial services can ride.

KENYA COUNTRY FACTORS: UNMET NEEDS, FAVORABLE MARKET CONDITIONS

The growth of M-PESA is a testament to Safaricom's vision and execution capacity. But Safaricom also benefited from launching the service under several enabling conditions for successful deployment of a mobile money service. These include strong latent demand for domestic remittances, poor quality of available financial services, a banking regulator that permitted Safaricom to experiment with different business models and distribution channels, a mobile communications market characterized by Safaricom's dominant market position and low commissions on airtime sales, and a reasonable amount of banking infrastructure.

Strong latent demand for domestic remittances

Safaricom based its launch of the M-PESA service on the very brief, but powerful, phrase: "send money home." In this, it capitalized on the fact that demand for domestic remittance services is greater in locations where migration has occurred, separating families, particularly when the breadwinner moves to an urban center and the rest of the family remains home. This was certainly the case in Kenya, where 17 percent of households depended on remittances as their primary income source as of 2006 (FSDT 2007a).

A recent study of M-PESA suggests that latent demand for domestic remittances is related to urbanization ratios (Ratan 2008), and that the most propitious domestic remittances markets are those in which the process of rural-urban migration is sufficiently rooted to produce large migration flows but not so advanced that rural communities are hollowed out. The study also finds that countries with mid-range urbanization ratios (20 to 40 percent), especially those that are urbanizing at a rapid rate, are likely to exhibit strong rural-urban ties requiring substantial transfer of value. This is the case in many African countries, such as Kenya and Tanzania, where the share of the population living in urban areas as of 2008 was 22 percent and 26 percent, respectively, according to the World Bank. On the other hand, where urbanization ratios exceed 50 percent, such as in the Philippines and several Latin American countries, remittances are likely to be more closely linked to international rather than domestic migration patterns.

Further, the study shows that in locations where entire nuclear families move, remittances are strongest when there is cultural pressure to retain a connection with one's ancestral village. In Kenya, migrants' ties with rural homes are reinforced by an ethnic (rather than a national) concept of citizenship. These links are expressed through burial, inheritance, cross-generational, social insurance, and other ties, even in cases where migrants reside more or less permanently in cities.[9] In countries where migrants have a stronger connection to national as opposed to local or ethnic identity, rural to urban migration may have diminished the significance of the rural "home" and hence dampened domestic remittance flows.

Poor quality of existing alternatives

Demand for mobile e-payments must be examined in the context of the accessibility and quality of alternative payment methods. If there are many good alternatives to mobile payments, as is typically the case in developed countries, it is difficult to convince users to switch to the new service. In the Philippines, for example, the G-Cash and Smart Money mobile payment services experienced low take-up in part because of the availability of a competitive alternative to mobile payments—an extensive and efficient semiformal retail network of pawnshops offering domestic remittance services at commissions of 3 percent.

In Kenya, by comparison, the most common channel for sending money before M-PESA was informal bus and *matatu* (shared taxi) companies. Because these companies are not licensed to transfer money, there is considerable risk that the money will not reach its final destination. Meanwhile, Kenya Post, Kenya's major formal remittance provider, is perceived by customers as costly, slow, and prone to liquidity shortages at rural outlets. M-PESA's popularity was also bolstered by the fact that Kenya's bank branch infrastructure (currently, there are 840 branches) is far too sparse to compete with M-PESA's 16,900 cash-in/cash-out outlets. Figure 20.6 illustrates how Kenyan households sent money before and after M-PESA. Of note is the dramatic reduction in the use of informal bus systems and Kenya Post to transfer money between 2006 and 2009.

As noted, M-PESA's early adopters were primarily banked customers, suggesting that M-PESA did not acquire its initial critical mass through competition with the formal sector but rather as a complement to formal services for clients who were wealthier, more exposed to formal financial service options, and less risk averse. As M-PESA services move deeper into the Kenyan market, however, unbanked users are increasingly driving M-PESA's expansion because of the competitive advantages of mobile banking offers over other options. This is one reason why Africa, with its high proportion of unbanked people, is seen as such a promising market for mobile money applications.

A supportive banking regulator

Regulation of mobile money can help secure trust in new mobile money schemes. At the same time, regulation may constrain the deployment of a mobile money application by limiting the scheme operator's freedom in structuring the business model, service proposition, and distribution channels. In the case of M-PESA in Kenya, Safaricom had a good working relationship with the central bank and was given regulatory space to design M-PESA in a manner that fit its market. Together, the Central Bank of Kenya and Safaricom worked out a model that provided sufficient prudential comfort to the central bank.

The Central Bank of Kenya insisted that all customer funds be deposited in a regulated financial institution and reviewed the security features of the technology platform, but it also allowed Safaricom to operate M-PESA as a payments system outside the provisions of the banking law.[10]

Figure 20.6 Money Transfer Behavior before and after M-PESA

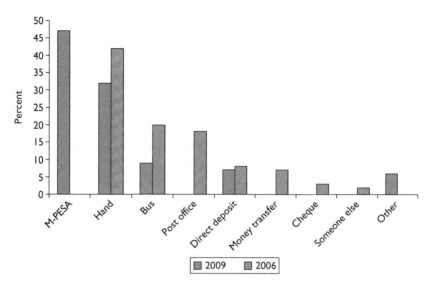

Source: FSDT 2007a, 2009b.

Safaricom has paid a certain price for this arrangement. For instance, interest earned on deposited balances must go to a not-for-profit trust and cannot be appropriated by Safaricom or passed on to customers. To address anti-money-laundering concerns, there are also limits on the size of M-PESA transactions. Fundamentally, however, Safaricom was able to design the M-PESA service without having to contort its business model to fit within a prescribed regulatory model.

The Central Bank of Kenya has continued to support M-PESA's development, even in the face of pressure from banks. In late 2008, following a lobbying effort by the banking industry to shut down the service, the Central Bank of Kenya performed an audit of the M-PESA service at the request of the Ministry of Finance and declared it safe and in line with the country's objectives for financial inclusion (see Okoth 2009 for information). Thus far, the central bank appears justified in its confidence in M-PESA—there have been no reports of major fraud. Although system downtime remains frequent, it has not been catastrophic.

A dominant mobile operator and low airtime commissions

The chances of a mobile money scheme taking root also depend on the strength of the mobile operator within its market, because a large market share is associated with a larger potential customer base for cross-selling the mobile money service, a larger network of airtime resellers that can

be converted into cash-in/cash-out agents, stronger brand recognition and trust among potential customers, and larger budgets to finance the heavy up-front investments needed to deploy a new service. With a market share of around 80 percent, Safaricom enjoyed all of these benefits when it launched M-PESA.

Successful deployment of a mobile money application also has a greater chance of success in countries where the commissions that mobile operators pay airtime resellers are relatively low. If commissions are too high, resellers will not be attracted by the incipient cash-in/cash-out business. In Safaricom's case, airtime commissions total 6 percent, of which 5 percent is passed on to the retail store. A commission of 1–2 percent on a cash-in/cash-out transaction is plausibly attractive—the store need only believe that the volume of the cash business will be five times the size of the airtime business. This seems reasonable, considering that the bulk of airtime sales are of low denominations (around $0.25).

A reasonable base of banking infrastructure

Finally, the ability of M-PESA stores to convert cash to e-value for customers depends on how easily they can rebalance their liquidity. If bank branch penetration is too low, rebalancing will be more difficult to achieve, because the agent channel is forced to develop alternative cash transport mechanisms. Thus, a mobile payment agent network must have at its disposal at least a minimal retail banking infrastructure. There appears to be a branch penetration "sweet spot" for mobile money, where penetration is not so high that it hampers demand for mobile money services but not so low that agents are unable to manage their liquidity. Because of the branch networks of Equity Bank and other banks and microfinance institutions, Kenya is reasonably well supplied with rural liquidity points. Even so, shortage of cash or electronic value for M-PESA agents is a problem in both rural and urban areas in Kenya. Mobile payment operators in some other Sub-Saharan African countries face more serious liquidity constraints, especially in rural areas. Such constraints are likely to be a major factor affecting the success of mobile services in specific country contexts.

M-PESA'S SERVICE DESIGN: GETTING PEOPLE ONTO THE SYSTEM

While M-PESA's rapid growth was fueled by certain country-specific enabling conditions, the success of such an innovative service hinged on the design of the service. Conducting financial transactions through a mobile phone is not an intuitive notion for many people, just as walking to a corner shop to make cash deposits and withdrawals may not at first seem natural to many. To overcome this adoption barrier, Safaricom designed M-PESA in a way that helped people immediately grasp how they might benefit from the service; removed barriers that might prevent people from experimenting with the service; and fostered trust in retail outlets that would be tasked with promoting the service, registering customers, and facilitating cash-in/cash-out services.

A simple message targeting a big point of concern among the population

In very early phases of conception, Vodafone developers thought that M-PESA would be used as a way for customers to repay microloans. However, as Safaricom market-tested the mobile money proposition, they shifted the core proposition from loan repayment to helping people make P2P transfers to their friends and family. In its commercial launch, M-PESA was marketed to the public with just three powerful words: "send money home." In an environment in which families were geographically split, this message tapped into a major concern for many Kenyans—the risks and high costs associated with sending money over long distances. Thus, a simple marketing message turned a basic "e-remittance" product into a must-have "killer" application and remains the main marketing message three

years later. Although people have proved creative in using M-PESA for their own needs, sending money home continues to be one of the most important uses, and the number of Kenyan households receiving money transfers has increased from 17 percent to 52 percent since M-PESA was introduced (FSDT 2009a).

A simple user interface

The simplicity of M-PESA's message is matched by the simplicity of its user interface. The service can be launched right from the main menu of a mobile phone, making it easy for users to find. And because the service resides on the phone and does not need to be downloaded from the network each time it is used, the menu loads very quickly and prompts the user for information step-by-step. For instance, for a P2P transfer, the user is asked to enter the destination phone number, the amount of the transfer, and the personal identification number (PIN) of the sender. Once the information is gathered, it is fed back to the customer for final confirmation. Once the customer hits OK on a mobile phone, the data is sent to the M-PESA server in a single text message. Consolidating all information into a single message reduces messaging costs as well as the risk that only part of the transaction data will be sent to the server. A final advantage is that the application can use the security keys in the user's SIM card to encrypt messages end-to-end, from the user's handset to Safaricom's M-PESA server.

Removing adoption barriers: free to register, free to deposit, no minimum balances

Safaricom designed M-PESA to make it as easy as possible for customers to try the service. Customer registration, which can be done at any M-PESA retail outlet, is quick, simple, and free. First, the retail clerk provides a paper registration form, where the customer enters his or her name, ID number (from Kenyan national ID, passport, military ID, diplomatic ID, or alien ID), date of birth, occupation, and mobile phone number. The clerk then checks the ID and inputs the registration information into the customer's mobile phone. SIM cards in Kenya are now preloaded with the M-PESA application. If the customer's SIM card is too old and does not contain the application, the clerk replaces it. The customer's phone number is not changed even if the SIM card is.

After Safaricom receives the application, it sends both the customer and the retail outlet an SMS confirming the transaction. The SMS provides the customer a four-digit start key (one-time password), which they use to activate their account. Customers enter the start key and their ID number, after which they are asked to input a secret PIN of their choice. This completes the registration process. In addition to leading customers through this registration process, retail clerks explain how to use the application and discuss the costs associated with each service. This customer support early in the process is particularly important in rural areas, where a significant percentage of the potential user base is unfamiliar with the functioning of mobile phones.

The minimum M-PESA deposit amount is approximately $1.25, but there is no minimum balance requirement. And because customers deposit money for free, there is no immediate barrier to taking up the service. M-PESA charges customers only for "doing something" with their money, such as making a transfer, withdrawing money, or buying prepaid airtime.

The ability to send money to anyone

M-PESA customers can send money to any GSM mobile phone subscriber on the Safaricom, Zain, Orange, or YU networks in Kenya, regardless of whether the receiving party is an M-PESA customer. When a transfer is sent, money is debited from the sender's account and the recipient receives a code by SMS, which is used to claim the monetary value at any M-PESA store. M-PESA is thus an account-to-cash service, with the receiver's experience being similar to the way Western Union works today. M-PESA's pricing, however, is quite different: customers pay a higher (roughly triple) P2P charge when sending money to a non-M-PESA customer, but at the other end the noncustomer is not charged to receive the cash, whereas registered customers pay a cash-out fee of at least $0.30. Safaricom developed this pricing scheme with the understanding that the sender has power over the recipient, and so it chose to put pressure on the sender to require the recipient to register with M-PESA. Furthermore, Safaricom hoped that providing noncustomers with a good, no-cost first experience with M-PESA would lure them to register for M-PESA.

Building trust in the retail network

Recognizing that M-PESA would not be rapidly adopted by the Kenyan population unless customers had enough trust in the M-PESA retail network that they were willing to conduct cash-in/cash-out transactions through those outlets, Safaricom employed several measures to build that trust. First, it closely linked the M-PESA brand with its own strong corporate brand. As the mobile operator in Kenya with the dominant share of the market (more than 80 percent at M-PESA's launch and almost as much in 2010), Safaricom was already a broadly respected and trusted brand, even among low-income customers. M-PESA retail outlets are required to paint their store "Safaricom green," a tactic that not only gives customers confidence that the store is acting on behalf of Safaricom but also makes it easier for customers to locate cash-in/cash-out points.

Second, by investing heavily in store training and on-site supervision, Safaricom ensured that customers can have a remarkably similar experience in any retail authorized outlet they use. This "sameness" has helped to build trust in both the platform and the outlets and gives customers a consistently positive view of the service. Rather than relying on its channel intermediaries to carry out these functions in retail shops, Safaricom chose to centralize the functions through a single third-party vendor, Top Image. Quality is maintained through a rating process. A Top Image representative visits each outlet at least once per month and rates each store on a variety of criteria, including visibility of branding and the tariff poster, availability of cash and M-PESA electronic value to accommodate customer transactions, and quality of record-keeping.

Third, the fact that M-PESA customers receive instant SMS confirmation of their transaction has helped them learn by experience to trust the system. Because the receipt confirming a money transfer includes the name and number of the recipient and the amount transferred, it allows the sender to confirm instantly that the money was sent to the right person—the most common source of error. In the case of an error, the receipt can then be used to resolve the situation.

Fourth, Safaricom requires its outlets to record all cash-in/cash-out transactions in a paper-based, Safaricom-created logbook. For each transaction, the store clerk enters the M-PESA balance, the date, agent ID, transaction ID, transaction type (customer deposit or withdrawal), value, customer phone number, customer name, and the customer's national ID number. Customers are then asked to sign the log for each transaction, which not only discourages fraud but also gives agents a way to offer first-line customer care for customers querying previous transactions. Each entry in the log is written in triplicate. The top copy is kept by the retail outlet for its own records, a second is passed on to the store's master agent, and the third is sent to Safaricom. Because all information contained in the logbook (except for the customer signature) is captured electronically by Safaricom when the transaction is made and is available to the master agents through a Web management system, the main purpose of the agent log is not for record-keeping but rather to provide comfort to customers who are accustomed to having transactions recorded on paper.

Simple and transparent pricing

M-PESA pricing is transparent and predictable. There are no customer charges for the SMSs that deliver the service. Instead, fees are applied to the actual, customer-initiated transactions. All customer fees are subtracted from the customer's account, and outlets cannot charge any direct fees. Thus, outlets collect their commissions from Safaricom

(through their master agents) rather than from customers. This arrangement reduces the potential for agent abuses. Customer fees are uniform nationwide, and they are prominently posted in all outlet locations in the poster shown in figure 20.7.

M-PESA chose to specify its fees in fixed currency terms rather than as a percentage of the transaction. This makes it easier for customers to understand the precise cost of each transaction and helps them think of the fee in terms of the transaction's absolute value (for example, sending money to grandmother). It also helps them compare the transaction cost against alternative and usually costlier money-transfer arrangements (for example, the *matatu* fare plus travel time).

Figure 20.7 M-PESA Tariff Structure

Transaction type	Transaction range (KShs)		Customer charge (KShs)
	Minimum	Maximum	
Value movement transactions			
Deposit cash	100	35,000	0
Send money to a registered M-PESA user	100	35,000	30
Send money to a nonregistered M-PESA user	100	2,500	75
	2,501	5,000	100
	5,001	10,000	175
	10,001	20,000	350
	20,001	35,000	400
Withdraw cash by a registered M-PESA user at an M-PESA agent outlet	100	2,500	25
	2,501	5,000	45
	5,001	10,000	75
	10,001	20,000	145
	20,001	35,000	170
Withdraw cash by registered M-PESA user at PesaPoint ATM	200	2,500	30
	2,501	5,000	60
	5,001	10,000	100
	10,001	20,000	175
Withdraw cash by a non-registered M-PESA user	100	35,000	0
Buy airtime (for self or other)	20	10,000	0
Pay Bill Transactions	-	-	0–30
Information transactions			
Show balance			1
Change secret word			0
Change PIN			20
Update menu			0
Change language			0
SIM replacement			20

Source: Safaricom.

M-PESA deposits are free to customers. Withdrawals of less than $33 cost around $0.33. Withdrawal charges are "banded" (that is, larger transactions incur a larger cost) so as not to discourage smaller transactions. ATM withdrawals using M-PESA are slightly more expensive than withdrawals at a retail outlet ($0.40 versus $0.33).

P2P transfers using M-PESA cost a flat rate of around $0.40. These transfers are where Safaricom makes the bulk of its revenue. Thus, for a purely electronic transfer, customers pay more than double the price they pay for the average cash transaction ($0.17), even though the cost of providing purely electronic transactions is lower than cash transactions. This model reflects a notion of optimal pricing that is based less on cost and more on customer willingness to pay. M-PESA is still cheaper, though, than the other available mechanisms for making remote payments, such as money transfer by the bus companies, Kenya Post's Postapay, or Western Union.[11]

Notably, M-PESA has maintained the same pricing for transactions in its first three years of operation. This strategy has helped establish customer familiarity with the service. Safaricom has changed, however, the price of two types of customer requests that do not involve a financial transaction: balance inquiries (because the initial low price generated a burdensome volume of requests) and PIN changes (because customers are far more likely to remember their PIN if the fee to change it is higher). The volume of both types of requests decreased substantially after these price changes. As previously noted, the SMS confirmation of a transaction contains the available balance, which also helps cut down on the number of balance inquiries.

Liquidity of last resort at bank branches and ATMs

From very early on, M-PESA signed up banks as agents, so M-PESA customers could walk into any branch of those banks to conduct cash-in/cash-out transactions. One year after its launch, M-PESA went further and partnered with PesaPoint, one of the largest ATM service providers in Kenya. The PesaPoint network includes more than 110 ATMs scattered in all eight provinces of the country. Customers can now retrieve money from any PesaPoint ATM. To do so, they select "ATM withdrawal" from the M-PESA menu on their mobile phone, after which they receive a one-time ATM authorization code. They then enter that code on the ATM keyboard to make the withdrawal. No bank card is needed for the transaction.

M-PESA's liquidity system is not without its challenges, however. Because of cash flow constraints, M-PESA retail outlets cannot always meet requests for withdrawals, especially large ones. Furthermore, the agent commission structure discourages outlets from handling large transactions. As a result, customers are sometimes forced to spread large withdrawals over several days rather than withdraw a lump sum, at an added cost and inconvenience. Cash flow constraints also undermine customer trust in M-PESA as a mechanism for high-balance, long-term saving. Use of bank branches and ATMs to give customers a sort of liquidity mechanism of last resort has bolstered the credibility of the M-PESA system, however,

M-PESA'S EXECUTION STRATEGY: QUICKLY REACHING CRITICAL MASS

Although strong services design has been a major factor in the success of M-PESA, an appropriate execution strategy has also been a key factor. Importantly, Safaricom recognized that it would be difficult to scale M-PESA incrementally, because it had to overcome three significant obstacles common to any new electronic payment system, namely, adverse network effects, the chicken-and-egg trap, and trust. First, in regard to adverse network effects, the value to the customer of a payment system depends on the number of people connected to and actively using it. The more people on the network, the more useful it becomes.[12] While network effects can help a scheme gain momentum once it reaches a critical mass of customers, they also make it difficult to attract early adopters of the new technology. Second, to grow, M-PESA had to attract customers and stores in tandem. It is difficult, however, to attract customers when there are few stores to serve them, and equally hard to convince stores to sell the service when there are few customers to be had (thus, the chicken-and-egg trap). Thus, M-PESA needed to drive both customer and store acquisition aggressively. Third, a company will be successful in attracting customers only when prospective customers have confidence in the reliability of the new system. In the case of M-PESA, customers had to be comfortable with three elements that were new at the time in Kenya: a payment system operated by a mobile operator, using a nonbank retail outlet to meet cash-in/cash-out needs, and using mobile phones to access account information and initiate transactions.

In the early stages of development of a payments system, the three problems described above reinforce each other, creating a significant hurdle to growth. In many cases, this hurdle helps explain why many other mobile money deployments remain subscale. M-PESA, however, overcame this hurdle through very forceful execution on two key fronts: Safaricom made significant up-front investments in building a strong service brand for M-PESA, and it effectively leveraged its extensive network of airtime resellers to build a reliable, consistent retail network that served customers' liquidity needs.

Aggressive up-front investment in promoting the M-PESA brand

From the beginning, Safaricom sought to foster customer trust in M-PESA and relied on existing customers to be the prime mechanism for drawing in new customers. The task was all the more difficult because Safaricom was not only introducing a new product, but an entirely new product category, to a market that had little experience with formal financial services. Safaricom's initial target for M-PESA was about 1 million customers within one year of the launch of the service, equal to 17 percent of Safaricom's customer base of about 6 million customers at the time, according to Safaricom company results for the year ending March 2007.

NATIONAL LAUNCH AT SCALE. After small pilots involving less than 500 customers,[13] M-PESA launched nationwide, increasing the likelihood that the service could reach a critical mass of customers in a short time frame. At launch, Safaricom had 750 stores that covered all of Kenya's 69 district headquarters. The launch was a massive logistical challenge that led to a great deal of customer and store confusion and, during the first few months, delays of several days in reaching customer service hotlines. User and store errors were frequent since everyone was new to the service. But the gamble paid off. Logistical problems subsided after a few months, leaving strong brand recognition and top-of-mind awareness among large segments of the population. The service outran first-year growth targets, quickly turning network effects in its favor as new customers begat more customers and turned M-PESA into a compelling business proposition for more stores.

AN APPROPRIATE MARKETING MIX. Initial M-PESA marketing featured and targeted urban, relatively wealthy city dwellers with a need to "send money home." The choice of this demographic as the initial customer created an aspirational image for prospective customers and avoided giving the impression that M-PESA was a low-value product aimed at the poor. Over time, the marketing moved from young, up-market urban dwellers with desk jobs to more ordinary Kenyans with lower-paid professions.

M-PESA's launch was associated with significant up-front investment in television and radio marketing,[14] but there was also intense outreach through road shows, in which company agents traveled around the country signing people up, explaining the product, and demonstrating how to use it. Over time, as people became more familiar with M-PESA, it was no longer necessary to do this kind of hands-on outreach. Television and radio marketing was largely replaced by the omnipresent M-PESA branding at all outlets, supported by a few large billboards. Newer ads feature a general emotional appeal, with a wider range of services indicated.

A scalable distribution channel

From the time Safaricom launched M-PESA, it understood that the primary role of the mobile phone is to enable the creation of a retail outlet–based channel for cash-to-digital value conversion. It also understood that for this cash-to-digital conversion to be broadly available to the bulk of the population, Safaricom had to develop a channel structure that could support thousands of M-PESA stores spread across a broad geographical area. To achieve this, Safaricom built four elements into its channel management execution strategy: engaging intermediaries to help manage the individual stores, thereby reducing the number of direct contacts it had to deal with, ensuring that outlets received sufficient incentives to actively promote the service, maintaining tight control over the customer experience, and developing several different methods for stores to rebalance their stocks of cash and e-value.

TWO-TIER CHANNEL MANAGEMENT STRUCTURE. Safaricom created a two-tier structure with individual stores (subagents, in Safaricom's parlance) that depends on master agents (referred to by Safaricom as agent head offices). Agent head offices maintain all contact with Safaricom, and perform two key functions: liquidity management (buying and selling M-PESA balance from Safaricom and making it available to individual stores under their responsibility), and distribution of agent commissions (collecting the commission from Safaricom based on the overall performance of the stores under them and remunerating each store). Individual stores are either directly owned by an agent head office or working for one under contract.

GIVING STORES INCENTIVES. Retail outlets will not maintain sufficient stocks of cash and electronic money unless they are adequately compensated for doing so. Hence, Safaricom pays commissions to agent head offices for each cash-in/cash-out transaction conducted by stores under their responsibility. Although Safaricom does not prescribe the commission split between agent head offices and stores, most agent head offices pass on 70 percent of commissions to the store.[15] For deposits under $33, Safaricom pays a $0.133 commission, of which $0.074 goes to the store after tax. For withdrawals, Safaricom pays $0.200, of which $0.111 goes to the store. So, assuming equal volumes of deposits and withdrawals, the store earns $0.092 per transaction. Assuming the store conducts 60 transactions per day, it earns around $5.50—almost twice the prevailing daily wage for a clerk in Kenya.

Recall that Safaricom charges customers $0.333 on a round-trip savings transaction (free deposit plus $0.33 for the withdrawal), which is in fact equal to what the channel receives ($0.13 on the deposit plus $0.20 for the withdrawal). So, assuming equal volumes of deposits and withdrawals, Safaricom does not make money on cash transactions. It merely "advances" commissions to the channel when customers make deposits and recoups them when customers withdraw. As noted, Safaricom generates the bulk of its revenue from services for which customer willingness to pay is the highest—electronic, P2P transactions.

Because store revenues are dependent on the number of transactions they facilitate, Safaricom has been careful not to flood the market with too many outlets, lest it depress the number of customers per agent. Instead, it has maintained balanced growth in the number of outlets relative to the number of active customers, resulting in an incentivized and committed agent base.

MAINTAINING TIGHT CONTROL OVER THE CUSTOMER EXPERIENCE. Safaricom also recognized early on that customers need to have a good experience at the retail stores offering M-PESA services, where the bulk of transactions take place. To ensure that it maintained control over the customer experience, it has not relied on agent head offices to perform all channel management functions. Instead, it concentrated the evaluation, training, and on-site supervision of stores in a single outsourcing partner, Top Image. The more routine and non-customer-facing store support activities, such as liquidity management and distribution of store commissions, are left to a large pool of agent head offices. Through its contract with Top Image, however, Safaricom retained direct, centralized control over key elements of the customer experience: store selection, training, and supervision.

DEVELOPING MULTIPLE STORE LIQUIDITY MANAGEMENT METHODS. By far the biggest challenge faced by M-PESA stores is maintaining enough liquidity, in terms of both cash and e-float,[16] to be able to meet customer requests. If they take too many cash deposits, stores will find themselves running out of e-float with which to facilitate further deposits. If they do too many withdrawals, on the other hand, they will accumulate e-float but will run out of cash. Thus, stores frequently undertake liquidity management efforts.

The M-PESA channel management structure was conceived to offer stores three methods for managing liquidity. Two of these place the agent head office in a central role, with the expectation that it will "recycle" e-float between locations experiencing net cash withdrawals (that is, accumulating e-float) and locations with net cash deposits (that is, accumulating cash). In the first method, the agent head office provides direct cash support to stores. The store clerk comes to the agent head office to deliver or offload cash, or the agent head office sends cash runners to the store to perform these functions.

In the second method, the agent head office and stores use their respective bank accounts. If the store has excess cash and wants to buy M-PESA e-float from the agent head office, the store deposits the cash into the account of the agent head office at the nearest bank branch or ATM. Once the agent head office confirms receipt of the funds into its account, it transfers M-PESA e-float to the store's M-PESA account. If the store wants to sell e-float to obtain cash, the store transfers M-PESA e-float to the agent head office. The agent head office then deposits (or transfers) money into the store's bank account, after which the store can withdraw the cash at the nearest branch or ATM.

In the third method, stores interact directly with a bank that has registered as an M-PESA "superagent." Under this method, the agent head office does not get involved in liquidity management. Instead, stores open an account with a participating superagent bank. To rebalance their cash, stores deposit and withdraw cash against their bank account at the nearest branch or ATM of the bank. The store then electronically buys and sells e-float in real time against its bank account. From a store's perspective, one drawback of using a bank-based superagent mechanism is that it can only be used during banking business hours.

In all cases, the e-float–cash nexus will remain the key constraint to further development of M-PESA, because it requires the physical movement of cash around the country and is thus the least scalable part of the system.

M-PESA'S FUTURE EVOLUTION

The experience of M-PESA demonstrates how powerful a payment network that offers convenience at an affordable cost can be once a critical mass of customers is reached. It also shows that achieving critical mass requires a service design that removes as many adoption barriers as possible, together with significant investment in marketing, branding, and agent network management. The Kenyan experience also suggests that several country-level factors must be aligned to set the scene for successful mobile money development, including the labor market profile (demand for remittances generated by rural-urban migration), the quality of available financial services, support from the banking regulator, and the structure of the mobile communications market (dominant mobile operator and low airtime commissions).

While M-PESA has been more successful than anyone could have imagined at its launch, the model still has substantial room for development. A threefold wish list for M-PESA could be delineated as follows: further mainstreaming of M-PESA's regulatory treatment, pricing that opens up a much larger market of microtransactions, and expanding M-PESA so that customers have access to a broader range of financial services.

Mainstreaming M-PESA's regulatory treatment

M-PESA's regulatory treatment as a payments vehicle needs to be formalized so that it can become regulated in the most appropriate way. To this end, the Central Bank of Kenya is backing a new payments law that would cover M-PESA transactions (as of this writing, the draft had not yet been approved by the Kenyan parliament). The Central Bank of Kenya is also in the process of finalizing agent banking regulations that would allow commercial banks to use retail outlets as a delivery channel for financial services. Banks are quite reasonably complaining that they could not replicate the M-PESA service themselves because they are not currently allowed to undertake customer transactions through agent networks on their own. Allowing both banks and M-PESA to operate such agent networks would level the playing field.

Pricing that enables smaller payments

M-PESA's current pricing model is not conducive to small transactions. The fee for a $10 P2P transfer plus withdrawal, for example, is approximately 7 percent of the amount of the transaction ($0.40 for the transfer plus $0.33 for the withdrawal). Adjusting M-PESA's current pricing model to account for smaller-denomination transactions would have two advantages. First, it would make the service more accessible to the poor, for whom pricing is now too high given their transactional needs. Such a reduction would allow Safaricom to maintain customer growth once saturation starts to set in at current pricing. Second, a pricing adjustment would allow customers to use M-PESA for their daily transaction needs, and in particular to save on a daily basis, which would be beneficial to those who are paid daily.

A reduction in customer prices could come about in several ways. There is room for "tranching" the P2P fee of $0.40, for example, so that the price of smaller, or more frequent, transactions becomes more affordable. For cash transactions, one way to enable lower fees would be to establish street-level M-PESA subagents who would offer lower costs and commissions than store-based agents. Subagents would be a kind of "e-susu collector," operating with small working capital in order to aggregate small customer transactions. Subagents would use normal M-PESA retail outlets to rebalance their cash and M-PESA stored value. The key principle here is that segmentation of customers would go hand-in-hand with segmentation of agents.

Linking with banks and other institutions

While some customers use M-PESA as a saving device, the service still falls short of being a useful method of saving for most poor people. The fact that the average balance of M-PESA accounts was less than $3 in early 2009 is partly a "large number" problem: if 900,000 people used M-PESA to save, that means 10 percent of users use the service to save, and that the average savings balance is diluted because it takes into account all M-PESA users rather than only users who save. But the fundamental problem is that there is still a lot of conversion of electronic value back into cash. This can be attributed to a combination of factors:

- *Lack of marketing.* Safaricom does not want to publicly promote using M-PESA as a saving tool for fear of provoking the Central Bank Kenya to regulate it more tightly.
- *Customer pricing.* The flat fee of around $0.33 for withdrawals under $33 means that small withdrawals carry a large relative fee.
- *Product design.* M-PESA works very much like an electronic checking account and does not offer structured

saving products that may help people build discipline around savings.

- *Inflation.* M-PESA does not pay interest. In an environment with 15 percent inflation (during its first full year of operation in 2008), saving may be too onerous for much of the Kenyan population.
- *Trust.* M-PESA deposits are not supervised by the Central Bank of Kenya. And unlike payments, where trust can be validated experientially in real time, saving requires garnering the trust of customers over a longer period of time.
- *Privacy.* People may want more privacy for their saving behavior than an agent provides.
- *Excess liquidity.* The 16,000 M-PESA cash-in points in Kenya are also 16,000 cash-out points. The ubiquity of M-PESA agents may make it too easy for customers to cash out their funds, thus limiting their ability to accumulate large balances.

Rather than expecting Safaricom to develop and market more comprehensive savings services, M-PESA should support saving by linking to banks. M-PESA could then become a massive transaction acquisition network for banks rather than an alternative to them. That said, Safaricom is beginning to connect with banks. In September 2009, for example, Family Bank and M-PESA established a connection allowing customers to transfer money from M-PESA to their Family Bank account using M-PESA's bill pay function. This connection follows a successful pilot of loan repayments via M-PESA's bill pay function.

M-PESA would also benefit from establishing further links with institutions beyond banks, such as billers, distributors, and employers. By promoting M-PESA as a mechanism for distributing salaries and social welfare payments, enabling payments across supply chains, and paying bills, the need for cash-in and cash-out services would be minimized, and, as a result, a key component of transaction costs could be reduced. Savings balances may also be higher if people received payments directly into their accounts rather than in cash, and if they had other useful things to do with their money in electronic form.

CONCLUDING THOUGHTS: HOW M-PESA CAN REINVIGORATE FINANCIAL INCLUSION EFFORTS

Imagine a world where there are no banks where you live. The nearest branch is 10 kilometers away, and it takes you almost an hour to get there by foot and bus. With waiting times at the branch, a trip to the bank and back may take two hours—approximately a quarter of your working day. A bus fare of only $0.50 to get to the bank may well represent one-quarter of your income on a good day. With the bank fees included, each banking transaction costs you the equivalent of almost half a day's wages. It would be like charging someone with an average income in the United States something like $50 for each ATM transaction. Then, imagine a world without credit instruments or electronic payments. No checks, no credit cards, no money orders, no direct debits, no Internet banking. All your transactions are done in cash or, worse, by bartering goods. All exchanges are physical, person-to-person, hand-to-hand. Consider the hassle and the risk of sending money to distant relatives, business partners, or banks.

How would you operate in such a world? A recent book, *Portfolios of the Poor*, documents how poor people cope (Collins et al. 2009). Some people save to "push" excess money from today to tomorrow, some people borrow to "pull" tomorrow's money to fund necessary expenses today. They store cash in the home to meet daily needs, they leave it with a trusted friend for emergencies, they buy jewelry because that represents a future for their children, they pile up bricks for the day when they can build an extra room in their house. They make contributions to a savings group with a circle of friends to build up a pot of money, and one day it will be their turn to take that pot home to buy new clothes. They borrow from friends, seek advances from their employers, pawn their jewelry, and borrow from a high-interest moneylender.

Lack of good financial options is undoubtedly one of the reasons why poor people are trapped in poverty. In many cases, poor people cannot sustain themselves or aspire to earn higher incomes because they are not able to invest in better farming tools and seeds to enhance their productivity, start a microenterprise, or even take the time to search for better-paying employment opportunities. Their income is volatile, often fluctuating daily, and without reliable ways of pushing and pulling money between good days and bad days, they face stark choices such as pulling their children out of school or putting less food on the table during bad patches. Without good financial tools, they also may not be able to cope with shocks that periodically set them back. Most of these shocks are foreseeable, if not entirely predictable: a drought, ill health, and lifecycle events such as marriage and death.

Cash is the main barrier to financial inclusion. As long as poor people are able to exchange value only in cash—or worse, physical goods—they will remain too costly for formal financial institutions to address in significant numbers. Few banks are willing to build the costly infrastructure necessary for collecting low-value cash deposits and redeeming savings back into small sums of cash in low-income or rural areas. But once poor people have access to cost-effective electronic means of payments such as M-PESA, they could, in principle, become profitable to financial institutions. Although M-PESA itself does not constitute financial inclusion, it does provide a glimpse of a commercially sound, affordable, and effective way to offer financial services to all.

NOTES

1. See Hughes and Lonie (2009) for a historical account of the M-PESA service, Mas and Morawczynski (2009) for a fuller description of the service, and Mas and Ng'weno (2009) for the latest accomplishments of M-PESA.

2. A SIM card is a smart card found inside mobile phones that are based on the Global System for Mobile communications (GSM) family of protocols. The SIM card contains encryption keys, secures the user's persona identification number on entry, and drives the phone's menu. SMS is a data messaging channel available on GSM phones.

3. These amounts use an exchange rate of $1 to 75 Kenyan shillings.

4. Kenya has a population of nearly 40 million. GDP per capita is $1,600, 78 percent of people live in rural areas, and 19 percent of adults have access to a formal bank account. See FSDT (Financial Sector Deepening Trust) (2009a) for financial access data derived from the FinAccess survey, a nationally representative survey of 6,600 households conducted in early 2009.

5. The 2009 FinAccess survey (FSDT 2009a, p. 16) confirms that 40 percent of adults have used M-PESA.

6. See Safaricom (2009) for key monthly M-PESA statistics. Additional figures are taken from Safaricom's published half-year results for the period ending September 2009 and Central Bank of Kenya reports.

7. Although the number of P2P transactions per customer has been rising steadily, it remains quite low, probably still less than two transactions per month.

8. For more detailed accounts of the M-PESA story, see Heyer and Mas (2009) on the country factors that led to M-PESA's success, Mas and Morawczynski (2009) on M-PESA's service features, Mas and Ng'weno (2010) on Safaricom's execution, and Mas (2009) on the economics underpinning branchless banking systems.

9. For a fuller analysis of the use of mobile money for domestic remittances in Kenya, see Ratan (2008) and Morawczynski (2008).

10. Although the Central Bank of Kenya Act was amended in 2003 to give the central bank broad oversight of payment systems, the operational modalities for this oversight have not been implemented; they are pending approval of a new National Payments System Bill that has languished in parliament.

11. Morawczynski and Pickens (2009) find that sending K Sh 1,000 through M-PESA is 27 percent cheaper than the post office's PostaPay and 68 percent cheaper than sending it by a bus company.

12. Network effects are commonly illustrated with reference to fax machines: the first set of people who bought a fax machine did not find them very useful, because they were not able to send faxes to many people. But as more people bought fax machines, everyone's faxes became increasingly useful. Network effects are sometimes called demand-side economies of scale to emphasize that scale affects the *value* of the service to each customer. This distinguishes it from supply-side economies of scale, which refer to situations in which the average *cost* per customer fall as volume increases. Davidson (2009) discusses implications of network effects for mobile money.

13. Safaricom's earliest pilot project conducted in 2004–05 revolved around microloan repayments and involved the Commercial Bank of Africa, Vodafone, Faulu Kenya, and MicroSave.

14. In a survey of 1,210 users in late 2008, 70 percent of respondents claimed they first heard about M-PESA from television or radio advertisements (FSDT 2009b).

15. Safaricom would like the split to be 20 percent/80 percent, meaning that more of the commission is passed on to the retail outlet.

16. E-float is the balance of money that an agent has in his M-PESA account, which he can electronically transfer to customers in exchange for cash.

REFERENCES

Camner, Gunnar, and Emil Sjöblom. 2009. "Can the Success of M-PESA be repeated? A Review of Implementations in Kenya and Tanzania." Valuable Bits. http://mobileactive.org/files/file_uploads/camner_sjoblom_differences_ke_tz.pdf.

Collins, Daryl, Jonathan Morduch, Stuart Rutherford, and Orlanda Ruthven. 2009. *Portfolios of the Poor: How the World's Poor Live on $2 a Day.* Princeton, NJ: Princeton University Press.

Davidson, Neil. 2009. "Tactics for Tipping Markets: Influence Perceptions and Expectations." Mobile Money for the Unbanked Blog, GSM Association, November 15.

Financial Sector Deepening Trust (FSDT). 2007a. "Financial Access in Kenya: Results of the 2006 National Survey." FSDT, Nairobi.

———. 2007b. "Key Findings of the FinScope Survey in Tanzania in 2006." FSDT, Nairobi.

———. 2009a. "FinAccess National Survey 2009: Dynamics of Kenya's Changing Financial Landscape." FSDT, Nairobi.

———. 2009b. "Research on Mobile Payments Experience: M-PESA in Kenya." Unpublished paper, FSDT, Nairobi.

GSM Association. 2009. "Wireless Intelligence Database." http://www.wirelessintelligence.com.

Heyer, Amrik, and Ignacio Mas. 2009. "Seeking Fertile Grounds for Mobile Money." Unpublished paper.

Hughes, Nick, and Susie Lonie. 2009. "M-PESA: Mobile Money for the Unbanked." *Innovations* (special edition for the Mobile World Congress 2009).

Isaacs, Leon. 2008. IAMTN presentation. MMTA Conference, Johannesburg, May.

Jack, William, and Tavneet Suri. 2009. "Mobile Money: the Economics of M-PESA." Unpublished paper.

Juma, Victor. 2009. "Family Bank Offers New Service Linking Accounts to M-PESA." *Business Daily*, December 18.

Kimenyi, Mwangi, and Njuguna Ndung'u. 2009. "Expanding the Financial Services Frontier: Lessons from Mobile Phone Banking in Kenya." Washington, DC: Brookings Institution.

Kinyanjui, Kui. 2009. "Yu Launches New Mobile Cash Transfer Platform." *Business Daily*, 16 December.

Mas, Ignacio. 2008a. "M-PESA vs. G-Cash: Accounting for their Relative Success, and Key Lessons for other Countries." Unpublished paper, CGAP, Washington, DC.

———. 2009. "Exploring the Usage and Impact of Transformational M-banking: The case of M-PESA in Kenya." Unpublished paper.

Morawczynski, Olga, and Gianluca Miscione. 2008. "Examining Trust in Mobile Banking Transactions: The Case of M-PESA in Kenya." *In Social Dimensions of Information and Communication Technology Policy: Proceedings of the Eighth International Conference on Human Choice and Computers (HCC8), IFIP TC 9, Pretoria, South Africa, September 25–26, 2008.* ed. C. Avgerou, M. Smith, and P. van den Besselaar, 287–298 (Boston, MA: Springer).

Morawczynski, Olga, and Mark Pickens. 2009. "Poor People Using Mobile Financial Services: Observations on Customer Usage and Impact from M-PESA." CGAP Brief, CGAP, Washington, DC. http://www.cgap.org/p/site/c/template.rc/1.9.36723/.

Okoth, Jackson. 2009. "Regulator Gives M-PESA a Clean Bill of Health." *The Standard*, 27 January.

Okuttah, Mark. 2009. "Safaricom Changes Method of Recruiting M-PESA Agents." *Business Daily*, December 223.

Ratan, A. L. 2008. "Using Technology to Deliver Financial Services to Low-Income Households: A Preliminary Study of Equity Bank and M-PESA Customers in Kenya." Microsoft Research Technical Report.

Safaricom. 2009. "M-PESA Key Performance Statistics." http://www.safaricom.co.ke/fileadmin/template/main/images/MiscUploads/M-PESA%20Statistics.pdf.

Suri, Tavneet, and William Jack. 2008. "The Performance and Impact of M-PESA: Preliminary Evidence from a Household Survey." Unpublished paper.

CHAPTER 21

Independent Power Projects in Sub-Saharan Africa: Determinants of Success

Anton Eberhard and Katharine Nawal Gratwick

A t the beginning of the 1990s, virtually all major power generation providers in Sub-Saharan Africa were financed by public coffers, including concessionary loans from development finance institutions (DFIs). These publicly financed power generation assets were considered one of the core elements of state-owned, vertically integrated power systems. A confluence of factors, however, brought about a significant change in the ensuing years.

With insufficient public funds for new power generation and decades of poor performance by state-run utilities, African countries began to adopt a new model for their power systems, influenced by pioneering reformers in Chile, Norway, the United Kingdom, and the United States.[1] Urged on by multilateral and bilateral development institutions, which were withdrawing funding from state-owned projects, a number of countries adopted plans to unbundle their power systems and introduce private participation and competition. Independent power projects (IPPs)—privately financed, greenfield generation supported by nonrecourse or limited-recourse loans and with long-term power purchase agreements (PPAs) with the state utility or another off-taker—thus became a priority in overall power sector reform (World Bank 1993; World Bank and USAID 1994). IPPs were considered a solution to persistent supply constraints, and they also

had the potential to benchmark state-owned supply to gradually introduce competition (APEC Energy Working Group 1997).

In 1994 Côte d'Ivoire became one of the first African countries to attract a foreign-led IPP to sell power to the national grid under long-term contracts with the state utility. Ghana, Kenya, Nigeria, Senegal, Tanzania, and Uganda, among others, opened their doors to foreign and local investors in their power sectors shortly thereafter.

Although IPPs were considered part of larger power sector reform programs in Sub-Saharan Africa, the reforms were not far-reaching. In most cases, state utilities remained vertically integrated and maintained a dominant share of the power generation market, while private investors were allowed to operate only on the margin of the sector.[2] Policy frameworks and regulatory regimes, necessary to maintain a competitive environment, were limited. International competitive bids (ICBs) for IPPs were often not conducted because of tight time frames, resulting in limited competition *for* the market and, because of the long-term PPAs, no competition *in* the market. These long-term PPAs, along with government guarantees and security arrangements such as escrows and liquidity facilities, exposed countries to significant exchange rate risks. Finally, while Africa has seen continued private participation in greenfield electricity projects, that progress has been erratic, with 2007 representing

---

Anton Eberhard is a professor and Katharine Nawal Gratwick is a PhD graduate at the University of Cape Town Graduate School of Business.

the zenith, largely because of the financial close of one large project, Bujagali.

Several factors explain the recent trends in investment in Africa's power sector. First, private sector firms were deeply affected by the Asian and subsequent Latin American financial crises in the late 1990s and early 2000s. The Enron collapse and its aftershocks also influenced U.S.- and European-based firms to reduce risk exposure in developing-country markets and to refocus on core activities at home. The financial crisis of 2008 and 2009 has also had a toll. Furthermore, DFIs began to reconsider their position of restricted infrastructure investment, a model that was predominant throughout the 1990s.[3] As concessionary funding became available again, many countries opted for a hybrid solution—part public, part private. Kenya represents one of the clearest examples of such a hybrid, with KenGen, the state-owned generator, building alongside IPPs, with support from DFIs.

Despite this revival of concessionary lending, power sector investments have been insufficient in addressing Sub-Saharan Africa's power needs. Only 25 percent of the population currently has access to electricity, and poor supply is the rule, not the exception. The cost of meeting Africa's power sector needs is estimated at $40.8 billion per year, equivalent to 6.35 percent of Africa's 2005 gross domestic product (GDP). Approximately two-thirds of the spending needed is for capital investment ($26.7 billion per year), and the remainder for operations and maintenance (O&M). Current spending on power infrastructure totals approximately $11.6 billion per year. Approximately 80 percent of existing spending is domestically sourced from taxes or user charges. The remainder is split among official development assistance (ODA) financing (6 percent of the total); other sources, mainly China (9 percent); and private sector investment (4 percent). Tackling existing utility inefficiencies, including system losses, underpricing, undercollection of revenue, and overstaffing, would make an additional $8.24 billion available, but a funding gap of about $21 billion would still remain (Eberhard and Shkaratan 2010).

Closing Africa's power infrastructure funding gap inevitably requires undertaking reforms to reduce or eliminate system inefficiencies. This will help existing resources go farther and create a more attractive investment climate for external and private finance, which still has growth potential. With the original drivers for market reform still present, future private sector involvement appears inevitable.

Approximately 20 grid-connected IPPs, each in excess of 40 megawatts (MW) and with long-term PPAs with the largely state-run utilities, have been developed in Sub-Saharan Africa as of early 2010 (table 21.1). In total, about four gigawatts (GW) of IPP capacity has been added. With few exceptions,[4] these IPPs represent a small fraction of total power generation capacity and have mostly complemented incumbent state-owned utilities.

Nevertheless, IPPs are an important source of new investment in the power sector in a number of African countries. In Togo, for example, Centrale Thermique de Lomé, the country's first IPP, will triple the country's installed capacity.

The majority of IPP contracts in Sub-Saharan Africa have been upheld (namely, CIPREL and Azito in Côte d'Ivoire, Takoradi II in Ghana, Iberafrica, Tsavo, OrPower 4, and Rabai in Kenya, Afam VI and Aba Integrated in Nigeria, and Namanve in Uganda). Although the contracts of the two Senegalese projects, GTi Dakar and Kounoune I, remain largely intact, there are reports of changes in fuel supply arrangements. A number of other IPPs, such as Bui Hydro in Ghana, Bujagali in Uganda, and Centrale Thermique de Lomé in Togo, have reached financial closure and are under construction.[5] Kenya is in the process of negotiating three more IPPs after an international competitive tender.

For all of this progress, however, there have been several high-profile IPP mishaps in Sub-Saharan Africa. Two projects—AES Barge in Nigeria and Independent Power Tanzania Limited (IPTL) in Tanzania—are in arbitration. The costs of Songas, in Tanzania, meanwhile, have escalated as a result of the unplanned, and later disputed, contracting of IPTL; Songas's capacity charges were later reduced after the government agreed to buy down the accumulated allowance for funds used during construction costs. A dispute about escalating investment costs also marked the Okpai project in Nigeria. In Kenya changes may be made in the contracts of OrPower 4, which reduced its tariff for the second phase of the plant. Another Kenyan project, Westmont, had an initial seven-year contract that was not renewed. The other early IPP in Kenya, IberAfrica, had its contract renewed but with much lower capacity charges.

Following contract changes, IPPs have generally gone on to make a significant contribution to the countries' power generation—the main exceptions being Westmont, which ceased operation, and IPTL, which has operated intermittently during its arbitration proceedings. Another high-profile failure was the nontransparent procurement process surrounding the Richmond/Dowans plant in Tanzania, which has not been allowed to operate since corruption charges were filed. Furthermore, there is evidence of stalling

Table 21.1 General Project Specifications of Sub-Saharan African IPP Projects

Country/ project	Size (MW)	Fuel/cycle	Contract type	Length of contract (years)	Project tender	Commercial operating data
East Africa						
Kenya						
Westmont	46	Kerosene/gas condensate/gas Turbine (barge-mounted)	BOO	7	1996	1997
Iberafrica	109[a]	HFO/medium-speed diesel engine	BOO	7/15/25	1996, 1999, 2008	1997, 2000, 2009
OrPower 4	48	Geothermal	BOO	20	1996	2000, 2009
Tsavo	75	HFO/medium-speed diesel engine	BOO	20	1995	2001
Rabai	90	HFO	BOOT	20	2006	2009
Tanzania						
IPTL	100	HFO/medium-speed diesel engine	BOO	20	1997	1998
Songas	180	Natgas/open cycle	BOO	20	1994	2004
Uganda						
Namanve	50	HFO	BOOT	6	—	2008
Bujagali	250	Hydro	BOT	30	2005[b]	—
West Africa						
Côte d'Ivoire						
CIPREL	210	Natgas/open cycle	BOOT	19	1993	1995
Azito	288[c]	Natgas/open cycle	BOOT	24	1996	2000
Ghana						
Takoradi II	220[d]	Light crude/single cycle	BOOT	25	1998	2000
Sunon Asogli	200	Combustion engine	BOO	20	2007	—
Bui Hydro[e]	400	Hydro	BOO	—	2005	—
Nigeria						
AES Barge	270	Natgas/open cycle (barge-mounted)	BOO	20 (2 parts)	1999	2001
Okpai	450	Natgas/combined cycle	BOO	20	2001	2005
Afam VI	630	Natgas/combined cycle	BOO	20	2000	2007
Aba Integrated[f]	140	Natgas/open-cycle	BOO	20/15	2005	—
Senegal						
GTi Dakar	52	Diesel/Nafta	BOOT	15	1996	1999
Kounoune 1	68	HFO	BOO	15	2003	2008
Togo						
Centrale Thermique de Lomé	100	Triple fuel (natgas/HFO/diesel)	BOOT	25	—	2010

Source: Authors.

Note: Projects included here are greater than 40 MW; have reached financial close; and are under construction, operational, or concluded. BOO = build-own-operate contract; HFO = Heavy fuel oil. — = Not available.

a. Iberafrica has been developed in three stages, with 44, 12 and 52.3 MW, totaling 109 MW at time of writing.

b. The first phase of Bujagali's conceptualization, spanning the mid-1990s until 2003 and involving AES, is not covered in this article. It should be noted that the project did not reach financial close during this time. Authors report only on the project from its second phase, starting in 2005.

c. The initial project concept included specifications to raise capacity to 420 MW.

d. Although the initial project concept included specifications to add a second phase of 110 MW and convert to combined cycle, lack of funding has limited the completion of this phase.

e. The Bui project was initiated in the 1960s but aborted after the coup in Ghana in 1966. The project was reconsidered several times in the decades that followed. In 2005 the government of Ghana signed a memorandum of understanding with the Chinese firm Sino Hydro, and the plant is expected to be online in 2012.

f. Aba Integrated is privately financed but is not a classic IPP in that ownership will extend to the off-taker.

in Takoradi II's second phase and in Sunon Asogli, which as of early 2010 had no gas supply—although efforts to rectify this situation are under way.

COUNTRY-LEVEL FACTORS AFFECTING THE IPP MARKET

Several elements have contributed to the success of IPP projects in Sub-Saharan Africa: a favorable investment climate; new policy frameworks and regulation; the linking of planning, procurement, and contracting; and low-cost fuel and secure fuel contracts.

Favorable investment climate

Even though a investment climate is not the only factor in influencing IPP outcomes, it sets the stage for negotiations and contract terms and helps explain the initial imbalance in some of the Sub-Saharan African cases. Host countries with a strong investment profile attracted more investors and ultimately were able to negotiate deals with more favorable terms than countries with weak investment conditions. Because all countries and entities compete for capital, a risk-reward balance needs to be offered that will attract investors and lenders. That "balance" starts with a stable and predictable investment environment (Rudo 2010a).

Of the Sub-Saharan countries whose IPPs are examined in this chapter, none has an investment-grade sovereign credit rating. Of the five countries that have received a speculative rating (Ghana, Kenya, Nigeria, Senegal, and Uganda), all except Ghana received their rating after the first IPP deals were signed. Kenya's investment climate was defined, at the time, by its aid embargo in the mid-1990s. Tanzania is also worth mentioning in this context. Throughout the 1990s, all export credit agencies were off-cover in Tanzania. Foreign commercial banks were not willing to lend, because there was no track record of successful repayment of commercial loans. Consequently, traditional, project-financed IPP deals in this climate were limited. In contrast in North Africa, the Arab Republic of Egypt, Morocco, and Tunisia have all attained either a credit rating of investment grade or one notch below and have experienced successful IPPs (Gratwick and Eberhard 2008a). While credit enhancements and security arrangements have differed broadly between North and Sub-Saharan Africa, interestingly, incentives offered to investors in IPPs were relatively similar in both regions, though there was some variety with regard to tax breaks. For instance, nearly all projects appear to have benefited from both customs and value added tax (VAT) exemptions during construction, as well as the right to full repatriation of profits. Currency conversion was also provided for virtually all projects. In East Africa, Tanzania provided a tax holiday of five years, but Kenya extended this benefit only until plants were commissioned. Although one would expect investment incentives to increase with perceived risk, such a pattern is not apparent.

New policy frameworks and regulation

While all eight Sub-Saharan African countries examined in this chapter have introduced legislation allowing for private sector power generation, few have actually formulated and implemented a clear and coherent policy framework for procuring IPPs. Thus, there is abundant evidence of tentative experimentation with private power that does not always lead to a sustained opening of the market for private investment. Furthermore, long-term power purchase agreements have the potential to constrain future wholesale competition, although means to transition to wholesale competition with IPPs have been identified (Woolf and Halpern 2001). In addition, state-owned utilities are rarely exposed to market costs of capital, and direct comparisons of state-owned utilities' costs and IPPs' costs are often difficult to discern.

The standard reform model for power sector reform—namely, unbundling of generation, transmission, and distribution; as well as the introduction of competition and private-sector participation at both the generation and distribution level—is not being fully adopted anywhere in Sub-Saharan Africa (UNEP and UNECA 2006; Malgras, Gratwick, and Eberhard 2007a; Gratwick and Eberhard 2008b). Most incumbent national utilities are state-owned[6] and in a dominant position. However, elements of the reform model have been adopted: for example, Kenya has unbundled power generation from its national transmission and distribution utility; Uganda and Ghana have unbundled generation, transmission, and distribution; and Uganda and Côte d'Ivoire have introduced private concessions. The private sector has also invested in IPPs in many countries. In general, there has been competition *for* the market, but not ongoing competition *in* the market in terms of customer choice. In effect, hybrid power markets have emerged across Africa, and in other developing regions. As such, the incumbent state-owned utility typically continues to play a key role in the sector, but because of inefficiencies and inadequate investment resources, IPPs are gradually being introduced. These hybrid power markets are giving rise to new challenges that need explicit attention if private investment is to be accelerated.

In addition to introducing legislation allowing for private power generation, the eight countries examined in this chapter also have established independent regulators. In Kenya the presence of the regulator, together with the adoption of International Competition in Bidding (ICB) practices, helped reduce PPA charges radically between the first set of IPPs and the second. A similar trend may be observed in Senegal, where the first IPP (GTi Dakar) was not overseen by the independent regulatory body and the second (Kounoune I) was (Regulatory Commission of Senegal 2010; IFC 2010b). Kenya's Energy Regulatory Commission (ERC) has also been instrumental in helping set tariffs and manage the overall interface between private and public sectors. In Uganda sponsors note the benefits of having the regulator involved from project inception, particularly in helping to increase overall transparency, especially in the case of Bujagali. An ERC staff member affirms that the commission's "presence has helped to focus minds on the requirements for setting up power supply projects so that investors coming in are clear of what is expected of them from the beginning and hence align their bids to these requirements. As a result, we have increasing numbers of investors applying to set up IPP projects" (ERC 2010a).

In Côte d'Ivoire, Ghana, Nigeria, and Tanzania, however, regulatory agencies have come into force only after IPPs have been negotiated, and as yet the agencies have had little impact on new investment. In general, the mere presence of a regulator does not appear to be a defining factor in attracting IPPs. An independent regulator may have positive, negative, or no impact on IPP outcomes. If, however, regulatory governance is transparent, fair, and accountable, and if regulatory decisions are credible and predictable, there is greater potential for positive outcomes for both the host country and investor alike. Evidence also suggests that effective regulatory oversight may lead to a reduction in the stated capital costs of projects and improved efficiency for selectively bid projects (Phadke 2007; Eberhard and Shkaratan 2010).[7]

In Nigeria and Tanzania efforts have been made to exploit stranded gas as part of the IPP program.[8] In Nigeria a reduction in gas flaring is central to the push for gas-fired power, while in Tanzania the IPP program commercialized previously stranded (although not flared) gas through Songas and Mtwara (a small private concession in the south of the country). Although these two countries have a distinct set of challenges,[9] in general the larger policy of involving stranded gas has insulated projects from intense public scrutiny, with project sponsors and policy makers alike able to point to the benefits of the commercialized gas and the reduction in fuel imports.

Finally, DFIs are behind many countries' power sector policy frameworks; notably the World Bank has had a hand in nearly all power sector reform programs in Africa. DFIs have been particularly instrumental in advancing private sector participation in generation. And as many of those same institutions began reconsidering publicly funded infrastructure investments at the end of the 1990s, countries' policies have followed—from state to market and back again, albeit with some changes to accommodate the more hybrid market that has emerged.

Linking planning, procurement, and contracting

Intricately connected to sound policy frameworks are coherent power sector plans. Ideally, planning, procurement, and contracting follow from sound policy frameworks and include a number of core components: setting a reliability standard for energy security, completion of detailed supply and demand forecasts, development of a least-cost plan with alternative scenarios, clarification of how new generation production will be split between the private and public sectors, and identification of requisite bidding and procurement processes for new projects. One important aspect of coherent power sector planning is vesting planning and procurement in one empowered agency to ensure that implementation takes place with minimal mishaps (Eberhard and Malgas forthcoming).

While that planning and procurement arrangement may be ideal, the reality is often quite different. As one stakeholder at Ghana's Public Utilities Regulatory Commission (PURC) notes about the recent past, "A crisis arises, and everybody panics; anybody who comes in [to propose generation] is listened to" (PURC 2010). Indeed, in the eight countries examined here, there have been several noteworthy planning mishaps that subsequently affected procurement and contracting. In some cases, demand and supply were not being accurately forecast partly because of weather conditions such as extended droughts, which in turn necessitated fast-tracking IPPs—that is, plans for IPPs were sped through to meet immediate power shortages. The first two plants in Kenya (Westmont and Iberafrica), the first plant in Nigeria (AES Barge), and Ghana's Takoradi II IPP were all negotiated during drought conditions. Although both the Westmont and Iberafrica plants came online within 11 months, they were later investigated for suspicious bidding practices and what were perceived as unnecessarily expensive charges. Furthermore, public stakeholders' unwillingness to make concessions over a tariff resulted in Westmont not securing a second PPA. The AES Barge project in Nigeria took nearly two years to come online because of a renegotiation of the PPA, despite the project being fast-tracked. In Ghana, no agreement was reached over the second phase of the Takoradi II project.

Inability to estimate demand and supply accurately or to set a clear reliability standard has also led to several cases in which emergency power units needed to be leased for one to two years with the purpose of plugging a short-term crisis. In 2009 approximately 750 MW of emergency power was in operation in Sub-Saharan Africa (Foster and Briceno-Garmendia 2010). The governments of Ghana, Kenya, Tanzania, and Uganda all have been forced to address drought and black-outs in recent years, often turning to emergency power suppliers (see box 21.1 for an example). Kenya harnessed 100 MW of emergency power twice: in 1999, 2000, and 2001, and again in 2006 (supplied by Aggreko, Cummins, and Deutz in the first instance and Aggreko alone in the second). In 2007 Aggreko's contract was extended for an additional two years, and in 2009 Aggreko was selected to provide a further 140 MW for a total of 250 MW of emergency power.[10] In Ghana emergency power was instrumental in reducing the impact of the 1998 drought, but as drought conditions reversed, the state failed to honor its contracts with SIIF Accra; as of 2007 those contracts were still in dispute. The cost of emergency power, at approximately 30 to 40 cents a kilowatt hour (kWh), is high (IFC 2005). Tanzania, for example, has estimated that it saves around $1 for every kWh of outage averted (or about 5 to 10 times the ordinary cost of generating electricity).[11]

COMPETITIVE INTERNATIONAL BIDDING PRACTICES. Although it is easy, in hindsight, to accuse IPP stakeholders of acting imprudently in the face of emergencies, the actual conditions of load-shedding and shortages in the power sector appear to have provided few alternatives. Two studies highlight the importance of the international competition in bidding practices in reducing up to 60 percent of the capital cost of plants (Deloitte Touche Tohmatsu Emerging Markets Ltd. and Advanced Engineering Associates International 2003; Phadke 2007). There is also evidence for selective bidding proving effective in certain instances, provided there is regulatory scrutiny. Of the 21 IPPs examined here, ICBs are known to have been conducted for nine. Six of the projects in East Africa (OrPower 4, Tsavo, Rabai, Songas, Namanve, and Bujagali) conformed to these bidding practices, as did three projects in

---

Box 21.1   Poor Planning Led to Significant Delays for Tanzania's Projects

The quick and obscure process through which IPTL (Tanzania) was negotiated resulted in the highest-profile IPP mishap on the continent to date. The project's total investment costs were estimated at $150 million ($163 million including fuel conversion), an amount the government and the World Bank later argued was inflated by 40 percent. This dispute led to a three-year arbitration process during which another project in Tanzania, the Songo Songo gas-to-electricity project, was also put on hold, mainly through pressure from the World Bank, its largest donor, because of alleged corruption. Although the IPTL arbitration reduced its estimated costs it was still well above the price the government sought to pay. In addition, since both IPPs were unavailable until 2002 and 2004 respectively, the state had to negotiate with another company, Richmond/Dowans, for emergency power, a contract that came with its own inflated costs and controversies. Furthermore, because of the delays, Songo Songo accumulated $100 million in interest charges on owner's equity.

In this project, critical planning elements are missing, namely, a clear reliability standard, an accurate demand and supply forecast, a detailed plan for privately powered and publicly powered generation, and, most important, timely initiation of procurement and effective conclusion of contracts.

Source: Authors.

West Africa (Azito, GTi Dakar, and Kounoune I). Of the projects examined here that have faced renegotiation, four were not bid through an ICB (IPTL, Iberafrica, AES Barge, and Okpai); the two exceptions were Songas and OrPower 4. Absence of regulatory scrutiny is also noteworthy in each of these four projects. Furthermore, Westmont, which was selectively bid, quit the country after its first seven-year PPA expired. Other non-ICB projects have also encountered difficulties. For example, Ghana's Takoradi II has not been able to raise financing for the second phase of the plant. Although reasons for these stumbling blocks may be traced well beyond the presence or absence of an ICB, the correlation is nonetheless revealing.

Furthermore, the success of the ICB process is intricately linked to the number of bids received, with more bidding driving down prices,[12] as evidenced by IPPs in North Africa, where the number of bids submitted to ICBs has been generally double to triple those submitted to ICBs in East and West Africa. That said, the time and cost required to complete an international competitive bid should not be underestimated. In Sub-Saharan Africa, drought-related energy crises are often cited as the reason why ICBs have not been pursued. In Togo, for example, the drought conditions of 2006 prompted a move to discontinue a rehabilitate-own-transfer contract with Electro Togo to manage the Centrale thermique de Lomé. Rather than launching an ICB, the government chose to negotiate directly with an existing player, Contour Global, which was already in discussions with the utility. In this case, time and project familiarity proved more important than complying with international bidding practices, which risked extending the project development timeline (Ministry of Energy of Togo 2010).[13]

The reason for these planning and contracting mishaps seems to lie in the changing nature of power markets across Africa and other developing regions. In addition, as power markets continue to include private sector participation, it is not always clear who has responsibility for maintaining security of supply. Often, the planning function is shifted from the state-owned utility company to the energy ministry, which does not have the capacity, resources, or experience to undertake detailed power sector planning. Alternatively, planning is contracted to consultants who produce master plans that quickly become outdated as global equipment, fuel costs, and other key parameters change (Eberhard and Malgas forthcoming). Absence of regulatory control and institutional capacity is evident in more areas than just planning. In many instances, there are no clear criteria for allocating power plant building opportunities to either the incumbent state-owned utility or the private sector.

Often, it is not clear whether plans are merely indicative, whether unsolicited proposals may be considered, or whether plans have legal force in determining which plants the regulator may license. Too often, plans do not translate into timely initiation of competitive bid processes for new plants. Similarly, there is often insufficient capacity to negotiate with winning bidders or to conclude sustainable contracts. Transaction advisers may be appointed, but often there is little continuity and the overall policy framework is lacking information about security packages or credit enhancement measures being offered by government. Despite past planning deficiencies and forced reliance on emergency power generation, Kenya provides an interesting recent example in which progress is being made in dealing

with these planning, procurement, and contracting challenges (box 21.2).

Abundant, low-cost fuel and secure fuel contracts

The availability of competitively priced fuel supplies has also emerged as a key factor in how IPPs are perceived and ultimately whether there is public appetite for such projects, in large part because fuel is generally a pass-through cost to the utility and, in many cases, also to the final consumer. Thus, if the IPP uses a different fuel than other plants, and if that fuel is more expensive, there is greater potential for disputes surrounding the new project.

In several Sub-Saharan African countries—Ghana, Kenya, Senegal, Tanzania, and Togo—low-priced hydropower was the dominant fuel source for power production, but IPPs were thermal powered, using a combination of imported fuel

---

Box 21.2   Planning, Procurement, and Contracting Challenges in Kenya

Recognizing that it does not have the internal capacity, resources, or planning tools to develop detailed and up-to-date electricity plans, Kenya's Energy Regulatory Commission (ERC) has delegated this function to the Kenya Power and Light Company (KPLC), guided by a government committee chaired by the ERC. KPLC ceased being an electricity-generating company in 1997, and thus has a neutral stance between the state utility, Kenya Electricity Generating Company (KenGen), on one hand and private IPPs on the other. KPLC has also been assigned responsibility for managing the procurement and contracting process for IPPs. As described by one project sponsor in Kenya, commenting in May 2010, "Kenya has an IPP structure that is working. It has a track record. It can structure new projects based on experience gained from previous projects. And it has a very capable set of teams working in KPLC, the Ministry of Energy/Finance and KenGen. It understands project finance and is not surprised when a developer requests a comfort letter, as one example." The fruits of this approach are evident. Kenya is about to add three new IPPs to its existing five, maintaining its lead position in Sub-Saharan Africa in terms of IPP investments.[a]

a. Kenya also has been cited by public stakeholders in Ghana and Tanzania as having processes that should be emulated (PURC 2010; EWURA 2010).

---

oil and domestically procured natural gas. These same countries witnessed a series of debilitating droughts during the 1990s and 2000s, during which existing hydropower infrastructure proved insufficient, and thermal power, provided almost entirely by IPPs, was increasingly integrated into the fuel supply mix (from 10 percent to 60 percent in Tanzania, for example), forcing up the price of power. Although more thermal power may be required, the public perception has been that IPPs drive up the price of power. OrPower 4, Kenya's geothermal IPP, deserves special mention in the context of hydro-dominant systems that have been diversified with (largely imported) fuel oil (box 21.3).

The number of IPPs in Sub-Saharan Africa with secure, low-cost fuel sources is still relatively few. In Tanzania, although natural gas from the Songo Songo field is cheaper than the imported fuel oil currently powering IPTL,[14] disputes continue to surround its use, and IPTL's diesel units have yet to be converted to gas. In Ghana the Sunon Asogli Power Plant is completed but awaits fuel. Ghana's Volta River Authority (VRA), the state-owned generator, is a foundation customer for the West African Gas Pipeline (WAGP), from which it has been receiving gas since February 2010, but the recently completed Shenzhen IPP will receive gas only when the pipeline is pressurized and higher volumes of gas flow. In short, an IPP's access to abundant, low-cost fuel is not only a matter of whether such fuel is available in a country, but whether the supply of such fuel is guaranteed through contracts well into the future. Fuel sourcing and other country-level elements that contribute to successful IPPs are summarized in table 21.2.

PROJECT-LEVEL FACTORS CONTRIBUTING TO SUCCESSFUL IPPS

Investors in IPPs in Sub-Saharan Africa must navigate changing investment climates, national policies, and planning frameworks. Starting with an evaluation of equity arrangements, this section examines trends in investor behavior and how investors secured revenue to service debt and reward equity, particularly in the face of exogenous stresses.

Favorable equity arrangements

In assessing the project-level factors contributing to the success of IPPs, it is useful to ask several questions. Does the presence of local equity shareholders make a difference in project outcomes? Are projects with such participation less likely to face pressure from host-country governments to change their contract terms? How does a firm's previous experience with a country play out in making or breaking deals? Does the presence of DFI or firms with international development experience, such as Industrial Promotion Services (IPS), Globeleq, and Aldwych International, affect the likelihood of an IPP's success? Table 21.3 shows the country origin of Sub-Saharan African IPP sponsors, along with their respective equity share, whether the project faced a change in contract terms, and whether there was turnover of the majority equity partner.

Unlike in China and Malaysia, where local investors in IPPs abound, foreign firms have long been dominant players in Sub-Saharan African IPPs (Woodhouse 2005). Given the limited availability of capital in Sub-Saharan African countries in the sample, this is not surprising. Foreign involvement, however, raises the issue of foreign exchange exposure.[15] Only 3 of the 21 projects examined here have local majority stakeholders: Nigeria's Okpai, Afam VI, and Aba Integrated. In two of these cases, however, the stakeholder was either the national utility or the Nigerian National Petroleum Company (NNPC).

Several observers (for example, Hoskote 1995; Woodhouse 2005) have cited local participation in IPPs as a possible means of reducing risk. Ten of the 21 projects have local equity participation—namely, Sunon Asogli, Iberafrica,[16] IPTL, Songas, Takoradi II, AES Barge, Okpai, Afam VI, Aba Integrated, and Bujagali. As noted, six of these

---

| Box 21.3 | Petroleum-Fired Versus Natural Gas-Fired IPPs |

As indicated in a press release from Ormat (2009), "At a price of US$29 per barrel of petroleum crude oil, [a] 48 MW geothermal plant is cheaper to operate than a heavy fuel oil fired plant. This means that at the current oil prices still above US$40 per barrel, OrPower 4 is providing cheaper electricity to the national grid than any existing oil fired plants in Kenya." In contrast, Nigeria has relied entirely on domestically procured natural gas to fuel its IPPs, and gas is the incumbent fuel. Until recently, although a series of issues affected project outcomes, most notably the investment climate and bidding procedures, fuel had not been an issue; however, civil unrest in the Niger Delta led to a disruption in the fuel supply in 2007–09, albeit with improved conditions as of 2010.

Source: Authors.

Table 21.2 Elements within Purview of Host Governments Contributing to Successful IPPs

Element	Details
Favorable investment climate	■ Stable macroeconomic policies ■ Legal system that allows contracts to be enforced, laws to be upheld, and arbitration ■ Good repayment record and investment-grade credit rating ■ Requires less (costly) risk mitigation techniques to be employed, translating into lower cost of capital, lower project costs, and more competitive prices ■ Potentially more than one investment opportunity
Clear policy framework	■ Policy framework enshrined in legislation ■ Framework clearly specifies market structure and roles and terms for private and public sector investments (generally for single-buyer model, as wholesale competition does not yet exist in African context) ■ Framework is led and implemented by reform-minded "champions," concerned with long-term power sector conditions
Clear, consistent, and fair regulatory oversight	■ Oversight improves general performance of private and public sector assets ■ Transparent and predictable licensing and tariff framework improves investor confidence ■ Cost-reflective tariffs ensure revenue sufficiency ■ Consumers protected
Coherent power sector planning linked to procurement and contracting	■ Energy security standard in place; planning roles and functions are clear ■ Power planning vested with lead, appropriate (skilled, resourced, and empowered) agency ■ Power sector planning takes into consideration the hybrid market (public and private stakeholders and their respective real costs of capital) and fairly allocates new building opportunities among stakeholders ■ Planning has built-in contingencies to avoid emergency power plants or blackouts ■ Responsibility for procurement is clearly allocated; plans are linked to procurement and bids are initiated in time ■ Procurement process is transparent and competition ultimately drives down prices ■ Capacity is built to contract effectively
Abundant, low- cost fuel and secure contracts	■ Cost-competitive with other fuels ■ Contract safeguards affordable and reliable; fuel supply sufficient for duration of contract

Source: Authors.

projects have encountered some form of change to their contract, and in four of the six, either the state utility or another government entity held an equity share, indicating that the existence of a local partner might not be critical in preserving the original financing balance.

As for renegotiating contract terms, it is unclear whether having a local partner makes a difference. Kenya's Westmont and Iberafrica, for example, were negotiated at the same time under similar policy frameworks, although Iberafrica had local participation and Westmont did not. Iberafrica first voluntarily reduced its tariff and then went on to negotiate a second 15-year PPA, in contrast to Westmont, which stopped production after failing to come to an agreement on a second PPA. Although the presence of a local partner may have helped Iberafrica create a long-term solution, with just one example, the evidence is not conclusive. Togo's Centrale thermique de Lomé, due to be online in July 2010, may provide a more sustainable method for balancing investment and development outcomes. In this project, 25 percent of the project equity must be sold to local investors within the first five years (Ministry of Energy of Togo 2010).

Table 21.3　Equity Participation in IPPs in Sub-Saharan Africa

Project	Equity partners (country and percent of equity held)	Change in contract terms	Majority equity partner turnover (number of times)
Westmont (Kenya)	Westmont (Malaysia, 100%); has sought to sell plant since 2004	—	—
Iberafrica (Kenya)	Union Fenosa (Spain, 80%), KPLC Pension Fund (Kenya, 20%) since 1997	yes	0
OrPower 4 (Kenya)	Ormat (United States/Israel, 100%) since 1998	yes	0
Tsavo (Kenya)	Cinergy (United States) and IPS (international) jointly owned 49.9%, Cinergy sold to Duke Energy (United States) in 2005; CDC/Globeleq (United Kingdom, 30%), Wartsila (Finland, 15%), IFC (international, 5%) have retained remaining shares since 2000	no	1
Rabai (Kenya)	Aldwych-International (Netherlands, 34%), BWSC (Denmark, but owned by Mitsui of Japan, 25.5%), FMO (Netherlands, 20%), IFU (Denmark, 20%)	no	0
IPTL (Tanzania)	Mechmar (Malaysia, 70%), VIP (Tanzania, 30% in kind); both have sought to sell shares, and actual equity contribution is currently disputed	yes	—
Songas (Tanzania)	TransCanada sold majority shares to AES (United States) in 1999, and AES sold majority shares to Globeleq (United Kingdom) in 2003.[a] All preferred equity shares were converted into "loan notes" in June 2009, only common shares remain	yes	2
Bujagali (Uganda)	Sithe Global (United States, 58%), IPS-AKFED (32%), government of Uganda (10%)	no	0
Namanve (Uganda)	Jacobsen (Norway, 100%)	no	0
CIPREL (Côte d'Ivoire)	SAUR International (88%). This is a joint venture between French SAUR Group owned by Bouygues (65%), and Electricité de France (35%). The remaining 12% was owned by a combination of BOAD (West African Bank for Development); the Investment and Promotions Company for Economic Cooperation, a subsidiary of AFD; and IFC. In 2005 98% of the shares were sold to Bouygues (France); BOAD retained 2%.	no	1
Azito (Côte d'Ivoire)	Cinergy (65.7%; joint venture between Swiss ABB and Globeleq), CDC/Globeleq (11%), and IPS-AKFED (23%)	no	1
Takoradi II (Ghana)	CMS (United States, 90%), VRA (Ghana, 10%); CMS sold shares to TAQA (UAE, 90%) in 2007	yes	1
Sunon Asogli (Ghana)	Shenzhen (China), Togbe Afede XIV (Ghana/local strategic investor)	no	0
Bui hydro (Ghana)	Sinohydro (China)	no	0
AES Barge (Nigeria)	Enron (United States, 100%; sold to AES (United States, 95%) and YFP (Nigeria, 5%) in 2000	yes	1
Okpai (Nigeria)	Nigerian National Petroleum Corporation (Nigeria, 60%), Nigerian Agip Oil Company (Italy, 20%), and Phillips Oil Company (United States, 20%) have maintained equity since 2001	yes	0
Afam VI (Nigeria)	Nigerian National Petroleum Corporation (Nigeria, 55%), Shell (United Kingdom/Netherlands, 30%), Elf (Total) (France, 10%), Agip (Italy, 5%)	no	0
Aba Integrated (Nigeria)	Geometric Power Limited (Nigeria)	no	0
GTi Dakar (Senegal)	GE Capital Structured Finance Group (SFG) (USA), Edison (Italy), IFC	no	0
Kounoune (Senegal)	Mitsubishi (Japan), Matelec S.A.L (Lebanon)	no	0
Centrale thermique de Lomé (Togo)	Contour Global (United States, 80%) IFC (20%)	no	0

Source: Authors.

Note: — = Pending developments.

a. Turnover within the Songas project has been complex: Ocelot (Canada), TransCanada (Canada), Tanzania Petroleum Development Corporation, TPDC (Tanzania), TANESCO (Tanzania), Tanzania Development Finance Company, TDFL (Tanzania, sponsored by European Investment Bank), IFC (multilateral), DEG (Germany), and CDC (United Kingdom) were shareholders by 1996, with TransCanada the majority shareholder. IFC and DEG sold their shares to CDC in 1997/98; TransCanada sold its shares to AES (United States) in 1999; Ocelot/PanOcean sold shares to AES in 2001; and AES sold majority shares to Globeleq (United Kingdom) and FMO (the Netherlands) in 2003. After the AES sale, equity shares and associated financial commitments in Songas were as follows: Globeleq, $33.8 million (56 percent); FMO, $14.6 million (24 percent); TDFL, $4 million (7 percent); CDC, $3.6 million (6 percent); TPDC, $3 million (5 percent); and TANESCO, $1 million (2 percent). The amount given for Globeleq does not reflect the additional $50 million that the company committed for the expansion of the project.

ORIGINS, EXPERIENCE, AND MANDATES OF PARTNERS. From a global perspective, IPP investments during the 1990s were led by a host of American and European investors who saw returns in their home markets diminishing. A wave of investors originating from developing countries, however, particularly from Malaysia, was also present. Although it would be inaccurate to say that investors based in developing countries overlooked the risk involved in African countries (or did not ultimately charge higher returns), they may have had a greater willingness to consider IPP investments in Sub-Saharan Africa in the first place.

While the number of developing-country-based investors in IPPs appears to be growing, three such firms are trying to sell their shares (Mechmar, VIP, and Westmont). Thus, the home country of the firm does not mean that project equity is permanent, or that firms based in developing countries are best positioned to service debt and reward equity.

An aspect more important than the nationality of the investing firm appears to be a firm's experience and mandate. Across the pool of IPPs examined in table 21.3, several firms were actively involved in the country before making an IPP investment. Union Fenosa, for example, the parent company of Iberafrica, had previous experience in Kenya through an information-technology contract. IPS, a major shareholder in Tsavo (Kenya), Azito (Côte d'Ivoire), and Bujagali (Uganda), has operated in Kenya since 1963 and in Côte d'Ivoire since 1965. For certain projects, it may be argued that long-term relationships, particularly those with strong local management, appear to have contributed to the staying power of firms and often the rebalancing of contract terms.

In addition to the terms of the deal, the mandate of the investing firm appears to play a central role in firms' decisions about whether to invest in IPP projects. Although Globeleq, IPS, and Aldwych, for example, are commercial entities, they emerged from agencies with a strong commitment to social and economic development. Until recently, the two firms that were increasing their stakes were Globeleq and IPS. Globeleq holds a 43 percent share in Côte d'Ivoire's Azito, 30 percent equity in Kenya's Tsavo, and 56 percent in Tanzania's Songas. IPS holds a 23 percent share in Azito, and together with Duke Energy, a 49.9 percent share in Tsavo. IPS is also leading development of Uganda's Bujagali project and is a 35 percent shareholder in equity. Although a smaller player than either Globeleq or IPS, Aldwych International has also made significant inroads via Rabai in Kenya and is evaluating further expansion.

With the exception of Tanzania's Songas, none of the Sub-Saharan African IPP projects with involvement of firms with development origins examined here has had any changes in contract terms, which may signal that they were better balanced from inception in terms of investors and had a better ability to withstand public pressure. Furthermore, in terms of the Songas change, although the $103 million buy-down of the allowance for funds used during construction resulted in a reduction in the capacity charge, the firm received full payment upon the buy-down—a different case from many of the contract changes cited earlier. Alongside companies with development origins, foreign investors remain directly involved in IPP investments. Indeed, DFI equity shares have increased in recent years for at least five IPPs. With the exception of Songas, no project with DFI involvement has seen any contract changes. Box 21.4 provides further insights on IPP projects concerned with their developmental impacts.

EQUITY TURNOVER. Of the 46 original equity partners in the 21 projects considered here, 7 have exited (from 5 projects). This ratio, however, tells only part of the story. First, as previously indicated, shareholders in Westmont (Kenya) and IPTL (Tanzania) have been trying for several years to

---

Box 21.4 Two IPPs with Development and Investment Mandates

Development is perhaps more important for Industrial Promotion Services (IPS) than for any other firm investing in IPPs in Sub-Saharan Africa. As a rule, IPS invests only in projects with a substantial developmental impact and a reasonable internal rate of return. For the Tsavo project, that rate is 17–18 percent, and for Bujagali, 19 percent—considerably lower than typical internal rates of return for IPP projects in Sub-Saharan Africa (IPS 2010).

Aldwych International, on the other hand, requires that its project investments both make commercial sense and serve a clear developmental function for the country and local community. The company's experience in the Rabai in Kenya helps to illustrate this point. The firm has faced three major hurdles as part of its involvement in the project—legal trouble during the tendering process, national postelection civil unrest in late 2007, and the global financial crisis. Despite the challenges, the project reached financial close successfully in 2008; it even won the Project Finance International's deal of the year award.

Source: Authors.

sell their assets. In the case of IPTL, Mechmar, the lead shareholder, has indicated that the sale has been driven by an arbitration settlement that hurt its equity partners. VIP, the minority shareholder, cites oppression by the majority shareholder, fraud by Mechmar in inflating the IPTL capital cost, and failure by Mechmar to pay its equity contribution (that is, the project was 100 percent debt financed) as reasons behind its desire to sell its stake. For this and other projects, investors repeatedly say that their motivation to sell stakes in IPPs is driven primarily by changing circumstances in home markets or corporate strategy—that is, the desire to sell has little to do with host-country actions and reactions or with poor investment outcomes, namely, the ability to service debt adequately and reward equity.

While investment outcomes may be partially motivating sales, turnover does not in and of itself appear to be challenging the long-term sustainability of contracts, since in nearly all cases sellers have found willing buyers to take over the original or recently renegotiated PPAs. The two exceptions, again, are Westmont, in which the first PPA expired and was shrouded in controversy, and IPTL, which has been embroiled in lawsuits. Under such circumstances, it may therefore be understandable that the plants have not attracted buyers. One stakeholder went so far as to assert that "[equity turnover is a] healthy factor in a maturing market. It is a good sign when investors come and go—not a bad or threatening thing." The return of the government as a shareholder, as planned in the case of Tanzania's IPTL, would, however, signal that some markets are less mature than initially expected.

Debt arrangements: Global and local

With debt financing often representing more than 70 percent of total project costs, competitively priced financing has emerged as a key factor in successful projects. How and where to get this low-cost financing is a challenge, but possible approaches in the case of Sub-Saharan Africa are DFIs, credit enhancements, and flexibility in repayment terms and conditions, including possible refinancing.[17] The goal for sustainable financing should be that the risk premium demanded by financiers or capped by the off-taker matches the actual country risk and that project risks and risk premiums are not inflated.

While there is no uniform pattern in the debt financing for the projects considered here, observation of several trends in terms of how investors handled costs may contribute to the success of other projects. Although

nonrecourse project financing is the norm for privately financed electric power plants in developing regions, the 21 projects examined here represent several notable exceptions: Nigeria's Okpai and Afam VI, which were 100 percent financed by the balance sheet of equity partners, and the second phase of Songas, which was largely refinanced by a World Bank loan in 2009 (Globeleq 2010a). Until recently, Westmont, Iberafrica, and OrPower 4 were all financed entirely with the balance sheets of their sponsors. For Westmont and Iberafrica, the reason cited for this arrangement was insufficient time to arrange project finance, because plants had to be brought online within 11 months. For OrPower4, the reason was linked to lack of a security package, which was not finalized until 2006.

THE IMPACT OF DFIS ON PROJECTS. With limited appetite for IPPs among commercial banks, DFIs provide a substantial amoung of credit to projects. Indeed, DFIs such as the World Bank, International Finance Corporation (IFC), European Investment Bank, DEG, FMO, African Development Bank, PROPARCO, the Emerging Africa Infrastructure Fund, and European Financing Partners, KfW, and Agence Française de Développement have participated in nearly every IPP. Beyond these institutions' long history of activity in Sub-Saharan Africa, their involvement is attributable to real and perceived risks by private investors, which keep them from filling the financing gap, and to the DFIs' interest in participating in the broader mandate of power sector reform.

Although projects with DFI funding tended to take longer to reach financial closure than those financed through private sources, project sponsors in Kenya say that multilateral and bilateral development institutions helped them maintain contracts and resist renegotiation in the face of external challenges such as droughts, when developers were pressured to reduce tariffs. A particularly revealing contrast is between the two Kenyan plants, OrPower 4 and Tsavo. Although the two projects were negotiated under the same policy framework, the former initially had no multilateral involvement in either its equity or debt,[18] whereas the IFC arranged all the debt for Tsavo and took a 5 percent equity stake. Tsavo has since resisted KPLC pressure to reduce its tariffs. OrPower 4, on the other hand, ultimately reduced its tariff for the second phase of the plant. Tanzania's Songas project, for which the World Bank and European Investment Bank financed all project debt, also deserves special mention here. The project took almost a decade to reach financial closure; the World Bank played an instrumental role in, among other things, pressuring the

IPTL arbitration, which ultimately led to more balanced contract terms.

LOCALLY SOURCED FINANCE. While observers argue that local financing is key to increasing sustainable foreign investment, capital markets in many Sub-Saharan African countries are underdeveloped and illiquid, hence unable to provide financing for all projects. Three exceptions in the project sample are Kounoune I of Senegal, Geometric of Nigeria, and Namanve of Uganda. The Kounoune I project received financing from both the West African Bank for Development (BOAD), based in Togo, and the Banking Company of West Africa (CBAO), a private bank based in Senegal. Funding for Geometric has been provided by Diamond Bank and Stanbic IBTC Bank Plc, both of Nigeria. Similarly, for Uganda's Namanve project, financing was provided by Standard Chartered Bank of the United Kingdom through Stanbic Bank of Uganda. By contrast, in North Africa, all of the €213 million debt of Tahaddart, a 384 megawatt combined-cycle gas turbine plant in Morocco, was financed by local banks. Local financing was aided by a number of factors, including the state utility's prominent role in the plant (it holds nearly 50 percent of total equity) and the fact that Morocco's commercial banks have a significant degree of state involvement. With or without state involvement, however, no other country in Sub-Saharan Africa has yet been able to manage to arrange this level and depth of local financing for IPPs.

One main drawback for IPPs without local finance is the impact of macroeconomic shocks and local currency devaluation. Since the late 1990s, Ghana, Kenya, and Tanzania have experienced substantial depreciation, with their currencies losing more than 100 percent, 200 percent, and 400 percent of their value against the U.S. dollar, respectively. Inevitably, these currency shifts have led to pressure to reduce capacity charges and to countries reconsidering IPP development.

Securing revenue: The PPA

All 21 of the projects examined here had a long-term power purchase agreement with the incumbent state-owned utility to ensure a market for the power produced and to secure revenue flows for debt and equity providers. In addition to stating who would buy the power, the PPAs detailed how much power capacity would be available and how much buyers would be charged. Provisions concerning fuel metering, interconnection, insurance, *force majeure*, transfer, termination, change of legal provisions, and refinancing were generally also addressed. Nearly all the contracts specified some form of international dispute resolution and minimum power availability.

For each project, sponsors negotiated or were granted PPAs in U.S. dollars, thereby reducing their exposure to currency devaluation. Over time, the bulk of project contracts have been upheld, but not without changes. Box 21.5 reviews PPA renegotiations in Kenya, Nigeria, and Tanzania.

Credit enhancements and security arrangements

The underlying credit risk of IPP projects in Sub-Saharan Africa has been dealt with largely through a suite of credit enhancements, namely, guarantees, insurance, and cash (the latter of which took the form of escrow accounts, liquidity facilities, and letters of credit of varying amounts and tenures). The Tsavo project in Kenya, for example, has an escrow account equivalent to one month's capacity charge and a standby letter of credit from KPLC covering three months' billing (approximately $12 million). At least 12 of the 21 projects examined in this chapter had some form of cash security arrangement, with typical terms of between one and four months' capacity charge in reserve.

Not surprisingly, the number of credit enhancements appears to diminish as a country's risk profile improves. There are, however, noticeable exceptions such as the first wave of IPPs in Kenya (Westmont and Iberafrica), for which risk appears to be entirely reflected in the higher capacity payments negotiated. That said, corruption was also alleged in both these plants.[19] Thus, the "security arrangement" may lie not in a letter of credit but in an informal agreement among sponsors.

Of the many different credit enhancements used in connection with IPPs, sovereign guarantees are most common. Such guarantees are known to have been extended for at least nine of the pool of 21 projects: Tanzania's IPTL, Nigeria's AES Barge, Côte d'Ivoire's Azito, Ghana's Takoradi II (phase I), both GTi Dakar and Kounoune I in Senegal, Togo's Centrale thermique de Lomé, and Bujagali and Namanve in Uganda. Several of the projects without guarantees—Tsavo and Rabai, for example—were, however, given assurances by the government in the form of comfort or support letters, through which political risk is assumed. In the case of the Okpai plant in Nigeria, security was extended in the form of the state-owned oil company's revenues. Thus, if the off-taker defaults, NNPC, among the most liquid firms in the country, is liable. Partial risk guarantees (PRGs) issued by the World Bank were used

In Kenya's first wave of IPPs, costs were inflated in part due to the short duration of contracts—only seven years. With Iberafrica facing ongoing pressure to reduce its tariff, coupled with an interest in negotiating another contract, the sponsor voluntarily reduced the capacity charge enshrined in the PPA. (Iberafrica's second and third PPAs are for a considerably longer time frame than its first, and tariffs have been reduced significantly.) Westmont, on the other hand, did not negotiate a second contract after it failed to obtain the same terms—in particular, those related to capacity charges—spelled out in its first PPA. Likewise, changes in Kenya's OrPower 4 and Tanzania's Songas PPA agreements are related in part to the final amount of the capacity charge (as originally spelled out in the PPA).[a]

In the case of Nigeria's AES Barge, initially sponsored by Enron, renegotiations in 1999–2000 brought about several changes in the PPA, including a change in the fuel specifications (from liquid fuel to natural gas), which led to a major reduction in the fuel charge for the off-taker. The current arbitration with AES Barge involves, among other things, reconsideration of the availability-deficiency payment as well as the tax exemption. In each of the cases reviewed here, the original terms of the PPA have been viewed as unsustainable for the host country and therefore challenged.

The case of Tanzania's IPTL is slightly different, however. Although the contract was considered initially unsustainable due to the added capacity of Songas, the IPTL arbitration was prompted by what was deemed a breach in the PPA, namely, the project sponsors' substitution of medium-speed for slow-speed engines without passing on the capital cost savings to the utility, as per the PPA.[b]

a. It is, however, worth reiterating in this context that failure to agree on the security package and the capacity charge contributed to delays in the development of OrPower 4's additional 36 megawatts of production capacity.
b. Although this dispute was resolved, a subsequent and prevailing dispute relates to the level of actual equity in the project, which in turn affects WACC and the allowed rate of return.

for two of the projects, Azito and Bujagali.[20] In these instances, the PRG covered all debt of the commercial banks. In the case of default by the project company, the PRG (backed by World Bank) would pay the commercial lenders, and the World Bank would then claim repayment from the government (World Bank 1997, 1999). For other IPPs, political risk insurance was provided by the Overseas Private Investment Corporation (OPIC), whereas guarantees relating to currency inconvertibility, expropriation, and political violence were issued by the World Bank's Multilateral Investment Guarantee Agency (MIGA).

In several cases, these credit enhancements have improved the sustainability of projects and attracted or assuaged lenders. The Bujagali project's PRG, for example, was instrumental in motivating and solidifying the involvement of four commercial banks, which contributed a combined $115 million at very competitive pricing. Some have likened the PRG to a hammer effect, with the World Bank guaranteeing what the government has already guaranteed and thus making the government's commitment twofold. That said, PRGs are not appropriate for all Sub-Saharan African IPPs because they are typically used for large projects in countries that are in an early stage of reform and when commercial lenders are also present. Furthermore,

the government of the country must request a PRG; thus, the project must be significant in the eyes of both the government and the World Bank. For projects without PRGs security arrangements and credit enhancements are similar, with the DFIs generally accepting the political risks, such as in the Azito and Songas projects.

In Kenya, the only country among those in Sub-Saharan Africa examined here to extend sovereign guarantees to IPPs, stakeholders in Tsavo indicated that, without such a guarantee, the presence of the IFC became critical, both to help arrange debt and share in equity. In Ghana, lack of sovereign guarantees has been cited as the main obstacle to developing the second phase of the Takoradi II project.

Other credit enhancements have been used in abundance in Kenya, including a suite of escrow facilities, which have contributed to KPLC's cash-strapped position. Although government guarantees were recently debated by officials, it looks as if the government will retain its no-guarantee policy going forward, providing only letters of support to IPPs. KPLC cites the absence of sovereign guarantees as hampering its ability to raise private finance, while ERC counters that IPPs have been introduced to help commercialize the sector. Government guarantees work against this goal, however.

Notably, sovereign guarantees, political risk insurance policies, and PRGs have not been invoked in any of the 21 projects examined here, including in those projects that ultimately faced a change in the contract (AES Barge, IPTL, OrPower 4, and Takoradi II). Recourse to international arbitration has occurred only in the case of IPTL. Additionally, it is helpful to reflect on the overall application of security arrangements and credit enhancements. Although there is some variation in the project sample, by and large the variation is limited, with the size of the project, the track record of the regulatory regime (including its stability and credibility), and the creditworthiness of the off-taker being the main determinants. While there is resistance to government guarantees on the part of some country stakeholders, project developers and multilaterals typically support them. As one World Bank (2010) official noted, "the first level of support has to come from the government."

Furthermore, there has been very little evolution in the credit arrangements used for IPPs in Sub-Saharan Africa. All projects are supported by a PPA and their credit risk largely carried by a government guarantee. In countries in which the market for power is not developed, a PPA, along with a government guarantee, is generally required, particularly where the off-taker is not creditworthy (IFC 2010a; Rudo 2010a). This situation is quite different than that in other developing regions. In Latin America, for example, PRGs and other credit enhancements and security arrangements are virtually nonexistent because power markets are operational and local lenders are "in the driver's seat and generally very comfortable with local developers and regulation."[21]

Positive technical performance

Virtually all IPPs among the 21 considered here have shown positive technical performance. Exceptions include Nigeria's plants (which have had problems with fuel supply) and, more recently, Kounoune I in Senegal (Nigeria Electricity Regulatory Commission 2010; IFC 2010b). In general, IPPs' technical performance is superior to that of state-owned plants. An argument for extending gas from the West African Gas Pipeline to the Sunon Asogli Power Plant in Ghana, for example, is being made in part because Sunon's technical performance is superior to that of the Volta River Authority (PURC 2010). The Ministry of Energy of Togo (2010), meanwhile, has indicated that Centrale thermique de Lomé is expected to be more efficient than its state-owned counterpart. In terms of availability, IPPs in Kenya had an average availability of approximately

95 percent between 2004 and 2006, versus 60 percent for KenGen's thermal plants. When asked generally about his most favorable IPP experience to date, one public stakeholder simply indicated, "their technical performance" (ERC 2010).

Strategic management and relationship building

Once 20-year contracts are in place, it would seem that the deal is set and the revenue secured, with clear provisions to ensure debt repayment and reward equity. Several other interrelated actions deserve mention, however. One involves relationship building, including with local partners and communities. Another relates to how sponsors handle the onset of stresses, including those presented by capacity charges and refinancing.

Numerous IPP sponsors have adopted outreach programs to improve relations with local communities. In Kenya, for example, Tsavo set up a $1 million community development fund for the duration of the 20-year PPA, from which grants of $50,000 each are disbursed each year to benefit environmental and social activities in Kenya's Coast Region. Iberafrica maintains a social responsibility program, and IPTL also is an active donor to its immediate community. In Ghana CMS's social responsibility involvement (before it sold its shares to TAQA in 2007) included providing scholarships for secondary and tertiary education and supporting medical clinics and the construction of drainage systems. Bujagali also has a suite of social outreach programs. Although the sums are not significant, these programs, particularly when well advertised, have the potential to win allies and counter the stereotype of IPPs.

Another, perhaps more significant, action is how sponsors cope with stresses such as macroeconomic shocks, currency depreciation, and pressure from host governments to reduce costs. Anecdotal evidence suggests that strategic management helped put Kenya's Iberafrica back on track, in contrast to Westmont, where there is no evidence of such action. Iberafrica, in fact, has had to cope with two major stresses, drought and alleged corruption. According to stakeholders at Iberafrica, the IPP voluntarily reduced its capacity charge when KPLC was operating at a loss (due in part to a drought-related recession), to show its support for the country and signal its interest in a second contract. Iberafrica later secured a second contract, albeit after even further reductions were negotiated and passed by the electricity regulator.[22] For Rabai, another project in Kenya, sponsors chose to continue work on the project in the midst of countrywide protests following the election in December 2007 (Aldwych International 2010a).

Project refinancing

A final area in which IPPs may yield greater balancing in terms of development and investment outcomes is in the refinancing of projects, evidence for which can be seen in the Songas project in Tanzania. Possible refinancing in the case of IPTL, with the government of Tanzania proposing to buy the project's outstanding debt equity, could also lead to what may be perceived as a more balanced outcome. A government buyback of IPTL would make a one-time payment on behalf of the utility and then transfer ownership of the asset to TANESCO, which may subsequently decide to convert the plant to run on natural gas. Through this transaction, the capacity charge will fall to a token amount, and following conversion to gas, the energy charge will drop from $9 million–$12 million to $1 million–$1.5 million a month. The PPA would also be terminated and a new agreement drafted, one that would offer customers discounted tariffs.

Project refinancing has limited application and must be dealt with carefully during the project negotiation. As one banker candidly indicated, "If project finance bankers are expected to finance projects with the understanding that periodically it will be necessary to have a restructuring, the outcome of which is uncertain, the result will be to eliminate the availability of nonrecourse financing." Given the already low level of availability of financing in Africa, this should be avoided.

A host-country government's willingness to share risks over the life of an IPP may thus be pivotal to the long-term sustainability of projects. That said, strategic management does not occur in a vacuum. Often, the government is not only an active counterparty but may even, as evidenced in the refinancing of IPTL, initiate strategic management. Other government-led initiatives include the government of Tanzania's buying down of Songas' allowance for funds used during construction. The myriad project-level factors are summarized in table 21.4.

LESSONS LEARNED FROM IPPs IN SUB-SAHARAN AFRICA

Despite numerous challenges, a number of Sub-Saharan African countries have managed to attract and sustain private investments in IPPs. More than 20 large IPPs have taken root in eight countries, and a number of smaller, private projects have also been developed. While some IPPs

Table 21.4 Elements Contributing to Successful IPP Investments

Element	Details
Favorable equity partners	■ Local capital/partner contribution, where possible ■ Risk appetite for project ■ Experience with developing-country project risk ■ Involvement of a DFI partner and/or host-country government ■ Reasonable, fair return on equity ■ Firms with development origins
Favorable debt arrangements	■ Competitively priced financing or involvement of DFIs ■ Local capital/markets to mitigate foreign exchange risk ■ Flexibility in terms and conditions (possible option to refinance)
Secure and adequate revenue stream	■ Commercially sound metering, billing, and collections by the utility ■ Robust PPA (stipulates capacity and energy charges as well as dispatch, fuel metering, interconnection, insurance, *force majeure*, transfer, termination, change of law provisions, refinancing arrangements, dispute resolution)
Credit enhancements and security arrangements	■ Guarantees: sovereign guarantees, partial risk guarantees ■ Insurance: political risk insurance ■ Cash: escrow accounts, letters of credit, liquidity facilities
Positive technical performance	■ High level of technical performance (including availability) ■ Sponsors anticipate and mitigate potential conflicts (especially related to O&M and budgeting)
Strategic management and relationship building	■ Sponsors work to create good image in country through political relationships, development funds, and effective communications and strategically manage their contracts, particularly in the face of exogenous shocks and other stresses

Source: Authors.

CHAPTER 21: INDEPENDENT POWER PROJECTS IN SUB-SAHARAN AFRICA: DETERMINANTS OF SUCCESS

have encountered some contract changes, nearly all have survived and are countributing to social and economic development.

At the country level, factors such as a favorable investment climate, clear policy and regulatory frameworks, and local availability of cost-competitive fuels clearly help create successful IPPs. Of growing importance are effective planning, procurement, and contracting policies and practices. Kenya provides an example of how responsibilty for these functions can be effectively allocated and institutionalized.

Although evidence is not conclusive, strategic management on behalf of IPP sponsors and governments, as well as strong technical performance, have been used to strengthen projects. The role of firms with development origins, such as Aldwych, Globeleq, and IPS, and development finance institutions such as the IFC is increasingly important in the successful development and operation of new IPPs in Sub-Saharan Africa. Projects with participation of these firms

and DFIs were less likely to unravel, leading to one of two conclusions: these projects may have been more balanced from the outset and when an exogenous stress struck, or they may have been better equipped to resist host-country government pressure.

In Sub-Saharan African countries in which an imbalance between development and investment outcomes is perceived, there is evidence that IPP contracts are more unlikely to unravel. The incidence of such unraveling, however, does not necessarily signal the end of a project's operation. In all cases, efforts to close the initial gap between investors and host-country governments' perceptions and treatment of risks must continue. Finally, the means of closing this gap may not be only, or mainly, through increasing new protections such as PRGs or political risk insurance. Rather, the solution may lie in systematic treatment of the numerous elements contributing to success at the country and project level defined in this chapter.

ANNEX 21A   PROJECT SPECIFICATIONS

Detailed specifications are presented for each IPP discussed in this chapter. Information is first grouped into regions with East Africa followed by West Africa. Countries within each of the regions are presented in alphabetical order. Under each country, IPPs are then presented in chronological order, based on the date when the IPP first came online.

East Africa	
Kenya (1 of 5 projects)	
Project	Westmont
Size	46 MW
Cost	US$65 million
$ per kW	US$1,413
Fuel/technology	Kerosene/gas condensate/gas turbine (barge mounted)
ICB	None, but selective international tender conducted
Contract	BOO, 7 years
Debt/equity	—
DFI in equity and debt	None
Local participation in equity and debt	None
Equity partners (country of origin; % of each shareholder)	Westmont (Malaysia, 100%) has sought to sell plant since 2004
Lenders	—
Credit enhancements, security arrangements	None
Project tender, COD	1996, 1997
Contract change	Not a contract change per se, but firm failed to negotiate a second contract after its 7 year contract ended in 2004 due to failure to agree on tariffs
Fuel arrangement	Originally Westmont to procure fuel and then pass through to utility, however, following dispute with fuel supplier about taxes after the first year of operation, utility took over procurement
Kenya (2 of 5 projects)	
Project	Iberafrica
Size	108.3 MW (44, 12, 52.3 brought on, respectively)
Cost	US$35 million (only for first 56 MW)
$ per kW	NA
Fuel/technology	HFO/medium speed diesel engine
ICB	None
Contract	BOO, 7 years, 15 years, 25 years
Debt/Equity	72/28
DFI in equity and debt	None
Local participation in equity and debt	Yes (equity and debt)
Equity partners (country of origin; % of each shareholder)	Union Fenosa (Spain, 80%), KPLC Pension Fund (Kenya, 20%) since 1997
Lenders	Union Fenosa (US$12.7 million in direct loans and guaranteed US$20 million); KPLC Staff Pension Fund (US$9.4 in direct loans and guaranteed US$5 million through a local Kenyan bank).
Credit enhancements, security arrangements	None
Project tender, COD	1996, 1997/1999, 2000/2008, 2009
Contract change	Yes, Iberafrica reduced the capacity charge of its first PPA by 37% in April 2002 and then to 59% of the original PPA in September 2003.[a]
Fuel arrangement	Iberafrica buys fuel and passes cost through to KPLC based on the units generated and specific consumption parameters agreed on in the PPA
Kenya (3 of 5 projects)	
Project	OrPower 4
Size	13 MW + 35 MW
Cost	US$105[b] million
$ per kW	NA
Fuel/technology	Geothermal
ICB	Yes

(continued next page)

Contract	BOO, 20 years
Debt/equity	NA
DFI in equity and debt	DEG
Local participation in equity and debt	None
Equity partners (country of origin; % of each shareholder)	Ormat (100%) from 1998 to 2008.
Lenders	—
Credit enhancements, security arrangements	MIGA guarantee, a stand-by letter of credit, covering several months billing (although only finalized at end-2006)
Project tender, COD	1996, 2000–2009
Contract change	Yes, tariff for the second phased (35 MW) reduced
Fuel arrangement	The only fuel arrangement per se is that OrPower 4 was granted a Geothermal Resource License from the government, to which it pays a royalty of sorts (of US$0.004/kWh or USc 0.4/kWh)

Kenya (4 of 5 projects)

Project	Tsavo
Size	75 MW
Cost	US$86 million
$ per kW	US$1,133
Fuel/technology	HFO/medium speed diesel engine
ICB	Yes
Contract	BOO, 20 years
Debt/equity	78/22
DFI in equity and debt	Yes (equity and debt)
Local participation in equity and debt	None
Equity partners (country of origin; % of each shareholder)	Cinergy and IPS jointly owned 49. 9%, Cinergy sold to Duke Energy in 2005, CDC/Globeleq (U.K., 30%), Wartsila (Finland, 15%), IFC (5%) retain remaining shares since 2000
Lenders	IFC own account (US$16.5 million), IFC syndicated (US$23.5 million); CDC own account (US$13 million), DEG own account (€11 million), DEG syndicated (€2 million)
Credit enhancements, security arrangements	Letter of comfort provided by government, and escrow account, equivalent to 1 month capacity charge, and a stand-by letter of credit, equivalent to 3 months billing
Project tender, COD	1995, 2001
Contract change	None, but was pressured to lower tariff
Fuel arrangement	Tsavo buys fuel and passes cost through to KPLC based on the units generated and specific consumption parameters agreed on in the PPA

Kenya (5 of 5 projects)

Project	Rabai
Size	90 MW
Cost	US$155 million
$ per kW	US$1,722
Fuel/technology	HFO
ICB	Yes
Contract	BOOT, 20 years
Debt/equity	75% debt, (5% subordinated debt, 25% equity)
DFI in equity and debt	Yes
Local participation in equity and debt	No
Equity partners (country of origin; % of shareholder)	Aldywch: 34%, BWSC (Danish, but owned by Mitsui of Japan): 25.5%, FMO: 20%, IFU (Danish bilateral lender): 20%
Lenders	DEG: 15%, FMO: 25%, EAIF: 25%, Proparco: 25%, EFP (European Financing Partners): 10%
Credit enhancements, security arrangements	Support letter from government of Kenya (covers political risk but falls short of being an outright guarantee), and KPLC-issued letter of credit equivalent to 5 months of capacity (debt service, fixed costs and equity returns) payments and 2 months of fuel payments
Project tender, COD	2006, 2009
Contract change	None
Fuel arrangement	Fuel supply agreement with Kenol of Kenya

(continued next page)

Tanzania (1 of 2 projects)

Project	IPTL
Size	100 MW
Cost	US$120 million
$ per kW	US$1,200
Fuel/technology	HFO/medium speed diesel engine
ICB	None
Contract	BOO, 20 years
Debt/equity	70/30 (albeit ratio disputed)
DFI in equity and debt	None
Local participation in equity and debt	Yes (in-kind equity participation)
Equity partners (country of origin; % of each shareholder)	Mechmar (Malaysia, 70%), VIP (Tanzania, 30% in kind), both have sought to sell shares
Lenders	Two Malaysian-based banks (Bank Bumiputra Malaysia Berhad—now Bank Bumiputra Commercial Bank—and SIME Bank) auctioned debt to Standard Chartered Bank
Credit enhancements, security arrangements	Sovereign guarantee, liquidity facility equivalent to 4 months capacity charge (but not yet established)
Project tender, COD	1997, 2002
Contract change	Yes, postarbitration, monthly capacity charges lowered from US$3.6 million to US$2.6 million
Fuel arrangement	IPTL imports fuel, which is a pass-through to the utility

Tanzania (2 of 2 projects)

Project	Songas
Size	180 MW[c]
Cost	US$316 million[d]
$ per kW	US$2,313 (for first 115 MW) and US$769 (for 65 MW expansion)
Fuel/technology	Natural gas/open cycle
ICB	Yes
Contract	BOO, 20 years
Debt/equity	70/30 for 115 MW 100% equity financed for 65 MW expansion, which has since been refinanced
DFI in equity and debt	Yes
Local participation in equity and debt	Yes (TANESCO, TDFL)
Equity partners (country of origin; % of each shareholder)	TransCanada sold majority shares to AES (USA) in 1999 and AES sold majority shares to Globeleq (UK) in 2003.[e] All preferred equity shares were converted into "Loan Notes" in June 2009. Only common shares remain.
Lenders	World Bank (US$136 million), EIB (US$55 million), Sida (US$15 million)
Credit enhancements, security arrangements	Escrow account: for first 115 MW, with the government matching every US$1 spent by the project company; liquidity facility equivalent to 4 months capacity charge for the first 3 years, declining to 2 months starting in year 4 through the remaining years of the contract
Project tender, COD	1994, 2004
Contract change	The changes to Songas' PPA include: US$103 million AFUDC buy-down; the use of escrow funds to buy down the AFUDC; freezing the liquidity facility, which was meant to be replenished and accessed only in the case of partial or nonpayment by TANESCO; and preferred equity conversion to "loan notes"
Fuel arrangement	Songo Songo gas provided to project company at a rate of US$0.55/MMBtu for turbines I–V and at US$2.17 MMBtu for turbine VI

Uganda (1 of 2)

Project	Namanve Power Plant/Jacobsen Uganda Power Plant Limited
Size	50 MW
Cost	US$74 million at inception
$ per kW	US$1,488
Fuel/technology	HFO
ICB	Yes

(continued next page)

Contract	BOOT, 6 year
Debt/equity	—
DFI in equity and debt	Yes (debt)
Local participation in equity and debt	Yes (debt)
Equity partners (country of origin; % of each shareholder)	Jacobsen Elektro (Norway, 100%)
Lenders	Loan from Standard Chartered Bank UK, partly guaranteed by GIEK (the Norwegian guarantee agency), commercial loan from Stanbic Bank (Uganda) Ltd. (backstopped by Standard Chartered Bank UK); subordinate loan from parent company Jacobsen Elektro AS; NORAD grant
Credit enhancements, security arrangements	GIEK guarantee backed up by government of Uganda
Project tender, COD	COD 2008
Contract change	None
Fuel arrangement	Openly bid for contract; not part of license (plant availability should be >90%)
Uganda (2 of 2)	
Project	Bujagali
Size	250 MW
Cost	US$860 million
$ per kW	US$3,440
Fuel/technology	Hydro
ICB	Yes
Contract	BOT, 30 years
Debt/equity	78/22
DFI in equity and debt	Debt
Local participation in equity and debt	Yes, government of Uganda
Equity partners (country of origin; & % of each shareholder)	Sithe Global (58%), IPS/Aga Khan (32% but 50.1% voting), government of Uganda (10%)
Lenders	African Development Bank, EIB, PROPARCO, AFD, DEG, KfW, FMO, and IFC as DFIs, NedBank, Absa Capital, Standard Chartered Bank, and Fortis as commercial banks covered by the PRG
Credit enhancements, security arrangements	Government guarantee, MIGA, PRG/IDA
Project tender, COD	2005, expected 2012
Contract change	None
Fuel arrangement	—

West Africa

Côte d'Ivoire (1 of 2)	
Project	Compagnie Ivoirienne de Production d'Electricité (CIPREL)
Size	210 MW
Cost	US$105.6 million[f]
$ per kW	US$503
Fuel/technology	Natural gas/open cycle
ICB	None
Contract	BOOT, 19 years
Debt/equity	—
DFI in equity and debt	Yes (equity and debt)
Local participation in equity and debt	None
Equity partners (country of origin; % of each shareholder)	SAUR International, with 88% joint venture (JV) between French SAUR Group owned by Bouygues, 65% and EDF, 35%) BOAD, PROPARCO, and IFC holding the remaining 12%; in 2005 all shares sold to Bouygues (France, 98%), except BOAD (2%)
Lenders	World Bank
Credit enhancements, security arrangements	None
Project tender, COD	1993, 1995
Contract change	None
Fuel arrangement	Government procures fuel

(continued next page)

Côte d'Ivoire (2 of 2)

Project	Azito
Size	288 MWg
Cost	US$225 million
$ per kW	US$781
Fuel/technology	Natural gas/open cycle
ICB	Yes
Contract	BOOT, 24 years
Debt/equity	70/30
DFI in equity and debt	Yes (debt)
Local participation in equity and debt	None
Equity partners (country of origin; % of each shareholder)	Cinergy (JV between Swiss ABB, 50% and French EDF, 50%) Holds 65.7% of shares, CDC/Globeleq (11%), and IPS (23%)
Lenders	IFC, CDC, FMO, DEG, AfDB, Societe Generale, and other European commercial banks
Credit enhancements	World Bank partial risk guarantee Sovereign guarantee
Security arrangements	Escrow account equivalent to 1 month capacity charge
Project tender, COD	1996, 2000
Contract change	None
Fuel arrangement	Government procures fuel

Ghana (1 of 3)

Project	Takoradi II
Size	220 MWh
Cost	US$110 million
$ per kW	US$500
Fuel/technology	Light crude oil/single cycle
ICB	None
Contract	BOOT, 25 years
Debt/Equity	Financed exclusively with balance sheet of sponsors
DFI in equity and debt	No
Local participation in equity and debt	Yes (equity)
Equity partners (country of origin & % of each shareholder)	CMS (U.S., 90%), VRA (Ghana, 10%), CMS sold shares to TAQA (UAE, 90%) in 2007
Lenders	Financed exclusively with balance sheet of sponsors
Credit enhancements	Sovereign guarantee
Security arrangements	US$3 million letter of credit provided by government
Project tender, COD	1998, 2000
Contract change	Failure to develop second phase (110 MW), investors cite the lack of government guarantees (granted in the first phase of Takoradi II), meanwhile government has indicated that the EPC costs are too high and further development remains at standstill
Fuel arrangement	Government procures fuel

Ghana (2 of 3)

Project	Sunon Asogli Power Plant
Size	200 MW
Cost	—
$ per kW	—
Fuel/technology	Combustion engine
ICB	No
Contract	BOO, 20 years
Debt/equity	—
DFI in equity and debt	None
Local participation in equity and debt	Local strategic investor, Togbe Afede XIV
Equity partners (country of origin; % of each shareholder)	Shenzhen (China, 100%)
Lenders	—
Credit enhancements, security arrangements	—
Project tender, COD	—

(continued next page)

Contract change	Related to fuel
Fuel arrangement	Inability to reach conclusion about fuel agreement, which has prevented plant from coming online

Ghana (3 of 3)

Project	Bui hydro
Size	400 MW
Cost	US$622 million
$ per kW	US$1,555/kW
Fuel/Technology	Hydro
ICB	No
Contract	—
Debt/Equity	—
DFI in equity and debt	None
Local participation in equity and debt	—
Equity partners (country of origin & % of each shareholder)	Sinohydro (China, 100%)
Lenders	—
Credit enhancements and security arrangements	—
Project tender, COD	2005, expected online in 2012
Contract change	None
Fuel arrangement	Hydro

Nigeria (1 of 4)

Project	AES Barge Limited
Size	270 MW
Cost	US$240 million
$ per kW	US$888
Fuel/technology	Natural gas/open cycle (barge mounted)
ICB	None
Contract	BOO, 13 years
Debt/equity	—
DFI in equity and debt	None
Local participation in equity and debt	Yes (equity)
Equity partners (country of origin; % of each shareholder)	Enron (U.S., 100%) sold to AES (95%) and YFP (Nigeria, 5%) in 2000
Lenders	—
Credit enhancements, security arrangements	OPIC political risk insurance Sovereign guarantee, US$60 million letter of credit from Ministry of Finance
Project tender, COD	1999, 2001
Contract change	Yes, initial plant size increased from 90 MW to 270 MW (9 units of 30 MW each) and change in the fuel from liquid fuel to natural gas, both of which had the effect of reducing the capacity charge, current contract changes under discussion involve among other things the availability of deficiency payment, meanwhile tax exemption certificate has been withheld by government for the duration of the project
Fuel arrangement	Utility arranges fuel

Nigeria (2 of 4)

Project	Okpai
Size	450 MW
Cost	US$462[i]
$ per kW	—
Fuel/technology	Natural gas/combined cycle
ICB	None
Contract	BOO, 20 years
Debt/equity	100% equity financed
DFI in equity and debt	None
Local participation in equity and debt	Yes (equity and debt)
Equity partners (country of origin; % of each shareholder)	Nigerian National Petroleum Corporation (Nigeria, 60%), Nigerian Agip Oil Company (Italy, 20%), and Phillips Oil Company (U.S., 20%) maintained equity since 2001

(continued next page)

Lenders	Provided by equity partners
Credit enhancements, security arrangements	PPA backed by Nigerian Petroleum Development Company's oil revenues
Project tender, COD	2001, 2005
Contract change	Ongoing negotiations related to investment costs which rose by US$150 million, to US$462 million; although plant is producing power, due to the dispute, full payment is not being made by utility
Fuel arrangement	Project company provides fuel
Nigeria (3 of 4)	
Project	Afam IV
Size	630 MW
Cost	—
$ per kW	—
Fuel/technology	CCGT
ICB	No
Contract	BOO, 20 years
Debt/equity	100% equity
DFI in equity and debt	None
Local participation in equity and debt	Yes, NNPC
Equity partners (country of origin; % of each shareholder)	NNPC (Nigeria, 55%), Shell (U.K./Netherlands, 30%), Elf (Total) (France, 10%), Agip (Italy, 5%)
Lenders	
Credit enhancements, security arrangements	PPA backed by Nigerian Petroleum Development Company's oil revenues
Project tender, COD	2000, 2007
Contract change	No
Fuel arrangement	Project company provides fuel
Nigeria (4 of 4)	
Project	Aba Integrated Power Project
Size	140 MW
Cost	US$385
$ per kW	US$2,750/kW (includes distribution investment)
Fuel/t\Technology	Gas fired open-cycle power
ICB	No
Contract	BOO
Debt/equity	
DFI in equity and debt	No
Local participation in equity and debt	Yes (equity)
Equity partners (country of origin; % of each shareholder)	Geometric Power Limited (Nigeria)
Lenders	Diamond Bank, Stanbic IBTC
Credit enhancements, security arrangements	
Project tender, COD	2005, anticipated COD end-2010
Contract change	No
Fuel arrangement	
Senegal (1 of 2)	
Project	GTi Dakar
Size	52 MW
Cost	US$65 million
$ per kW	US$1,250/kW
Fuel/technology	Complete cycle/diesel/natfa
ICB	Yes
Contract	BOOT, 15 years
Debt/equity	75/25
DFI in equity and debt	Yes (both)
Local participation in equity and debt	None
Equity partners (country of origin, % of each shareholder)	GE Capital Structured Finance Group (U.S.), IFC, Edison (Italy)
Lenders	IFC and Credit Commercial de France

(continued next page)

Credit enhancements, security arrangements	Government guarantee, credit insurance through a guarantee program of SACE, the Italian export credit agency, and a partial interest subsidy through the Mediocredito Central Subsidy Department, escrow account
Project tender, COD	1996, 1999/2000
Contract change	None
Fuel arrangement	
Senegal (2 of 2)	
Project	Kounoune I
Size	68 MW
Cost	US$110 million
$ per kW	US$1617/kW
Fuel/technology	HFO diesel
ICB	Yes
Contract	BOO, 15 years
Debt/equity	
DFI in equity and debt	Yes (debt)
Local participation in equity and debt	Yes (debt)
Equity partners (country of origin; % of each shareholder)	Mitsubishi (Japan), Matelec S.A.L (Lebanon)
Lenders	IFC, Proparco, AfDB, BOAD, and CBAO
Credit enhancements, security arrangements	Government guarantee, a PRG although never signed by the government, a letter of credit from Senelec
Project tender, COD	2003, 2008
Contract change	None
Fuel arrangement	During the project negotiations, the structures of the FSA and PPA were changed to turn the PPA into a tolling agreement.
Togo (1 of 1)	
Project	Extension of Central Thermique de Lome (CTL)
Size	100 MW
Cost	US$196 million (including 18 km transmission lines rehabilitation and soil decontamination investment)
$ per kW	US$1,960
Fuel/technology	Triple fuel
ICB	No
Contract	BOOT, 25 years
Debt/equity	75/25
DFI in equity and debt	Yes (debt)
Local participation in equity and debt	None (but contract stipulates up to 25% of equity must be sold to local/Togolese)
Equity partners (country of origin; % of each shareholder)	Contour Global (U.S., 80%), IFC (20%)
Lenders	OPIC
Credit enhancements, security arrangements	Government guarantee, OPIC guarantee, escrow account for 1 month of full operation, letter of credit of 2 months of full operation, (which become one month after 2 years of no incident of payment, and ceases to exist after 4 years of no incident)
Project tender, COD	Due online in July 2010
Contract change	No
Fuel arrangement	The buyer (utility provides fuel)

Source: Authors.

Notes: — = Not available. BOT = build, own, transfer.

a. Furthermore, although not a contract change per se, the value of the capacity charge for Iberafrica's second PPA was 50 percent that of the first PPA.

b. US$105 includes only the loan portion for the 35 MW part of the plant (Ormat, personal communication, 2010).

c. There was considerable evolution in terms of the planned capacity for the plant, from 60 MW to the current 180 MW.

d. Songas project costs include refurbishment of gas wells, a new gas processing facility, pipeline construction and fuel conversion of the existing power station (Ubungo), in total amounting to US$266 million, and an additional US$50 million for expansion in terms of two additional turbines (total 65 MW) and related infrastructure. The expansion was financed entirely by equity. A rough estimate for the electricity generation component would be 40 percent of project costs or US$130 million, based on US$35 million for refurbishment and fuel conversion of existing turbines, US$45 million assumed loans on existing turbines, and US$50 million for expansion.

(continued next page)

e. Due to complexity, turnover is detailed in this footnote: Ocelot (Canada), TransCanada (Canada), Tanzania Petroleum Development Corporation, TPDC (Tanzania), TANESCO (Tanzania), Tanzania Development Finance Company, TDFL (Tanzania, sponsored by EIB), IFC (multilateral), DEG (German), CDC (UK) were shareholders by 1996, with TransCanada the majority shareholder; IFC and DEG sold shares to CDC in 1997/8; TransCanada sold shares to AES (USA) in 1999; Ocelot/PanOcean sold shares to AES in 2001; AES sold majority shares to Globeleq (UK) and FMO (Holland) in 2003. After the AES sale, equity shares and associated financial commitments (expressed in US$ million) in Songas were as follows: Globeleq: US$33.8 (56%); FMO: US$14.6 (24%); TDFL: US$4 (7%); CDC: US$3.6 (6%); TPDC: US$3 (5%) and TANESCO: US$1 (2%). This does not reflect the additional US$50 million that Globeleq committed for the expansion.

f. Investment cost €87.8m or 57.6 billion CFA, with the average 1994 conversion of US$ to CFA, 545,100.

g. The initial project concept included specifications to raise capacity to 420 MW.

h. The initial project concept included specifications to add a second phase of 110 MW and convert to combined cycle, however, lack of funding has limited the completion of this phase.

i. Project costs include the gas infrastructure.

NOTES

1. The standard model for power sector reform has been roughly defined as a series of steps that move vertically integrated utilities toward competition, generally including the following activities: corporatization, commercialization, passage of the requisite legislation, establishment of an independent regulator, introduction of IPPs, restructuring/unbundling, divestiture of generation and distribution assets, and introduction of competition (Bacon 1999; Adamantiades and others 1995; Besant-Jones 2006; Williams and Ghanadan 2006). Although this model, based largely on the early power sector reforms carried out in Chile, Norway, and the United Kingdom, came to represent a standard, it is arguable that not all steps were relevant to conditions on the ground in most developing countries (Gratwick and Eberhard 2008b).

2. Exceptions are Côte d'Ivoire and Tanzania, where IPPs are contributing more than 50 percent to overall electricity production. Togo's first IPP, Centrale thermique de Lomé, will also supply the majority of electricity for that country.

3. Two different categories of DFIs should be distinguished, namely, those that lend on commercial terms and largely to private companies (for example, FMO, PROPARCO, DEG, and IFC), and the multilateral development banks (such as the World Bank and the African Development Bank) that lend on concessionary terms and primarily to public sector projects. It is the latter that refocused on infrastructure (Rudo 2010a).

4. Although Mauritius has four IPPs (which, at approximately 200 MW combined, account for about 37 percent of installed capacity and a little less than 25 percent of production, as of end-2005), the country has not been included in this sample. The IPPs, which are all cogeneration plants, provide power and steam to the country's sugar mills throughout the crop season, reducing their contribution to the state-owned utility by about 30 percent. During this time, the shortfall in production is made up by seven continuous power producers, privately owned by the sugar mills. With installed capacity of 40 MW, roughly equal to the IPP shortfall, these continuous producers also have long-term take or pay contracts with the state (Bergesen 2007; World Bank 2007a).

5. Centrale thermique de Lomé is a preexisting 90 MW facility for which a rehabilitate-own-transfer contract was provided to Electro Togo in 2001. In 2006, however, when a power crisis intensified and the rehabilitation had not yet been completed, the government of Togo opted to terminate Electro Togo's contract and initiate a BOOT directly with Contour Global, which had previously been involved in discussions with Electro Togo (Ministry of Energy of Togo 2010).

6. A portion of the shares of the two Kenyan utilities, KPLC and Kengen, however, are listed on the Nairobi Stock Exchange. Côte d'Ivoire's state utility has been under a private concession contract since 1990—an arrangement that is expected to continue until 2020. TANESCO in Tanzania and KPLC in Kenya also have had private management contracts. In Senegal, there was an attempt (albeit aborted) to privatize Senelec in 1999 through a concession with Hydro-Québec and Elyo (the concession was annulled by the president in 2001). Uganda unbundled its national utility into separate generation, transmission, and distribution companies and entered into long-term private concession in generation (Eskom) and distribution (Umeme-Globeleq). Finally, Nigeria has expressed an intention to unbundle and privatize but has not yet fully realized this ambition.

7. Alternatives to strictly independent regulation that may provide a better match to a country's regulatory commitment and institutional and human resource capacity (for example, regulatory contracts, outsourcing of regulatory functions, expert panels, and regional regulators) are increasingly being considered (Eberhard 2007).

8. Domestic gas reserves were used for IPPs in Côte d'Ivoire. Unlike for the other countries, however, this use

did not represent the establishment of a new gas infrastructure. An attempt, led by the government, was also made to exploit stranded gas reserves in Ghana's Osagyefo Barge project.

9. Stakeholders in Nigeria have seen costs escalate, causing the utility to withhold payments. In Tanzania costs have also escalated, but for reasons unrelated to the project itself.

10. At the time of writing, Kenya had only 60 MW still in service, and that was expected to be retired by November 2010.

11. In terms of international norms, however, it should be noted that Tanzania's cost of unserved energy (CUE) is low. South Africa's CUE is approximately US$10/kWh, which is in line with the CUE in many industrialized countries (Global Energy Decisions 2007).

12. On the other hand, given the high cost of mounting a bid, having an excessive amount of bidders would also not be desirable as some will not bid if they perceive their chances to be low (Rudo 2010a).

13. Togo's next IPP, a 24 MW wind farm, is being procured through an ICB (Ministry of Energy of Togo 2010).

14. Tanzania used the net-back calculation method to establish the gas price for the first 142 MW owned by Songas. Although it is viewed to be low ("US$0.55/Mcf"), most of the costs associated with the gas infrastructure are paid separately as part of the capacity charge. In typical projects, these would have been part of the gas price (i.e., US$4.20/Mcf). The same gas price is not offered to IPTL. Under the IPTL PPA, fuel is a pass-through. TANESCO has negotiated with PanAfrican Energy and TPDC to book 100 MMcfd at negotiated wellhead prices (in favor of the additional 40 MW owned by Songas, 145 MW owned by TANESCO, and the next 100 MW plant, which may be IPTL or any other plant) starting at US$1.98/Mcf, escalated at 2.2 percent annually for the first five years from July 2007, then to US$3.5/Mcf thereafter, escalated at USCPI. In summary, the gas prices are discounted market prices of an alternative fuel (EWURA 2010a).

15. Projects such as Osagyefo Barge in Ghana and Ibom and Omoku in Nigeria are sometimes loosely termed IPPs. In Ghana, private participation was expected (but not achieved), and in Nigeria, projects, although independent of the national utility, have been led entirely by the Rivers and Akwa Ibom state governments, respectively. All of these projects are excluded from the analysis presented here.

16. At the time of writing, the level of equity (including local equity) is under dispute in Tanzanian court.

17. The emergence of two Chinese firms, Shenzhen and Sinohydro, in Sunon Asogli and Bui hydro, respectively, in Ghana could represent a new element and be a significant source of investment for other African IPPs. Foster and Briceno-Garmendia (2010) report on the general phenomenon of non-OECD funders, including the emergence of increasingly significant funding flows from China to Sub-Saharan Africa.

18. In 2009, 10 years after financial close, DEG arranged a $105 million loan (Ormat 2009).

19. In 2005, it was found that the then managing director of KPLC, Samuel Gichuru, received $2 million from Westmont.

20. In addition, a PRG for Kounoune I was approved by the World Bank but was ultimately not signed by the government of Senegal, because the lender that the PRG would have covered was willing to fund the project without the PRG (IFC 2010a).

21. World Bank 2010. For IPPs in Central Asia, however, and for cross-border projects such as those in Laos and Thailand (Nam Theum II), a PRG or other "strong" credit enhancements would be employed. In the middle-income Latin American countries cited above, privatization trajectories meant there were few IPPs, and in those few cases (for example, Colombia), bilateral and multilateral institutions helped back investments (Rudo 2010a).

22. The fact that Iberafrica was not project-financed meant that the company had greater flexibility to change the payment streams.

REFERENCES

Adamantiades, A. G., et al. 1995. "Power Sector Reform in Developing Countries and the Role of the World Bank." Paper prepared for 16th Congress of the World Energy Council, Tokyo. World Bank, Industry and Energy Department, Washington, DC.

Africa Electra. 2005. "The Role of Local Banks in Financing Power Projects." Africa Electra 30.

Aldwych International. 2010a. Personal communication, May 5–6.

———. 2010b. Personal communication, June 9.

APEC (Asia-Pacific Economic Cooperation) Energy Working Group. 1997. "Manual of Best Practice Principles for Independent Power Producers." APEC Secretariat, Canberra.

Bacon, R. 1999. "A Scorecard for Energy Reform in Developing Countries." World Bank, Finance Private Sector and Infrastructure Network, Washington, DC.

Bergesen, C. 2007. *Mauritius*. Columbus, OH: McGraw Hill.

Besant-Jones, J. E. 2006. "Reforming Power Markets in Developing Countries: What Have We Learned?" Energy and Mining Sector Board Discussion Paper 19, World Bank, Washington, DC.

Deloitte Touche Tohmatsu Emerging Markets Ltd. and Advanced Engineering Associates International. 2003. "Energy Program South Asia Generation Pricing Study."

South East Asia Regional Initiative for Energy, USAID, Washington, DC.

Eberhard, A. 2007. "The Independence and Accountability of Africa's Infrastructure Regulators: Reassessing Regulatory Design and Performance." Paper presented at AFUR Annual Conference, Livingstone, Zambia, April 25–26.

Eberhard, A., and I. Malgas. Forthcoming. "Hybrid Power Markets in Africa: Generation Planning, Procurement and Contracting Challenges." *Energy Policy.*

Eberhard, A., and M. Shkaratan. 2010. "Africa's Power Infrastructure: Improving Investment, Connectivity, Reliability and Efficiencies." Africa Infrastructure Country Diagnostic, World Bank, Washington, DC.

EDF (Électricité de France). 2005. Personal communication, January 11.

ERC (Energy Regulatory Commission of Kenya). 2010a. Personal communication, May 18. Nairobi, Kenya.

———. 2010b. Personal communication, May 26. Nairobi, Kenya.

EWURA (Energy and Water Utilities Regulatory Authority). 2010. Personal communication, May 18. Dar es Salaam Tanzania.

Foster, V., and C. Briceño-Garmendia, eds. 2010. *Africa's Infrastructure: A Time for Transformation.* Washington, DC: Agence Française de Développement and World Bank.

Global Energy Decisions. 2007. "Electrical Resource Needs Analysis: Adequate Reserve Margin for Development of Third National Integrated Resource Plan for South Africa." Pretoria.

Globeleq. 2006. "Enabling Electricity Growth in Africa: Some Experiences." In *Financing Electricity for Growth in Africa.* Tunis: Infrastructure Consortium for Africa.

———. 2010a. Personal communication, May 5.

———. 2010b. Personal communication, June 1.

Gratwick, K. N., and A. Eberhard. 2008a. "An Analysis of Independent Power Projects in Africa: Understanding Development and Investment Outcomes." *Development Policy Review* 26 (3): 309–38.

———. 2008b. "Demise of the Standard Model for Power Sector Reform and the Emergence of Hybrid Power Markets." *Energy Policy* 36: 3948–60.

IFC (International Finance Corporation). 2005. Personal communication, January 24.

———. 2010a. Personal communication, May 21. Washington, DC.

———. 2010b. Personal communication, June 12. Washington, DC.

IPS (Industrial Promotion Services). 2010. Personal communication, May 24. Nairobi, Kenya.

Hoskote, M. 1995. "Independent Power Projects (IPPs): An Overview." Energy Note 2. In *Energy Themes,* ed. R. English. Washington, DC: World Bank.

International Energy Agency. 2006. *World Energy Outlook 2006.* Paris: OECD/IEA.

Malgas, I., K. N. Gratwick, and A. Eberhard. 2007a. "Moroccan Independent Power Producers: African Pioneers." *Journal of North African Studies* 13 (1): 15–36.

———. 2007b. "Two of a Kind: Lessons from Tunisian Independent Power Projects." *Journal of North African Studies* 12 (4): 395–415.

Matsukawa, T., R. Sheppard, and J. Wright. 2003. "Foreign Exchange Risk Mitigation for Power and Water Projects in Developing Countries." Energy and Mining Sector Board Discussion Paper 9, World Bank, Washington, DC.

Ministry of Energy of Togo. 2010. Personal communication, June 10–11. Lome, Togo.

Nigeria Electricity Regulatory Commission. 2010. Personal communication, May 21. Abuja, Nigeria.

Ormat. 2009. "Ormat Technologies Announces Closing of $105 Million Long-Term Senior Debt Financing for the Olkaria III Geothermal Power Project in Kenya." Press release, March 6, Reno, Nevada.

———. 2010. Personal communication, May 17.

Phadke, A. 2007. "Mark-ups in the State Capital Cost of Private Power Projects in Developing Countries." Energy and Resources Group, University of California, Berkeley.

PURC (Public Utilities Regulatory Commission of Ghana). 2010. Personal communication, May 19–21. Accra, Ghana.

Regulatory Commision of Senegal. 2010. Personal communication, June 11. Dakar, Senegal.

Rudo, D. 2010a. Personal communication, May 14. Washington, DC.

———. 2010b. Personal communication, June 10. Washington, DC.

Sinclair, S. 2007. "The World Bank Group Risk Mitigation Instruments." Paper presented at Private Sector Participation in Power Conference, Dead Sea, Jordan.

UNEP (United Nations Environment Programme) and UN Economic Commission for Africa. 2006. *Making Africa's Power Sector Sustainable: An Analysis of Power Sector Reforms in Africa.* New York: United Nations.

Williams, J. H., and R. Ghanadan. 2006. "Electricity Reform in Developing and Transition Countries: A Reappraisal." *Energy* 31: 815–44.

Woodhouse, E. J. 2005. "The Experience with Independent Power Projects in Developing Countries: Interim

Report." Program on Energy and Sustainable Development, Stanford University, Stanford, CA.

Woolf, F., and J. Halpern. 2001. "Integrating Independent Power Producers into Emerging Wholesale Power Markets." Policy Research Working Paper 2703, World Bank, Washington, DC.

World Bank. 1993. *The World Bank's Role in the Electric Power Sector: Policies for Effective Institutional, Regulatory, and Financial Reform.* Washington, DC: World Bank.

———. 1997. "Morocco's Jorf Lasfar Power Station." In *Project Finance and Guarantees.* World Bank, Washington, DC.

———. 1999. "Sub-Saharan Africa Benefits from the first IDA Guarantee for Azito." In Project Finance and Guarantees. Washington, DC: World Bank.

———. 2007. Private Participation in Infrastructure Database. http://ppi.worldbank.org.

———. 2010. Personal communication, May 17.

World Bank and USAID. 1994. "Submission and Evaluation of Proposals for Private Power Generation Projects in Developing Countries." IEN Occasional Paper 2. World Bank, Washington, DC.

PART VI

Improving Human Development Outcomes with Innovative Policies

CHAPTER 22

Innovative Financing for Health in Rwanda: A Report of Successful Reforms

C. Sekabaraga, A. Soucat, F. Diop, and G. Martin

Rwanda has been moving very rapidly to expand health service delivery. It has dramatically accelerated the trend of progress on health indicators, putting it back on track to reach the health Millennium Development Goals (MDGs). Three interrelated innovative reforms contributed to improvement: community-based health insurance, performance-based financing within a broader framework of reform of management of human resources for health, and fiscal decentralization. This chapter examines these reforms, showing how they worked together to improve health outcomes in Rwanda.

Health indicators in Rwanda improved dramatically in recent years, and projections for the coming years are positive. After an initial surge following the genocide, under-five mortality (the probability of death per 1,000 live births) significantly decreased, falling from 196 in 2000 to 152 in 2005 and 103 in 2007 (figure 22.1). The infant mortality rate decreased from 107 per 1,000 live births in 2000 to 86 in 2005 and 62 in 2007. Improvements were particularly significant among the poor, with the under-five mortality rate among the poorest quintile declining by 50 deaths per 1,000 between 2005 and 2008 compared with 38 deaths per 1,000 live births among the richest quintile. The annual rate of decrease achieved between 2005 and 2008 was 12.2 percent—far greater than the 9.7 percent needed to meet the MDG 4 target of 50 in 2015. Rwanda is thus back on track to reach the health MDGs.

Since 2000 the maternal mortality ratio has declined at an annual rate of 12.1 percent to reach 383 per 100,000 in 2008, ranking it among the best-performing countries in the world (figure 22.2). This rate of decline far exceeds the 5 percent rate needed to meet the MDG target of reducing the maternal mortality ratio by three-quarters between 1990 and 2015.

These achievements have been the result of innovative strategies to address some of the key challenges affecting maternal mortality. The share of women delivering their babies in health facilities has steadily increased, rising from 28 percent of pregnant women in 2000 to 45 percent in 2008. Many challenges remain, but preliminary data from the Ministry of Health for 2010 suggest that this figure has risen to two-thirds of all pregnant women; the finding should be validated by the 2010 Demographic and Health Survey.

These successes can be attributed largely to an increase in the use of essential health interventions, particularly high-impact interventions that are critical in reducing disease burden in developing countries, including immunization, assisted deliveries, family planning, and the use of insecticide-treated bed nets to prevent malaria. Rwanda has maintained a very high and equitable coverage of vaccination against avoidable childhood diseases since 2000: immunization rates, at 95 percent in 2008, are among the highest in Sub-Saharan Africa. Major progress has also been made in extending the coverage of vitamin A supplementation among children and women, through a mass campaign and integration into routine health facility services. Treatment of acute respiratory infections of children has also increased, including among the poor.

Figure 22.1   Under-five Mortality Rate in Rwanda, 1990–2015

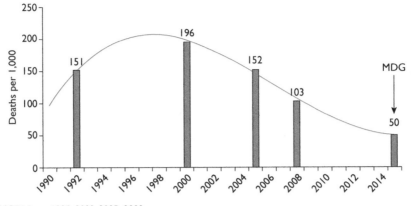

Sources: Measure DHS and ICF Macro 1995, 2000, 2005, 2008.

Figure 22.2   Maternal Mortality Ratio and Facility-based Deliveries in Rwanda, 2000–15

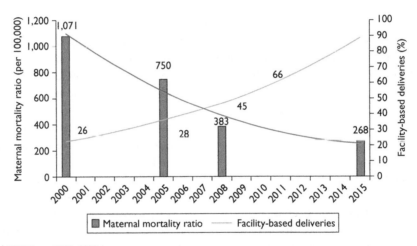

Sources: Measure DHS and ICF Macro 2005, 2008.

Improvements in the use of women's health services are also evident, with significant increases in the proportion of assisted birth deliveries and the number of emergency obstetrical cases referred. The use of modern contraceptives increased from 3 percent in 2000 to 27 percent in 2007, one of the fastest increases ever observed. The proportion of women having at least one antenatal consultation rose from 58 percent in 1995–2000 to 96 percent in 2000–07. The proportion of assisted deliveries increased from 39 percent in 2005 to 52 percent in 2007.

Major progress has also been made in controlling communicable diseases—including malaria, a prime cause of morbidity and mortality in Rwanda—and containing the HIV/AIDS epidemic. Malaria incidence and mortality have declined dramatically, largely as the result of increased use of insecticide-treated nets, which among children under five rose from 11 percent in 2005 to 56 percent in 2007. As a result, malaria-specific mortality was cut in half. Rwanda has thus moved from being a country where malaria was endemic to one focusing on eliminating malaria as a public health problem. The HIV/AIDS epidemic has been contained, with 3 percent of the population affected and more than 60 percent of patients needing treatment receiving highly active antiretroviral therapy. Knowledge of HIV/AIDS is better in Rwanda than in any other Sub-Saharan African country: nationwide 54 percent of women and 58 percent of men had comprehensive knowledge of HIV/AIDS in 2005.[1]

This progress occurred in a context in which annual total per capita health expenditures doubled, from $17 to $34 between 2003 and 2006. In 2006 total health expenditures reached 10.7 percent of gross domestic product (GDP) (one of the highest levels of health expenditures observed in low-income countries), up from 3 percent in 2002.

The overall share of public expenditures allocated to health has remained stable, with most of the increase coming from donors. Private expenditures were about $9.40 per capita, and domestic public expenditure about $6.30 per capita, with donors contributing $17.70 per capita, one of the highest levels of donor dependency in Sub-Saharan Africa. Much of this donor funding is earmarked funding for HIV/AIDS.

Despite the increase in funding, resources are not sufficient to meet the country's health care needs. Rwanda has therefore pioneered profound reforms, including an innovative health system and a financing model grounded in grassroots initiatives and institutions. Three prominent reforms were adopted to boost both the demand for and the supply of health services: health microinsurance (*mutuelles*), performance-based financing, and fiscal decentralization. Those reforms have transformed the fiscal space landscape. Revenues generated by health facilities have increased significantly as a result of increased use of health services and health insurance coverage, and an increasing share of domestically generated revenues is captured by health centers, strengthening front-line providers.

In 2007 the Rwandan government adopted its second Poverty Reduction Strategy Paper (the Economic Development and Poverty Reduction Strategy). Its goals for the health sector are to maximize preventive health measures and build the capacity to provide high-quality and accessible health care services to the entire population in order to reduce malnutrition, infant and child mortality, and fertility and to control communicable diseases. The strategy also supports strengthening institutional capacity, increasing the quantity and quality of human resources, ensuring that health care is accessible to the entire population, increasing geographical accessibility, increasing the availability and affordability of drugs, improving the quality of services in the control of diseases, and encouraging the demand for such services. It also sets ambitious targets for slowing population growth, calling for innovative measures in the strengthening of reproductive health services and family planning and ensuring free access to information, education, and contraceptive services.

REFORM STRATEGIES: COMMUNITY-BASED HEALTH INSURANCE, PERFORMANCE-BASED FINANCING, AND FISCAL DECENTRALIZATION

Rwanda has pioneered major programmatic, organizational, and health financing reforms, which are increasing the accountability of major actors in the health sector. Rwanda has a long history of centralized management structures with a clear hierarchy and a relatively low level of corruption. It has progressively moved toward a modern health system design, including full autonomy of facilities, decentralization, third-party payment, and strategic purchasing through performance-based financing. It has transitioned from a faith-based service delivery model in the colonial era to a model guided by the Bamako Initiative, which sought to expand access to health services through the development of local models of primary health care that are managed and financed by communities. Both public and private not-for-profit health facilities charge fees that are locally retained and managed to cover the costs of health services and improve the quality of care.

To improve financial access, the government pioneered a microinsurance scheme and supported its expansion and subsidization. It then introduced a mechanism of performance-based financing to provide incentives to health facilities to deliver high-impact interventions and ensure quality of services. In 2006 it established a fiscal decentralization policy and a legal framework that delineated a clear role for central and local governments and service providers.

Together these three reforms constitute strategies to strengthen accountability for services to citizens as part of Rwanda's 2006 national decentralized service delivery policy (Government of Rwanda 2006). Fiscal decentralization has been accompanied by measures to strengthen citizen participation and accountability, including mechanisms for establishing accountability links between citizens and local government officials, contractual performance between health services providers and local governments or national policy makers, and contractual approaches between communities and health providers. This policy can be visualized by using the accountability framework laid out in the *World Development Report 2004* (World Bank 2004). Accountability of health providers to clients ("client's power") is strengthened through micro–health insurance funds that claim and fund health services on behalf of households. Accountability of providers to the government (the "compact") is strengthened thanks to performance-based financing mechanisms. Accountability of government to citizens ("voice") is strengthened through decentralization, citizen report cards, and the possibility of recourse to the ombudsman (figure 22.3).

Rwanda has finally settled into its current decentralized model of care, in which health facilities are fully autonomous entities responsible for the management of financial resources, health service delivery, and human resources for health. Community-based health insurance schemes, which have been established and scaled up nationally, have evolved in response to low levels of utilization of health services. Partly to encourage community members to buy in to these health *mutuelle* schemes, the government developed performance-based financing as a complementary scheme to boost the performance and motivation of staff to deliver higher-quality services as well as to increase the delivery of preventive services.

Mutuelles and performance-based financing are two complementary schemes. Both aim to shift health financing mechanisms from inputs-based mechanisms toward output- or results-based contractual mechanisms. The interactions between the two strategies are therefore strong. Whereas *mutuelles* emphasize personal curative care services, performance-based financing emphasizes high-impact preventive services and the quality of services.

The nationwide expansion of both strategies has occurred rapidly since the pilot schemes were launched, thanks largely to government ownership and commitment,

which have propelled these strategies forward. The nationwide implementation of *mutuelles* was closely followed by the implementation of performance-based financing. *Mutuelles* revealed the need for improvements in staff motivation and incentives to deliver high-quality health services, which in turn served as the driving force for performance-based financing. As the implementation of performance-based financing in the pilot districts proved successful in improving staff motivation and health outcomes, performance-based financing became a major pillar within the Ministry of Health Strategic Plan (2005–09). In 2006 the government, with the support of external partners, expanded performance-based financing to the entire health sector (table 22.1).

Rwanda has continuously learned from and adapted its health service delivery strategies. The ability of the government to adapt strategies—as evident in the scaling up of successful pilot schemes to the national level, in light of the changing macroeconomic and health sector environment—was also essential to strengthen health services. Independent controls and quality checks under contractual arrangements have been essential for the monitoring and evaluation of health facility performance. Performance-based financing is a prime example of a system in which independent controls on performance are in place to ensure proper monitoring and reporting of health centers and district hospitals on the quantity and quality of services delivered, which in turn drive facilities' reimbursement.

Figure 22.3   Decentralization of and Accountability for Health Services in Rwanda

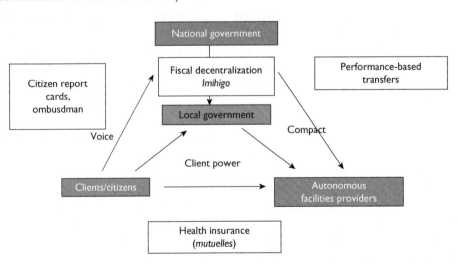

Source: Government of Rwanda 2006.
Note: Imihigo are performance contracts in which the region and its districts promise the president of Rwanda that they will implement the measures outlined in the annual plans.

Table 22.1 Health Financing Reforms in Rwanda, 1999–2008

Reform	1999	2000	2001	2002	2003	2004	2005	2006	2007	2008
Enrollment in *mutuelles* (percent)	0	1.6	2.6	4.7	7	27	44	73	75	85
Number of districts with performance-based financing	0	0	0	2	5	7	7	14	23	30
Assisted deliveries (percent)							39		52	
Key policy milestones		Rwandaise d'Assurance Maladie (RAMA) created; fiscal decentralization policy						Fiscal decentralization law passed; decentralized service delivery policy includes performance-based financing and *mutuelles*		Health insurance law passed
Key implementation milestones	Community-based health insurance pilots launched in three health districts since July 1999		RAMA established	Performance-based financing pilots launched in four districts			Integration of performance-based financing and subsidies to *mutuelles* in national budget		Fiscal decentralization	Full autonomy given to public health facilities, including over hiring and firing National guarantee fund established
Per capita health expenditures (National Health Account)				$15			$37			

Source: Authors.

Note: RAMA = Rwandaise Assurance Maladie.

Community mobilization and intersectoral collaboration have contributed significantly to the implementation of health reforms. Cultural and social factors, particularly solidarity within communities, have contributed to the success of several health service delivery innovations. The rapid proliferation of health *mutuelles* was made possible by the strong solidarity within Rwandan society, in which community members encouraged one another to join. This solidarity has been long-standing in Rwanda, evident even before the start of health *mutuelles*. In the case of health *mutuelles*, cultural barriers initially thwarted implementation, particularly because Rwandans were used to seeking care from traditional healers and because patients of traditional healers were able to pay in kind rather than making cash payments.

Figure 22.4   Use of Health Services in Rwanda in Event of Illness, by Health Insurance Coverage, 2005

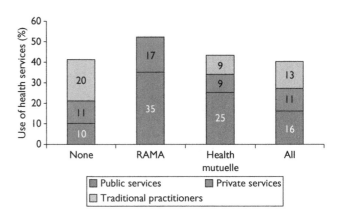

Source: Government of Rwanda 2005.

Community-based health insurance

Health insurance has been scaled up at the national level on the basis of community-based health insurance schemes, with strong support from the government of Rwanda. Coverage of health *mutuelles* increased dramatically between 2003 and 2008, rising from less than 7 percent to 85 percent of the population in just five years.

Health *mutuelles* have had a significant positive impact on health service utilization, income protection, and household health behaviors (Sekabaraga, Diop, and Soucat 2010). Health insurance coverage increased the use of modern health services by children under five between 2000 and 2007. In the general population, use of modern services by the insured population is nearly twice as high as use by the uninsured (figure 22.4). In addition, health *mutuelles* seem to protect against expenditure caused by unexpected illness, because uninsured households spend directly twice as much as insured households for illness-related expenditure. Health insurance coverage has thus significantly reduced household out-of-pocket health expenditures (Ministry of Health of Rwanda and World Bank 2011). Among women who gave birth during the period 2000–05, 77 percent were affiliated with Rwandaise d'Assurance Maladie (RAMA). About 42 percent of women affiliated with a health *mutuelle* were assisted by a skilled health professional during delivery compared with 35 percent of women with no insurance (Sekabaraga, Diop, and Soucat 2010).

Before 1996 health services in Rwanda were free. Given problems associated with the quality of services and the financial sustainability of the health system, cost-recovery mechanisms were reintroduced in 1996, while policy debates continued over alternative financing mechanisms for reconciling internal resource mobilization and access to

health services, including prepayment mechanisms through health insurance schemes. In view of the significant scope of poverty following the war of 1994, the reintroduction of user fees in the health sector in 1996 was accompanied by an exemption policy that allowed for free health care coverage in health facilities for people identified by the local administrative authorities as indigent. Coverage of the poor and vulnerable groups has been integrated in the development of health *mutuelles* since they were first piloted in 1999.

In 2000 Rwandaise d'Assurance Maladie, the first health insurance scheme for the formal sector, was established for civil servants. Membership in RAMA soon became compulsory in order to increase coverage. To complement insurance schemes such as RAMA and a few private insurance schemes that target the formal sector, health *mutuelles* covering rural communities and the informal sector were expanded to promote equitable access to quality health services. Health *mutuelles* were designed to pool or spread the financial risk of seeking care across their membership base. The goal was to respond to the low use of health services (caused in part by user fees) by improving financial access to health services, particularly for underserved populations. The package of services reimbursed by health *mutuelles* to health facilities has expanded over time and currently covers all services delivered within a health center as well as drugs from the national essential drug list. Health *mutuelles* also cover most costs for health services and drugs delivered at district and referral hospitals when *mutuelle* members receive referrals for these higher levels of care.

These schemes have been extended to empower citizens and communities in the health sector and to change their interactions with health care providers. Through contractual relations between health *mutuelles* and health care providers, communities and citizens have a tool with which to hold health care providers accountable for services provided. In essence, health *mutuelles* in Rwanda reflected a bottom-up strategy, driven largely by local communities. The success of the initial pilot schemes motivated the central government to scale up this strategy. Currently, the central government sets national guidelines and policies, including benefit packages and contribution policies. In 2008 it instituted a national guarantee fund for providing general subsidies to support the extension of the benefit packages of health *mutuelles*. Since 2009 the government has also built on the national network of health *mutuelles* to elaborate and implement demand-based targeted subsidies, through which the government, donors, and nongovernmental organizations (NGOs) are providing health insurance coverage to poor people, vulnerable groups, and people living with HIV/AIDS. At the operational level, health *mutuelles* are run and organized by community representatives and local health care providers. They also serve as a forum for promoting dialogue between the community and providers on the quality and range of health services offered. In this way, community members are better able to hold providers accountable for services delivered.

For the majority of the population employed in the rural and informal sectors, an incremental approach was followed in developing mechanisms for pooling health risk. The process of cumulative building of national capacities is a hallmark of the incremental development of *mutuelles* in Rwanda. Capacity building for local actors involved in setting up, managing, and monitoring health *mutuelles* began in 1999, with the establishment of *mutuelles* in three pilot health districts.[2] The geographic extension of the *mutuelles* was accelerated in 2004, after the adoption of a national strategic framework for their development. The number of health *mutuelles* grew by a factor of 2.5 in a single year, climbing to 226 nationwide. In 2007 each of Rwanda's 403 health centers had a partner health *mutuelle* or "health *mutuelle* section," and all of the country's 30 districts had a district health *mutuelle*, which, on average, was linked to 13 health *mutuelle* sections.

The period of experimentation, which started in 2001, was followed by attempts to adapt the institutional arrangements for health *mutuelles* to the environment of administrative and political decentralization and by early efforts to expand the *mutuelles* to other districts of the country. In the absence of an explicit policy framework for coordinating the initial efforts of adaptation and expansion, a variety of local policies and incentives proliferated, initiated by local authorities of all categories (political groups, associations, and so forth) to motivate the population to join health *mutuelles* (by, for example, linking membership to civil status services, microcredit, and so forth). These initiatives helped develop the health *mutuelles* and contributed to the growth of social demand for their expansion nationwide.

Current levels of contributions to health *mutuelles* are affordable for all but the poorest 10 percent of Rwandans. Affordability of enrollment in health *mutuelles* is assessed based on the percentage of contributions in household total expenditures and household nonfood expenditures. The cost of membership rises with family size (for many reasons, including high disease burden in large families and the externalities of insurance benefits). Male-headed households have a higher proportion of enrollment than female-headed households, partly because of the income difference between the two groups. Family heads that completed primary school or received some vocational training tend to have the highest rate of enrollment among the least-educated and best-educated households. This trend is also reflected in the enrollment rate by income (expenditure) category, so that middle-income and middle-rich people tend to have the highest participation rates in health *mutuelles*. Out-of-pocket illness-related expenditures among households enrolled in health *mutuelles* are twice as high as those of members. Households that live very close to health centers spend more than those living far away. Households that are not covered by health *mutuelles* spent nearly twice as much for illness-related services as people who were insured.

Information has played an important role in the operational management and monitoring of the development of health *mutuelles* at the local level and in their strategic management at the central level. Indeed, Rwanda is one of the few African countries where an information system to support health *mutuelle* management has been developed to permit monthly monitoring of performance. It is also one of the few countries that has adapted training manuals on health *mutuelle* development, management, and monitoring in line with the local context, including availability in the local language. Numerous other activities to promote and raise awareness of health *mutuelles* are carried out around the country and at the national level. The Ministry of Health occasionally organizes an annual event on mutual organizations at which prizes are awarded to the best performing health *mutuelles*.

Performance-based financing and reforms of human resources management

Based on a positive evaluation of a three-year pilot phase in two provinces, Rwanda has implemented a national program since 2005; it has scaled up performance-based financing since 2006 (Rusa et al. 2009).[3] Performance-based financing is currently implemented at three levels: health centers, hospitals, and community levels.

The performance-based financing model is based on the principle of separating purchaser and provider functions in health service delivery (figure 22.5). By distinguishing between and maintaining a split between bodies purchasing services and bodies providing services, this model promotes accountability and avoids conflicts of interest. The model consists of a family of methods and approaches that aim, through differing levels of intervention, to link incentives to performance. In the national model for health centers, payments for performance are based on the quantity of outputs achieved conditional on the quality of services delivered. Through performance-based financing, the central

government purchases 13 quantitative indicators and 13 qualitative measurements from health facilities (tables 22.2 and 22.3).[4] At the hospital level, performance is assessed through a peer-evaluation mechanism.

Low intake of preventive services and poor quality of care in health centers served as the impetus for introducing performance-based financing strategies. Quality of care became a particularly salient issue as expansion of health *mutuelles* increased utilization rates dramatically at all health centers, adding to the workload of health personnel who, at the time, had little or no incentive to take on the additional work. The impetus for the performance-based financing strategy in Rwanda first came from external actors; additional resources and incentives were provided to health workers to improve efficiency and outcomes, under pilot schemes implemented in 2001–05. As a result of the pilots' success, performance-based financing became a major pillar within the Ministry of Health strategic plan and was implemented nationally.

Rwanda's institutional performance-based financing model can be classified as "output-based financing," because

Figure 22.5   Rwanda's Performance-Based Health Care Financing Model

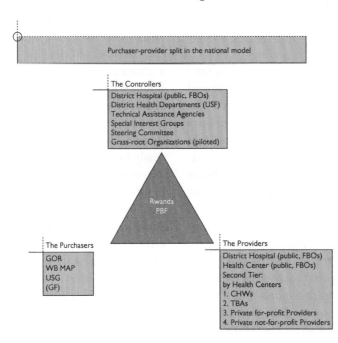

Source: Rusa et al. 2009.
Note: Purchasers are those who pay for services. They include NGOs, which purchase services with their own funds and act as fundholders or pass-through mechanisms for other donors; the government of Rwanda (in the case of the national model); the U.S. government, through collaborative agencies such as Management Science for Health and Family Health International; World Bank MAP funding, NGOs in the Cyangugu and Butare pilots and purchasing performance through the new national model; and the Global Fund to Fight AIDS, Tuberculosis and Malaria, which is expected to start purchasing through the new national model. Providers can include public and faith-based managed health facilities (health centers and hospitals) and private for-profit health facilities. Controllers are those who control the level of performance, such as district health teams in the Ville de Kigali pilot, who certify a mix of quantity and quality deliverables in health centers and hospitals. District health teams were used in Butare for random quantity control and in Cyangugu l for a quality measure in health centers. A peer-evaluation mechanism for district hospitals was piloted in Cyangugu and partially in Butare.

Table 22.2   Output Indicators and Unit Payments under Performance-Based Financing Formula

Output indicators	Amount paid per unit (US$)
Visit indicators (number of)	
Curative care visits	0.18
First prenatal care visits	0.09
Women who completed 4 prenatal care visits	0.37
First time family planning visits (new contraceptive users)	1.83
Contraceptive resupply visits	0.18
Deliveries in the facility	4.59
Child (0–59 months) preventive care visits	0.18
Content of care (number of)	
Women who received tetanus vaccine during prenatal care	0.46
Women who received malaria prophylaxis during prenatal care	0.46
At-risk pregnancies referred to hospital for delivery	1.83
Emergency transfers to hospital for obstetric care	4.59
Children who completed vaccinations (child preventive care)	0.92
Malnourished children referred for treatment	1.83
Other emergency referrals	1.83

Source: Basinga et al. 2009.

Table 22.3   Quality Indicators Services and Weights Used in the Performance-Based Financing Formula

Service	Weight	Share of weight allocated to structural components	Share of weight allocated to process components	Means of assessment
General administration	0.052	1.00	0.00	Direct observation
Cleanliness	0.028	1.00	0.00	Direct observation
Curative care	0.170	0.23	0.77	Medical record review
Delivery	0.130	0.40	0.60	Medical record review
Prenatal care	0.126	0.12	0.88	Direct observation
Family planning	0.114	0.22	0.78	Medical record review
Immunization	0.070	0.40	0.60	Direct observation
Growth monitoring	0.062	0.15	0.85	Direct observation
HIV services	0.090	1.00	0.00	Direct observation
Tuberculosis service	0.028	0.28	0.72	Direct observation
Laboratory	0.080	1.00	0.00	Direct observation
Pharmacy management	0.060	1.00	0.00	Direct observation
Financial management	0.050	1.00	0.00	Direct observation
Total	1.000			

Source: Basinga et al. 2009.

it pays on a fee-for-service or case reimbursement basis to improve outputs. Although performance-based financing incentives are generally meant to induce providers (the supply side), supply-side incentives in Rwanda work through supplier-induced demand, whereby suppliers actively seek to convince people to use more of certain kinds of services. Such incentives are necessary in Rwanda, where the goal is not to limit excessive supply and unnecessary demand (as is the case in richer health systems) but rather to induce

providers to provide more services while also increasing financial revenues at the health facility level.

As of 2006 the government transferred about $1.80 per capita from the Treasury directly to health facilities at the basic health service level on the basis of a performance-based formula. The program channels funds directly from Treasury to the bank accounts of the more than 400 health clinics in Rwanda (40 percent of them faith based, 60 percent of them public) on the basis of performance agreements.

These funds are flexible and may be used for facility expenditures, including performance-linked salary bonuses, partially substituting for revenues from user fees. Rwanda implemented a three-tier performance-based financing model—including hospitals, health centers, and ultimately the community level—in order to make health services more community oriented.

One of the key objectives of performance-based financing was to introduce bonuses to health workers as incentives for good performance, based on a range of agreed indicators. This system was designed to allow for better monitoring of health personnel activities and hence to enable district and central levels to track staff performance over time. Although the central government determines the overall performance-based financing budget envelope that the health facility receives, based on a formula involving the quantity and quality of services provided, it is the committee within the health facility itself that determines how these funds should be used.

In 2008 Rwanda decentralized wages. As a result, financing and payments for health personnel are increasingly linked to performance in which block grants from the government and donors can be used as salary. Direct spending on wages and salaries by the central administration and transfers to public institutions for salaries of health workers have declined. In contrast, funds channeled to human resources for health through provinces and districts that come from both the government (including performance-based financing) and user fees collected directly by facilities have risen dramatically in recent years (figure 22.6).

It is the policy of the Ministry of Health, in collaboration with development partners, to harmonize the framework for compensation packages of health professionals. The objective is to avoid introducing distortions in the distribution of health workers, which occurs when health workers move from the public sector to donor projects where the pay is higher. In light of this concern, donors, such as the Global Fund, have begun to use national pay scales and to fully integrate staff within the health system at large.

Results-based block grants in Rwanda have contributed significantly to the increase in assisted birth deliveries as well as the intake of child health services; the grants have also increased the quality of services. Clinics that received performance-based financing (of about $1.80 per capita per year) performed more assisted deliveries and more post-natal visits than clinics receiving the same funding without a performance contract (figure 22.7). The quality of care of antenatal services was 15 percent higher in performance-based financing clinics than in control clinics (figure 22.8).

The results achieved—in service supply and the enthusiastic participation of all stakeholders—after a few years of experience point to a promising future. However, because it is a dynamic strategy, performance-based financing adjusts to innovative ideas that benefit the population and health care providers. The remaining challenges are related to the permanent oversight requirements, the accuracy of data, and the delicate balance of the pricing of the various indicators. The future of performance-based financing will depend on finding appropriate solutions to these issues.

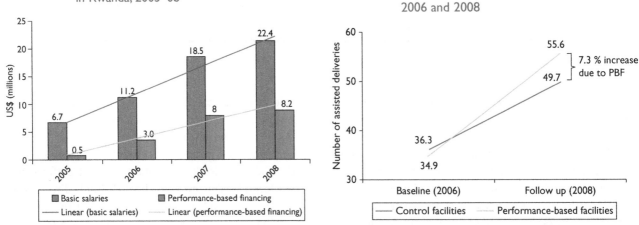

Figure 22.6 Financing for Human Resources for Health in Rwanda, 2005–08

Source: Authors.

Figure 22.7 Number of Assisted Deliveries in Rwanda under Performance-Based and Nonperformance-Based Financing, 2006 and 2008

Source: Basinga et al. 2009.

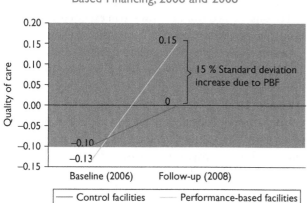

Source: Basinga et al. 2009.

Fiscal decentralization

A strong commitment to bring services closer to the people resulted in rapid fiscal decentralization, increased citizen participation, and increased autonomy of health facilities. Fiscal decentralization (adopted as policy in 2001 and enacted into law in 2006) served as an essential component of Rwanda's decentralization agenda to devolve authority to the district level. As was to be expected, given the presence of such a strong state, a mindset change was needed to move forward on many of these reforms. As in the case of decentralization, some officials at the central level felt disempowered and were initially unwilling to relinquish their control at the outset. Officials at the local level had to adapt to accept their new responsibilities, and donors had to adjust to working with local governments.

The decentralization of authority across sectors was planned through an incremental, three-phased approach. The first phase (2001–05) focused on administrative and political decentralization; it aimed to institutionalize decentralized governance by establishing democratic and community development structures, delineating policies, establishing legal frameworks, and strengthening institutional capacity at local levels. Phase two, which began in 2006 and ran through 2008, focused on making local governments responsible for bringing health services closer to beneficiaries. The devolution of responsibilities in health services and the transfer of resources under fiscal decentralization are the backbone of relationships between the national government and districts in the health sector. It aimed to reorganize roles and responsibilities within local

government under the decentralization framework and further strengthen district authority while allowing for greater community participation and facilitating resource allocation to local government. Central government responsibilities in this phase remained regulation and development of policy frameworks, capacity building of local government, and monitoring and evaluation.

Finally, phase three, which began in 2008, granted autonomy to health facilities and transferred fiscal responsibilities and financial resources from the central and local government to facilities. This reform has resulted in relative autonomy in budgeting and financial management within facilities, because health care providers are now contracted with and managed by health facilities.

Fiscal decentralization in Rwanda was government owned and driven, with strong support and collaboration of development partners. The objective was to bring services closer to the people, and to improve the financial viability of districts. The infrastructural changes needed may not have been in place (until June 2007 districts lacked accounting software to manage financial transactions, and local capacity in managing financial and human resources still remains limited), but overall success was striking. The strategy was organized by the central government, which from the outset determined the degree of authority delegated to local levels and delineated relevant policies and standards. In these efforts, the central government received significant technical assistance and guidance from development partners, which organized their support in the form of a sector-wide policy to ensure government ownership over decision making and policy setting; increase coherence between policy, spending, and actual results; reinforce the government's management systems; and harmonize donor support.

Decentralized units at local levels were given the authority to manage the flow of funds (once received) as well as the delivery of health services. Decentralization transformed health facilities into autonomous entities, with the ability to manage financial and human resources as they deem most appropriate, according to local needs. The process gave them complete control over the hiring and firing of health personnel.

The accountability links between local governments and national policymakers are strengthened through inspections, audits, and *Imihigo*—performance contracts in which the region and its districts promise the president of Rwanda that they will implement the measures outlined in the annual plans.[5] Decentralization reforms have resulted in increased responsibilities of local governments in many areas and are increasing space for community participation and community-driven development initiatives. Satisfaction with service delivery is measured through citizen report cards.

CONCLUSION

Fiscal decentralization, performance-based financing, and the expansion of health insurance have led to a dramatic increase in resources for frontline providers. Between 2002 and 2007, public resources flowing to health facilities more than tripled (figure 22.9). The increase in resources took place at all levels, showing no higher priority given to the primary care level. An increasing number of donors are channeling their assistance through on-budget support, and major efforts are under way toward coordinating and harmonizing aid. Most of the increase in publicly managed resources flowed to human resources and to performance-based financing; resources directly managed by donors funded HIV/AIDS activities. On the domestic front, internally generated revenues of health facilities increased significantly as a result of increased utilization of health services and health insurance coverage; an increasing share of internally generated revenues is captured by health centers, strengthening frontline providers.

Rwanda chose to develop a mixed health care financing model, combining decentralization and performance-based financing with a strategy to pool private spending through the building of grassroots, community-based microinsurance. Key reforms included provisions for financial protection and other support for poor people.

Lessons learned from the Rwandan experience provide a strong base for future action. As financial barriers to access to health services are being reduced significantly through health care financing reforms, improving the quality and sustainability of health services will remain among the main challenges facing Rwanda in the coming years.

The success of Rwanda in improving health outcomes, particularly for women, children, and the poor, can be linked to both increased resources and implementation of reforms. Rwanda used the inflow of resources to strengthen its country system, including its public finance and health systems. It designed its own brand of reforms, staying away from donor fads and looking realistically and opportunistically at the balance between sustainability and equity. Reforms focused on results, and results attracted more funding, both domestic and external. Increased resources and reforms mutually reinforced each other as part of a virtuous cycle. Efficient and equitable use of resources required reform, and the success of reforms needed resources.

The success of the health financing innovations is critically linked to the institutional context. Decentralization reforms coupled with performance-based financing ensure that health facility managers have not only the incentives but also the power to ensure that these innovations translate

Figure 22.9   Financial Transfers to Districts for Priority Programs, 2006–10

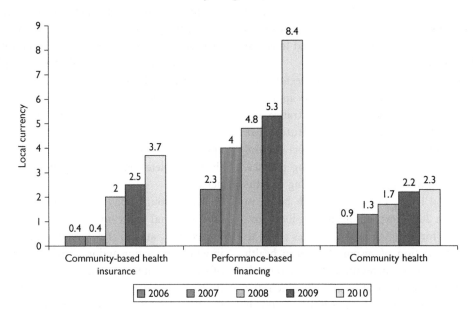

Source: World Bank 2010.

CHAPTER 22: INNOVATIVE FINANCING FOR HEALTH IN RWANDA: A REPORT OF SUCCESSFUL REFORMS

into changes in the delivery of services. The performance-based financing system is now being extended to provide incentives to community health workers providing outreach services and demand-side incentives to women to continue the increased utilization of key maternal health services.

Strong government leadership, vision, and the step-by-step building of a policy and regulatory framework at all levels have fostered the short- and long-term sustainability of health sector reforms. The Rwandan government showed flexibility and was able to adapt strategies in light of the changing macroeconomic and international health environment. Government coordination of donor funding was critical to ensure that aid was used effectively and aligned with national priorities. Systems for improved accountability, including contractual arrangements, independent controls, and quality checks, were essential for monitoring and evaluating health facility performance. Cultural and social factors, particularly solidarity within communities, also contributed to the success of several health service delivery innovations.

A particularly important feature of the Rwanda experience is the integration of strong mechanisms to evaluate the impact of its policies. Rwanda's experience, as well as that of other low-income countries, in introducing pro-poor financing policies needs to be systematically evaluated using rigorous metrics and standardized benchmarks. It is possible for countries to nest impact evaluation designs when introducing new policies at scale. The donor community needs to support these evaluations if it wants to improve aid effectiveness.

A key issue for the future is sustainability and the necessary evolution of the institutional support for the health financing approach of Rwanda. Like many Sub-Saharan African countries, Rwanda is highly dependent on aid and will remain so for the next decade. Sustained support from the donor community is therefore needed to support the health system strengthening agenda. *Mutuelles* provide one way to ensure more sustained domestic funding. They represent an efficient way to pool private out-of-pocket spending, but there is a need for the government—with the help of donors—to subsidize the enrollment of the poorest Rwandans and to regulate the package of benefits as well as the provider payments mechanisms to ensure equitable access to quality services.

NOTES

1. Comprehensive knowledge of HIV/AIDS, which can be used as a tracer indicator of general health knowledge in the country, means knowing that use of condoms and having a single, uninfected, faithful partner can reduce the chances of contracting HIV, knowing that a healthy-looking person can have HIV/AIDS, and rejecting the two most common local misconceptions about HIV/AIDS transmission and prevention.

2. At the time, the districts were called Byumba, Kabgayi, and Kabutare. They are now called Gicumbi, Muhanga, and Save.

3. This program has been supported by a broad consortium of donors, including the World Bank, the U.K. Department for International Development, the European Union, Sweden, the African Development Bank, the Netherlands, and Germany.

4. A separate contract channels earmarked funds of global HIV/AID programs for another 16 indicators.

5. *Imihigo* are also monitoring instruments designed to help local authorities plan and act realistically.

REFERENCES

Basinga, P., P. Gertler, A. Binagwaho, A. Soucat, J. Sturdy, and C. Vermeersch. 2010. *Paying Primary Health Care Centers for Performance in Rwanda.* World Bank, Washington, DC.

Government of Rwanda. 2005. "Enquete Integrale sur les Conditions des Menages." Kigali.

———. 2006. *Decentralized Service Delivery.* Kigali.

May, J. F., and A. Kamurase. 2009. *Demographic Growth and Development Prospects in Rwanda: Implications for the World Bank.* World Bank, Washington, DC.

Measure DHS and ICF Macro. 1995. *Demographic and Health Survey, Rwanda.* Calverton, MD. http://www.measuredhs.com/.

———. 2000. *Demographic and Health Survey, Rwanda.* Calverton, MD. http://www.measuredhs.com/.

———. 2005. *Demographic and Health Survey, Rwanda.* Calverton, MD. http://www.measuredhs.com/.

———. 2007. *Demographic and Health Survey, Rwanda.* Calverton, MD. http://www.measuredhs.com/.

———. 2008. *Demographic and Health Survey, Rwanda.* Calverton, MD. http://www.measuredhs.com/.

Ministry of Health of Rwanda, and World Bank, 2011. *Country Status Report on Health, Health Systems and Poverty.* Human Development Series. World Bank, Washington, DC.

Rusa, Louis, Miriam Schneidman, Gyuri Fritsche, and Laurent Musango. 2009. "Rwanda: Performance-Based Financing in the Public Sector" In *Performance Incentives for Global Health: Potential and Pitfalls,* eds. Rena Eichler, Ruth Levine, and the Performance-Based

Incentive Working Group. Washington, DC: Center for Global Development.

Sayinzoga, K., A. Soucat, A. Kjellgren, and P. Musafiri. 2010. *From Reconstruction to Development: Budgeting for Performance in Rwanda.* Human Development Series, World Bank, Africa Human Development, Washington, DC.

Sekabaraga, C., F. Diop, and A. Soucat. 2010 "Can Innovative Health Financing Policies Turn the Tide on the Health MDGs? Evidence from Rwanda." Communication to the International Symposium on Health Systems Research, Montreux, Switzerland.

World Bank, 2004. *World Development Report 2004: Making Services Work for Poor People.* Washington, DC: World Bank.

———. 2010. *Country Status Report on Health, Health Systems and Poverty.* Washington, DC: World Bank.

CHAPTER 23

The Malaria Control Success Story

Anne-Maryse Pierre-Louis, Jumana Qamruddin,
Isabel Espinosa, and Shilpa Challa

Malaria is both preventable and treatable. Yet
more than 220 million cases of malaria are estimated to occur each year, and approximately
785,000 people die from the disease annually. Half of the
world's population—some 3.3 billion people living in 109
countries—are at risk of malaria (Roll Back Malaria 2008).
Worldwide, malaria is the fifth-leading cause of death
from infectious diseases (after respiratory infections,
HIV/AIDS, diarrheal diseases, and tuberculosis). The disease is life threatening and needs early, accurate diagnosis
and treatment, which can be difficult in remote areas that
lack clinics, trained health care providers, technical assistance, or medicine.

Malaria is caused by *Plasmodium* parasites, which are
spread to humans through infected *Anopheles* mosquitoes,
called *malaria vectors*, which bite mainly between dusk and
dawn.[1] Ninety percent of the world's malaria deaths occur
in Sub-Saharan Africa, where the most severe form of the
disease prevails, making malaria the second-leading cause of
death in the region after HIV/AIDS (Roll Back Malaria
2008). The disease is one of the leading causes of death of
children under the age of five in Sub-Saharan Africa and a
major cause of complications, including maternal death and
low birth weight, in pregnancy.

Malaria is not only a health problem in Africa; it is also a
development problem. Death and disability (both short-
and long-term) from malaria have enormous social and
economic costs, costing African countries an estimated $12
billion a year in lost productivity (Gallup and Sachs 2001).

Treatment of severe episodes, which can cost up to one-
quarter of a household's monthly income, accounts for up
to 40 percent of public sector health expenditures in the
worst-affected countries (WHO 2007). Other direct costs
include the costs of insecticide-treated nets and indoor
residual house spraying to prevent malaria, antimalarial
drugs, transportation to clinics, and hospital fees. Operating
in a vicious cycle, malaria is both a cause and a consequence
of poverty.

Malaria keeps countries as well as households in poverty:
annual economic growth in countries with high malaria
transmission has historically been lower than in countries
without malaria. Economists have estimated that malaria is
responsible for an "economic growth penalty" of up to 1.3
percent a year in malaria-endemic African countries (Gallup
and Sachs 2001). The disease discourages local and foreign investment and tourism, affects land use patterns and
crop selection (resulting in suboptimal agricultural production), and reduces labor productivity through lost work days
and diminished on-the-job performance. It affects learning
and academic achievement through frequent absenteeism of
teachers and students. In children who suffer severe or frequent infections, it can cause cognitive impairment and in
some cases permanent neurological damage. Other indirect
costs include loss of income and work, including the unpaid
work carried out largely by women who take care of the sick
and support them at home or in the hospital.

Expenditures on malaria control drain already fragile
economies through the deterrent effect on investment

(private businesses are reluctant to expand in areas where the disease is affecting the workforce and creating gaps in the production line). Economic and social decision making at all levels is affected. Travelers are hesitant to visit countries with a high incidence of malaria, reducing tourism revenues and leading to losses of job opportunities and income.

A global effort to help countries control the disease that was revitalized in 2005 is showing signs of success. In countries in which control measures have been intensified, there have been clear and positive results. Eleven countries and one territory in Africa show reductions of more than 50 percent in either confirmed malaria cases or malaria admissions and deaths in recent years (WHO 2010b). This progress is a direct result of the scaling up and acceleration of measures against the disease. Other positive outcomes include parallel declines in child mortality in some countries.

This chapter examines progress in Sub-Saharan African countries on key malaria indicators as well as in funding for the fight against malaria between 2005 and 2010. The first section examines the four main interventions for preventing and treating malaria (insecticide-treated nets, antimalarials, artemisinin-based combination therapy, indoor residual spraying). The second section looks at prevention among and treatment of pregnant women and children under five. The third section discusses partnership and coordination in the fight against malaria. The fourth section describes success stories in four African countries (Eritrea, Ethiopia, Rwanda, and Zambia). The last section identifies lessons learned and discusses the way forward.

INTERVENTIONS FOR PREVENTING AND TREATING MALARIA

Between 2000 and 2008 malaria control efforts in Africa were measured against targets set in the 2000 Abuja Declaration.[2] Since 2008 progress has been measured against the universal coverage targets set forth in the Roll Back Malaria Global Malaria Action Plan 2010. These targets include the following:

- Eighty percent of people at risk from malaria are using locally appropriate vector control methods, such as long-lasting insecticidal nets, indoor residual spraying, and, in some settings, other environmental and biological measures.
- Eighty percent of malaria patients are diagnosed and treated with effective antimalarial treatments; in areas of

high transmission, 100 percent of pregnant women receive intermittent preventive treatment.
- The global malaria burden is reduced by 50 percent from 2000 levels, to less than 175 million–250 million cases and 500,000 deaths annually.

This section looks at progress on key malaria indictors in Africa based on an analysis of nationally representative surveys in countries in which the data were available for a particular indicator. A subset of countries for which data were available is used to illustrate progress on key indicators.

Insecticide-treated nets

The promotion and distribution of insecticide-treated nets has long been recognized internationally as a key cost-effective intervention to control malaria (Statesmen's Forum 2010 (box 23.1). This intervention has been the primary focus for scale-up over the past few years. Beginning in 2008, some countries in Africa made a policy shift from providing insecticide-treated-net coverage only for populations at greatest risk (including children under five and pregnant women) to seeking coverage for the entire population at risk. This shift has largely been the result of a global effort to increase progress toward the Millennium Development Goals (MDGs) and a call for action from the UN Secretary General in 2008. Given that the policy changed fairly recently, the shift to implementation has not yet been seen on a large scale across the continent.

Figure 23.1 illustrates progress toward coverage with insecticide-treated nets across a number of countries in Africa. At first glance, the story appears discouraging, as many countries are well below the 80 percent coverage target for this key intervention. Many of the data used, however, come from representative surveys in countries conducted in 2006 and 2007—around the same time that malaria control efforts on the continent started ramping up. Among countries in which coverage is 50 percent or greater (Ethiopia, Madagascar, Rwanda, Senegal, Zambia, and Zanzibar), most surveys were conducted between 2007 and 2009. The most recent 2010 Malaria Indicator Survey in Zambia (not illustrated in the figure) shows an increase in the share of households with at least one insecticide-treated net rising to 64 percent.

Since 2006 coordinated efforts have supported the "catch-up, keep up" approach to bed net distribution in countries with low coverage. During the "catch-up" phase, bed nets are distributed through either stand-alone or integrated bed net campaigns to increase coverage

Box 23.1   Cost-Effective Tools in the Fight against Malaria

A variety of antimalarial tools are starting to produce results in Africa. They include artemisinin-based combination therapies (ACTs), long-lasting insecticidal-treated nets, indoor residual spraying, intermittent preventive treatment, and rapid diagnostic tests.

Artemisinin-based combination therapies

Artemisinin-based combination therapies are produced by combining compounds from the *Artemisia annua* plant with various antimalarial partner drugs. They are recognized by the World Health Organization (WHO) and the scientific community as the most effective therapy for treating *Plasmodium falciparum* malaria, the predominant form in Africa and the most deadly. ACTs are thought to delay the development of drug-resistant strains of the disease. They are also active against gametocytes, the sexual stage of the parasite cycle, effectively reducing disease transmission. For these reasons ACTs have become the first line of therapy for many countries struggling to control malaria infection and transmission. The treatment is fast acting and produces minimal side effects, making it possible for patients to return quickly to their daily routines. The challenge is to ensure that prompt and effective treatment with ACT is available as a critical intervention to complement prevention activities.

Long-lasting insecticidal nets

WHO policy recommends long-lasting insecticidal mosquito nets (a type of insecticide-treated net), which offer protection against malaria. If used by at least 80 percent, in an affected area, these nets can help break the malaria transmission cycle, thus reducing the risk for all who live nearby. Woven from insecticide-bound fibers, the nets kill the potential disease-carrying mosquitoes on contact and offer protection from bites. Unlike insecticide-treated nets that require redipping every few months, long-lasting insecticidal nets remain effective for at least three years. The nets provide protection at night, when individuals are most vulnerable. They are safe for children and simple to hang up.

Indoor residual spraying

Indoor residual spraying is the application of long-acting chemical insecticides on the walls and roofs of all houses and domestic animal shelters in a given area to kill the adult vector mosquitoes that land and rest on these surfaces. Indoor residual spraying shortens the life span of vector mosquitoes so that they can no longer transmit malaria parasites from one person to another, and reduces the density of the vector mosquitoes.

Intermittent preventive treatment

Intermittent preventive treatment given to pregnant women at routine antenatal care visits has been shown to promote healthier pregnancies and yield benefits for both mothers and developing fetuses. It can significantly reduce the proportion of low birthweight infants and maternal anemia. Intermittent preventive treatment in infants may also play a major role in malaria prevention at the public health level; however, additional research is needed to confirm this hypothesis.

Rapid diagnostic tests

Rapid diagnostic tests for malaria, also known as dipsticks or malaria rapid diagnostic devices, have the potential to greatly improve the quality of management of malaria infections when high-quality microscopy is not readily available. The tests detect specific antigens (proteins) produced by malaria parasites that are present in the blood of infected individuals. Some rapid diagnostic tests detect only one species (*P. falciparum*), others also detect other species of the parasite. Blood for the test is commonly obtained from a finger prick. WHO (2010) now recommends that all cases of suspected malaria be confirmed with a diagnostic test before treatment. As the incidence of malaria continues to decrease in Africa, the need to differentiate between malaria from nonmalarial fevers becomes more pressing, especially given the need to avoid drug resistance and increase efficiency of resources. Implementation of the WHO recommendations will require a more integrated approach to childhood illnesses (to address the question of what to do if the fever is not caused by malaria).

Figure 23.1 Coverage of Insecticide-Treated Nets in Africa, by Country

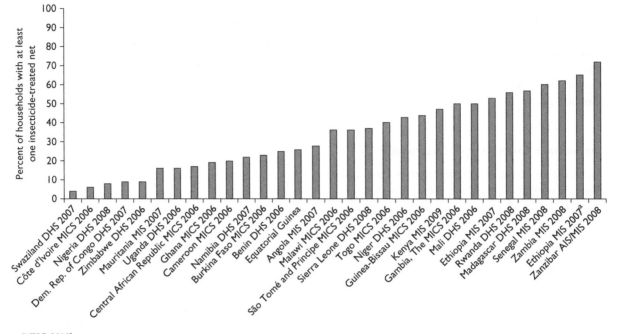

Source: WHO 2010b.
Note: DHS is Demographic Health Survey. MICS is Multiple Indicator Cluster Survey. MIS is Malaria Indicator Survey. AIS is AIDS Indicator Survey. Data for Equatorial Guinea are from a national survey.
a. Updated since original DHS.

quickly. During the "keep-up" phase, bed nets are distributed through mechanisms such as routine antenatal care visits, child wellness weeks, routine immunization completion, and school health programs. This approach has been proven to work in countries such as Ethiopia, Zambia, and Zanzibar, where high coverage of bed nets is correlated with sharp declines in malaria prevalence. Other countries that are lagging behind, such as the Democratic Republic of Congo (where just 4 percent of the population has bed nets) and Nigeria (3 percent), have been focusing efforts on increasing coverage of bed nets. The Democratic Republic of Congo plans to launching a large-scale bed net campaign in 2011 to ramp up coverage rates. In Nigeria the government has been working with partners to implement a "catch-up, keep-up" approach to increasing bed net coverage. The catch-up phase has been under way since 2008, through a phased-in nationwide mass campaign whose ultimate goal is to distribute 70 million nets (providing every household with at least two long-lasting insecticidal nets) by the end of 2011. In Nigerian states in which the bed net campaigns have been completed, data from a Lot Quality Assurance Sampling (LQAS) survey conducted in 2010 show coverage of bed nets of more than 70 percent.[3]

USE OF INSECTICIDE-TREATED NETS AMONG VULNERABLE GROUPS

Two of the many vulnerable population groups in the malaria epidemic are pregnant women and children under age five. To help safeguard these populations, a number of countries in Africa made the strategic choice to focus key prevention and promotion activities on these two groups. Despite the recent policy shift to universal coverage, many countries are still targeting these groups, given constrained budget envelopes for health in general and for malaria in particular. Examining use of LLINs among pregnant women and children under five thus still provides a good indicator of progress on use of bed nets (figure 23.2). Among these groups, the rates of usage are more encouraging, with Equatorial Guinea, Ethiopia, The Gambia, São Tomé and Principe, Zambia, and Zanzibar reaching at least 40 percent usage.

Analysis of usage rates among pregnant women indicates that, despite some progress, there is much room for improvement. Figure 23.2 highlights two key issues in this context: the lack of data for this indicator and the relatively low level of use among pregnant women compared with children under five. Ethiopia and Zambia[4] are the highest performers with 43 percent of pregnant women sleeping under an insecticide-treated net.

420   CHAPTER 23: THE MALARIA CONTROL SUCCESS STORY

Figure 23.2   Use of Insecticide-Treated Nets in Africa by Children under Five and Pregnant Women, by Country

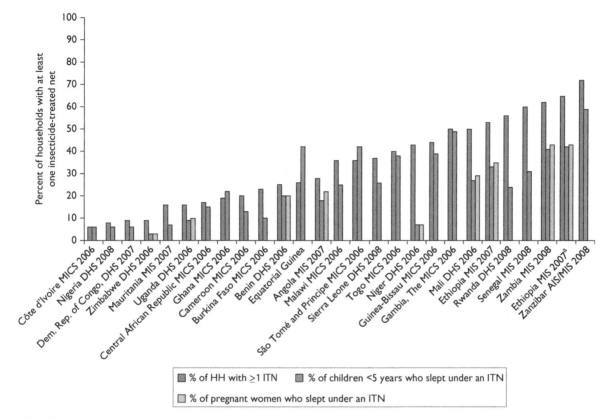

Source: WHO 2010b.

Note: DHS is Demographic Health Survey. MICS is Multiple Indicator Cluster Survey. MIS is Malaria Indicator Survey. AIS is AIDS Indicator Survey. Data for Equatorial Guinea are from a national survey.

a. Updated since original DHS.

Antimalarials

Fever is internationally recognized as one of the main indicators of malaria. Prompt access to treatment of malaria, especially among children under five, is one of the key indicators of effective malaria treatment.[5] The percentage of children under five receiving any antimalarial treatment (including artemisinin-based combination therapy, or ACT) through public and private channels varies by country (figure 23.3), but across the board there is vast room for improvement. In several countries, access to antimalarial treatment is much higher in the public sector than in the private sector, although many seek treatment first in the private and informal sectors.

Artemisinin-based combination therapy

In response to increasing levels of antimalarial resistance, in 2001 WHO began recommending that countries experiencing resistance to conventional monotherapies, such as chloroquine, amodiaquine, or sulfadoxine-pyrimethamine, use combination therapies, preferably those containing artemisinin derivatives for *p. falciparum* malaria. In 2006 it developed standard guidance on artemisinin-based combination therapy for countries to adopt into policy. As of 2010, 43 countries in Africa had adopted ACTs, several as first-line treatment and a few as second-line treatment. The rollout of this policy is being implemented in stages across Africa (table 23.1).

ACTs retail for $6–$10 a course in the private sector, making the drug prohibitively expensive; even the $1 paid by the public and nonprofit is 10 times the price of cholorquine. In addition, a number of factors, including procurement and supply chain issues, theft, and counterfeiting have made the availability of quality-assured ACTs through public and private sectors challenging (figure 23.4). But innovative solutions to access to ACTs are being implemented at the global and country level. The Affordable Medicines Facility for Malaria mechanism aims to reduce the unit cost of ACTs (box 23.2). In Zambia, a supply chain intervention has dramatically increased the

Figure 23.3   Percentage of Children under Five with Fever Receiving Any Antimalarial Medication in the Public and Private Sector, by Country

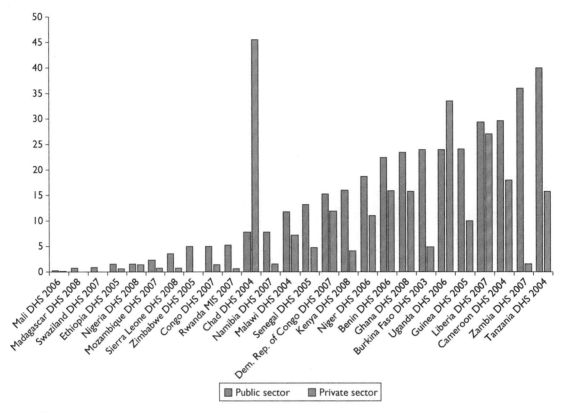

Source: WHO 2010b.
Note: DHS is Demographic Health Survey. MIS is Malaria Indicator Survey. AIS is AIDS Indicator Survey.

Table 23.1   Adoption of Policies for Malaria Treatment in Africa

Policy	Number
Number of endemic countries and territories	43
Number of *P. falciparum* endemic countries and territories	42
Artemisinin-based combination therapy (ACT) used for treatment of *P. falciparum*	42
ACT provided free of charge in public sector for all age groups	24
ACT provided free of charge in public sector only for children under five	5
ACT delivered at community level	25
Pre-referral treatment with quinine/artemether IM	32
Artesunate suppositories	25

Source: WHO 2010.

availability of ACTs and other essential drugs in health facilities (box 23.3).

Indoor residual spraying

Indoor residual spraying is recommended for control of malaria in 71 countries, 32 of them in Africa. It is the primary vector control intervention in Botswana, Mozambique, Namibia, South Africa, Swaziland, and Zimbabwe.

The number of people benefiting from indoor residual spraying rose from 10 million in 2005 to 73 million in 2009, or about 10 percent of the population at risk for malaria (WHO 2010b). In countries that have seen a rapid decline in malaria within the past five years, bed net distribution has been complemented with indoor residual spraying in the areas of the countries where it is epidemiologically justified.

Figure 23.4   Percentage of Children under Five with
                Fever Receiving Artemisinin-Based
                Combination Therapy in the Public and
                Private Sector, in Selected Countries

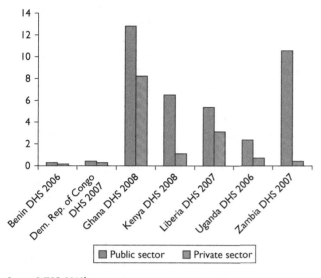

Source: WHO 2010b.
Note: DHS is Demographic Health Survey.

**Box 23.2   The Affordable Medicines Facility
for Malaria**

Most malaria cases are treated with an over-the-counter drug such as chloroquine. Resistance to this drug has increased, however, making it increasingly ineffective. As a result, in 2004 WHO recommended that all countries use ACTs as first-line treatment for malaria. ACTs are not widely available at private pharmacies and other medical distribution centers because of their high cost.

The Affordable Medicines Facility for Malaria (AMFM) is a financing mechanism, managed by the Global Fund to Fight AIDS, Tuberculosis and Malaria, designed to subsidize ACTs. The initiative negotiates a lower price with pharmaceutical producers. It aims to make ACTs even more affordable through a co-payment and subsidy system that will allow first-line buyers, including in-country private sector wholesalers, hospitals, and nongovernmental organizations, to pass on the benefit to patients, who will pay $0.20–$0.50 for ACTs—comparable to what they currently pay for less effective alternatives.

Source: Authors.

The data also point to deficiencies in the use of intermittent preventive treatment of pregnant women. In three countries (Malawi, Senegal, and Zambia), at least 70 percent of pregnant women reported having received SP/Fansidar during an antenatal care visit (figure 23.5).[6] In contrast, less than 10 percent of pregnant women in Benin, Niger, and Nigeria and less than 20 percent of women in the Democratic Republic of Congo reported receiving intermittent preventive treatment during an antenatal care visit.

PARTNERSHIP AND COORDINATION FOR RESULTS

During the past decade governments, communities, donors, and individuals have been working under growing consensus and coordinated action. Since 2005 partners and malaria-endemic countries have placed greater emphasis on strengthening coordination of technical and human resources at global, regional, and country levels. This intense collaboration, under the umbrella of the Roll Back Malaria Partnership (box 23.4), has been a key component of the success on the ground in Africa. These partnerships have helped reduce duplication in efforts, increase resource mobilization, raise awareness of the problem at the global and regional level, and create a network of technical and implementation experts for countries to draw on as they implement strategies to control malaria.

Funding for malaria control has increased dramatically since 2005 (figure 23.6). Evidence-based advocacy efforts have led to a number of notable achievements, including increased funding from partners such as the President's Malaria Initiative, the World Bank, and the Global Fund to Fight AIDS, Tuberculosis and Malaria. As a direct result of these efforts, in 2008 the Global Fund increased its funding to malaria to the historic level of $1.62 billion worldwide. In addition, the Roll Back Malaria Partnership formed the Harmonization Working Group, which seeks to harmonize donor resources to support countries with costed national malaria control plans. Partners also joined forces to develop the Global Malaria Action Plan, which provides a framework for current and future malaria control effort worldwide.

Aid harmonization for malaria has improved, and malaria disbursements rose to $1.5 billion in 2009. But new commitments for malaria control plateaued in 2010 at $1.8 billion. Government spending for health in high-burden countries remains low, with far less than 15 percent of budgets spent on the health sector in more than 90 percent of countries. The level of spending for malaria falls far short of the resources needed to control the disease, which the RBM

Box 23.3   Improving Access to ACTs in Zambia

Recognizing that access to proper treatment needed to be improved, the World Bank, the United Kingdom's Department for International Development, and the U.S. Agency for International Development (USAID) joined forces to try out new drug distribution methods in 16 districts in Zambia. The results from this pilot, evaluated through a rigorous impact evaluation, have been exceptionally encouraging. Simple but smart steps to grease the supply chain for lifesaving drugs— including hiring district-level planners to help manage orders and deliver them more efficiently—have proved very effective.

Two models were tested. Under Model A drug stock continues to be held at the district level. The new position of commodity planner (CP) at the district level, designed to enhance planning capacity, is responsible for coordinating orders from the health facilities and stock management at the district. The CP also ensures that requisitions requests are sent every month by each health facility to the district store and performs picking and packing operations at the district level to fulfill the order requisitions of health facilities under that district. The CP also estimates the overall requirements and places orders to Medical Stores Limited (MSL)[1] for the stock needed to maintain the desired inventory level at the district store. CPs were recruited to hold the logistics responsibilities in 12 of the intervention

districts, while the remaining 4 districts relied on pharmacy technologists.

Model B eliminates the intermediate storage of drugs at the district level. The district store is converted into a "cross-dock," a point of transit that receives shipments from MSL that are pre-packed for individual health facilities. Under this option, the district does not carry any stock or perform any secondary picking and packing. This system has the potential to reduce the scope for pilferage and leakages because it enables better shipment tracking.[2] However, it hinges on the health facilities transmitting their order requisitions to MSL every month to allow for the assembling of packages to individual health facilities. As in Model A, a CP was added to the district store under this option to ensure the smooth flow of order information from the health facilities to MSL.

Remarkable improvement in access to essential drugs has occurred at the health facility level, particularly in districts in which Model B was implemented. In districts implementing Model A (panel a of figure B23.3), 38 percent of health facilities were out of stock of DepoProvera (a contraceptive) at baseline. At the end of the pilot program, the stock-out rate had fallen to 17 percent. Reductions in stock-out rates of the same magnitude are observed for amoxicillin and ACT for adults. Reductions in stock-out rates were even more dramatic in districts

Figure B23.3   Baseline and Endline Stock-Out Rates following Implementation of Pilot Program

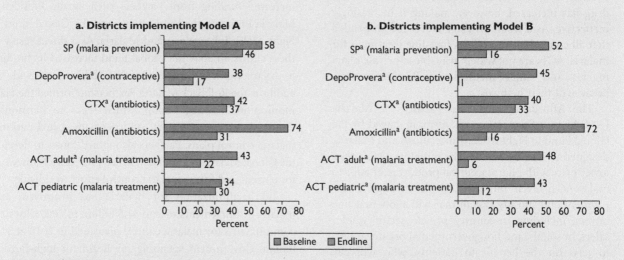

Source: Authors.
Note: Figures show the percentage of health facilities that were out of stock of the drug indicated. The intervention had similar impacts on almost all essential drugs tracked.
a. Reduction in stock-out rate is statistically insignificant compared with observed change in control districts.

Box 23.3   *(continued)*

implementing Model B (panel b of figure B23.3), where decreases in stock-out rates exceeded 40 percentage points for SP, DepoProvera, amoxicillin, and ACT for adults.

Zambia is in the process of scaling up Model B nationwide. A conservative estimate suggests that this effort could decrease under-five mortality by 21 percent and over-five mortality by 25 percent. These reductions would avert 3,320 under-five deaths and 448 over-five deaths from malaria each year. In economic terms, the aggregate household income loss averted as a result of the national scale-up of Model B is estimated to exceed $1.6 million a year.

Source: World Bank 2010.

1. The receipt, storage, and primary distribution of drugs and other health commodities from Lusaka to approximately 120 districts stores and hospitals are managed by a parastatal agency called Medical Stores Limited (MSL), currently under the management of Crown Agents. Improvements of MSL have been observed in recent years as a result of large capital investments and management reforms. Consequently, primary distribution is quite reliable and effective.

2. Zambia already had a very similar arrangement in place that has eliminated stock-outs of antiretrovirals at almost all antiretroviral therapy sites.

Figure 23.5   Treatment of Pregnant Women with SP/Fansidar during Antenatal Visit in Selected African Countries

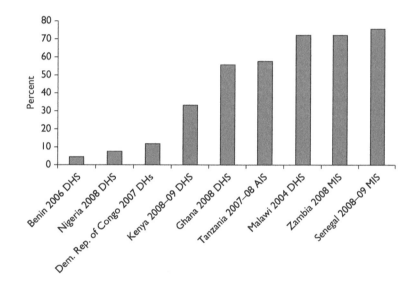

Source: Authors' compilation based on data from national household surveys.
Note: DHS is Demographic Health Survey. MIS is Malaria Indicator Survey. AIS is AIDS Indicator Survey.

Global Malaria Action Plan estimates at about $5 billion a year in 2010–15 and $4.75 billion in 2020–25. The shortfall underscores the need for policy makers and development partners to continue to work collaboratively to ensure that adequate resources are mobilized to scale up and sustain control efforts over the long term.

SUCCESS STORIES

This section highlights four countries that are showing significant progress in their malaria control efforts. The profiles show that with a combination of effective prevention and treatment tools, country leadership, and partner coordination, controlling malaria in Africa is possible.

Eritrea

In 1997 and 1998 Eritrea experienced a series of malaria epidemics that produced more than 424,000 cases; more than 500 inpatient malaria deaths were recorded in 1998 alone (RTI 2005). A 2002 Demographic Health Survey revealed

Box 23.4   The Roll Back Malaria Partnership

The Roll Back Malaria (RBM) Partnership is the global framework for implementing coordinated action against malaria. It mobilizes resources and forges consensus among more than 500 partners, including malaria-endemic countries, their bilateral and multilateral development partners, the private sector, nongovernmental and community-based organizations, foundations, and research and academic institutions.

RBM's strength lies in its ability to form effective partnerships globally and nationally. Partners work together to scale up malaria control efforts at the country level, coordinating their activities to avoid duplication and fragmentation and to ensure optimal use of resources.

Source: Authors.

RBM's overall strategy aims to reduce malaria morbidity and mortality by reaching universal coverage and strengthening health systems. The Global Malaria Action Plan defines three stages of malaria control: scaling up for impact of preventive and therapeutic interventions, sustaining control over time, and elimination.

The RBM Partnership was launched in 1998 by WHO, UNICEF, the United Nations Development Programme, and the World Bank, in an effort to provide a coordinated global response to the disease. It is served by a secretariat, hosted by WHO in Geneva, that works to facilitate policy coordination at the global level.

Figure 23.6   Commitments and Disbursements for Antimalaria Activities in Malaria-Endemic Countries in Africa, 2000–09

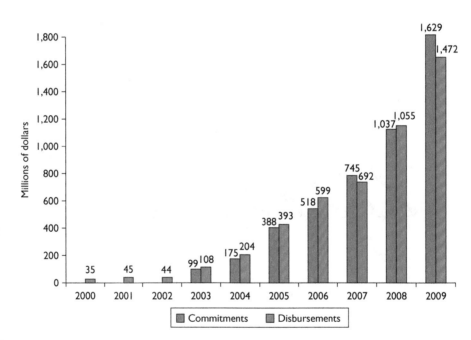

Source: WHO 2010b.

that less than 20 percent of households had at least one mosquito net, just 7 percent of pregnant women slept under a mosquito net the night before the interview, and less than half of those used an insecticide-treated net. The report also indicated low use of antimalaria drugs by pregnant women, with just 5 percent of women who had given birth in the five years preceding the survey reporting having received

antimalarial treatment for the last birth. Twelve percent of children under five were reported as having slept under a mosquito net the night before the interview, and just a third of them used an insecticide-treated net; 30 percent had a fever in the two weeks preceding the survey, but only 4 percent were treated with antimalarial medication—mostly chloroquine (NSEO and ORC Macro 2003).

EFFORTS. The alarming condition in the country, coupled with the rise of HIV/AIDS in Africa, triggered the Eritrean Ministry of Health to establish a new strategy and program to control HIV/AIDS, malaria, sexually transmitted diseases, and tuberculosis in 2000. The program, dubbed HAMSET, supplemented the National Malaria Control Program (NMCP), established in 1998. The technical strategy of NMCP sought to reduce and better target indoor residual spraying to the highest-risk areas and scale up rapid diagnosis and effective treatment for fever cases, environmental management activities, and use of insecticide-treated nets. At the core of this strategy was the strengthening of disease surveillance and operational research activities, data from which would be used to select and refine the mix of strategies and geographically target control activities. During 1999–2005, the NMCP introduced a first-line antimalarial drug and implemented an integrated vector control program using insecticide-treated nets, indoor residual spraying in selected areas, and other interventions. In 2005 the Ministry of Health articulated a clear strategic plan, with the goal of "reducing malaria to such low levels that it is no longer a public health problem in the country" (Ministry of Health 2008).

Through support from the World Bank, the Global Fund, and other donors, Eritrea has been able to employ a comprehensive strategy against malaria through a centralized approach. This approach involves targeting the use of indoor residual spraying in the highest-risk areas, carrying out environmental management of malaria vector breeding sites, increasing distribution of insecticide-treated mosquito nets, and expanding diagnostic and treatment services.

RESULTS. The fact that about 60 percent of Eritrea's population of 3.5 million people live in malaria- endemic or epidemic-prone areas where disease is seasonal, highly focal, and unstable puts the country in a disadvantageous position in terms of malaria control. Despite these odds, through the support of the World Bank and other donors, in only a few years Eritrea has been able to introduce new first-line antimalarial drugs and implement an integrated vector control program using insecticide-treated nets, indoor residual spraying in selected areas, and other interventions. Through these efforts, Eritrea has reduced malaria mortality by more than 80 percent, malaria inpatient cases by 90 percent, and malaria outpatient cases by 68 percent (WHO 2009). It also met the target set at the Africa Summit on Roll Back Malaria in April 2000 of reducing the incidence of malaria by at least 60 percent before 2010.

As a result of the strong commitment of the government, Eritrea has come a long way in 10 years. Through

implementation of prevention activities, diligent environmental management of malaria vector breeding sites, and widespread diagnostic and treatment services, it has reduced overall malaria morbidity from about 100,000 cases in 2000 to about 8,000 in 2008 (Ministry of Health 2008) These achievements have led to an overall decrease in maternal and infant mortality and a healthier population.

Ethiopia

Malaria was responsible for the deaths of nearly 29,000 children—about 80 children a day—in Ethiopia in 2000 (WHO 2002). In 2003 Ethiopia had more than half a million reported malaria cases. According to a 2005 Demographic Health Survey, malaria was the primary cause of health problems, accounting for 17 percent of outpatient visits, 15 percent of hospital admissions, and 29 percent of in-patient deaths (Central Statistical Agency [Ethiopia], and ORC Macro 2006). During this period only 5.7 percent of households owned at least one bed net, and less than 4 percent had an insecticide-treated net. The situation for children under five years of age was dire, with only 2.3 percent sleeping under any net the night before the survey and less than 2 percent sleeping under an insecticide-treated net. During the two weeks preceding the survey, about 19 percent of children under five were reported as having had a fever, and only 3 percent of these received antimalarial drugs. Among pregnant women, only 1.6 percent slept under any bed net the night before the survey and only about 1 percent slept under an insecticide-treated net. Less than 5 percent took any antimalarial drug, and only 0.5 percent received any intermittent preventive treatment. Just one-tenth of all households reported occupying a dwelling that was ever sprayed with insecticide to prevent malaria.

EFFORTS. Ethiopia has been trying to control and eliminate malaria for more than 60 years. The Malaria Eradication Service was established in 1959, making Ethiopia one of the pioneering countries in Africa to embark on a malaria eradication effort. In 2000 the country became a cosignatory to the Abuja Declaration, committing itself to the declaration's aims of increasing coverage of malaria interventions and reducing malaria mortality by half by 2010.

The Ethiopian government has implemented a centralized approach to bringing the disease under control, with significant success. In 2009, after analysis of the results of the 2007 Malaria Indicator Survey as well as the discussions and recommendations that followed a consultative meeting held in Ethiopia in 2009, Ethiopia developed a six-year

(2010–15) National Strategic Plan for Malaria Prevention, Control, and Elimination. In the new strategic plan, top priorities among malaria control strategies are given to community empowerment and social mobilization. These priorities were based on the results of the 2007 Malaria Indicator Survey, which showed substantial differences between the coverage and utilization of key malaria interventions by the population at risk of malaria. Malaria diagnosis, case management, disease surveillance, and epidemic control will all be geared to serve Ethiopia's goal of shrinking malaria-endemic areas by 2015 and eliminating the disease throughout the country by 2020 (USAID and PMI 2010).

Donors such as the World Bank, the Global Fund, the U.K. Department for International Development, UNICEF, and the Canadian International Development Agency have been providing coordinated support to the Ethiopian government in its fight against malaria by offering flexible and pragmatic funding to ensure that the country's efforts have been scaled up and sustained. Together they have contributed more than $151 million—for malaria control efforts in the country. Partner resources have supported the procurement and free distribution of long-lasting insecticidal nets, antimalarial drugs, and indoor residual spraying as well as the strengthening of the supply chain. Other components have included capacity building for other functions, especially procurement and monitoring and evaluation.

RESULTS. The effort by the Ethiopian government and its partners has resulted in remarkable improvements in malaria control and overall health in Ethiopia. Recent data suggest sharp declines in the number of malaria cases as well as declines in malaria outbreaks and deaths (Global Fund 2009). These efforts correlated with an overall decrease in under-five mortality by more than 20 percent between 1990 and 2008, and maternal mortality declined by nearly 60 percent, from 968 maternal deaths per 100,000 live births to 590.

Given the scope of the problem in Ethiopia—about 68 percent of the population of 73 million lives in areas at risk of malaria—the government has accomplished extraordinary results.

Rwanda

Rwanda has made remarkable progress in malaria control. In 2005, according to the Demographic Health Survey, only one-fifth of households reported having at least one once-treated mosquito net. Sixteen percent of children under five, 20 percent of pregnant women, and 13 percent of all women reported having slept under any mosquito net the night before the survey. Only 5.8 percent of women reported having taken any antimalarial drug to prevent or treat malaria during an antenatal care visit during their last pregnancy, and just 0.3 percent of women reported having received intermittent preventive treatment during their last antenatal care visit.

EFFORTS. Acting on the recommendation of its ministry of health, the Rwandan government adopted two major strategies to reduce malaria: promoting the use of insecticide-treated nets for prevention, particularly among vulnerable groups, including pregnant women and children under five, and providing early diagnosis and timely treatment with combination therapy of amodiaquine and sulfdoxine/pyrimethamine (Concern Worldwide, International Rescue Committee, and World Relief 2004). The prevention component of malaria transmission was moving along steadily. In contrast, as a result of rapid widespread resistance to older first-line treatment antimalarial drugs, the country was no longer able to effectively combat the disease, forcing it to change its national treatment policy. In 2005 the Rwandan government made ACT the official first-line antimalarial drug (Friends of the Global Fight against AIDS, Tuberculosis, and Malaria 2008). To support the intense efforts of the Rwandan government to control malaria and strengthen health systems, development partners such as the World Bank, the Global Fund, the President's Malaria Initiative, the Roll Back Malaria Partnership, WHO, Malaria No More, the Bill & Melinda Gates Foundation, nongovernmental organizations, and others contributed grants and loans to step up funding of programs across the country.

In addition to providing assistance for prevention activities such as bed net distribution and indoor residual spraying and funding for antimalarial treatment, some donors have provided grants to finance the overall strengthening of Rwanda's health system. In 2005 the Global Fund approved a grant of $33.9 million to finance health systems strengthening activities. The grant reduced the cost of health services, improved the quality of care offered at health centers, and financed training for more than 100 healthcare administrators in health financing and management for health information systems.

RESULTS. Rwanda was once a country with extremely high malaria prevalence and large numbers of deaths from malaria, particularly among children. As a result of its efforts, the number of malaria illnesses attended at health facilities declined from 1.5 million people in 2005 to 800,000 in 2008, and the mortality rate from malaria dropped from 41 percent in 2006 to 16 percent in 2008. In 2008 malaria was the third-leading cause of morbidity and mortality, after pneumonia and diarrhea. The 2008 interim Demographic Health Survey indicated a child mortality rate of 103 deaths per 1,000 live births, a 32 percent reduction from the 2005 rate of 152 (USAID and PMI 2009).

The percentage of households with at least one ever-treated net increased by nearly 40 percent, from 18.1 percent in 2005 to 57.2 percent in 2007–08. The percentage of children under five that slept under an ever-treated net the night before the Demographic Health Survey increased by 42 percentage points, from 15.7 percent in 2005 to 58.0 percent in 2007–08, and the share of children under five with fever in the two weeks preceding the survey decreased by nearly 5 percentage points, from 26.2 percent in 2005 to 21.4 percent in 2007–08. By 2008 the use of health centers had increased by 10.0 percent and the use of district hospitals had increased by 16.8 percent over 2005 (Malaria Free Future 2008).

Rwanda—a country whose entire population was once at risk of malaria—is now one of Africa's frontrunners in the fight against the disease. With increasing use of bed nets, long-lasting insecticidal-treated mosquito nets, antimalarial drugs, and intermittent preventive treatment during pregnancy, Rwanda has significantly reduced the number of malaria transmissions, malaria cases being reported at health facilities, and deaths from malaria. These achievements have contributed to a decrease in infant and maternal mortality and a healthier Rwanda. The Rwandan National Malaria Control Program is continuing to pursue its very ambitious goals, which include universal coverage of long-lasting insecticidal-treated mosquito nets, expansion of indoor residual spraying, subsidization of ACTs nationwide, and better monitoring and evaluation to tackle epidemics (Malaria Free Future 2008).

Zambia

In 2001–02 Zambia had about 3.5 million cases and 50,000 deaths a year from malaria, making the disease the leading cause of morbidity and the second-highest cause of mortality. Disease prevalence was highest among pregnant women and children under five, making Zambia one of the countries with the highest malaria-related maternal mortality in Africa and one with an extremely high under-five mortality rate (168 deaths per 1,000 live births) (DHS 2002). During this time, only 14 percent of households in Zambia owned an insecticide-treated net, 7 percent of children under five slept under a mosquito net the night before the survey, and

43 percent of children under five suffered from fever or convulsions in the two weeks preceding the survey, among whom about half received antimalarial drugs for their symptoms. Among pregnant women, just 8 percent slept under an insecticide-treated net, and only 36 percent received antimalarial drugs during pregnancy (DHS 2002).

EFFORTS. To control and reverse the deteriorating situation, the Zambian Ministry of Health identified malaria control as one of its main public health priorities and included it in both the National Development Plan 2006–10 and the National Health Strategic Plan 2006–10. Through the National Malaria Control Centre, the Ministry of Health developed a detailed national malaria strategic plan, which aimed to drastically reduce the malaria burden—by scaling up malaria control interventions—with a vision of achieving a malaria-free Zambia. This plan was the backbone for support by the country and its partners.

The strategy adopted a two-pronged approach, aiming to bring malaria under control with key malaria control interventions while at the same time supporting broader improvements in health systems, including decentralizing budgeting and planning, building capacity throughout the supply chain for procurement and forecasting of commodities, and strengthening monitoring and evaluation and program management. As a result of these combined efforts, 3.6 million long- lasting insecticide-treated bed nets were distributed throughout the country between 2006 and 2008, raising the percentage of households with one long-lasting insecticidal-treated net from 48 to 72 percent. Indoor residual spraying coverage increased from 15 districts in 2006 to 36 districts in 2008.

RESULTS. The impact of Zambia's efforts has been felt countrywide. In just two years the number of malaria deaths declined 47 percent, and nationwide surveys showed a decline in parasite prevalence of 53 percent (from 21.8 percent in 2006 to 10.2 percent in 2008). The percentage of children with severe anemia declined 68 percent (from 13.3 percent in 2006 to 4.3 percent in 2008). The percentage of children under five with malaria parasite prevalence fell by half (from 22 percent in 2006 to 10.2 percent in 2008) and the percentage of children under five with severe anemia fell from 14 percent in 2006 to 4.3 percent in 2008 (MIS 2008). These successes reduced the overall under-five mortality from 168 in 2002 to 148 in 2008 (UNICEF 2008). The successful scale-up of Zambia's malaria program contributed to a 29 percent drop in the overall mortality rate for children under five between 2002 and 2008, saving an estimated

75,000 lives over that period. The capacity of the malaria program as well as supporting critical health systems interventions was strengthened for better management.

FRAGILE PROGRESS. Zambia's success illustrates one of the most important issues associated with malaria control efforts. Delayed external financing slowed execution of all of the necessary malaria control interventions between June 2009 and December 2010, causing a significant decline in malaria outcomes in some provinces of the country. Data from the 2010 Zambia National Malaria Indicator Survey indicates a resurgence in malaria between 2008 and 2010. Most of this increase was in rural areas, among the poorest segments of the population. In three of the country's nine provinces, about half of the decrease in malaria cases between 2006 and 2008 was lost by 2010. In Luapula and the Northern Provinces, there were marked declines in ownership and use of mosquito nets between 2008 and 2010, which alone could explain the increase in malaria cases. Zambia's experience shows that once the disease is under control, efforts have to be sustained if gains are not to be reversed or even worsened, because malaria can have an even deadlier impact on a population that has lower immunity to the disease.

LESSONS LEARNED AND THE WAY FORWARD

Effective tools for malaria prevention and treatment exist. With concerted and collaborative efforts, implementation of these tools is starting to show results in Africa. Progress in the past few years has shown that success in Africa is possible. The results of WHO's 2010 *World Malaria Report* are very encouraging. Since 2000, 11 countries have shown decreases in malaria cases after widescale implementation of malaria control activities in the population at high risk. In Botswana, Cape Verde, Eritrea, Madagascar, Rwanda, Zambia, and other countries, the number of cases has fallen by more than half. By the end of 2010, about 289 million insecticide-treated nets were to have been delivered to Sub-Saharan Africa, enough to cover 76 percent of the 765 million people at risk of malaria there. Global malaria control efforts have resulted in a reduction in the estimated number of deaths from nearly 1 million in 2000 to 781,000 in 2009. The international community has played an important role in supporting government efforts to reduce the impact of malaria through substantial financial and technical support in the past decade.

These emerging successes notwithstanding, more remains to be done. Sustained support is needed to replace nets and scale up other proven interventions (access to effective diagnosis and treatment, indoor residual spraying). Gaps in increased coverage and use of malaria control activities remain substantial in many countries. To continue and intensify the fight against malaria, increased funding is required for activities that prevent and treat malaria. In countries where there has been significant progress, resources must be sufficient to, at the very minimum, maintain efforts, so that the disease does not resurface.

It is critical that political will and financing be sustained. Failure to protect and expand on the fragile progress taking place in Africa will lead to a resurgence of malaria cases and deaths. Learning from early successes is critical to avoiding such a prospect. Several lessons emerge from African countries' experience:

- The high level of external funding, coupled with in-country ownership, has proven to be extremely successful in combating malaria. Government ownership and initiative to work with partners in support of established policy in the malaria control programs at the country level is essential.
- Bed net coverage has rapidly increased, but other key interventions are lagging, and the gaps are becoming increasingly more critical. There needs to be more focus on use of key interventions, monitoring of drug resistance, deployment of rapid diagnostic tests, and access to ACTs.
- At a minimum, maintaining current levels of funding in order to ensure prevention and treatment activities is essential in the short and medium term to protect the progress that has been achieved to date. To reach the Abuja targets of the Roll Back Malaria Partnership—coverage of 80 percent for insecticide-treated nets for people at risk, treatment with appropriate antimalarial drugs for people with probable or confirmed malaria, indoor residual spraying for households at risk, and intermittent treatment in pregnancy in high-transmission areas—funding needs to be about four times the current level. This estimate does not take into account the resource needs to reach the universal coverage target of the population at risk by the end of 2010 set by the Secretary-General of the United Nations and highlighted in the RBM Global Malaria Action Plan.
- Without continued and additional resources in the short and medium term, countries may risk a resurgence of malaria cases in the coming years. Zambia highlights this issue by showing that significant progress is possible but that it is fragile and needs a sustained effort.

- To achieve long-term financial sustainability in national health systems, national malaria control funding as well as the national health budget of countries will need to increase. In the long run, malaria control efforts will need to be covered more substantially by those sources. Both governments and partners need to address financial sustainability.
- Financing should focus on supporting countries that have not yet scaled up their prevention and treatment efforts while maintaining support to those that have.
- Support needs to be provided to countries ready to move toward eliminating malaria. In this context, more attention will have to be placed on cross-border and regional activities.
- Strengthening health system aspects such as supply chains and human resources as well the interface between health systems and disease control will be needed to sustain gains.

NOTES

1. There are four types of human malaria: *Plasmodium falciparum*, *Plasmodium vivax*, *Plasmodium malariae*, and *Plasmodium ovale*. *Plasmodium falciparum* and *Plasmodium vivax* are the most common. *Plasmodium falciparum*, the most deadly form of the disease, is the predominant type of malaria in Sub-Saharan Africa.

2. The original Abuja targets were set and agreed to by 53 African heads of state in the Abuja Declaration on Roll Back Malaria in Africa on April 25, 2000. They included the following targets: at least 60 percent of those suffering from malaria have prompt access to and are able to use correct, affordable, and appropriate treatment within eight hours of the onset of symptoms; at least 60 percent of those at risk of malaria, particularly pregnant women and children under five years of age, benefit from the most suitable combination of personal and community protective measures, such as insecticide-treated mosquito nets and other materials to prevent infection and suffering; at least 60 percent of all pregnant women who are at risk of malaria, especially those in their first pregnancies, have access to chemoprophylaxis or presumptive intermittent treatment.

3. Lot Quality Assurance Sampling (LQAS) was developed in the 1920s as a quality control technique for goods produced on a factory assembly line. It was used to examine a small number of units randomly selected from each lot. If the number of defective items in that small sample exceeded a predetermined number, the lot was examined more closely and either repaired or discarded; otherwise the lot was accepted. The number of units tested and the maximum allowable number of defects were determined to ensure that there was a high probability that the lots accepted contained no more than a specified proportion of defective goods and that the lots rejected contained a relatively high proportion of defective goods. Since the 1980s, use of LQAS in health assessment has increased. In 1991 WHO identified LQAS as one of the more practical rapid assessment methods and encouraged further study. (For examples of LQAS application in the health field, see Robertson 1997.) LQAS has been employed for a range of purposes, including monitoring immunization program performance in Southeast Asia, Peru, and the United States and assessing immunization coverage. To monitor immunization, supervisors sample records to assess compliance with immunization protocols. The number of "defective" or incorrect procedures allowed per lot is set to determine whether a facility (or lot) is accepted or rejected. LQAS can also be used to assess compliance with a policy, such as patient screening practices or immunization administration; identify areas of high incidence of specific diseases; or assess program impact.

4. According to the Zambia MIS carried out in 2010, the percentage of women sleeping under an insecticide-treated net rose from 43 percent to 46 percent.

5. Once a diagnosis of malaria is established, effective treatment should be started within 24 hours of the onset of symptoms, to avoid progression to severe malaria, for which the case fatality rate is high.

REFERENCES

Central Statistical Agency (Ethiopia), and ORC Macro. 2006. *Ethiopia Demographic and Health Survey 2005.* Addis Ababa and Calverton, MD.

Concern Worldwide, International Rescue Committee, and World Relief. 2004. *Baseline Survey of the Rwanda Community Distribution of Anti-Malarials Pilot Program.* http://www.concernusa.org/media/pdf/2007/10/Rwanda _Baseline_Malaria.

Friends of the Global Fight against AIDS, Tuberculosis and Malaria. 2008. *Country Profile: Rwanda.* http://www.the globalfight.org/view/resources/uploaded/Rwanda_Coun try_Profile.pdf.

Gallup, J. L., and J. Sachs. 2001. "The Economic Burden of Malaria." *American Journal of Tropical Medicine and Hygiene* 64 (Suppl. 1): 85–96.

Global Fund to Fight AIDs, Tuberculosis and Malaria. 2009. *Early Evidence of Sustainable Impact on Malaria.* http://www.theglobalfund.org/documents/publica tions/onepagers/Malaria.pdf.

Hogan, Margaret C., Kyle J. Foreman, Mohsen Naghavi, Stephanie Y. Ahn, Mengru Wang, Susanna M. Makela, Alan D. Lopez, Rafael Lozano, and Christopher J. L. Murray.

2010. "Maternal Mortality for 181 Countries, 1980–2008: A Systematic Analysis of Progress towards Millennium Development Goal 5." *Lancet* 375 (9726): 1609–23.

Malaria Free Future. 2008. *Rwanda: Winning the Fight against Malaria.* http://www.malariafreefuture.org/rwanda/success.php.

Ministry of Health of Rwanda. 2008. *Integrated Approach to Reducing Malaria Related Morbidity and Mortality in Rwanda.* Kigali.

NSEO (National Statistics and Evaluation Office Eritrea), and ORC Macro. 2003. *Eritrea Demographic and Health Survey 2002.* Calverton, MD.

Robertson, S. E., M. Anker, A. J. Roisin, N. Macklai, K. Engstrom, and F. M. LaForce. 1997. "The Lot Quality Technique: A Global Review of Applications in the Assessment of Health Services and Disease." *World Health Statistics Quarterly* 50: 199–209.

Roll Back Malaria Partnership. 2008. *The Global Malaria Action Plan—for a Malaria-Free World.* http://www.rbm.who.int/gmap/.

———. 2010. "Roll Back Malaria Report Confirms Aid for Malaria Is Working But Predictable Long-Term Funding Is Essential to Achieve Millennium Development Goals." http://www.rollbackmalaria.org/globaladvocacy/pr2010-03-18.html.

RTI International. 2005. *Combating Malaria in Eritrea.* http://www.rti.org/brochures/rti_Eritrca_malaria_brochure.pdf.

Statesmen's Forum. 2010. *Global Health Initiative: Integration and Innovation for Better Outcomes.* June 29. UNICEF (United Nations Children's Fund), New York.

UNICEF (United Nations Children's Fund). 2008. *Zambia.* http://www.unicef.org/infobycountry/zambia_statistics.html.

USAID (United States Agency for International Development), and PMI (President's Malaria Initiative). 2010a. *Country Profile Rwanda.* http://www.fightingmalaria.gov/countries/profiles/rwanda_profile.pdf

———. 2010b. *Malaria Operational Plan Ethiopia FY 2010.* http://www.fightingmalaria.gov/countries/mops/fy10/ethiopia_mop-fy10.pdf.

WHO (World Health Organization). 2007. Fact Sheet 94. http://www.who.int/mediacentre/factsheets/fs094/en/.

———. 2009. *World Malaria Report 2009.* Geneva: World Health Organization.

———. 2010a. *Basic Malaria Microscopy. Part 1, Learner's Guide,* 2nd ed. Geneva: World Health Organization.

———. 2010b. *World Malaria Report 2010.* Geneva: World Health Organization.

World Bank. 2007. *The World Bank Booster Program for Malaria Control in Africa: Scaling Up for Impact. A Two-Year Progress Report.* Washington, DC. www.worldbank.org/afr/malaria.

———. 2010. *World Bank Policy Note: Enhancing Supply Chain Management in Zambia.* Africa Health Unit, Washington, DC.

Zambia NMCC (National Malaria Control Center). 2008. *Zambia Malaria Indicator Survey 2008.* Ministry of Health, Lusaka.

———. 2010. *Zambia Malaria Indicator Survey 2010.* Ministry of Health, Lusaka.

CHAPTER 24

Health Extension Workers in Ethiopia: Improved Access and Coverage for the Rural Poor

Nejmudin Kedir Bilal, Christopher H. Herbst, Feng Zhao, Agnes Soucat, and Christophe Lemiere

Health systems in Sub-Saharan African countries often suffer from weak infrastructure, lack of human resources, and poor supply chain management systems. Access to health services is particularly low in rural areas, where the majority of the population still lives. The few private outlets that are available usually favor urban or wealthy areas. Together with an uneven distribution of health workers, this pattern often results in little availability and poor quality of health services in rural areas.

Ethiopians' access to services was particularly low before the government came up with innovative ways of scaling up the delivery of essential health interventions, in particular through its Health Extension Program (HEP). The HEP was designed and implemented in recognition of the fact that the major factor underlying poor health services in Ethiopia is the lack of empowerment of households and communities to promote health and prevent disease. This chapter reviews Ethiopia's experience in producing and deploying health extension workers and summarizes some of the key factors that made the program a success.[1]

THE PROBLEM: SHORTAGE OF HEALTH CARE PROVIDERS IN RURAL AREAS

With a population of 80 million people, Ethiopia is the second-most populous country in Africa. Throughout the 1990s poor nutritional status, infections, and a high fertility rate, together with poor access to basic health services, contributed to one of the highest maternal and child mortality ratios in the world. Moreover, their use of available health facilities was low. In 2005 almost all births took place at home, with only 6 percent of women delivering in a clinic or hospital (CSA and Macro International 2005). Major causes of morbidity and mortality for children under age five were preventable. Extrapolations from the 2005 Demographic and Health Survey showed malnutrition to be the underlying cause of more than half of deaths of children under five (CSA and MACRO International 2005). In 2005 only 1 percent of households owned a bed net, of which less than 18 percent were insecticide treated.

The brunt of poor health falls on the rural poor, most of whom live out of reach of health providers. In 2005 only 40 percent of the population lived within 10 kilometers of a clinic or other health service delivery point. The number of trained health workers has historically been inadequate in Ethiopia, with shortages of almost all cadres of workers, particularly in rural areas. Throughout the early 1990s, universities and health professional training colleges focused on clinically oriented training rather than on more relevant rural-oriented community health training. Although more than 85 percent of the population lives in these rural areas, doctors and nurses preferred to work in urban hospital settings, where professional opportunities were better.

ADDRESSING THE PROBLEM: THE HEALTH EXTENSION PROGRAM

To address these problems, Ethiopia launched the HEP in 2003. The program's objectives were to reach the poor and deliver preventive and basic curative high-impact interventions to all of the Ethiopian population. The HEP is an ambitious government-led community health service delivery program designed to improve access to and utilization of preventive, wellness, and basic curative services.

At the heart of this program is the production and deployment of more than 30,000 front-line community health workers. These health extension workers are posted to rural communities across Ethiopia, where they provide better and more equitable access to health services for the poor, women, and children in a sustainable manner (Assefa et al. 2010; Ghebreyesus 2010). The program focuses on four major areas and provides 17 different packages to reach the poor and address inequities (table 24.1).

Training and deployment of health extension workers

Since 2003 the HEP has been rolled out step by step to reach full coverage of all rural villages by the end of 2010 (table 24.2; figure 24.1). As a result of the program, the ratio of health extension workers to people increased from 1: 23,775 in 2004/05 to 1: 2,437 in 2008/09.

Health extension workers are recruited from the communities in which they will work according to specific criteria: they are female (except in pastoralist areas), at least 18 years old, have at least a 10th grade education, and speak the local language. Females are selected because most of the HEP packages relate to issues affecting mothers and children; thus communication is thought to be easier between mothers

and female health extension workers and female workers are thought to be more culturally acceptable. In addition, their selection is seen as empowering women. Selection is done by a committee made up of members nominated by the local community and representatives from the district (*woreda*) health office, the district capacity building office, and the district education office (FMOH 2007b). Upon completion of training, pairs of health extension workers are assigned as salaried government employees to *kebeles* (neighborhoods), where they staff health posts and work directly with individual households. Each *kebele* has a health post that serves 5,000 people and functions as an operational center for a health extension worker. Five health posts and a health center work in collaboration and for the Primary Health Care Unit (PHCU) that serves 25,000 people. The health center serves as a referral center and logistic hub for a health post and also offers technical support. The health post is under the supervision of the district health office and the *kebele* administration and receives technical and practical support from the nearby health center.

Health extension workers are trained to manage operations of health posts; conduct home visits and outreach services to promote preventive health actions; refer cases to health centers and follow up on referrals; identify, train, and collaborate with voluntary community health workers; and provide reports to district health offices.

Upon assignment, health extension workers conduct a baseline survey of the village, using a standardized tool. They map households and the population by age category. They also prioritize health problems of the village, set targets with respect to the 17 packages of services, and draft a plan of action for the year. The draft plan of action is then submitted to the village council and approved. The plans are

Table 24.1 Major Areas and Packages of Health Extension Program

Hygiene and environmental sanitation	Disease prevention and control	Family health services	Health education and communication
1. Proper and safe excreta disposal system	1. Prevention and control of HIV/AIDS	1. Maternal and child health	1. Health education and communication
2. Proper and safe solid and liquid waste management	2. Prevention and control of tuberculosis	2. Family planning	
3. Water supply safety measures	3. Prevention and control of malaria	3. Immunization	
4. Food hygiene and safety measures	4. First aid	4. Adolescent reproductive health	
5. Healthy home environment		5. Nutrition	
6. Arthropod and rodent control			
7. Personal hygiene			

Source: FMOH 2005.

Table 24.2   Number of Health Extension Workers Trained and Deployed in Ethiopia, by Region, 2005/06–2009/10

Region	2005/06	2006/07	2007/08	2008/09	2009/10	Total
Afar	0	0	164	148	196	572
Amhara	3,500	2,631	680	382	330	7,342
B. Gumuz	0	59	120	315	403	924
Dire Dawa	0	33	0	0	63	142
Gambella	0	47	0	410	0	457
Harari	0	0	0	0	8	47
Oromia	1,296	3,524	2,884	4,526	524	13,487
SNNPR	1,500	2,666	2,650	800	627	8,542
Somali	0	0	420	545	327	1,427
Tigray	840	0	0	134	73	1,442
National	7,136	8,960	6,918	7,260	2,551	34,382

Source: FMOH 2009.

Figure 24.1   Number of Health Extension Workers Deployed, 2004/05–2009/10

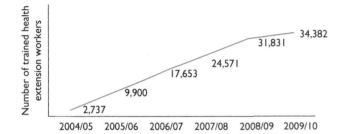

Source: HSDP Annual Performance Report 2009/2010.

also disseminated to the district and regional councils and health offices.

The basic philosophy of the HEP is to transfer ownership of and responsibility for maintaining their own health to individual households by transferring health knowledge and skills to households. Health extension workers spend 75 percent of their time visiting families in their homes and performing outreach activities in the community. The house-to-house activity starts by identifying households to serve as role models. These households have earned the respect and credibility of the community because of their extraordinary performance in other social aspects, such as agricultural production. They are willing to change and, upon completion of the training, are able to persuade and convince other households to follow appropriate health practices. The model households are considered early adopters of health practices in line with heath extension packages. They help diffuse health messages, leading to the adoption of the desired practices and behaviors by the rest of the community.

Two health extension workers are expected to train 360 model households a year. The training lasts 96 hours, after which the household "graduates" receive a certificate as

recognition. Health extension workers also work with communities through traditional associations, such as *idir* (community-level volunteer organizations that collect money on a regular basis to cover funeral costs and give some money to the family of the deceased), *mehaber* (professional and religious organizations), *ekub* (a scheme in which people regularly contribute money, which at a specified time is given to one group member; this process is repeated until all members receive a contribution), schools, women's associations, and youth associations. These institutions help communicate health messages and mobilize the community to help with environmental cleanup, health post construction, and other efforts.

The health extension workers' remaining time is spent providing services, including immunizations and injectable contraceptives, at the health posts. They are trained to provide first aid; conduct safe and clean deliveries; diagnose and treat malaria, diarrhea, and intestinal parasites. In 2010 the government added the diagnosis and treatment of pneumonia to the HEP, following an evidence-based analysis of the potential impact of different packages of high-impact interventions. The addition represents a significant step toward tackling a primary cause of child mortality.

Health extension workers also participate in local politics and are part of the multisectoral local decision-making process. One of the two health extension workers in a village sits on the village council, along with an elected village chairman, a teacher, an agricultural development agent, and a community representative. The council is the political administration of the village that serves to prioritize the work of the HEP, provide support to health extension workers, and review their regular performance reports.

Various institutions have well-defined roles in supporting the work of health extension workers once they are deployed. The Federal Ministry of Health provides medical equipment and supplies, such as vaccines, cold chain equipment, contraceptives, and insecticide-treated bednets. Regional health bureaus and district health offices pay the salaries of the health extension workers and provide technical support and political leadership. Health centers play a crucial role in providing referral care and technical and practical support. In addition, volunteer community health workers work closely with health extension staff.

Impact of the intervention

More than 9 million households in Ethiopia (some 63 percent of all households) have completed their training on the 17 packages of the HEP. Training and "graduation" of households is an output indicator for monitoring the performance of health extension workers (table 24.3).

Health conditions, including the proportion of households with access to sanitation, improved disproportionately in HEP villages. A case control study conducted in HEP and non–HEP villages between 2005 and 2007 indicated that the proportion of households with access to improved sanitation reached 76 percent in the intervention villages (from 39 percent at baseline). In contrast, access to improved sanitation in the control villages increased from 27 percent at baseline to just 36 percent during the follow-up survey period (Center for National Health Development in Ethiopia 2008.) Awareness of HIV/AIDS also improved, with the level of knowledge of condoms as a means of

preventing HIV increasing by 78 percent in HEP villages and 46 in control villages.

Vaccination coverage improved significantly. A study by Admassiea, Abebaw, and Woldemichael (2009) finds that a significantly larger proportion of children in villages where health extension workers were deployed were vaccinated against diphtheria, polio, and tetanus (DPT); measles; polio; tuberculosis; and main antigens. A study by the Center for National Health Services indicates that more than 96 percent of health posts in the three largest regions of the country provide immunization services. A routine report from the Ministry of Health indicates that child vaccination is increasing in Ethiopia: by June 2010, 86 percent of children had received Penta 3/DPT 3 vaccine, 82 percent had received measles vaccine, and 62 percent had been fully immunized (FMOH 2010a), an average annual increase in the number of fully immunized children of 15 percent since 2006. A household survey in the four largest regions finds that 64 percent of children received Penta 3 and 68 percent of children 12–23 months had been vaccinated against measles, one of the indicators in the Millennium Development Goals (MDGs) (The Last Ten Kilometers Project 2009). Although the routine report and the household survey differ in terms of immunization coverage, both results indicate significant improvement.

Coverage of maternal health services also improved: 85 percent of health posts could provide family planning services, 83 percent could provide antenatal care, 59 percent could perform clean deliveries, and 47 percent could provide postnatal care (Center for National Health Services 2007). Health posts had also become the major source for current users of contraceptives, as reported by about 60 percent of women from the four largest regions; 22 percent of women cited heath centers. A household survey conducted by the Last Ten Kilometers Project in the four largest regions documents that 32 percent of married women were practicing family planning; about 54 percent of these women received antenatal care services and 20 percent received focused antenatal care (four or more visits). Some 42 percent of women received at least two doses of *Tetanus Toxoid* vaccine (TTII), and 54 percent were inoculated against tetanus. The increase in the use of any contraceptive method among currently married women was also higher in HEP villages (where it rose from 31 percent to 46 percent) than in control villages (where it rose from 30 percent to 34 percent).

Ethiopia has made significant efforts in expanding coverage of key malaria interventions. Major scale-up efforts began in 2004/05, with the introduction of artemisinin-based

Region	Number of households eligible, as of September 2009	Number of households "graduating," as of June 2010	Coverage (percent)
Addis Ababa	0	n.a.	0
Afar	258,572	130	0
Amhara	4,209,129	2,508,472	63
Benishangul Gumuz	158,156	15,604	10
Dire Dawa	80,041	2,400	9
Gambella	72,304	–	0
Harari	49,488	2,159	11
Oromia	6,011,967	4,300,287	72
SNNP	3,272,573	2,417,012	74
Somali	708,028	30,490	17
Tigray	1,030,199	703,152	66
National	15,850,457	9,072,040	63

Table 24.3 Number of Households "Graduating" from the HEP, as of June 2010

Source: FMOH 2010a.

Note: n.a. = Not applicable. – = Not available.

combination therapy (ACT) as the first line of treatment, expanded use of rapid diagnostic tests, and enhanced vector control and prevention through the wide distribution of long-lasting insecticide-treated nets coupled with targeted indoor residual spraying. Coverage with insecticide-treated nets has increased significantly since 2004/05 (figure 24.2). The 2007 Malaria Indicator Survey documents that overall coverage increased by a factor of 15 between 2004/05 and 2009/10, with 68 percent of households in malaria-affected areas protected by at least one net or indoor residual spraying. Use of insecticide-treated nets by children under five and pregnant women increased to nearly 45 percent in malaria-affected areas and to more than 60 percent in households that owned at least one net (FMOH 2007a). A case control study indicates that from roughly similar levels of coverage at baseline, ownership of nets increased more in HEP villages (87 percent) than in control villages (62 percent) during the follow-up period (Center for National Health Development in Ethiopia 2008). With this momentum, reaching universal coverage appears feasible.

Residents in HEP and control villages showed a marked difference in seeking treatment for malaria. In HEP villages, about 53 percent of patients with fever or malaria sought treatment with antimalaria drugs the day of or the day after the onset of symptoms. In control villages, only 20 percent of patients sought treatment under similar conditions. The baseline values were 33 percent and 26 percent.

A report published in 2009 indicates that in-patient malaria cases fell by 73 percent and deaths in children under five fell by 62 percent (Otten and others 2009). Another study reports a 48 percent reduction in morbidity, a 54 percent reduction in admission, and a 55 percent reduction in mortality related to malaria.

In contrast to the progress made fighting malaria, postnatal care and assisted delivery coverage remain low. The recently completed third round of the HEP evaluation shows that less than 10 percent of women in Ethiopia receive postnatal care. Despite some improvements, many of them associated with the increased availability of health extension workers, more than 90 percent of women still give birth at home (Last Ten Kilometer Project 2009). The main underlying factor for the low rate of attended births is the low skill levels of health extension workers in assisting deliveries and to some extent the cultural barriers to delivering at a modern health facility (FMOH 2009). To deal with the problem, in 2009 HEP provided practical training to 5,000 health extension workers on performing clean and safe deliveries.

ELEMENTS OF SUCCESS FOR HEP

Several factors contributed to the success of the HEP. This section examines these factors.

Government leadership and political commitment

Ethiopia's national health policy and strategies clearly indicate that accelerated training of human resources for health and expansion of infrastructure and supplies are the priority vehicles for achieving the health MDGs. The national Health Sector Development Plan is a mechanism for translating Ethiopia's health policy into action. It serves as a guidebook for all stakeholders regarding priorities and operation modalities in the health sector.

Ethiopia's health policy focuses on providing quality promotive, preventive, and basic curative health care services in an accessible and equitable manner to reach all segments of the population, with special attention to mothers and children. The policy emphasizes establishing an effective and responsive health delivery system for rural residents.

The health strategy indicates the need for an adequate number of midwives and other required staff in order to tackle the leading causes of neonatal and maternal mortality. The Health Sector Strategic Plan III (HSDP-III) set a target of training and deploying 30,000 health extension workers at the community level and 5,000 health officers at health

Figure 24.2   Number of Health Extension Workers and Number of Insecticide-Treated Nets Distributed in Ethiopia, 2004/05–2009/10

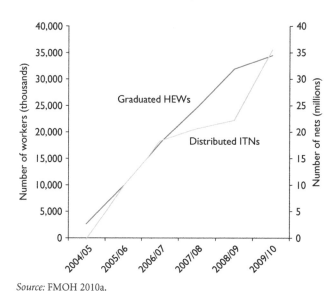

Source: FMOH 2010a.

centers and primary hospitals to address both the preventive and curative aspects of morbidity and mortality.

The HEP features at the top of the agenda of health sector leaders at all levels of the health system and in their discussions with stakeholders. In the bimonthly meeting of the Federal Ministry of Health (FMOH) with development partners—known as the Joint Consultative Forum (JCF) between the Ministry of Health and development partners—issues related to these priority areas are at the top of the agenda. The forum also regularly reviews the status of implementation of priorities and collectively tackles challenges.

The other important governance structure is the bimonthly meeting of the FMOH and the regional health bureaus. The meeting is chaired by the minister of health and includes the heads of the bureaus and the agencies and departments in the Ministry of Health. The main purpose of this steering committee is to align federal and regional stakeholders around priorities, review progress, identify challenges, share best practices, and agree on mitigation measures and actions. The HEP always comes at the top of the agenda of the steering committee. The priorities also appear as key messages in the opening remarks made by leaders and officials from the minister of health to district health officers during health sector–related meetings.

The key principle underpinning the scaling up of the HEP was ensuring ownership by the local community for meaningful and sustainable change. Local governments at the village and district levels, together with community representatives, formed a committee that selects candidate health extension workers for training based on nationally agreed upon criteria. Local communities also contribute to the construction of health posts, by providing construction materials and labor. One of the two health extension workers sits on the village council, which discusses the performance and challenges facing HEP and provides support to mitigate challenges on a regular basis. For the construction of health centers, local governments were given the authority to choose the site of construction so that it is within walking distance to about 25,000 people.

Effective intersectoral collaboration has been demonstrated in the last few years. Scaling up of health extension workers and health officers would not have happened had it not been for the strong collaboration between the Ministry of Health and the Ministry of Education, which provided the technical and vocational educational training (TVET) and resources, including teachers. Strong collaboration with the Ministry of Works and Urban Development (MWUD) and its offices at the subnational level facilitated the construction

of more than 2,500 health centers. MWUD's support in providing contractors, supervision, and quality assurance of construction has been one of the key critical success factors in this area.

The most important success factor has been the increase in expenditure allocated to implement the HEP (figure 24.3). Total per capita health expenditure in Ethiopia was $7.13 per capita in 2005 (FMOH 2005), 28 percent of it borne by the government. The MDG needs assessment conducted in 2004 recommended an additional $3.48 per capita per year on average over the period 2005–15 from all sources, peaking at $4.55 per capita in 2015 just for scaling up the HEP. To meet this guideline, the government committed to at least double its share of health expenditure over the life of HSDP-III (2005–10). By 2008 total health expenditure had reached $16.10 per capita, following an increase in government expenditure to health of 77 percent over three years, indicating that the government is on track to fulfill its commitment over five years (FMOH/Abt 2010).

In addition to increasing expenditure, the federal government negotiated with the regional governments to share the cost of implementing the national health strategy. Roles and responsibilities were clarified and agreed upon by the FMOH and the subnational health authorities (FMOH 2009). Local governments (regions, zones, and districts) took responsibility for covering the full cost of constructing health posts, partially covering the cost of construction of health centers ($230 million), and fully covering the salaries of health extension workers and health officers ($143 million) over five years. The government supports these activities, through a commitment of Br 275 million (about $21 million) a year for the salaries of health extension workers. The agreement defining the roles of different levels of the health system in scaling up health interventions is signed by the minister of health and the heads of the 11 regional

Figure 24.3   Total Health Expenditure in Ethiopia, 1995/96–2007/08

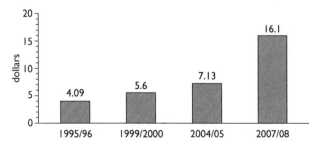

Source: FMOH/Abt Associates 2010.

health bureaus each year at the annual review conference. This system set a model for using development partner funds as a catalytic fund to provide incentives to different levels of health authorities to allocate more resources to agreed-upon priorities in the health sector.

Multifaceted, systemwide approach

A multipronged strategy that would address systemic weaknesses was at the heart of the development of the HEP. Simply increasing the number of health extension workers was not viewed as likely to be effective in isolation. The increase had to be implemented together with improvements in other system requirements.

One important factor in the success of the HEP in rural areas was the strategic commitment of regions and districts to address complementary and supportive factors, including the availability of other health cadres; the availability of health infrastructure (health posts and health centers) together with adequate supplies of equipment and pharmaceuticals; and health information systems. All of these strategic elements have been addressed, with various degrees of success.

INFRASTRUCTURE. One of the components of the sector strategy was the construction and rehabilitation of health facilities. The number of health posts staffed by health extension workers increased from 6,191 in 2004 to 14,192 in 2010 (FMOH 2009) (figure 24.4). Funds were secured from development partners to equip all health posts. As of 2009, health posts were present in 70 percent of the *kebeles* of Ethiopia's four largest regions (Last Ten Kilometer Project 2009).

As of 2007 about 94 percent of villages had health posts built by the local communities or the government (Center for National Health Development in Ethiopia 2007). The majority of these health posts were equipped with basic furniture. However, access to other important services (clean water, electricity, telephone, and means of transportation) was generally low in all regions.

MEDICAL CADRES FOR SUPERVISION, SUPPORT, AND REFERRAL OF HEALTH EXTENSION WORKERS. The training of health extension workers was part of a larger government effort to increase the number, distribution, and performance of health workers. Over the past few years, there has been a significant increase in the intake and output of health training colleges and universities for other categories of health workers (table 24.4). The output of nurses has

Figure 24.4 Cumulative Number of Health Posts Constructed in Ethiopia, EFY 2004–09

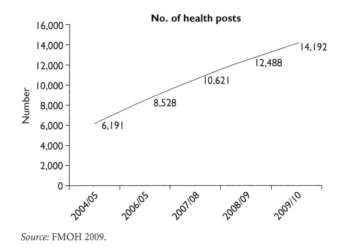

Source: FMOH 2009.

Table 24.4 Ratio of Health Human Resources in Public Sector to People in Ethiopia, 2001/02–2008/09

Category	2001/2002	2004/2005	2008/2009
All physicians	1:35,603	1:35,604	1:34,986
General practitioners	1:54,385	1:58,203	1:76,302
Health officers	1:138,884	1:104,050	1:20,638
Nurses (excluding midwives), BSc and diploma	1:5,613	1:4,980	1:4,895
Midwives (senior)	1:77,981	1:55,782	1:57,354
Health extension workers	n.a.	1:23,775	1:2,437

Source: FMOH.
Note: n.a. = Not applicable.

increased, boosted by the proliferation of private training institutes. The number of universities involved in training of medical doctors also increased, from three to six, over a decade, raising the average annual output of doctors from 90 to 350. One of the most significant achievements of these universities was the production of cadres with intermediate skill mixes adapted to the Ethiopian context.

In 2005 the government began preparing a new midlevel health cadre called health officers. Health officers provide most of the curative care services at the first level of clinical services (health center) level. The program was launched with the financial support of the U.S. Agency for International Development and the technical support of the Carter Center. A network of 5 universities (Jimma, Haramaya, Hawassa, Mekelle, and Gondar) and 21 hospitals in

7 regions was strengthened to provide theoretical and practical training to trainees. The accelerated training of health officers lasts five years, including three years at university and two years in training hospitals. After completion of their training, health officers are supposed to provide support to the HEP by working in health centers with other health team members in providing curative, preventive, promotive, and rehabilitative health care. Their duties include the following:

- Assess community health needs
- Plan, implement, and evaluate activities and resources of the primary health care unit
- Collect, organize, and analyze health and health-related data from health institutions, communities, and other relevant areas and use and disseminate the information to the community and other concerned bodies
- Conduct and provide on-the-job training to the staff of the primary health care unit and to community health workers
- Provide comprehensive outpatient care and in-patient services
- Perform minor surgical procedures
- Refer difficult cases and follow up on return to ensure continuity of care
- Mobilize individuals, families, and communities for health action
- Promote and be engaged in intersectoral activities
- Undertake essential and operational health research
- Document and report all primary health care unit activities
- Oversee the equity and efficiency of health services

Public health officers can go on to become physicians or public health specialists, or they can pursue master's level training on emergency surgery.

The health officers program has more than tripled the uptake and production of health officers training in Ethiopia (see table 24.4). More than 5,500 health officer students have entered the training program. By August 2010, 3,871 (71 percent) of the overall target had graduated.

An independent study of graduating students (Carter Center 2009) reveals the following:

- 90–97 percent feel prepared to diagnose and manage or refer common adulthood infectious diseases and common chronic illnesses.
- 80–90 percent feel prepared to diagnose, manage, or refer surgical emergencies (acute abdominal problems) and

perform minor surgical procedures (wound and trauma management).

- 80–95 percent feel confident to provide antenatal and postnatal care and to diagnose and manage or refer normal labor and common gynecologic problems.
- 55–65 percent feel confident to perform common obstetric and gynecologic procedures, such as manual removal of placenta, instrumental delivery (vacuum), safe abortion, and postabortion care. The low level of confidence is attributable mainly to inadequate on-the-job training caused by a shortage of obstetricians, surgeons, and surgical equipment and supplies.

ACCOUNTABILITY STRUCTURE FOR HEALTH EXTENSION WORKERS. A supportive accountability mechanism was established to support health extension workers. Supervisors were trained and deployed in 3,200 health centers. Each supervisor supports 10 health extension workers in 5 satellite health posts, which together form a primary health care unit. An independent survey indicates that two-thirds of the health posts were supervised during the three months preceding the survey and that 75 percent of these health posts received feedback from supervisors (Carter Center 2009).

ADEQUATE SUPPLIES AND EQUIPMENT. Ensuring continuous logistics supply—equipment, contraceptives, vaccines, insecticide-treated nets, delivery kits, and so forth—is a crucial area of support to health extension workers. At the federal level, FMOH engaged in a continuous dialogue with development partners to improve aid effectiveness by supporting priorities (such as the HEP) and improving harmonization and alignment to reduce transaction costs. Two pooled fund arrangements, Protection of Basic Services and the MDG Performance Fund, were established and made functional at the federal level. The establishment of these funds contributed significantly to financing the procurement of contraceptives, vaccines, insecticide-treated nets, and equipment. In addition, funds from global health initiatives, particularly the Global Fund to Fight AIDS, Tuberculosis and Malaria (GFATM) and the Global Alliance for Vaccines and Immunisation (GAVI), contributed to the financing and procurement of equipment and pharmaceutical supplies as part of their support to health system strengthening.

Ensuring timely and continuous logistic supply requires an efficient procurement and distribution system. Building such a system takes time. Ethiopia had to come up with a quick transitional mechanism while building sustainable capacity of the health sector in supply chain management through the implementation of the logistic master plan. One mechanism it adopted to do so was the use of development partners with comparative advantage in procurement and distribution of commodities to the health posts. FMOH negotiated with UNICEF and the United Nations Population Fund (UNFPA) for the procurement and distribution of vaccines, cold chain equipment, insecticide-treated nets, contraceptives, and health post kits. This partnership provided a remarkable short-term solution to the logistic challenges associated with the HEP.

INFORMATION SYSTEMS. Information systems that facilitate the collection, analysis, use, and dissemination of data were perceived as significantly improving the support provided to the HEP as well as the quality and relevance of the HEP to beneficiary communities. Accordingly, the FMOH designed a robust, simplified, and standardized health management information system contextualized to the Ethiopian setting. Family folders were developed based on the 17 packages of health interventions, and health extension workers and HEP supervisors were trained on the system's application and use. Each household has a family folder that records the status of its members (for family planning, antenatal care, expanded program of immunization, and so forth) and the household in general (ownership and use of a latrine, clean water supply and use, waste disposal, and so forth) in terms of completing the desired changes indicated in the HEP. The Ministry of Health is printing family folders to make sure that all households in Ethiopia have a formal medical record.

Innovative training strategy

Training more than 30,000 health extension workers could not have been done through traditional means. Innovative approaches were applied through the use of existing TVET for theoretical training and health centers for practical training. FMOH provided training materials; regional health bureaus provided the stipend and transportation services for the students.

Health extension workers must complete a 12-month course of theoretical and field training. One-quarter of the period is allocated to theoretical teaching at TVET institutions; three-quarters of the period is spent in a practicum in the community. The average monthly cost of the program per health extension worker was about $234 for training, $178 for apprenticeships, and $83 for salaries.

The TVET institutions are run by the Ministry of Education. The number of institutions involved in the training of health extension workers grew every year, reaching 36 by 2007. The same year, 140 TVET tutors were given trainers instruction in HEP teaching methodology as well as an integrated refresher training course. Appropriate education materials were developed, printed, and distributed to the TVET institutions.

Mobilizing financial support from development partners

The progressive increase in domestic resource allocation to priorities was key to ensuring sustainability. With regard to the HEP, an agreement was reached between FMOH and regional health bureaus under which the ministry mobilizes funds from development partners to provide support to the TVET institutions for printing the HEP training manuals and tools and for procuring and distributing medical equipment, insecticide-treated nets, contraceptives, and other supplies; subnational governments allocate domestic resources for stipends to health extension workers during training, pay their full salary on deployment, and cover the costs of building the health posts.

FMOH mobilized resources from development partners to provide teaching materials, transportation services, and other relevant supplies for the accelerated training of health officers. To put in place 3,200 health centers by the end of 2010, the regional health bureaus agreed that subnational authorities would construct one matching health center for every health center the FMOH constructed using donor funds. As part of this agreement, FMOH covers the required medical equipment while the regional health bureaus cover the cost of furnishing the centers.

Significant support was mobilized from various development partners to support the new initiatives. GFATM and GAVI provided financial support for the construction of 512 health centers and procurement of medical equipment for 7,340 health posts and 300 health centers (table 24.5). Development partners that contributed to the Protection of Basic Services program—the World Bank, the United Kingdom's Department for International Development (DFID)], RNE, Irish Aid, Canadian International Development Association (CIDA) , Italian Cooperation— also provided support for the procurement of medical equipment for 2,295 health centers and 7,000 health posts, contraceptives worth $37 million, essential drugs worth $10 million, and insecticide-treated nets worth $7.9 million. These contributions helped provide the required inputs to maintain HEP basic services.

Table 24.5 Support from Development Partners in Key Areas of Scaling Up of Health Interventions, 2006–2010

Development partner/area	Support (millions of dollars)
Global Alliance for Vaccines and Immunisation (GAVI)	
Health center construction (212)	25.8
Health center equipment (300)	6.8
Health post equipment (7,340)	20
Subtotal	52.6
Global Find to Fight AIDS, Tuberculosis and Malaria (GFATM)	
Health center construction (300)	55.4
Protection of Basic Services I and II (World Bank, DFID, RNE, Irish Aid, Canadian CIDA, Italian Cooperation)	
Health center equipment (1,999)	31.2
Health post equipment (7,000)	5.6
Contraceptives	43.6
Insecticide-treated nets	31.6
Vaccines and cold chain equipment	9.8
Artemisinin-based combination therapy (ACT)	2.4
Essential drugs	18.5
Subtotal	142.7
MDG Performance Fund	
Health center construction	15
Health management Information system printing	6.5
Contraceptives	3.1
Vaccines	5
Advocacy and training	2.3
Insecticide-treated nets	4.8
Subtotal	36.7
USAID	
Accelerated training of health officer (5 universities and 21 teaching hospitals)	11.8
Total	287.4

Source: Authors' compilation, based on data from FMOH and Financial Resource Mobilization Directorate.

In addition to their own financial support, UNICEF and UNFPA helped in the bulk procurement and distribution of health commodities to the service delivery points by using the funds provided by the Global Fund, GAVI, the World Bank protection of basic services (PBS), and the MDG Performance Fund. UNICEF provided support in procuring and distributing insecticide-treated nets, vaccines, and health post kits to health facilities. UNFPA supported the government by procuring and distributing contraceptives.

LESSONS LEARNED

The HEP has been successful largely because of the strong political commitment to strengthening health systems, with the ultimate goal of improving coverage of and access to health services by the rural poor. Investment in health extension workers has been part of a wider package of support services that is showing promising results.

Some weaknesses remain, and not all regions show a similar level of success. Incentive packages for health human resources are lacking, and the link between compensation and performance is weak. The capacity of the district health offices to provide supervision, monitoring, and evaluation is low. These and other constraints need to be addressed if gaps in coverage are to be filled and access scaled up even further.

A number of lessons can be drawn from the implementation of the HEP, which can be replicated in other countries:

First, political leadership and champions at higher levels are a critical success factor in improving health outcomes. Adoption of the HEP as a major political agenda of the government at various levels of the health system tightened the focus and galvanized the involvement of various stakeholders. Beyond the general increase in its fiscal space to finance the HEP, the government made sure that such increments happened at local levels. Accordingly, salaries of health extension workers, construction of health posts, and the basic running cost of the HEP are financed mainly by subnational health authorities (regions, districts, and zones), creating the foundation for local ownership and sustainability of the program.

Second, delivery of services and management of programs should be integrated into existing systems. Vertical programs and projects can be successful in the short term, but they are often unsustainable. What HEP has demonstrated is that vertically mobilized resources can be used for systemwide interventions that make disease-specific programs successful while strengthening health systems. Adopting this approach avoids creating parallel systems and procedures in the delivery of services and management of programs, averting unnecessary administrative burdens, transaction costs, and inefficiencies.

Third, community ownership is a key to sustainable impact. The major principle underpinning the HEP is transferring the right knowledge and skills to communities and households so that they are able to adopt behaviors that improve their own health. Households are trained and certified, after which they take responsibility for promoting behaviors that lead to positive health outcomes.

Fourth, all components of the health system need to be addressed to make a program work. The HEP does not merely train and deploy health extension workers. Significant investment is made in setting up and equipping health posts to serve as formal institutional hubs for the program. A health information system has been adapted, and HEP supervisors have been trained and deployed to enhance supportive supervision and continuous improvement in quality of program management and service delivery. Continuous assessment and in-service training have been conducted to fill the gap in capacity of health extension workers. Referral levels (to health centers, health officers, and so forth) have been expanded to ensure delivery of a complete package of essential services. A major shift in the amount and modality of financing of the sector has been undertaken to support the key components of the program.

Fifth, buy-in and involvement of key stakeholders is crucial. A unique model for partnership and collaboration has evolved in Ethiopia between the government and various actors in the health system, including the community, development partners, and other sectors. The growing trust among these stakeholders has resulted in harmonization of financing, program implementation, monitoring, and evaluation, leading to further strengthening of health systems.

Sixth, a program needs to be flexible and adaptable to various contexts. The HEP has been implemented in settings with significant diversity in socioeconomic, cultural, and geographic conditions without compromising the basic principles that led to its success. Ethiopia designed three versions of the HEP (agrarian, urban, and pastoralist) to modify and fit key aspects of program implementation in these widely varying contexts. This flexible nature of the program provides key lessons that are unique to the different environments, facilitating replication in other countries.

Seventh, success of a program or an intervention should be assessed by concrete and measurable improvements in health outcomes. Implementation of HEP has shown encouraging results in a short time in increasing coverage of essential interventions and reducing morbidity and mortality related to communicable health diseases.

NOTE

1. Certain criteria were applied to identify an intervention as successful. An intervention is considered successful if it addresses diseases of public health importance; is owned and financed by the government (to ensure sustainability); fits into the country's conventional health system without creating parallel structures and systems; is flexible enough to be applied in different socioeconomic, cultural, and geographic settings; is embraced and supported by development partners, nongovernmental organizations, and other stakeholders; is delivered at low cost; and shows concrete results in terms of improving health outcomes.

BIBLIOGRAPHY

Admassiea, A., D. Abebawa, and A. Woldemichael. 2009. "Impact Evaluation of the Ethiopian Health Services Extension Program." *Journal of Development Effectiveness* 1 (4): 430–49.

Assefa, A., Alebachew, H. Fassil, N. Haniko, M. Ihalainen, A. Zwandor, and B. Kinfegebriel. 2010. "HIV/AIDS and the Health-Related Millennium Development Goals. The Experience in Ethiopia." *Lancet.*

Carter Center. 2009. *Evaluation of the Quality of Training of Health Officers and Quality and Utilization of Health Learning Materials.* Report of an Independent Assessment. Addis Ababa.

Center for National Health Development in Ethiopia. 2008. *Ethiopia Health Extension Program Evaluation Study, 2005–2007,* vol. I. *Household Health Survey.* Addis Ababa.

Center for National Health Services, 2007. *Functioning of Health Posts.* Addis Ababa.

CSA (Central Statistical Authority), and MACRO International. Ethiopia *Demographic and Health Survey, 2005.* Addis Ababa.

FMOH (Federal Ministry of Health). 2005. *Third National Health Account Report.* Addis Ababa.

———. 2007a. Ethiopian National Malaria Indicator Survey. Addis Ababa

———. 2007b. Health Extension Program in Ethiopia Profile. Addis Ababa.

———. 2009. *Report of the Joint Review Mission of HSDP III.* Addis Ababa.

———. 2010a. *Annual Performance Report of HSDP.* Addis Ababa.

———. 2010b. *Ethiopian National Malaria Indicator Survey.* Addis Ababa.

FMOH (Federal Ministry of Health), and Abt Associates. 2010. *Fourth National Health Account Report.* Addis Ababa.

Ghebreyesus, A. T. 2010. "Achieving the Health MDGs: Country Ownership in Four Steps." *Lancet* 376 (9747): 1127–28. http://www.lancet.com/journals/lancet/article/PIIS0140-6736(10)61465-1/fulltext?_eventId=login.

Last Ten Kilometers Project. 2009. *Baseline Household Health Survey: Amhara, Oromiya, SNNP and Tigray.* JSI Research & Training, Inc., Addis Ababa.

Otten, Mac, Maru Aregawi, Wilson Were, Corine Karema, Ambachew Medin, Worku Bekele, Daddi Jima, Khoti Gausi, Ryuichi Komatsu, Eline Korenromp, Daniel Low-Beer, and Mark Grabowsky. 2009. "Initial Evidence of Reduction of Malaria Cases and Deaths in Rwanda and Ethiopia Due to Rapid Scale-Up of Malaria Prevention and Treatment." *Malaria Journal* 8 (14).

Family Planning Trends in Sub-Saharan Africa: Progress, Prospects, and Lessons Learned

Mona Sharan, Saifuddin Ahmed, John May, and Agnes Soucat

Sub-Saharan Africa has the highest average fertility rate in the world. In 2009 the total fertility rate (TFR), or the average number of births per woman, was 5.1—more than twice that in South Asia (2.8) or Latin America and the Caribbean (2.2) (World Bank 2009). The average contraceptive prevalence rate (22 percent) is less than half that of South Asia (53 percent) and less than a third that of East Asia (77 percent) (World Bank 2009). Population in the region continues to grow at a faster rate (2.3 percent) than in other regions, including both Asia and Latin America (1.1 percent each) (UN DESA 2008).

These dismal indicators at the aggregate level conceal ongoing and imminent fertility transitions that are taking place at the country level. Contrary to the popular perception, there is evidence of progress in fertility decline in many countries across Africa (Cohen 1998). Emerging research shows that fertility transition has already begun in Sub-Saharan Africa and that some countries are undergoing dynamic and unprecedented changes in fertility patterns.

Acceptance of family planning in the region has traditionally been low and cultural resistance to family planning high (Caldwell and Caldwell 1987). Nevertheless, over the past two decades, contraceptive use increased in several countries. Its impact, along with that of changes in other determinants of fertility, is leading the onset of fertility decline in the region.

This chapter examines contraceptive use and fertility trends in Sub-Saharan African countries between 1986 and 2009. It is based on an analysis of household survey data from Demographic and Health Surveys in 45 countries (all countries with more than one survey during the reference period were included). Data from the World Bank's *World Development Indicators* and the United Nations were also used for additional analyses. The chapter discusses the impact of micro and macro level factors, that have contributed to changes in the dynamics of contraceptive use and fertility decline. It highlights national policies, institutional frameworks, and service delivery strategies in selected countries in which the greatest progress has been made.

TRENDS IN CONTRACEPTIVE USE

Contraceptive use indicators—including the contraceptive prevalence rate (CPR), method mix, and unmet need—are showing encouraging progress in some countries of the region. Such changes are often precursors of fertility decline.

Changes in the contraceptive prevalence rate

The modern contraceptive prevalence rate—the proportion of women of reproductive age who are using a modern contraceptive method—varies widely across the region. Among women of reproductive age, CPRs for modern methods ranged from 1.2 percent in Somalia to 60.3 percent in South Africa (figure 25.1). Geographic variations in family planning use were apparent in the findings, with countries in Southern Africa reporting the highest levels of contraceptive

Figure 25.1 Modern Contraceptive Prevalence Rates in Sub-Saharan Africa, by Country

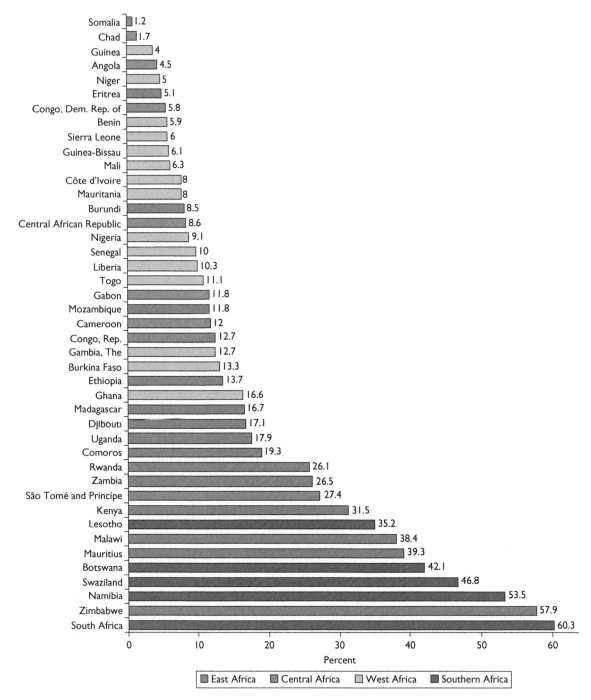

Source: United Nations Population Division 2009.

use, followed by countries in East Africa. With a few exceptions, West and Central African countries report very low rates of family planning use. Some of the lowest contraceptive prevalence rates in the world exist in these two subregions of Africa.

Levels of fertility were high throughout Sub-Saharan Africa during the 1970s. Some indication of fertility transition began to emerge in the 1980s in some parts of Africa. Evidence was accumulating that fertility was falling or expected to fall and contraceptive prevalence was high in

CHAPTER 25: FAMILY PLANNING TRENDS IN SUB-SAHARAN AFRICA: PROGRESS, PROSPECTS, AND LESSONS LEARNED

Southern Africa, at least in comparison with the levels for Africa as a whole in the 1970s (Lucas 1992). Parts of East Africa were also showing signs of change. Surveys carried out in the mid-1980s reported pockets of high contraceptive prevalence in Botswana, Kenya, and Zimbabwe and an increasing desire among more than one-third of women in these countries to stop childbearing—a proportion that was above the 10 percent average for the region (Way, Cross, and Kumar 1987).

More recent data corroborate the onset of fertility decline in parts of the region. Wide variation in contraceptive prevalence persists across countries, suggesting that country-level contexts and policies may underlie these differentials.

Although overall progress is only modest, the experience of a few countries in increasing contraceptive prevalence stands out. An analysis of fertility trends in 23 countries of Sub-Saharan Africa from 1980 to 1995 showed evidence of fertility decline in two-thirds of the countries, with a particularly rapid decline in Kenya and Zimbabwe (Kirk and Pillet 1998).

Trend data on modern CPR over the past 20 years show that some countries have made remarkable progress (figure 25.2). Countries such as Namibia and Zimbabwe started out with high levels of contraceptive prevalence in the 1990s and saw their rates climb steeply over the next two decades. Other countries, such as Malawi, Madagascar, and Mozambique, began with relatively lower CPRs in the early 1990s, but these rates sharply increased in the following years. Progress was apparent not only in Southern Africa but also in countries in East Africa, where increases in Zambia, Uganda, and Tanzania were particularly noteworthy.

CPRs between the first and the most recent Demographic and Health Survey during the study period were compared to examine the rate of change over time. The findings reveal that some countries experienced dramatic increases in contraceptive prevalence within relatively short periods of time. The increases in CPR in Namibia, Tanzania, Zambia, and Zimbabwe were particularly rapid. Mozambique experienced the steepest increase in modern CPR within the shortest time frame in the region: between 1997 and 2003 its CPR increased more than fourfold, from 5.6 to 25.5 percent. Although other countries reported larger increases, changes there occurred over longer time periods. Data show that between the first and the most recent Demographic and Health Survey, all countries reported increases in CPR. Malawi, Mozambique, Namibia, Zambia, and Zimbabwe made the greatest progress.

Analysis comparing African countries with countries in other regions shows that the rate of percentage change in CPRs in Malawi, Mozambique, Namibia, and Zambia was far greater than in many South Asian, East Asian, and Latin American countries. Although fertility transition began late in Africa, the increase in CPR occurred from a very low base, thus there was scope for a greater magnitude of change relative to countries in other regions that had already attained high levels of coverage (figure 25.3).

Changes in the choice of contraceptive method

An indicator of progress in family planning adoption is the change in the type of contraceptive methods used by family planning acceptors. The use of traditional methods tends to be higher in settings where acceptance of family planning is low and use of family planning programs is weak. Traditional methods have a high failure rate compared with modern methods and are therefore not considered an effective mode of contraception.

Trends in contraceptive choice show that in many countries of the region, use of traditional methods has declined and use of modern methods increased (figure 25.4). The use of modern methods has increased most markedly in countries that had the greatest increases in CPR (Madagascar, Malawi, Namibia, Zambia, and Zimbabwe). Use of traditional methods in these countries has either remained stagnant or has decreased. Ghana, Kenya, Tanzania, and Uganda showed increases in use of modern methods while maintaining use of traditional methods. In West African countries such as Benin, Burkina Faso, Cameroon, Senegal, and Togo, traditional method use declined and relatively modest gains in modern method use were observed.

Family planning programs that have been successful in Africa have promoted birth spacing. Marriage patterns in Africa differ from those in Asia, possibly accounting for a cultural preference for spacing methods. Various studies in the region document African cultural preferences for spacing rather than limiting births (Cohen 1998). In contrast to Asian family planning programs, which have emphasized permanent contraceptive methods, such as sterilization and abortion, programs in Africa rely on temporary methods, such as pills, injectables, and implants (Caldwell and Caldwell 1988). It has been suggested that successful program strategies in Africa must promote methods that are temporary, can be used covertly by women, and do not have to be stored at home (Caldwell and Caldwell 2002).

Figure 25.2   Trends in Modern Contraceptive Prevalence Rates in Selected Countries in Sub-Saharan Africa

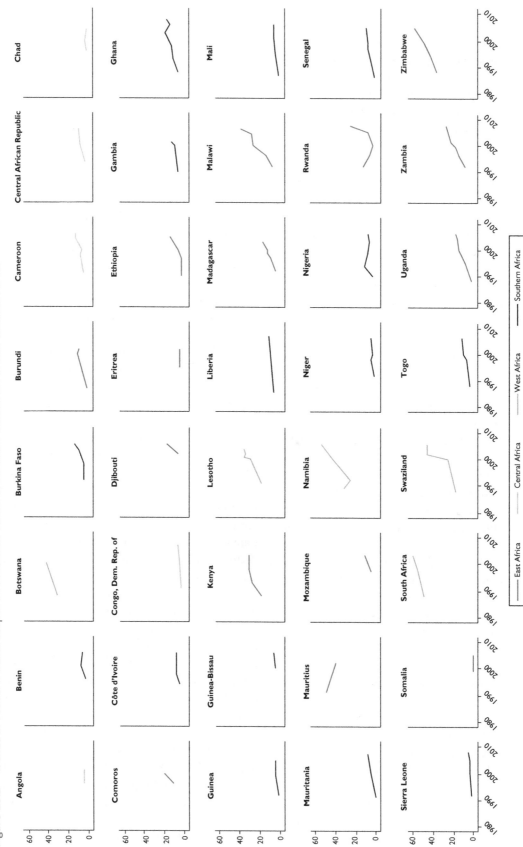

Source: Demographic and Health Surveys, various years.

Figure 25.3   Annual Rate of Change in Modern Contraceptive Use in Selected Countries between First and Last Rounds of Demographic and Health Surveys

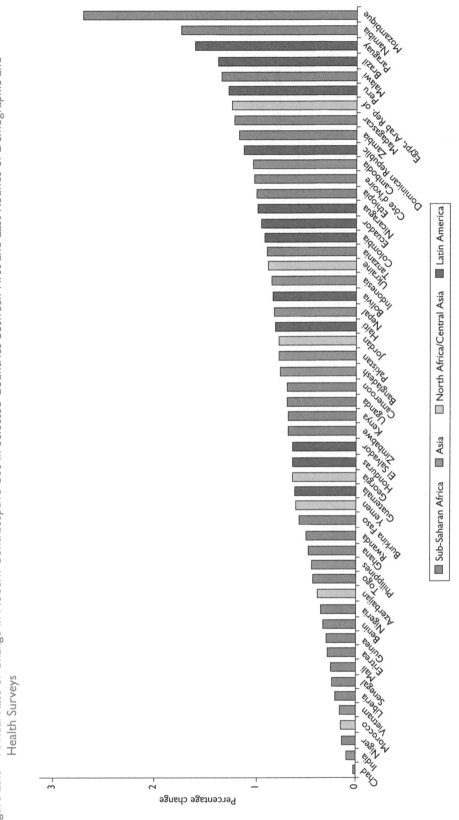

Source: Demographic and Health Surveys, various years.

Figure 25.4 Trends in Modern and Traditional Contraceptive Prevalence Rates in Selected Countries in Sub-Saharan Africa

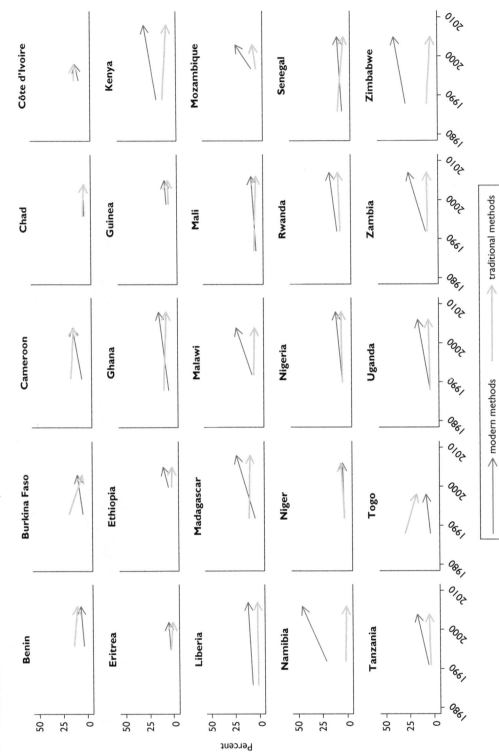

Source: Demographic and Health Surveys, various years.

The use of family planning methods depends not just on users' preferences but also on health system characteristics. Strong family planning programs rely on effective family planning service delivery strategies, such as those that offer methods tailored to the needs of users, provide family planning counseling and medical expertise for administering methods, and follow up on users' response to the method. Countries in the region with frail health systems are faced with the challenge of improving contraceptive method choice within existing constraints. There is growing evidence that new methods such as injectables are being readily accepted by women in the region; these methods accounted for 62 percent of modern contraceptive users in Malawi and 66 percent in Ethiopia (National Statistical Office Malawi and ORC Macro 2005; Central Statistical Agency and ORC Macro 2006).

Changes in unmet need and satisfied demand

Unmet need measures the gap between demand for family planning and use of contraception. Expressed as the percentage of sexually active women who do not want additional children but are not using any family planning method, this measure is often considered a precursor of fertility decline, because it indicates that demand for family planning services exists but is not being met.

Changes in unmet need can be influenced by a variety of factors related to fertility preferences or family planning acceptance, which may or may not be related to the effectiveness of family planning programs. Nevertheless, when examined in relation to contraceptive prevalence, these changes provide an estimate of the gap between demand and utilization of family planning.

Trends in modern CPR and unmet need indicate that in countries such as Kenya, Madagascar, Malawi, and Zambia, decline in unmet need has corresponded with an increase in family planning (figure 25.5) suggesting a convergence of demand and supply of family planning. In contrast, in other countries, such as Eritrea, Ghana, Mali, and Senegal, the gap has remained wide and consistent.

Satisfied demand for contraception is defined as the percentage of sexually active women who do not want additional children and are practicing family planning. Increases in satisfied demand corresponded with a decrease in the unmet need for family planning in certain countries in the region. The percentage change in satisfied demand increased most in countries such as Madagascar, Mozambique, Tanzania, and Zambia where contraception prevalence rates are increasing (figure 25.6).

TRENDS IN TOTAL FERTILITY RATES

Another set of analyses examined trends in total fertility rates, or the average number of children per woman. In most countries the TFR declined over time; in some countries it remained stagnant (figure 25.7). The steepest declines in average fertility were observed in Ghana, Kenya, Liberia, Namibia, and Zimbabwe. Other countries, such as Madagascar, Senegal, and Togo, also showed promising declines. The TFR increased or remained constant in a few countries, including Mozambique, Niger, and Nigeria.

Despite increases in contraceptive prevalence in many countries, fertility decline has been slow. As there tends to be a time lag between changes in contraceptive use behavior and a corresponding decline in average fertility, it is likely that subsequent rounds of surveys will show greater fertility declines in countries in which CPRs have risen. Fertility decline also tends to be correlated with demographic and socioeconomic factors, such as the level of urbanization, women's education, women's labor force participation, and economic growth. Studies in Africa have shown that differentials in fertility trends across countries are associated with women's education, child survival (Kirk and Pillet 1998), and exposure to modern roles and behaviors linked with growing urbanization (Garenne and Joseph 2002).

Trends in actual and wanted TFR were examined in each of the countries for which data were available. Actual TFR exceeded wanted TFR in all countries (figure 25.8), indicating that women were not able to regulate their fertility preferences. In countries such as Uganda, that have high unmet need, the gap between the actual and wanted TFR widened, suggesting a growing demand for small family size and the failure of family planning programs to meet the latent demand for services. Countries, such as Kenya and Zimbabwe, that have had strong family planning programs and have improved contraceptive prevalence showed a narrowing of the gap between desired and actual fertility.

Some countries that made progress in the 1990s started to falter at the beginning of the 2000s. Stagnation on contraceptive prevalence and total fertility rate, was evident (see figures 25.2, 25.7). Uganda, Tanzania, Malawi, Kenya, and Ghana underwent large increases in contraceptive prevalence in the 1990s but stagnated after 2000. Stagnation in satisfied demand was evident in Kenya, Malawi, Tanzania, and Zambia. Total fertility rates also stagnated in the 2000s, especially in Cameroon, Ghana, Kenya, and Zimbabwe. In some countries, such as Rwanda, Tanzania and Uganda, the gap between actual and wanted fertility widened after 2000, a

Figure 25.5 Unmet Contraceptive Need and Modern Contraceptive Prevalence Rate in Selected Countries in Sub-Saharan Africa

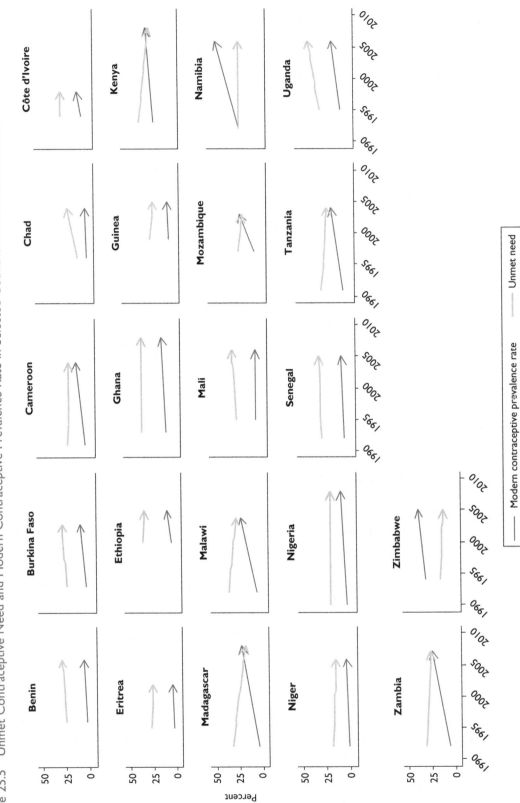

Source: Demographic and Health Surveys, various years.

Figure 25.6 Satisfied Demand for Contraception in Selected Countries in Sub-Saharan Africa

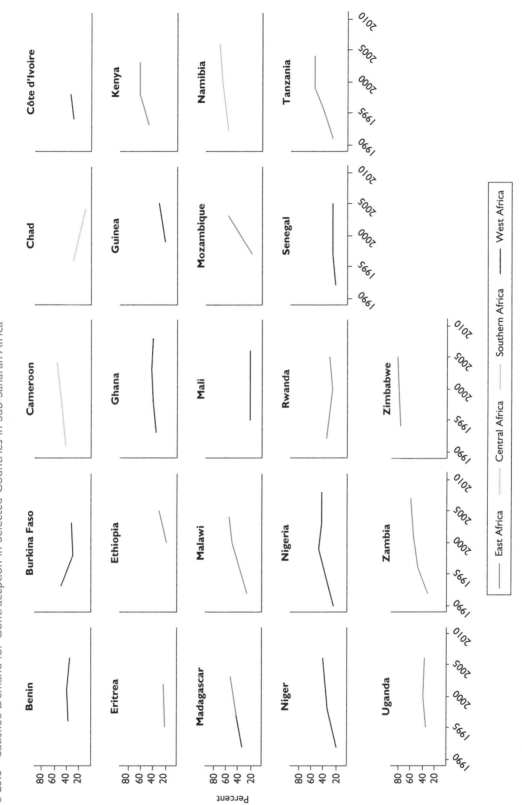

Source: Demographic and Health Surveys, various years.

Figure 25.7 Total Fertility Rates in Selected Countries in Sub-Saharan Africa

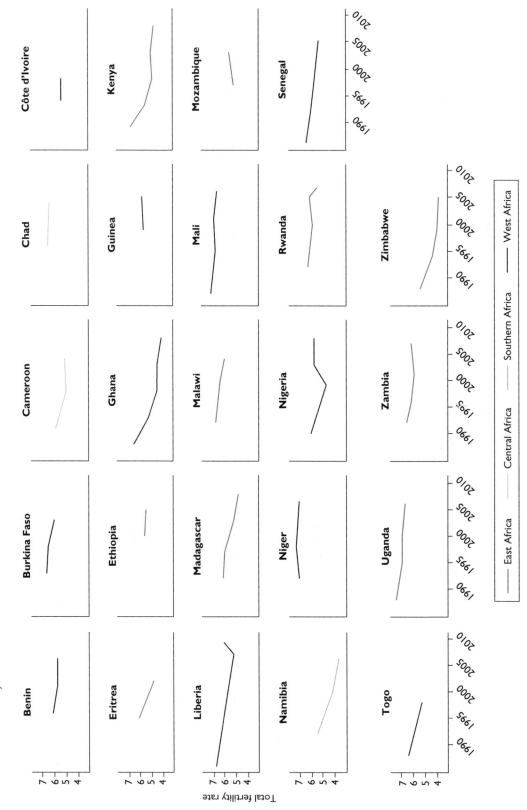

Source: Demographic and Health Surveys, various years.

Figure 25.8 Actual and Wanted Total Fertility Rates in Selected Countries in Sub-Saharan Africa

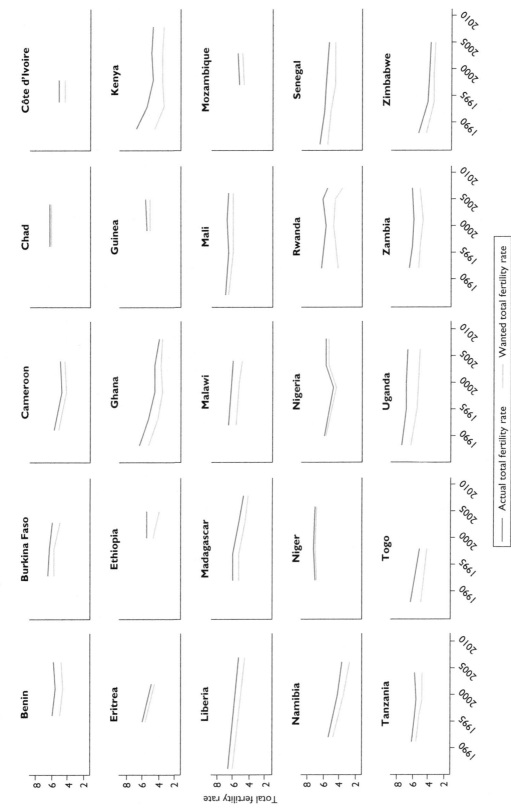
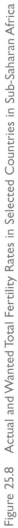

Actual total fertility rate   Wanted total fertility rate

Source: Demographic and Health Surveys, various years.

probable consequence of the weakening of the family planning program or a shift in desired family size (figure 23.8).

Although conclusive evidence on the reasons for the stagnation remains elusive, some explanations include changes in the international policy arena and contextual changes at the country level. A key policy factor is purported to be the reduced priority of reproductive health and family planning after its exclusion from the Millennium Development Goals as well as competition for resources from diseases such as tuberculosis, malaria, and HIV (Gillespie 2004). Country-level studies (for example, in Kenya) attribute the faltering of the fertility decline to dwindling donor support for family planning and a greater emphasis on HIV/AIDS and other sexually transmitted diseases (Blacker and others 2005). A regional study on the stagnation of fertility decline in Eastern Africa concludes that changes in socioeconomic variables, the family planning program environment, and reproductive behavior models are associated with the decline in contraceptive use and increases in unmet need, preferences for larger families, and adolescent fertility (Ezeh, Mberu, and Emina 2009).

The HIV/AIDS epidemic has also impacted fertility levels in Sub-Saharan Africa. The region has the highest prevalence of HIV/AIDS and the largest number of people living with HIV/AIDS in the world. Stagnation in fertility decline over the past 10 years has been related to the increase in HIV prevalence. In Zimbabwe, for example, estimated total fertility was 8.5 percent lower than it would have been in the absence of HIV, and HIV-associated changes in fertility behavior accounted for one-quarter of the drop in fertility since the 1980s (Terceira, Simon, and Gregson 2003). In South Africa, where the prevalence of HIV is among the highest in the region, the spread of HIV is expected to accelerate fertility decline (Moultrie and Timaeus 2003).

DETERMINANTS OF FERTILITY DECLINE

Fertility patterns tend to be influenced by proximate and socioeconomic determinants of fertility. Findings indicate that changes on both fronts are taking place in Africa.

The proximate determinants of fertility are the biological and behavioral factors through which socioeconomic and environmental variables operate to influence the rate of childbearing in a population (Bongaarts 1987). These determinants have been classified into two broad categories: fertility-enhancing trends (shortening of breast-feeding periods and postpartum abstinence, decline in pathological sterility) and fertility-reducing trends (rise in age at first union, higher prevalence and effectiveness of contracep-

tion) (Bongaarts, Frank, and Lesthaeghe 1984). In countries in which fertility reduction is most pronounced, there is evidence that fertility-reducing variables such as age of marriage have risen (Cohen 1998). However, comparison of the proximate determinants of fertility in countries in which the fertility transition is more advanced and those in which it is delayed indicates that contraceptive use is by far the most important factor accounting for intercountry differences (Kirk and Pillet 1998).

Increases in induced abortion—suspected to be a major method of contraception in urban areas of Africa—are associated with recent declines in fertility (Garenne and Joseph 2002). Abortion is the most likely explanation for the drop in fertility, from 6.9 in 1980 to 5.5 in 2010, in Western Africa, where contraceptive use remains very low (Cleland, Ndugwa, and Zulu 2011). An estimated 14 million unintended pregnancies occur in Sub-Saharan Africa every year (Hubacher, Mavranezouli, and McGinn 2008). Consequently, the demand for medical abortion is expected to be very high. Because abortion remains illegal in all but a few countries in the region, women have to seek unsafe abortions from illegal practitioners. It is estimated that more than 4 million unsafe abortions are performed in Africa every year (Brookman-Amissah and Moyo 2004). Abortion is a major risk factor underlying the high levels of maternal mortality in Africa.

The main socioeconomic determinants of fertility include socioeconomic status, women's education, and urban residence. The negative association between women's education and fertility level observed in other settings is apparent in Africa as well (figure 25.9). Analysis of the relationship between economic growth and fertility indicates that increases in GDP are associated with higher rates of contraceptive prevalence (figure 25.10). The direction and pathways of causality between fertility and economic growth remain debatable. In general, socioeconomic change is believed to modify the incentives to have children, diffuse new ideas about childbearing through society, and provide women with better access to contraceptive methods (Bryant 2007). Emerging economic growth prospects in the region indicate potential for future fertility decline.

Other covariates of fertility, such as infant mortality rates, have declined in the region. A plot of the relationship between contraceptive prevalence rates and infant mortality rates indicates the negative correlation between the two variables (figure 25.11). Fertility decline in countries such as Botswana, Kenya, and Zimbabwe, which had lower levels of infant mortality than other countries in the region, provides evidence that improved rates of child

Figure 25.9 Relationship between Women's Secondary Education and Contraceptive Prevalence Rates in Sub-Saharan Africa

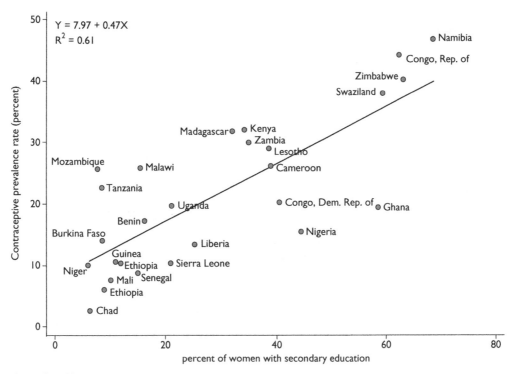

Source: Demographic and Health Surveys, 2000–08.

Figure 25.10   Relationship between Annual Percentage Change in GDP and Contraceptive Prevalence Rate in Sub-Saharan Africa, 1990–2009

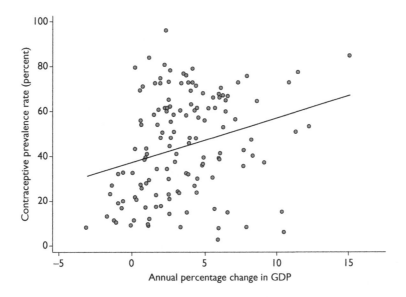

Source: World Bank 2009.

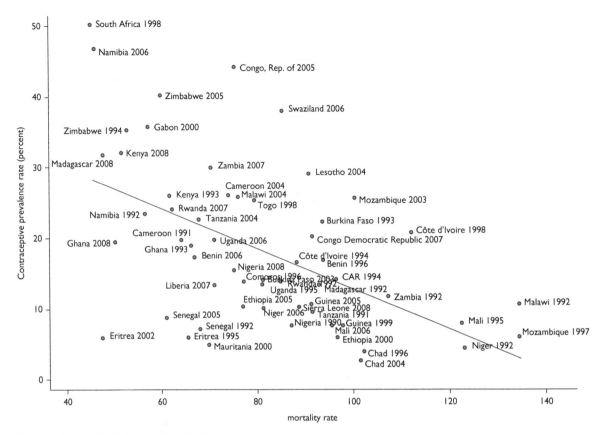

Source: Demographic and Health Surveys, 1986–2009.

survival may be a necessary condition for fertility decline in Africa (Caldwell, Orubuloye, and Caldwell 1992).

FAMILY PLANNING POLICIES AND PROGRAMS

Some studies have tried to identify reasons why certain countries in the region underwent fertility decline whereas others did not. One study compares Kenya, where total fertility fell about 40 percent between 1980 and 2000, with neighboring Uganda, where fertility declined by 10 percent. It finds that both economic development and a strong national family planning program were associated with lower fertility in Kenya (Blacker and others 2005) (box 25.1).

A comparative analysis of Zimbabwe, where the fertility rate fell more rapidly than in Zambia, reveals that a strong family planning program in Zimbabwe backed by high-level political commitment and institutional and financial stability were key ingredients of success (Lee et al. 1998) (box 25.2). Emerging evidence from Rwanda suggests that

major strides in improving family planning uptake can be made if political commitment exists (box 25.3).

Some observers have argued that high rates of fertility in the region can be linked with the lack of policy level commitment for family planning programs. During the 1960s and 1970s, African governments were reluctant to institute effective family planning programs; political support for family planning in the public sector was weak throughout the continent. Since the 1974 and 1984 World Population Conferences, however, governments in several African countries have acknowledged high levels of fertility and initiated family planning programs (Kalipeni 1995). Africa has lagged other regions on fertility decline because family planning programs were introduced relatively late in the region. Family planning programs in Africa are not as strong or as old as those in other parts of the world, but as the experience of many African countries reveals, if strong and high-quality family planning programs are developed, people will use them and fertility will decline (Mbacke 1994). Relatively better progress on

Box 25.1   Kenya Case Study

Kenya was the first country in Sub-Saharan Africa to adopt a population policy, with the launch of a national family planning program in 1967. Initially, the promotion of the program was halfhearted and ineffective: fertility appeared to be rising rather than falling. In the 1980s, however, the government rapidly expanded the number of outlets from which contraceptives could be obtained and the number of health workers trained in family planning. By the end of the century, more than half of the country's 3,500 (governmental and nongovernmental) health facilities were offering maternal and child health and family planning services.

In 1996, the National Council for Population and Development published its *National Population Advocacy and IEC Strategy for Sustainable Development, 1996–2010*, which aimed to promote the use of modern contraceptive methods among less educated women (Blacker and others 2005). Modern methods of contraception have been available in Kenya since 1957 through the facilities of the Ministry of Health and the private sector, including nongovernmental organizations. Community-based distribution and

social marketing of contraceptives have been effective in increasing coverage.

The combined program efforts of public and private agencies facilitated Kenya's transformation from the country with the highest fertility level in the world in the late 1970s to one in which significant fertility decline has been achieved. The rate of contraceptive use among married women increased from 17 percent in 1984 to 39 percent in 1998, one of the highest rates in Sub-Saharan Africa (Magadi and Curtis 2003). The main driving force behind the success was the government's effort in increasing the number of family planning service delivery points and an intensified and focused information, education and communication strategy (Aloo-Obunga 2003). The leveling off in the fertility decline after 2000 may have been caused by problems in the supply of contraceptives, weaknesses in the quality of care, and changes in the contraceptive method mix (Pathfinder International 2005). Another factor may have been the HIV/AIDS program, which gradually pushed family planning off the agenda as it became a priority for funding and strategic programming considerations (Aloo-Obunga 2003; Pathfinder International 2005).

Source: Authors.

---

family planning indicators in Eastern Africa compared to Western Africa has been attributed to stronger family planning efforts that ensured wider availability of modern contraceptive methods (Cleland, Ndugwa, and Zulu 2011).

Although family planning programs in the region have been weak overall, some encouraging progress in program implementation began to emerge in the 1980s. A study of family planning program effort finds that the greatest improvement among all regions of the world between 1982 and 1989 occurred in Sub-Saharan Africa, where there was a sharp increase in family planning program effort indicators, albeit from a low base (Mauldin and Ross 1991). Policy-level support in countries in which strong commitments existed translated into successful national family planning programs.

Certain family planning program management strategies have been found to be particularly effective in the region. Countries such as Kenya and Zimbabwe had strong family planning associations that spearheaded policy changes and program implementation. A unified institutional structure responsible for program implementation was found to be effective in Zimbabwe. In Zambia the

separation of institutions responsible for policy formulation and implementation resulted in a weaker family planning program (Lee and others 1998).

A few countries have tried community-based distribution of contraceptives to extend family planning to hard-to-reach populations, particularly in rural areas. Community depots, mobile clinics, women's groups, and both paid and volunteer village health workers are some modes of service delivery used by such programs. Countries such as Ghana, Kenya, Nigeria, and Zimbabwe have implemented large community-based distribution programs at the national level. Although conclusive evidence on the effectiveness of such programs is not available, these programs provide good examples of successful bottom-up approaches that have been applied in the region (Phillips, Greene, and Jackson 1999).

LESSONS LEARNED

Notwithstanding the high levels of aggregate fertility in Sub-Saharan Africa, some countries in the region have made significant progress on fertility decline. Ongoing

Box 25.2   Zimbabwe Case Study

After independence, in 1980, the government of Zimbabwe reformed and expanded the family planning program with great success. The family planning program was spearheaded by the Zimbabwe National Family Planning Council, a body created in the early 1980s and backed by high-level leadership from Sally Mugabe, the president's wife, and Ester Boohene, his sister-in-law. The Zimbabwe National Family Planning Council built consensus for family planning among opinion leaders including religious groups, the business community, mass media, nongovernmental organizations, and civil servants (Lee, and others 1998).

Initially, Zimbabwe's family planning program was clinic-based. A community-based distribution system was launched in 1983 and it was considered among the most successful programs of its type in the region (Way, Cross, and Kumar 1987). Distributors were selected by the communities they served and paid government salaries and benefits. They were responsible for making household visits to deliver modern contraceptives, recruit new acceptors, follow up on dropouts, and make referrals where necessary (Phillips, Greene, and Jackson 1999). Mobile clinics covered about 29 percent of the rural population (Koblinksy 2003). Groups of men and women were recruited to motivate and educate people in communities about family planning. Other innovative approaches included the mobilization of farmers' wives to provide contraceptives to workers on their farms and the launching

of a large national information, education, communication campaign that promoted family planning with messages targeting men. The number of service delivery points was increased, particularly in rural areas; the number of family planning personnel more than doubled in some units; and the government made health care free to lower-income groups, thereby removing a major barrier to contraceptive use (Zinaga 1992).

The availability and quality of family planning and health services in the community was a key determinant of higher rates of adoption of modern contraceptives (Thomas and Muvandi 1994). The impact of community-based distributors was associated with increased adoption of modern methods. Mobile family planning clinics had a powerful impact on adoption, as did the presence of a general hospital in the area. These two investments in infrastructure had an above-average impact on women with little education. The program also provided a range of contraceptive methods, including Norplant, the female condom, and emergency contraception (Koblinksy 2003). Family planning was positioned as an integral part of the maternal and child health program. The primary health care strategy adopted by the government included both maternal and child health and family planning. All service delivery units were instructed to provide family planning as an integral part of their maternal and child health services (Zinaga 1992).

Source: Authors.

transformations in contraceptive use and fertility behavior signal the onset of fertility declines in more countries in the years to come. Despite tumultuous political situations several success stories in family planning policy formulation and program implementation have emerged. Lessons drawn from countries that have made progress attest to the importance of political commitment, institutional arrangements, and service delivery strategies in increasing the use of family planning methods and lowering fertility.

Many countries that were successful in reducing fertility adopted population policies and instituted family planning programs relatively early. Programs in Botswana, South Africa, and Zimbabwe have been considered particularly successful in this regard (Lucas 1992). High-level policy commitment and political ownership of the population program was a key ingredient for success. Political com-

mitment is not enough, however; the leadership must provide contraceptives and appropriate outlets for obtaining them and create an environment that is conducive to adoption of family planning (Caldwell, Orubuloye, and Caldewell 1992).

The existence of strong family planning programs is a prerequisite to reducing fertility. Family planning programs that have delivery points throughout the country; provide a range of contraceptive methods; ensure easy availability of contraceptives; adopt a reproductive health approach; and reach adolescents, men, and unmarried people are most likely to accelerate progress toward fertility decline in Africa (Caldwell and Caldwell 2002). Some specific service delivery strategies that have been found to be effective in Africa are those that promote spacing methods, give women the means to assume responsibility over contraceptive adoption, and allow women to use contraception

Box 25.3 Rwanda Case Study

In the 1980s Rwanda had one of the highest levels of fertility in the world (8.6). The availability of family planning service was very limited, and cultural attitudes dictated the desire for a large family. As a result, contraceptive prevalence rate was extremely low, at 3–4 percent in 1988 (May, Mukamanzi, and Vekemans 1990).

The National Office of Population (ONAPO) was established in 1981 to increase demand for and improve the supply of family planning services. It made some initial progress, but its gains were lost during the genocide of 1994. After the recovery, the government introduced sweeping reforms that have resulted in dramatic progress on health and family planning indicators, with the contraceptive prevalence rate increasing several-fold, skyrocketing from 4.3 percent in 2000 to 26.1 in 2007.

The importance of providing family planning services as a rationale for national development found strong support at the top leadership level of the government. A number of innovative strategies were applied to improve access and quality of health services. Some successful strategies included the introduction of a performance-based financing mechanism at various levels. Performance contracts were established between the presidency and district mayors (*Imihigo*) that included an indicator on family planning. Performance incentives were also given to health workers to improve their motivation levels and to health centers for providing quality care. Universal health insurance schemes (*mutuelles de santé*) further enhanced the coverage of health care and encouraged community involvement in health provision. Other strategies included decentralizing health services, strengthening contraceptive supply systems, training health workers for family planning provision, and establishing secondary posts as an alternate means for providing modern contraceptives to circumvent that religiously affiliated health facilities were not allowed to do so (Solo 2008). Rwanda's remarkable turnaround from its conflict-torn past to current achievements serves as a model for other countries in the region.

Source: Authors.

---

without their partners' knowledge (Caldwell, Orubuloye, and Caldwell 1992).

Policies that go beyond simply increasing contraceptive prevalence to address the proximate determinants of fertility can accelerate fertility decline in significant ways. Increasing the age of marriage through legislation and behavior change, encouraging natural child spacing through promotion of exclusive breastfeeding, and reducing the risk of unsafe abortion by removing legal restrictions will be key factors underlying fertility decline in Africa (Guengant and May 2002). Improvements in health, education, and socioeconomic factors can also catalyze fertility reduction in the region. For example, experiences from Botswana, Kenya, and Zimbabwe show that countries that are making improvements in child survival and women's education have the greatest potential for reducing fertility (Caldwell, Orubuloye, and Caldwell 1992).

Although fertility transition has begun in Africa, it is limited to a few countries; fertility decline across the region remains a distant goal. Even in countries in which contraceptive prevalence is increasing, huge differentials exist by socioeconomic strata, urban-rural residence, and correlates such as female education and autonomy. The stagnation in recent years provides compelling evidence that faltering policy and resource commitments can easily reverse the gains that have been made in the past.

Family planning remains an unfinished agenda in the region, because high fertility and rapid population growth present a great threat to the achievement of the Millennium Development Goals (Cleland and others 2006). A greater thrust in this direction will be required to sustain and improve the prospects for health and development in Sub-Saharan Africa in the coming decades.

REFERENCES

Aloo-Obunga, C. 2003. *Country Analysis of Family Planning and HIV/AIDS: Kenya.* Policy Project, Washington, DC.

Blacker, J., C. Opiyo, M. Jasseh, A. Sloggett, and J. Ssekamatte-Ssebuliba. 2005. "Fertility in Kenya and Uganda: A Comparative Study of Trends and Determinants." *Population Studies* 59 (3): 355–73.

Bongaarts, J. 1987. "The Proximate Determinants of Fertility." *Technology in Society* 9 (3–4): 243–60.

Bongaarts, J., O. Frank, and R. Lesthaeghe. 1984. "The Proximate Determinants of Fertility in Sub-Saharan Africa." *Population and Development Review* 10 (3): 511–37.

Brookman-Amissah, E., and J. B. Moyo. 2004. "Abortion Law Reform in Sub-Saharan Africa: No Turning Back." *Reproductive Health Matters* 12 (24): 227–34.

Bryant, J. 2007. "Theories of Fertility Decline and the Evidence from Development Indicators." *Population and Development Review* 33 (1): 101–27.

Caldwell, J. C., and P. Caldwell. 1987. "The Cultural Context of High Fertility in Sub-Saharan Africa." *Population and Development Review* 13 (3): 409–37.

———. 1988. "Is the Asian Family Planning Program Model Suited to Africa?" *Studies in Family Planning* 19 (1): 19–28.

———. 2002. "Africa: The New Family Planning Frontier." *Studies in Family Planning* 33 (1): 76–86.

Caldwell, J. C., I. O. Orubuloye, and P. Caldwell. 1992. "Fertility Decline in Africa: A New Type of Transition?" *Population and Development Review* 18 (2): 211–42.

Central Statistical Agency, and ORC Macro. 2006. *Ethiopia Demographic and Health Survey 2005.* ORC Macro, Calverton, MD.

Cleland, J., S. Bernstein, A. Ezeh, A. Faundes, A. Glasier, and J. Innis. 2006. "Family Planning: The Unfinished Agenda." *The Lancet* 368 (9549): 1810–27.

Cleland J., R. P. Ndugwa, and E. M. Zulu. 2011. "Family planning in sub-Saharan Africa: Progress or Stagnation." *Bulletin of the World Health Organization* 89: 137–143.

Cohen, B. 1998. "The Emerging Fertility Transition in Sub-Saharan Africa." *World Development* 26 (8): 1431–61.

Ezeh, A. C., B. U. Mberu, and J. Emina. 2009. "Stall in Fertility Decline in Eastern African Countries: Regional Analysis of Patterns, Determinants and Implications." *Philosophical Transactions of the Royal Society Biological Sciences* 364 (1532): 2991–3007.

Garenne, M., and V. Joseph. 2002. "The Timing of the Fertility Transition in Sub-Saharan Africa." *World Development* 30 (10): 1835–43.

Gillespie, D. G. 2004. "Whatever Happened to Family Planning and for That Matter, Reproductive Health?" *International Family Planning Perspectives* 30 (1): 34–38.

Guengant, J. P., and J. M. May. 2002. *Impact of the Proximate Determinants on the Future Course of Fertility in Sub-Saharan Africa: Prospects of Fertility Decline in High Fertility Countries.* New York: United Nations.

Hubacher, D., I. Mavranezouli, and E. McGinn. 2008. "Unintended Pregnancy in Sub-Saharan Africa: Magnitude of the Problem and Potential Role of Contraceptive Implants to Alleviate It." *Contraception* 78 (1): 73–78.

Kalipeni, E. 1995. "The Fertility Transition in Africa." *Geographical Review* 85 (3): 286–300.

Kirk, D., and B. Pillet. 1998. "Fertility Levels, Trends, and Differentials in Sub-Saharan Africa in the 1980s and 1990s." *Studies in Family Planning* 29 (1): 1–22.

Koblinksy, M. 2003. *Reducing Maternal Mortality: Learning from Bolivia, China, Egypt, Honduras, Indonesia, Jamaica, and Zimbabwe.* Washington, DC: World Bank.

Lee, K., L. Lush, G. Walt, and J. Cleland. 1998. "Family Planning Policies and Programmes in Eight Low-Income Countries: A Comparative Policy Analysis." *Social Science & Medicine* 47 (7): 949–59.

Lucas, D. 1992. "Fertility and Family Planning in Southern and Central Africa." *Studies in Family Planning* 23 (3): 145–58.

Magadi, M. A., and S. L. Curtis. 2003. "Trends and Determinants of Contraceptive Method Choice in Kenya." *Studies in Family Planning* 34 (3): 149–59.

Mauldin, W. P., and J. A. Ross. 1991. "Family Planning Programs: Efforts and Results, 1982–89." *Studies in Family Planning* 22 (6): 350–67.

May, J. F., M. Mukamanzi, and M. Vekemans. 1990. "Family Planning in Rwanda: Status and Prospects." *Studies in Family Planning* 21 (1): 20–32.

Mbacke, C. 1994. "Review: Family Planning Programs and Fertility Transition in Sub-Saharan Africa." *Population and Development Review* 20 (1): 188–93.

Moultrie, T. A., and I. M. Timaeus. 2003. "The South African Fertility Decline: Evidence from Two Censuses and a Demographic and Health Survey." *Population Studies* 57 (3): 265–83.

National Statistical Office Malawi, and ORC Macro. 2005. *Malawi Demographic and Health Survey 2004.* ORC Macro, Calverton, MD.

Pathfinder International. 2005. *Community-Based Family Planning in Kenya: Meeting New Challenges.* Nairobi and Watertown, MA.

Phillips, J. F., W. L. Greene, and E. Jackson. 1999. *Lessons Learned from Community-Based Distribution of Family Planning in Africa.* No. 121, Population Council, New York.

Solo, J. 2008. "Family Planning in Rwanda: How a Taboo Topic Became Priority Number One." IntraHealth International, Chapel Hill, NC.

Terceira, N., G. Simon, and S. Gregson. 2003. "The Contribution of HIV to Fertility Decline in Rural Zimbabwe, 1985–2000." *Population Studies* 57 (2): 149–64.

Thomas, D., and I. Muvandi. 1994. "The Demographic Transition in Southern Africa: Another Look at the

Evidence from Botswana and Zimbabwe." *Demography* 31 (2): 185–207.

UNDESA (United Nations Department of Economic and Social Affairs). 2008. *World Population Prospects, the 2008 Revision.* New York: United Nations.

United Nations Population Division. 2009. *World Contraceptive Use.* Nw YorK; United Nations Department of Economic and Social Affairs.

Way, A. A., A. R. Cross, and S. Kumar. 1987. "Family Planning in Botswana, Kenya and Zimbabwe." *International Family Planning Perspectives* 13 (1): 7–11.

World Bank. 2009. *World Development Indicators.* Washington, DC: World Bank.

Zinaga, A. F. 1992. "Development of the Zimbabwe Family Planning Program." Policy Research Working Paper, World Bank, Washington, DC.

CHAPTER 26

Achieving Universal Primary Education through School Fee Abolition: Some Policy Lessons from Uganda

B. Essama-Nssah

In 1997 the government of Uganda abolished school fees for primary education. Immediately, primary enrollment rates skyrocketed, with gross enrollment rates rising from 77 percent in 1996 to 137 in 1997 and net enrollment rising from 57 percent to 85 percent.[1] Enrollment remained high over the following decade, with poor children, girls, and rural residents benefiting disproportionately from the increase in access.

The quantitative success of the government's universal primary education (UPE) initiative put significant stress on the country's educational infrastructure, however, with a consequent toll on the quality of primary schooling. Increased enrollment led to overcrowding, multiple shifts, shortages of teachers and material, and an increase in over-age students.[2] This chapter analyzes the outcomes of UPE in Uganda in order to draw policy lessons from the experience.

THE NEED FOR REFORM

Uganda's education sector achieved considerable progress following independence, but that progress was reversed as a result of various sociopolitical crises in the 1970s and 1980s. In 1985 the level of government expenditure on education was about 27 percent that of the 1970s (Appleton 2001). Partly as a result of the high costs of education to families, the gross primary enrollment rate stood at 50 percent in 1980—the same rate as in 1960. Significant improvement was observed in 1985, when the gross primary enrollment rate increased to 73 percent, but it remained stagnant at that level until 1995.

In 1996 the government committed itself to providing UPE. It abolished school fees at the primary level starting in January 1997. The policy was not adopted overnight. It is an integral part of a broader reform program, which can be traced back to the creation in 1987 of the Education Policy Review Commission (see discussion later in chapter).

Education contributes directly to human development and is an investment in economic prosperity. In recognition of the fact that it has both intrinsic and instrumental value for development, the government placed education at the center of its Poverty Eradication Action Plan (PEAP). The current 2010–15 five-year National Development Plan also recognizes the importance of education for sustained economic growth and social transformation.

OUTCOMES OF REFORM

The goal of Uganda's primary education policy is to ensure that every child enrolls at the appropriate age and successfully completes the full cycle of education.[3] Achievement of this objective requires expanding educational opportunities and improving educational outcomes. The review of the results of reform presented in this section focuses on four outcomes: school enrollment and its cost, age at enrollment, completion rates, and equity considerations.

School enrollment

Between 1996 (the year of the policy announcement) and 1997 (the first year of implementation), primary school enrollment in Uganda increased from about 3.1 million (a gross enrollment rate of 77 percent) to 5.3 million (a gross enrollment rate of 137 percent), a 58 percent increase. The net enrollment rate rose from 57 percent in 1996 to 85 percent in 1997 and 90 percent in 1999 (MOES 1999).

To what extent are these changes in enrollment a result of the UPE policy? The 1997 education policy reform can be viewed as a natural experiment in which a sharp change in government policy is an exogenous variation in a treatment variable to which only a segment of the population (that is, primary school students) is exposed. Deininger (2003) estimates a linear probability model for primary school enrollment among three age groups: 6–12, 6–8, and 9–12 (see annex 26A for technical details). To control for unobserved effects of factors associated with a common economic environment, he estimates the same equation for secondary school enrollment (the 12–18 age group). All primary school regressions show a positive and significant time trend, implying that the probability of primary school enrollment increased for everyone in the sample. When all other variables are set to their mean levels, the probability of a child being enrolled in primary school in 1999 is about 60 percent higher than it was in 1992. Deininger finds no significant effect of UPE on secondary school enrollment. Essama-Nssah, Leite, and Simler (2008) replicate this analysis using data for 1992 and 2005. They find similar results.

The surge in enrollment associated with the reduction in the cost of primary schooling is evidence that this cost was a significant impediment to primary school enrollment by the poor (Deininger 2003). Indeed, lack of interest and the cost of enrollment are the two major determinants of nonenrollment.

As a result of these reforms, the importance of cost as a reason for not enrolling in school declined significantly: in 1992, 42 percent of households cited cost as a factor. This figure fell to just 13 percent by 2005 (Essama-Nssah, Leite, and Simler 2008). This constraint did not change in urban areas, and it declined by less in the central region, where it fell from about 46 percent in 1992 to about 36 percent in 2005, than elsewhere in Uganda. Lack of interest, which increased from 49 percent in 1992 to 56 percent in 2005, remains a severe constraint to enrollment.

To what extent have increases in enrollment been sustained over time? Total enrollment increased steadily, from 5.4 million in 2000 to about 7.4 million in 2010 (figure 26.1). The gross enrollment ratio dropped from about 128 percent in 2000 to about 104 percent in 2004 (figure 26.2). After a slight increase in 2005, it has been hovering around 115 percent since 2006. After peaking at 100 percent in 2003, the net enrollment ratio has shown an upward trend, rising from 90 percent in 2004 to 96 percent in 2010. These trends suggest that the sustained efforts of the government to improve education policy led to and maintained an increase

Figure 26.1   Boys' and Girls' Enrollment in Public Primary Schools in Uganda, 2000–10

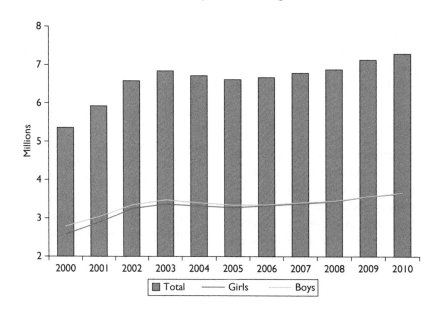

Source: MOES 2010.

Figure 26.2   Gross and Net Primary Enrollment Rates in Uganda, 2000–10

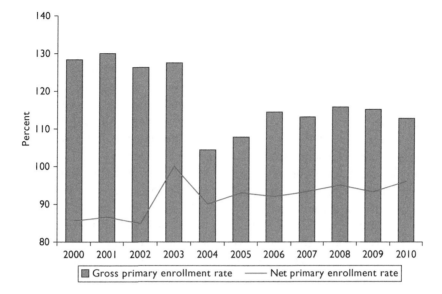

Source: MOES 2010.

Note: The gross primary enrollment rate (GER) is the ratio between the number of children enrolled in primary school and the number of children of primary school age. The net primary enrollment rate (NER) is the ratio between the number of children of primary school age enrolled in primary school and the number of children of primary school age. See note 1 for more information.

in enrollment not only for over-age but for under-age children as well.

Essama-Nssah, Leite, and Simler (2008) study the impact of the policy shift on the cost of enrollment using a linear regression model with interactive terms (analogous to the linear probability model discussed above). The dependent variable is the logarithm of school fees paid (as reported in the 1992 and 2005 surveys). The specification accounts for the fact that school fees are observed only for students who are enrolled and not for those who are not enrolled in school. This potential selection bias calls for the application of Heckman's (1976) two-step estimator. This approach, which is analogous to instrumental variable estimation, requires simultaneous modeling of both exposure to policy intervention and the associated outcome. Identification therefore hinges on an exclusion restriction—that is, the variation of at least one exogenous variable that affects participation (enrollment) but not the outcome (fees paid).

Essama-Nssah, Leite, and Simler apply this methodology to both the primary and secondary levels of education, using community-level costs and peers' enrollment rates in the identifying restriction. Thus at the household level, the construction of these variables excludes the information pertaining to the household under consideration. This construction ensures that the instrumental variables used for identification are not directly related to the outcome variable. They find

that over time there has been a significant increase in school fees paid by families at all levels of schooling. However, students in public primary schools were paying less in 2005 than they paid in 1992, suggesting that UPE may have reduced the cost of enrolling in public primary schools. A comparison of the policy impact at the primary and the secondary levels suggests that the policy shift may indeed have moderated the increase in school fees at the primary level but that there was no spillover effect to the secondary level. Their results show that in 2005, fees paid at the secondary level of education were higher in public than in private schools. UPE did lower the cost of primary education.

Age at enrollment and completion rates

Deininger (2003) finds that mother's education is the most important factor influencing timely enrollment (that is, enrollment between the ages of 6 and 8). It does not affect children who enroll between the ages of 9 and 12.

Grogan (2009) uses data from the 1995 and 2000 Demographic and Health Surveys (DHS) along with the 2001 DHS EdData survey for Uganda to assess the impact of UPE on the likelihood of enrolling in school before the age of nine—a key factor in preventing drop-out.[4] She shows that starting school before age nine is associated with a 16–26 percent increase in the probability of completing at least seven years of schooling. Using the regression discontinuity framework from the program evaluation literature, she shows that elimination of school fees associated with the UPE policy had a positive albeit small effect on the propensity to enroll in primary school before age nine (the overall effect is estimated at 3 percent). This finding is consistent with the conclusion reached earlier, on the basis of the evolution of enrollment rates, that UPE led to an increase in the enrollment of under-age children.

Essama-Nssah, Leite, and Simler (2008) analyze the impact of the policy shift on primary school completion. In particular, they focus on the probability of completing the seventh year of primary school (P7), the last grade of primary school in Uganda. As in the case of enrollment, household income, age, parental education, and urban residence are key determinants of the likelihood of completing primary school. These factors have a positive and significant effect on the probability of completing P7. Essama-Nssah, Leite, and Simler find that the policy shift may not have improved the chances of completing P7. They also find that the income constraint on the chances of completing P7 has become more severe.

The overall completion rate fell continuously between 2004 and 2007, from 62 percent to 47 percent (figure 26.3). This trend seems to support the results of the analysis based on the 2005 household survey discussed earlier. The completion rates for girls and boys follow the same pattern, with rates for boys consistently above those for girls. Improving completion rates thus remains a challenge to policy makers.

Equity

The achievement of equity is increasingly seen as an important goal of socioeconomic development. Identifying winners and losers is therefore an important concern for policy makers. Doing so depends fundamentally on the response of socioeconomic agents to the incentives of the policy under consideration.

The distributional implications of an intervention depend on the variation in the impacts across groups or individuals. Such impact heterogeneity stems from both treatment heterogeneity (if the dose received depends on some unit attributes) and heterogeneity in individual circumstances (which determine the response to treatment). The same heterogeneity that must be controlled for in identifying causal effects must be accounted for in identifying winners and losers. Models that include interaction between the treatment indicator and covariates offer a framework for the analysis of systematic variation in mean impacts across socioeconomic groups. Interactive models focus on differences in subgroup means.

The regression framework used by Deininger (2003) is suitable for the analysis of the distributional implications of the UPE policy. In 1992, before the introduction of UPE,

Figure 26.3   Boys' and Girls' Primary School Completion Rates in Uganda, 2001–10

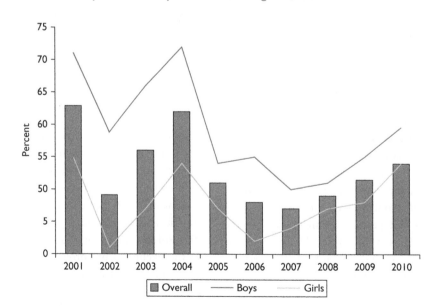

Source: MOES 2010.

CHAPTER 26: ACHIEVING UNIVERSAL PRIMARY EDUCATION THROUGH SCHOOL FEE ABOLITION

there was a strong bias against girls in Uganda, and parental income had a strong impact on the probability of enrollment. The probability of enrollment, which increases with parental income, was 5 percent higher for boys than for girls. The relationship between parental education and the probability of primary school enrollment was also positive and significant. Fixing all variables at their mean level and increasing the father's education by one year would lead to an increase in the probability of enrollment of about 3 percent; an additional year of education by the mother would increase the probability of her child enrolling in school by 4 percent. The baseline results show significant regional disparities.

Interacting the policy variable with a variety of household characteristics, Deininger (2003) shows that UPE has been pro-poor. The positive impact of parental income on the probability of enrollment is significantly lower after reform. Comparing 1992 and 2005, Essama-Nssah, Leite, and Simler (2008) find a significant increase in enrollment of the poor. At the bottom quintile, enrollment increased by more than 28 percentage points (from 50.2 percent in 1992 to 78.8 percent in 2005). However, the gap between the bottom and the top quintile does not seem to have narrowed. The gap between boys and girls that was evident in 1992 disappeared in 2005, with the gap in the gross enrollment rate for girls (23.5 percent) somewhat higher than that for boys (20.4 percent). These results confirm the trends observed by Deininger (2003).

The achievement gap between boys and girls narrowed as well. In 2001 the primary school completion rate was 71 percent for boys and 63 percent for girls. The two groups almost achieved parity in 2008, when the completion rate was 51 percent for boys and 49 percent for girls. For 2010 the gap is estimated at 6 percentage points.

Convergence in achievement by boys and girls is evident from figure 26.4, which shows the success rate on the Primary School Leaving Examination over the past decade. In 2000, 90 percent of male candidates but only 63 percent of female candidates passed the examination. In 2010, 92 percent of boys and 90 percent of girls who take the exam were expected to pass.

Another dimension of gender inequality deserves special attention. The 2010–15 five- year national development plan notes that the largest proportion of out-of-school children are girls. Girls are also more likely than boys to drop out of school or repeat grades.

The *World Development Report 2006* argues for the pursuit of equity on both intrinsic and instrumental grounds. It defines equity in terms of a level playing field on which individuals have equal opportunity to freely pursue chosen life plans and are spared from extreme deprivation in outcomes. The equitable distribution of educational resources is one of the best ways to try to equalize opportunity across socioeconomic groups. Observed inequality of outcomes among groups defined on the basis of circumstances beyond their

Figure 26.4 Boys' and Girls' Success Rates on Uganda's Primary School Leaving Examination, 2000–10

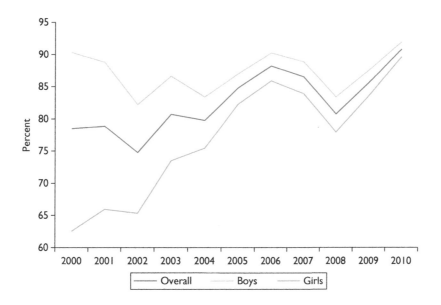

Source: MOES 2010.

control is one potential indicator that current policies have not fully achieved equality of opportunity.

Regional differences in resource allocations are wide in Uganda (figure 26.5). Of the country's four regions, the eastern and the northern have the highest pupil-teacher and pupil-classroom ratios. These data suggest that children in these regions do not have the same learning opportunities as their counterparts in the central and western regions.

POLICY FRAMEWORK

The abolition of primary school fees and the associated measures adopted in the context of the UPE reform led to a significant and lasting expansion of educational opportunities and an improvement in equity in Uganda. The policy process that underpins these achievements has been held up as a leading example of the crucial role played by country ownership and donor cooperation within a sectorwide approach to policy reforms.

The success or failure of a policy is usually assessed in terms of its objectives. But to understand the observed outcomes one needs to consider the policy-making process. The UPE reform sought to expand educational opportunities and improve teaching and learning outcomes. There is evidence that the gains in access and equity have not been fully matched by improvement in educational outcomes. This section considers the policy framework in order to identify key determinants of these outcomes and draw policy lessons from the Ugandan experience.

Figure 26.5   Pupil-Classroom and Pupil-Teacher Ratios in Uganda, by Region, 2008

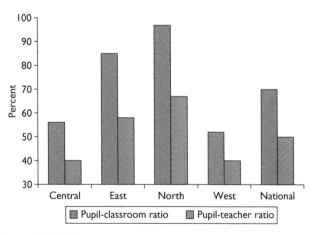

Source: MOES 2008.

Vision and political commitment

A clear strategic vision focused on the role of education in poverty reduction as well as strong political commitment at various levels of government backed by a sound policy framework underpinned the "big bang" approach adopted in Uganda and contributed to its success. In 1996–97 the top political leadership in Uganda showed its commitment to poverty reduction by spearheading the formulation of the Poverty Eradication Plan. Uganda was among the first low-income countries to prepare a comprehensive and participatory national strategy for poverty reduction; its experience inspired the design of the Poverty Eradication Plan in Uganda and the Poverty Reduction Strategy Program (PRSP) approach (Mackinnon and Reinikka 2000). The government placed education at the center of this action plan, in recognition that education has both intrinsic and instrumental value for development. To show its determination, the government quickly translated the action plan into a budget and medium-term expenditure framework.

Nature and scope of education policy reform

The *World Development Report 2004* (World Bank 2003) argues that the effectiveness of social services in developing human capital depends fundamentally on the method of delivery and the behavior of key actors, including policy makers, service providers, and potential beneficiaries.[5] Outcomes are thus jointly determined by supply- and demand-side factors and the interactions among them. Supply-side interventions seek to increase the level and quality of services provided. Such interventions usually entail building and staffing facilities, providing inputs, implementing institutional reforms, and strengthening the incentives facing services providers. On the demand side, typical interventions seek to improve the ability of participants to benefit from the service provided. Some interventions include incentives for potential beneficiaries to provide the requisite level of effort to achieve the desired outcome. One way of stimulating demand for services is to make them more affordable. Other incentive-based interventions make resource transfers conditional on some desired behavior. For example, a conditional transfer program may seek to promote human capital accumulation by making cash or in-kind transfers to poor families provided that their school-age children stay in school and young children and pregnant and nursing women participate in some health-enhancing activities.

The education policy reform in Uganda is broadly consistent with this framework. The sudden increase in the demand for public primary education created a series of challenges for the government, related mainly to financing the reform, improving the quality of primary education, ensuring equitable access to primary education, and planning beyond primary school. To improve the quality of primary education, the government has focused on five areas: curriculum development, provision of basic learning materials, teacher development, language of instruction for lower primary pupils, and establishment and maintenance of standards.

It took some time for reform in these areas to significantly improve the quality of teaching and learning in Uganda. Test results from the National Assessment of Progress in Education between 1996 and 2000 showed deterioration in student performance in math, reading, science, and social studies (Bategeka 2005). The key factors explaining the decline outcome were lack of coherence and consistency within the system and changes in teaching and learning methods (Penny and others 2008).

Over time the situation has improved, for both boys and girls. Between 2003 and 2010, the overall numeracy rate for students in P3 rose from 42 percent to 72 percent, with similar increases for girls and boys (figure 26.6). These gains were more dramatic than were gains in literacy (figure 26.7).

Uganda uses two types of grants to increase equitable access to primary education: capitation grants and school facilities grants. The purpose of the capitation grant is to shift some of the burden of school fees from parents to the government and to provide schools with some of the resources necessary to run the school and support teaching and learning.[6] The capitation grant is meant to cover tuition only; families remain responsible for writing materials, uniforms, and lunches. This grant is paid to schools in nine monthly installments, at an annual rate of U Sh 5,000 (about $3.00) per pupil in P1–P3 and U Sh 8,100 (about $4.75) per pupil in P4–P7 (Penny and others 2008).[7]

The school facilities grant is designed to assist schools in the neediest communities in building classrooms, latrines, and teachers' houses and procuring furniture. After a favorable review in 1999, it became the only mechanism through which public funds are channeled for the construction of school facilities. Both grants are conditional, to the extent that funding is given to districts or municipalities under strict guidelines and regulations and under the supervision of the Ministry of Education and Sports (MOES).[8]

Planning

The success of a policy initiative like Uganda's UPE requires background analytical work, identification of financing sources, and the development of implementation and monitoring capacity. Analytical work could take the form of an overall assessment of the performance of the current

Figure 26.6   Numeracy Rates for Boys and Girls in P3 in Uganda, 2003–10

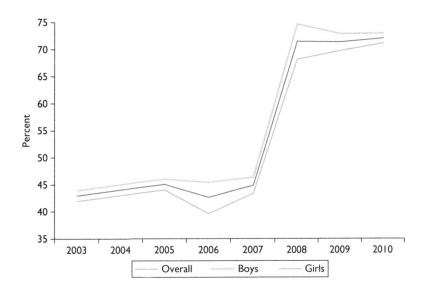

Source: MOES 2010.

Figure 26.7   Literacy Rates for Boys and Girls in P3 in Uganda, 2003–10

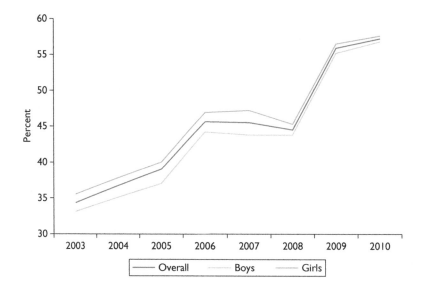

Source: MOES 2010.

system. Such an assessment would identify constraints that must be addressed and consider the feasibility and desirability of a variety of policy options. In an environment in which parents value education, as is the case in Uganda, abolition of school fees will normally lead to a surge in enrollment. It is therefore important to assess the expected increase in demand for schooling and plan for the additional resources (teachers, facilities, and teaching and learning material) needed to cope with the surge.

The UPE reform in Uganda followed the "big bang" approach to policy reform, but adoption of the reform followed a long gestation period, and it benefited from many critical prior actions, starting with the creation of the Education Policy Review Commission in 1987. In its 1989 report to the government, the commission set an ambitious goal for primary education, recommending that education policy ensure that every child enroll in school at the appropriate age and successfully complete the full cycle (P1–P7) (Grogan 2009).[9] The first response to this recommendation came in 1993, in the form of the Primary Education and Teacher Development Project, supported by the World Bank and the U.S. Agency for International Development (USAID). The project, which sought to introduce a countrywide evaluation framework for overall progress in education, led to the establishment of a Teacher Development and Management System and the creation of an Instructional Material Unit. Under the Teacher Development and Management System, all public schools (also known as government-aided schools) were organized into clusters of 18

schools. One school in each cluster serves as the coordinating center school, in the sense that it had a trained teacher (the outreach tutor) in charge of helping parents, community leaders, teachers, and principals in each school in the cluster coordinate their efforts for improving teaching and learning outcomes. Outreach tutors are supervised and supported by outreach administrators from core primary teacher colleges. By 1998, 18 core primary teacher colleges were supervising about 550 outreach tutors (MOES 1999).

In 1994 the National Curriculum Development Center lost its monopoly on the production of instructional materials. The role of the Instructional Material Unit is to help districts acquire instructional materials (including books) and to ensure that the process is consistent with government regulation designed to ensure transparency.

In 1995 a monitoring and evaluation program, the National Assessment of Progress in Education was set up to attempt to determine the amount of and type of knowledge acquired by pupils relative to the objectives of the curriculum.

Partnerships

The outcome of a policy intervention hinges critically on individual behavior and on the rules that govern interaction among stakeholders. In the context of the provision of public services, the *World Development Report 2004* argues that there is a need for a governance framework that defines accountability for results between policy makers and providers, between policy makers and beneficiaries, and between providers and beneficiaries. The UPE reform was embedded in Uganda's national Poverty Eradication Plan, which is consistent with the key principles underlying the PRSP approach of accountability based on partnership. In the context of education reform, now a strategic component of the National Development Plan, the central government is engaged in a two-tier partnership involving development partners and domestic stakeholders.

The government of Uganda and its development partners adopted a sectorwide approach to deal with resource mobilization and aid coordination. The common vision binding this partnership stems from both the adoption of the PRSP approach toward the end of the 1990s and the principles voiced at the World Education Forum held in Dakar in 2000. The government agreed with its development partners that 31 percent of the recurrent discretionary budget would go to education and that at least 65 percent of that amount would be allocated to primary education (Higgins and Rwanyange 2005). The World Education Forum led to a commitment by the international community to support any developing country that seriously engaged in the pursuit of policies aimed at securing quality education for all (Eilor 2004).

The sectorwide approach started with the Education Strategic Investment Plan (ESIP) 1998–2003. At the end of the ESIP funding agreement, the Medium-Term Budget Framework became the common budget support modality (Penny and others 2008). The sectorwide approach emphasized actions designed to enhance local leadership and the integration of development partner and government efforts. Budget support was thus conditioned on a few key outputs, and outcomes related fiduciary integrity and progress toward improving service delivery and equitable access. The Heavily Indebted Poor Country Initiative led to an increase in funds available to the education sector. The effectiveness of this institutional arrangement was significantly enhanced by the use of sector reviews and budget working groups. These mechanisms, along with an effective and reliable Education Management Information System, are now playing a fundamental role in the education planning and budgeting processes (Penny and others 2008).

The partnership between the government of Uganda and the aid community is often cited as a success story. This partnership is based on a common vision about the effectiveness of poverty reduction strategies. It pursues a holistic approach, putting the country in the driver's seat. Both sup-

ply and demand constraints to service delivery are addressed within a common sector policy and planning framework supported by well-functioning mechanisms for the flow of funds and information.

The same cannot be said of the partnership between the central government and domestic stakeholders. Higgins and Rwanyange (2005) present results from a qualitative assessment of the education reform process in Uganda focusing on ownership and accountability in the sector. Based on data collected between 1997 and 2004, the study finds that officials at the district level acknowledge improvements in the transfer of funds but feel that they lack the autonomy to adjust the use of funds to the particular needs of the districts and that the process is designed to cater to the needs of the central government and the donor community.

At the school level, according to the same study, parents and teachers are excluded from the decision-making process for the utilization of funds allocated to schools. Some observers consider this lack of involvement and alienation a serious constraint to the performance of schools and students (Higgins and Rwanyage 2005). In the survey underlying the study, respondents cited the lack of integrity of head teachers among the factors that impede effective learning and school management. Some head teachers reportedly fail to post capitation grants on public notice boards, as required by the rules.

All stakeholders are concerned about the quality of entrants to primary teachers' colleges and the training they receive there. Teachers themselves feel marginalized, because they have little say in decisions that affect their working conditions. These considerations suggest that domestic partnerships for education in Uganda may not be as effective as they could be, because of imbalance in influence and capacity. Education reform in Uganda continues to evolve, however, and coordination mechanisms have been improving. Starting in 2007, for instance, the participation in sector reviews and discussions of the Education Sector Consultative Committee have been opened up to representatives of teachers and head teachers, local authorities, and parent teacher associations.[10]

CONCLUSION

Uganda's success in increasing access and equity in primary education stems from the following institutional factors:

- Strong political commitment to a development strategy centered on building human capital

- A comprehensive approach to policy making based on careful planning and implementation of critical prior actions
- Effective and sustained domestic and international partnerships supportive of country ownership and donor cooperation within a sectorwide approach
- Efficiency gains from measures designed to improve transparency and accountability at the school level in the use of available resources.

Reform initially put enormous stress on the country's educational infrastructure, reducing the quality of education as well as completion rates. Significant improvements have been achieved over the past few years. Policymakers in Uganda must now consolidate and expand these improvements if they are to successfully link the country to the global economy, which pays a premium for knowledge and skills.

ANNEX 26A DIFFERENCE-IN-DIFFERENCES IDENTIFICATION OF POLICY IMPACT

When repeated cross-section data are available, the impact of a policy can be identified and estimated using a two-step procedure known as difference-in-differences (DID) or double difference. The first stage involves the reflexive (or before and after) change in average outcomes of the treatment and control groups. This difference eliminates the selection bias associated with permanent group differences, leaving intact the bias as a result of the time trend. The bias that remains after the first step is removed by the difference in the second stage, in which the change in the average outcome of the comparison group is subtracted from that of the treated group.[11] Alternatively, the treatment effect can be obtained by measuring the difference in the change in average outcomes across groups (that is, comparing with- and without-treatment groups) before and after treatment. The DID method can thus be said to be path independent, because the same result is achieved regardless of the sequence in which these two differences are computed. DID estimation can be implemented within a regression framework, which also offers a convenient way to obtain the relevant estimates and the associated standard errors. This framework also makes it easier to add more groups and time periods using dummy variables (Angrist and Pischke 2009).[12]

Deininger (2003) applies a regression model that is consistent with the double difference approach to two nationally representative household surveys: the 1992 Uganda Integrated Household Survey (UIHS) and the 1999 Uganda National Household Survey (UNHS). Given that UPE took effect in 1997, observations for 1992 represent the base case; schooling outcomes observed in 1999 presumably reflect continued implementation of UPE.

To see clearly what is involved, let S_{it} stand for an indicator of enrollment status (enrolled or not enrolled) of child i in year $t = 1992$ or 1999. Think of this outcome as a function of individual, household, and community characteristics (X_{it}) such as gender, income, and parental education. This indicator also depends on a time trend (T) and unobservables (e_{it}) assumed to be independently and identically distributed. The time variable T is a dummy variable that is equal to one for 1999 (to mark exposure to UPE regime) and zero for 1992 (indicating no exposure). Deininger's (2003) regression is of the following form:

$$S_{it} = \alpha + \beta X_{it} + \gamma T + \delta X_{it} T + \varepsilon_{it}.$$

The interaction terms in this equation play a crucial role in the assessment and interpretation of various effects of the shift to the UPE regime. One can think of the dummy variable T (representing the shift in policy regime) as having a moderating influence on the effects of the individual and household characteristics on the schooling outcome (here the probability of enrollment). The dummy variable T is a moderator variable.[13] The coefficient (g) associated with the moderator variable represents the effect of any secular trend captured by T. The other coefficients in the model are easily interpreted within the logic of difference-in-difference estimation.

NOTES

1. The net primary enrollment ratio is the ratio between the number of children of primary school age enrolled in primary school and the number of children of primary school age. By definition, this ratio cannot exceed 100 percent. The gross primary enrollment ratio is the ratio between the number of children enrolled in primary school and the number of children of primary school age. It can exceed 100 percent if children above (or below) primary school age are in primary school (because, for example, of repetition or delayed entry).

2. The pupil-teacher ratio rose from 38 pupils per teacher in 1996 to about 52 in 1997. The situation has improved since 2000, with the pupil-teacher ratio falling steadily from 65 in 2000 to an estimated 47 in 2010, the pupil-classroom ratio falling from 106 in 2000 to an estimated 66 in 2010, and the proportion of untrained teachers declining continuously (MOES 2010).

3. This section relies heavily on earlier work by the author and two of his colleagues (Essama-Nssah, Leite, and Simler 2008).

4. The 2001 DHS EdData survey collected information on the age at which children started and finished schooling, educational attainment, reasons for nonenrollment, the extent to which parents and guardians were aware of the UPE program. The survey also contains information about the assessment by parents and guardians of the quality of local schools.

5. Such methods include central government provision, contracting out to the private or nongovernmental sector, decentralization to local governments, community participation, and direct transfers to households (World Bank 2003).

6. Parents paid up to 90 percent of recurrent and capital expenditure for primary education in 1991 (Oketch and Rolleston 2007).

7. For students in P7, the government also pays the registration fees for the National Examination Board (Bategeka 2005).

8. For instance, guidelines from the MOES require primary schools to spend capitation grant as follows: 50 percent on instructional material, 30 percent on co-curricular activities such as sports and clubs, 15 percent on utilities and maintenance, and 5 percent on school administration (Bategeka 2005).

9. According to the commission, primary school completion is the minimum level of education that all citizens need to be able to live a full life. It noted that society would benefit a great deal from this outcome, which would probably increase national unity, moral standards, and prosperity (MOES 1999).

10. Communication with Luis Benveniste, World Bank, May 24, 2010.

11. The first stage relies on the assumption of time invariance of the group effects; the second is justified by assuming that, in the absence of treatment, the average outcome of the treated would follow the same time path as the average outcome of the control group. When combined with the fact that both groups are observed before treatment, the assumption of common time trend makes it possible to frame the DID method within the logic of the traditional counterfactual approach. The treatment effect can thus be identified and measured by comparing the observed outcome of the treated with the counterfactual predicted on the basis of the evolution of the average outcome of the control group.

12. The double difference approach (in which impact is defined by the difference in the change of outcomes for the treated and untreated group) can be implemented by a linear regression that includes a constant, a group dummy variable, a time dummy, and an interaction term between the two dummies. Impact is measured by the coefficient associated with this interaction term.

13. By definition, a moderator is a qualitative or quantitative variable that affects the direction or strength of the relationship between a response variable and a predictor or independent variable (Baron and Kennedy 1986). For instance, the shift in policy regime (the moderator) may affect the impact of gender (a predictor) on schooling outcomes (response variables).

REFERENCES

Angrist, Joshua D., and Jörn-Steffen Pischke. 2009. *Mostly Harmless Econometrics: An Empiricist's Companion.* Princeton, NJ: Princeton University Press.

Appleton, Simon. 2001. "What Can We Expect from Universal Primary Education?" In *Uganda's Recovery: The Role of Farms, Firms and Government*, ed. Ritva Reinikka and Paul Collier. Washington, DC: World Bank.

Avenstrup, Roger. 2006. "Reducing Poverty through Free Primary Education: Learning from the Experiences of Kenya, Lesotho, Malawi, and Uganda." In *Attacking Africa's Poverty: Experience from the Ground*, ed. Louise Fox and Robert Liebenthal. Washington, DC: World Bank.

Avenstrup, Roger, Liang Xiaoyan, and Nellemann Soren. 2004. "Kenya, Lesotho, Malawi and Uganda: Universal Primary Education and Poverty Reduction." Paper presented at the conference "Scaling Up Poverty Reduction: A Global Learning Process and Conference," Shanghai, May 25–27.

Baron, Reuben M., and David A. Kennedy. 1986. "The Moderator-Mediator Variable Distinction in Social Psychological Research: Conceptual, Strategic and Statistical Considerations." *Journal of Personality and Social Psychology* 51 (6): 1173–82.

Bategeka, Lawrence. 2005. *Universal Primary Education (UPE) in Uganda: Report to the Inter-Regional Inequality Facility.* Institute of Development Studies, University of Sussex, UK.

Deininger, Klaus. 2003. "Does Cost of Schooling Affect Enrollment by the Poor? Universal Primary Education in Uganda." *Economics of Education Review* 22: 291–305.

Devarajan, Shantayanan, and Ritva Reinikka. 2004. "Making Services Work for Poor People." *Journal of African Economies* 13 (1): i142–i166.

Dixit, Avinash, K. 1996. *The Making of Economic Policy: A Transaction-Cost Politics Perspective.* Cambridge, MA: MIT Press.

Eilor, Joseph. 2004. *Education and Sector-Wide Approach in Uganda.* International Institute for Educational Planning, UNESCO, Paris.

Essama-Nssah, B., Phillippe G. Leite, and Kenneth R. Simler. 2008. "Achieving Universal Primary and Secondary Education in Uganda Access and Equity Considerations." World Bank, Poverty Reduction and Equity Group, Washington, DC.

Government of Uganda. 2010. *National Development Plan, 2010/11–2014/15.* Kampala.

Grogan, Louise. 2006. "Who Benefits from Universal Primary Education in Uganda." Department of Economics, University of Guelph, Ontario.

———. 2009. "Universal Primary Education and School Entry in Uganda." *Journal of African Economies* 18 (2): 183–211.

Heckman, James J. 1976. "The Common Structure of Statistical Models of Truncation, Sample Selection and Limited Dependent Variables and a Simple Estimator for such Models." *Annals of Economic and Social Measurement* 5 (4): 475–92.

Higgins, Liz, and Rosemary Rwanyange. 2005. "Ownership in the Education Reform Process in Uganda." *Compare: A Journal of Comparative and International Education* 35 (1): 7–26.

Ingram, Gregory K. 2004. "Overview." In *Evaluation and Development: The Partnership Dimension*, ed. Andres Liebenthal, Osvaldo N. Feinstein, and Gregory K. Ingram. New Brunswick, NJ: Transactions Publishers.

Mackinnon, John, and Ritva Reinikka. 2000. "Lessons from Uganda on Strategies to Fight Poverty." Policy Research Working Paper 2440, World Bank, Washington, DC.

MOES (Ministry of Education and Sports, Uganda). 1999. *The Ugandan Experience of Universal Primary Education.* Kampala.

———. 2010. *The Education and Sports Annual Performance Report. ESAPR. for the Financial Year 2008/09.* Kampala.

Nelson, Jane, and Simon Zadek. 2000. *Partnership Alchemy: New Social Partnerships in Europe.* Copenhagen Centre, Copenhagen.

Nishimura, Mikiko, Yamano Takashi, and Sasaoka Yuichi. 2008. "Impacts of the Universal Primary Education Policy on Educational Attainment and Private Costs in Rural Uganda." *International Journal of Educational Development* 28: 161–75.

Oketch, Moses O., and M. Rolleston Caine M. 2007. "Policies on Free Primary and Secondary Education in East Africa: A Review of the Literature." Research Monograph 10, Consortium for Research on Educational Access, Transitions and Equity, Institute of Education, University of London.

Penny, Alan, Michael Ward, Tony Read, and Hazel Bines. 2008. "Education Sector Reform: The Uganda Experience." *International Journal of Educational Development* 28: 268–85.

Picciotto, Robert. 2004. "The Logic of Partnership." In *Evaluation and Development: The Partnership Dimension*, ed. Andres Liebenthal, Osvalso N. Feinstein, and Gregory K. Ingram. New Brunswick, NJ: Transactions Publishers.

Reinikka, Ritva, and Jakob Svensson. 2004. "Local Capture: Evidence from a Central Government Transfer Program in Uganda." *Quarterly Journal of Economics* 119 (2): 679–705.

———. 2007. "The Returns from Reducing Corruption: Evidence from Education in Uganda." CEPR Discussion Paper 6363, Center for Economic Policy Research, Washington, DC.

World Bank. 2003. *World Development Report 2004: Making Services Work for Poor People.* Washington, DC: World Bank.

World Bank, and UNICEF (United Nations Children's Fund). 2009. *Abolishing School Fees in Africa: Lessons from Ethiopia, Ghana, Kenya, Malawi and Mozambique.* Washington, DC: World Bank.

CPSIA information can be obtained at www.ICGtesting.com
Printed in the USA
LVOW010435130912

298632LV00001B/1/P